BEHAV[illegible] SCIENC[illegible]
FOR [illegible] PROFES[illegible]

BEHAVIOURAL SCIENCES FOR HEALTH PROFESSIONALS

V. AITKEN, DMU TDCR PgD MSc

Senior Lecturer, Medical Education,

King's College School of Medicine & Dentistry,

London

H. JELLICOE, DCR BA MSc PhD

Clinical Psychologist,

Kingston Hospital,

Kingston Upon Thames,

London

With contributions from:
G. Jordan BA Msc MCSP Dip DT, Programme leader, University of Greenwich, Faculty of Human Sciences, London, who played a major role in the conception of the book and provided invaluable advice.

G.W. Roberts, MA DiP Cot SROT, Course Leader, Director of Fieldwork Studies, School of Occupational Therapy Department of Rehabilitation, St Bartholomews and Royal London School of Medicine & Dentistry, Queen Mary and Westfield College: University of London and **P. Cherry,** Head of Radiotherapy, Department of Radiography, City University, London, who assisted in the learning exercises.

W B Saunders Company Ltd
London Philadelphia Toronto Sydney Tokyo

W.B. Saunders Company Ltd 24–28 Oval Road
London NW1 7DX

The Curtis Center
Independence Square West
Philadelphia, PA 19106–3399, USA

Harcourt Brace & Company
55 Horner Avenue
Toronto, Ontario M8Z 4X6, Canada

Harcourt Brace & Company, Australia
30–52 Smidmore Street
Marrickville, NSW 2204, Australia

Harcourt Brace & Company, Japan
Ichibancho Central Building, 22–1 Ichibancho
Chiyoda-ku, Tokyo 102, Japan

This book is printed on acid free paper

A catalogue record for this book is available from the British Library

ISBN 0–7020–1964X

Typeset by J&L Composition Ltd, Filey, North Yorkshire, UK
Printed in Great Britain by The Bath Press

CONTENTS

SECTION IV INTERPERSONAL ISSUES

SECTION V COGNITIVE PROCESSES

SECTION VI ETHICS

SECTION VII RESEARCH AND EVALUATION

CONTRIBUTORS LIST

Armando Barrientos BA PhD	Principal Lecturer in Economics, Business School, University of Hertfordshire, Hertford.
Pamela Cherry MSc TDCR	Section Head-Radiotherapy, Department of Radiotherapy, City University, London.
Martin F Davis MA PhD CPsychol	Senior Lecturer, Department of Psychology, Goldsmiths College, London.
Robert J Edelmann BSc MPhil PhD FBPsS CPsychol	Senior Lecturer, Department of Psychology, University of Surrey, Guildford.
Lindsay S M Fraser BSc	Department of Psychology, University College, London.
Sebastian P Garman BSc MSc PhD PGCE	Department of Health Sciences, Brunel University, Isleworth.
Roger Gomm BSc MSc Dip Soc Studies PhD FRAI	Lecturer in Health and Social Welfare, Department of Health and Social Welfare, Brunel University, Ilseworth.
Jorg Hüber Diplpsych MSc PhD	School of Life Sciences, Roehampton Institute, London.
Valerie Kent PhD	Senior Lecture in Social Psychology, Department of Psychology, Goldsmiths College, London.
Helen Jellicoe DCR BA MSc PhD	Clinical Psychologist, Department of Psychology, Kingston Hospital Trust, Kingston.
Athena S Leoussi MPhil PhD	Lecturer in Sociology, Department of Sociology, Reading University, Reading.
Jennie Lindon BA MPhil CPsychol	Chartered Psychologist, People Consulting Ltd, London.
Andrew D Worthington BSc MSc CPsychol	Senior Clinical Neurochologist, Rayners Hedge Rehabilitation Centre, Aylesbury.
David Marsland MA PhD FRSH	Professor of Social Sciences & Director, Centre for Evaluation Research, Brunel University, Isleworth.
Sheina Orbell PhD	Lecturer, Department of Psychology, Sheffield University, Sheffield.
Nigel Reeve BSc PGCE PhD	Senior Lecturer, School of Life Sciences, Roehampton Institute, London.
Frances A Reynolds BSc Dip Psych Counselling PhD	Senior Lecturer in Psychology, Department of Health Studies, Brunel University, Isleworth.
Kate Ridout MSc CPsychol RGN	Consultant Clinical Psychologist, Department of Pain Management, University College, London.
Gwilym Wyn Roberts MA DipCotSrot	Course Leader, School of Occupational Therapy, Department of Rehabilitation, University of London, London.

Nikki Rochford MSc MCSP SRP GD Biomech	Senior Lecturer, Department of Health Studies, West London Institute of Higher Education, London.
Carol Sherrard CPsychol	Department of Psychology, University of Leeds, Leeds.
Jane Singleton BA DPhil	Senior Lecturer in Philosophy, Division of Humanities, University of Hertfordshire, Watford.
Léonie Sugarman BSc MSc PhD	Chartered Occupational Psychologist, Senior Lecturer in Psychology, Department of Applied Social Sciences, University College of St Martin, Lancaster.
Lesley Vernon MSc DipNEd RGM RHU	Senior Lecturer, School of Midwifery and Family Health, Middlesex University, London.

PREFACE

This book provides a comprehensive overview of behavioural sciences for health professionals. As a single text it will support courses primarily at undergraduate level but it will also be for use as a primer for Masters degrees. It will be helpful to radiographers, physiotherapists, occupational therapists, dieticians, podiatrists and speech therapists.

The book aims to show how the behavioural sciences are specifically relevant to health care by linking theories to the clinical experience of health professionals. Each chapter provides a core text, learning activities, current references and summary points. The learning activities allow the reader to relate key topics to their specialist experience and to reflect on the relevance of the information to their working environment.

The book is divided into seven major sections:

Section I examines health from a psychological perspective. Models of health and illness provide a conceptual framework for the succeeding chapters which discuss the topics of stress, pain and disability in more detail. Each chapter discusses conceptual issues as well as providing guidelines for clinical management.

Section II takes a sociological perspective. The impact of changing patterns and perceptions of disease on health care are examined providing an important discussion on the way that health and illness are defined and negotiated. The succeeding chapters look at the effects of health on a society increasingly polarized by age and gender.

Sections III and IV provide a core of psychological knowledge important to working effectively and compassionately with people. Section III examines the processes of development from birth to old age and death. Section IV is an introduction to social psychology, looking at interpersonal perception and attitudes. With this deeper knowledge base, the health professional should learn to engage in richer communication and be more likely to influence attitudes and behaviour where these are relevant to good health and effective treatment.

Section V gives a comprehensive and clear outline of the highly specialised area of neuropsychology. Although complex, this topic is important to all professionals working with people who have suffered brain damage. It is particularly useful to those professionals directly involved in neurological rehabilitation.

Section VI discusses the ethics of health care. The principles and theories underlying ethics form a conceptual framework for the justification of ethical principles and their application to a clinical setting.

Section VII examines two important areas for clinical practice: research and evaluation. It includes a concise introduction to research, first looking at different approaches and then giving an outline of the research process itself. Health promotion is discussed allowing the reader to evaluate strategies and to see how these can be put into practice. The last two chapters continue the theme of evaluation looking at how healthcare systems are analysed and the performance of professionals can be monitored when professional competence and quality assurance are under consideration.

The book forms a coherent whole enabling the reader to see that a particular topic can be approached from several different perspectives. Its strength lies in the fact that health topics are discussed in psychological, sociological, political and economic terms thus helping the reader to gain a depth and breadth of knowledge and to appreciate a perspective as a point of view and not a point of fact. Whilst there are many links between chapters, each chapter stands alone and provides a comprehensive coverage of theory and practice in its own field.

The authors come from different backgrounds, some work in academic settings, others work as health practitioners thus allowing the editors to strike a balance between theory and practice. This core text, written especially for the professions allied to medicine provides a behavioural science foundation from which clinical excellence might develop.

Vickie Aitken
Helen Jellicoe

ACKNOWLEDGEMENT

We would like to acknowledge the support and encouragement in the development of this project from the Divisions of Physiotherapy and Radiography at the University of Hertfordshire.

SECTION I

Psychological Concepts

1

Models of Health and Illness

Frances Reynolds

LEARNING OBJECTIVES

After studying this chapter you should:

- Appreciate various conceptual models of health and illness
- Be able to identify facets of health, distinguishing between physical state and psychological well-being
- Be able to compare several psychological models of well-being
- Understand the extent to which psychosocial factors influence subjective well-being, physical health and recovery from illness
- Understand psychoimmunological processes
- Appreciate the treatment implications of biomedical and biopsychosocial models

INTRODUCTION

Contemporary healthcare is rooted firmly in medical science. However, in the later part of the twentieth century, in Western societies, the main threats to life are posed by lung cancer, cardiovascular disease, drug and alcohol abuse and road traffic accidents (Matarazzo, 1982). Such diseases and damage are viewed as potentially preventable as their development and course are open to influence by psychological and behavioural factors.

This chapter looks at the extent to which psychological factors may influence the onset and experience of illness, and the biological bases of these relationships. It explores some implications for clinical practice. There is a wealth of evidence about the role of psychosocial factors in health and illness, and this chapter links selected research issues to the diversity of models of health and well-being which shape current understanding and treatment approaches.

MODELS OF HEALTH AND DISEASE

Because health and illness profoundly affect the conduct and enjoyment of their lives, people have always striven to understand and control these states. Throughout history a variety of causal influences have been put forward as likely to contribute to ill-health, including transgression of moral codes, climatic conditions, pathogens, and possession by evil spirits (see Brannon and Feist (1992) for one discussion). These suggested causes imply very different models of health and illness and imply very different treatments or 'cures'.

What are conceptual models?

In order to make sense of observations in any field of enquiry they need to be related to each other by a theory or model. According to Popper (1959), 'Theories are nets cast to catch what we call "the world", to rationalise, to explain and to master it.' Until, for example, Darwin developed his theory of natural selection, numerous observations about animal biology, behaviour, extinctions and fossils remained disparate and puzzling. This theory, while still debated, offers linkages and explanation.

In the field of science and medicine, it is recognized that health and disease are complex biological states about whch there are a huge number of disparate observations and opinions. As with any complex phenomenon, a map, model or conceptual framework guides understanding of causal influences, and allows questioning and interpretation of evidence. A model inevitably acts as a conceptual lens for observations, focusing attention on some aspects of the phenomenon rather than others and highlighting some causal relationships for particular attention.

Kuhn (1962), in his account of scientific paradigms, emphasizes that scientific observations may fit *alternative* frames of reference. Choosing one model rather than another partly depends on the weight of confirming evidence, but also reflects researchers' acceptance of the *promise* of the chosen conceptual framework. Not only does a given model put forward certain questions as worth asking and offer a restricted set of explanatory concepts, but it is likely to exclude some issues. It is particularly important for health practitioners to consider their favoured model of health and disease, as this will be reflected in their chosen treatments and relationships.

In summary, a scientific model can be seen as a broad system of assumptions, beliefs and concepts, which gain plausibility both from empirical evidence and from the wider cultural and historical context. Previously accepted models may be queried and perhaps rejected if incompatible evidence accumulates. However, acceptance is based also on the more intuitive features of models such as their consistency, fertility (or problem-solving 'promise') and applicability.

The biomedical model

Over the last hundred years or so, the biomedical model has had enormous influence over medical research and practice. The key assumptions of the biomedical model are that:

- the body can be understood as a complex machine – with parts and processes that can malfunction;
- health and disease are contrasting states of the body machine, with health defined as the machine in good working order and with disease representing a deviation from normal biological functioning;
- illness is typically generated by assault from pathogens (viruses, bacteria, noxious chemicals and so on) although malfunctions may also be inherent in the body machinery (e.g. from 'faulty' genes);
- effective treatment for disease rectifies physiological functioning (usually by chemical means) or eliminates faulty parts by surgery or radiation.

These features characterize a mechanistic model of the person. It arguably suits the long-standing Western acceptance of mind–body dualism. The model also reflects late nineteenth century/early twentieth century confidence in the power of science to locate causal mechanisms, and to break down complex phenomena into simpler, more readily understandable and controllable parts. It is self-evidently a *powerful* model which has enabled the development of effective medical treatments, and has had a significant impact on commonsense concepts of illness (Engel, 1977). By attributing disease largely to environmental pathogens, the model has a humane aspect, taking blame and responsibility away from the 'victims' of disease.

However, there has been increasing argument over the last twenty or so years that the biomedical model is not entirely adequate (e.g. Ader, 1980; Engel, 1977). The criticisms can be summarized as follows:

- Some illnesses have psychological components, for example being triggered or exacerbated by emotional stress.
- Lifestyle and personality factors are increasingly regarded as playing a role in chronic diseases such as cardiovascular disease and cancers.
- Only some people become ill after exposure to pathogens, with susceptibility to infection heightened by stress.
- Efforts to promote personal responsibility for keeping fit and healthy and other preventative measures have influenced disease (especially cardiovascular) and decreased morbidity.

Research studies illustrating the above points can be found reprinted in Steptoe and Wardle (1994).

Biopsychosocial models of health and disease

The biopsychosocial model of health and illness – proposed by Engel (1977) and elaborated, for example, by Schwartz (1984) – goes beyond viewing the person as a complex physical machine but argues that behaviour, thoughts, and feelings may influence a physical state. This model accepts the role of pathogens in disturbing health, but additionally considers the role of behavioural, psychological and social influences on the person's well or ill state. In some ways it returns to an historically earlier acceptance of the interplay of biological and psychological factors in disease.

The remainder of this chapter explores in more detail the likely pathways of influence between psychological and physical state. However, in summary, the main assumptions of the biopsychosocial model are that the individual's susceptibility to disease, subjective experience of illness and recovery pattern are influenced by:

- *psychosocial factors* such as patterns of consumption, personality, coping resources, and lifestyle;
- *social and environmental* support or stress;
- *quality of relationships* with health professionals and healthcare systems;
- *immune functioning* which is open to modification by psychological factors.

Nevertheless, as with any model, acknowledgement is needed that the biopsychosocial model of health and illness can be misapplied:

- In emphasizing the role of personality and lifestyle in staying healthy, the individual's personal control over factors such as stress may be overestimated.
- A more active role in coping and rehabilitation may place an unacceptable burden on the ill person.
- Stronger norms for 'healthy' weight control, exercise, limited drug use and stress control may create less tolerance for those whose behaviour is regarded as health-jeopardizing.
- In a climate that regards individuals as having some influence over their health, the chronically ill may be portrayed as incurring cost to the health system rather than as deserving of care.

Once again, it is important to reiterate that models contain assumptions and values that shape one's perspective on complex processes.

PSYCHOLOGICAL MODELS OF HEALTH AND WELL-BEING

Whilst a biomedical framework has traditionally viewed health as the absence of disease, and treatment as the pursuit of a cure, as far back as 1946 the World Health Organization defined health as 'a state of complete physical, mental and social well-being, and not merely the absence of disease or infirmity'. This definition may be criticized for a certain lack of realism, but is useful in emphasizing health as a positive state, not only of physical but psychological well-being.

Downie *et al.* (1990) argue that well-being and health can usefully be regarded as *separate* concepts. Whilst acknowledging that individuals in poor physical health are less likely to experience psychological well-being, Downie *et al.* note that some individuals remain psychologically robust even in the face of debilitating disease. Conversely, some people experience distressing physical or psychological problems without an identifiable physical disease. In terms of total health, therefore, psychological well-being becomes a significant factor, open to influence by healthcare professionals.

What is psychological well-being?

If health professionals accept that psychological well-being is relevant to physical health, and may be a legitimate focus of therapy, it would be useful to have a conceptual model of 'psychological health' on which to base interventions. Rather different conceptualizations of well-being are suggested by the four main psychological models of the person, namely the psychoanalytic, humanistic, behavioural and cognitive.

All of these perspectives have been influenced by practitioners engaged in psychological therapy, and consequently have more to say about the conditions under which human beings become distressed or disturbed rather than well-adjusted and content. Despite these limitations, each model identifies some factors associated with well-being and suggests practical actions that health professionals may take to improve the quality of a person's care and well-being. A necessarily brief synopsis is presented here, but readers interested in pursuing this topic may find Cramer (1991) helpful.

It should be noted that most models take for granted that the person has an adequate environment, physical mobility and freedom from pain, when specifying the foundations of psychological well-being.

The psychoanalytic perspective

Freud was the founder of psychoanalysis, although the perspective has been modified by later analysts. Freud's theories were developed over time on the basis of his clinical experiences and self-insights, in order to provide some understanding of the development of neurotic preoccupations and behaviours. Given his focus on distress and neurosis, he presents a pessimistic view of the human mind, portraying it as beset by psychological forces largely beyond control (Schulz, 1990). The psychoanalytic model of the person recognizes the power of the unconscious in shaping behaviour and feelings – in both healthy and disturbed individuals.

Freud argued that disparities between inner needs and outer reality can generate anxiety against which the individual may erect defence mechanisms. Denial, repression ('burying' anxiety-provoking material in the unconscious mind) and regression (displaying more infantile behaviour) are understood as ways of coping with unacceptable threats. These may be adequate ways of coping in the short term but are often costly to psychological health in the longer term because active avoidance leads to failure to find solutions and perhaps a continued preoccupation with the source of stress. Freud saw the psychologically healthy person as relatively free from emotional conflict. When freed from conflict, the person experiences less need for defence mechanisms against anxiety and hence enjoys greater creativity and effective use of mental energy.

PSYCHOSOMATICS

In health settings, the psychoanalytic model has considerable relevance. The model suggests that some illnesses have a psychosomatic basis (Kaplan, 1985). Repressed emotions are viewed as associated not only with subjective distress but also with physical symptoms (somatizing). Freud noted many in whom physical problems (such as inability to swallow) were relieved once the underlying psychological conflict had been discovered (see Cramer (1991) for one discussion). Founding researchers in psychosomatic medicine, such as Alexander (1950), attempted to link specific diseases with particular personality characteristics. Although this approach is not quite as popular today, there remains a recognition that emotional trauma may be somatized. For example, a person may present with chronic abdominal pain or breathing difficulties following childhood sexual abuse (Draucker, 1992). The physical symptoms may be more effectively treated and the person more adequately returned to health if the deeper symbolic roots of some disorders are acknowledged.

The psychoanalytic model also provides some understanding of the individual's decision process to consult health professionals. The decision to seek medical help may be influenced not only by physical illness symptoms but also by emotional factors, particularly those about which the individual has little awareness (see Pitts (1991) for one discussion). Furthermore, once in the consulting room the person may select for description only the physical problems that seem 'safe' to disclose. Emotional concerns may be left until later in the consultation or omitted entirely. Unless the health professional is sensitive to this inner conflict, then the person may be unable to voice concerns of potential relevance to treatment and recovery.

The psychoanalytic model also highlights the power of emotional responses to illness and injury, which may interfere with physical recovery. Any condition which involves the loss of a body part or function (as in spinal or head injury, amputation or stroke), as well as terminal illness, may present with overwhelming anxiety. Denial, or regression (including crying, rocking and angry outbursts) may be triggered and it seems important that such reactions are acknowledged and worked with. Listening and relationship skills may be as helpful in the task of coping with the trauma as medical expertise. However, health professionals have an alarming tendency to 'treat normal, predictable emotional processes as if they were bacterial infections, that is, something to do battle with and "put down"' (Nichols, 1989). Health professionals also need to be alert to their own emotional responses to the predicaments or behaviour of others, for their psychological health and professional effectiveness may be jeopardized by continued denial or repression (Maslach and Jackson, 1982).

The main criticisms of the psychoanalytic approach concern its essential irrefutability (as so much concerns the unconscious mind) and its evidence, drawn from case studies of people in analysis. Nevertheless, it may help health professionals to take a more 'depth' view of a person's concerns and difficulties, and help them to acknowledge that recovery from illness may require more than physical repair.

Learning Activity 1 ◆ ◆ ◆

◆ The aim of this and the following activities is to analyse the situation of an ill person from different psychological perspectives. Consider the case of Mrs Kelly who is 32 years old and has multiple sclerosis. The symptoms have exacerbated since her pregnancy. Despite the assistance of carers to look after the baby, therapists find her angry, poorly motivated and continually complaining about the baby's safety. In turn, they regard her as a difficult, unrewarding person.

What features of this situation do you think the psychoanalytic perspective might emphasize and hope to change?

The behaviourist perspective

In contrast with the clinical basis of psychoanalysis, behaviourism originally drew upon experimental methods, particularly experiments with animals, which sought to tease out the factors that govern learning. However, in more recent years, the behaviourist perspective has been further developed through therapeutic work with people. Typically, the behavioural legacy is represented as a technology for changing behaviour, rather than a clear conceptualization of the basis of psychological health. It seems compatible with the biomedical model in viewing people as complex machines with rather little self-insight and capacity for self-direction. Nevertheless, it may be argued that the behaviourist model is in some ways optimistic about the capacity for change, whilst recognizing the extent to which this change may be under the influence of the environment rather than simply chosen by the individual.

The behaviourist perspective suggests that much behaviour is learned through the processes of classical and operant conditioning (see Gross (1992) for further introduction). Through classical conditioning, emotional and physical reflex responses may become triggered through a process of association with preceding events. For example, if severe back pain is experienced when walking to the railway station, the person may through association experience increased pain when waiting at the station in the future, or even when thinking about travelling by train. Such anticipatory pain (or anxiety) can place great restrictions on the person's daily activities and reduce well-being.

Operant conditioning refers to a process whereby behaviour is shaped by its consequences. Rewarding consequences tend to make the previous response more likely whereas unpleasant consequences tend to extinguish the behaviour in question. Many health-jeopardizing behaviours, being pleasurable, are positively reinforced. For example, 'unhealthy' foods are commonly enjoyed more than healthy substitutes; smoking may be valued as a stress reliever or as a means of social acceptance (e.g. among teenagers). Conversely, the person may find it difficult to persevere with medication or exercises that are followed by unpleasant side-effects.

HEALTH BEHAVIOUR

Researchers in health promotion have long recognized that little behavioural change occurs simply from education, but rather from providing people with 'know-how'; this ought to include identifying the immediate steps that must be taken in order to give up habits such as smoking or to adopt new habits such as exercise, and scheduling small reinforcements (self-treats or social praise) at regular intervals to maintain new habits. See the final chapter of Gatchel *et al.* (1989) for one discussion of behaviour modification of health-relevant beliefs and behaviours; also see Chapter 28 of this book.

The behavioural model also exposes the potentially rapid conditioning of negative behaviours such as sick role, dependency, or passivity by the reinforcing behaviours of health personnel. For example, the clinician who interrupts, who ignores non-verbal cues, or asks closed rather than open questions is soon likely to be relating to a person who offers brief, inadequate answers, asks few questions, and who feels dissatisfied with the encounter. Likewise a person discharged back to a family that reinforces dependence rather than independence may soon lose skills acquired in physiotherapy or occupational therapy, and may become, through an increasing sense of helplessness, vulnerable to depression (Seligman, 1975).

As with other models, the behaviourist perspective has limitations. The person is presented as a rather passive victim of circumstance. Furthermore, it is possible to overestimate the role of behavioural factors in illness, when aetiology reflects a multiplicity of interacting factors.

Although the behaviourist perspective does not explicitly specify the foundations of health and well-being, it nevertheless has relevance through providing a view of the person as open to change through experience, rather than fixed in personality and behaviour. Through its perspectives on learning, health professionals may find that behavioural interventions have a role to play in multifaceted approaches to treatment (for example, in pain management – see Blanchard and Andrasik (1985) for one discussion).

Research into behaviour modification has also provided a rationale and evidence for the effectiveness of behavioural strategies of stress management, as described in the next chapter.

Learning Activity 2 ◆ ◆ ◆

Continuing the case example above (Mrs Kelly): What features of her situation would a behaviourist approach emphasize and hope to change?

The humanistic perspective

In contrast to the rather pessimistic psychoanalytic and behaviourist theories of personality, which focused on the basis of emotional and behavioural disturbance, the humanistic theorists such as Rogers (1957) and Maslow (1954) placed more emphasis on the person's resources and capacity for well-being. Both Maslow and Rogers argued that people have an innate drive to self-actualize – that is, develop their potential skills and capacities – if the conditions in which they live are favourable. Specifically, people are said to flourish to the extent that they experience unconditional acceptance, respect, or love. In such conditions of tolerance, the person is free to choose and move towards a state of psychological growth and satisfaction with life.

However, because the need for love and acceptance is very great, people may be very sensitive to others' expectations and may behave in inauthentic ways in order to be accepted, losing touch with their own needs and feelings in the process. The human capacity and need to be creative can easily be stifled, to the detriment of psychological well-being.

THERAPEUTIC ALLIANCE

The humanistic vision of psychological health emphasizes that people have great resources for adapting and healing, if they are nourished in a psychological sense. The biomedical model which envisages the ill person as a complex machine awaiting repair ignores this vision. The humanistic model sees the psychologically healthy person as empowered to make personally meaningful choices, if listened to without judgement, and treated as an active partner in therapy. The humanistic model of therapy (originally applied to counselling but arguably more widely applicable) emphasizes the 'therapeutic alliance' (e.g. Dryden, 1989); in establishing an alliance, the therapist, as well as bringing his or her own expertise, needs to listen carefully in order to see the person's concerns, hopes and fears. It is only with respectful (non-judgemental) listening that the therapist can work *with* rather than *on* people, empowering rather than disempowering them, mobilizing their resources rather than leaving them unused.

Furthermore, the concept of the therapeutic alliance places emphasis on the qualities of respect and trust in therapy and the development of *shared* goals. People using the health service frequently complain that they are not treated as full partners, but are, for example, denied full information about their diagnosis, treatment options, drug side-effects and so on (see Stewart *et al.* (1995) for one discussion). However, the increasing use of psychological treatments such as counselling (Trijsburg *et al.*, 1992) and visualization (and other supportive treatments) in cancer and other therapies (Wells and Tschudin, 1994) indicates some move to encouraging individuals to play a more active role in their recovery/adjustment.

The humanistic perspective may be criticized as underestimating the influence of social and environmental factors in limiting an individual's choices and coping (see Gross (1992) for further discussion). It appears that not all individuals thrive on self-direction; indeed, research shows differences in patients' coping styles, with control and partnership not sought by everyone (Burger, 1989). Sensitivity to a person's needs is required; the humanistic perspective certainly encourages listening to, and acceptance of, their views and experiences.

Learning Activity 3 ◆ ◆ ◆

Continuing the case example above (Mrs Kelly): What features of her situation would a humanistic approach emphasize and hope to change?

The cognitive perspective

The cognitive perspective has grown in influence since the 1960s. It shares the above assumptions that people are open to change. Indeed, some cognitive theorists argue that people are at their psychologically most healthy when actively managing change and challenge. People are seen as information processors, living in a world of meaning which they construct (see Bannister and Fransella (1986) for further discussion). In this model, psychological well-being follows from holding relatively benign models of reality which serve to account well for experiences.

However, the person's model of reality can be bleak and self-defeating, holding little hope for the future and little prospect of pleasure. Cognitive therapists such as Beck (1976) argue that disturbances such as depression and anxiety result from these negative patterns of thinking.

HEALTH BELIEFS

The cognitive perspective argues that people live in a personally constructed world of meaning. Their beliefs and expectations about their illness or disability may be very different from that of the health professional, not least because the changes associated with the illness are personal rather than impersonally experienced. People have a need for information that is attuned to their concerns and questions, so alleviating anxiety and assisting problem-focused coping. Unstated catastrophizing thoughts about an illness can be more harrowing than reality-based information. Whilst recognizing that not everyone wants to be given control over decisions, the cognitive model of the person suggests that people usually benefit from realistic hope and some sense of influence over events (Steptoe, 1991). Those who feel that their condition is beyond their control soon feel hopeless and helpless, which bodes poorly for recovery (e.g. in cancer – Greer *et al.* (1979); also see Affleck *et al.* (1987)).

In conjunction with humanistic approaches, the cognitive perspective emphasizes the likely enhancement of well-being when people experience active and empathic listening, and are offered increased information and control over decision-making. As with the humanistic view, cognitive models of the person possibly underestimate the impact of social, environmental and genetic influences upon the individual. Nevertheless, cognitive–behavioural interventions are increasingly used to help individuals manage a range of psychological and physical conditions (see Bennet (1994) for discussion in the context of cardiovascular disease).

Learning Activity 4 ◆ ◆ ◆

Continuing the case example above (Mrs Kelly): What features would a cognitive approach emphasize and hope to change?

Review

The psychological models of the person introduced above are not mutually exclusive in practice. Their applicability depends upon factors such as the nature of a person's presenting problems, as well as the personal values of health professionals and their organization's philosophy. Psychological care of the person is likely to require multifaceted interventions and an appreciation of the varied foundations of well-being.

PSYCHOSOCIAL INFLUENCES ON HEALTH AND ILLNESS

Psychological models help to explain the foundations of well-being and also enhance understanding of why individuals differ in their susceptibility to particular diseases, their experience of illness, and in their physical recovery or adjustment following ill-health.

Susceptibility to disease: psychological and social factors

Since the rise of psychoanalysis and psychosomatic medicine, there has been interest in the influence of psychological and behavioural factors on the development of disease and disability. These factors may be grouped into:

- *behavioural and lifestyle influences on health*, such as patterns of exercise and smoking;
- *cognitive factors and attitudes*, such as appraisal of control, assessments of risk and vulnerability;
- *dispositional influences*, including personality and coping styles;
- *social factors*, such as support;
- *chronic stress* (considered in Chapter 2).

There have been several lengthy reviews of these areas of research in recent years (e.g. papers by Rodin and Salovey (1989), Taylor (1990); and textbooks by Brannon and Feist (1992), Sarafino (1994), Sheridan and Radmacher (1992)). There is only space here to discuss some key issues.

The influence of psychological factors upon health and susceptibility to disease can be indirect, via health-promoting or health-jeopardizing behaviour for example. Such influences will be explored below. They may also directly affect the functioning of the immune system, and the topic of psychoimmunity will be discussed later in the chapter.

BEHAVIOURAL AND LIFESTYLE FACTORS IN DISEASE SUSCEPTIBILITY

There are great methodological difficulties in establishing the risk to health of certain behaviours and lifestyles. Diseases have multivariate causation, with behavioural habits, genetic susceptibility, and exposure to environmental pathogens all involved. Moreover, behaviour which protects the individual from one type of disease may, by lengthening life, expose the individual to an elevated risk of other diseases.

Nevertheless, there is substantial evidence that unhealthy lifestyles are contributory factors in the two main killers in affluent societies – cancer and coronary heart disease (CHD).

It is recognized that the individual's susceptibility to coronary heart disease is increased by factors such as hypertension, smoking and high cholesterol. A middle-aged man with all risk factors faces a sixfold increase of the risk of heart attack (Syme, 1984). Susceptibility to stroke is increased by the same factors. These factors are unlikely to represent simple causes (as not all people at high risk develop disease), but longitudinal studies reveal that parental CHD history, chronic stress and Type A personality are common predictors (Rosenman *et al.*, 1975).

Some cancers, in particular lung cancer, are thought to relate to lifestyle and behaviour. It is estimated that about 30% of cancers are associated with tobacco use (Doll and Peto, 1981), and that diet also accounts for elevated incidence of digestive system cancers in Britain and US societies. More research is needed to establish whether (and to what extent) lifestyle and health behaviours can increase or decrease the individual's susceptibility to other chronic diseases such as Alzheimer's disease or rheumatoid arthritis.

Whilst it has been possible to identify health-jeopardizing behaviours (e.g. Farquhar *et al.*, 1984), knowledge of risks is not always enough to motivate people to change their behaviour. Some difficulties in changing health-relevant behaviour are as follows:

- 'Consuming' behaviours such as smoking, alcohol over-use and unwise eating are frequently viewed as highly pleasurable activities, providing immediate reinforcement and used as stress buffers.
- Some consuming behaviours such as smoking and drinking alcohol may be driven by physiological addiction.
- Individuals who feel healthy 'enough' may not give health a great priority when making behavioural choices, especially those in their teens embarking upon high-risk behaviour (Jessor and Jessor, 1982).
- The behaviour may have an important value to the individual for non-health reasons – for example, teenage smokers may follow the norms of their peer group in order to gain acceptance.
- There may be difficulties involved in adopting new behaviour, because it involves repeated decision-making (e.g. to cope with stressful events with a different strategy), altered self-image, and possibly social rejection.

Although health promotion activities can be considered as benign attempts to improve people's health, they can degenerate into 'healthism' – it may be regarded as an oppressive and disempowering requirement for the individual to consider health as a priority over other values.

So if the health professional is to avoid punitive victim-blaming (Crawford, 1977), how may a model of health and disease which acknowledges behavioural factors be used positively? Essentially this knowledge can motivate health professionals to conduct health education; to teach stress management strategies, reducing reliance on unhealthy stress buffers; and to recommend other interventions such as support groups which encourage and support behavioural change. If people are successfully motivated to change behaviour, they may not only reduce health risk factors but also increase their sense of control over the course of illness, which is an important contributor to psychological well-being. Moreover, an increase in physical well-being (reduction in pain and other symptoms, increased mobility) may result from practice of healthy behaviours (e.g. exercise in MS – Cioffi (1991)). Thus, not only can behavioural change reduce susceptibility to disease, it may contribute to recovery as well.

COGNITIVE FACTORS IN SUSCEPTIBILITY TO DISEASE

Evidence that behaviour patterns influence health does not necessarily cast doubt on the biomedical model. It is easy to see that poor quality fuel (i.e. consumption of tobacco, drugs, poor food) and lack of regular maintenance (e.g. in the form of exercise) may cause the body machine to work less than optimally. However, the biomedical model copes poorly with evidence that cognitive and dispositional factors also influence health.

Cognitive models suggest that people respond very differently according to the meanings that they place on events. So how may people's attitudes, beliefs and concepts affect their health and susceptibility to disease? Researchers have focused on several issues, including how people appraise stressful events and personal risk, whether they perceive themselves to be in control, and their sense of self-efficacy and self-esteem.

Appraisals of stressful events

More detailed discussion of appraisal processes in stress is provided in Chapter 2. Essentially, different individuals may experience objectively similar situations (such as examinations or clinical investigations) in different ways according to whether they evaluate the event as threatening and their coping strategies as adequate. Where values and appraisals lead to long-term stress and physiological changes, health is likely to be at risk.

Appraisals of risk

Behaviour such as smoking, drinking and eating in excess is continued by many people despite some knowledge that it damages health. It appears that simple information about health risks is not enough to prompt people into changing behaviour. The Health Belief Model (Becker, 1974; Janz and Becker, 1984) argues that people only tend to act on information about health risks if:

- they judge themselves to be at personal risk of a particular disease;
- they assess the likely disease as serious;
- they feel that the rewards outweigh the costs of changing their behaviour.

Personal appraisal of risk is known to be highly overoptimistic, with most healthy people (especially youngsters) feeling invulnerable (e.g. Weinstein, 1987) and so unlikely to engage in preventive behaviour.

People also tend to believe that their personal habits follow the norm. This has been termed the 'false consensus bias' (Ross *et al.*, 1977). Feeling socially supported in one's behaviour (smoking, drug use, workaholic habits) may further reduce the perceived need for change (see also Chapters 16 19).

Perceived control

Cognitive therapists have argued that a common cognitive feature of negative states such as depression and anxiety is lack of perceived control (learned helplessness or learned hopelessness). Conversely, those who experience a firm sense of internal control typically achieve a higher degree of psychological well-being (Scheier *et al.*, 1989; Taylor *et al.*, 1984). Many constructs such as internal locus of control (Rotter, 1966), hardiness (Korbasa, 1982) and optimism (Scheier and Carver, 1985) may be describing this key sense of control over events. There is evidence from both animal and human studies that a chronic sense of helplessness may predate poor health (Seligman, 1975), perhaps via poor self-care, sensitization to stress, and direct immune system damage.

Self-efficacy beliefs

Self-efficacy refers to a belief in one's own capability of achieving a desired outcome by performing appropriate behaviour (Bandura, 1977, 1986). High self-efficacy beliefs tend to be associated with successful behavioural change, treatment compliance and coping (for example, with pain – Bandura *et al.* (1987)). Perhaps this is because such beliefs are based realistically on knowledge of previous successes and failures. However, dispositional optimism and pessimism, and the attitudes of others, also shape self-efficacy beliefs. Low self-efficacy beliefs (self-defeating expectations) may be based on recall of past failures, misperceptions, or the negative and perhaps faulty appraisals of others. There is increasing acknowledgement that unless people believe that they can accomplish a target, they may rapidly give up the difficult task of behaviour change. Negative self-efficacy beliefs can thus sabotage a person's efforts to change behaviour (e.g. smoking cessation) or comply with long-term medical treatment. Focused attempts to improve self-efficacy contribute to successful behaviour management (Damrosch, 1991).

Self-esteem

High self-esteem appears to confer resilience against stress (Hobfoll and Lieberman, 1987). Low self-esteem, perhaps through association with a poor body image, may contribute to health-jeopardizing behaviour such as over-consumption or addiction. There has been some evidence that self-esteem can be improved in conjunction with physical health, by increasing levels of exercise (Sonstroem, 1984). Exercise may influence self-concept in several ways, such as increasing levels of energy, enhancing a sense of control and mastery, improving body image, and elevating mood through direct effects on brain biochemistry (Hogan, 1989).

In summary, cognitive factors may increase or decrease the individual's commitment to healthy behaviours. For further discussion of cognitive issues related to health, see Marteau (1989).

PERSONALITY AND EMOTIONAL FACTORS IN SUSCEPTIBILITY TO DISEASE

Long-term personality factors are recognized to have a role in disease, and these long-term dispositions would seem even harder to modify than specific habits such as smoking. Early researchers in psychosomatic medicine attempted to locate prototypical personalities for each major disease (e.g. Alexander, 1950). This approach has declined in popularity, but there is a remaining interest in whether certain personality traits may act as risk factors for specific diseases, and debate about the likely causal pathways.

Large numbers of traits have been the subject of investigation, but most attention has been given to whether there are coronary-prone and cancer-prone personalities or behaviour patterns.

The Type A personality or behaviour pattern (TABP)

This refers to a complex of behaviours and emotions, including muscle tension, rapid movements and speech, competitiveness, impatience, aggressiveness and hostility. Anger and hostility may be the traits most damaging to cardiovascular health (Dembroski and Costa, 1987). TABP was originally considered as a rather stable trait constellation, but more recent investigations indicate that such personality traits rarely occur persistently, in all circumstances, but may be elicited by stressful circumstances. Thus Type A persons tend to:

- manifest their tendencies to hostility and competitiveness to a marked degree only when under stress (Rosenman *et al.*, 1988);
- show greater autonomic reactivity to stress (Matthews *et al.*, 1986);
- show greater susceptibility to heart disease only when stress is prolonged.

See the review by Booth-Kewley and Friedman (1987) for further details.

Cancer-prone personality

Personalities very different from the impatient, aggressive, striving TABP seem to have a greater susceptibility to cancer. In some studies, passive, emotionally repressed personalities have been shown to experience comparatively high rates of death from cancer, in both older and younger samples; a pattern even more marked in stressed groups (Grossarth-Maticek *et al.*, 1986).

How personality traits and emotional style affect future health remains debated. Possible links include:

- a direct impact on physiology such as the immune system;
- participation in health-jeopardizing behaviours (e.g. increasing 'oral' habits);
- illness behaviours (e.g. encouraging infantile dependency).

A word of caution is needed, because prospective studies of personality and disease are few. It remains possible that some personality traits and emotional styles may represent responses to long-standing, perhaps insidious, disease processes rather than causal factors.

What are the implications of evidence which links personality and emotional styles to disease susceptibility? Certainly it is unlikely that health professionals have time or inclination to strive for major psychotherapeutic change. However, they may find ways of alerting people to their vulnerability in the face of stress, perhaps directly teaching stress management techniques which modify habitual but dysfunctional coping patterns, or referring them to a professional counsellor to assist them in working through the difficult emotions which may be impeding recovery or increasing susceptibility to further illness.

PSYCHOSOCIAL FACTORS IN DISEASE VULNERABILITY

Research has shown that a person who experiences a good measure of acceptance and a number of valued social roles is likely to enjoy greater self-esteem and resilience compared with the isolated individual. Lack of social support is known to be associated with depression (Brown and Harris, 1978). Furthermore, the sudden loss of a valued social relationship (for example, through bereavement) increases the likelihood of physical illness (Parkes *et al.*, 1969). However, there is considerable debate regarding the key elements of social support and the circumstances in which it contributes to health (Wallston *et al.*, 1983). This is covered in more detail in Chapter 2.

There are many influences on health from the person's immediate social environment (ignoring for the moment the larger cultural context). Families provide social role models and reinforcements for health-relevant behaviour such as smoking and eating patterns. Individual decisions to change behaviour, and to seek medical help, can be influenced by the family to good or poor effect. For example, in cardiac rehabilitation, relatives may need to learn how to interpret the somatic effects of exercise in positive ways, in order to help catastrophizing thoughts which will sabotage the rehabilitation programme (Taylor *et al.*, 1985).

Learning Activity 5 ◆ ◆ ◆

In the light of the biopsychosocial relationships discussed so far, reflect on what 'being healthy' means to you.

PSYCHOIMMUNITY

The discussion above favours the biopsychosocial model in indicating that cognitions, personality, behaviour patterns and interpersonal experiences may all influence physical as well as mental health. Various mechanisms have been suggested whereby psychosocial factors may promote or undermine biological health:

- health-relevant behaviours (e.g. adequate exercise) which affect metabolism;
- consumption patterns (e.g. diet, smoking, alcohol and drug use) which alter general metabolism or specific organ functions;
- chronic stress, leading to reactivity of the autonomic nervous system and wear and tear on specific organs (see Chapter 2);
- direct psychological effects on the immune system (via the central nervous and endocrine systems).

This section looks at the emerging field of psychoimmunology, considering the processes whereby psychological factors can influence immunity. This perspective is somewhat incompatible with the biomedical model of health and disease, with its focus upon the body as a complex machine. At most, the biomedical model regards psychological influences as indirect, operating on bodily functions through influences such as long-standing patterns of consumption or chronic stress. However, more direct connections between biological, psychological and social processes have been identified by research into the immune system (Baker, 1987).

The immune system is composed of many body organs and cells acting together, including the lymphatic system, bone marrow, thymus and spleen. The body's defences occur at several levels (see Figure 1.1):

- *outer barriers* (skin and mucous membranes to trap incoming particles);
- *nonspecific immune system responses*, including (i) inflammation (increased blood flow to damaged or infected parts, and enzyme production to destroy invaders and damaged body cells), and (ii) phagocytosis (enveloping and ingesting of foreign particles by white blood cells or macrophages);
- *specific* (acquired) *immune system responses.*

The body learns to recognize invaders in order to destroy them more rapidly on subsequent exposure,

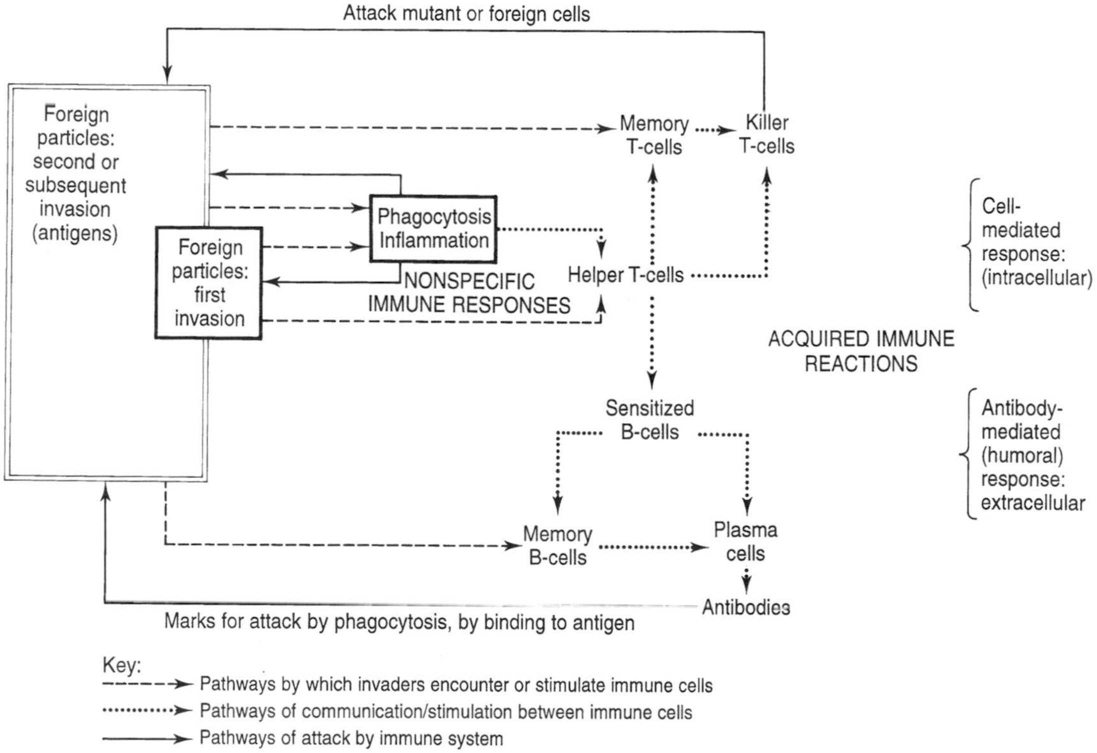

Figure 1.1 *Simplified nonspecific and specific immune pathways (adapted from Starr and Taggart, 1984)*

using two systems (cellular and humoral/antibody-mediated immunity).

Essential to the immune response is the lymphatic system, which interconnects with the blood circulation, and bathes tissues with lymph. Lymph is mainly plasma fluid and white blood cells (lymphocytes), more selective than macrophages, and classified into several types, including T-lymphocytes, B-lymphocytes, killer (K) cells and natural killer (NK) cells. These operate a search and destroy mission on foreign particles as well as on damaged body cells. The debris from this mission is cleaned from the lymph in the lymph nodes and tonsils.

On first contact with invading particles such as bacteria or fungi, the nonspecific immune system is triggered to deal with and destroy the foreign material. Macrophages attempt to engulf and destroy the invaders. T-lymphocytes in contact with the invader become sensitized and develop recognition sites on their surfaces. As indicated in Figure 1.1, the helper T-cells release chemical messengers, including interleukins and interferons, stimulating the production of killer T-cells to attack the invader. Some of these T-cells remain as memory T-cells awaiting the subsequent arrival of the particular foreign substance. This process is termed 'cell-mediated immunity', and is most effective against intracellular disturbances (from viruses, parasites, fungi or mutated body cells). It is the system thought to be more alert to and active against the presence of cancerous body cells.

Helper T-cells, when sensitized to the presence of a foreign substance, also trigger B-cell lymphocytes to differentiate into plasma cells which secrete antibodies (each specific to a particular invader). Antibodies are proteins called immunoglobulins which attach to invading particles, signalling the presence of the invader and contributing to its destruction. After the infection has been overcome, some of these plasma cells remain as vigilant memory B-cells. If the body is again exposed to the substance (now regarded as an antigen), the secondary immune response is triggered, with the antibodies 'recognizing' and binding to the particles, therefore speeding the destruction process. The antibody-mediated (or humoral) immune response is more effective against invaders in the bloodstream and body fluids, rather than those which have penetrated cells.

The immune system not only has a vital role in repelling and dealing with invading organisms, but is also thought to be involved in immune surveillance – that is, detecting and destroying cancerous cells through responding to antigens on their surfaces (Antoni, 1987). Patients with compromised immunity are more likely to face the growth of tumours. In people with AIDS, for example, Karposi's sarcoma is a common occurrence. Cancer cells appear to be particularly targeted by K and NK cells.

Traditionally, the immune system is portrayed as a property entirely of the body, so how may psychological factors affect it?

Considerable research has been carried out to investigate the impact of psychological state with immune system function, and the role of immune function in disease onset. However, it is rarely possible to show conclusively that psychologically compromised immunity increases vulnerability to disease, as disease onset is not likely immediately to follow immune compromise and may also reflect a complex array of factors including genetic susceptibility and exposure to specific pathogens. (For a discussion of factors contributing to onset of rheumatoid arthritis, see McFarlane and Brooks (1990).)

Several studies confirm that immune system competence (whether measured by T-cell, NK-cell, B-cell or antibody activity) declines during periods of chronic stress. For example, antibody levels have been shown to decline during term-time for students (Jemmott *et al.*, 1983). Medical students show a variety of negative immunological changes during examination periods (Glaser *et al.*, 1985, 1986). Such changes are particularly significant given medical students' considerable familiarity with examinations and hence opportunity to develop coping strategies. Kiecolt-Glaser *et al.* (1987) have shown immune decline during other, less chosen forms of chronic stress – for example, among carers of relatives with Alzheimer's disease. Experiences such as bereavement which are likely to provoke long-term feelings of helplessness are commonly associated with immunosuppression (Bartrop *et al.*, 1977; Jemmott and Locke, 1984; Irwin *et al.*, 1987).

However, research indicates that objective stress may have less biological impact than perceived stress. For example, academic or examination stressors seem to provoke greater immune suppression and likelihood of infection in those individuals who lack social support (Kiecolt-Glaser *et al.*, 1984) and those with higher motivation, parental pressure or previously poor academic records (Jemmot *et al.*, 1983, 1990). On the other hand, immune function is more likely to be maintained in those who react to stress with active coping strategies rather than passive helplessness (Kiecolt-Glaser and Glaser, 1988).

This evidence is crucial to the argument that personality, cognitive and emotional variables (rather

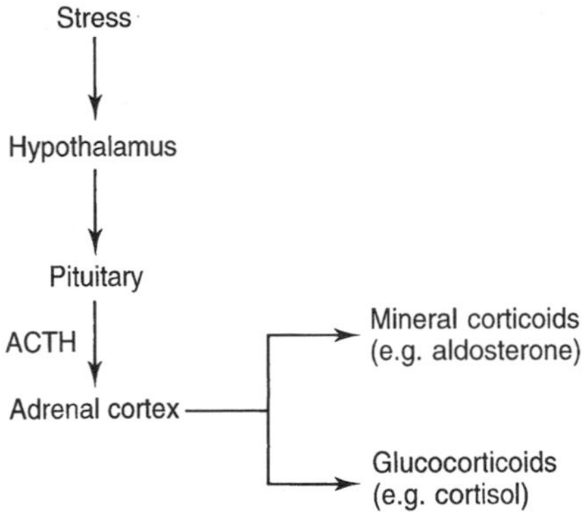

Figure 1.2 *The hypothalamic–pituitary–adrenocortical system*

than environmental events alone) influence the immune system, and hence susceptibility to disease.

The hypothalamus may provide a critical connection between central nervous system functioning, the endocrine system and the immune system (Sarafino, 1994). In cases of inescapable stress (associated with helpless behaviour), the hypothalamic–pituitary–adrenocortical system is activated (see Figure 1.2). Mineralocorticoids regulate blood pressure, for example by controlling the balance of sodium and potassium in body fluids; glucocorticoids are anti-inflammatory and control blood pressure, regulate blood glucose, and have an immunosuppressive effect.

Under chronic stress, the feedback loop appears disrupted and the body seems to adapt to high levels of cortisol (hyperadaptosis). High levels of cortisol have several adverse effects on the immune system, depressing phagocytosis, natural killer cell activity, and T-lymphocyte function.

There are likely to be additional pathways connecting neurological, endocrine and immune function. For example, activity in the autonomic nervous system (reactive to perceived stress) can affect the thymus gland, thereby affecting immunity as the thymus is implicated in the maturation of T-cells (Jemmott and Locke, 1984).

Research into psychoimmunity carries implications for treatment and preventive work (Glaser *et al.*, 1985). For example, combating stress reactions, by relaxation, visualization or other methods, may allow the immune system to recover by eliciting parasympathetic autonomic nervous system activity, decreased release of cortisol and the repair of damaged tissues. This argument is taken seriously by many with HIV who attempt to maintain psychological well-being and physical fitness in order to provide the best possible support to the compromised immune system. However, evidence is mixed concerning the effectiveness of psychosocial interventions in delaying onset of AIDS (Kiecolt-Glaser and Glaser, 1988).

IMPLICATIONS OF BIOPSYCHOSOCIAL PERSPECTIVES FOR PROMOTING RECOVERY

Psychological and behavioural factors have been shown to influence the body's susceptibility to illness and recovery. Psychological interventions are relevant, therefore, in promoting positive health and well-being as well as in alleviating illness.

Biopsychosocial models see the person not as a passive machine in need of manipulation but as a self-aware partner in his or her own care. If adopting the biopsychosocial model, health professionals attempt to engage in holistic treatment of a *person* who is ill rather than a defective body part or process. Holistic care tends to emotional and cognitive hurt as well as physical problems. The psychological aspects of health care are always important whether or not physical health is likely to be restored. Helping people to *feel* better is worthwhile in itself as illness and injury commonly elicit emotional conflict, anxiety, changes in social roles and reduced self-esteem. Health professionals need to develop, as an integral part of assessment and treatment, an understanding of how people perceive their illnesses and their coping strategies. Research into psychoimmunity supports a further argument that psychological experiences may affect *biological* processes, and hence that psychological care may affect physical recovery processes.

Health professionals can contribute to psychological care and objective recovery through good communication with more deliberate and empathic listening; providing appropriate and honest information; enhancing the person's control over decision-making; and by acknowledging the cognitive and emotional aspects of physical illness (Bennett, 1994; Stewart *et al.*, 1995).

Appropriate and honest information

This needs to be given with sensitivity as to the person's state of mind and questions; in comprehensible terminology; in suitable amounts, repeated as necessary, given that anxiety tends to block understanding and recall (Ley, 1988; Nichols, 1984,

1989; Mazzucca, 1982). Different media can be used to repeat information; for instance, verbal explanation may be supplemented by written material that can be reconsidered later.

Being listened to

Failure to listen to a person's concerns is a common source of dissatisfaction (MacLeod-Clark, 1985; Maguire, 1985). Health professionals may moderate their own stress levels by disregarding others' distress, but with the result that people feel uncared for, more anxious or depressed, burdened with feelings of shame and isolation, and less likely to cope. Interview schedules need to include questions about worries, social support, coping strategies and so on, and time is needed for exploration of these issues. If there is any doubt about a persons' state of mind, then a request for a more detailed psychological assessment may be made with a view to more specialized psychological treatment.

Enhanced perceived control

Opportunities to participate in treatment decisions, skills for managing practical tasks, and strategies for managing stress reactions all contribute to a sense of control and self-esteem. Training in practical skills such as use of a wheelchair, or adapted equipment, forms an important, clearly accepted element of many treatment programmes. However, introduction of the need for such skills needs to be handled sensitively. It is inappropriate for an aid such as a wheelchair, for example, to be produced almost directly after a diagnosis, before any time has been allowed for processing the information and adjustment. Cognitive and emotional strategies also contribute to perceived control, adjustment and the reintegration of a new identity. See Stewart *et al.* (1995) for further evidence regarding the impact of 'patient-centred' communication on recovery.

More specific options for psychosocial intervention may be based on any of the psychological perspectives outlined previously. The choice of approach depends in part on the main problems identified during assessment. For example, health-jeopardizing behaviour, anxiety or pain might be effectively managed through a cognitive–behavioural approach which would help to identify new coping strategies. People experiencing the distress of grief (in the face of chronic or terminal illness, for example) would probably be helped by a less directive, counselling approach in which painful feelings are acknowledged and explored. On some occasions, a 'mixed' approach may be most appropriate (e.g. see Trijsburg *et al.* (1992) on evaluating the psychological treatment of people with cancer.

Some specific interventions associated with the behavioural perspective (relaxation training), humanistic/psychoanalytic perspectives (counselling) and cognitive perspective (cognitive reframing) are described below.

Thus relaxation skills can help to control anxiety, and pain, and appear to promote recovery. Emotional disclosure in the context of a trusted relationship can significantly reduce stress. Cognitive distraction and cognitive reframing (where the patient is supported in finding some positive aspect to a negative experience, or in challenging catastrophizing thoughts) are skills from cognitive behaviour therapy that have wide application in the treatment of physical illness. Readers interested in details of psychological and 'alternative' adjuncts to medical treatment are recommended to Wells and Tschudin (1994).

Relaxation training

Physiologically it is impossible to be both anxious and deeply relaxed at the same time. Hence relaxation training is a behaviour therapy which seeks to reduce anxiety by practice of releasing muscle tension. There are several methods (Wells and Tschudin, 1994). Progressive relaxation invites the person to tense briefly and then relax for longer the main muscle groups of the body, usually starting with the feet and progressing up to the head. With practice, the technique may combat generalized anxiety as well as specific fears (e.g. of surgery). Systematic deep breathing provides another route to relaxation. Biofeedback may also encourage sensitivity to body tension and help the person modify stress reactions.

Relaxation skills seem to work both on a biological level, increasing parasympathetic nervous system activity, and at a cognitive–emotional level, increasing a sense of control. Well-practised relaxation responses help in the control of pain as well as anxiety management, and may assist the person to cope not only with illness symptoms but with unpleasant treatment side-effects (as in chemotherapy). Some practitioners teach relaxation in conjunction with meditation or visualization to increase the sense of psychological control and self-awareness.

Research indicates that relaxation may have effects not only on subjective distress but also immune function, for example in the elderly (Kiecolt-Glaser *et al.*, 1985) and in examination students (Kiecolt-Glaser *et al.*, 1986). In the last study, individuals varied considerably in the time they devoted to relaxation practice, and it was found that higher levels of T-lymphocytes occurred in those who practised for longer.

Relaxation training may also improve NK cell activity – shown in some studies to decline in people with active rheumatoid arthritis, and increased by relaxation training (Kiecolt-Glaser *et al.*, 1985). Use of audio tapes to promote relaxation (with guided imagery) has been associated with reduced anxiety, cortisol levels and improved wound healing following surgery (Holden-Lund, 1988). Relaxation with guided imagery has also been shown to reduce nausea and anxiety of people awaiting chemotherapy for cancer (Burish *et al.*, 1987). Relaxation training may be an important first step in pain management although not all individuals find sufficient pain relief through this method alone (Blanchard and Andrasik, 1985).

Counselling interventions

It is unlikely that health professionals have the time or inclination to offer formal counselling or psychotherapy. However, this does not preclude using counselling skills in the care of people who are ill.

Good communication, characterized by active listening, warmth, and acceptance of emotional expression, can help the person (and carers) to feel heard and supported (Stewart *et al.*, 1995). This cathartic experience may be helpful at a psychological level in controlling stress, reducing anxiety and a sense of isolation. For people facing terminal illness or any condition involving the loss of a body part or function, grief is a likely response. Not only may valued abilities and functions be mourned, but also there may be grief at the loss of inner peace, dignity, valued roles and future expectations (see Wilson (1989) for additional discussion). Individuals differ in their grief reactions and do not necessarily pass through a fixed sequence of stages. Nevertheless it may be useful for health professionals to be aware of the psychological tasks (termed 'griefwork') that assist in adjustment and well-being.

According to Worden (1991), there are four major tasks in adjusting to loss or bereavement:

- accepting the reality of the loss;
- experiencing the pain of grief;
- adjusting to a world in which the valued person (or function or body part) is absent (which may involve learning new skills or adapting to new roles);
- construction of a new identity by reinvesting emotional energy in new relationships and roles.

Health professionals often have difficulty accepting intense and lengthy griefwork. For them, the medical condition may be encountered routinely, and its symptoms, treatment and prognosis well known. For the person concerned, the experience is far from routine and may provoke considerable emotional, social and identity upheaval (e.g. Hersen and Van Hasselt, 1990). Therapeutic listening that facilitates griefwork can be as helpful to the task of coping as medical expertise.

Some research indicates that disclosure of emotional pain is not only subjectively helpful but also brings about biological benefits. For example, Pennebaker (1988) reported how immune system functioning and subsequent health in students were measurably enhanced through writing about previously undisclosed traumatic experiences, even though the initial release of feelings was upsetting.

Counselling which included relaxation training has been demonstrated to contribute to reduced disease activity in rheumatoid arthritis as well as decreasing pain and anxiety (Bradley *et al.*, 1987). People in this study also appeared to gain a long-term coping strategy in that improvement was maintained over a six-month follow-up period. It is accepted by psychoanalytic models of the person that repressed emotions may lead not only to distress but physical symptoms. Psychoimmunity research provides further impetus for studying biological responses to counselling interventions.

Cognitive interventions

Illness always has a cognitive dimension. It commonly provokes worry which can exacerbate pain or other physical symptoms, and the person may experience uncertainty, a lack of information, and an altered self-image. Cognitive therapy attempts to challenge the negative and self-defeating thoughts that fuel depression and anxiety. Cognitive distraction (refocusing of attention away from distressing thoughts or sensations) and cognitive reframing (where the person is supported in finding some positive aspect to a negative experience, or in challenging catastrophizing thoughts) are skills from cognitive behaviour therapy that have wide application. Such skills may be needed beyond the initial adjustment period, and may reduce the likelihood of 'anticipatory disability' – self-imposed restrictions on activity through fear of worsening the symptoms or the disease itself (Cioffi, 1991).

For example, in cardiac rehabilitation, a person may be reluctant to engage in exercise if interpreting sensations of exertion as life-threatening. If such catastrophizing thoughts are identified and challenged, the rehabilitation process is facilitated.

Cognitive approaches are often combined with behavioural techniques (e.g. for enhancing coping with pain) and there is some evidence for long-term benefits following cognitive–behavioural therapy (e.g. Kerns *et al.*, 1986; also see Chapters 3 and 4).

Further details about cognitive behaviour therapy and applications may be found in Dryden and Rentoul (1991) and Dobson and Craig (1996).

Learning Activity 6 ◆ ◆ ◆

Practise taking a broader psychological approach to people who are physically ill. What psychological issues might be relevant in the examples given below:

a a person who is attending regularly because of a degenerative non-life-threatening condition
b a person who becomes panicky/hysterical during a necessary diagnostic procedure
c a person who attends regularly but whose mood seems to be getting lower and lower with each visit
d a person who seems well-adjusted and has enjoyed reasonable health, but who is now attending for what to you is a relatively simple and routine procedure
e a person who knows they are attending for investigation to see whether they have a serious malignant condition
f a person who has just been told they have a life-threatening condition
g a person who is failing to make the progress expected for the treatment being offered
h a person who seems not to want to help themselves get better
i a person attending for a health check for insurance purposes

In the context of your normal clinical setting, what could you do to go beyond your technical role (i.e. assessment, examination, treatment) and manage the *person* rather than simply their medical condition. (In some, not necessarily all, of the examples above, failure to acknowledge the person would undermine your technical effectiveness.)

SUMMARY

This chapter has suggested some possible pathways of influence between the psychological, social and biological aspects of the person, elaborating the biopsychosocial model of health and disease. Some suggestions are offered for psychological interventions as treatments in their own right or as adjuncts to medical treatment. There are many research studies that reveal the biological as well as psychological impact of good communication.

Psychologically oriented interventions may support physical therapies in several ways. They may help to control anxiety reactions, so modifying endocrine secretions and other biological stress responses. They may also be regarded as promoting psychological well-being through increasing a sense of control, over symptoms or future health state. Perceived control provides a key underpinning to psychological well-being according to cognitive models of the person. A therapeutic alliance may also create a sense of support or 'holding' (Winnicott, 1965), offering opportunities for people to be honest about their fears and other feelings, reducing conflict and shame, and preserving self-esteem. Behavioural interventions can provide additional coping strategies, through reinforcing health-enhancing behaviour.

The chapter has emphasized the relevance of models of health and illness to health care. The preferred model adopted by health professionals will determine their treatment options as well as their relationships with people who are ill.

Thus in the case of a person given the diagnosis of myalgic encephalopathy (ME), a practitioner adopting the biomedical model might recommend rest to a body that is viewed as fatigued by a viral infection. A practitioner adopting a biopsychosocial view may be additionally concerned by social and behavioural influences over the onset and course of the condition. There would be some examination of the reinforcers which may maintain the person in the 'sick role'. The cognitive dimensions of the illness such as assumptions, goals and self-image would be deemed relevant to treatment plans. Such considerations, facilitated by the practitioner's model of health and illness, might lead to the view that a graded programme of activity would be more effective than rest in reducing symptoms (see Mechanic (1993) for further discussion about interventions).

The many models of health and well-being available in medicine and psychology encourage health professionals to view illness and disease from a more person-centred perspective. Unconscious processes, behavioural habits, perceived stress, coping styles, social roles and support all play a part in the illness experience and recovery process. When health professionals harness the person's psychological and social resources, the therapeutic alliance so established may be more effective than passive biomedical treatment, particularly in managing chronic conditions.

Key Points

- Biopsychosocial models of health and illness have greater fertility and applicability than biomedical models for some conditions.
- Psychological well-being can be described in different ways by different models of the person.
- Physical health and psychological well-being can be related or independent.
- Psychological, social and biological processes can be linked indirectly (through behaviour) or directly (through the immune system).
- Chronic stress and lack of coping are not only distressing but also adversely affect the endocrine and immune systems.
- Psychological interventions can be used as treatments in their own right or as adjuncts to medical treatment.
- Good communication, relaxation and counselling have biological as well as psychological effects.

References

Ader, R. (1980). Psychosomatic and psychoimmunologic research. *Psychosomatic Medicine,* **42**: 307–21.

Affleck, G., Tennen, H., Pfeifer, C. and Fifield, J. (1987) Appraisals of control and predictability in adapting to a chronic disease. *Journal of Personality and Social Psychology,* **53**: 273–9.

Alexander, F. 1950: *Psychosomatic Medicine.* New York: Norton.

Antoni, M. (1987). Neuroendocrine influences in psychoimmunology and neoplasia: a review. *Psychology and Health,* **1**: 3–24.

Baker, G. (1987). Invited review: psychological factors in immunity. *Journal of Psychosomatic Research,* **31**: 1–10.

Bandura, A. (1977). Self-efficacy: towards a unifying theory of behavioural change. *Psychological Review,* **84**: 191–215.

Bandura, A. (1986). *Social Foundations of Thought and Action: A Social Cognitive Theory.* Englewood Cliffs, NJ: Prentice Hall.

Bandura, A., O'Leary, A., Taylor, C., Gauthier, J. and Gossard, D. (1987). Perceived self-efficacy and pain control: opioid and nonopioid mechanisms. *Journal of Personality and Social Psychology,* **53**: 563–71.

Bannister, D. and Fransella, F. (1986). *Inquiring Man,* 3rd edn. London: Croom Helm.

Bartrop, R., Lazarus, L., Luckhurst, E., Kiloh, L. and Penny, R. (1977). Depressed lymphocyte function after bereavement. *Lancet,* **1**: 834–6.

Beck, A. (1976). *Cognitive Therapy and the Emotional Disorders.* New York: International Universities Press.

Becker, M. (1974). The health belief model and personal health behaviour. *Health Education Monographs,* **2:** 324–508.

Bennett, P. (1994). *Counselling for Heart Disease.* Leicester: BPS Books.

Blanchard, E. and Andrasik, F. (1985). *Management of Chronic Headaches: A Psychological Approach.* New York: Pergamon Press.

Booth-Kewley, S. and Friedman, H. (1987). Psychological predictors of heart disease: a quantitative review. *Psychological Bulletin,* **101**: 343–62.

Bradley, L., Young, K., Anderson, R. *et al.* (1987). Effects of psychological therapy on pain behaviour in rheumatoid arthritis patients. *Arthritis and Rheumatism,* **30**: 1105–14.

Brannon, L. and Feist, J. (1992). *Health Psychology: An Introduction to Behaviour and Health,* 2nd edn. Belmont, CA: Wadsworth.

Brown, G. and Harris, T. (1978). *Social Origins of Depression.* London: Tavistock.

Burger, J. (1989). Negative reactions to increases in perceived control. *Journal of Personality and Social Psychology,* **56**: 246–56.

Burish, T., Carey, M., Krozely, M. and Greco, F. (1987). Conditioned side-effects induced by cancer chemotherapy: prevention through behavioural treatment. *Journal of Consulting and Clinical Psychology,* **55**: 42–8.

Cioffi, D. (1991). Beyond attentional strategies: a cognitive–perceptual model of somatic interpretation. *Psychological Bulletin,* **109**: 25–41.

Cramer, D. (1991). *Personality and Psychotherapy: Theory, Practice and Research.* Buckingham: Open University Press.

Crawford, R. (1977). You are dangerous to your health: the ideology and politics of victim-blaming. *Journal of Health Services,* **7**: 663–80.

Damrosch, S. (1991). General strategies for motivating people to change their behaviour. *Nursing Clinics of North America,* **26**: 833–43.

Dembroski, T. and Costa, P. (1987). Coronary prone behaviour: components of the Type A pattern and hostility. *Journal of Personality,* **55**: 211–35.

Dobson, K. and Craig, K. (1996). *Advances in Cognitive–Behavioural Therapy.* London: Sage.

Doll, R. and Peto, R. (1981). *The Causes of Cancer.* New York: Oxford University Press.

Downie, R., Fyfe, C. and Tannahill, A. (1990). *Health Promotion: Models and Values.* New York: Oxford University Press.

Draucker, C. (1992). *Counselling Survivors of Childhood Sexual Abuse.* London: Sage.

Dryden, W. (1989). The therapeutic alliance as an integrating framework. In: Dryden, W. (ed.), *Key Issues For Counselling in Action.* London: Sage, 1–15.

Dryden, W. and Rentoul, R (eds) (1991). *Adult Clinical Problems: A Cognitive Behavioural Approach.* London: Routledge.

Engel, G. (1977). The need for a new medical model: a challenge for biomedicine. *Science,* **196**: 126–9.

Farquhar, J., Fortmann, S., Maccoby, N. *et al.* (1984). The Stanford Five City Project: an overview. In: Matarazzo, S. *et al.* (eds),

Behavioural Health: A Handbook of Health Enhancement and Disease Prevention. New York: Wiley, 1154–65.

Gatchell, R., Baum, A. and Krantz, D. (1989). Prevention and health promotion. In: *An Introduction to Health Psychology*. New York: McGraw-Hill, 290–314.

Glaser, R., Rice, J., Sheridan, J. *et al.* (1985). Stress-related immune suppression: health implications. *Brain, Behaviour and Immunity,* **1**: 7–20.

Glaser, R., Rice, J., Speicher, *et al.* (1986). Stress depresses interferon production by leukocytes concomitant with a decrease in natural killer cell activity. *Behavioural Neuroscience,* **100**: 675–8.

Greer, S., Morris, T. and Pettingale, K. (1979). Psychological response to breast cancer: effect on outcome. *Lancet,* **2**: 785–7.

Grosarth-Maticek, R., Eysenck, H., Vetter, H. and Frentzek-Beyme (1986). The Heidelberg prospective intervention study. In: Eylenbasch, W et al. (eds), *Primary Prevention of Cancer.* New York: Raven Press, 199–212.

Gross, R. (1992). *Psychology: The Science of Mind and Behaviour*, 2nd edn. London: Hodder & Stoughton.

Hersen, M. and Van Hasselt, V. (eds) (1990). *Psychological Aspects of Developmental and Physical Disabilities: A Casebook*. London: Sage.

Hobfoll, S. and Leiberman J. (1987). Personality and social resources in immediate and continued stress resistance among women. *Journal of Personality and Social Psychology,* **52**: 18–26.

Hogan, J. (1989). Personality correlates of fitness. *Journal of Personality and Social Psychology,* **56**: 284–8.

Holden-Lund C. (1988). Effects of relaxation with guided imagery on surgical stress and wound healing. *Research in Nursing and Health,* **11**: 235–44.

Irwin, M., Daniels, M., Smith, T., Bloom, E. and Weiner, H. (1987). Impaired natural killer cell activity during bereavement. *Brain, Behaviour and Immunity,* **1**: 98–104.

Janz, N. and Becker, M. (1984). The health belief model: a decade later. *Health Education Quarterly,* **11**: 1–47.

Jemmott, J.B., Borysenko, J., Borysenko, M. *et al.* (1983). Academic stress, power motivation, and decrease in secretion rate of salivary secretory immunoglobulin A. *Lancet,* **i**: 1400–2.

Jemmott, J.B., Hellman, C., McClelland, D. *et al.* (1990). Motivational syndromes associated with natural killer cell activity. *Journal of Behavioural Medicine,* **13**: 53–73.

Jemmott, J.B. and Locke, S. (1984). Psychosocial factors, immunologic mediation and human susceptibility to infectious diseases: how much do we know? *Psychological Bulletin,* **95**: 78–108.

Jessor, R. and Jessor, S. (1982). Adolescence to young adulthood: a twelve-year prospective study of problem behaviour and psychosocial development. In: Mednick, A. and Harway, M. (eds), *Longitudinal Research in the United States*. Boston: Martinus Nijhoff, 34–61.

Kaplan, H. (1985). Psychological factors affecting physical conditions (psychosomatic disorders). In: Kaplan, H. and Saddock, B. (eds), *Comprehensive Textbook of Psychiatry,* vol. 4. Baltimore: Williams & Wilkins, 1106–13.

Kerns, R., Turk, D., Holzman, A. and Rudy, T. (1986). Comparison of cognitive–behavioural and behavioural approaches to the outpatient treatment of chronic pain. *Clinical Journal of Pain,* **1**: 195.

Kiecolt-Glaser, J., Garner, W., Speicher, C., Penn, G. and Glaser, R. (1984). Psychosocial modifiers of immunocompetence in medical students. *Psychosomatic Medicine,* **46**: 7–14.

Kiecolt-Glaser, J. and Glaser, R. (1988). Psychological influences on immunity: implications for AIDS. *American Psychologist,* **43**: 892–8.

Kiecolt-Glaser, J. and Glaser, R. (1989). Psychoneuroimmunology: past, present and future. *Health Psychology,* **8**: 677–82.

Kiecolt-Glaser, J., Glaser, R., Dyer, C., Shuttleworth, E., Ogrocki, P. and Speicher, C. (1987). Chronic stress and immunity in family caregivers of Alzheimer's disease victims. *Psychosomatic Medicine,* **49**: 523–35.

Kiecolt-Glaser, J., Glaser, R., Strain, E., Stout, J., Tarr, K., Holliday, J. and Speicher, C. (1986). Modulation of cellular immunity in medical students. *Journal of Behavioural Medicine,* **9**: 5–21.

Kiecolt-Glaser, J., Glaser, R., Williger, D. *et al.* (1985). Psychosocial enhancement of immunocompetence in a geriatric population. *Health Psychology,* **4**: 25–41.

Korbasa, S. (1982). The hardy personality: toward a social psychology of stress and health. In: Sanders, G. and Suls, J. (eds), *Social Psychology of Health and Illness*. Hillsdale, NJ: Erlbaum, 3–32.

Kuhn, T. (1962). *The Structure of Scientific Revolutions*. Chicago: University of Chicago Press.

Ley, P. (1988). *Communicating with Patients*. London: Croom Helm.

Macleod-Clark, J. (1985). The development of research in interpersonal skills in nursing. In: Kagan, C. (ed.), *Interpersonal Skills in Nursing: Research and Applications*. London: Croom Helm.

Maguire, P. (1985). Deficiencies in key interpersonal skills. In: Kagan, C. (ed.), *Interpersonal Skills in Nursing*. London: Croom Helm.

Marteau, T. (1989). Health beliefs and attributions. In: Broome, A. (ed.), *Health Psychology: Processes and Applications*. London: Chapman & Hall, 1–23.

Maslach, C. and Jackson, S. (1982). Burnout in health professionals: a social psychological analysis. In: Sanders, G. and Suls, J. (eds), *Social Psychology of Health and Illness*. Hillsdale, NJ: Erlbaum.

Maslow, A. (1954, 1970). *Motivation and Personality,* 2nd edn. New York: Harper & Row.

Matarazzo, J. (1982). Behavioural health's challenge to academic, scientific and professional psychology. *American Psychologist,* **37**: 1–14.

Matthews, K., Weiss, S., Detre, T., Dembroski, T., Falkner, B., Manuch, S. and Williams, R. (eds) (1986). *Handbook of Stress, Reactivity and Cardiovascular Disease*. New York: Wiley.

Mazzuca, S. (1982). Does patient education in chronic disease have therapeutic value? *Journal of Chronic Diseases,* **35**: 521–9.

McFarlane, A. and Brooks, P. (1990). Psychoimmunology and rheumatoid arthritis: concepts and methodologies. *International Journal of Psychiatry in Medicine,* **20**: 307–22.

Mechanic, D. (1993). Chronic fatigue syndrome and the treatment process. *Ciba Foundation Symposium,* **173**: 318–27.

Nichols, K. (1984). *Psychological Care in Physical Illness*. Beckenham: Croom Helm.

Nichols, K. (1989). Institutional versus client-centred care in general hospitals. In: Broome, A. (ed.), *Health Psychology: Processes and Applications*. London: Chapman & Hall, 103–13.

Parkes, C.M., Benjamin, B. and Fitzgerald, R. (1969). Broken heart: a statistical study of increased mortality among widowers. *British Medical Journal,* **1**: 740–3.

Pennebaker, J. (1988). Confiding traumatic experiences and health. In: Fischer, S. and Reason, J. (eds), *Handbook of Life Stress, Cognition and Health*. New York: Wiley.

Popper, K. (1959). *The Logic of Scientific Discovery.* London: Hutchinson.

Pitts, M. (1991). The medical consultation. In: Pitts, M. and Phillips, K. (eds), *The Psychology of Health*. London: Routledge.

Rodin, J. and Salovey, P. (1989). Health psychology. *Annual Review of Psychology,* **40**: 533–79.

Rogers, C. (1957). The necessary and sufficient conditions of therapeutic personality change. *Journal of Consulting Psychology,* **21**: 95–103.

Rosenman, R., Brand, R., Jenkins, C., Friedman, M., Straus, R. and Wurm, M. (1975). Coronary heart disease in the Western Collaborative Group Study: final follow-up experience of 8 and a half years. *Journal of the American Medical Association,* **233**: 872–7.

Rosenman, R., Swan, G. and Carmelli, D. (1988). Definition, assessment and evolution of the Type A behaviour pattern. In: Houston, B. and Snyder, C. (eds), *Type A Behaviour Pattern: Current Trends and Future Directions*. New York: Wiley.

Ross, L., Green, D. and House, P. (1977). The false consensus phenomenon: an attributional bias in self-perception and social perception processes. *Journal of Experimental Social Psychology,* **13**: 279–301.

Rotter, J. (1966). Generalised expectancies for internal versus external control of reinforcement. *Psychological Monographs,* **30**: 1–26.

Sarafino, E. (1994). *Health Psychology: Biopsychosocial Interactions*, 2nd edn. New York: Wiley.

Scheier, M. and Carver, C. (1985). Optimism, coping and health: assessment and implications of generalised outcome expectancies. *Health Psychology*, **4**: 219–47.

Scheier, M., Matthews, K., Owens, J. *et al.* (1989). Dispositional optimism and recovery from coronary artery bypass surgery: the beneficial effects on physical and psychological well-being. *Journal of Personality and Social Psychology*, **57**: 1024–40.

Schulz, D. (1990). *Theories of Personality*. Belmont, CA: Wadsworth.

Schwartz, G. (1984). Psychobiology of health: a new synthesis. In: Hammonds, B. and Scheirer, C. (eds), *Psychology and Health: The Master Lecture Series*, vol 3. Washington, DC: American Psychological Association, 149–93.

Seligman, M. (1975). *Helplessness: On Depression, Development and Death*. San Francisco: W.H. Freeman.

Sheridan, C. and Radmacher, S. (1992). *Health Psychology: Challenging the Biomedical Model*. New York: Wiley.

Sonstroem, R. (1984). Exercise and self-esteem. *Exercise and Sport Sciences Reviews*, **12**: 123–55.

Starr, C. and Taggart, R. (1984). *Biology: The Unity and Diversity of Life*. Belmont, CA: Wadsworth.

Steptoe, A. (1991). Psychological coping, individual differences and physiological stress responses. In: Cooper, C. and Payne, R. (eds), *Personality and Stress: Individual Differences in the Stress Process*. New York: Wiley, 205–33.

Steptoe, A. and Wardle, J. (1994). *Psychosocial Processes and Health: A Reader*. Cambridge: Cambridge University Press.

Stewart, M., Brown, J., Weston, W., McWhinney, I., McWilliam, C. and Freeman, T. (1995). *Patient-Centred Medicine: Transforming the Clinical Method*. London: Sage.

Syme, S. (1984). Sociocultural factors and disease etiology. In: Gentry, W. (eds), *Handbook of Behavioural Medicine*. New York: Guilford.

Taylor, S. (1990). Health psychology: the science and the field. *American Psychologist*, **45**: 40–50.

Taylor, S., Bandura, A., Ewart, C. *et al.* (1985). Raising spouse's and patient's perception of his cardiac capabilities after clinically uncomplicated myocardial infarction. *American Journal of Cardiology*, **55**: 635–8.

Taylor, S., Lichtman, R. and Wood, J. (1984). Attributions, beliefs about control and adjustment to breast cancer. *Journal of Personality and Social Psychology*, **46**: 489–502.

Trijsburg, R., Van Knippenberg, C. and Rijpma, S. (1992). Effects of psychological treatment on cancer patients: a critical review. *Psychosomatic Medicine*, **54**: 489–517.

Wallston, B., Alagna, S., DeVellis, B. and DeVellis, R. (1983). Social support and physical health. *Health Psychology*, **4**: 367–91.

Weinstein, N. (1987). Unrealistic optimism about susceptibility to health problems; conclusions from a community-wide sample. *Journal of Behavioural Medicine*, **10**: 481–500.

Wells, R. and Tschudin, V. (1994). *Wells' Supportive Therapies in Health Care*. London: Baillière Tindall.

Wilson, C. (1989). Terminal care: using psychological skills with the terminally ill. In: Broome, A. (ed), *Health Psychology: Processes and Applications*. London: Chapman & Hall.

Winnicott, D. (1965). *The Maturational Process and the Facilitating Environment*. New York: International Universities Press.

World Health Organization (1946). *Constitution*. New York: WHO.

Worden, W. (1991). *Grief Counselling and Grief Therapy*, 2nd edn. London: Tavistock.

Further Reading ▲ ▲ ▲

Brannon, L. and Feist, J. (1992). *Health Psychology: An Introduction to Behaviour and Health*, 2nd edn. Belmont, CA: Wadsworth.

Broome, A. (ed.). *Health Psychology: Processes and Applications*. London: Chapman & Hall.

Sarafino, E. (1994). *Health Psychology: Biopsychosocial Interactions*, 2nd edn. New York: Wiley.

Steptoe, A. and Wardle, J. (1994). *Psychosocial Processes and Health: A Reader*. Cambridge: Cambridge University Press.

Stewart, M., Brown, J., Weston, W., McWhinney, I., McWilliam, C. and Freeman, T. (1995). *Patient-Centred Medicine: Transforming the Clinical Method*. London: Sage.

2

Stress

Robert J. Edelmann

LEARNING OBJECTIVES

After studying this chapter you should:

- Understand the concept of stress with regard to trigger events, appraisal of those events, and subsequent responses
- Understand the relationship between stress and illness
- Understand the variables that can moderate the relationship between stress and illness, with regard to coping style, social support, and stress management procedures

INTRODUCTION

Stress is at the centre of the debate concerning the mind–body relationship. The symptoms of stress can be disruptive and unpleasant, signalling inability to cope and, at worst, the onset of serious disease. This chapter discusses prominent theories and methods of measuring stress before debating the relationship between stress and illness. It ends by describing strategies for coping with stress and some common approaches to its management.

WHAT IS STRESS?

Defining stress exactly is one of the most difficult problems for researchers and clinicians. Indeed, the term 'stress' has been used in at least three different ways within the psychological literature (Baum, 1990) (see Figure 2.1).

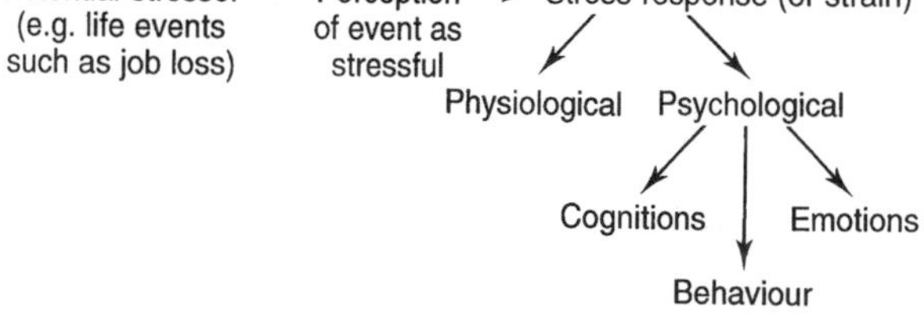

Figure 2.1 *Approaches to stress*

- Stress can be defined as a particular event or set of circumstances in the environment that are perceived as potentially harmful (i.e. stressors).
- Stress can be defined in terms of the person's reaction or response to the stressful event. This response can be described in physical and psychological terms.
- Stress is neither merely an event, nor merely a response to that event. Rather, it is a process involving an appraisal by the person of the extent to which they have the resources available to meet the emotional demands placed upon them by the event.

The third definition is the one most widely accepted in current stress research. Lazarus and Folkman (1984) have provided one of the most useful definitions:

> '[Stress is] a particular relationship between the person and the environment that is appraised by the person as taxing or exceeding his or her resources and endangering his or her well-being.'

Stress is thus dependent on a transaction between the person and his or her environment. If the person feels able to deal with a difficult situation then little stress may be felt; if, on the other hand, resources are perceived as insufficient to meet the demands of a situation, the person may well experience a great deal of stress.

In thinking about stress it is therefore necessary to

Learning Activity 1 ◆ ◆ ◆

Reflect for a moment on a time in your life when you felt unable to cope – when you felt stressed in the sense defined by Lazarus and Folkman.

take account not only of the types of events or situations that might be defined as stressful, and reactions to these events, but also factors influencing the person's perception of and reaction to the events. The chapter goes on to look in detail at these three aspects of stress: stressors; responses; and appraisal.

STRESSORS

Sources of stress (i.e. stressors) include major life events such as bereavement, divorce or job loss; involvement in major incidents such as road traffic accidents; and environmental circumstances such as noisy neighbours or crowded living conditions. Indeed, the range of stressors is so diverse that no listing would be comprehensive, so a number of classification systems have been devised.

Sarafino (1994) categorizes stressors on the basis of the system from which they come. He argues that sources of stress can be generated from within the person (e.g. illness or conflict), in the family (e.g. a new member, illness or death in the family), in the community (e.g. work demands; lack of control or poor relationships with colleagues; unemployment) or in society (e.g. noise or overcrowding).

Such a description of stressors has helped to define which conditions or events are more likely than others to produce a stress response. However, this type of classification has limitations because simply specifying events does not adequately explain the actual experience of stress. Why, for example, do supposedly stressful events produce a stressful response in some people but not in others? It is clear that many situations are only stressful because of the way in which they are appraised by the person (e.g. lack of control at work or work overload).

Learning Activity 2 ◆ ◆ ◆

As a health professional, could you ever be described as a stressor? If so, how could you act differently to reduce the stress you might cause?

This is recognized by Taylor (1991) who seeks to identify the particular dimensions of events which serve to make them more or less stressful. This notion of appraisal is central to most current theories of stress (e.g. Lazarus and Folkman, 1984). Taylor, for example, suggests that events are more likely to be stressful if they are perceived as negative, uncontrollable, ambiguous or overwhelming.

Assessment of stressors

Just as stress can be defined in terms of its sources, it can be measured by determining the occurrence of particular stressors. This has mainly been done either by measuring the number of major life events or by measuring the accumulation of minor daily irritations.

LIFE EVENTS

One of the most frequently used measures of life events is the Social Readjustment Rating Scale (SRRS; Holmes and Rahe, 1967). This consists of a list of 43 life events with values assigned to each on the basis of pre-testing to indicate the extent to which they would involve people making changes in their lives. The greater the amount of change, the greater the degree of stress each event is assumed to occasion. At the top of the list is 'death of a spouse', which is assigned a value of 100, while at the bottom of the list is 'minor violations of the law', which is assigned a value of 11. Respondents are asked to indicate which events they have experienced within a specified period of time, usually not more than the previous two years. The total stress score is the sum of the values for the items ticked by the respondent.

The SRRS includes a relatively wide range of events and is easy and quick to administer. The values assigned to the events were determined from the responses of a large sample of people and seem to provide a reasonable estimate of the relative impact of events. It has been used in a number of both retrospective and prospective studies examining the relationship between stress/life events and illness (Rahe and Arthur, 1978). However, the general finding from these studies is that scores on the SRRS only show a moderate correlation with illness (about 0.3). Whilst one might argue that this merely reflects the fact that stress is only one factor leading to the development of disease, others have argued that the SRRS is not a particularly sensitive measure of stress for the following reasons:

- The SRRS rates events without taking account of their meaning for the individual (Lazarus and Folkman, 1984; Schroeder and Costa, 1984). For example, while divorce or separation may indeed be stressful events (assigned values of 63 and 75 on the SRRS), they may be viewed in a very different light by two people, one of whom sees it as a welcome release from an abusive partner, the other of whom sees income and status loss resulting from the loss of an apparently previously supportive partner.
- The SRRS does not differentiate between desirable and undesirable events (Suls and Mullen, 1981). Few people would regard an 'outstanding personal achievement' as anything other than desirable. Similarly, few would regard a 'major personal injury or illness' as anything other than undesirable. While positive events can involve effort and worry which may well lead to illness, few would regard them in the same light as negative events. Indeed, research suggests that sudden, negative, unexpected and uncontrollable events are more likely to relate to illness than events which build gradually, are positive, expected and under a degree of personal control (Glass, 1977).
- Some of the items in the SRRS are vague and ambiguous (Hough *et al.*, 1976). For example, major change in financial status (assigned a value of 38) does not indicate the direction or degree of change. The meaning assigned to events and their desirability is of particular importance given that studies tend to find a relationship between illness and undesirable life events while there is no such link with desirable life events (Sarason *et al.*, 1985).

Such concerns have led to the development of other scales such as the Unpleasant Events Schedule (UES; Lewinsohn *et al.*, 1985), although these too are not without their difficulties. Indeed, one problem with all such life-event scales is that they are concerned with major life events when many stressors take the form of minor annoyances or daily hassles. It is then the cumulative impact of these individually relatively trivial events that gives rise to illness.

DAILY HASSLES

The Hassles Scale (HS; Kanner *et al.*, 1981) has been designed to provide a measure of minor annoyances and irritations. This consists of 117 events ranging from minor annoyances, such as 'silly practical mistakes', to major problems or difficulties, such as 'not enough money for food'. Respondents indicate which events have occurred within the past month and rate each event for its severity (somewhat, moderately, or extremely). One hundred adults assessed over a nine-month period reported that their most frequently experienced hassles were 'concerns about weight', 'health of a family member', 'rising prices of common goods', and 'too many things to do'.

As a counterpoint to the Hassles Scale, Kanner *et al.* (1981) also developed an Uplifts Scale. This lists 135 desirable events likely to bring peace, happiness or joy, which make hassles more bearable and hence reduce their potential impact upon health. The uplifts reported most frequently by the 100 subjects who had also completed the Hassles Scale were 'relating well to a spouse or lover', 'completing a task', and 'feeling healthy'.

A number of studies have examined the relationship between hassles, uplifts and health and have found a positive relationship between measures (e.g. DeLongis *et al.*, 1982; Weinberger *et al.*, 1987). DeLongis *et al.* (1982) administered the Hassles and Uplifts Scales, a life-events scale and a measure of health status to an adult population. They found that both hassles and life-events scores were weakly associated with health status, although hassles were more strongly associated than life events with the health status measure; uplifts had little relationship with health status. It could be, therefore, that this is not measuring the appropriate aspect of stress and/or that stress is only one factor leading to ill-health.

Learning Activity 3 ◆ ◆ ◆

With a group of others, brainstorm a list of typical life events. Identify those you have experienced personally, and then rank these in terms of the amount of stress (if any) they seemed to be associated with at the time. Compare your rank ordering with others in the group to see whether some events are associated with more relative stress than others for different people. (If time permits, discuss reasons why an event was more stressful for you than for others, or why some events were more stressful than others.)

Repeat the exercise using a list of daily hassles.

RESPONSES TO STRESS

Physiological/biological, cognitive, emotional and behavioural responses can occur either as involuntary reactions to a potentially stressful event or as part of a deliberate strategy for dealing with it. The combination of psychological and physiological responses to stress is generally referred to as 'strain'.

Physiological/biological response

The physiological/biological stress response involves sympathetic nervous system activity. Blood pressure, heart rate, pulse rate, skin conductance and respiration all increase. The sympathetic nervous system impacts on the endocrine system, leading the adrenal medulla to produce the catecholamines, epinephrine and norepinephrine.

In addition, stress affects the pituitary gland which stimulates the adrenal cortex, which in turn releases corticosteroids such as cortisol (see Chapter 1). Stress also triggers the release of glucocorticoids which help to dampen down initial arousal.

The earliest contributions to stress focused almost exclusively on these bodily reactions occurring in response to a threatening event.

FLIGHT-OR-FIGHT

Cannon (1929) proposed that, when humans and animals perceive danger, the sympathetic nervous system stimulates the adrenal glands of the endocrine system to secrete epinephrine so that the body is rapidly aroused. Heart rate speeds up; blood pressure, blood sugar and respiration increase; the circulation of the blood to the skin is reduced; and circulation to the muscles is increased. Because this prepares the person or animal to attack or flee, it has been called the 'fight-or-flight response. In the short term it is clearly an adaptive reaction as it enables the person or animal to respond rapidly to threat. However, if such a reaction is maintained over a longer period of time it can be harmful to emotional well-being and health.

SELYE'S GENERAL ADAPTATION SYNDROME

What happens to the body when it is exposed to prolonged stress was one of the questions which intrigued Hans Selye. He noticed that the fight-or-flight response was actually just the first of a series of reactions the body makes when exposed to prolonged stress (1956, 1976). He called this series of physiological reactions the 'general adaptation syndrome' (GAS). This consists of three stages (see Figure 2.2). Selye's model has had a major impact on stress research because:

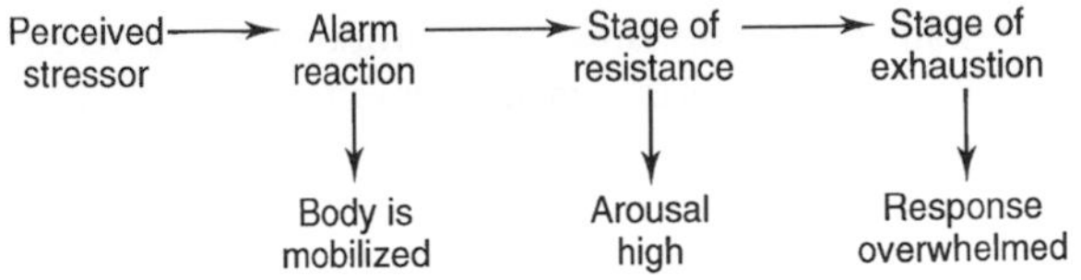

Figure 2.2 *Selye's general adaptation syndrome*

- it provides a general theory of physiological reactions to a wide range of stressful situations over time;
- it offers a physiological mechanism linking stress and illness.

The first stage, the alarm reaction, is like the flight-or-fight response, mobilizing glucoids and adrenaline, which quickly energize the body. In time, the body's reserves become depleted leading to fatigue. At this time the second stage of the GAS, resistance, occurs. In this stage the body tries to adapt to the stressor, physiological arousal declining although remaining higher than normal. Selye argued that, at such time, ability to resist new stressors was impaired, so that the individual became vulnerable to health problems resulting from impaired immune function, as well as ulcers, high blood pressure and asthma. Finally, chronic stress results in a stage of exhaustion, when cellular response and immune function are overwhelmed. If stress continues, death may occur.

Seyle's model has, however, been criticized for a number of reasons:

- It places too little emphasis on psychological factors and it is known that psychological appraisal plays an important role in determining reactions to stress (Lazarus and Folkman, 1984).
- Physical responses to stress do not seem to be as uniform as the model implies (Hobfoll, 1989). How a person responds to stress is influenced by his or her constitution, personality and perceptions (Lazarus and Folkman, 1984).
- Selye's argument is somewhat circular (Hobfoll, 1989). He regarded stress as a state that was inferred from biological changes, and it was this response which defined the stimulus as stressful rather than the stimulus itself. Thus a stimulus is stressful only if there is a physiological response and vice versa.

Despite these criticisms, and although more recent models of stress place greater emphasis on psychological appraisal, Selye's model remains influential.

ASSESSING PHYSIOLOGICAL RESPONSE

Just as stress can be defined in terms of the physiological response, it can also be measured along physiological and biological parameters. Thus physiological aspects such as blood pressure, heart rate or perspiration (galvanic skin response – GSR), or biochemical aspects such as corticosteroids or catecholamines, can serve as markers of stress. Physiological responses, in particular, provide direct and objective measures and a quantifiable index of stress. In one study, for example, Goldstein *et al.* (1992) found that ambulance personnel had higher blood pressure when they were in the ambulance or at hospital (and presumably under stress) than during other work activities or at home.

It is widely recognized, however, that assessing physiological parameters is not without its difficulties. For example, major problems arise in the selection of measures (i.e. which individual parameters or multiple set of parameters should be assessed), the reliability of the equipment, intrusiveness of the techniques, and interpretation of the data (Ney and Gale, 1988).

Emotional responses

A number of different emotions can occur in response to stress, including fear, anger, anxiety and depression. Although there is some commonality of responses across situations, the type of response may well vary according to the nature of the stressor experienced. For example, difficulties with a colleague at work may initially provoke anger; however, if the problem is not resolved then anxiety about work and depression about the possible consequences of the conflict may become the predominant emotions.

Behavioural responses

A number of behavioural reactions can occur from stress, including confrontation ('fight') or withdrawal ('flight'). Again, although there is some commonality of responses across situations, the type of response can also vary according to the nature of the stressor experienced. For example, if the stressor is associated with anger at others for one's predicament, then irritability and aggressive outbursts are not uncommon. In other instances, withdrawal and shutting oneself away from others may predominate.

Cognitive responses

As with other responses to stress, cognitions or patterns of thinking can either reflect an involuntary reaction to a potentially stressful event or be a deliberate strategy for dealing with it. Involuntary cognitive responses frequently associated with stress include memory and concentration difficulties and unwanted intrusive thoughts. Indeed, the general pattern of perceiving events can be greatly influenced by stress. On the other hand, purposeful cognitive responses are closely related to the processes of appraisal and coping which are described in detail in the next section.

Learning Activity 4 ◆ ◆ ◆

Try recognizing stress responses at different psychological levels. Choose a time in your lfe (maybe the one mentioned in activity 1) when you felt stressed. Imagine yourself back in that situation and analyse your physiological and psychological responses at that time:

- What were your typical physical responses (i.e. how did your body feel)?
- What were some of your main emotional responses (i.e. what did you feel)?
- How did you behave at the time in response to the situation (i.e. what did you do)?
- What were some of your thoughts at the time (i.e. what did you think)?

APPRAISAL OF EVENTS AS STRESSFUL

It is evident that the same event may be perceived as stressful by one person but not by another. One person may feel they have the resources to cope with, or meet, the demands of a particular situation, while another person might not. The central role of such cognitive appraisal in determining stress has been emphasized by Lazarus and his colleagues (Folkman, 1984; Folkman and Lazarus, 1985; Lazarus and Folkman, 1984). Cognitive appraisal includes two components, primary and secondary (see Figure 2.3).

Potential stressor →	Primary appraisal: →	Secondary appraisal: →	Stress response
	Is the event positive, negative or neutral? If negative, is it likely to be harmful, a future threat or a challenge?	Are coping resources sufficient to deal with the harm, threat or challenge?	

Figure 2.3 *Appraisal of events as stressful*

Primary appraisal

When a person is exposed to a potentially stressful situation, the first task is to assess the meaning of the situation for that individual's own well-being. Through primary appraisal the person judges whether the situation is:

- *irrelevant* (i.e. of no significance to their well-being); or
- *good* (referred to as benign positive – i.e. a good outcome is signalled); or
- *stressful* (i.e. characterized by threat or harm).

Events perceived as stressful are then subject to further appraisal for three implications: harm/loss, threat, or challenge. Harm/loss refers to the amount of damage already done (e.g. the loss of a limb); threat is the expectation of future harm; and challenge is the opportunity to develop one's potential for growth, mastery or gain. Thus, even if an event is perceived as potentially stressful it could nevertheless be interpreted positively; i.e. as a challenge.

Appraisal of events is influenced by two factors, those relating to the person and those relating to the situation. *Personal factors* include beliefs and commitments (e.g. religion), personality and motivation. For example, people who have high self-esteem are more likely to perceive a stressful event as challenging than threatening (Cohen and Lazarus, 1983).

Situational factors include ambiguity, familiarity and clarity, desirability and controllability. Highly ambiguous situations are those in which the likelihood of harm or availability of resources to meet the demands of the situation remains unclear. An example might be when facing some painful or debilitating chronic condition in which the long-term course is unclear. In such circumstances it is more likely that the stressfulness of the situation will be influenced by personality and beliefs. Similarly, whilst undesirable events such as job loss are generally perceived as more stressful than desirable ones, such as marriage or the birth of a child, the latter can also be stressful because of their inherent ambiguity. Finally, uncontrollable events are generally appraised as being more stressful than controllable ones.

Secondary appraisal

This is the assessment of one's coping resources and of the options available to reduce the chances of harm, threat or challenge. Coping resources include physical assets (a person's health, energy and stamina), social assets (the individual's social network and support systems), psychological assets (beliefs, problem-solving skills, self-esteem and morale), and material assets (money, equipment) (Folkman, 1984; Schaefer *et al.*, 1981).

Learning Activity 5 ◆ ◆ ◆

This activity is intended to make explicit the process of cognitive appraisal. Tick any of the following situations that you might find stressful:

- ◆ Final exams
- ◆ Driving test
- ◆ Loss of someone very dear to you
- ◆ Unemployment
- ◆ Diagnosis of progressive disease
- ◆ Giving a lecture to your colleagues
- ◆ Looking after a relative with dementia
- ◆ Loss of a leg

Now choose one of those ticked as potentially stressful and carry out an analysis of why this might be so using the ideas of cognitive appraisal:

Primary appraisal
Assuming that the situation is neither irrelevant to you nor good for you, analyse *why* it is potentially stressful by considering to what extent it implies: (i) harm or loss; (ii) threat; (iii) challenge.

Secondary appraisal
Now analyse your coping resources to see how these might increase or reduce the stressfulness of this situation, by identifying: (i) your physical assets; (ii) your social assets; (iii) your psychological assets; (iv) your material assets.

Box 2.1 *Subscales of the Ways of Coping Questionnaire*

Subscale	*Description*	*Example*
Confrontive	Aggressive efforts to alter the situation	Stood my ground and fought for what I wanted
Distancing	Efforts to detach oneself	Went on as if nothing had happened
Self-control	Efforts to regulate one's own feelings	Tried to keep myself to myself
Seeking social support	Efforts to seek information support	Talked to someone to find out more about the situation
Accepting responsibility	Acknowledgement of one's role in the problem	Criticized or lectured myself
Escape/avoidance	Wishful thinking and behavioural efforts to escape or avoid the situation	Wished the situation would go away
Planful problem-solving	Deliberate problem-solving efforts to alter the situation	Made a plan of action and followed it
Positive reappraisal	Efforts to create positive meaning by focusing on personal growth	Changed or grew as a person in a good way

COPING

Coping has been defined as the process of executing the response evaluated during secondary appraisal. It refers to the cognitive and behavioural efforts to manage (master, reduce, or tolerate) specific external and/or internal demands that are appraised as taxing or exceeding the resources of the person (Folkman, 1984; Folkman and Lazarus, 1980; Lazarus and Folkman, 1984; Lazarus and Launier, 1978).

An important feature of this definition is that coping is defined independently of outcome. It refers to attempts to manage the demands of the situation and is independent of the success of these attempts.

Coping is also a process that changes over time rather than being a one-off response to an event.

Assessment of coping

Because appraisal is important in defining stress, it is also important to measure how people are likely to cope under stress. A measure of coping that has been widely used in research is the Ways of Coping Checklist (Folkman and Lazarus, 1988). This consists of 66 items describing possible coping responses. The respondent rates each from 0 (never) to 4 (very often) to describe whether they have used a particular coping action in relation to the most stressful episode they have experienced in the past week or month. Research using the scale suggests that there may be a number of different coping dimensions. One study by Folkman *et al.* (1986) suggests eight coping dimensions, as shown in Box 2.1.

The Ways of Coping Checklist is not without its critics, and a number of alternative coping measures have been devised. However, the one consistent finding across a range of populations and with a number of different scales is the emergence of two broad types of coping efforts:

- *Problem-focused coping* involves attempts to do something that is active, practical and constructive to deal with the stressful situation.
- *Emotion-focused coping* involves doing something to deal with the emotional consequences of the stressor.

Inevitably, each of these dimensions is likely to consist of several components such as those shown in Box 2.1.

A further dimension of coping considered in some studies contrasts strategies that *confront* the problem with those that *avoid* it.

A great deal of effort has been expended in investigating the extent to which a particular coping style may or may not be more effective in dealing with stress. There is some evidence, for example, that avoidance coping is more effective in the short term but becomes ineffective if maintained over time. In contrast, confrontation seems more effective in dealing with long-term threats (Holahan and Moos, 1987). However, many factors influence how individuals cope with problems; these include situational demands, individual variability, and personal resources such as social support.

Learning Activity 6 ◆ ◆ ◆

Continue the analysis of your own stress response in the last activity.

- Can you now identify what coping strategies you might use?
- Are these common strategies for you?
- Were there particular reasons in your appraisal that led you to choose any given strategies?
- How effective were the strategies in reducing stress?

If you have assessed another person's stress, try to identify which coping strategy or strategies they used.

Factors affecting coping

PERSONALITY

It has been suggested that certain personality traits such as optimism (Scheier and Carver, 1985), self-esteem (Leventhal and Nerenz, 1982) and an easy-going disposition (Holohan and Moos, 1987) facilitate effective coping. There may well be some degree of stability in an individual's style of appraising and coping, although there also seems to be a tendency to use different coping strategies from encounter to encounter. The strategy used will be shaped to some extent by the individual's appraisal of the situation, which may be influenced to some degree by personality characteristics, as well as the resources available.

SOCIAL SUPPORT

Support types can include informational, emotional, material, personal, formal and professional, and can vary both in terms of quantity and quality. Schaefer *et al.* (1981), for example, refer to social networks as an index of the quantity of support, and perceived social support as an index of quality. A social network is the set of relationships of one individual and can be defined in terms of either its composition and structure (number of people known and the number who know each other), or the particular type of relationship (family or friends).

Perceived social support is an assessment of the individual's views and beliefs about how helpful the interactions or relationships within the network actually are. Cohen and colleagues (e.g. Cohen and Wills, 1985) have argued that it is perceived social support that provides stress-buffering effects. Further, they propose that stress-buffering only occurs when there is a match between the needs elicited by the stressful event and the functions of support that are perceived to be available. For a review of stress-buffering, see Cohen (1988).

Dimensions of perceived support proposed by Cohen and colleagues are:

- *appraisal support* (i.e. having people to talk to about problems);
- *self-esteem support* (i.e. having people who make us feel better about ourselves);
- *tangible support* (i.e. having people who provide economic aid);
- *belonging to a network* (i.e. having real social ties) (Cohen *et al.*, 1985).

Clearly there are difficulties with self-report measures of perceived social support because people may be unwilling to admit to inadequate social support, loneliness and feelings of rejection.

The way in which social support is perceived will determine its effect on the coping process. Thus, support can be seen as beneficial or negative, as providing sympathy or as irritating and leading to resentment, or as providing helpful or misleading information (Suls, 1982). Cohen and McKay (1984) suggest a number of mechanisms by which support may affect one's ability to cope:

- Members of one's support system may provide information, possibly providing alternative coping strategies based upon their own past experiences.
- A social support system may facilitate certain kinds of behaviour (e.g. exercise, diet) which would increase the individual's ability to resist or overcome stress.
- Social support can provide tangible aid in dealing with a stressor.
- Support may operate by encouraging the person to focus more on the positive and less on the negative aspects of the distressing situation.
- A support system may enhance the individual's feeling that their present coping abilities are adequate to handle the demands of the situation, but that if they should fail, then others will be available to provide assistance.

Appraisal of support in addition to appraisal of the situation is thus important in determining coping ability. Taken together with internal coping resources, including aspects of personality and individual flexibility, these factors interact to build up coping activity (e.g. Lazarus and Folkman, 1984).

Learning Activity 7 ◆ ◆ ◆

Continuing your example from activities 1 and 3, can you identify both positive and negative aspects of social relationships during this period of stress?

THE RELATIONSHIP BETWEEN STRESS AND ILLNESS

The presence of stress has been implicated in many illnesses, including ulcers, asthma, headaches and skin disorders, in the development of hypertension, coronary heart disease and cancer and, more recently, in the development of infectious diseases (e.g. Bakal, 1975; Cohen and Williamson, 1991; Shapiro and Goldstein, 1982; Sklar and Anisman, 1981). A number of models have been proposed to explain how stress affects health (see Figure 2.4).

The stress/illness relationship is complex, so there is likely to be an interplay between factors such as those described below.

BEHAVIOUR CHANGE

Stress can affect health indirectly by altering a person's behaviour patterns. During periods of stress, people are likely to sleep less, eat poorly, consume more alcohol, or smoke, each of which is likely to affect health.

BIOLOGICAL VULNERABILITY

Some have argued that stress may only lead to illness in those who are biologically vulnerable. For example, stress may give rise to hypertension only in those who already have elevated blood pressure.

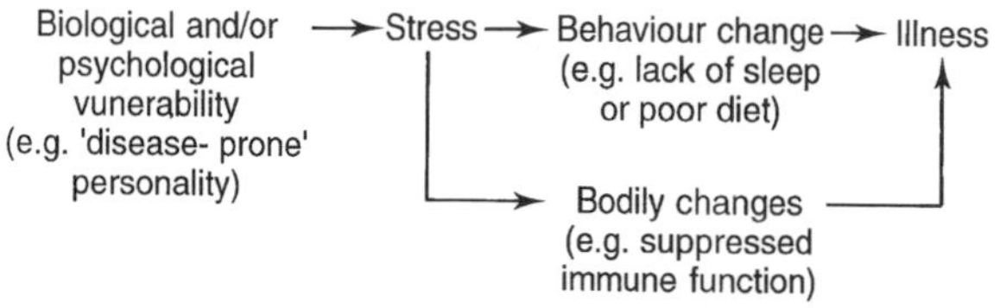

Figure 2.4 *Potential links between stress and illness*

PREDISPOSING PERSONALITY

It has been argued that some people are high in negative affectivity; that is, they are by nature predisposed to view things negatively. In a review of the literature, Friedman and Booth-Kewley (1987) found a small but consistent relationship between the occurrence of negative emotions (depression, anger, hostility, anxiety) and five diseases (asthma, arthritis, ulcers, headaches, coronary artery disease). They argue that these negative emotions form the basis for a 'disease prone' personality that predisposes people to develop illnesses. Indeed, Friedman (1990) has commented that 'there should be little doubt that personality, stress and health are interrelated. There is solid evidence for associations among individual personality differences, emotional reactions, health-related behaviours, physiological responses and disease' (p. 283).

Others, however, have interpreted the data rather more cautiously, suggesting that while personality factors may be predictive of somatic complaints or healthcare utilization, they are not necessarily associated as causal agents in organic disease (e.g. Stone and Costa, 1990). Thus, Watson and Pennebaker (1989) found that, although negative affectivity was related to self-reported stress and health complaints, it was not related to a range of illness variables.

Negative affectivity may thus influence the tendency to *report* stress and illness rather than influencing illness *per se*. Indeed, because stress is associated with a variety of symptoms such as insomnia, anxiety and depression, people under stress are much more likely to seek medical care (Gortmaker *et al.*, 1982), even though these conditions are not in themselves signs of physical illness.

SOCIAL SUPPORT

It has been assumed that adequate support will offset or moderate the detrimental health effects of stress (Cohen, 1988). Indeed, a number of authors have noted that social support seems to facilitate coping and is implicated in positive health outcomes. Singer and Lord (1984) hypothesize four links between social support and health: social support protects against stress-induced disorders; lack of social support itself is a stressor; loss of social support is a stressor; social support is beneficial.

SUPRESSED IMMUNITY

Stress may cause illness directly via changes in the body's physical systems. There is increasing evidence that stress suppresses immune functions in some way, leaving people open to infectious diseases (Cohen and Williamson, 1991), cancer (Levy, 1983), and varieties of the human herpes virus (Kiecolt-Glaser and Glaser, 1987). The impact of stress and other psychological processes on the immune system forms an area of recent study referred to as psychoneuroimmunology. This is covered in more detail in Chapter 1, where there is also a discussion of the broader relationship between psychological factors and health.

Learning Activity 8 ◆ ◆ ◆

Either reflect on the example you are already working on (activity 1), or another stressful episode in your life when you felt that you became unwell as a result of stress. How did this 'illness' manifest itself (e.g. tired, run down, pain, ulcer)? What were the likely mechanisms through which you became ill (e.g. behaviour change, biological vulnerability, predisposing personality, social support, suppressed immunity)? Support your conclusions with evidence if you can.

Box 2.3: *Managing stress*

Stage 1a: Education/learning
(i) What is stress?
(ii) What are the stressors in your life?

Stage 1b: Self-monitoring/recording
(i) Circumstances you find stressful
(ii) Your physiological, emotional and behavioural responses to those stressors
(iii) Any inappropriate coping efforts (e.g. eating or drinking too much)

Stage 2: Skills acquisition/learning techniques for managing stress
(i) Set goals or targets to meet in reducing the experience of stress (e.g. to manage work more effectively)
(ii) Identify behaviours to meet these goals (e.g. better organization of work and thoughts)
(iii) Learn to engage in strategies to help achieve one's goals (e.g. time management)

Stage 3: Practice
Practice stress management techniques in the targeted stressful situations and monitor their effectiveness

MANAGING STRESS

Bearing in mind that stress is a complex state involving an ongoing appraisal of the situation and one's ability to cope with it, it is perhaps not surprising that there are numerous strategies for managing stress (see Box 2.2). For further information on any of these techniques see for example, Poppen (1988), Ellis (1977), Meichenbaum and Cameron (1983).

Box 2.2: *Techniques for managing stress*

(i) *Managing stressors*
Time management
Improving personal control

(ii) *Changing the way one thinks about the situation*
Cognitive restructuring
Stress innoculation training
Rational–emotive therapy

(iii) *Managing the stress responses*
Relaxation
Biofeedback

(iv) *Improving coping resources*
Coping skills training
Enhancing social support

Stress management programmes are likely to include elements of each of these strategies (see Box 2.3). The first phase of any such programme is to learn what stress is and to identify stressors in one's life. The

Learning Activity 9 ◆ ◆ ◆

The aim is to practise devising a stress-management programme for people suffering serious physical disease. Imagine that as part of a patient-focused initiative in an outpatient department, you have been asked to run such a programme to help people cope with a recent diagnosis of diabetes. Devise an outline programme for eight weekly 1-hour sessions to be run on an outpatient basis. Remember that stress management works best if it is centred on the participant rather than 'taught'. Also think how you might evaluate the effectiveness of your programme.

second is to learn the skills necessary to deal with each of the different facets of stress and then to practise these skills. The third phase is to put this into practice in real life and carefully monitor whether the techniques are effective. A complex problem requires complex solutions. For more details see Fontana (1989) and Meichenbaum (1985).

SUMMARY

Stress can be described as events or situations, as a range of responses to these, or as the feeling of being unable to cope. Stress has been assessed in ways that reflect these different levels of analysis. As far as an individual's health is concerned, it is the *relationships* between these levels that is important – events may prompt an inability to cope, which in turn can lead to a breakdown in healthy lifestyle or may even have a direct effect on the functioning of the immune system. Multilevel assessments of stress permit the development of a broad range of strategies to alleviate it.

Key Points ■ ■ ■

❑ Stress can be defined in different ways.

❑ Measurement of stress depends on how it is defined.

❑ Cognitive appraisal is central to the experience of stress.

❑ Coping is affected by certain psychosocial factors.

❑ Stress may be related to illness indirectly through a number of psychosocial mechanisms.

❑ The management of stress can be directed towards the individual and his or her environment.

References ▼ ▼ ▼

Bakal, D.A. (1975). Headache: a biopsychological perspective. *Psychological Bulletin*, **82**: 369–82.

Baum, A. (1990). Stress, intrusive imagery, and chronic distress. *Health Psychology*, **9**: 653–75.

Cannon, W. (1929). *Bodily Changes in Pain, Hunger, Fear and Rage*, 2nd edn. New York: Appleton.

Cohen, F. and Lazarus, R.S. (1983). Coping and adaptation in health and illness. In: Mechanic, D. (ed.), *Handbook of Health Care and the Health Professions*. New York: Free Press.

Cohen, S. (1988). Psychosocial models of the role of social support in the aetiology of physical disease. *Health Psychology*, **7**: 269–97.

Cohen, S. and McKay, G. (1984). Social support, stress and the buffering hypothesis: a theoretical analysis. In: Baum, A *et al.* (eds), *Handbook of Psychology and Health. Vol 4: Social Psychological Aspects of Health*. Hillsdale, NJ: Lawrence Erlbaum.

Cohen, S., Mermelstein, R., Kamarck, T. and Hoberman, H. (1985). Measuring the functional components of social support. In: Sarason, I.G. and Sarason, B. (eds), *Social Support: Theory, Research and Applications*. The Hague: Martinus Nijhoff.

Cohen, S. and Williamson, G.M. (1991). Stress and infectious disease in humans. *Psychological Bulletin*, **109**: 310–57.

Cohen, S. and Wills, T.A. (1985). Stress, social support and the buffering hypothesis. *Psychological Bulletin*, **98**: 310–57.

DeLongis, A., Coyne, J.C., Dakof, G., Folkman, S. and Lazarus, R.S. (1982). Relationship of daily hassles, uplifts and major life events to health status. *Health Psychology*, **1**: 119–36.

Ellis, A. (1977). The basic clinical theory of rational emotive therapy. In: Ellis, A. and Grieger, R. (eds), *Handbook of Rational–Emotive Therapy*. New York: Springer.

Folkman, S. (1984). Personal control and stress, and coping processes: a theoretical analysis. *Journal of Personality and Social Psychology*, **46**: 839–52.

Folkman, S., Dunkel-Schetter, C., DeLongis, A. and Grues, R.J. (1986). Dynamics of a stressful encounter: cognitive appraisal, coping and encounter outcomes. *Journal of Personality and Social Psychology*, **50**: 992–1003.

Folkman, S. and Lazarus, R.S. (1980). An analysis of coping in a middle-aged community sample. *Journal of Health and Social Behavior*, **21**: 219–39.

Folkman, S. and Lazarus, R.S. (1985). If it changes it must be a process: a study of emotion and coping during the stages of a college examination. *Journal of Personality and Social Psychology*, **48**: 150–70.

Folkman, S. and Lazarus, R.S. (1988). *Manual for the Ways of Coping Questionnaire*. Palo Alto, CA: Consulting Psychologists Press.

Fontana, D. (1989). *Managing Stress*. London: Routledge/British Psychological Society.

Friedman, H.S. (ed.) (1990). *Personality and Disease*. New York: Wiley.

Friedman, H.S. and Booth-Kewley, S. (1987). The 'disease-prone personality': a meta-analytic review of the construct. *American Psychologist*, **42**: 539–55.

Glass, D.C. (1977). *Behavior Patterns, Stress, and Coronary Disease*. Hillsdale, NJ: Erlbaum.

Goldstein, I.B., Jamner L.D. and Shapiro, D. (1992). Ambulatory blood pressure and heart rate in healthy male paramedics during a workday and a nonworkday. *Health Psychology*, **11**: 48–54.

Gortmaker, S.L., Eckenrode, J. and Gore, S. (1982). Stress and utilization of health services: a time series and cross-sectional analysis. *Journal of Health and Social Behavior*, **23**: 25–38.

Hobfoll, S.E. (1989). Conservation of resources: a new attempt at conceptualizing stress. *American Psychologist*, **44**: 513–24.

Holahan, C.J. and Moos, R.H. (1987). Personal and contextual determinants of coping strategies. *Journal of Personality and Social Psychology*, **52**: 946–55.

Holmes, T.H. and Rahe, R.H. (1967). The social readjustment rating scale. *Journal of Psychosomatic Research*, **11**: 213–18.

Hough, R.L., Fairbank, D.T. and Garcia, A.M. (1976). Problems in the ratio measurement of life stress. *Journal of Health and Social Behavior*, **17**: 70–82.

Kanner, A.D., Coyne, J.C., Schaefer, C. and Lazarus, R.S. (1981). Comparison of two modes of stress measurement: daily hassles and uplifts versus major life events. *Journal of Behavioral Medicine*, **4**: 1–39.

Kiecolt-Glaser, J.K. and Glaser, R. (1987). Psychosocial influences on herpesvirus latency. In: Kurstak, E. *et al.* (eds), *Viruses, Immunity and Mental Disorders*. New York: Plenum.

Lazarus, R.S. and Folkman, S. (1984). *Stress, Appraisal, and Coping*. New York: Springer.

Lazarus, R.S. and Launier, R. (1978). Stress-related transactions between person and environment. In: Pervin, L.A. and Lewis, M. (eds), *Internal and External Determinants of Behavior.* New York: Plenum.

Leventhal, H. and Nerenz, D.R. (1982). A model for stress research and some implications for the control of stress disorders. In: Meichenbaum, D. and Jaremko, M. (eds), *Stress Prevention and Management: A Cognitive Behavioral Approach.* New York: Plenum.

Levy, S.M. (1983). Host differences in neoplastic risk: behavioral and social contributors to disease. *Health Psychology,* **2**: 21–44.

Lewinsohn, P.M., Mermelstein, R.M., Alexander, C. and MacPhillamy, D.J. (1985). The unpleasant events schedule: a scale for the measurement of aversive events. *Journal of Clinical Psychology,* **41**: 483–98.

Meichenbaum, D. (1985). *Stress Inoculation Training.* New York: Pergamon Press.

Meichenbaum, D. and Cameron, R. (1983). Stress inoculation training: toward a general paradigm for training coping skills. In Meichenbaum, D. and Jaremko, M.E. (eds), *Stress Reduction and Prevention.* New York: Plenum.

Ney, T. and Gale, A. (1988). A critique of laboratory studies of emotion with particular reference to psychophysiological aspects. In: Wagner, H.L. (ed.), *Social Psychophysiology and Emotion.* Chichester: Wiley.

Poppen, R. (1988). *Behavioral Relaxation Training and Assessment.* New York: Pergamon Press.

Rahe, R.H. and Arthur, R.J. (1978). Life change and illness studies: Past history and future directions. *Journal of Human Stress,* **4**: 3–15.

Sarafino, E.P. (1994). *Health Psychology: Biopsychosocial Interactions,* 2nd edn. New York: Wiley.

Sarason, I.G., Sarason, B.R., Potter, E.H. and Antoni, M.H. (1985). Life events, social support, and illness. *Psychosomatic Medicine,* **47**: 156–63.

Schaefer, C., Coyne, J.C. and Lazarus, R.S. (1981). The health-related functions of social support. *Journal of Behavioral Medicine,* **4**: 381–406.

Scheier, M.F. and Carver, C.S. (1985). Optimism, coping and health: assessment and implications of generalized outcome expectancies. *Health Psychology,* **4**: 219–47.

Schroeder, D.H. and Costa, P.T. (1984). Influence of life event stress on physical illness: substantive effects or methodological flaws. *Journal of Personality and Social Psychology,* **46**: 853–63.

Selye, H. (1956). *The Stress of Life.* New York: McGraw-Hill.

Selye, H. (1976). *Stress in Health and Disease.* Reading, MA: Butterworth.

Shapiro, D. and Goldstein, I.B. (1982). Biobehavioral perspectives on hypertension. *Journal of Consulting and Clinical Psychology,* **50**: 841–58.

Singer, J.E. and Lord, D. (1984). The role of social support in coping with chronic life-threatening illness. In: Baum, A. et al. (eds), *Handbook of Psychology and Health. Vol 4: Social Psychological Aspects of Health.* Hillsdale, NJ: Lawrence Erlbaum.

Sklar, L.S. and Anisman, H. (1981). Stress and cancer. *Psychological Bulletin,* **89**: 369–406.

Stone, S.V. and Costa, P.T. (1990). Disease-prone personality or distress-prone personality? The role of neuroticism in coronary heart disease. In: Friedman, H.S. (ed), *Personality and Disease.* New York: Wiley.

Suls, J. (1982). Social support, interpersonal relations, and health: benefits and liabilities. In: Sanders, G. and Suls, J. (eds), *Social Psychology and Health.* Hillsdale, NJ: Lawrence Erlbaum.

Suls, J. and Mullen, B. (1981). Life change in psychological distress: the role of perceived control and desirability. *Journal of Applied Social Psychology,* **11**: 379–89.

Taylor, S.E. (1991). *Health Psychology,* 2nd edn. New York: McGraw-Hill.

Watson, D. and Pennebaker, J.W. (1989). Health complaints, stress and distress: exploring the central role of negative affectivity. *Psychological Review,* **96**: 234–54.

Weinberger, M., Hiner, S.L. and Tierney, W.M. (1987). In support of hassles as a measure of stress in predicting health outcomes. *Journal of Behavioral Medicine,* **10**: 19–31.

Further Reading ▲▲▲

Bailey, R.O. and Clarke, M. (1989). *Stress and Coping in Nursing.* London: Chapman & Hall.

Cooper, C.L. and Payne, R. (eds) (1988). *Causes, Coping and Consequences of Stress at Work.* Chichester: Wiley.

Fontana, D. (1989). *Managing Stress.* London: Routledge/British Psychological Society.

Moos, R.H. (1986). *Coping with Life Crises: An Integrated Approach.* New York: Plenum Press.

Ross, R.R. (1994). *Intervention in Occupational Stress: A Handbook of Counselling for Stress.* London: Sage.

3

Acute Pain

Lindsay S.M. Fraser

LEARNING OBJECTIVES

After studying this chapter you should:

- Understand a conceptual model of pain which includes the role of psychological factors
- Be able to identify individual differences in the psychological components of pain and understand the origins of these differences
- Understand the basic approaches to measuring pain and be able to assess psychological factors that can influence pain behaviour and pain assessment
- Have a basic knowledge of some of the psychological interventions that can be used in the management of acute pain
- Be able to identify misconception and mismanagement of acute pain in clinical practice
- Recognize the important role played by health professionals in instigating adaptive or maladaptive reactions to acute pain

INTRODUCTION

Pain is one of the most common symptoms in ill-health; it is important in diagnosis and in evaluating repsonse to treatment. Pain that is not well controlled is not only unpleasant and disruptive but is known to hinder physical recovery and psychological well-being. Whilst medication has an important role to play, the purpose of this chapter is to explain the role of psychological factors in the experience of acute pain. It will also outline psychological interventions that may be useful in maximizing relief from pain.

DEFINITION OF ACUTE PAIN

Acute pain is defined as any pain which is of recent onset and which is expected to be relatively brief in its duration – for example, as a result of traumatic injuries, burns, surgery, medical procedures and childbirth (International Association for the Study of Pain, IASP, 1992). It is usually symptomatic of actual (or impending) tissue damage and serves a protective role by immobilizing the injured area. Typically, the intensity of the pain is greatest at the time of onset and gradually subsides as healing takes place.

The fundamental issue that must be grasped is that there is more to pain than sensation alone, as verified by the lack of one-to-one correspondence between a painful stimulus and pain experience. 'There is no direct relationship between physical pathology and the intensity of pain' (IASP, 1993, p. 1). Pain also has an emotional component. This dual nature of pain is reflected in the IASP's (1979) definition of pain as 'An unpleasant sensory and emotional experience associated with actual or potential tissue damage, or described in terms of such damage' (p. 250).

Pain is a complex, subjective phenomenon that can only be directly perceived by the sufferer. Whilst individuals do not vary greatly in their ability to detect a sensation (sensation thresholds appear to be fairly constant), they nevertheless show great variability in the level at which they judge a stimulus to be painful (pain threshold) and in their ability to withstand pain (pain tolerance) (Melzack and Wall, 1988). 'For any given amount of visible tissue damage, there are differing magnitudes of pain complaints and analgesic requirements' (IASP, 1992,

p. 6). This diversity in responding, both between different people and within the same person exposed to the same pain at different times (Wells *et al.*, 1988), should immediately alert health professionals to the potential dangers of treating pain as though each person's pain experience is identical. 'Treatment needs to be individualized for each patient' (Justins and Richardson, 1991, p. 561).

Traditionally, acute pain has been viewed as a normal and harmless consequence of tissue damage. However, the presence of unrelieved acute pain may have detrimental consequences in both the short and long term (Cousins, 1989). Not only does pain cause unnecessary suffering, but it inevitably disrupts appetite and sleep, further weakening already debilitated people and dramatically eroding their quality of life. Pain may also hinder immediate recovery by interfering with deep breathing, mobility and compliance with treatment (Lewis *et al.*, 1994). There is also some evidence to suggest that the suboptimal management of acute pain may be connected with the development of a chronic, or long-term, pain condition (Philips and Grant, 1991; Niv and Devor, 1993).

Learning Activity 1 ◆ ◆ ◆

Reflect on the emotional aspect of the experience of acute pain. Choose a clinical situation where you commonly encounter acute pain in another person. Describe how different people react to this situation.

Now reflect on a time (however brief) when you have experienced acute pain in a medical setting and identify the most memorable features of the experience.

PROBLEMS IN THE CONVENTIONAL MANAGEMENT OF ACUTE PAIN

ADULTS

Many people attending hospital experience a considerable amount of pain despite the availability of drugs and techniques to relieve it (Justins and Richardson, 1991). Indeed, there has been a tendency for health professionals to regard inadequate pain relief as acceptable (Rankin and Snider, 1984; Weiss *et al.*, 1983; Brose, 1994), 'resulting in the needless suffering of countless millions of patients' (IASP, 1992, p. 3).

Analgesic prescriptions are often written up in a formulaic fashion according to how painful or otherwise a medical condition or procedure is *expected* to be, with little consideraton of an individual's needs (Whipple *et al* 1995). 'The human being at the centre of the suffering can easily be neglected' (IASP, 1992, p. 6). Often people are not asked if they are in pain (Donovan, 1989), and doctors have been found to consistently under-prescribe analgesia (Marks and Sachar, 1973; Bingle *et al.*, 1991). Even when analgesia has been prescribed people may not be given it, or its effectiveness may not be properly assessed (Cohen, 1980). Paradoxically, whilst the presence of severe pain is often underestimated by health professionals, pain relief tends to be overestimated (Zalon, 1993; Choiniere *et al.*, 1990).

CHILDREN

Inadequate pain control in children has been compounded by the erroneous belief that children, particularly the very young, do not feel as much pain as adults (McGrath and Craig, 1989). 'The view that the nervous system of neonates and infants is

Learning Activity 2 ◆ ◆ ◆

The aim is to recognize mismanagement of acute pain within your own clinical context. Try to recall the phrases most commonly heard relating to acute pain used by members of *your* profession (e.g. 'This isn't too painful'; 'It shouldn't hurt'; 'Most people don't find it too bad'). Now add your own and listen out for others as you go about your work. Choose a couple of the most popular phrases and rate these along the following dimensions:

|-----------------------------------|

Based on sound knowledge — Based on conventional wisdom of fellow professionals

|-----------------------------------|

Considered — Mindless

|-----------------------------------|

For the benefit of the listener — For the benefit of the speaker

|-----------------------------------|

As part of a conversation — Standard schpiel

developmentally immature has been used to support the practice of providing little or no anaesthesia or analgesia for painful invasive procedures' (Pounder and Steward, 1992, p. 970).

This has been shown to be untrue. Pre-term and full-term babies exhibit acute distress in response to tissue damage (Fitzgerald and Anand, 1992). In fact, very young babies may feel more pain than adults because pain inhibitory mechanisms are not fully developed (Fitzgerald, 1991). Yet many paediatric anaesthetists remain reluctant to prescribe anaesthesia or analgesia (Purcell-Jones *et al.*, 1988; McLaughlin *et al.*, 1993). The belief that children feel less pain than adults persists, leading to under-assessment and under-medication (Gonzalez *et al.*, 1993). Any potential long-term consequences of repeated exposure to painful procedures in infancy have yet to be addressed (Grunau *et al.*, 1994).

Evidence of neglect at the other end of the age spectrum is also not hard to find: pain in the elderly attracts little medical and research attention (Melding, 1991) and is often poorly managed (Brockopp *et al.*, 1993).

DISCUSSION OF THE ISSUES

The inadequate management of acute pain has been condemned as being 'morally and ethically unacceptable' (Joint Report of the Royal College of Surgeons and the College of Anaesthetists, 1990, p. 3). Nevertheless, conventional therapy for the treatment of pain is often ineffective (Kuhn *et al.*, 1990). Professional reticence in managing acute pain more aggressively has been fuelled by concerns about the side-effects of pain-relieving drugs (notably, sedation, nausea and respiratory depression) and exaggerated fears of drug addiction (Lander, 1990; Tucker, 1990).

In fact, acute pain can often be successfully controlled without unacceptable side-effects, for example through the use of adjuvant drugs (Reigler, 1994). Moreover, drug addiction is extremely rare: the risk is less than 1%, unless the person was a previous drug abuser (Porter and Jick, 1980). Significant improvements in pain control could be achieved by raising standards of professional education in the use of drugs and other techniques currently available (Max, 1990; IASP, 1991; McCaffery, 1992; Mackintosh, 1994).

The picture is not entirely bleak. Progress is being made in the development of in-hospital services committed to improving the management of acute pain (Rawal and Berggren, 1994). Also, there has been an upsurge in acute pain research which, so far, has lagged behind chronic pain research. 'The tolerant acceptance of unrelieved pain by the patient and by the staff is disappearing' (Alexander and Gardner, 1994, p. 1).

Alongside medical research into improved pain control, the recognition of the importance of psychological factors in the acute pain experience has led to a shift towards more person-centred approaches to pain management (Nichols, 1993). Clinical and research interest into psychological interventions has been gaining momentum. Here the emphasis is on managing the emotional component of pain. Much is already known about the psychology of acute pain which, if implemented, could make a significant contribution to its effective management.

A MODEL OF PAIN

An influential model of pain which gives psychological factors a credible role in the acute pain experience is Melzack and Wall's 'gate-control' theory (Melzack and Wall, 1965, 1988). This can best be imagined as a spinal 'gateway' which has the capacity to modulate pain sensations arriving from the periphery (Figure 3.1). When the gate is open, pain signals are transmitted up to the brain. When the gate is closed, pain transmission is inhibited. This hypothetical gating mechanism can be influenced by both sensory input from the periphery and descending control from the brain.

Activity in large touch-sensation nerve fibres can inhibit the transmission of pain (A). For example, think of 'rubbing a pain better' following an injury with minor tissue damage. This is often effective in reducing the perceived intensity of the pain. In addition, descending influences from central cortical areas may either inhibit (B) or potentiate (C) pain transmission. Psychological factors interact with sensory input to moderate the perception of pain (Turk *et al.*, 1993). For example, mood has been found to influence people's experience of pain: elevated mood appears to increase pain tolerance whilst depressed mood reduces it (Zelman *et al.*, 1991).

Various counter-irritation procedures used to alleviate pain – such as transcutaneous electrical nerve stimulation (TENS) and acupuncture – are believed to close the pain gate, either through their stimulation of afferent fibres or by blocking spinothalamic pathways (Abram, 1992). Interestingly, in recent clinical studies neither TENS nor acupuncture were found to be any more useful in the treatment of acute pain than placebo treatments (Herman *et al.*, 1994; Grabow, 1994). The placebo effect is where a beneficial

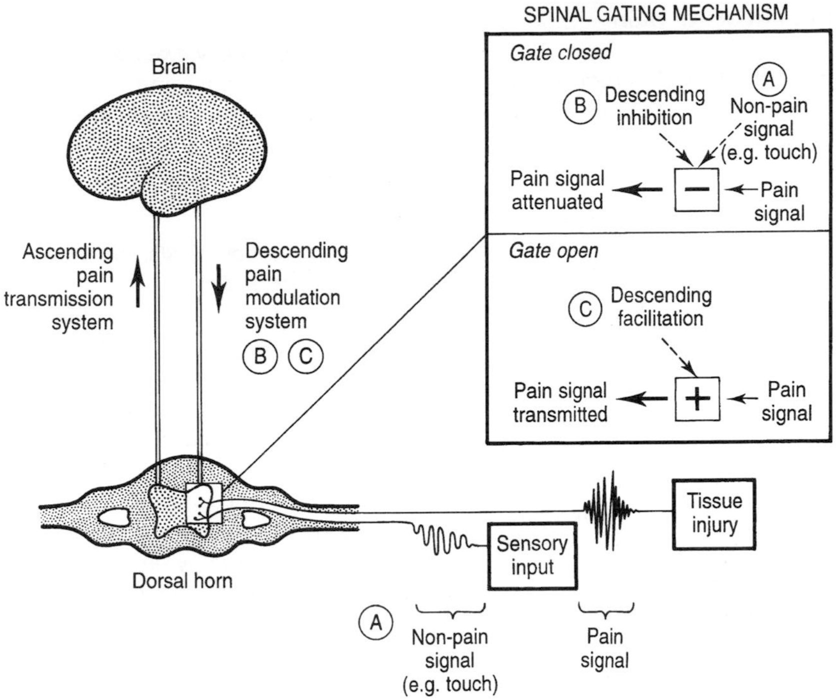

Figure 3.1 *Schematic of simplified gate control mechanism*

therapeutic change takes place in the absence of any active agent. The placebo effect in pain probably reflects the inhibitory roles of expectation and reduced anxiety on spinal gating mechanisms (Turner *et al.*, 1994; Richardson, 1995). 'The potency of the 'placebo' effect provides very strong evidence for a major psychological component in the experience of pain' (Weinman, 1987, p. 9).

Gate-control theory clearly implies that there is no strict distinction between the physical and psychological components of pain, since all pain contains elements of both, although one or the other may predominate in a particular situation. Whilst the specific special gating mechanisms proposed by gate-control theory have not been identified, the theory continues to provide a rational and structured approach to the development of methods of pain control (Melzack, 1993).

PSYCHOLOGY OF ACUTE PAIN

'Psychological factors are always present, whether or not they are acknowledged by patients or therapists. They can be ignored, although their effect on pain may be powerful, or they can be systematically managed in such a way as to maximize pain relief' (IASP, 1992, p. 6).

Pain is never experienced in a contextual vacuum. It always has a meaning to the sufferer and this meaning is influenced by a host of personally relevant factors, including:

- cultural background;
- previous pain history;
- current mood;
- *the person's understanding* of the reason for the pain (which may or may not be accurate);
- its immediate *impact on lifestyle* and relationships;
- its *implications* for the future.

These factors affect the way a person thinks about their pain and, ultimately, their ability to cope with it (Hapidou and DeCatanzaro, 1992; Dar *et al.*, 1995). For example, whilst most people would be unconcerned about experiencing a low level of pain when the cause was both understood and viewed as non-threatening (for example, the aching muscles that typically follow an overly enthusiastic workout), an equivalent amount of discomfort that arises for no apparent reason and which may be feared as a signal of disease, would probably be experienced as distressing and therefore 'more' painful.

Individual differences in acute pain

People differ in terms of their psychological make-up, which explains why they differ in their experience of pain. Differences can be seen in three psychological domains:

- *cognition*: how thoughts influence the experience of pain;
- *affect*: how the emotional state influences pain;
- *behaviour*: the response to being in pain.

It is almost impossible to discuss any one of these areas in isolation from the other two as the three are inextricably linked (Box 3.1). The contents of a person's thoughts are likely to influence their emotional state and vice versa, and both thought and emotion will have a bearing on behaviour. The challenge for the health professional is to tease out the subtle ways in which each person differs in these dimensions and to use the insight gleaned to select the most effective intervention.

COGNITION

Thoughts can be viewed as mediators between pain-evoking sensations and emotional or behavioural reactions (Turk *et al.*, 1983). There are two key cognitive concepts to consider, each of which must be addressed at the outset of treatment.

Pain locus of control (Wallston and Wallston, 1982; Lefcourt and Davidson-Katz, 1991)

Does the person want to play an active role in managing their own pain? Who does the person believe can alleviate the pain? Some people believe they have a role to play and the capacity to reduce pain; they would be said to have an 'internal locus of control'. Others are inclined to hand over responsibility for their care to the health team; they are described as having an 'external locus of control'. In reality there are degrees of internality and externality, and locus of control scales reflect this (Lefcourt, 1981; Penzien *et al.*, 1989).

There is ample evidence to suggest that a perceived lack of personal control is associated with feelings of helplessness (Seligman, 1975), which increases the fearfulness of a painful experience, leading to reduced

Box 3.1 *Relationship between thought, emotion and behaviour*

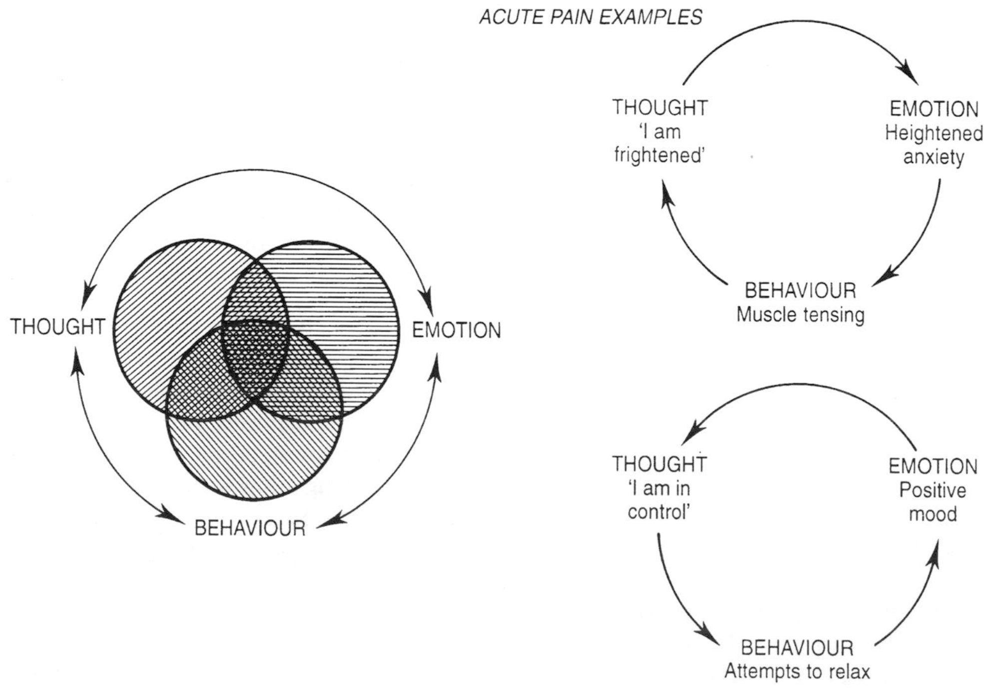

pain tolerance (Thompson, 1981). Those who express a high need for control, but who are denied it, are likely to experience the greatest levels of distress (Logan *et al.*, 1991).

The degree to which a person may adopt an active or passive role may be partially determined by situational factors. The opportunity to pursue an active role may not be available, for example due to the constraints imposed by inflexible hospital regimes. Although staffed by caring health professionals, many hospitals are 'characterized by psychological neglect' of the person (Nichols, 1993, p. 100), because of an institution-centred approach. It is not enough for a person to want to be involved in their own pain management; the opportunity for them to pursue such a role must also be provided.

Coping strategy (Lazarus and Folkman, 1984)

How is the person going to cope with pain? People's spontaneous coping strategies in response to hospitalization have been studied frequently (for a review, see Salmon (1994)). In potentially threatening circumstances (and the prospect of pain would be considered by many as threatening), there appear to be two broad styles of coping:

- 'monitors' who seek out relevant information and think through the implications;
- 'blunters' who avoid information and prefer distraction (Miller, 1987).

Cognitive avoidance appears to be the best strategy in the immediate term. Postoperatively, blunters, or avoiders, appear to fare better than their monitoring counterparts on indices of pain report and consumption of analgesia (Mathews and Ridgeway, 1981), and brief episodes of procedural pain are also better tolerated when the person is distracted from the pain. Importantly, research suggests that interventions should be matched to a person's usual coping style (Miller and Mangan, 1983; Martelli *et al.*, 1987), as a mismatched intervention may reduce coping ability (Rokke and al'Absi, 1992; Fanurik *et al.*, 1993).

A distinction needs to be made between 'cognitive avoidance' which can be an adaptive coping strategy, and 'behavioural avoidance' which is not. A reluctance to mobilize following injury or surgery is likely to hinder a return to normal functioning (Feifel *et al.*, 1987). Behavioural avoidance and feelings of helplessness are characteristic features of those suffering from chronic pain (Philips, 1987). Encouraging people to use more adaptive strategies during the acute pain phase may protect vulnerable individuals from going on to develop a chronic pain condition (Philips and Grant, 1991), or at least help them to cope more effectively with chronic pain should the condition arise.

AFFECT

'For people suffering from painful injuries or diseases, emotional distress provides the most salient, disruptive and undesirable qualities of the experience' (Craig, 1994, p. 261). The predominant emotion associated with acute pain is fear. Emotional arousal is associated with sympathetic excitation and increased muscle tension, which intensify pain (Chapman and Turner, 1986). 'Fear of the unknown' is the most common response to novel medically related procedures (Johnson, 1983). Even intrinsically painless diagnostic or therapeutic procedures may be frightening and indirectly provoke pain and distress (Brennan *et al.*, 1988).

Fear is the core emotion in anxiety (Izard, 1991). Anxiety may be both a precursor of pain and a constant companion to unrelieved acute pain. When acutely painful episodes punctuate an underlying chronic pain condition (such as myofascial pain and rheumatoid arthritis) or a relapsing medical condition (for example, sickle cell crisis and some cancer pain), depression is also likely to be present.

Personality

'Research shows a linear relationship between anxiety and pain, with higher levels of reported pain associated with increased anxiety' (IASP, 1992, p. 19). In the study of anxiety, a distinction has been made between *trait* and *state* anxiety (Spielberger *et al.*, 1970; Edelmann, 1992). Trait anxiety is thought to be an enduring feature of personality, unlike state anxiety which is temporary and results from a situation perceived to be anxiety-provoking. It might therefore be assumed that a person with an anxious personality (trait anxiety) will necessarily experience more pain. In fact, state anxiety appears to be a better predictor of pain experience. This suggests that identifying people who are likely to become anxious in a potentially pain-related situation (state anxiety) will be more helpful in the management of acute pain than simply identifying someone as having an anxious personality (Salmon, 1994). Moreover, it is *attention* rather than *anxiety* that should be the focus of any intervention.

The role of attention

Attention appears to modulate the relationship between anxiety and pain: paying attention to pain heightens pain perception, while distraction decreases it (Arntz *et al.*, 1991). Given that people cannot attend as much to pain when they are concentrating on something else, a number of pain-reducing strategies have been designed which are aimed at displacing the processing of pain by the brain (Turk *et al.*, 1983).

BEHAVIOUR

The term 'pain behaviour' refers to any observable and potentially measurable acts by which a person communicates, intentionally or otherwise, that they are experiencing pain. These include explicit verbal complaints of pain or requests for analgesia, and non-verbal indicators such as sighing, moaning or crying, or reduced activity.

How inhibited (or otherwise) people are in expressing their pain is largely determined by familial and cultural influences (Koopman *et al.*, 1984; Bates, 1987; Neimeyer, 1990; Thomas and Rose, 1991; Bernstein and Pachter, 1992). A child may be rewarded, ignored, or punished for complaining about pain and by adulthood this pattern of behaviour may be well ingrained (Weisenberg, 1977; Turnquist and Engel, 1994). Despite the popular conception that women have lower pain tolerances than men, (Lautenbacher and Rollman, 1983) this view has not been validated in clinical studies (Lander *et al.*, 1990; Fowler and Lander, 1991).

How much pain a person is willing to express may also depend on situational factors. Children may be reluctant to report pain if they associate pain relief with a dreaded painful injection (Eland and Anderson, 1977; Jacox, 1992), whilst adults may be constrained in requesting analgesia in the belief that 'good patients' do not complain of pain, or that other people are more deserving of care (Ward *et al.*, 1993). Conversely, listening to another person's cries of pain can provoke anticipatory anxiety and heighten pain reporting (Craig, 1978). Clearly, then, a number of issues motivate or inhibit pain behaviour. In order to unscramble these, an effective two-way process of communication is required between the individual and the health professional.

Learning Activity 3 ◆ ◆ ◆

Below is a component analysis of the acute pain experience of a young, fit woman undergoing a hystero-salpingogram as an outpatient.

- *Pain intensity*: unbearable/reducing to very intense after 45–60 minutes
- *Feelings*: fear/resentful and cross
- *Thoughts*: it's more pain than it should be/ they're so callous/I wish they'd stop/I can't walk
- *Behaviour*: silence/weak smiles/polite/obedient/ left after 15 minutes
- *Coping strategy*: told self it would soon be over/ told self they had never bothered to find out how painful it was
- *Situational factors*: told by professionals it would not be very painful and would quickly pass off/ no other communication about pain/polite/ informed of findings during the examination/ private cubicle for 10-minute rest

In the light of the previous section, reflect on the implications of this woman's experience both for her and for the professionals concerned.

Repeat this type of analysis on an acute pain experience of your own, or perhaps on one which you have witnessed in your professional capacity.

ASSESSMENT AND MEASUREMENT OF PAIN

'A lack of communication is a major problem in the relationship between patient and healthcare professionals' (King, 1991, p. 127). The person knows what he feels, but may have difficulty in adequately expressing his pain. The health professional, in turn, must accurately interpret the person's pain behaviour. This is a difficult process as adequate behaviour measures are hard to find and are subject to many other influences (Beyer *et al.*, 1990).

It is important to recognize potential sources of bias in the interpretation of pain behaviour by health professionals and in the subsequent action taken to alleviate pain. What is considered a normal and appropriate response to pain by an individual may be perceived as excessive pain-reporting by a health professional accustomed to less emotive behaviour. This may go some way to explain why nurses, for example, have consistently been found to under-assess the severity of people's pain (Zalon, 1993).

Assessment measures

In view of these difficulties, the person's self-report should always be used as the primary source of assessment. A pretreatment measure of pain will

Box 3.2 *Pain intensity scales suggested by the Acute Pain Management Guideline Panel (1992)*

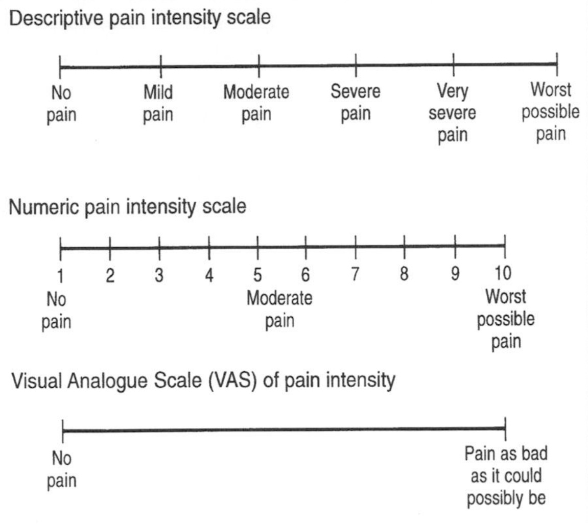

Box 3.3 *Pain distress scales suggested by the Acute Pain Management Guideline Panel (1992)*

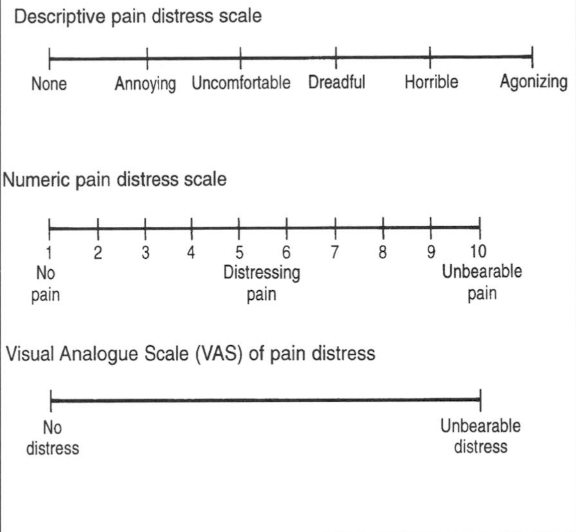

provide a baseline against which to assess the impact, successful or otherwise, of treatment, and pain should continue to be assessed at regular intervals. All of the assessment measures described below have been well-validated and are easy to administer (Turk and Melzack, 1992).

The most commonly used measures of pain in clinical settings (Box 3.2) are the Descriptive Pain Intensity Scale, the Numeric Pain Intensity Scale and the Visual Analogue Scale (VAS). People mark a point on the scale which best describes their pain. These scales can be used to measure how someone estimates their pain in general but, more usually, they are used to record how much pain is being experienced at that point in time. These estimations cannot be done from memory, they have to be done in real time (Beese and Morley, 1993). The scales can also be modified to assess the emotional component of pain (Box 3.3).

The McGill Pain Questionnaire (Melzack, 1987) is useful in assessing the sensory, emotional and evaluative components of the pain experience and in differentiating clinical pain syndromes. People select descriptions from a multiple adjective checklist to describe their pain. People in acute pain tend to score higher on the sensory descriptors, while those with chronic pain score more highly on the emotional words (Melzack *et al.*, 1982; Reading, 1982).

Valuable insight into the nature of a person's pain can be gained by assessing its sensory and emotional features. Consider the example of somebody who undergoes the same painful medical procedure on two separate occasions. During one the pain is described as 'moderate' and during the other as 'severe'. The use of scales which distinguish between pain intensity and pain distress can be helpful in understanding why the two reports differ. Whilst the rating of the sensory component of the pain may be almost identical on both occasions, the person's rating of pain distress may be elevated (perhaps by a perceived lack of ability to control the pain or heightened anxiety). Thus, once identified, the source of that person's distress can be explored in more detail. The person's thoughts, feelings and reactions can be explored as well as an assessment of contributing factors which may have added to the distress.

Measures which simultaneously assess the physical and psychological components of the pain experience provide a level of detail about an individual's pain that can be helpful in tailoring treatment to their needs.

Assessing children's pain

Assessment of young, pre-verbal children's pain requires the use of scales that have been specifically tailored to the developmental level of the child (Lincoln, 1992; Mathews *et al.*, 1992; IASP, 1995). As children's cognitive skills increase, assessment can move from observer-generated pain scales (facial expression, crying) to picture-based pain scales, say a 'hurt thermometer',

Learning Activity 4 ◆ ◆ ◆

Try using the pain scales in a variety of ways to appreciate the subjective nature of pain and to break the habit of ignoring other people's pain. For example:

a Ask people to rate pain intensity and/or pain distress *before* a painful procedure: during it; and afterwards. Reflect on the results.
b Ask people to describe their acute pain using the McGill Pain Questionnaire. Compare the relative strengths of the sensory, emotional and cognitive (evaluative) components across different individuals.
c Using pain scales, ask people to rate their pain three times a day between treatments. Then look at the effect of the treatment.
d Ask some people to rate pain regularly, as in (c), and work out the difference between pretreatment pain and posttreatment pain by comparing the average of the first week's scores with that of the last week's scores.
e Take another set of people and ask them to rate pain only for the first week and last week of treatment. See whether the differences in pain levels after treatment is similar to that for people who rated pain every week. Reflect on whether pain scales might have a therapeutic value in their own right.

'pieces of hurt', or the 'Oucher Scale' (Beyer, 1989; Hester, 1990; McGrath, 1990).

MANAGEMENT OF ACUTE PAIN

An important assumption underpinning psychological approaches to pain management is that a pain response is a learned response and, as such, is amenable to change. Thus, it should be possible to alleviate pain by teaching people new ways of interpreting and coping.

At the outset it should be explained that effective control of acute pain is an important goal. Potential barriers to accurate pain-reporting should be discussed and the use of pain-rating scales explained.

The level of pain reported should not be ignored or challenged. Instead, the health professional should try to establish the magnitude of the psychological factors involved, identify appropriate psychological interventions, and encourage the use of adaptive coping strategies. 'The techniques which appear to have the greatest application are those which increase a patient's sense of control, provide psychological support, permit relaxation, or modify cognitive activity' (IASP, 1992, p. 6).

Psychological interventions are an important part of a multimodal approach to pain management, aimed primarily at increasing pain tolerance levels by reducing distress. Such interventions do not replace analgesics, but are used in conjunction with the appropriate pain-killing drugs, thereby adopting a biopsychosocial approach to management (Engel, 1992; see also Chapters 1 and 4). The interventions discussed here can be performed by most health professionals with minimal training. These include:

- the provision of information;
- behavioural instructions;
- cognitive methods.

For a more detailed description of the use of psychological techniques in the management of acute pain, the reader is referred to Van Dalfsen and Syrjala, 1990; Gil, 1992; Syrjala, 1993; Horne *et al.*, 1994a, b; Tearnan and Ward, 1994; Pain Management Guideline Panel, 1994).

Other techniques of demonstrable clinical value which require specialized clinical expertise such as hypnosis (Hart and Alden, 1994) or the provision of psychotherapy (Fawzy *et al.*, 1990; Nichols, 1993) are not considered here. However, health professionals should recognize the need to refer people on for more extensive psychological counselling when it becomes apparent that the extent of their psychological needs exceeds the support which health carers are equipped to provide (Derogatis *et al.*, 1982; Trijsburg *et al.*, 1992).

Provision of information

People who have little information about a forthcoming medical procedure typically react with anxiety. Studies have shown that people can benefit from two types of preparatory information (Johnson, 1973, 1975):

- *procedural information*: what will be done, the surroundings, and how long it will take;
- *sensory information*: what it will feel like.

Knowing what to expect can be very reassuring and alleviates anxiety and uncertainty (Chapman and Turner, 1986; Wilson-Barnett, 1992).

However, not all people (especially young children) want to know about what is going to happen in advance, and being told can make the situation more difficult for them to cope with. Not surprisingly, 'monitors' appear to derive greater benefit from receiving information than 'blunters' (Mathews and Ridgeway, 1984). For practical purposes, the simplest way of identifying those people who will benefit from receiving information may be to ask (Salmon, 1992)! In the case of young children, parents can be consulted about how their children usually cope in stressful situations (Patterson and Ware, 1988).

Behavioural instructions

Anticipation of pain can be very anxiety-provoking and an anxious person is likely to be both mentally and physically tense. Teaching simple relaxation techniques can help people manage brief episodes of pain. They do not require any specialized equipment or staff training, are easy to learn, and are readily accepted (Davis *et al.*, 1988; Syrjala, 1990; Payne, 1995). Muscle tension can be relieved in a number of ways:

- by taking a deep breath and holding it until tension is felt in the chest and then breathing out;
- by sequentially clenching and unclenching sets of muscles throughout the body, starting with the legs and arms and gradually moving up the body to the shoulders, neck and face (progressive muscle relaxation);
- through the use of slow rhythmic breathing when the person is encouraged to breathe deeply 'from the stomach' rather than shallowly 'from the chest'.

The most profound state of relaxation can be achieved when both body and mind are at ease. The choice of technique depends on the context in which it needs to be used. Muscle tensing, for example, might not be appropriate during a painful procedure or treatment.

Cognitive methods

How people think about their pain affects how they feel towards it; therefore changing how they think about pain can change their sensitivity to it and their feelings and reactions toward it (McGrath, 1990).

Any intervention in which the person plays an active rather than a passive role is to be encouraged, such as the use of distraction, relaxation, or patient-controlled analgesia (PCA). PCA is a drug delivery system that allows people to administer their own analgesia (Heath and Thomas, 1993). People using PCA after surgery report less pain and use less opioid analgesia than those receiving nurse-administered intramuscular injections (Thomas *et al.*, 1993). In addition to these short-term benefits, ensuring that a person does not perceive themselves as a helpless onlooker in their treatment may facilitate their transition back to normal non-hospitalized life (Keefe *et al.*, 1992).

Cognitive interventions can also produce mental relaxation and increase feelings of control (Turner and Romano, 1990). Pain-associated fear and anxiety can be eased by 'cognitive restructuring' which encourages people to use calming 'self-talk' (Tan and Poser, 1982). People replace negative thoughts about the prospect of pain ('I will feel pain and I don't think I will be able to cope with it') with a more positive attitude ('I anticipate that it will be uncomfortable, but I will try to relax and it will soon be over').

A person's misconceptions about pain management can often undermine effective pain control. For example, many people under-report pain in the belief that taking painkillers when the pain is bearable will necessarily mean that pain relief will not be as effective when the pain is severe (Wilder-Smith and Schuler, 1992). In fact it is known that pain is more difficult to control once established, and that analgesia given in anticipation of pain occurring (pre-emptive analgesia) is likely to be more effective in providing good pain control (McQuay and Dickenson, 1990). Misconceptions of this sort need to be clarified at the outset.

Involvement in purposeful mental activity which focuses attention away from the pain can improve pain tolerance (Heck, 1988). Attention to pain can be targeted either directly through the use of distraction techniques, or indirectly through the use of anxiety-reduction techniques.

- *Distraction techniques*: Recreating a pleasant memory, reminiscing, listening to music, or listening to a favourite story (for children) may be used alone to manage mild pain or as an adjunct to analgesic drugs to manage brief episodes of severe pain (Beck, 1991; Syrjala, 1993). The more absorbing the mental activity, the more successful it will be in distracting the person from the pain (McCaul and Malott, 1984).
- *Anxiety-reduction techniques*: Positive emotion induction – for example the use of imagery that

evokes feelings of calm and happiness – is likely to be effective in reducing pain, fear and anxiety (Bruehl *et al.*, 1993). The use of pleasant mental imagery can be used alone or in conjunction with physical methods of relaxation, both of which have been shown to decrease self-reported pain intensity and distress (Graffam and Johnson, 1987; McCaffery and Beebe, 1989).

Recognizing that hospital working practices are not easily modified (Contrada *et al.*, 1994) and that personal control may be unavoidably restricted, it is helpful to know that a person's ability to cope can be enhanced by receiving emotional support from health professionals. This has been shown to reduce anxiety and lower analgesic use (Egbert *et al.*, 1963; Elsass *et al.*, 1987; Schwartz-Barcott *et al.*, 1994). Emotional support can come in many guises, ranging from a willingness to listen to a person's anxieties, a touch, or a genuine smile (Dodds, 1993).

After demonstrating the non-pharmacological interventions available, a person can be given the opportunity to identify factors they have found to increase or decrease their own pain (Booker, 1994) before selecting the appropriate psychological intervention. In this way, people come to recognize that their active participation in their pain management is both possible and desirable.

Many of the techniques mentioned have the advantage of being instant but, to use them effectively, people should be given as much time as possible to practise any chosen strategy before it is needed (for example, listening to a tape-recording of relaxation exercises, either at home prior to admission or on the ward). It is unlikely that any single technique used by a person to reduce pain (such as relaxation) will be sufficient; instead, a combination of strategies (for example, relaxation and a compatible distraction technique) will probably be more effective; or different techniques might be appropriate at different times during the period of acute pain.

Learning Activity 5 ◆ ◆ ◆

Practise identifying psychologial strategies for the management of acute pain in typical clinical settings. Suggest psychological strategies that might be used in the following clinical situations:

a a painful clinical procedure such as the hysterosalpingogram (above); traction, walking; micturating cystogram; radiotherapy
b a non-painful clinical procedure to be undertaken in someone with acute pain as a result of surgery, trauma or disease.

Choose a painful situation which you have personally encountered or often encounter professionally, and repeat the exercise to try to incorporate psychological management of the pain.

MALADAPTIVE REACTIONS TO PAIN

A maladaptive reaction can be viewed as one that either interferes with the effective management of current pain or that places the individual at risk of developing a chronic pain condition. Learning to relax and being able to distract attention away from movement-associated pain during the period of recovery and rehabilitation is an adaptive coping strategy, whereas avoiding movement owing to the fearful prospect of pain that the person feels unable to control is not (Philips, 1987; Rose *et al.*, 1992). In children, the emotional release afforded by crying during a painful procedure is not maladaptive, whereas physical resistance that prolongs a procedure (thereby heightening pain perception) is (Patterson and Ware, 1988).

From acute to chronic pain

There is some evidence to suggest that if pain is not effectively managed at the acute stage, people are put at an increased risk of developing a chronic pain problem (Weiser and Cedraschi, 1992; Klenerman *et al*, 1995). Recovery has been assessed in prospective, longitudinal studies from the time of pain onset up to six months in people with back pain (Philips and Grant, 1991) and up to 12 months in people with herpes zoster (Dworkin *et al.*, 1992). In both studies, 33% of people went on to develop a chronic pain condition. Examination of the data revealed that, at the time of the first assessment, those who subsequently developed a chronic pain condition had reported not only higher pain intensity, but also higher pain distress, higher anxiety, higher avoidance behaviour and more negative, helpless thinking about their pain. Moreover, most of the maladaptive reactions to the pain occurred in the first three months. 'The evolution of a chronic problem appears not to be a process of growth, but one of maintenance or limitation of decline' (Philips and Grant, 1991, p. 440).

Learning Activity 6 ◆ ◆ ◆

How might the following clinical practices (i) encourage or (ii) discourage maladaptive pain responses?

a an information leaflet on procedural and sensory aspects of a procedure
b minimal eye contact during the interaction
c stock phrases and introductions
d piped music
e lack of privacy and space
f busy schedules.

Have you ever experienced these in your clinical work? Can you suggest any changes that might prevent (b), (c), (e) and (f) (inadequate management strategies) from persisting?

These findings suggest that it is equally important to effectively manage both the intensity of pain and the person's reaction to pain during the acute pain phase. Professionals have a role in teaching people the skills required to cope effectively with acute pain in order to minimize the risk of future long-term pain (Klenerman *et al*, 1995). Once established, maladaptive coping patterns are difficult and time-consuming to reverse. 'The implication is that the ever-increasing resources being funnelled into chronic pain management might be more effectively spent on prevention at a very early stage' (Philips *et al.*, 1991, p. 450).

When in regular contact with somebody during a painful episode, professionals are ideally positioned to encourage adaptive pain reactions. Through an understanding of the psychological factors involved in the acute pain experience, their skilled intervention can lessen suffering, assist recovery and rehabilitation, and may also serve to protect vulnerable individuals from the development of chronic pain. 'It does not necessarily take more time or a special expertise for the therapist to put many helpful forms of non-pharmacologic treatment to effective use; it does take awareness, sensitivity, and willingness to approach patients and pain management from a broad perspective' (IASP, 1992, p. 6).

SUMMARY

People vary in their experience of pain because it consists of physical and psychological components. Models that attempt to integrate these components are still evolving and are essential to effective pain management. Measures have been developed to help in the assessment of psychosocial factors in an individual's pain, as have methods which directly manipulate psychological processes. Approaching acute pain management from a broad biopsychosocial perspective is the way forward.

Key Points ■ ■ ■

- ❒ Pain is a subjective experience made up of sensory and psychological components.
- ❒ The 'gate-control' theory of pain justifies the role of psychological factors in acute pain.
- ❒ Situational and management factors can be instrumental in increasing the degree of pain by ignoring or aggravating the psychological components of pain.
- ❒ Assessment of acute pain is not simply the measurement of how much pain exists (quantity), but of ascertaining the nature (quality) of the overall pain experience.
- ❒ Active participation and partnership in the management of acute pain promotes recovery and rehabilitation and reduces the risk of maladaptive patterns becoming established.
- ❒ Management is aimed at increasing the person's sense of control and encouraging adaptive coping strategies, whether or not analgesics are a part of the overall management strategy.

References ▼ ▼ ▼

Abram, S.E. (1992). 1992 Bonica Lecture. Advances in chronic pain management since gate control. *Regional Anaesthesia*, **18**(2): 66–81.

Alexander, J.I. and Gardner, F.V. (1994). Prevention and management of postoperative pain. In: Gibson, H.B. (ed.) *Psychology, Pain and Anaesthesia*. London: Chapman and Hall, 1–24.

Arntz, A. Dreessen, L. and Merkelbach, H. (1991). Attention, not anxiety, influences pain. *Behaviour Research and Therapy*, **29**(1): 41–50.

Bates, M.S. (1987). Ethnicity and pain: a biocultural model. *Social Science Medicine*, **24**(1): 47–50.

Beck, S.L. (1991). The therapeutic use of music for cancer-related pain. *Oncology Nursing Forum*, **18**(8): 1327–37.

Beese, A. and Morley S. (1993) Memory for acute pain experience is specifically inaccurate but generally reliable. *Pain* **53**(2): 183–189.

Bernstein, B.A. and Pachter, L.M. (1992). Cultural considerations in children's pain. In: Schechter, N.L. Berde, C.B. and Yaster, M.

(eds.) *Pain in Infants, Children, and Adolescents*. Baltimore, MD: Williams and Wilkins, 113–22.

Beyer, J.E. (1989). The Oucher Scale: a pain intensity scale for children. In: Funk, S.G. *et al.* (eds.), *Key Aspects of Comfort.* New York: Springer, 65–71.

Beyer, J.E., McGrath, P.J. and Berde, C.B. (1990). Discordance between self-report and behavioral pain measures in children aged 3–7 years after surgery. *Journal of Pain and Symptom Management*, **5**(6): 350–6.

Bingle, G.J., O'Connor, T.P., Evans, W.O. *et al.* (1991). The effect of 'detailing' on physicians' prescribing behaviour for postsurgical narcotic analgesia. *Pain*, **45**(2): 171–3.

Booker, C.K. (1994). Rehabilitation of the chronic pain patient. In: Gibson, H.B. (ed.) *Psychology, Pain and Anaesthesia*. London: Chapman and Hall, 25–56.

Brennan, S.C., Redd, W.H., Jacobsen, P.B. *et al.* (1988). Anxiety and panic during magnetic resonance scans. *Lancet*, **2**(8609): 512.

Brockopp, D.Y., Warden, S., Colclough, G. *et al.* (1993). Nursing knowledge: acute postoperative pain management in the elderly. *Journal of Gerontological Nursing*, **19**(11): 31–7.

Brose, W.G. (1994). Health outcomes (editorial). *Clinical Journal of Pain*, **10**(2): 89–94.

Bruehl, S., Carlson, C.R. and McCubbin, J.A. (1993). Two brief interventions for acute pain. *Pain*, **54**(1): 29–36.

Chapman, C.R. and Turner, J.A. (1986). Psychological control of acute pain in medical settings. *Journal of Pain and Symptom Management*, **1**(1): 9–20.

Choiniere, M., Melzack, R., Girard, N. *et al.* (1990). Comparisons between patients' and nurses' assessment of pain and medication efficacy in severe burn patients. *Pain*, **40**(2): 143–52.

Cohen, F.L. (1980). Postsurgical pain relief: patients' status and nurses' medication choices. *Pain*, **9**(2): 265–74.

Contrada, R.J., Leventhal, E.A., and Anderson, J.R. (1994). Psychological preparation for surgery: marshalling individual and social resources to optimize self-regulation. In Maes S., Leventhal H. and Johnston M. (eds) International Review of Health Psychology, **3**: 219–66. Chichester: Wiley.

Cousins, M.J. (1989). John J. Bonica distinguished lecture. Acute pain and the injury response: immediate and prolonged effects. *Regional Anaesthesia*, **14**(4): 162–79.

Craig, K.D. (1978). Social modelling influences on pain. In: Sternbach, R.A. (ed.), *The Psychology of Pain*. New York: Raven Press, 73–109.

Craig, K.D. (1994). Emotional aspects of pain. In: Wall, PD and Melzack, R. (eds.) *Textbook of Pain*. London: Churchill Livingstone, 261–74.

Dar, R., Ariely, D. and Frenk, H. (1995). The effect of past injury on pain threshold and tolerance. *Pain*, **60**(2): 189–93.

Davis, M., Eshelman, E.R. and McKay, M. (1988). *The Relaxation and Stress Reduction Workbook*, 3rd edn. Oakland, CA: New Harbinger.

Derogatis, L.R., Morrow, G.R., Fetting, J. *et al.* (1982). The prevalence of psychiatric disorders among cancer patients. *Journal of the American Medical Association*, **249**: 751–7.

Dodds, F. (1993). Access to the coping strategies: managing anxiety in elective surgical patients. *Professional Nurse*, **9**(1): 45–52.

Donovan, M.I. (1989). Relieving the pain: the current bases for practice. In: Funk, S.G. *et al.* (eds.), *Key Aspects of Comfort.* New York: Springer, 25–31.

Dworkin, R.H., Hartstein, G., Rosner, H.L. *et al.* (1992). A high-risk method for studying psychosocial antecedents of chronic pain: the prospective investigation of herpes zoster. *Journal of Abnormal Psychology*, **101**(1): 200–205.

Edelmann, R.J. (1992). *Anxiety: Theory, Research and Intervention in Clinical and Health Psychology.* Chichester: Wiley.

Egbert, L.D., Battit, G.E., Turndorf, H. *et al.* (1963). The value of the preoperative visit by an anaesthetist. *Journal of the American Medical Association*, **185**: 553–5.

Eland and Anderson (1977). The experience of pain in children. In: Jacox, A.K. (ed.), *Pain: A Source Book for Nurses and Other Health Care Professionals*. Boston: Little, Brown, 453–73.

Elsass, P., Duedahl, H., Friis, B. *et al.* (1987). The psychological effects of having a contact-person from the anaesthetic staff. *Acta Anaesthesiologica Scandinavica*, **31**(7): 584–6.

Engel, G.L. (1992). The need for a new medical model: a challenge for biomedicine. *Family Systems Medicine*, **10**: 317–31.

Fanurik, D., Zeltzer, L.K., Roberts, M.C. *et al.* (1993). The relationship between children's coping styles and psychological interventions for cold pressor pain. *Pain*. **53**(2): 213–22.

Fawzy, F.I., Cousins, N. Fawzy, N.W. *et al.* (1990). A structured psychiatric intervention for cancer patients. I: Changes over time in methods of coping and affective disturbance. *Archives of General Psychiatry*, **47**(8): 720–25.

Feifel, H. Strack, S. and Nagy, V.T. (1987). Coping strategies and associated features of medically ill patients. *Psychosomatic Medicine*, **49**(6): 616–25.

Fitzgerald, M. (1991). Development of pain mechanisms. *British Medical Bulletin*, **47**(3): 667–75.

Fitzgerald, M. and Anand, K.J.S. (1992). Developmental neuroanatomy and neurophysiology of pain. In: Schechter, N.L. *et al.* (eds.), *Pain in Infants, Children and Adolescents*. Baltimore, MD: Williams and Wilkins, 11–31.

Fowler, K.S. and Lander, J. (1991). Assessment of sex differences in children's and adolescents' self-reported pain from venipuncture. *Journal of Pediatric Psychology*, **16**(6): 783–93.

Gil, K.M. (1992). Psychologic aspects of acute pain. In: Sinatra, R.S. *et al.* (eds.), *Acute Pain: Mechanisms and Management*. London: Mosby YearBook, 58–69.

Gonzalez, J.C., Routh, D.K. and Armstrong, F.D. (1993). Differential medication of child versus adult postoperative patients: the effect of nurses' assumptions. *Children's Health Care*, **22**(1): 47–59.

Grabow, L. (1994). Controlled study in the analgetic effectivity of acupuncture. *ArzneimittelForschung*, **44**(4): 554–8.

Graffam, S. and Johnson, S. (1987). A comparison of two relaxation strategies for the relief of pain and its distress. *Journal of Pain and Symptom Management*, **2**(4): 229–31.

Grunau, R.V.E., Whitfield, M.F., Petrie, J.H. *et al.* (1994). Early pain experience, child and family factors, as precursors of somatization: a prospective study of extremely premature and fullterm children. *Pain*, **56**(3): 353–9.

Hapidou, E.G. and DeCatanzaro, D. (1992). Responsiveness to laboratory pain in women as a function of age and childbirth pain experience. *Pain*, **48**(2): 177–81.

Hart, B.B. and Alden, P.A. (1994). Hypnotic techniques in the control of pain. In: Gibson, H.B. (ed.), *Psychology, Pain and Anaesthesia*. London: Chapman and Hall, 120–45.

Heath, M.L. and Thomas, V.J. (1993). *Patient-Controlled Analgesia: Confidence in Postoperative Pain Control*. Oxford: Oxford University Press.

Heck, S.A. (1988). The effect of purposeful activity on pain tolerance. *American Journal of Occupational Therapy*, **42**(9): 577–81.

Herman, E., Williams, R., Stratford, P. *et al.* (1994). A randomized controlled trial of transcutaneous electrical nerve stimulation (CODETRON) to determine its benefits in a rehabilitation program for acute occupational low back pain. *Spine*, **19**(5): 561–8.

Hester, N.O. (1990). Measuring children's pain: the convergent and discriminant validity of the pain ladder and the poker chip tool. *Journal of Pain and Symptom Management*, **4**: S6.

Horne, D.J., Vatmanidis, P. and Careri, A. (1994a). Preparing patients for invasive medical and surgical procedures. 1: Adding behavioral and cognitive interventions. *Behavioral Medicine*, **20**(1): 5–13.

Horne, D.J., Vatmanidis, P. and Careri, A. (1994b). Preparing patients for invasive medical and surgical procedures. 2: Using psychological interventions with adults and children. *Behavioral Medicine*, **20**(1): 15–21.

International Association for the Study of Pain (1979). Subcommittee on Taxonomy. II: Pain terms: a current list with definitions and notes on usage. *Pain*, **6**: 249–52.

International Association for the Study of Pain (1992). In: Ready, L. B. and Edwards, W.T. (eds), *Task Force on Acute Pain. The Management of Acute Pain: A Practical Guide*. Seattle: IASP Publications.

International Association for the Study of Pain (1993). *Pain:*

Clinical Updates. Vol. 1(3): Assess the Person, Not Just the Pain. Englewood, CO: Postgraduate Institute for Medicine, 1–4.

International Association for the Study of Pain (1995). *Pain: Clinical Updates. Vol. 3(2): Pain Measurement in Children.* Englewood, CO: Postgraduate Institute for Medicine, 1–4.

Izard, C.E. (1991). *The Psychology of Emotions.* London: Plenum Press.

Jacox, A. (1992). Clinicians' quick reference guide to acute pain management in infants, children, and adolescents: operative and medical procedures. *Journal of Pain and Symptom Management,* **7**: 229–42.

Johnson, J.E. (1973). Effects of accurate expectations about sensations on the sensory and distress components of pain. *Journal of Personality and Social Psychology,* **27**(2): 261–75.

Johnson, J.E. (1975). Stress reduction through sensory information. In: Speilberger C.D. and Sarasson I.G. (eds) *Stress and Anxiety,* Washington DC: Hemisphere Publishing Corporation.

Johnson, J.E. (1983). Preparing patients to cope with stress while hospitalised. In: Wilson-Barnett, J. (ed.), *Patient Teaching: Recent Advances in Nursing Service,* vol. 5. Edinburgh: Churchill-Livinstone, 19–37.

Joint Report of the Royal College of Surgeons and the College of Anaesthetists (1990). *Commission on the Provision of Surgical Services: A Report of the Working Party on Pain After Surgery.* London: RCSE/CA.

Justins, D.M. and Richardson, P.H. (1991). Clinical management of acute pain. *British Medical Bulletin,* **47**(3): 561–83.

Keefe, F.J., Salley, A.N. and Lefebvre, J.C. (1992). Coping with pain: conceptual concerns and future directions (editorial). *Pain,* **51**(2): 131–4.

King, P.E. (1991). Communication, anxiety, and the management of postoperative pain. *Health Communication,* **3**(2): 127–38.

Klenerman, L., Slade P.D., Stanley I.M. *et al* (1995) The prediction of chronicity in patients with an acute attack of low back pain in a general practice setting. *Spine,* **20**(4): 478–84.

Koopman, C., Eisenthal, S. and Stoeckle, J.D. (1984). Ethnicity in the reported pain, emotional distress and requests of medical outpatients. *Social Science and Medicine,* **18**(6): 487–90.

Kuhn, S., Cooke, K., Collins, M. *et al.* (1990). Perceptions of pain relief after surgery. *British Medical Journal,* **300**: 1687–90.

Lander, J. (1990). Fallacies and phobias about addiction and pain. *British Journal of Addiction,* **85**(6): 803 9.

Lander, J., Fowler, K.S. and Hill, A. (1990). Comparison of pain perceptions among males and females. *Canadian Journal of Nursing Research,* **22**(1): 39–49.

Lautenbacher, S. and Rollman, G.B. (1993). Sex differences in responsiveness to painful and non-painful stimuli are dependent upon the stimulation method. *Pain,* **53**(3): 255–64.

Lazarus, R.S. and Folkman, S. (1984). *Stress, Appraisal and Coping.* New York: Springer.

Lefcourt, H.M. (ed.) (1981). *Research with the Locus of Control Construct. Vol. 1: Assessment Methods.* London: Academic Press.

Lefcourt H.M. and Davidson-Katz K. (1991) Locus of control and health. In Snyder C.R. and Forsyth D.R. (eds) *Handbook of Social Clinical Psychology: The Heath Perspective.* Pergamon General Psychology series, **162**: 246–66. New York: Pergamon Press.

Lewis, K.S., Whipple, J.K., Michael, K.A. *et al.* (1994). Effect of analgesic treatment on the physiological consequences of acute pain. *American Journal of Hospital Pharmacy,* **51**(12): 1539–54.

Lincoln, L.M. (1992). Children's response to acute pain: a developmental approach. *Journal of the American Academy of Nurse Practitioners,* **4**(4): 139–42.

Logan, H.L., Baron, R.S., Keeley, K. *et al.* (1991). Desired control and felt control as mediators of stress in a dental setting. *Health Psychology,* **10**(5): 352–9.

Mackintosh, C. (1994). Do nurses provide adequate postoperative pain relief? *British Journal of Nursing,* **3**(7): 342–7.

Marks, R.M. and Sachar, E. (1973). Undertreatment of medical inpatients with narcotic analgesics. *Annals of Internal Medicine,* **78**: 173–81.

Martelli, M.F., Auerbach, S.M., Alexander, J. *et al.* (1987). Stress management in the health care setting: matching interventions with patient coping styles. *Journal of Consulting and Clinical Psychology,* **55**(2): 201–7.

Mathews, A. and Ridgeway, V. (1981). Personality and surgical recovery: a Review. *British Journal of Clinical Psychology,* **20**(14): 243–60.

Mathews A. and Ridgeway V. (1984) Psychological preparation for surgery. In Steptoe A. and Mathews A. (eds) *Health Care and Human Behaviour,* 231–59. London: Academic Press.

Mathews, J.R., McGrath, P.J. and Pigeon, H. (1992). Assessment and measurement of pain in children. In: Schechter, N.L., Berde, C.B. and Yaster, M. (eds), *Pain in Infants, Children and Adolescents.* Baltimore: Williams and Wilkins, 97–111.

Max, M.B. (1990). Improving outcomes of analgesic treatment: is education enough? *Annals of Internal Medicine,* **113**(11): 885–9.

McCaffery, M. for the World Health Organization Expert Committee on Cancer Pain Relief and Active Supportive Care, Pain control: barriers to the use of available information. *Cancer,* **70**(5 suppl.): 1438–49.

McCaffery, M. and Beebe, A. (1989). *Pain: Clinical Manual for Nursing Practice.* St Louis: C.V. Mosby.

McCaul, K.D. and Malott, J.M. (1984). Distraction and coping with pain. *Psychological Bulletin,* **95**(3): 516–33.

McGrath, P.A. (ed.) (1990). *Pain in Children: Nature, Assessment and Treatment.* New York: Guilford Press.

McGrath, P.J. and Craig, K.D. (1989). Developmental and psychological factors in children's pain. *Pediatric Clinics of North America,* **36**(4): 823–35.

McLaughlin, C.R., Hull, J.G., Edwards, W.H. *et al.* (1993). Neonatal pain: a comprehensive survey of attitudes and practices. *Journal of Pain Symptom Management,* **8**(1): 7–16.

McQuay, H.J. and Dickenson, A.H. (1990). Implications of nervous system plasticity for pain management. *Anaesthesia,* **45**(2): 101–2.

Melding, P.S. (1991). Is there such a thing as geriatric pain? (editorial) *Pain,* **46**(2): 119–21.

Melzack, R. (1987). The short-form McGill Pain Questionnaire. *Pain,* **30**(2): 191–7.

Melzack, R. (1993). Pain: past, present and future. *Canadian Journal of Experimental Psychology,* **47**(4): 615–29.

Melzack, R. and Wall, P.D. (1965). Pain mechanisms: a new theory. *Science,* **150**: 971–9.

Melzack, R. and Wall, P.D. (1988) *The Challenge of Pain,* 2nd edn. London: Penguin Books.

Melzack, R., Wall, P. and Ty, T. (1982). Acute pain in an emergency clinic: latency of onset and descriptor patterns related to different injuries. *Pain,* **14**: 33–43.

Melzack R. and Wall D. (1994) Pain mechanisms: a new theory. In Steptoe A. and Wardle J. (eds) *Psychosocial Processes and Health: A Reader.* 112–31. Cambridge: Cambridge University Press.

Miller, S.M. (1987). Monitoring and blunting: validation of a questionnaire to assess styles of information-seeking under threat. *Journal of Personality and Social Psychology,* **52**(2): 345–53.

Miller, S.M. and Mangan, C.E. (1983). The interacting effects of information and coping style in adapting to gynaecological stress: should the doctor tell all? *Journal of Personality and Social Psychology,* **45**(1): 223–36.

Neimeyer, L.O. (1990). Psychologic and sociocultural aspects of responses to pain. *Occupational Therapy Practice,* **1**(3): 11–20.

Nichols, K.A. (1993). *Psychological Care in Physical Illness,* 2nd edn. London: Chapman and Hall.

Niv, D. and Devor, M. (1993). Does the blockade of surgical pain preempt postoperative pain and prevent its transition to chronicity? In: *IASP Newsletter,* Nov/Dec. Seattle: IASP Publications.

Pain Management Guideline Panel (1994). *Management of Cancer Pain. Nonpharmacologic Management: Physical and Psychosocial Modalities* (Clinical Practice Guideline 9, AHCPR Publication 94-0592). Rockville, MD: Agency for Health Care Policy and Research, 75–87.

Park, G. and Fulton, B. (1991). *The Management of Acute Pain.* Oxford: Oxford University Press.

Patterson, K.L. and Ware, L.L. (1988). Coping skills for children undergoing painful medical procedures. *Issues in Comprehensive Pediatric Nursing,* **11**(2–3): 113–43.

Payne, R.A. (ed.) (1995). *Relaxation Techniques: A Practical Handbook for the Health Care Professional.* London: Churchill Livingstone.

Penzien, D.B., Mosley, T.H., Knowlton, G.E. *et al.* (1989).

Psychometric properties of the Pain Locus of Control Scale (abstract). *Proceedings of the American Pain Society*, **8**: 68.

Philips, H.C. (1987). Avoidance behaviour and its role in sustaining chronic pain, Special issue: chronic pain. *Behaviour Research and Therapy*, **25**(4): 273–9.

Philips, H.C. and Grant, L. (1991). The evolution of chronic back pain problems: a longitudinal study. *Behaviour Research and Therapy*, **29**(5): 435–41.

Philips, H.C., Grant, L. and Berkowitz, J. (1991). The prevention of chronic pain and disability: a preliminary investigation. *Behaviour Research and Therapy*, **29**(5): 443–50.

Porter, J. and Jick, H. (1980). Addiction rare in patients treated with narcotics. *New England Journal of Medicine*, **302**: 123.

Pounder, D.R. and Steward, D.J. (1992). Postoperative analgesia: opioid infusions in infants and children. *Canadian Journal of Anaesthesia*, **39**(9): 969–74.

Purcell-Jones, G., Dormon, F. and Sumner, E. (1988). Paediatric anaesthesists' perceptions of neonatal and infant pain. *Pain*, **33**: 181–7.

Rankin, M.A. and Snider, B. (1984). Nurses' perceptions of cancer patients' pain. *Cancer Nursing*, **7**: 149–55.

Rawal, N. and Berggren, L. (1994). Organization of acute pain services: a low-cost model. *Pain*, **57**(1): 117–23.

Reading, A.E. (1982). A comparison of the McGill Pain Questionnaire in chronic and acute pain. *Pain*, **13**: 185–92.

Reigler, F. (1994). Update on perioperative pain management. *Clinical Orthopaedics*, **305**: 283–92.

Richardson, P.H. (1995). Placebos: their effectiveness and modes of action. In: Broome, A.K. and Llewelyn, S. (eds.), *Health Psychology: Process and Applications*, 2nd edn. London: Chapman and Hall, 35–51.

Rokke, P.D. and al'Absi, M. (1992). Matching pain coping strategies to the individual: a prospective validation of the Cognitive Coping Strategy Inventory. *Journal of Behavioral Medicine*, **15**(6): 611–25.

Rose, M.J., Klenerman, L., Atkinson, L. *et al*. (1992). An application of the fear avoidance model to three chronic pain problems. *Behaviour Research and Therapy*, **30**(4): 359–65.

Salmon, P. (1992). Psychological factors in surgical stress: implications for management. *Clinical Psychology Review*, **12**: 681–704.

Salmon, P. (1994). Psychological factors in surgical recovery. In: Gibson, H.B. (ed.), *Psychology, Pain and Anaesthesia*. London: Chapman and Hall, 229–58.

Schwartz-Barcott, D., Fortin, J.D. and Kim, H.S. (1994). Client–nurse interaction: testing for its impact in preoperative instruction. *International Journal of Nursing Studies*, **31**(1): 23–35.

Seligman, M.E.P. (1975). *Helplessness: On Depression, Development and Death*, San Francisco: Freeman.

Spielberger, C.D., Gorsuch, R.L. and Lushene, R.E. (1970). *The State–Trait Anxiety Inventory*. Palo Alto, CA: Psychologist Press.

Syrjala, K.L. (1990). Relaxation techniques. In: Bonica, J (ed.), *The Management of Pain*, vol. 2, 2nd edn. Philadelphia: Lea and Febiger, 1742–50.

Syrjala, K.L. (1993). Integrating medical and psychological treatments for cancer pain. In: Chapman, C.R. and Foley, K.M. (eds.), *Current and Emerging Issues in Cancer Pain: Research and Practice*. The Bristol Myers Squibb Symposium on Pain Research. New York: Raven Press, 393–409.

Tan, S.Y. and Poser, E.G. (1982). Acute pain in a clinical setting: effects of cognitive–behavioral skills training. *Behaviour Research and Therapy*, **20**(6): 535–45.

Tearnan, B.H. and Ward, C.H. (1994). Psychological management of malignant pain. In: Tollison, C.D. (ed.), *Handbook of Pain Management*, 2nd edn. London: Williams and Wilkins, 431–46.

Thomas, V.J. and Rose, F.D. (1991). Ethnic differences in the experience of pain. *Social Science and Medicine*, **32**(9): 1063–6.

Thomas, V.J. Rose, F.D., Heath, M.L. *et al*. (1993). A multidimensional comparison of nurse and patient controlled analgesia in the management of acute postsurgical pain. *Medical Science Research*, **21**(10): 379–381.

Thompson, S.C. (1981). Will it hurt less if I can control it? A complex answer to a simple question. *Psychological Bulletin*, **90**(1): 89–101.

Trijsburg, R.W., van-Knippenberg, F.C. and Rijpma, S.E. (1992). Effects of psychological treatment on cancer patients: a critical review. *Psychosomatic Medicine*, **54**(4): 489–517.

Tucker, C. (1990). Acute pain and substance abuse in surgical patients. *Journal of Neuroscience Nursing*, **22**(6): 339–49.

Turk, D.C. and Melzack, R. (eds) (1992). *Handbook of Pain Assessment*. London: Guilford Press.

Turk, D.C., Meichenbaum, D. and Genest, M. (1983). *Pain and Behavioural Medicine: A Cognitive–Behavioural Perspective*. New York: Guilford Press.

Turk, D.C. and Melzack, R. (eds) (1992). *Handbook of Pain Assessment* London: Guilford: Guildford Press.

Turk, D.C., Rudy, T.E. and Boucek, C.D. (1993). Psychological aspects of pain. In: Warfield, C.A. (ed.), *Principles and Practice of Pain Management*. London: McGraw-Hill, 43–52.

Turner, J.A. and Romano, J.M. (1990). Cognitive–behavioural therapy. In: Bonica, J.J. (ed.), *The Management of Pain*, 2nd edn. Philadelphia: Lea and Febiger, 1711–21.

Turner, J.A., Deyo, R.A., Loeser, J.D. *et al*. (1994). The importance of placebo effects in pain treatment and research. *Journal of the American Medical Association*, **271**(20): 1609–14.

Turnquist, K.M. and Engel, J.M. (1994). Occupational therapists' experiences and knowledge about pain in children. *Physical and Occupational Therapy in Pediatrics*, **14**: 35–51.

Van Dalfsen, P.J. and Syrjala, K.L. (1990). Psychological strategies in acute pain management. *Critical Care Clinics*, **6**(2): 421–31.

Wallston, K.A. and Wallston, B.S. (1982). Who is responsible for your health? The construct of health locus of control. In: Sanders, G. and Suls, J.M. (eds.), *Social Psychology of Health and Illness*. Hillsdale, NJ: Erlbaum.

Ward, S.E., Goldberg, N., Miller-McCauley, V. *et al*. (1993). Patient-related barriers to management of cancer pain. *Pain*, **52**(3): 319–24.

Weinman, J. (1987). *An Outline of Psychology as Applied to Medicine*, 2nd edn. Bristol: Wright.

Weis, O.F., Sriwatanakul, K., Alloza, J.L. *et al*. (1983). Attitudes of patients, housestaff and nurses toward post-operative analgesic care. *Anaesthesia and Analgesia*. **62**: 70–4.

Weisenberg, M. (1977). Pain and pain control. *Psychological Bulletin*, **84**(5): 1008–44.

Weiser, S. and Cedraschi, C. (1992). Psychosocial issues in the prevention of chronic low back pain: a literature review. *Baillière's Clinical Rheumatology*, **6**(3): 657–84.

Wells, P.E., Frampton, V. and Bowsher, D. (eds.) (1988). *Pain: Management and Control in Physiotherapy*. London: Heinemann Medical.

Whipple, J.K., Lewis, K.S., Quebbman, E.J. *et al*. (1995) Current patterns of prescribing and administering morphine in trauma patients. *Pharmacotherapy*, **15**(2): 210–5.

Wilder-Smith, C.H. and Schuler, L. (1992). Postoperative analgesia: pain by choice? The influence of patient attitudes and patient education. *Pain*, **50**(3): 257–62.

Wilson-Barnett, J. (1992). Psychological reactions to medical procedures. *Psychotherapy and Psychosomatics*, **57**(3): 118–27.

Zalon, M.L. (1993): Nurses' assessment of postoperative patients' pain. *Pain*, **54**(3): 329–34.

Zelman, D.C., Howland, E.W., Nichols, S.N. *et al*. (1991). The effects of induced mood on laboratory pain. *Pain*, **46**(1): 105–11.

Further Reading ▲ ▲ ▲

Davis, M., Eshelman, E.R. and McKay, M. (1988). *The Relaxation and Stress Reduction Workbook*, 3rd edn. Oakland, CA: New Harbinger.

Melzack, R. and Wall, P.D. (1988). *The Challenge of Pain*, 2nd edn. London: Penguin Books.

Park, G. and Fulton, B. (1991). *The Management of Acute Pain*. Oxford: Oxford University Press.

Schechter, N.L., Berde, C.B. and Yaster, M. (eds) (1992). *Pain in Infants, Children, and Adolescents*. Baltimore, MD: Williams and Wilkins.

Turk, D.C. and Melzack, R. (eds.) (1992). *Handbook of Pain Assessment*. London: Guilford Press.

4

Chronic Pain

Kate Ridout

LEARNING OBJECTIVES

After studying this chapter you should:

- Appreciate the biopsychosocial nature of chronic pain
- Be able to recognize and describe psychosocial processes associated with chronic pain
- See and assess aspects of chronic pain that might be amenable to change
- Understand strategies within the clinical setting that optimally manage chronic pain

INTRODUCTION

Chronic pain is a condition that frequently has no visible signs, may not be readily explained in terms of underlying pathology, and all too often does not respond to active treatment. It is poorly understood by professionals and non-professionals, so that once the acute phase turns into long-term pain and all the investigations are complete, treatment dwindles away and the person is left to 'learn to live with it'. This chapter looks at chronic pain as a biopsychosocial phenomenon and shows how the management of certain psychological processes can provide much-needed relief.

WHAT IS CHRONIC PAIN?

Chronic pain is defined quite literally as pain (excluding cancer-related pain) that continues to be experienced for more than three months from the time of its original onset. This definition makes no assumptions about causality or the mechanisms behind pain of this sort. However, there are widely held beliefs amongst health professionals and the public which raise important conceptual issues. These are:

- There is some sort of direct relationship between pain and pathology.
- There are specified levels or ranges of pain.
- There is a healing time.

The phenomenon of chronic pain challenges these beliefs, leading to a distinction being made between 'real' physical pain and 'psychogenic' or 'functional' pain (i.e. that which is psychological or imagined). 'Psychogenic pain' is a term sometimes used to describe the situation where there is no known pathology, or the reported pain outweighs the level of abnormality detected, or healing of the original damage is thought to be complete. The person in pain can then face the added distress of not being taken seriously, not actually helped, and sometimes labelled as malingering or even mad. The consequences for the individual can be disastrous.

The International Association for the Study of Pain defines pain not just as a physical sensation but as 'an unpleasant sensory and emotional experience associated with actual or potential tissue damage, or described in terms of such damage' (IASP, 1986). Thus a mind–body split of this sort is conceptually misleading, empirically wrong and clinically unhelpful.

PREVALENCE OF CHRONIC PAIN

The most common types of chronic pain are back and neck pain, headache and migraine, neuralgias, post-surgical scar pain, facial pain, and pain associated with inflammatory conditions. Current estimates suggest that about 11% of the adult population in the UK experience chronic pain. Sixty per cent of the population suffer back pain at some time in their life. A government advisory group on back pain (CSAG, 1995) estimated a loss of 106 million working days in 1993/94 (compared with 81 million days in 1991/92); a cost of £480m to the NHS and £5.2bn to the benefits system. Chronic pain is, therefore, a serious problem and one that is getting worse.

The demand for medically based hospital treatment for back pain, for example, increased fivefold over a 10-year period, yet it has been estimated that only 5–10% of back problems need specialized hospital services. Hospital treatment may not be appropriate for most people, and 'the trouble is that when this happens, people get trapped in chronic pain and disability, they can't work, they suffer psychological distress and they get caught in the DSS system' (CSAG, 1995).

Data on people admitted to a Pain Management Programme in the UK (Williams *et al.*, 1993) suggest that, on average, they have already experienced chronic pain for 10 years (median 8 years). Over that period they have become involved in a process which also encompasses other people, including family, friends, health professionals and society in general. As the process gains momentum, a number of consequences are commonly recognized that add to the overall suffering of the individual, and this is referred to as the 'chronic pain syndrome' (see below).

MODELS OF CHRONIC PAIN

Various models have been proposed to explain why people continue to experience very real and disabling pain in the absence of well-recognized diagnostic signs.

Neurophysiological models

No single neurophysiological 'pain mechanism' accounts for the experience of chronic pain. The nervous system is not a series of separate compartments each designed to deal with a specific problem. Current knowledge favours the view that injury-produced afferent signals pass through a 'gate control, where they are influenced by other peripheral events and by the sensory posture set by the central nervous system itself' (Wall, 1989; also see Chapter 3).

Wall has proposed that pain might more usefully be considered as a phenomenon associated with 'output' (i.e. what the individual does) since it is 'invariably associated with a disruption of activity and a substitution of activity related to the prevention of further damage and to cure and recovery. Such 'activity' might include increased rest, medication-taking, and seeking help from health professionals.

Psychological models

Chronic pain has been addressed from the usual psychological perspectives (see Chapter 1), including psychoanalytic and cognitive–behavioural approaches as well as personality theory. Their scope ranges from describing psychological mechanisms involved in coping with pain, to causal theories which argue that the source of current pain can be purely psychological.

PERSONALITY THEORY

Theorists have attempted to identify personality types or traits most likely to be found in people suffering chronic pain (e.g. Sternbach, 1974). However one problem with trying to link pain to personality is the implication of weakness in the individual, suggesting, for example, that unresolved and high intensity of pain may be explained by notions such as a 'low pain threshold' or, worse, a 'pain-prone personality'. Furthermore, no consistent data have been reported to support a relationship between 'personality' and experience of chronic pain (Fordyce, 1976).

From a clinical standpoint, personality theory implies that the sufferer is in some way *responsible* for his or her difficulties; and, since 'personality' is assumed to be reasonably stable, it could also be assumed that little can be done to alter the situation.

PSYCHODYNAMIC THEORY

According to the psychoanalytic perspective, 'intractable pain which defies organic explanations is a defence against unconscious psychic conflict' (Gamsa, 1994). Studies aim to show that people with chronic pain suffer from unresolved conflicts of which they are unaware, and that pain serves to express this unconscious conflict. Gamsa (1994) details examples of this, including repressed hostility and aggression, guilt, defence against loss or threatened loss, early childhood trauma, and masked depression.

Psychodynamic ideas are often based on anecdotal accounts and sometimes on individual case studies. Elaborate theoretical ideas can be based on very small numbers of cases with poor control procedures (Merskey and Spear, 1967). With some exceptions (e.g. Adler *et al.*, 1989), the accumulated evidence does not support the psychoanalytic proposition that, in general, emotional conflict gives rise to bodily pain – although there are undoubtedly instances where this might be seen as a valid formulation.

One of the most useful roles of the psychoanalytic or psychodynamic approach to chronic pain may have been to highlight the importance of psychological factors at a time when the medical model of treatment predominated. There is, however, an uncomfortable legacy; as with personality theories of pain, psychodynamic perspectives encourage 'all in the mind' (i.e. psychogenic) explanations.

BEHAVIOUR THEORY

In the 1970s, behavioural and cognitive theories were elaborated to explain the role of psychological factors in the experience of chronic pain and to provide a conceptual framework for treatment. In contrast to psychoanalytic theory, behaviour theory studies only observable behaviours which can, according to Skinner (1953), be 'shaped, altered, weakened or strengthened as a direct result of environmental manipulation'.

Fordyce *et al.* (1968) were the first to apply the behavioural model to chronic pain. They described the presence of 'pain behaviours' (Fordyce, 1976, 1986) such as wincing, moaning, limping, taking analgesic medication. As with all models based on *learning theory*, behavioural explanations of pain fail to take into account what people think and feel, and deny any self-determination in behaviour or any of the subtleties of social/psychological and systemic influences (for a general discussion of this, see Mersky (1985)).

PAIN AS A REWARD

There has been some argument that chronic pain might persist because it is reinforcing or rewarding for the sufferer. The notion of 'secondary gain' is sometimes proposed, but the clinical evidence does not seem to support this. Whilst people can often recognize possible benefits such as the shedding of major responsibility for a job or family, it is most unusual, when working clinically, to find individuals who actually believe that such benefits outweigh the costs involved.

Similarly, there is no good evidence for financial gain. A recent review by Mendelson (1992) repudiated the existence of 'compensation neurosis' (whereby it is proposed that a person's suffering is unlikely to improve until a pending compensation case is settled). Considerable stress is associated with the lengthy legal process, however, and it is therefore not surprising if someone shows considerable relief when the process is complete.

COGNITIVE THEORY

Cognitive theory takes account of the fact that experience and behaviour are the result of psychological processes. In particular it is concerned with the person's evaluation or understanding of their pain. It is argued that 'modifications of a person's beliefs, such as, for example, unrealistic fears about what the pain means, will generate changes in the experience of pain and in maladaptive behaviour' (Gamsa, 1994).

Some cognitive theories go beyond psychological coping responses to pain, and argue for psychological factors in their own right as the source of pain. In this manner they account for pain in the absence of any sensory (i.e. physical) input or pathology. In the cognitive tradition, Leventhal (1984) elaborates an information-processing model which proposes that environmental stimuli may, via a sort of automatic processing (see Chapter 17), trigger the experience of pain without any physiological signals.

Systemic approaches

More recently it has been argued that, in some instances, the person in pain is the symptom-bearer for a system of which they are a part. Possible systems of which an individual might be a part, and which might be maintaining their pain problem, include the family, the workplace, the medical model, or the healthcare system (Ramsay, 1989).

In summary, different models emphasize different aspects of the experience of pain. Thus a number of components can be identified, such as sensory, behavioural, evaluative, affective and social or contextual (e.g. see Karoly, 1985). Any of these may be more or less prominent at different times such that the experience of pain is not fixed or static. Whilst it may be tempting to seek a straightforward, unitary explanation of chronic pain, it is more prudent to adopt an integrative, multicomponent approach. At the clinical level it is the interactions between the components which define chronic pain. Indeed, the multicomponent models developed in the field of chronic pain are good examples of the biopsychosocial approach in action (see next section).

Learning Activity 1 ◆ ◆ ◆

The aim of this activity is to recognize the different components of pain.

Mary is a 45-year-old divorced woman with two teenage sons. She tripped over a loose floorboard at her workplace two years ago and has severe low back pain and sciatica. She has had to take prolonged periods of sick leave from her job as branch manager and her employer is now suggesting medical retirement. Her claim for industrial injury compensation continues and looks likely to offer a favourable compensation settlement. Investigations show mild degenerative changes in her lumbar spine. She is no longer able to enjoy family sporting and camping activities and has stopped attending her badminton club. She hardly manages those light jobs around the house which her family have not taken over; indeed any degree of sustained activity can only be obtained by reliance on high doses of painkillers. Her sleep is disturbed, she gets headaches, panics if she gets increased pain whilst out, feels lonely and trapped with 'no light at the end of the tunnel'.

Carry out a component analysis of Mary's pain by sorting the problems listed below in terms of the component they represent:

Loss of status as successful career woman	Lost role as mother, homemaker
High pain	Activity extensively reduced
Given up sports	High medication use
Low self-confidence	Panic and anxiety
No social life	Lowered self-image
Reduction in finances	Unfit
Disturbed sleep	Stiff and tense body
Weight gain	Isolated and lonely
Low mood	

INTEGRATION: CHRONIC PAIN PROCESSES

The search for a cure

When a person in pain decides to seek medical help, he or she is likely to be referred for a number of investigations to try to establish the cause. Often the process is one of elimination. This can be lengthy and requires frequent contact with a range of health professionals. There are two possible outcomes of the process:

- A diagnosis is confirmed and treatment instigated. The treatment (medication, physiotherapy, etc. – see below) may or may not provide relief and such relief may or may not be long-lasting. Where one treatment fails to provide substantial relief, another may be tried. The quest for what becomes perceived to be the 'magic cure' can become a full-time occupation and may be very costly in both emotional and financial terms for the individual. Further, there is evidence to suggest that repeated treatments may in certain circumstances have iatrogenic effects, such as additional scar tissue from repeated surgery (Pither and Nicholas, 1991).
- No diagnosis is confirmed, so the quest here becomes that of looking for an 'answer' – which, it is assumed, will lead to the 'magic cure'. The individual may thus go from specialist to specialist having more and more investigations, often resulting in the same unsatisfactory results.

These outcomes have similar consequences: they both involve repeated disappointment and often contribute to a growing sense of helplessness. Over time, this can result in a lowering of mood (Fordyce, 1976) and decreased self-efficacy (Dolce, 1987). Disillusionment with health professionals is common because it is often felt that medicine has 'let me down'.

Where a medical explanation of the problem remains elusive, health professionals and lay people alike can begin to 'blame' the sufferer. The individual may be placed in a position of apparently shouldering the burden of proof. Most people in pain report that, at some time or another, they have questioned their own sanity and wondered whether they were indeed imagining their pain, or else contributing to it in some way. When this is compounded by messages being given by health professionals, the effects for the individual can be devastating, especially if these result in reduced family support or even rejection.

When physical investigations continue to supply little new information, many people find themselves referred for a psychiatric assessment. For the most part, a psychiatrist can validate their experiences as 'real' and hence prove to be tremendously helpful to them. However, the abiding message from such a referral may be that 'the doctor does not believe me', and this can do lasting damage to their relationship with the doctor.

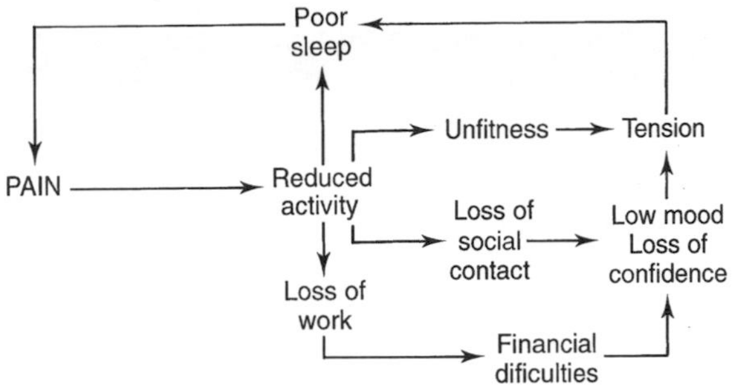

Figure 4.1 *Example of interactions of biopsychosocial variables in chronic pain*

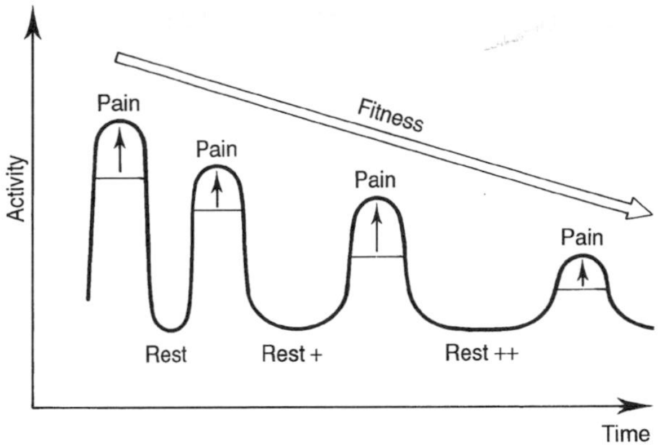

Figure 4.2 *The overactivity/underactivity cycle, or 'roller-coaster'*

Chronic pain as loss

Alongside the lengthy process of repeated investigations and treatments, it is common for the individual's quality of life to be gradually deteriorating. In effect there are many losses, mostly interrelated. Figure 4.1 shows some of the ways in which these losses compound each other. The pattern of interrelationships is not fixed for all individuals, although the example given is fairly typical.

The overactivity/underactivity cycle (or 'roller-coaster')

Pain itself is only a part of the overall picture of what has come to be recognized as the 'chronic pain syndrome'. Loss of fitness and mobility are directly related to disuse; a person often starts to rest more and more in an attempt to carry on a normal life, but excessive resting is now understood to compound the problem in the longer term.

Initially, many people with chronic pain push themselves to do things and stoically carry on. They then have to take prolonged periods of rest in order to bring the level of pain back within more manageable limits. These periods of rest contribute to loss of fitness. This pattern of activity (the 'overactivity/underactivity cycle') is cumulative (see Figure 4.2).

As problems and limitations increase, individuals develop ways of thinking about their situation which feed into their increasing disability. Often these interpretations serve to increase fear and anxiety and encourage helplessness. An unhelpful way of thinking might be to habitually over-react to situations, so exaggerating the negative consequences. This is referred to as 'catastrophizing' (Rostensteil and Keefe, 1983) and its effects on feelings and behaviour are illustrated in Figure 4.3. Unhelpful thoughts clearly contribute to the development of depressed mood, which in turn makes it more difficult to cope (Blackburn and Davidson, 1990).

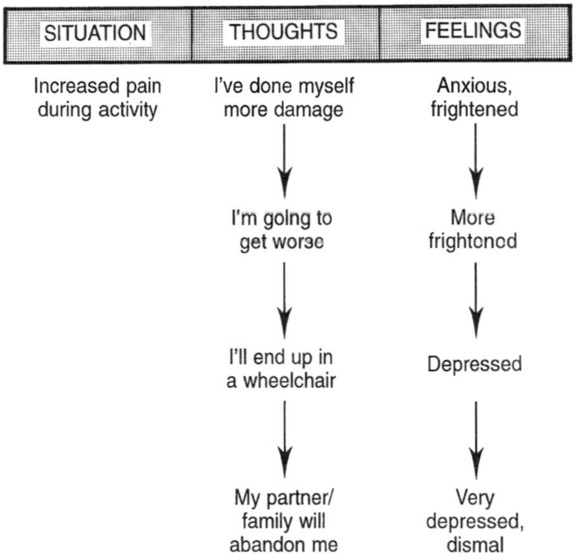

Figure 4.3 *Example of the effects of downward spiralling negative thoughts*

Learning Activity 2 ◆ ◆ ◆

The aim is to understand the relationships between components of the pain problem which maintain chronic pain. Select any of the aspects of Mary's pain problem listed in Activity 1 and show in a diagram how they might be interlinked.

ASSESSMENT OF CHRONIC PAIN

Acute pain is often monitored for its intensity and frequency over a number of days or weeks. This can provide useful information where the types of treatment being offered are aimed at reducing or alleviating the existing level of pain. In chronic pain, however, the focus needs to be much broader in order to understand the person who is in pain, not just the pain itself. This means looking at intensity of pain and its patterns, but then going on to understand these in the context of the person in their environment. This identifies aspects of the person's pain problem which may be amenable to change.

Broadly speaking, chronic pain assessment needs to cover the areas listed below. Some of the common measuring instruments are included in parentheses, although quite a lot of this information can be gleaned from a discussion or semistructured interview with the person.

- Current levels and patterns of pain (diaries, visual analogue scales)
- The pain and medical history (notes, interview)
- Environmental or social context (interview)
- Effects of pain on mood (diaries/interview, Hospital Anxiety and Depression scale (HAD) – Zigmond and Snaith (1983))
- Effects of pain on activity (Sickness Impact Profile (SIP) – Bergner *et al.* (1981))
- Effects of pain on thoughts (Pain Cognitions Questionnaire – Boston *et al.* (1990))
- Effects of pain on relationships (interview, SIP)
- Psychological coping strategies (Coping Strategies Questionnaire – Rosensteil and Keefe (1983))
- Some measure of physical functioning (self-report, objective assessment)
- Measures of self-efficacy (Pain Self-Efficacy Questionnaire (PSEQ) – Nicholas (1989))

Numerous assessment instruments have been developed to look at pain and associated disability, and further details of these can be found in, for example, Karoly and Jensen (1987), where methodological issues are also fully explored. However, for everyday clinical care, simple but carefully worded questions exploring the functional relationships between pain variables are valuable and more practicable.

> **Learning Activity 3 ◆ ◆ ◆**
>
> Practice assessing the person in pain following a biopsychosocial component analysis. What five questions might you ask Mary to begin a multicomponent assessment of her pain?

MANAGEMENT STRATEGIES

Corresponding to the various components of chronic pain, intervention can be aimed at one or more of these. The main intervention strategies are summarized in Box 4.1.

Physical methods

Some people can be helped significantly by physical treatments, usually when chronic pain has been relatively short-lived. Many of these treatments are extensions of the methods used for acute pain relief, and as such they fail to accommodate the more complex chronic pain processes. In acute pain, medication, rest and being treated are justifiable; however, where pain is prolonged these methods can make matters worse, for the reasons outlined earlier.

EPIDURAL INJECTION

Injection of an anti-inflammatory agent and/or nerve block may be performed by clinicians (usually anaesthetists) if this is thought to be appropriate.

MEDICATION

Medication is likely to be reviewed and analgesics may be initiated or modified accordingly. Certain anticonvulsants may also be utilized, and low doses of some antidepressants are considered to have analgesic properties.

PHYSIOTHERAPY

Physiotherapy is often offered. This may be 'active' (usually involving exercises to encourage mobilization) or 'passive' (involving, for example, manipulation). Frost and Klaber-Moffett (1992) describe a progressive exercise programme, for chronic low back pain sufferers, which encourages patients to be more active

Box 4.1 *Chronic pain management strategies*

Underlying model	*Focus of intervention*	*Methods*
Neurophysiological	To change or block pain sensation	• Local anaesthetic blocks • TENS • Physiotherapy • Acupuncture • Medication • Surgery
Psychodynamic	To resolve emotional conflict underlying pain	• Long-term or brief psychotherapy
Behavioural	To replace pain behaviours (e.g. limping, medication, inactivity) with well behaviours	• Graded exposure to activity • Reinforcement
Cognitive	To identify and modify irrational negative thoughts	• Cognitive therapy
Systemic	To alter dynamics of the system to release person from sick role	• Family therapy • Clinical audit
Biopsychosocial	Chronic pain processes and traps	• Multimodal, multidisciplinary pain management

and responsible for their own management. They suggest that physiotherapists should be aware that passive treatment may, for some people, lead to reduced activity and fear of spinal movement.

ACUPUNCTURE

This is now widely used in pain clinics as a treatment for chronic pain, despite continuing debate as to how and why it is effective. Possible physiological and psychological explanations for the mechanism of acupuncture as a treatment for chronic pain are proposed in a paper by Lewith and Kenyon (1984). Although the precise mechanism is as yet unclear, there is good evidence that reproducible neurological and chemical changes are initiated by this treatment, and these almost certainly modify the perception of, and response to, pain.

TRANSCUTANEOUS NERVE STIMULATION

TENS as a treatment for chronic pain has been questioned. Several studies have looked at the relative effectiveness of therapies for chronic pain (Deyo *et al.*, 1990; Huitt *et al.*, 1991). Deyo and co-workers concluded that, for chronic low back pain, treatment with TENS was no more effective than treatment with a placebo. Marchand *et al.* (1993) suggest that TENS reduces both the sensory-discriminative (intensity) and the motivational-affective (unpleasantness) components of low back pain in the short term, but that much of the reduction in the affective component may be a placebo effect. This suggests that TENS may be most effective when used as a short-term analgesic.

Psychosocial management strategies

Many people derive very little or no benefit from the standard physical treatments just described. A broader psychosocial approach to management is required, because the consequences of the ongoing experience of pain continually add to the individual's difficulties, and it is these chronic pain processes which need to be the focus of attention. The objective thus changes from alleviating pain to helping the individual manage its consequences more effectively.

BEHAVIOUR

Interventions based on cognitive and behavioural approaches in combination aim to help people restructure the way they think about their pain as well as to foster their 'well behaviours', such as increased activity levels (Box 4.1).

The aim of treatment based on the behavioural or operant model is to abolish pain behaviours and substitute 'well behaviours', such as an increase in the level of physical functioning. By gradually increasing fitness with planned, regular exercise, and by breaking the pattern of overactivity/underactivity with systematic 'pacing', involving regular changes of position and frequent, short rests, the individual can gradually become increasingly able to resume many of the activities previously found to be impossible. The focus here is not on getting rid of the pain but on managing it more effectively and limiting its detrimental effects on quality of life.

Whilst a number of studies have demonstrated the effectiveness of treatment based on this model (for a review, see Fordyce *et al.* (1985)), critics have said that outcome does not recognize a person's suffering (Merskey, 1985) nor take account of the variables that may be influencing pain behaviour within the person's environment.

THOUGHTS

A further aspect of the problem of chronic pain which is amenable to change, and particularly important in terms of maintenance of change, focuses on the kind of things people are saying to themselves (Lefebvre, 1981; Keefe *et al.*, 1992). Recognition of, and the gradual development of skills for challenging unhelpful thoughts, and then learning to replace them with more helpful, and often more realistic ones, is an especially important area for attention. An example of this process involves replacing feelings of helplessness and hopelessness with a renewed sense of control (Blackburn and Davidson, 1990).

Behavioural and cognitive–behavioural approaches have been used extensively and with some success in pain management programmes during the last 15 years (Turk *et al.*, 1983; Nicholas *et al.*, 1992), but are equally relevant to general clinical practice. Effective pain management, however, does not depend solely on the application of techniques. These need to be used in the context of a therapeutic or counselling relationship which can accommodate issues such as grief, personal development, or perhaps transition to a life in which there may always be pain or at least the potential for pain.

Management that is based on a biopsychosocial approach needs to be eclectic, combining ideas from different perspectives in the name of pragmatism. Modification of one component will have repercussions for the other components; thus tablets and injections might encourage beliefs that there may be a cure or that the person cannot manage the pain without these. Alternatively, behavioural change in terms of increased activity may improve emotions and self-efficacy as well as other beliefs and pain-related behaviours.

Evaluation

Outcome measures are used to assess changes that may occur as the result of any intervention directed specifically at the chronic pain problem. The methods most commonly used for assessing pain intensity and frequency are pain diaries involving simple visual analogue scales (Karoly, 1985; Williams, 1988). For measures of psychosocial disability associated with pain, see the pain assessment section above. Measures should be used before the intervention, immediately after it, and on at least one occasion as a follow-up.

Learning Activity 4 ◆ ◆ ◆

Practice devising a pain management strategy with someone in chronic pain (to directly address some aspect(s) of the pain process). Describe how might Mary tackle the following problems:

a reduced activity
b dependency on medication
c poor sleep
d high tension and anxiety
e low mood and low confidence.

How might you ensure that Mary took part in devising the strategies to deal with these problems?

Learning Activity 5 ◆ ◆ ◆

You need to carry out a lengthy investigation/treatment (unrelated to their chronic pain) which involves someone lying down for longer than they feel they can manage because of 'unbearable' pain. Would you personally prefer to:

a ignore protestations and carry on anyway, scowling when they move at the wrong moment?
b try to get the investigation over with as quickly and effectively as possible, being as kind as possible?
c explain the procedural details and allow the person to have control over breaks for movement where the quality of the investigation would not be compromised?
d try to get the person engaged in a conversation or problem-solving task as a distraction from the pain?
e abandon the procedure, writing back to the referrer explaining that the person found it impossible to cooperate?
f teach the person a relaxation technique?

Briefly justify your choice. Which of these options is more likely or realistic in the situations in which you are likely to be working?

SUMMARY

Chronic pain is a widespread problem, the effects of which can be devastating for the individual and their family. Distressing consequences can be compounded by lack of understanding from both health professionals and lay people. Multicomponent assessment based on broad biopsychosocial models has encouraged the development of effective psychological approaches to management. These can easily be adapted to a variety of clinical settings. Chronic pain is an area where considerable development in theory and practice may be anticipated in the future.

Key Points ■ ■ ■

- ❑ A distinction between physical and psychological pain is theoretically and clinically misleading.

- ❑ Chronic pain is an extensive problem that is often mismanaged by health professionals.

- ❑ Psychological models of pain identify different components of chronic pain.

- ❑ Multicomponent descriptions best fit chronic pain phenomena.

- ❑ Chronic pain is a biopsychosocial process.

- ❑ Assessment needs to be broad-based.

- ❑ Effective management needs to address the psychosocial processes that are maintaining the pain problem.

References ▼ ▼ ▼

Adler, R.H., Zlot, S. Hurny, C. and Minder, C. (1989). Engel's 'Psychogenic pain and the pain-prone patient': a retrospective, controlled clinical study. *Psychosomatic Medicine*, **51**: 87–101.

Bergner, M., Bobbitt, R.A., Carter, W.B. and Gilson, B.S. (1981). The Sickness Impact Profile: developmen and final revision of a health status measure. *Medical Care*, **19**: 787–805.

Blackburn, I.-M. and Davidson, K. (1990). *Cognitive Therapy for Depression and Anxiety*. Oxford: Blackwell.

Boston, K., Pearce, S. and Richardson, P.H. (1990). The Pain Cognition Questionnaire. *Journal of Psychosomatic Research*, **34**: 103–9.

CSAG (1995). *Clinical Standards Advisory Group on Back Pain*. London: HMSO.

Deyo, R.A., Walsh, N.E., Martin, D.C., Schoenfeld, L.S. and Ramamurthy, S. (1990). A controlled trial of transcutaneous electrical nerve stimulation (TENS) and exercise for chronic low back pain. *New England Journal of Medicine*, **332**: 1627–34.

Dolce, J.J. (1987). Self-efficacy and disability beliefs in behavioural treatment of pain. *Behaviour Research and Therapy*, **25**: 289.

Fordyce, W.E. (1976). *Behavioural Methods for Chronic Pain and Illness*. St Louis: CV Mosby.

Fordyce, W.E. (1986). Learning processes in pain. In Sternbach, R.A. (ed.) *The Psychology of Pain*, 2nd edn. New York: Raven Press, 49–65.

Fordyce, W.E., Fowler, R.S., Lehmann, J.F. and De Lateur, B.J. (1968). Some implications of learning in problems of chronic pain. *Journal of Chronic Disability*, **21**: 179–90.

Fordyce, W.E., Roberts, A.H. and Sternbach, R.A. (1985). The behavioural management of chronic pain: a response to critics. *Pain*, **22**: 113–25.

Frost, H. and Klaber-Moffett, J.A. (1992). Physiotherapy management of chronic low back pain. *Physiotherapy*, **78**: 751–4.

Gamsa, A. (1994). The role of psychological factors in chronic pain. 1: A half century of study. *Pain*, **57**: 5–15.

Huitt, C., Rafii, A., Dunbar, A. and Price, D.D. (1991). Comparison of relative effectiveness of therapies for chronic pain: an 8-year experience of a multidisciplinary pain center. *Proceedings of the 11th International Conference of the World Confederation for Physical Therapy*. London: Proceedings Books.

International Association for the Study of Pain (IASP) Subcommittee on Taxonomy (1986). *Classification of Chronic Pain*. Amsterdam: Elsevier.

Karoly, P. (1985). The assessment of pain: concepts and procedures. In Karoly, P (ed.) *Measurement Strategies in Health Psychology*. New York: Wiley, 461–515.

Karoly, P. and Jensen, M.P. (1987). *Multimethod Assessment of Chronic Pain*. Oxford: Pergamon.

Keefe, F.J., Salley, A.N. and Lefebvre, J.C. (1992). Coping with pain: conceptual concerns and future directions. *Pain*, **51**: 131–4.

Lefebvre, M.F. (1981). Cognitive distortion and cognitive errors in depressed psychiatric and low back pain patients. *Journal of Consulting and Clinical Psychology*, **49**: 517–25.

Leventhal, H. (1984). A perceptual-motor theory of emotion. *Advances in Experimental Social Psychology*, **17**: 117–83.

Lewith, G.T. and Kenyon, J.N. (1984). Physiological and psychological explanations for the mechanism of acupuncture as a treatment for chronic pain. *Social Science & Medical.* **19**: 1367–78.

Marchand, S., Charest, M., Li, J., Chenard, J.-R., Lavignole, B. and Laurencelle, L. (1993). Is TENS purely a placebo effect? A controlled study on chronic low back pain. *Pain*, **54**: 99–106.

Mendelson, G. (1992). Compensation and chronic pain. *Pain*, **48**: 121–3.

Merskey, H. (1985). A mentalistic view of pain and behaviour. *Behavioural Brain Science.* **8**: 65.

Merskey, H. and Spear, F.G. (1967). *Pain: Psychological and Psychiatric Aspects*. London: Baillière Tindall/Cassell.

Nicholas, M.K. (1989). The Pain Self-Efficacy Questionnaire: self-efficacy in relation to chronic pain. Paper presented at the British Psychological Society Annual Conference, St Andrews, Scotland.

Pither, C.E. and Nicholas, M.K. (1991). The identification of iatrogenic factors in the development of chronic pain syndromes: abnormal treatment behaviour? In Bond, M.R. *et al.* (eds) *Proceedings of the VIth World Congress on Pain*. Amsterdam: Elsevier, 429–34.

Ramsay, C.N. (1989). *Family Systems in Medicine*. London: Guilford Press.

Rosensteil, A.K. and Keefe, F.J. (1983). The use of coping strategies in chronic low back pain patients; relationship to patient characteristics and current adjustment. *Pain*, **17**: 33–44.

Skinner, R. (1953). *Science and Human Behaviour*. New York: Macmillan.

Sternbach, R.A. (1974). *Pain Patients: Traits and Treatment*. New York: Academic Press.

Turk, D.C., Meichenbaum, D. and Genest, M. (1983). *Pain and Behavioural Medicine: A Cognitive–Behavioural Perspective*. New York: Guildford Press.

Wall, P.D. (1989). Introduction. In Wall, P.D. and Melzack, R. (eds) *Textbook of Pain*. Edinburgh: Churchill Livingstone, 1–18.

Williams, A.C., de C., Nicholas, M.K., Pither, C.E., Justins, D.M.,

Chamberlain, J.H., Harding, V.R., Ralphs, J.A., Jones, S.C., Dieudonne, I., Featherstone, J.D., Hodgson, D.R., Ridout, K.L. and Shannon, E.M. (1993). A cognitive–behavioural programme for rehabilitating the chronic pain patient: results of the first 200 cases. *British Journal of General Practice*, **43**: 513–518.
Williams, R.C. (1988). Toward a set of reliable and valid measures for chronic pain assessment and outcome research. *Pain*, **35**: 239–51.
Zigmond, A.S. and Snaith, R.P. (1983). The Hospital Anxiety and Depression Scale. *Acta Psychiatrica Scandinavica*, **67**: 361–70.

Further Reading ▲ ▲ ▲

Hanson, R.W. and Gerber, K.E. (1990). *Coping with Chronic Pain: a Guide to Patient Self-management*. London: Guildford Press.
Holzman, A.D. and Turk, D.C. (1986). *Pain Management: A Handbook of Psychological Treatment Approaches*. New York: Pergamon.
Shone, N. (1996). *Coping Successfully with Pain*. London: Sheldon Press.

5

Disability

Sheina Orbell

LEARNING OBJECTIVES

After studying this chapter you should:

- Appreciate the significance of disability to healthcare practice and research
- Understand three principal theoretical models of disability and explain their different implications for healthcare
- Be able to critically appraise existing measures of disability

INTRODUCTION

The notion of disability is most readily associated with people who have had serious accidents or who were born with a physical condition such as cerebral palsy. However, disability is associated with almost all diseases and the minimization of disability is an important concern to all those involved in health research and practice.

An holistic view of health acknowledges that the ability to perform ones' usual daily activities and to participate in a normal social life are critical aspects of human health. Indeed, it might be argued that demands for healthcare and the motivation to take action to prevent disease arise as much from threat to quality of life in terms of normal functioning as from threat to *quantity* of life. A doctor is consulted at least in part because pain or other symptoms interfere with the ability to work and live as normal (Nerenz and Leventhal, 1983). Viewed in this way, disability is clearly a valuable measure of health status and one which might be used both to assess the health of people in communities and the effectiveness of healthcare interventions.

EPIDEMIOLOGICAL CHANGES

Interest in disability as a concept and in methods of assessing and measuring disability has increased considerably in recent years. A number of factors may account for this. Firstly, the pattern of morbidity is changing; most of the morbidity in society now is due to chronic diseases, such as cardiovascular disease, stroke and rheumatoid arthritis, rather than the infectious and other acute diseases that were prevalent at the start of the century (Verbrugge, 1995). As a result, healthcare has become directed more towards the rehabilitation and promotion of health amongst those with chronic disease. This aspect of healthcare, which is termed 'tertiary prevention', necessitates measurement of the impact of disease on functional health (i.e. measurement of disability).

A second reason for concern with disability is related to changes in the demographic structure of the population. Larger numbers of people began surviving infancy and childhood during the earlier part of the twentieth century, and these people have reached middle and old age in ever-increasing numbers. In England and Wales, the number of people aged between 70 and 79 increased by 13% between 1976 and 1984, whilst a 24% increase occurred in the numbers of people aged 80 and over (Grundy, 1987). In Europe as a whole, it is expected that nearly a quarter of the total population will be aged over 60 by the year 2025, compared with just 13% of the total population in 1950 (Warnes, 1991).

It is not true to say that all adults over the age of 60 (or even 80) are disabled. Arber and Gilbert (1989) examined data from the 1980 *General Household Survey* in Britain (OPCS, 1982) and estimated that about 6% of those aged 65–74 years, 15% of those aged 75–84 years and 41% of those aged over 85 years had difficulty with walking outdoors and with self-care activities. Nonetheless it is the case that the rapid ageing of the population does indicate a growing concern with the maintenance of functional capacities and the assessment of incapacity and delivery of healthcare services to older adults.

MODELS OF DISABILITY

As the term implies, disability is generally understood to mean a lack of ability in some domain, such as self-care or mobility. In order to assess and perhaps modify the degree of disability, assumptions have to be made about why there are difficulties in performance. Traditionally there have been three main approaches to understanding the causes of disability:

- the *biological model*
- the *environmental constraints model*
- the *psychological model*.

Each model defines disability in different ways, thus having different implications for measurement and intervention. These are summarized in Box 5.1.

Before considering the models, it is important to

Box 5.1 *Models of disability*

Model type	*Assumptions about the cause of performance capacity*	*Implications for assessment and intervention*
Biological	Disability is caused by impairment of physiological or anatomatical structures	• Successful performance reflects extent of impairment • Two people with the same impairment will experience the same disability • Disability 'scores' reflect severity of impairment • Disability can be altered by altering impairment • Where impairment cannot be altered, healthcare focus is on providing help to substitute for disability
Environmental	Disability is caused by environmental structures which impede or facilitate performance; these environmental structures intervene to modify the impact of impairment on disability	• Successful performance reflects extent to which the environment facilitates performance • Two people with the same impairment will not experience the same disability • Two people with the same environmental facilitators will experience the same disability • Disability 'scores' reflect environmental facilitators • Disability can be altered by altering the environment • Assessment and intervention will focus on identifying and modifying aspects of the environment
Psychological/social	Disability is caused by beliefs about the self, the evaluative and affective significance of performance, and beliefs about social norms for performance; these beliefs intervene to modify the impact of impairment on disability	• Successful performance reflects the beliefs a person holds about successful performance • Two people with the same impairment will not experience the same disability • Two people with the same beliefs will experience the same disability • Disability 'scores' reflect motivational belief systems • Disability can be altered by altering belief systems • Assessment and intervention will focus on identifying and modifying belief systems

appreciate that disability may have more than one cause and the three models may not be mutually exclusive. For example, disability may arise from a combination of biological and psychological causes. In clinical practice, therefore, it would be important to consider the relative contribution of different causes to a person's performance and activity.

The biological model

The World Health Organization (Whiting and Lincoln, 1980) defines disability as 'any restriction or lack (resulting from an impairment) of ability to perform an activity in the manner or within the range considered normal for a human being'. The important feature of this definition is that disability is said to arise from an impairment. The same document defines impairment as 'any loss or abnormality of psychological, physiological or anatomical structure or function'. When parts or systems of the body do not work, disability is said to arise.

Whilst impairment refers to individual functions of parts of the body, disability is concerned with compound activities expected of the person or of the body as a whole. The WHO suggests that disability is represented by performative incapacity of tasks, skills or behaviours. For example, an impairment to a part of the eye may lead to a seeing disability, or an impairment to the musculoskeletal system may lead to a walking disability, or an impairment to the brain may lead to a speech disability. The extent to which a person can perform a given activity is assumed to be directly related to the severity of the underlying biological impairment.

Since it is often difficult to assess objectively the degree of impairment to a body part or process, measures of disability derived from the biological model often provide the next best thing to a measure of the severity of an impairment. Measures developed by Partridge *et al.* (1987) and the Office of Population Censuses and Surveys (OPCS) (1988) are examples of assessments based on biological models of disability.

The environmental constraints model

An environmental constraints model suggests that disability is not directly related to severity of impairment, but is moderated by the extent to which the environment facilitates or impedes performance of an activity (Verbrugge, 1995). According to this model, two people with the same biological impairment may demonstrate different degrees of disability because they occupy different environments. For example, two people with a similar degree of rheumatoid arthritis may differ in their ability to climb stairs because one person has a railing and the other does not. By providing the second person with a railing, the two people will become equal in their ability to climb stairs.

An important distinction between the biological and the environmental constraints models is that the biological model is concerned with being able to perform activities in the normal manner, whereas the environmental constraints model is concerned with enabling people to perform activities in *some* manner. The emphasis in assessment is on what a person needs in order to succeed at a given activity. Very many healthcare assessments are based on the environmental constraints model and use scoring systems that are intended to assess what a person is able to do with or without aids, or with or without the help of another person (e.g. Whiting and Lincoln, 1980; Lincoln and Gladman, 1992; Katz *et al.*, 1963; Mahoney and Barthel, 1965).

The psychological model

In common with the environmental constraints model, the psychological model suggests that disability does not arise simply and directly from impairment. However, an important distinction exists between these two models. According to the environmental constraints model, it is possible to modify a person's disability simply by altering the environment – for example by providing an aid. The psychological model, on the other hand, suggests that neither degree of impairment nor environmental conditions will provide an adequate explanation of a person's functional capacity because the psychological processes which give rise to a person trying to perform a particular activity have to be taken into account.

There are two principal accounts of the ways in which psychological processes might influence functional activity. Leventhal and colleagues (Nerenz and Leventhal, 1983) suggest that the ways in which people represent the nature of the disease they have and their beliefs about what will cure or control it will determine their response to disease. The 'illness representation' model suggests that people's beliefs concerning the symptoms, cause, consequences, time-course and cure for their condition will determine how they respond to it. For example, a person with arthritis who believes that the stiffness in his or her leg is caused by activity might gradually stop trying certain activities and become disabled as a result. According to Leventhal's approach, by investigating and modifying the beliefs people hold about their condition, disability can be reduced.

An alternative psychological approach to modifying disability comes from Bandura's (1977) Social Cognitive Theory. According to this perspective, functional activities can be viewed as goals which people will strive to achieve if they have a strong desire or need to achieve and feel confident of success (O'Leary *et al.*, 1988). Confidence is referred to by psychologists as belief in one's own self-efficacy, and it can be modified by giving people graded practice in performing particular tasks. Commitment to try a certain activity depends critically on the value a person attaches to it and their self-efficacy beliefs. It may also depend on the extent to which other people, such as friends and relatives, encourage or discourage activity by the things they say or the help they offer.

The psychological model is different from other conceptualizations of disability, because it has the potential to explain the processes by which one person with an impairment gradually becomes disabled where another strives to maintain independence. If a person is committed to a particular activity, say going to a club every week, he or she will strive to find a means of achieving this goal. This may involve engaging the support of others to accompany the person on outings, and success may therefore depend to some extent on available support and the social skills a person possesses to request assistance.

According to the psychological perspective, disability can be altered by interventions that directly alter beliefs, attitudes, feelings and behaviours. Assessments of these beliefs can be made before and after an intervention (e.g. see Leventhal and Nerenz, 1985; Schwarzer, 1994). In addition, it will be important to obtain valid assessments of what people actually do. This can sometimes be achieved by observation, or third-party reports, but often it will be based on self-reports. If self-reports are used, it is important to ask several questions about the same activity in order to test for reliability.

Relationships between the biological, environmental and psychological models

In practice, disability is probably best understood as a result of the combined influence of biology, psychology and environment, and it will often be the task of the health professional to identify the most important causes or to provide a package of care that addresses several causes. For example, a joint replacement operation will alter impairment to the hip, but the extent to which a person resumes activities after the operation may additionally depend on their sense of self-efficacy. (See Smith *et al.* (1991) and Lorig *et al.* (1989) for examinations of the interactions between disease activity, psychological state and disability.)

It is also important to recognize the possible ways in which interventions at one level may affect other levels of a person's functioning. For example, there is growing evidence that disease activity in arthritis may be affected by a person's mood (Anderson *et al.*, 1985). If this is the case, it is possible that the satisfaction a person gains from successfully doing something important to them could actually in turn alter their level of impairment. Giving a person a bath aid (an environmental intervention) might similarly alter both their psychological state and the impairment.

MEASURING DISABILITY

The foregoing discussion suggests that physical, environmental and psychological factors can be involved in the process of disability. Different conceptualizations of disability, such as the three just described, require different approaches to assessment. In order to evaluate existing measures of disability, it is necessary to appreciate the assumptions about cause on which the scales and measures are based. The underlying model dictates what needs to be measured and how; it is thereby predicting what needs to be targeted for intervention.

A critical approach to assessment is essential not only for good clinical practice but also as a means of testing the predictions of a given model of disability. For example, assessing someone for aids identifies certain items which should, according to an environmental constraints view, modify disability. The extent to which these aids actually reduce a person's disability is a measure of the power of this model to explain their disability. If disability is not particularly reduced, it would be sensible to take another perspective on the problem and, for instance, assess psychological factors, such as self-efficacy, which may be contributing to the overall degree of disability.

Most measures of disability in clinical use are measuring behaviour. However, the measurement of behaviour is not necessarily straightforward. It is important always to be aware of exactly what is being assessed and to take care to avoid obtaining unreliable information which might lead to misleading conclusions.

In most cases, practitioners or researchers will be interested in a specific set of behaviours. It is clearly important that the disability measure adopted contains items that refer to the behaviours of interest. The following subsections consider some of the key issues in disability assessment; the first is concerned with issues of measurement technique; the second is concerned with the content of disability measures in terms of the behaviours or activities they assess; the third considers the problem of how to combine a person's scores on different behaviours to produce a disability score.

Measurement technique

DEMAND EFFECTS

One difficulty in the assessment of disability concerns the distinction between what a person 'can' do, if asked to demonstrate, and what a person actually 'does' do in his or her normal life. If a person is asked by a health professional to demonstrate a particular movement or action, he or she might become subject to what in social psychology are referred to as experimenter demand effects (Orne, 1962; Rosenthal, 1966). In other words, a person's motivation to succeed in doing something may be altered by the mere fact that someone else has suggested doing it; particularly if this is someone perceived to be in a position of authority. As a consequence, the assessment reflects what the person 'can' do under those motivational conditions, in the supposedly protective presence of a health professional, rather than what they actually succeed in doing when alone. Conversely, a person may underachieve in the presence of a professional if, for instance, they feel in need of greater support at home.

Nonetheless, several assessments of disability rely on the observation of behaviour, particularly those used in physiotherapy to assess changes in flexibility (e.g. Partridge *et al.*, 1987). Such assessments use various scoring systems. These may be dichotomous (e.g. can perform/cannot perform) or dimensional (e.g. measuring the time taken to perform or sustain a given action).

SELF- AND OTHER-REPORTS

It can be useful to find out what activities people undertake when they are not motivated by a health professional, or where there is no one at all present who, for example, might protect them from the fear of falling. There are also circumstances in which assessment is required of activities which cannot be observed directly by a health professional, such as social activities. This can be achieved either by self-report (asking the individual to report what he or she does) or by third-party observation.

Where self-report measures are utilized, effort needs to be made to ensure that responses are valid. In other words, if someone reports that they have been shopping in the past week, it is necessary to make every effort to ensure that they have actually done so. One way to do this is to get a third party to answer the same questions and compare the two sets of answers. Another way might be to ask the same question in slightly different ways and examine the correlation between the two self-reports.

SPECIFIC QUESTIONS

Careful attention has to be given to the wording of questions. If questions are very specific (e.g. how many days last week did you use the bus?) the responses are more likely to be accurate than if the questions are very general and subject to interpretation by the respondent (e.g. how often did you use the bus last week?). Vaguely worded questions may be particularly subject to response bias due to mood. For example, people who are distressed by their disability may report doing things frequently in order to protect themselves from feelings of distress. There is some evidence that self-report disability measures are particularly vulnerable to this sort of bias (Spiegel *et al.*, 1988). Oppenheim (1992) or Rust and Golombok (1989) provide detailed guides to using self-report and observational techniques.

DIARIES

If measures are to be used to evaluate healthcare interventions, they will be administered before and after the intervention has taken place, and it is therefore particularly important that participants cannot recall what they said at the first time of testing. Measures that require people to detail exactly what they have done during a specific period may help overcome this problem. Seven-day diaries are probably the easiest and most widely used method, but these do pose problems for measuring change accurately as the information recorded in the diary has to be summated in some way. But they are adequate for individual case management where the person and professional have agreed specific targets for treatment and can therefore estimate how satisfactory the outcome has been. Box 5.2 shows how a diary might be designed for use in clinical assessment.

Box 5.2 *Example of a walking and activity diary*

DAY ONE: Day ______________________ Date ________________

Did you walk out-of-doors today? Write down all the walking you did today.

Where did you walk to?	How far was this?	Did you go alone or with someone?	How did you feel?

What else did you manage to do today? Write down everything you did today.	
What did you do?	Was this alone, or with help?

If you did not do all the things you hoped to do today, is there anything that would make it easier next time?

Learning Activity 1 ◆ ◆ ◆

The aim of this activity is to practise designing different ways of measuring disability. A middle aged man who lives with his wife who has agorophobia has suffered a left CVA haemorrhage and has dysphasia and right hemiplegia. He needs to keep as fit and mobile as possible because he has to do the shopping and other jobs outside the home. Devise three ways of assessing his walking at three levels of analysis:

a biological
b environmental constraints
c psychological

and using three methods of assessment:
(i) observation; (ii) self- and other-report; (iii) diary monitoring.

The content of disability

Considerable conceptual variability exists in the definition of the activities or movements that comprise disability. In its original definition, the *International Classification of Impairments, Disabilities and Handicaps* (WHO, 1980) drew a distinction between what are referred to as 'activities', which comprise the content of disability, and 'fulfillment of roles', which comprise the content of handicap.

The contents of these two domains are rarely clearly specified and often subject to confusion. The Office of Population Censuses and Surveys (OPCS, 1988), for example, suggests that mobility can be considered a handicap (p. 7). However, it would seem clear that 'mobility' does not constitute a social role. Social roles refer to the ability to occupy some socially constructed position, such as that of spouse or employee. The extent to which a limitation in performance of specific activities leads to a handicap will depend to a large extent on the attitudes and laws which members of society use to restrict or facilitate occupation of such roles (Russell, 1989).

Disability, then, refers only to specific definable tasks, skills or behaviours. However, the activities included in disability assessments are variable. Some of the main assessments are summarized in Box 5.3; some, such as those used to assess changes resulting from physiotherapy, include only assessments of body movements (e.g. Partridge *et al.*, 1987). But the most commonly used measures also include assessments of personal care activities, and activities performed within the house. Fewer measures include what might be referred to as activities of independent living, such as shopping, using public transport, or participation in leisure or social activities.

Given this diversity, what defines the content of disability? A person who can perform specific body movements but who is unable to go shopping is not disabled according to the Partridge *et al.* (1987) scale. Similarly, if assessments include only self-care activities, a person who cannot use public transport or who does not go out socially will not be assessed as disabled. But how exhaustive should the list of activities be? Most measures have been developed for specific purposes and the choice or development of a suitable measure will depend on the purpose for which it is intended. For example, measures that include only body movements were developed to assess changes in flexion following physiotherapy. Interventions that seek to change self-care activities, or mobility or social activities, should assess these activities specifically.

The content of the measure adopted should be specific to the purpose, and the technique of assessment should be appropriate for the model being tested. Thus, interventions that aim to modify leg or arm movements require assessments that involve demonstrations of arm movement, whilst interventions that aim to modify participation in social activities by modifying self-efficacy beliefs or skills in requesting assistance would require measures of social activity.

It is important to be aware of the range and type of activities being assessed and under what conditions they are being assessed, because these may reflect an inappropriate model of disability and lead to poor management of it. For example, it is unclear to what extent gains in flexion made in physiotherapy may generalize to other activities; in an exercise intervention amongst patients with arthritis, O'Leary *et al.* (1988) found that, although improvements in joint flexion were found, there was no change on a measure of functional activities of everyday living.

The structure of disability

The structure of functional assessments refers to the ways in which the activities or movements assessed relate to each other, or can be combined to produce an overall measure of disability. Most measures have adopted an hierarchical approach to disability assessment (see Box 5.3): a list of activities within a

Box 5.3 *The content and structure of disability in selected scales*

Authors	*Number of domains assessed*	*Content assessed*	*Structure*
Partridge *et al.* (1987)	2	Gross body movements Arm movements	Hierarchical within domains
Whiting and Lincoln (1980)	3	Self-care Household 1 Household 2	Hierarchical within domains Guttman = 0.79 Guttman = 0.68 Guttman = 0.92
Lincoln and Gladman (1992)	4	Mobility Kitchen Domestic Leisure	Hierarchical within domains Guttman = 0.88 Guttman = 0.81 Guttman = 0.88 Guttman = 0.89
Katz *et al.* (1963)	1	Self-care	Hierarchical
Mahoney and Barthel (1965)	1	Self-care	Hierarchical
Williams *et al.* (1976)	3	Self-care Domestic Transport	Hierarchical across domains Guttman = 0.71 (men) Guttman = 0.69 (women)
Patrick and Peach (1989)	12	Ambulation Body care and movement Mobility Household Management Recreation and pastimes Social interaction Emotion Alertness Sleep and rest Eating Communication Work	Severity weightings are attached to each item, indicating non-equivalent intervals. Domain scores are summed to produce total score
OPCS (1988)	13	Locomotion Reaching and stretching Dexterity Personal care Continence Seeing Hearing Communication Behaviour Intellectual functioning Consciousness Eating, drinking and digestion Disfigurement	Severity weightings are attached to each item, indicating non-equivalent intervals. Domains are combined by the equation: most severe + 0.3 times second severest + 0.4 times third severest

particular domain of activity, such as self-care, is developed; then, if a person can perform the most difficult activity on the assessment, this infers that he or she can also perform all the other activities on the assessment. A simple addition of all items the person can perform will then provide a disability score within the domain of activity being assessed.

Scales which use this additive hierarchical approach should have a reported coefficient of reproducibility (Guttman coefficients). If no coefficient is reported by

Learning Activity 2 ◆ ◆ ◆

Be aware of how questions or content of an assessment can reflect different models of disability. Continue with the case example in Activity 1, and assume that your initial assessments generated a lot of useful information:

- *Observation*: Walks slowly but very unsteadily without three-footed stick because of foot drop. Nervous and tense when walking.
- *Self-report*: Can walk around house pretty well because plenty to hold on to. Has walked in the back garden but otherwise not yet walked out of the house. Says he is very frightened of falling and making a fool of himself. Also embarrassed at not being able to ask for help.
- *Other-report*: Confirms above, but also notes that he gets very angry and frustrated at his clumsiness or bursts into tears.
- *Diary*: Shows that he has not carried out any activity outside the house but they have managed because relatives are doing their shopping.

What does this assessment tell you about the potential contributions to the man's level of disability of (i) impairment, (ii) environment and (iii) psychology? Which bits of information lead you to your various conclusions?

Finally, choose one level to pursue in a little more detail (e.g. the psychological factors). Devise assessment techniques appropriate to this level that would enable you to clarify the factors contributing to this disability.

the authors of the scale, it is not advisable to use it. The coefficient of reproducibility should have a value as near as possible to 1.0. The coefficient is a test of confidence that if someone performs the most difficult task, he or she also performs the easier tasks. If the value of this coefficient is too near to zero, it would not be statistically justified to add together the different tasks to produce an overall score.

One drawback of simply adding up items in an hierarchical manner is that this implies that the gap between items is equivalent, so that a person who scores 10 might be said to be twice as disabled as a person who scores 5. To avoid making this assumption, some scales attach a weighting to each item to reflect its relative severity (in Box 5.3, the OPCS scale and the Functional Limitations Profile (Patrick and Peach, 1989)).

In order to assess the structure of disability scales, it is necessary to reconsider the assumptions about the causes of disability on which they are based. If the model of disability is derived from the biological model, it is assumed that the hierarchical ordering of tasks reflects the extent to which the underlying impairment limits their performance. In other words, the ability to perform each task is directly related to the extent of biological impairment a person has.

If adopting a psychological approach, the underlying structure of activities within a domain might be derived from the motivational significance of the activities concerned. For instance, it may be assumed that people become competent or incompetent at particular activities not because they differ in the amount of biological function required to perform them but because they differ in terms of their importance to the person concerned.

In support of this, Williams *et al.* (1976) assessed the recovery of functional activity following surgery. The data showed that the order in which different activities were recovered differed for men and women, suggesting that the ability to perform each activity was more closely related to the evaluation of each task and the commitment to performing it, than it was to some underlying biological impairment. Whilst this study is rather old and may not reflect current gender variations in commitment to different tasks, it does underline the importance of assessing psychological determinants of disability as well as biological determinants. Similarly, it may be the case that some activities are particularly sensitive to environmental or social constraints, so that disability measures in part reflect the extent to which certain resources are available or the extent to which they interfere with particular activities.

Learning Activity 3 ◆ ◆ ◆

Practise relating interventions to levels or models of disability. Based on what you have been told already in Activities 1 and 2, identify interventions that might be useful for the man if you wished to address:

a the impairment
b the environmental constraints
c the psychological issues.

SUMMARY

The prevention and reduction of disability is an important aim of healthcare in a number of medical conditions. Disability in functional activity can result from physiological, psychological and environmental causes. Whilst there is a place for all levels of analysis, understanding of the psychosocial processes involved in disability opens up a wide range of intervention possibilities. Direct manipulation of psychosocial processes has been shown to be important in the management of disability. Intervention at one level can have consequences – helpful or detrimental – at other levels, so that broad-based assessment is essential to the optimal management of disability.

Key Points

- Disability may arise from biological impairment, limitations in the environment, or levels of motivation, or from combinations of all three.
- When using or designing measures of disability it is important to consider underlying theoretical assumptions.
- The measurement technique is determined by the model of disability being used.
- The content of the assessment is determined by the purpose for which it has been designed.
- The structure of disability describes how activities are related.
- Awareness of the conceptual basis of assessment will lead to a better understanding of the determinants of disability.
- Individual models may need to be combined in the management of disability.

References

Anderson, K.O., Bradley, L.A., Young L.D. and McDaniel, L.K. (1985). Rheumatoid arthritis: a review of psychological factors related to etiology, effects and treatment. *Psychological Bulletin*, **98**: 358–87.

Arber, S. and Gilbert, N. (1989). Men: the forgotten carers. *Sociology*, **23**: 111–18.

Bandura, A. (1977). Self-efficacy: toward a unifying theory of behaviour change. *Psychological Review*, **84**: 191–215.

Grundy, E. (1987). Community care for the elderly, 1976–84. *British Medical Journal*, **294**: 626–9.

Katz, S., Ford, A., Moskowitz, R., Jackson, B. and Jaffe, M. (1963). Studies of illness in the aged. *Journal of the American Medical Association*, **185**: 914–9.

Leventhal, H. and Nerenz, D. (1985). The assessment of illness cognition. In Karoly, P. (ed.). *Measurement Strategies in Health Psychology*. New York: Wiley, 517–55.

Lincoln, N. and Gladman, J. (1992). The extended activities of daily living scale: a further validation. *Disability and Rehabilitation*, **14**: 41–3.

Lorig, K., Seleznik, M., Lubeck, D., Ung, E., Chastain, R.L. and Holman, H. (1989). The beneficial outcomes of the arthritis self-management course are not adequately explained by behaviour change. *Arthritis and Rheumatism*, **32**: 91–5.

Mahoney, F. and Barthel, D. (1965). Functional evaluation: the Barthel Index. *Maryland State Medical Journal*, 21 April, 61–5.

Nerenz, D.R. and Leventhal, H. (1983). Self-regulation theory in chronic illness. In Burish, T.G. and Bradley, L.A. (eds). *Coping with Chronic Disease: Research and Applications*. New York: Academic Press, 13–37.

O'Leary, A., Shoor, S., Lorig, K. and Holman, H. (1988) A cognitive–behavioural treatment for rheumatoid arthritis. *Health Psychology*, **7**: 527–44.

OPCS (1982). *General Household Survey 1980*. London: HMSO.

OPCS (1988). *Disability in the Community*. London: HMSO.

Oppenheim, A.N. (1992). *Questionnaire Design, Interviewing and Attitude Measurement*. London: Pinter.

Orne, M.T. (1962). On the social psychology of the psychological experiment: with particular reference to demand characteristics and their implications. *American Psychologist*, **17**: 776–83.

Patrick, D.L. and Peach, H. (eds) (1989). *Disablement in the Community*. Oxford: Oxford University Press.

Partridge, C., Johnston, M. and Edwards, S. (1987). Recovery from physical disability after stroke: normal patterns as a basis for evaluation. *Lancet*, 14 Feb. 373–5.

Rosenthal, R. (1966). *Experimenter Effects in Behavioural Research*. New York: Appleton–Century–Crofts.

Russell, S. (1989). From disability to handicap: an inevitable response to social constraints? *Canadian Review of Sociology and Anthropology*, **26**: 276–93.

Rust, J.R. and Golombok, S. (1989). *Modern Psychometrics*. London: Routledge.

Schwarzer, R. (1994). *Self-Efficacy: Thought Control of Action*. Washington: Hemisphere.

Smith, C.A., Dobbins, C.J. and Wallston, K.A. (1991). The mediational role of perceived competence in psychological adjustment to rheumatoid arthritis. *Journal of Applied Social Psychology*, **21**: 1218–47.

Spiegel, J., Leake, B., Spiegel, T., Paulus, H., Kane, R., Ward, N. and Ware, J. (1988). What are we measuring? *Arthritis and Rheumatism*, **31**: 721–9.

Verbrugge, L.M. (1995). New thinking and science on disability in mid and late life. *European Journal of Public Health*, **20**(5): 20–8.

Warnes, A. (1991). The changing elderly population: aspects of diversity. *Reviews in Clinical Gerontology*, **1**: 185–94.

Whiting, S.E. and Lincoln, N. (1980). An activities-of-daily-living assessment for stroke patients. *Occupational Therapy*, Feb., 44–7.

Williams, R., Johnston, M., Willis, L. and Bennett, A. (1976). Disability: a model and a measurement technique. *British Journal of Preventive and Social Medicine*, **30**: 71–8.

World Health Organization (1980). *International Classification of Impairments, Disabilities and Handicaps*. Geneva: WHO.

Further Reading

Schwarzer, R. (1994). *Self-Efficacy: Thought Control of Action*. Washington: Hemisphere.

Skelton, J.A. and Croyle, R.T. (eds) (1991). *Mental Representation in Health and Illness*. New York: Springer Verlag.

SECTION II

Social Concepts

6

Social Models of Health and Illness

Sebastian Garman

LEARNING OBJECTIVES

After studying this chapter you should:

- Be aware of the differing definitions of health and illness from a social context;
- Understand the impact of biomedical and social approaches on health;
- Know how holism fits into today's models of health;
- Understand the concept of the disease model;
- Be able to discuss how different social groups perceive health.

INTRODUCTION

Individuals engaged in health-related employment, like the lay population around them, draw upon a common culture for the values and precepts to make sense of experiences. Health professionals are not, therefore, insulated from the world of lay beliefs and values about health, illness and disease but are better seen as taking part in a community-wide debate about these beliefs. Such notions of health and illness are subject to historical change and are constantly under negotiation. It is important for health professionals to show awareness of the normative factors that shape their professional judgements and decisions, as well as the sociological forces that dispose these to change.

This chapter starts by evaluating the use of language in the way health is viewed. This is followed by a short introduction to the normative aspects of illness, by reflecting on what is normal in terms of health and illness. This is then put into the context of the differing models of health and disease. The chapter ends with an analysis of how different social groups consider illness in relation to themselves.

HEALTH AND ILLNESS

Work on how people conceptualize health, illness, pain and disease has demonstrated that not only do different social class, status and culture groups perceive or construct such ideas differently, but also that the ideas themselves change over time (see Stacey (1988) and Helman (1990) for useful introductory discussions).

Consider first the difference in terms as suggested by English usage (Stacey, 1988). A 'disease' is generally presented as an objective condition, whilst an 'illness' is seen to be a subjectively felt experience: individuals are diagnosed as being ill (a felt experience) because of a disease (an objective condition). Indeed, a disease is often perceived to be the main cause – if not the sufficient cause – of the illness on the model of an alien invader that attacks the body from the outside. Such perceptions channel professional expectations and actions, but it should be remembered that these models are only aids to understanding. They change over time (McKeown, 1979; Kennedy, 1981; Scadding, 1988) and other people may see things differently.

The words 'health', 'healing', 'hale' and 'whole' derive from the same root. The connection made between health and wholeness has been dominant until fairly recently, with both physical and moral connotations (Stacey, 1988). It is interesting to note, also, that the words 'well' and 'wealth' are connected, and have moral connotations. The predominant connotation of the idea of 'ill' in the English language, through its long development, has been a moral one. Only since the eighteenth century has its dominant meaning of 'evil' been replaced by more morally neutral connotations (Granshaw and Porter, 1989).

Health, like cleanliness, has been next to godliness in

many traditional cultures (Douglas, 1966). Physical or mental impairment has been so often regarded as discrediting, grounds for being considered impure and for exclusion from religious communion. (Goffman, 1963; Douglas, 1966; Turner, 1986). Explanations of ill-health or bodily impairment in traditional agrarian communities tend to be conceptualized in either personalistic or naturalistic terms (Foster and Anderson, 1978). The former conceptual scheme tends to 'explain' such bodily misfortune as an act of aggression or punishment against the person by ancestors, witchcraft or a vengeful deity.

What, then, do contemporary professionals concerned with health mean by the word? This is not as easy to establish as might be supposed. Often, the books concerned with medicine and health assume the concept is too unproblematic to define. The *Heinemann Medical Dictionary* (Lennox and Lennox, 1986) is entirely typical in this regard. Medicine is defined with reference to disease. Disease is defined normatively as significant and named abnormality of body function. Health is not defined at all. This is perhaps not as surprising as might at first appear, for as the psychiatrist Anthony Clare observes in the introduction to a book by Payer (1990), 'a particular difficulty I encounter from time to time when I teach medical students is introducing them to or reminding them of the simple fact that medicine is not a science'. Medicine utilizes an impressive array of rigorous scientific techniques, but in itself is an art as much as a science that is concerned with a moral good, health. Health is a value embedded in culture and as such is negotiated felt experience and an ideal. Health professionals are dependent on philosophers, theologians, artists and the lay public for clarifying these values. Doctors and the lay public negotiate and to some extent share their perceptions of health (see Lock and Gordon (1988) for one discussion).

Definitions of health used by health professionals can be placed on a continuum (Box 6.1). At one end there are 'quantitative' definitions, trying to avoid the awkward ambiguity of cultural values by stressing that which can be measured. At the other end there are 'qualitative' definitions that try to reveal the moral good by describing the values suggested by the idea of health. Placed on a continuum between negative definitions, which stress what people are without, and positive definitions which attempt to describe the attributes of health, a number of definitions are possible.

The first two definitions in Box 6.1 tend to be associated with epidemiological, and what is sometimes referred to as biomedical, perspectives on health. They are 'positivist' in emphasis, attempting to recognize observable facts and restrict their concern to measurable phenomena. Positivism in its disproportionate application in medicine has many critics (Dubos, 1960; McKeown, 1976; Kennedy, 1981). But a positivistic approach has certain advantages too. By restricting definitions to a variable that can be observed and potentially measured enables common agreement about health concerns. People generally agree that longevity and freedom from discomfort and pain are often desired and may even be desirable. Increasing life expectancy among a population is generally accepted as evidence for increasing health. But the two concepts should not be interchanged. Measurable evidence of health, such as life expectancy, should not be mistaken for health itself.

Box 6.1 *A continuum of health definitions*

Quantitative

- The absence of death (mortality); survival for the full life span
- The absence of illness or disease (morbidity)
- Homeostasis or the ability to adapt to changing demands
- Immunity or the capacity to adapt to future challenges
- The facility to live to the full potential
- Resources with which to handle the personal and social demands of living
- An ideal state of complete physical, mental and social well-being
- A process engaging social, mental, spiritual and physical well-being
- 'Joie de vivre'
- Wholeness; a metaphysical and ecological balance of self with the social and material environment

Qualitative

It is the evaluative or qualitative dimensions missing from such definitions that have been increasingly influential among health professionals since the Second World War. Health is presented as a value, an ideal and a commitment and as such is embedded within the matrix of values, the design for living that anthropologists refer to as a culture. It is this awareness that informs definitions favoured by institutions concerned with caring and health, who for example have constructed models of care around Maslow's hierarchy of needs (Maslow, 1954) and the World

Health Organization (WHO) with its much quoted definition (WHO, 1946) stressing 'complete physical, mental and social well-being, and not merely the absence of disease'.

More recently, however, there has been a marked change in definition favoured by health professionals towards an emphasis on health as a process in community or even ecological 'settings' involving the active participation of populations. These tendencies can be illustrated from WHO initiatives, both in the preference for defining health as a process (WHO, 1988), and in the attempts through the healthy cities movement (WHO, 1990) to utilize 'a social rather than a narrowly medical concept, which meant that the improvements can only occur from a partnership of all institutions and organizations, as well as the inhabitants of a city.'

Learning Activity 1 ◆ ◆ ◆

- ◆ Consider what you mean by 'health'.
- ◆ Ask friends and colleagues for their definitions and compare them with yours. Discuss the different definitions.
- ◆ Be alert to the uses of the word 'health' and 'healthy' in the media, conversation and literature, and notice the variety of interpretations used and implied.

THE NORMATIVE ASPECTS OF ILLNESS

In contemporary English usage, illness is distinguished from disease by its subjective connotations. Illness is a felt experience judged against what is felt to be normal. Equally, however, illness involves social transactions in which moral and even political judgements are made. People often feel ill, but the social process of being recognized as 'ill' rather than as, say, a 'malingerer' or a 'hypochondriac' requires a process of negotiation during which official pronouncements are made.

This process of making judgements operates at two levels, the macro and the micro. *At the macro level*, certain physiological states are defined and categorized as illnesses and others are not. In the *Heinemann Medical Dictionary* (1986) an illness is defined in terms of disease ('a patient's perception of the effects of a disease') and a disease is defined in terms of a physiological model based on normative considerations ('the significant departure from normal bodily function'). The problem is, of course, that there is no consensus and people change their minds over time, about what is normal bodily functioning.

An interesting case in point is the debate that surrounds the felt experience myalgic encephalomyelitis (ME), because no one could describe the abnormal physiological processes involved. However, researchers seem to have demonstrated that ME sufferers experience a marked reduction in flow of oxygen to the brain (Schwartz *et al.*, 1994; Shepherd, 1995). If this is so, then evidence exists for more widespread official recognition of the condition.

However, with many felt and behaviour states the demonstration of 'significant' abnormality of body function is not enough. The uncomfortable questions have to be faced about for whom is the abnormality regarded as significant and why. Abnormality of bodily function is a judgement that depends on the demands of the culture in which people are placed. Body smell in Japan (Baker, 1976), homosexuality in America (Conrad and Schneider, 1992), masturbating in Victorian England (Szasz, 1970), have all been regarded as such 'significant' abnormalities. Too little head hair, too much body hair, excess subcutaneous fat, and a perceived dependency on alcohol are recently negotiated categories in industrial urban societies (Conrad and Schneider, 1992), whilst barrenness in women and the lack or excess of limbs and digits were regarded as highly inappropriate in many traditional agrarian societies (Foster and Anderson, 1978).

Learning Activity 2 ◆ ◆ ◆

- ◆ What are your definitions of 'illness' and 'disease'?
- ◆ Ask friends and colleagues for their definitions, and compare them.
- ◆ Watch out for how 'illness' and 'disease' are used in the media, and consider the variety of interpretations used and implied.

MODELS OF HEALTH: BIOMEDICAL AND SOCIAL APPROACHES

In his discussion of health, Dubos (1960) draws attention to the ceaseless oscillation in the West between two views of health, symbolized by the Greek hero Asclepius, who became god of healing and medicine, and his daughter Hygieia, goddess of health. The followers of the former sought out the techniques and art of curing disease, to correct the imperfections caused by accidents of circumstance or birth. The worshippers of the latter were seeking the laws of healthy living, itself, by which they thought they would achieve the wisdom necessary to achieve health and longevity.

McKeown (1979), who has done much to popularize the distinction, suggests that in seventeenth century Europe the turning point was reached in which the balance was tipped in favour of Asclepius, and that this has remained true for the next three centuries. In a seminal critique, McKeown lays out the essentials of this concept, which others have labelled biomedical, 'a concept which is rarely stated explicitly but on which medical activities largely rest, namely that human health depends essentially on a mechanistic approach based on understanding the structure and function of the body and the disease processes that affect it', a concept that informs and underpins the major research, teaching and practice-based institutions of modern medicine. The elements of the biomedical model are summarized in Box 6.2.

With hindsight it can be seen that Dubos and McKeown represent one part of a sustained and widespread movement expressing dissatisfaction with biomedicine. It is now often suggested that the pendulum swing is once more altering the balance of influence, this time in favour of Hygieia over Asclepius. Influential critiques include those of Fabrega (1975), Engel (1977), Capra (1982), Turner (1986), Stacey (1988), Lock and Gordon (1988) and Sheridan and Radmacher (1992).

Box 6.2 *Elements of the biomedical model*

- Health is the absence of disease or biological abnormality.
- The healer is the medical or professional or specialist.
- The focus of activities is the human body.
- The model or metaphor used is the machine.
- The knowledge base is biomedical science.
- The locus of activity is the clinic or hospital.
- The nature of the disorder is acute.
- The goal of activity is cure.
- The role of the individual is as passive recipient of treatment.

A model attempting to approach the wisdom of the followers of Hygieia is not so easily arrived at. The variety of intellectual critiques of biomedicine has been remarkable. Key references in the new thinking include emphasis on self-help (Hastings *et al.*, 1981; Shames and Shames, 1982) and symbiosis (Capra, 1982; Myers, 1985), ecology (Goldsmith and Hidyard, 1988; Last and Guidotti, 1990; Stokols, 1992) and empowerment (McNight, 1985; Rose and Black, 1985; Stevenson and Parsloe, 1993; Swain, 1993), political involvement (McKinley, 1985; Grace, 1991) or the stilling of the passions (Sobel, 1979), feminism (Rosser, 1988; Zola, 1991) or the fight against patriarchy (Witz, 1992). However, bearing in mind that models are only aids to understanding, it is perhaps worth attempting to suggest certain key features to contrast with those that we have isolated as paradigmatic of biomedicine.

Social models are united in agreement about the appropriate aetiology of health problems and the appropriate locus of activity, that prevention is better than cure. Proponents often refer to the story of the man who, with considerable expenditure of time and energy, devotes himself to rescuing a string of drowning people from a river until it occurs to him to go upstream to find out who is throwing them in. Elements of the 'social model' are summarized in Box 6.3.

Box 6.3 *Elements of the social model*

- Health is homeostasis, symbiosis and wholeness: personal, social and/or ecological.
- The healer is the person in conjunction with helpers (the healthcare team).
- The focus of activity is the whole person in a social setting (e.g. family, work, community).
- The model or metaphor used is that of a homeostatic system.
- The knowledge base draws on social sciences and traditional wisdom.
- The locus of activity is the person in the community.
- The nature of the disorder tends to be chronic.
- The goal of activity is welfare.
- The role of the patient is as active participant.

Thomas McKeown, who has questioned the validity of the dominant assumptions of biomedicine, traces the loss of balance between Asclepius and Hygieia to the seventeenth century when advances in understanding of the human body and the natural world were rapidly achieved using the metaphor of the machine – for example, Kepler's work on the dioptric mechanism for the eye's production of a retinal image and Harvey's discovery of the circulatory system of the blood. This mechanistic model of the human body is attributed to the French philosopher Descartes, who popularized this notion. Descartes is also attributed with the split between mind and body.

This emphasis on the body as machine suggests that ill-health will be the result of one of two causes: either faulty structure (physiological abnormality), the result of faulty design or damage through use, or the invasion of one organism by another which incapacitates the host. From this model the medical practitioner is seen as the person who acts upon the passive body (patient = enduring with composure) by altering it or casting out aliens. Disease theories of illness gain in popularity, and the locus of medical intervention tends to be seen as the clinic.

The remarkable improvements in the health of populations of urban industrial societies has been largely attributed to medical advances of knowledge and clinical activity. The reality, McKeown (1976) suggests, is very different because 'predominant influences which led to the improvement in health in the past three centuries were nutritional, environmental (particularly control of water and food) and behavioural; the last through the change in reproductive practices which limited population growth'.

In place of the individualist and mechanistic model of health that he suggests is typical of biomedicine, he demonstrates that the actual advances achieved in health have been mainly due to a collectivist and systems approach of aetiology and action that stresses both the 'environment' (e.g. the organization of water and sewerage) and communal behaviour (e.g. fertility).

On the continuum between the biomedical and the social models, this model suggested by McKeown (1976) represents a half-way stage that might be called the 'public health approach'. The person remains a passive recipient who is acted upon by forces beyond his or her control. A public health literature has emerged that questions this emphasis (Crawford, 1980; Knight, 1985; Baric, 1990a,b). The point of view has been sometimes dubbed 'the new public health' (see Ashton and Seymour, 1988), which suggests improvements are only likely to be sustained by exercise in empowerment of the person who becomes a participant in managing his/her own health (WHO, 1990; Baric, 1990a; Stokols, 1992).

Learning Activity 3 ◆ ◆ ◆

Look again at Boxes 6.2 and 6.3, the biomedical and social models of health.

- How do you, as a health professional, view your role?
- What is the role of the person in your care?
- If you and your patients/clients hold different views on health models, how might this affect your interactions?

TOWARDS A NEW MODEL?

This restless and multifaceted critique of biomedicine has led to much speculation about whether some more profound changes are taking place in Western urban industrial societies of which changing perceptions of health are only one part (Capra, 1982, 1986; Turner, 1987; Poynton, 1989). This is perhaps best explored by focusing on a key concept that seems strategic to a range of critical perspectives outlined above – that of *holism*.

Deriving from the work of the South African philosopher, Jan Christian Smuts, the idea of 'holism' recurs in the work of the last two decades in conscious opposition to the perceived 'reductionism' of biomedicine. Holism to its supporters projects a model of understanding of the world that stresses the interconnectedness of all animate, and, indeed, inanimate things. Understanding the phenomenon depends on exploring interconnections through systems and ecological approaches with environmental matters, and qualitative or empathic approaches to the understanding of human beings. Seminal to the development of holistic thinking among health professionals was the work of Engel (1977) and Gordon (1981). Theoretical discussions of practice based on holistic principles have followed by proponents in many health professions, including psychiatry (Gordon, 1981), occupational health nursing (Smith and Stenger, 1985), dentistry (Isaacs, 1987) and occupational therapy (Miller, 1993).

Critics have focused their concerns on a central paradox they see as being implicit within holistic health models (Crawford, 1980; McKee, 1988). On the one hand, explanations for health problems depend on a system or ecological approach that emphasizes interconnection, but on the other hand solutions to health problems are perceived at the level of individual action and self-help. Crawford (1980) associates the popularity of holistic health models with what he calls 'healthism', the widespread development in popular culture of a 'preoccupation with personal health as a primary focus for the definition and achievement of well-being'. On the one hand, people attempt to live longer and better lives by jogging, aerobics, high-fibre and low-fat diets, and on the other hand pollution, traffic congestion, poverty, crime and ecological devastation occur around them. The popularity of the holistic health movement is accounted for by providing easy and illusory solutions to health problems, and, therefore, allowing the political status quo of consumerism and market capitalism to go unchallenged (McKee, 1988).

Current usage of the concept of holism seems to reveal a convergence of several schools of thought concerned with health, including critiques of biomedicine (Engel, 1977), neo-Marxist critiques of the way political power operates through health discourses (McKee, 1988), feminist critiques of the way gender and power work within health and other professional settings (Rosser, 1988; Witz, 1992; Miller, 1993), and sociological critiques of the medical model (Stacey, 1988). The paradox of explanations that emphasizes personal control and self-advocacy, on the one hand, and a systems understanding on the other, in which the individual is locked into a global ecological network of apparently hostile forces, is very evident. Attempts at resolution are still emerging (St George, 1984; Poynton, 1989; Cassidy, 1994).

Learning Activity 4 ◆ ◆ ◆

One of the results of the popularity of concepts of holism has been a rise in the number of 'alternative' lifestyles and therapies promoted and practised.

- Make a list of the alternative therapies you know about and look out for mention of them in the media.
- Are you able to identify any alternative therapies that are gaining mainstream acceptance?
- How do you, as a health professional, view alternative medicine?

DISEASE MODELS OF HEALTH

Kennedy (1981) suggests that disease models of health encourage identification of disease so that human beings are reduced 'to ambulatory assemblages of parts'. Often, he points out, the doctor can only offer a diagnosis but no cure. Yet giving a felt experience of illness a name can be reassuring to patients because it can offer welcome relief from responsibility for the condition and protection against accusations of hypochondria, as sufferers of ME can bear witness.

Despite the large critical literature expressing reservations, both philosophical and scientific (see McKeown, 1979; Kennedy, 1981; Scadding, 1988; Foss, 1989; McCombie, 1989), disease models remain central to medicine. In appropriate contexts the idea of disease has its place. The problem comes when that place is exaggerated so that the disease is made the sufficient or only cause of the illness. Such aetiologies as these are guilty of what philosophers call the naturalistic fallacy, when an empirical description of what is the case cannot demonstrate what ought to be. As discussed, illness is among other things a normative concept, a judgement. A disease cannot cause the evaluative judgements called illness, although it can and does contribute to such judgements being made. In medical history there are numerous conceptual confusions, where medical specialists have sought to establish scientific credence to 'cures' for morally disapproved of behaviours of people by working on their bodies. The history of what has been aptly called the dustbin category, that of the 'psychopath', provides preposterous examples from Benjamin Rush's 'disease of the moral faculty' (1786) by way of Pritchard's 'moral insanity' of 1835, to the 'moral defective' category of the 1913 Mental Deficiency Act (Werlinder, 1978).

The disease theory has proved useful to many in the medical profession who, in the opinion of McKeown, have done much to promote it. Another powerful ally has been the pharmaceutical industry which, according to Kennedy (1981), has 'a vested interest in the continued vitality of the notion of specific disease entities'. Kennedy also points out that the two interests converge, particularly in the United States where wealth from petrochemical and pharmaceutical companies provides the main private source of funding for medical science and medical education.

A contemporary example of disease theory are American doctors who carry out many more diagnostic tests than European doctors; also their dosages of drugs are much higher, and they favour surgery far more often. Payer (1990) argues that in America 'the presence of a virus or bacteria is emphasized with little regard for host resistance'. Whereas American doctors like to cite the study of islanders who did not develop a particular disease until foreigners came to the island, Payer suggests French and German doctors would point out that whereas a virus is doubtless important, resistance obviously played a part since not everyone exposed got the disease.

Learning Activity 5 ◆ ◆ ◆

In clinical practice you will come across examples where the disease models of health are used.

- ◆ Make a list of any examples you come across.
- ◆ Discuss and compare these examples with colleagues and friends.

HEALTH AND ILLNESS AS SOCIAL REPRESENTATIONS

How, then, do people actually perceive health in themselves and others? Since the pioneering study of Herzlich (1973) on Parisian middle-class lay conceptions of health and illness, a series of studies in Britain has added to the body of knowledge. Herzlich argues that both lay groups and professionals alike draw upon common cultural assumptions which help to make sense of their health and illness experiences, a point reinforced more recently by Payer (1991). Herzlich's sample saw health in three different ways (see Box 6.4).

Box 6.4 *The three ways used by Herzlich's sample to describe health*

- The robustness of the body or a good constitution.
- Health as separate from the body and personal responsibility.
- An equilibrium of body and mind sustainable by the will of the individual.

A recent summary by Blaxter (1990) of the findings of the largest health and lifestyle survey in Britain to date found that people responded differently when they described health in others, which they saw in terms of either fitness or the absence of disease. When asked how people described health in themselves, however, psychological perceptions were resorted to, with people talking of feeling 'good', 'happy', 'able to cope'.

Cornwell (1984) found among working-class people in London's Bethnal Green area that material and social class factors influenced perceptions of health. Negative or functional perceptions of health tended to be emphasized by working-class respondents where financial and employment constraints were felt to be dominant. The experience of health as being within the control and responsibility of self tends to be found more in the middle classes, or at least among those members of the middle class who experience similar choice and self-determination in their career and financial circumstances.

The few studies of health perceptions of ethnic minority groups in Britain confirm the pattern. Among groups deriving from traditional agrarian societies, health tends to be viewed in terms of fate or the natural order and not as something within personal control to be aimed at or considered as one of life's goals (Helman, 1990). Moreover, studies demonstrate that less-educated respondents from working-class groups of both indigenous and ethnic minority backgrounds tend to somatize; that is to say, mental illnesses are described in terms of body-located physical symptoms, such as bodily aches and pains.

Aetiology or causation is important to all definitions or classifications of illness by both lay and professional observers. Cornwell (1984) found that her sample from Bethnal Green tended to distinguish between 'normal illnesses' such as infectious diseases of childhood, 'real illness' such as the major disabling and life-threatening conditions, and 'health problems' that are not perceived as illnesses – such as problems associated with reproduction, ageing and mental state. There is some evidence to suggest that, for neurotic disorders ar least, people are increasingly willing to accept abnormal

Learning Activity 6 ◆ ◆ ◆

Compare the coverage given by broadsheet and tabloid newspapers to any issue related to health or illness.

- ◆ Are you able to identify any differences in approach between the two types of newspaper?
- ◆ Can any differences be linked to the distinct social groups who read these publications?
- ◆ Do all health professionals read the same type of newspaper?

mental states as illnesses (see Miles (1988) for a discussion).

SUMMARY

It is important for health professionals to consider what they and the people in their care understand by health, illness and related concepts since judgements about who, when, where and how to treat individuals depends on these understandings.

Since the Cartesian revolution, a particular view of health, the human body and medical intervention has tended to dominate, which commentators have summarized under the label of 'biomedicine'. There is evidence that this dominance is giving way as various social models compete for influence with it.

Both lay groups and health professionals depend for their perceptions of health upon such constructs as a part of the culture, or design for living, with which people make sense of their experience. It is interesting, therefore, to look at the evidence for what is known about health professionals and other peoples beliefs about health and illness. The evidence seems to suggest that lay and professional people do not differ much in this: both groups conceptions have been shaped by the assumptions of biomedicine and both groups are now experimenting with different ways of approaching an understanding of the human body and its health status. From a sociological viewpoint, it seems to be true to say, moreover, that the way people construct and defend their different perceptions of health and illness is related to the material and social circumstances in which they find themselves.

Key Points

- Health and illness are defined by different models in numerous ways.
- These definitions can be placed on a continuum, using qualitative and quantitative attributions.
- Health professionals historically have subscribed to a biomedical model of health and illness.
- Illness has been based on normative considerations.
- The new public health model represents a half-way stage between the biomedical and social models of health.
- Holism acts as model which overarches between systems and ecological approaches to the environment and human beings.
- Models of disease have played an important role in the way that health and illness are perceived.
- Social representation of health and illness depends on the social group that holds them.

References

Ashton, J. and Seymour, H. (1988). *The New Public Health: The Liverpool Experience*. Milton Keynes: Open University Press.

Baker, J.R. (1974). *Race*. Oxford University Press.

Baric, L. (1990a). Primary Health Care and health promotion. *Journal of Institute of Health Education*, **28**: 1, 22–27.

Baric, L. (1990b). A healthy enterprise in a healthy environment. *Journal of Health Education*, **28**: 3, 84–91.

Blaxter, M. (1990). *Health and Lifestyles*. London: Tavistock/Routledge.

Capra, F. (1982). *The Turning Point: Science, Society and the Rising Culture*. London: Fontana.

Capra, F. (1986). Wholeness and health. *Holistic Medicine*, **1**: 145–59.

Cassidy, C.M. (1994). Unravelling the ball of string: reality, paradigms and the study of alternate medicine. *Advances: Journal of Mind–Body Health*, **10**: 5–31.

Conrad, P. and Schneider, J.W. (1992). *Deviance and Medicalization: From Badness to Sickness*, 2nd edn. London: C.V. Mosby.

Cornwell, J. (1984). *Hard Earned Lives: Accounts of Health and Illness from East London*. London: Tavistock.

Crawford, R. (1980). Healthism and the medicalization of everyday life. *International Journal of Health Services*, **100**: 367–80.

Douglas, M. (1966). *Purity and Danger*. Harmondsworth: Penguin.

Dubos, R. (1960). *Mirage of Health*. London: George Allen & Unwin.

Engel, G.L. (1977). The need for a new medical model: a challenge for biomedicine. *Science*, **196**: 129–36. Reprinted in *Holistic Medicine*, 1989, **4**: 37–54.

Fabrega, H. (1975). The need for an ethnomedical science. *Science*, **189**: Sept.

Foss, L. (1989). The challenge of biomedicine: a foundation perspective. *Journal of Medical Philosophy*, April, 165–91.

Foster, G. and Anderson, B. (1978). *Medical Anthropology.* London: Wiley.

Goffman, E. (1963). *Stigma: Notes on the Management of Spoiled Identity.* New York: Prentice Hall.

Goldsmith, E. and Hildyard, N. (ed.) (1980). *The Earth Report.* London: Mitchell Beazley.

Gordon, J.S. (1981). Holistic medicine: toward a new medical model. *Journal of Clinical Psychiatry,* **42**(3): 114–19.

Grace, V.M. (1991). The marketing of empowerment and the construction of the health consumer: a critique of health promotion. *International Journal of Health Services,* **21**: 329–43.

Granshaw, L. and Porter, R. (1989). *The Hospital in History.* London: Routledge.

Hastings, A.C., Fadiman, J. and Gordon, J.S. (1981). *Health for the Whole Person.* London: Bantam.

Helman, C. (1990). *Culture, Health and Illness: An Introduction for Health Professionals,* 2nd edn. London: Wright.

Herzlich, C. (1973). *Health and Illness.* London: Academic Press.

Isaacs, M. (1987). Holistic health for dentists. *Journal of Dental Practice Administration,* **4**(2): 70–5.

Kennedy, I. (1981). *The Unmasking of Medicine.* London: George Allen & Unwin.

Last, J. and Guidotti, T.L. (1990). Implications for human health of global ecological changes. *Public Health Review,* **18**: 49–67.

Lock, M. and Gordon, D. (1988). *Biomedicine Examined.* London: Kluwer.

Lennox, B. and Lennox, M. (eds) (1986). *Heinemann Medical Dictionary.* London: Heinemann.

Maslow, A. (1954). *Motivations and Personality,* 2nd edn. New York: Harper & Row.

McCombie, S.C. (1989). Folk flu and viral syndrome: an epidemiological perspective. *Social Science and Medicine,* **9**: 987–93.

McKee, J. (1988). Holistic health and the critique of western medicine. *Social Science and Medicine,* **26**: 775–84.

McKeown, T. (1976). *The Modern Rise of Population.* London: Edward Arnold.

McKeown, T. (1979). *The Role of Medicine: Dream, Mirage or Nemesis.* Oxford: Basil Blackwell.

McKinley, J.B. (ed.) (1985). *Issues in the Political Economy of Health Care.* London: Tavistock.

McNight, J.L. (1985). Health and Empowerment. *Canadian Journal of Public Health,* **76** (suppl.1): 37–88.

Miles, A. (1988). *The Mentally Ill in Contemporary Society,* 2nd edn. Oxford: Basil Blackwell.

Miller, R.J. (1993). Interwoven threads: occupational therapy, feminism and holistic health. *American Journal of Occupational Therapy,* **47**: 2688–9.

Myers, N. (ed.) (1985). *The Gaia Atlas of Planet Management.* London: Pan.

Payer, L. (1990). *Medicine and Culture: Notions of Health and Sickness.* London: Gollancz.

Poynton, J. (1989). Holistic thinking in medicine: pitfalls and possibilities. *Holistic Medicine,* **4**: 3.

Rose, S.M. and Black, B.L. (1985). *Advocacy and Empowerment: Mental Health Care in the Community.* London: Routledge & Kegan Paul.

Rosser, S.V. (1988). *Feminism Within the Science and Health Care Professions.* Oxford: Pergamon.

Ryan, J. and Thomas, F. (1987). *The Politics of Mental Handicap,* rev. edn. London: Free Association.

Scadding, J.G. (1988). Health and disease: what can medicine do for philosophy? *Journal of Medical Ethics,* **15**(5): 118–24.

Schwartz, R.B., Komaroff, A.L., Garada, B.M., Gleit, M. *et al.* (1994). SPECT imaging of the brain: comparison of the findings in patients with chronic fatigue syndrome, AIDS dementia complex, and major unipolar depression. *American Journal of Roentgenology,* **162**: 943–51.

Shames, R. and Shames, K. (1982). *The Gift of Health: A Holistic Approach to Higher Quality and Lower Cost Health Care.* London: Bantam.

Shepherd, C. (1995). Letter. *British Medical Journal,* **310**: 1330.

Sheridan, C. and Radmacher, S. (1992). *Health Psychology: Challenging the Biomedical Model.* New York: Wiley.

Smith, M.N. and Stenger, F. (1985). Holistic health in the occupational setting. *Occupational Health Nursing,* **33**: 291–3.

Sobel, D.S. (1979). *Ways of Health: Holistic Approaches to Ancient and Contemporary Medicine.* London: Harcourt Brace Jovanovich.

Stacey, M. (1988). *Sociology of Health and Healing: A Textbook.* London: Unwin Hyman.

Stevenson, O. and Parsloe, P. (1993). *Community Care and Empowerment.* York: Joseph Rowntree Foundation.

St George, D. (1984). The individual and the environment. *British Journal of Holistic Medicine,* **1**: 1.

Stokols, D. (1992). Establishing and maintaining healthy environments: towards a social ecology of health promotion. *American Psychologist,* **47**: 6–22.

Swain, J. (1993). *Disabling Barriers: Enabling Environments.* London: Sage/Open University.

Szasz, T. (1971). *The Manufacture of Madness.* London: Routledge & Kegan Paul.

Turner, B.S. (1987). *Medical Power and Social Knowledge.* London: Sage.

Walters, V. (1993). Stress, anxiety and depression: womens' accounts of their health problems. *Social Science and Medicine,* **36**: 393–402.

Werlinder, H. (1978). *Psychopathy: A History of the Concept.* Uppsala: Almquist & Wiksell International.

Witz, A. (1992). *Professions and Patriarchy.* London: Routledge.

World Health Organization (1946). *Constitution.* New York: WHO.

World Health Organization (1988). *From Alma-Ata to the Year 2000: Reflections at the Midpoint.* Geneva: WHO.

World Health Organization (1990). *WHO Healthy City Project: A Project Becomes a Movement.* Copenhagen: WHO Euro.

Zola, I.K. (1991). Bringing our bodies and ourselves back in. *Journal of Health and Social Behaviour,* **32**: 1–16.

Further Reading ▲ ▲ ▲

Stainton Rogers, W. (1991). *Explaining Health and Illness: An Exploration of Diversity.* Hemel Hempstead: Harvester Wheatsheaf.

Gabe, J., Kelleher, D. and Williams, G. (eds) (1994). *Challenging Medicine.* London: Routledge.

7

Inequality in Health

Sebastian Garman

LEARNING OBJECTIVES

After studying this chapter you should:

- Be able to explain the concept of inequality in health
- Be aware of the factors that contribute to inequality in health
- Understand the concepts and tools used for data collection
- Be able to describe the patterns of inequality and suggest reasons for them
- Be able to evaluate ethnicity and inequality in health

INTRODUCTION

In helping to assess the effectiveness of their practice, health professionals are encouraged to take note of the improvements, or otherwise, in the health statuses of the populations they serve. Although as a whole Britain's population has experienced steadily improving health for much of this century (measured by the usual morbidity and mortality criteria), it has become increasingly apparent since the 1970s that not all social groups and geographical regions have shared in these improvements. By becoming aware of the variations, socially and geographically, in the health status of populations, and by being familiar with the assumptions that underpin the recognition and measurement of these variations, health professionals are more able to plan and target effective practice.

This chapter commences with an overview of the concept of inequality. The differing patterns of inequality are then considered alongside national and international regional variations. The chapter then reflects on the causes of health inequalities, ending with a discussion on ethnicity and health.

THE CONCEPT OF INEQUALITY

The great Victorian surveys of the condition of the poor in England, including those of Engels (1846), Booth (1902) and Rowntree (1899), all drew attention to the fact that poverty and ill-health are correlated. In every part of the world the children of the rich are taller, heavier, and live longer than those of the poor; and with the return of large-scale unemployment to the advanced industrialized world in the 1980s, the difference has tended to become more marked even here (Whitehead, 1992; Fox 1989; Davey Smith *et al.*, 1990).

The transition from traditional agrarian societies to urban industrial societies has been accompanied by changes in value systems. The emphasis has shifted from ascribed status to those systems that stress achieved status and the pursuit of parity. Members of urban societies are used to making rational choices based on comparative accounting decisions of cost and benefit under the impetus of market competition and the production of commodities and services. In such societies traditional ascribed statuses, whether based on gender, ethnicity, age, religion, region or social class, tend to come under threat and have to be continually justified if they are to be sustained. Apartheid and nepotism are expensive and inefficient anomalies for advanced market economies, and the employment of men on higher wages than women is a cause for serious resentment and a stimulus to political action within them (Tawney, 1964; Brown, 1988; Boudon and Bourricaud, 1989).

In most traditional societies, status, wealth and health advantages accrue to males over females, town dwellers over rural dwellers, and – other things being equal – the mature over the young. In most traditional societies, therefore, the life chances of a female baby in a rural area of a peasant background were precarious – and female infanticide remains not unusual in such societies even today (Shorter, 1984). In contrast, the rapid transition to urban industrialism leads to a marked increase in the health status of women. Research has shown the sex advantage of women over men in terms of longevity is a recent phenomenon consequent upon the urban industrial process (Shorter, 1984; Graham, 1987). Moreover, in absolute terms as measured by mortality and morbidity, the health of people in such urban societies has shown a dramatic improvement (Kuh *et al.*, 1991; Whitehead, 1992; Macintyre, 1988).

The idea that people are born equal tends to be a core value of contemporary industrial societies, and institutions that sustain inequalities are a source of shame, embarrassment or resentment. With the arrival of a system where achievement is stressed rather than ascription, the more such anomalies stand out. Britain's health service is imbued with such expectations of parity, not only for the reasons outlined above, but also because it was founded in a postwar period, when the aspirations of citizens imposed special burdens upon it (Klein, 1989; Ham, 1992).

Concepts and tools for data collection

Epidemiologists and health statisticians emphasizing a biomedical model of health have tended to favour easily quantifiable, objective indicators of health status (Macintyre, 1986; Stacey, 1988; Townsend *et al.*, 1988). The most immediate indicators, in the sense of dramatic impact and availability, are those of adult and infant mortality plus height and weight measurements of infants and adults. Low birthweight has been promoted as a particularly useful indicator of future health status by sociologists (Townsend *et al.*, 1988; OPCS, 1992).

HEIGHT AS AN INDICATOR OF INEQUALITY

The use of height, both of children and of adults, as an indicator of health status has led to much discussion (Macintyre, 1988). Whilst there has been an increase of 1.09 cm per decade this century in the mean height of men (0.36 cm for women), on average men from non-manual occupations remain 1.97 cm taller than those from manual occupations (Kuh *et al.*, 1991). Regional analyses (Barker *et al.*, 1990) have shown how height in the counties of the UK is closely related to the pattern of mortality, populations of the north and west being shorter and living less long than those of the south and east. Yet height has its problems as an indicator of health status, for although counties with taller populations have significantly lower mortality rates from chronic bronchitis, rheumatic heart disease and stroke (see also Yarnell *et al.*, 1992), there is a clear inverse relationship between height and cancers of the breast, ovary and prostate (Barker *et al.*, 1990).

MEASUREMENT OF SOCIO-ECONOMIC STATUS

The tool most commonly used to measure socio-economic status in relation to health is the Registrar General's classification of occupational classes. This separates the population into five (since 1981, six) 'social classes' on the basis of occupations (see Table 7.1), ranked according to their supposed social standing in the community. Because of the widespread use of this classification, it is important to realize some of its strengths and weaknesses (Thomas and Elias, 1989).

For the 1991 Census, a major rationalization was attempted by the Office of Population, Censuses and Surveys (OPCS) to take into account the criticisms, in particular the compounding of social status categories with those of occupational class. A new categorization known as the Standard Occupational Classification (SOC) has been developed for use by departments of government. This moves away from linking occupation with social prestige, concentrating instead on education and training criteria – similarities of qualification, experience, skills and training (OPCS, 1990).

Table 7.1 *The Registrar General's classification of occupational classes*

Occupational classes		Examples
Social Class I:	Professional	Doctors, lawyers
Social Class II:	Intermediate non-manual	Teachers, nurses, most managers and service administrators
Social Class III N:	Skilled non-manual	Clerks, shop assistants
Social Class III M:	Skilled manual	Bricklayers, underground coalminers, bus drivers
Social Class IV:	Semi-skilled manual	Bus conductors, postmen
Social Class V:	Unskilled manual	Porters, cleaners, labourers

Table 7.2 *Occupations in SOC major groups*

Major groups	Occupations
1. Managers and administrators	General managers in NHS, production managers in manufacturing industries, managers and proprietors in service industries
2. Professional occupations	Doctors, lawyers, social workers
3. Associate professional and technical occupations	Nurses and midwives, driving instructors
4. Clerical and secretarial occupations	Secretaries, accountant clerks
5. Craft and related occupations	Miners (face workers), machine tool setters, fitters
6. Personal and protective service occupations	Police officers, railway station staff, traffic wardens
7. Sales occupations	Cashiers, roundsmen/women
8. Plant and machine operatives	Bus conductors, assembly-line workers
9. Other occupations	Postal workers, farm workers, window cleaners

Source: OPCS 1990.

The new SOC comprises nine major occupational groups (see Table 7.2). By incorporating occupational groupings where women predominate which have not been differentiated in previous classifications, and by making the classification applicable to paid jobs currently done by active persons, it is hoped the SOC will more accurately reflect the experience of women's employment.

Nevertheless it is intended that it will still be possible to aggregate individuals from the SOC into the more established six class categories (Thomas and Elias, 1989).

The association between socio-economic status and health status has been explored by using a variety of indicators, each providing its own insights into the way health status is patterned. The most commonly used correlates are:

- housing tenure, e.g. owner-occupier, private rented, public rented, and homeless;
- car ownership;
- income and/or wealth;
- educational attainment;
- employment status (e.g. categories of employed, unemployed and non-employed).

When these are put together in various combinations, a range of health and deprivation indicators are achieved which are widely used for health and health promotion data collection and research (Jarman, 1983; Townsend *et al.*, 1988; Hayes and Williams, 1990).

THE PATTERN OF INEQUALITY OF HEALTH STATUS

It became increasingly apparent during the 1970s that, despite the establishment of a national health service for some quarter of a century, and a steady improvement in mortality rates for the population as a whole (Table 7.3), the social class differences in mortality rates were not narrowing and might well be getting wider.

Townsend is typical of the concern expressed at that time. In an article in the *Lancet*, Townsend (1974) argued 'if its exact extent remains debatable the trend of growing inequality is securely established'. Townsend points out that:

- whilst the mortality rates for all men had fallen, those for men in Social Class V had actually risen in absolute terms;
- the mortality rate for Social class I was double that for Social class V;
- a similar regional disparity could be demonstrated for both infant and adult mortality;
- there had been no noticeable improvement in social class differences in children's physique since 1953.

Social class as a factor of inequality

Concerns about the widening gap in health status between the classes, and the long-term regional disparities, led in 1980 to a government-inspired review of the evidence, known as the Black Report (Townsend *et al.*, 1992). The findings of this report have since been updated and reassessed at the behest of the Health Education Council (Whitehead, 1987/1992) and reviewed in 1990 (Davey Smith *et al.*, 1990).

Since the Black Report, another OPCS decennial supplement has been published making available the standardized mortality ratios for the whole postwar period in Great Britain up to 1982 (see Table 7.4).

Table 7.3 *Age-specific death rates (by sex, 1992) and standardized mortality ratios*

	Deaths per 1000 population for specific age groups											SMR* (UK = 100)
	Under 1	0–4	5–14	15–24	25–34	35–44	45–54	55–64	65–74	75–84	85 and over	
Males												
United Kingdom	7.3	1.8	0.2	0.8	0.9	1.7	4.4	13.8	38.0	91.2	196.6	100
North	7.9	1.8	0.2	0.7	0.8	1.8	5.0	16.5	43.9	102.8	200.6	112
Yorkshire & Humberside	7.5	1.8	0.2	0.7	0.8	1.7	4.6	14.0	39.5	93.1	195.8	102
East Midlands	7.9	1.8	0.2	0.7	0.9	1.4	4.1	13.1	36.1	93.0	202.4	98
East Anglia	5.6	1.4	0.2	0.7	0.9	1.3	3.5	10.5	32.5	82.3	188.7	87
South East	6.8	1.7	0.2	0.7	0.9	1.8	4.0	12.1	34.7	86.2	189.1	93
Greater London	8.0	2.0	0.2	0.6	1.1	2.3	4.8	13.3	37.6	87.3	187.1	99
Rest of South East	6.0	1.4	0.2	0.7	0.8	1.4	3.6	11.5	33.2	85.7	190.1	90
South West	7.0	1.7	0.2	0.7	0.9	1.5	3.7	11.4	32.7	81.3	188.4	89
West Midlands	8.7	2.1	0.2	0.7	0.8	1.7	4.3	13.9	38.6	93.2	205.7	102
North West	7.4	1.7	0.2	0.8	1.0	1.9	4.9	15.8	41.9	99.2	198.4	109
England	7.3	1.7	0.2	0.7	0.9	1.7	4.2	13.3	37.0	90.0	193.9	98
Wales	6.3	1.6	0.2	0.9	0.9	1.7	4.2	14.3	38.8	90.2	190.7	100
Scotland	7.8	1.9	0.2	1.0	1.3	2.1	6.0	17.0	44.5	101.0	225.9	117
Northern Ireland	6.2	1.6	0.3	0.9	1.0	1.6	4.8	15.6	41.3	97.8	213.2	108
Females												
United Kingdom	5.7	1.4	0.1	0.3	0.4	1.1	2.8	8.1	22.0	57.7	150.7	100
North	6.1	1.5	0.2	0.3	0.4	1.1	3.2	9.7	25.5	65.5	154.4	111
Yorkshire & Humberside	5.6	1.3	0.1	0.3	0.5	1.1	2.8	8.6	22.7	57.7	147.4	100
East Midlands	5.6	1.3	0.1	0.3	0.4	1.1	2.7	7.8	21.6	58.6	149.1	99
East Anglia	3.6	1.0	0.1	0.3	0.4	1.0	2.3	6.4	18.5	55.5	145.2	92
South East	5.3	1.3	0.1	0.3	0.4	1.0	2.5	7.1	19.7	53.6	146.4	93
Greater London	6.4	1.6	0.1	0.3	0.4	1.1	2.6	7.5	21.2	53.9	140.2	94
Rest of South East	4.6	1.1	0.1	0.3	0.4	0.9	2.4	6.8	18.9	53.5	149.8	93
South West	4.2	1.0	0.1	0.3	0.4	1.0	2.4	6.7	18.1	52.2	147.9	91
West Midlands	7.3	1.7	0.1	0.3	0.5	1.2	2.8	8.2	22.1	58.4	151.6	101
North West	6.4	1.5	0.1	0.3	0.5	1.2	3.3	9.3	25.0	63.0	152.3	108
England	5.6	1.3	0.1	0.3	0.4	1.1	2.7	7.8	21.3	56.8	148.5	98
Wales	5.6	1.4	0.1	0.3	0.4	1.1	2.8	8.3	22.5	57.0	151.9	100
Scotland	5.7	1.5	0.1	0.3	0.6	1.3	3.7	10.0	26.7	65.3	170.1	116
Northern Ireland	5.5	1.4	0.2	0.2	0.4	1.0	3.0	8.2	23.0	61.9	164.4	106

* Standardized Mortality Ratio, i.e. adjusted for age structure of population.
Source: Office of Population Censuses and Surveys; General Register Offices for Scotland and Northern Ireland.

These statistics show that there has been a steady increase in class differences, so that by 1981 the death rates were twice as great for Social Classes IV and V combined as they were for Social Class I. If the occupational group defined as 'manual' by the Registrar General (IIIM, IV, V) is compared with the equivalent non-manual category (I, II, IIIN), then the former had a 44% higher death rate. Put another way, if the manual class experienced the same death rates as the non-manual class there would be 42 000 fewer deaths each year in the 16–74 age group (Jacobson *et al.*, 1991). By 1980 the expectation of life for children born in Britain to parents in Social Class V was seven years shorter than for children whose parents were in the Social Class I category. The differences are even more marked for children of single mothers outside paid employment (Judge and Benzeval, 1993). (On the statistical complexities of measuring changes over such long periods of time, see Wagstaff *et al.* (1991) and Devis (1993)).

This class-based experience of greater vulnerability to death is not confined to a few specific diseases or causes of death (Black, 1980; Marmott and MacDowall, 1986; Goldblatt, 1990). Therefore, it seems reasonable to suggest that the cause of this pattern could be sought in a variety of deprivation factors. When the major causes of death are considered, 65 of the 78 'major list' causes for men (62 out of 82 for women) were more common

Table 7.4 *Standardized mortality ratios for men aged 15–64, for England and Wales since 1945*

Social class	1945–53	1959–63[1]		1970–72		1979–80†
		Unadjusted	(Adjusted)*	Unadjusted	(Adjusted)*	1982–83
I Professional	86	76	(75)	77	(75)	66
II Managerial	92	81	(–)	81	(–)	76
III Skilled manual and nonmanual	101	100	(–)	104	(–)	94 106
IV Partly skilled	104	103	(–)	114	(–)	116
V Unskilled	118	143	(127)	137	(121)	165

* Occupations in 1959–63 and 1970–72 have been reclassified according to the 1950 classification of occupations.
† Men aged 20–64 (Great Britain).

Sources:
Townsend, P. and Davidson, N. (1982). Inequalities in Health. Harmondsworth: Penguin, 67.

among Social Classes IV and V combined than for Social Classes I or II (Whitehead, 1987/1992; Marmot and McDowall, 1986).

REGIONAL INEQUALITIES IN HEALTH

There are striking regional differences in death rates within Great Britain (Table 7.3). East Anglia has the best record for both infant and adult mortality rates, and going further north and west increases the death rates (Marmot and McDowall, 1986; Barker *et al.*, 1990). There is also a small but statistically significant difference in stature between the north and west and the south and east (Knight, 1984). These differences cannot be accounted for by the different social class composition of the different areas. Each social class benefits from the health experience of particular regions (Jacobson, *et al.*, 1991).

It is possible that natural factors, such as the climate or the hardness of the water, might have an influence (Britton, 1990). It is also likely that regional cultural factors such as diet may play a part (Blaxter, 1990), although comparative studies of diet do not conclusively support such a link (Cade *et al.*, 1988). There have been studies of health differences between local areas, such as wards within regions, which suggest that socio-economic factors are the primary cause (Carstairs and Morris, 1989; reviewed in Whitehead, 1992). It seems likely, therefore, that the regional variations are in some part due to social and economic advantages that benefit people from all occupational categories in the more prosperous regions.

Learning Activity 1 ◆ ◆ ◆

Over the next week or so, scan the newspapers for reports on issues relating to health and illness.

- Is it possible to determine from the details given the occupational statuses of the people mentioned?
- Does a pattern emerge?
- Can you draw any conclusions?

INTERNATIONAL COMPARISONS

Since the Black Report was published and the commitment, four years later, by the members of the European region of the World Health Organization (WHO) to reduce inequalities within and between regions of Europe by 25% by the year 2000, several studies have emerged comparing patterns of inequality across Europe. Conclusions from the findings must be tentative because of the difficulty of making social class comparisons between countries that do not use the same social class classifications. Nevertheless the relationship between mortality and occupation found in Britain seems to be a pattern that is Europe-wide, a relationship that is found also in New Zealand, Australia and Japan (Davey Smith *et al.*, 1990). Several studies of health in particular countries report an apparent widening in class differences in health during the 1970s (reviewed in Whitehead, 1992), although not in Scandinavia and the Netherlands. As yet there is no clear picture of European mortality patterns in relation to social class for the 1980s, but there are interesting comparative data on morbidity for Scandinavian countries which suggests that social class patterns persist, although not so dramatically as in Britain (Rahkonen *et al.*, 1993; Arber and Lahelma, 1993).

CAUSES OF HEALTH INEQUALITIES

The Black Report (1980) found that four different kinds of explanation have been offered to explain the pattern of health inequalities:

- artefact
- social and natural selection
- cultural or behavioural
- materialist.

Subsequent debate has tended to focus on these terms.

Artefact

These explanations defend the hypothesis that the social class differences in mortality are apparent not real, that the differences are the result of bias in the way the statistics are collected. Such explanations, popular in the early 1980s, are now far more difficult to sustain because it is becoming increasingly apparent that however the statistics are collected a consistent pattern of class inequality in mortality and morbidity is revealed. (For a different view, see Bloor *et al.* (1987).) For example, the claims about numerator/denominator bias have been shown to be untrue by different methods of data collection. It had been argued that social class was being assigned differently on the death certificate (numerator) than in the census (denominator). If a proportion of manual workers were being categorized differently on census forms during their lives than on death certificates, then the apparent difference of mortality between the classes could be artefactual. However, the OPCS longitudinal study (following a group over time) using the 1971 census social class categorization to categorize deaths found a similarly large mortality difference between the classes (Goldblatt, 1990).

It has also been proposed that as Social Class V has shrunk in size, it has been left with a higher proportion of people vulnerable to life-threatening illnesses. Yet by using alternative measures of socio-economic status, such as car ownership or housing tenure, similar findings occur. Men in rented accommodation and without access to a car have a standardized mortality ratio of 123, almost exactly the same as that for Social Class V (Davey Smith *et al.*, 1990) and much higher rates of morbidity (Haynes, 1991). Moreover, single-occupation studies such as those of the Civil Service (Marmot *et al.*, 1991) and the British Army (Lynch and Oelman, 1981) show clear health differences between higher and lower employment grades in terms of height, longevity and morbidity. Table 7.5 illustrates the pattern using census data on National Health Service employees.

Table 7.5 *Standardized mortality ratios for selected NHS occupations, 1979–85*

Dentists	66
Doctors	69
Opticians	72
Physiotherapists	79
Ambulance men	109
Male nurses	118
Hospital porters	151

Source: Balarajan, R. (1989).

Social and natural selection

These explanations tend to suggest that the cause of the correlation between mortality and class is the reverse of that which is commonly assumed. Instead of being more vulnerable to illness and death because of manual socio-economic status, people have manual status because of a greater prevalence of illness. The most favoured of these is the so-called 'downward drift' hypothesis, which suggests that as Social Class V has shrunk in size it has increasingly become a residual class of those who have lost socio-economic standing in the community owing to recurrent illness.

Alternatively, evidence has been cited to propose that people experiencing hardship in childhood are more likely to experience downward social mobility in later life (Lundberg, 1991).

Some favour genetic explanations. It is true that there is a statistically significant tendency for tall girls to marry upwards in socio-economic status (Knight, 1984). Again, the data from the longitudinal study (through time) have been compared with the census data (at one point in time) from the 1971 and 1981 censuses to demonstrate that such theories cannot explain the size of the differences between the classes (Goldblatt, 1990; Marmot *et al.*, 1991).

Cultural or behavioural

These explanations tend to focus causation at the level of learned behaviour patterns of different class or status groups. It is true that people on lower incomes of both sexes have a higher rate of cigarette smoking (Blaxter, 1990), eat fewer fruits, vegetables and high-fibre foods (MAFF, 1991), and probably eat more sweets. It is possible that differences in diet could account for some of the differences in mortality between both classes and regions, although the evidence as yet does not support this view (Cade *et al.*, 1988). It is also true that certain causes of death, notably accidents of children and young adults, could be linked with subcultural practices related to discipline, self-expression and child supervision.

The correlation of child accidents and parental occupation is very marked, with Social Class V suffering more than twice the child accident rate of any other class. Moreover, different social class groups demonstrate different attitudes to and knowledge of health-related matters (Blaxter and Paterson, 1982; Cornwell, 1984) which is likely to influence health-related behaviours. Middle-class groups are more likely to have a positive view of health, seeing strategies for health enhancement as being within their personal control. They are more likely to take regular exercise and seek out and attend services designed for illness prevention, such as maternity services and child welfare clinics. There also seems to be evidence of regional differences in physical fitness measures, with residents of Scotland and Wales (Blaxter, 1990) scoring unfavourably when compared with Britons from the south-east. On the other hand, manual workers experience more physical exercise at work.

Sociologists are cautious of causal explanations that isolate behavioural patterns from their social context in this way. The problem is that if causation is attributed to behaviour without taking into account the context in which behaviour occurs, then mistakes occur when it comes to illness prevention or health promotion strategies (Calnan, 1990; Brown and Harris, 1989; Blaxter, 1990). It can also have a labelling or stigmatizing effect which can compound a problem rather than help to solve it.

The Materialist

These explanations suggest that it is the circumstances people find themselves in – working environment, housing, income, wealth, exclusion from the labour market – that are the causes of their health-related behaviour and attitudes, and their different morbidity and mortality rates. There is a lot of circumstantial evidence to suggest this might be true. As seen previously, the expectation of life, infant mortality rates, and height improves in direct relation to the increasing standard of living of the regions of Britain, Europe and the world in which they grow up. Moreover, people moving from poorer regions of Britain to more prosperous ones tend to benefit from the improved life chances of the areas to which they move. The research on these links is considerable (Wilkinson, 1986; Wilkinson, 1992).

UNEMPLOYMENT

Until the late 1980s there was some dispute about the relationship between unemployment and health, but now there are studies of both local areas and cross-Europe comparisons. These demonstrate a clear correlation between morbidity rates, mortality rates and unemployment for men (Smith, 1991; Wilson and Walker, 1993). Moreover, studies suggest that notice of redundancy raises morbidity rates for men and dependent spouses. Despite some unusual features of the recession of the 1980s, it remains true that manual workers are far more likely to experience redundancy and unemployment as well as cycles of seasonal employment than are non-manual workers. There is some evidence to suggest that there is a relationship between unemployment of parents and the height of children (Rona and Chinn, 1991). The effect of youth unemployment on morbidity rates has been recently reviewed (Hammarstrom, 1994).

A characteristic of unskilled and some skilled categories of manual work, too, is that pay tends to peak when people are still young and fit, and to decline with age. This has important consequences for life chances and health in later life, because without cooperative strategies such as local authority housing and mutual aid schemes, manual workers cannot compete with other groups for health-giving goods such as home ownership and higher education. This is because people of higher socio-economic status can more easily mortgage their anticipated future high incomes to buy a house or to improve their children's education. Goldblatt (1990) suggests that census data and longitudinal study evidence show a clear correlation between mortality, morbidity and housing tenure. The National Child Development Study found that children brought up in owner-occupied homes had clear health advantages as measured by the five criteria of height, 'malaise', self-reported health, and psychiatric morbidity (Fogelman *et al.*, 1987).

ETHNICITY AND HEALTH INEQUALITY

Ethnicity refers to the identification of people by themselves or others with social groups assumed to have shared origins or descent claims. It has largely replaced the concept of 'race' in scientific discourse, because the assumptions of the genetic basis of the classifications of human types, which that word came to imply, have proved to be unfounded. Nevertheless, behavioural scientists and statisticians have to use categories that are understood by the populace they are sampling, hence the use of the terms 'black' and 'white' under the heading of 'ethnic' and the concentration on relatively recent New Commonwealth immigrants as distinct categories (Anthias and Yuval-Davis, 1992; Teague, 1993).

Migrants often have mental illness rates higher than that typical of the country where they settle, but the remarkably high rates of schizophrenia diagnosis in Britain for people of Afro-Caribbean origin of some three to five times that of the majority ethnic groups has led to much discussion (Lipsedge and Littlewood, 1988; Littlewood, 1992), the implication being that psychiatric diagnostic categories cannot be separated from political and cultural judgements (Helman, 1990).

In term of mortality, however, migrants to Britain seem to have lower rates than the average for their country of origin (Marmot *et al.*, 1984, Balarajan, 1991; Whitehead, 1992) which has been interpreted to mean that people healthier than average have migrated. The notable exception is that of the migrant Irish whose mortality is significantly higher than that for Eire or England and Wales.

In general terms, the health of the older established ethnic groups tends to match that of the regions already discussed – with health indicators suggesting the best health in the south (outside London) and east compared with the north and west. The standardized mortality rates indicate significantly lower expectation of life for Scots and Welsh, when compared with the English, particularly the southern English. This pattern is confirmed by height and birthweight indicators. Moreover, OPCS data indicate that Scottish and Irish migrants to England have a markedly raised mortality rate (Balarajan, 1991), and high rates of drinking and smoking (Balarajan and Yuen, 1986).

Evidence of disease patterns for more recently established ethnic groups is perhaps best revealed from the Immigrant Mortality Study in England and Wales (Marmot *et al.*, 1984). All immigrant groups were found to have higher mortality rates than the average for tuberculosis and accidents but lower than average rates for obstructive lung conditions including bronchitis. Migrants from the Indian subcontinent had low mortality from several cancers, including lung cancer, but high mortality from ischaemic heart disease, liver cancer and diabetes, a pattern that has been confirmed elsewhere (Balarajan *et al.*, 1984). Migrants from African Commonwealth countries and the Caribbean tend to suffer much higher mortality rates from hypertension and strokes.

Recent evidence has led to much discussion of infant mortality rates. Many migrant groups seem to experience higher neonatal mortality rates (Britton, 1990), except babies born to women deriving from the Caribbean and Pakistan where the neonatal mortality rate was lower than the average of the UK population as a whole. The causes of these variations has yet to be fully understood and the findings of the 1991 Census should add much. There are, however, some interesting indicators.

Bhopal (1988) warns against focusing on the differences in health experience of ethnic minority groups rather than on the similarities. Men from both the Indian subcontinent and those born in England and Wales share major fatal diseases (i.e. coronary heart disease, stroke, bronchitis, and lung cancer). Since migrants are particularly prone to periods of unemployment, housing problems and low incomes, which in themselves are major health hazards, a large part of the differences in mortality and those of morbidity (Ahmad *et al.*, 1989) might be due to such 'structural' factors.

Learning Activity 2 ◆ ◆ ◆

Undertake a review of two or three different aspects of inequality and its causes and then relate those to practice. For example, access to health services for the elderly or ethnic groups.

SUMMARY

Although Britain's population has experienced marked improvements in health status throughout this century, certain social groups and geographical sectors have not benefited from these improvements. Moreover, it can now be demonstrated that the recession of the 1980s and the accompanying widening of economic disparities between rich and poor was accompanied by larger health status differences between population groups in the UK and probably Europe as a whole. The recognition and measurement of the extent of these differences has brought new considerations into debates about effective professional practice in health services.

Key Points ■ ■ ■

❑ There is considerable sociological evidence to link poverty with ill-health.

❑ Inequalities in health are attributable to multiple causes.

❑ The most commonly used tool to measure socio-economic status in relation to health is the Registrar General's Classification of Occupational Classes.

❑ Inequality of health status can be shown to have set patterns in relation to class, geographical distribution, gender and ethnicity.

❑ The Black Report proposed four different kinds of explanation for the pattern of health inequalities.

References ▼ ▼ ▼

Ahmad, W.I., Kernohan, E.E. and Baker, M.R. (1989). Influence of ethnicity and unemployment on the perceived health of a sample of general practice attenders. *Community Medicine*, **11**: 148–56.

Anthias, F. and Yuval-Davis, N. (1992). *Racialized Boundaries*. London: Routledge.

Arber, S. and Lahelma, E. (1993). Inequalities in women's and men's ill-health: Britain and Finland compared. *Social Science and Medicine*, **37**: 1055–68.

Balarajan, R. (1989). Inequalities in health within the Health Sector. *British Medical Journal*, **299**: 822–5.

Balarajan, R. (1991). Ethnic difference in mortality from IHD and CVD in England and Wales. *British Medical Journal*, **302**: 237–9.

Balarajan, R. *et al.* (1984). Patterns of mortality among immigrants in England and Wales. *British Medical Journal*, **289**: 1188–7.

Balarajan, R. and Yuen, P. (1986). British smoking and drinking habits: variations by country of birth. *Community Medicine*, **8**: 237–9.

Barker, D.J., Osmond, C. and Golding, J. (1990). Height and mortality in the counties of England and Wales. *Annals of Human Biology*, **17**: 1–6.

Bhopal, R.S, (1988). Health care for Asians in equity: a prerequisite for health. Presented at the 1987 Summer Conference, Geneva, WHO.

Black, D. (1980). *Inequalities in Health: Report of a Research Working Group Chaired by Sir Douglas Black*. London: DHSS.

Blaxter, M. (1990). *Health and Lifestyles*. London: Tavistock/ Routledge.

Blaxter, M. and Paterson, L. (1982). *Mothers and Daughters*. London: Heinemann.

Bloor, M., Samphier, M. and Prior, L. (1987). Artefact explanations of inequalities in health: an assessment of the evidence. *Sociology of Health and Illness*, **9**: 231–64.

Booth, C. (1902). *Life and Labour of the People of London*. London: Macmillan.

Boudon, R. and Bourricaud, F. (1989). Egalitarianism. In: *A Critical Dictionary of Sociology*. London: Routledge.

Brown, H.P. (1988). *Egalitarianism and the Generation of Inequality*. Oxford: Clarendon Press.

Brown, G.W. and Harris, T. (1989) *Life Events and Illness*. London: The Guildford Press.

Britton, M. (ed.) (1990). *Mortality and Geography, OPCS Series DS9*. London: HMSO.

Cade, J.E., Barker, D.J.P., Martetts, B.M. and Morris, J.A. (1988). Diet and inequalities in health in three English towns. *British Medical Journal*, **296**: 1359–62.

Calnan, M. (1990). Food and health: a comparison of beliefs and practices in middle-class and working class households. In: Cunningham-Barely, S. and McKeganey, N.P. (eds), *Readings in Medical Sociology*. London: Routledge.

Carstairs, V. and Morris, R. (1989). Deprivation: explaining differences in mortality between Scotland, England and Wales. *British Medical Journal*, **299**: 886–9.

Cornwell, J. (1984). *Hard Earned Lives – Accounts of Health and Illness from East London*. London: Tavistock.

Davey Smith, G., Bartley, M. and Blane, D. (1990). The Black Report on Socioeconomic Inequalities in Health – ten years on. *British Medical Journal*, **301**: 373-7.

Devis, T. (1993). Measuring mortality differences by cause of death and social class defined by occupation (OPCS). *Population Trends*, **73**. London: HMSO.

Engels, F. (1846/1892) *The Condition of the English Working Class in 1844*. London: Allen and Unwin.

Fogelman, K., Fox, J. and Power, C. (1987). *Class and Tenure Mobility: National Child Development Study*. Working Paper 21, Social Statistics Research Unit, City University, London.

Fox, J. (1989). *Health Inequalities in European Countries*. Aldershot: Gower.

Goldblatt, P. (ed.) (1990). *Longitudinal Study 1971–1981: Mortality and Social Organization* (OPCS LS Series 6). London: HMSO.

Graham, H. (1987). Women, health and illness. *Social Studies Review*, **3**: 15–20.

Ham, C. (1992). *Health Policy in Britain: The Politics and Organization of the National Health Service*, 3rd ed. London: Macmillan.

Hammarstrom, A. (1994). Health consequences of youth unemployment – review from a gender perspective. *Social Science and Medicine*, **38**: 699–709.

Hayes, M. and Williams, R. (1990). Healthy community indicators. *Health Promotion International*, **5** (2), 54–60.

Haynes, R. (1991). Inequalities in health and health service use: evidence from the General Household Survey. *Social Science and Medicine*, **33**: 361–8.

Helman, C. (1990). *Culture, Health and Mental Illness: An introduction for health professionals*. 2nd edn. London: Wright.

Jacobson, B., Smith, A. and Whitehead, M. (1991). *The Nation's Health: A Strategy for the 1990s*, 2nd edn. London: King's Fund.

Jarman, D. (1983). Identification of underprivileged areas. *British Medical Journal*, **286**: 1705–9.

Judge, K. and Benzeval, M. (1993). Health inequalities: new

concerns about the children of single mothers. *British Medical Journal*, **306**: 677– 80.
Knight, I. (1984). *The Height and Weight of Adults in Great Britain* (OPCS). London: HMSO.
Klein, R. (1989). *The Politics of the National Health Service*, 2nd ed. Harlow: Longman.
Kuh, D.L., Power, C. and Rodgers, B. (1991). Secular trends in social class and sex difference in height. *International Journal of Epidemiology*, **20**: 1001-9.
Lipsedge, M. and Littlewood, R. (1988). Psychiatric illness among Afro-Caribbeans. *British Medical Journal*, **296**: 950–1.
Littlewood, R. (1992). Psychiatric diagnosis and racial bias: empirical and interpretive approaches. *Social Science and Medicine*, **34**: 141–9.
Lundberg, O. (1991). Causal explanations for class inequalities in health: an empirical analysis. *Social Science and Medicine*, **32**: 385–93.
Lynch and Oelman (1981). Mortality from CHD in the British Army compared with the civilian population. *British Medical Journal*, **283**, 405–7.
Macintyre, S. (1986). Health and illness. In: Burgess, R. (ed.), *Key Variables in Social Investigation*. London: Routledge and Kegan Paul.
Macintyre, S. (1988). A review of the social patterning and significance of measures of height, weight, blood pressure and respiratory function. *Social Science and Medicine*, **27**: 327–37.
MAFF (1991). *Household Food and Consumption Expenditure 1990*. London: HMSO.
Marmot, M.G., Adelstein, A.M. and Bulusu, L. (1984). *Immigrant Mortality in England and Wales, 1970–78* (OPCS Studies on Medical and Population Subjects 47). London: HMSO.
Marmot, M.G. and MacDowall, M.E. (1986). Mortality decline and widening social inequalities. *Lancet*, **2**: 274–6.
Marmot, M.G., Davey Smith, G., Stansfield, S., Patel, C., North, F. *et al.* (1991). Health inequalities among British civil servants: the Whitehall II Study. *Lancet*, **337**: 1387–93.
Office of Population, Censuses and Surveys (OPCS) (1990). *Standard Occupational Classification*, vol. 1. London: HMSO.
Office of Population, Censuses and Surveys (1992). *Mortality Statistics: Perinatal and Infant Mortality: Social and Biological Factors, 1989 and 1990*. London: HMSO.
Rahkonen, O., Lahelma, E., Karisto, A. and Manderbacka, K. (1993). Persisting health inequalities: social class differentials in illness in the Scandinavian countries. *Journal of Public Health Policy*, **14**: 66–81.
Rona, R.J. and Chinn, S. (1991). Fathers' unemployment and height of primary school children in Britain. *Annals of Human Biology*, **18**: 441–8.
Rowntree (1899/1901). *Poverty: A Study of Town Life*. London: Nelson.
Shorter, E. (1984). *A History of Women's Bodies*. Harmondsworth: Penguin.
Smith, R. (1991). Unemployment: here we go again. *British Medical Journal*, **302**: 607–8.
Stacey, M. (1988). *Sociology of health and healing: a textbook*. London: Unwin Hyman.
Tawney, R. (1964). *Inequality*, 5th edn. London: Allen and Unwin.
Teague, A. (1993). Ethnic group: first results from the 1991 Census (OPCS). *Population Trends*, **72**. London: HMSO.
Townsend P. (1974). Inequalities in health. *Lancet*, 7868, i, 15 June: 1179–1190.
Townsend, P., Phillimore, P. and Beattie, A. (1988). *Health and Deprivation: Inequality in the North*. London: Croom Helm.
Townsend, P., Davidson, N. and Whitehead, M. (1992). *Inequalities in Health*, 2nd edn. reprinted with revisions. Harmondsworth: Penguin.
Wagstaff, A., Paci, P. and Doorslaer, E. (1991). On the measurement of inequalities in health. *Social Science and Medicine*, **33**: 545–7.
Whitehead, M. (1987/92). The health divide. In: Townsend, P., Davidson, N. and Whitehead, M. (eds), *Inequalities in Health: The Back Report*. Harmondsworth: Penguin.
Wilkinson, R.G. (ed.) (1986). *Class and Health: Research and Longitudinal Data*. London: Tavistock.
Wilkinson, R.G. (1992). Income distribution and life expectancy. *British Medical Journal*, **304**: 165–8.
Wilson and Walker (1993). Unemployment and health: a review. *Public Health*, **107**: 153–62.
Yarnell, J.W., Limb, E.S., Layzell, J.M. and Baker I.A. (1992). Height: a risk marker for ischaemic heart disease: prospective results from the Caerphilly and Speedwell heart disease studies. *European Heart Journal*, **13**: 1602–5.

Further Reading ▲ ▲ ▲

Benzeval, M., Judge, K. and Whitehead, M. (1995). *Tackling Health Inequalities: An Agenda for Action*. Dorest: King's Fund and BEBC.
Blackburn, C. (1991). *Poverty and Health*. London: Open University Press.

8

Gender and Health

Sebastian Garman

LEARNING OBJECTIVES

After studying this chapter you should:

- Be able to discuss the issues underlying the differences in gender and health
- Understand the nature of bias towards women
- Be aware of the different patterns associated with gender
- Be able to discuss the gender mortality and morbidity patterns
- Understand the factors that socially influence gender and health

INTRODUCTION

One of the features of urban industrial societies in the late twentieth century is an increasing emphasis on gender parity in terms of education and occupational status. Such socio-political changes have resulted in a reappraisal of health studies from a gender perspective. Consideration of the issue of gender, therefore, is particularly pertinent for health professionals, not least because the majority of health workers – formal and informal carers – are women. Moreover, gender perspectives and issues are likely to gain in significance in the health professions over the next thirty years owing to demographic changes, particularly the ageing structure of the population, which ensure that women's health is seen to be a major policy issue.

The role of gender in health is discussed in this chapter to give an insight into the effects gender has been found to have in the provision of health care. The distinction between genders is considered first, and this is followed by a short introduction to the bias that exists against women. The chapter then moves on to reflect on the patterns associated with gender and to consider the reasons for these patterns. Finally, attention is given to the issue of men and health.

GENDER AND HEALTH CARE

For sociological perspectives the distinction between sex and gender is of key analytic importance.

- 'Sex' refers to the unchanging and universal binary classification of male and female based on biological difference.
- 'Gender' refers to the socially constructed and culturally acquired normative expectations and roles that are associated with sex differences, and which are subject to continuous change and negotiation.

There has been a marked increase of interest in gender as a focus for health related-research in the last decade. The issue of gender and health is important because women provide the main targets for health promotion and health education messages. They constitute the main workforce in health-related activities, both as formal carers and as informal carers – roles that are going to continue to grow in importance with the demographic changes of the next decade. Moreover, they can be shown to perceive health differently from men (Miles, 1991; Stacey and Olesen, 1993).

In the USA, recent government directives have been issued to focus federally supported health research on women's needs (Stacey and Olesen, 1993). Within the social sciences the interest has undoubtedly been stimulated by the fact that an increasing proportion of researchers interested in health matters are women, and that the issue of the care and control of women's bodies has been an important one for feminist movements everywhere. It is worth noting, also, that the intellectual critiques of 'biomedicine' fit well with the preoccupations of the green movement and ecological philosophies where the active participation of women is evident.

Learning Activity 1 ◆ ◆ ◆

- ◆ Review the newspapers for the last two weeks to see if you are able to identify examples of incorrect use of the words 'sex' and 'gender'.
- ◆ Are you able to identify why this misuse occurs?
- ◆ Do certain papers use this incorrect terminology more than others?

Bias against women

Recent histories of medicine and the social organization of healthcare systems have had to contend with the fact that there has been a long history of bias against women. Elements of this discussion are worth noting.

- There has been a systematic bias against the recruitment of women into the medical profession in both Britain and the USA, a bias that has only recently begun to be rectified (Davies and Rosser, 1986)
- Women have been neglected in medical research. Indeed, it has been not at all uncommon for researchers to make generalizations about health matters from all-male samples (Matlin, 1993).
- There has been an inheritance of gender stereotypes in medicine and the presentation of medical knowledge. These have influenced the way health is perceived and how illness has been dealt with (Ehrenreich & English, 1979).
- The doctor–patient relationship has often exaggerated and helped to maintain the subordinate status of women in society (Miles, 1991).
- The medical care provided for women is sometimes inappropriate and, by some accounts, sometimes even irresponsible because of gender attitudes and expectations (Matlin, 1993).

Patterns associated with gender

If health is measured by death rates, then from conception to extreme old age females are more advantaged and live longer than males. In the UK in 1991, newborn girls could expect to live longer than newborn boys by approximately six years (78.8 compared with 73.2 years), and there were higher proportions of male deaths in every age group through to adulthood. The pattern is noticeable even before birth, leading some to suspect a strong female predisposition to greater chances of survival.

Matlin (1993) gives dramatic illustration of the point by summarizing the data for the USA in a chronological progression. There, 125 male fetuses are conceived for every 100 females and about 106 live males are born for every 100 females. The difference persists in childhood – almost one-third more boys die in the first year of life, and an equal sex ratio does not occur until 18 years of age. Thereafter the ratio decreases, so that by 87 years of age there is one man for every two women and by 100 years there is one man for every five women. This pattern is widespread, leading some to argue that in evolutionary terms females are predisposed to survival and that nature compensates by arranging for more males to be conceived.

Nevertheless, in historical terms the pattern is a recent one and is by no means universal. Even today it is largely restricted to urban industrial societies with high material standards of living. In traditional agrarian societies, both past and present, women have tended to live less long than men owing to their harsh life experiences of recurrent childbirth, manual work, and dietary and other physical disadvantages consequent upon low social status (Shorter, 1984). There is, therefore, a strong correlation between economic development and female advantage in life expectancy. (Waldron, 1983). Countries with large peasant populations such as India, Bangladesh, Nepal and Papua New Guinea still record a greater male life expectancy. Moreover, although it is entirely likely that there are some biological reasons for gender differences in life expectancy of populations in industrial countries with high living standards, these cannot be the only reasons.

Stacey and Olesen (1993) cite WHO evidence from 27 countries to demonstrate that rankings for mortality and risk factors are not highly correlated, the rankings being different for women and men. Nevertheless, for young adult males under 35 in Britain and the USA, accidents and violence account for the majority of deaths, with heart diseases

Table 8.1 *Age-adjusted mortality rates (per 100 000 population) by cause and gender, 1993**

	All circulatory diseases			All respiratory diseases			All injuries and poisonings				
	Total	Ischaemic heart disease	Cerebro-vascular disease	Total	Bronchitis and allied conditions	Cancer†	Total	Road traffic accidents	Suicides and open verdicts	All other causes	All causes
Males											
United Kingdom	496	319	92	165	69	293	42	9	16	114	1 109
Northern	539	360	101	177	79	337	41	9	15	113	1 207
Yorkshire	503	339	90	171	72	286	38	10	14	109	1 106
Trent	511	333	95	163	70	305	41	11	16	116	1 136
East Anglia	498	306	99	158	58	287	43	12	15	115	1 101
North West Thames	386	241	67	149	56	240	36	6	13	106	917
North East Thames	427	272	74	158	65	272	36	6	12	120	1 013
South East Thames	489	296	90	173	73	301	41	7	15	119	1 123
South West Thames	462	279	88	172	66	281	32	6	13	109	1 056
Wessex	494	318	88	150	60	287	35	8	14	119	1 085
Oxford	362	228	66	135	55	237	38	9	14	96	869
South Western	544	339	103	163	66	301	37	6	14	126	1 171
West Midlands	493	317	92	160	73	291	39	8	15	108	1 090
Mersey	511	337	93	185	75	316	39	8	14	107	1 157
North Western	541	358	99	190	87	299	44	7	16	111	1 185
England	485	311	89	165	69	289	39	8	14	113	1 090
Wales	560	371	97	179	77	325	43	8	15	115	1 223
Scotland	561	361	123	153	67	320	62	11	27	134	1 231
Northern Ireland	439	292	81	156	55	235	55	13	15	85	970
Females											
United Kingdom	518	259	151	186	44	257	24	3	5	157	1 142
Northern	560	302	156	200	57	286	25	3	5	159	1 230
Yorkshire	524	277	154	193	50	251	23	4	5	161	1 152
Trent	516	261	146	178	43	253	21	3	4	160	1 128
East Anglia	495	237	149	164	30	246	25	5	5	171	1 102
North West Thames	398	197	111	169	34	215	19	2	5	132	933
North East Thames	438	220	122	175	35	241	21	3	4	159	1 033
South East Thames	535	249	153	202	40	268	23	3	6	161	1 190
South West Thames	521	235	152	205	40	260	21	4	6	166	1 173
Wessex	507	244	150	186	35	257	22	3	4	175	1 147
Oxford	393	185	116	156	31	212	18	3	4	133	912
South Western	559	263	173	172	34	275	24	4	5	180	1 211
West Midlands	500	251	142	174	43	242	22	3	5	151	1 089
Mersey	542	280	147	215	56	274	21	4	4	143	1 195
North Western	582	303	168	215	66	265	24	3	5	162	1 248
England	507	252	146	186	43	253	22	3	5	158	1 126
Wales	584	297	161	200	47	278	24	3	4	150	1 236
Scotland	605	302	202	175	51	285	36	5	9	169	1 270
Northern Ireland	436	230	128	181	35	209	24	5	4	96	946

* Adjusted for the age structure of the population. The 1993 data are not comparable with injuries for 1992 and earlier years as published in previous editions of *Regional Trends* because of changes to the coding rules. Deaths at ages under 28 days occuring in England and Wales can no longer be assigned an underlying cause of death.

† Malignant neoplasma only.

Source: CSO (1995) Regional Trends London: HMSO Table 7.10, p. 109.

becoming increasingly important with age. For women in the USA, malignant neoplasms are the major cause of death in both young and middle age. It is only for the over-65 age group that heart disease becomes the dominant cause of death. In England and Wales, on the other hand, coronary heart disease is the main cause of death of women. Breast cancer is the second most important cause, and trends show an increase for the older age groups which has yet to be reversed (see Table 8.1).

Gender morbidity patterns

It is widely believed in the health professions that, although men experience higher mortality, women suffer more illness. However, this apparent truism cannot be taken for granted. How people perceive, describe and present illness and health leaves health professionals with problems of interpretation which must be explored.

As already shown, newborn girls can expect to live nearly six more years in Britain than newborn boys, yet it is also true that surveys repeatedly find that women report more illness at all ages than men (Blaxter, 1990). This apparent contradiction is to some extent resolved when factors such as the type of illness, social class, and employment status are taken into consideration, both separately and in combination (Whitehead, 1992).

- When the different age groups were related to social class, the National Survey of Health and Development found that serious illness in 21–25 year olds was significantly more common in young men (15.8%) than in young women (11.8%) and the relationship held within each social class (Wadsworth, 1986).
- When people report their illnesses there is not a very great sex difference in the age groups between 16 and 64 years of age. The notable difference emerges in the over-75 group, where 70% of women and 61% of men had long-standing illnesses (OPCS, 1991).

The highest consultation rates for both sexes are for skin disorders, respiratory disorders (including asthma) and hypertension (CSO, 1995a). Psychiatric symptoms, such as depression and anxiety, on the other hand, are far more prevalent for women. Perhaps the most interesting difference, both because of its size and its possible implications, is the consultation rate for problems defined by the International Classification of Diseases as 'symptoms, signs and ill-defined conditions' which includes experiences such as headaches, dizziness, chest pains, fatigue, tiredness, nausea, and skin eruptions. Here there is a marked difference between the sexes in Britain, especially among the younger age groups (Miles, 1991).

Verbrugge (1986), using data from the US, reports a similar pattern. For both sexes respiratory disorders dominate with younger adults and musculoskeletal problems for older adults. Moreover, women in the USA apparently report more daily symptoms than men and higher rates of all types of acute conditions, except injuries at younger ages. They also report more hospital stays.

Learning Activity 2 ◆ ◆ ◆

From within your own clinical practice, are you able to identify any gender differences in the way staff or patients are treated?

Explaining gender mortality and morbidity patterns

There are three possible causes (or as is more likely, a combination of the three causes) for the sex differences in morbidity and mortality:

- artefact,
- genetic and
- social.

ARTEFACT

The issues of interpretation upon which artefact explanations depend tend to focus on evidence about the way perceptions of gender influence the collection of statistics about gender-related health (Clarke, 1983). For example, there is some evidence to suggest that doctors' diagnoses might be influenced by the sex of their patients, and it has been suggested that recording of the causes of death might be influenced by the sex of the deceased (for a discussion, see Miles (1991)). Women's attitudes to health are thought by some to influence the way gender-related data on mortality are collected. Women are more likely to take note of symptoms, more likely to seek treatment, and may be more willing to cooperate with surveys into health-related problems (Waldron, 1983; Ansen *et al.*, 1993).

GENETIC

The probable genetic factors have been widely discussed. The differences in reproductive anatomy and physiology between the sexes has led many to expect more complexity in health problems for women and a consequent difference in the reporting of symptoms. It has also been suggested that women may be endowed with greater resistance to infectious diseases owing to genes affecting immunity being carried by the x chromosome, and that endogenous oestrogens may reduce women's illness rates for ischaemic heart disease (Waldron, 1976) – although recent research on the latter cited by Stacey and Olesen (1993) casts doubt on this. The recent controlled administration of oestrogen to men raised their incidence of coronary heart disease, leading to cancellation of the trials.

The higher fetal mortality of males can be amenable to reduction by improved maternal health and obstetric skills, although the causes of the sex differences in fetal vulnerability remain a matter for speculation.

SOCIAL

The obvious sociological categories of class, social support, employment and marital status can all be shown to shape the health experience of women and affect their rates of illness.

Risk

Perhaps the single most important social factor affecting mortality and morbidity differences between the sexes is their attitude to risk. Studies have shown that females engage in less dangerous activities at all ages and that, where male and female lifestyles are very similar, such as on *kibbutzim*, differences in morbidity and mortality are much reduced. Nevertheless, even here there are still noticeable differences, as shown by Leviatan and Cohen (1985).

Marital status

The relationship between marital status, mortality and morbidity has long been noted and has generated much discussion. In general terms, marital status is good for the health of both sexes. Married people have lower death rates than those who have never married or who are divorced or widowed, although the benefits in terms of mortality rates are greater for men than women at all ages. Moreover, married men report better health than do single men, although no such benefits are reported by women (Macintyre, 1986; Blaxter, 1990).

Companionship in itself is a factor that seems to improve health. Several studies have shown that people who live alone suffer greater health problems and that even the presence of a pet improves their health status (Ornstein and Sobel, 1988). Under the influence of companionship people eat more regularly and improve the quality of their diet, note each other's illness symptoms, and nurse each other when ill – although such benefits are much more marked for men than women (Graham, 1984). Moreover, marriage affects the level of wider social support and community involvement. People living alone are often more socially isolated, and divorced or widowed women find greater difficulties in establishing and sustaining social networks (Stark, 1987).

Material deprivation

There is a direct correlation between material deprivation and women's health. Whatever deprivation indicators used, whether car ownership, occupation, housing tenure or education, the research findings consistently reinforce the same picture (Moser *et al.*, 1988). Moreover married woman's health can be shown to be related to the occupation of her spouse. Material hardship is particularly noticeable with single mothers, about half of whom rely on state benefits, a rate that is ten times as great as that for two-parent families. The mortality rate of children of single mothers is by far the highest of any social group, some 42% worse than that of Social Class V (Judge and Benzeval, 1993). Male single parents are likely to be more secure in terms of finance and housing tenure, not only because they have a statistically better chance of sustaining a career, but also because they can more easily claim tax exemption and state help for child support services (Miles, 1991). They are also significantly older yet remarry in a shorter space of time.

Lone mothers

Lone mothers have a poorer health record than mothers living with their spouses (Miles, 1991), and the evidence indicates that they evaluate their health at a lower level and report more health-related symptoms. Much recent attention has focused on the health problems of the children of young, particularly teenage, single mothers living alone, who in 1990 made up nearly one-quarter of the total (Judge and Benzeval, 1993). Interesting recent research indicates, however, that a high proportion of children referred to psychiatric and psychological services (Tripp and Crockett, 1994) come from reordered or reconstituted families of which those with lone parents form only a part.

These factors, however, are strongly influenced by class and, perhaps, ethnic status. Social support for women by spouses in marriage markedly improves women's health, and several studies have shown that such support in marriage is correlated with class (Brown and Harris, 1978; Webb, 1986; Miles, 1988). Women without such support are particularly prone to suffer from stress-related disorders (Gove, 1979) and depression (Brown and Harris, 1978).

Employment

Although women represent an increasing proportion of the workforce in nearly all industrialized countries, and the majority of new jobs over the next decade are projected to be for women, too little is yet known about the effects of employment on women's health. Research on the health of unemployed women is complicated by the difficulties of distinguishing between 'unemployment' and 'non-employment', but the statistics for those women who are registered as unemployed seems to show they experience similar health problems as men in the same circumstances (Miles, 1991). Women in white collar employment and part-time jobs have lower mortality than those in full-time manual employment (Goldblatt, 1990). Moreover, women's health is adversely affected not only by the unemployment of a spouse but even by the advance notice of such unemployment (Beale and Nethercott, 1988).

Women in non-manual part-time jobs seem to have the highest health status, in terms of both mortality and morbidity. This is either because such jobs are more readily available to women who for socio-economic reasons have better life chances, or it could be a cause of that better health status (Moser *et al.*, 1990). Recent comparative studies of Britain and Scandinavian countries (Haavio-Manila, 1986; Arber and Lahelma, 1993; Rahkonen, 1993) suggest that women have higher rates of illness in countries and in regions where they have a greater propensity to stay at home as housewives and little chance of gaining non-manual occupations.

MEN AND HEALTH

The rapid and fairly steady increase in life expectancy at birth of roughly two years each decade for both sexes is often used as evidence for the improving health of the whole population (CSO, 1995a). Yet for men over 60 the increase has been under five years this century, and for men over 80 it actually fell in the first three decades, and even now is less than two years more than it was in 1901 (CSO, 1995a). But when the population is examined in terms of occupational class and region, the very uneven nature of these improvements becomes apparent. For the country as a whole, standardized mortality rates are markedly greater for men in manual occupations and those who are unemployed. The most favoured region, East Anglia, and the most favoured towns are in the south and south-east (CSO, 1995b). The further to the north and west, the greater is the rate of mortality for men but also the greater are the differences between the occupational classes in those mortality rates. Not only does the north of England, therefore, sustain the highest mortality rates, but male manual workers in some poorer areas show no improvement in health status over much of the last 50 years (Townsend *et al.*, 1988).

Heart disease remains by far the most important cause of premature death for men (see Table 8.1), and is significant for health professionals since the major risk factors are amenable to influence by changes in behaviour. The second most common cause of premature death for men is lung cancer. In 1992, the age-standardized mortality rates for lung cancer in women under 65 was roughly half that for men. Whereas the male death rates for lung cancer fell by nearly 50% in the last 20 years, that for women has actually increased by 16% in that same period. Again, it is recognized (CSO, 1995a) that the major risk factor (80% is attributable to tobacco smoke) is amenable to influence by behaviour changes.

For men in the younger age groups, the most common causes of death are suicides and accidents. Although the rates of accidents fell by some 37% between 1971 and 1992, they still remain the most common cause of death for people under 30 (see Table 8.1). Accident rates are far higher for men than for women. Of these, roughly one-third occur in the home, one-third on the road and one-third in work and other places (CSO, 1995a).

Suicide is three times more common for males than females (see Table 8.1). Whilst for women there has been a marked decline in deaths from suicide over the last decade in the older age groups, for men the rates have dramatically increased in the younger age groups. The usual pattern has been for suicide rates to increase with age, and indeed this pattern remains true for women. However, so steep has been the growth in suicide rates for younger men that, by the mid-1980s, men in the 25–44 age band became the most suicide prone.

The regional distribution of the most common causes of death shows a marked consistency of pattern. The most common causes of death for men (circulatory disease, respiratory diseases and malignant neoplasms) are lowest in the south and east of the country and increase to the north and west. They are also strongly related to occupational class and amenable to improvement by behaviour changes (CSO, 1995b).

Knowledge of male morbidity patterns has been much improved by the yearly *Health Surveys for England* commissioned by the Department of Health since 1991

(CSO, 1995a). Cholesterol levels and high blood pressure increases dramatically with age, as does the decline in rates of physical activity. Just over half of men (and just under half of women) recorded a body mass index (BMI) high enough to class them as overweight or obese.

There is evidence to suggest that men perceive health more positively in terms of valued quality-of-life parameters than women. When asked to describe health in someone else they tended to use terms such as 'fit, strong, energetic and physically active' whilst women favoured more negative perceptions such as 'never ill, no disease, never see a doctor' (Blaxter, 1990). It is perhaps significant to note that in the same survey, when asked to think of someone who was especially healthy, the majority of both sexes nominated a man rather than a woman.

This tendency to emphasize functional, negative, or coping definitions of health seems to be related to social class (Cornwell, 1984; Calnan, 1987) and on how much sense of control people have over their destinies. Where people felt powerless when confronted by employment, housing and welfare factors that had a direct bearing on their health, health tends to be defined in functional and negative terms, as the ability to cope (Calnan, 1987; Blaxter, 1990).

Such evidence has been used to suggest that part of the apparent difference between the morbidity rates of men and women is to be accounted for by gender differences in the amount of control people felt they have over their own lives (Miles, 1991). There is interesting recent evidence to suggest that this is true (Ansen *et al.*, 1993). In a study of patients with similar clinical status (mild hypertension) and under the same treatment regime (beta-adrenoceptor blocking agents), the men were found to be significantly advantaged in terms of social factors that affected their sense of being in control (more education, more in employment), they expressed much greater satisfaction with the coherence and stability of their lives, they experienced fewer symptoms than the women, and evaluated their own health more positively.

SUMMARY

By focusing on the distinction between sex and gender, sociologists are interested to explore how gender roles, cultural mores and political changes have contributed to women's health experience and the ways in which women's health is described and managed. In particular, the apparent paradox of women's greater morbidity rates but lower mortality rates when compared with men has been widely discussed. It is suggested that recent research is consistent with the view that much of the difference in gender morbidity rates can be accounted for by the greater social support and status men gain through marriage and paid employment, and that even the gender differences in mortality can be, in part, accounted for by gender-related behaviour.

Key Points

- ❒ Inequalities in health are attributable to multiple causes.
- ❒ There are three explanations for gender patterns in health: artefact, genetic and social.
- ❒ There is sociological evidence to link gender with mortality and morbidity.
- ❒ Gender provides a useful case study with which to review inequalities in health status.

References

Ansen, O., Paran, E., Neumann, L. and Chernichovsky, D. (1993). Gender differences in health perceptions and their predictors. *Social Science and Medicine*, **36**: 419–27.

Arber, S. and Lahelma, E. (1993). Inequalities in women's and men's ill-health: Britain and Finland compared. *Social Science and Medicine*, **37**: 1055–68.

Beale, N. and Nethercott, S. (1988). The nature of unemployment morbidity. *Journal of the Royal College of General Practitioners*, **38**: 200–2.

Blaxter, M. (1990). *Health and Lifestyles*. London: Tavistock/Routledge.

Brown, G.W. and Harris, T. (1978). *The Social Origins of Depression*. London: Tavistock.

Calnan, M. (1987). *Health and Illness: the lay perspective*. London: Tavistock.

Central Statistical Office (CSO) (1995a). *Social Trends*, **25**. London: HMSO.

Central Statistical Office (CSO) (1995b). *Regional Trends*, **30**. London: HMSO.

Clarke, J. (1983). Sexism, feminism and medicalization – a decade review of the literature on gender and illness. *Sociology of Health and Illness*, **5**: 62–4.

Cornwell, J. (1984). *Hard Earned Lives – Accounts of Health and Illness from East London*. London: Tavistock.

Davies, C. and Rosser, J. (1986). *Processes of Discrimination: A Study of Women Working in the National Health Service*. London: HMSO.

Ehrenreich, B. and English, D. (1979). *For Her Own Good: 150 Years of the Expert's Advice to Women*. London: Pluto.

Goldblatt, P. (ed.) (1990). *Longitudinal Study 1971–1981: Mortality and Social Organization* (OPCS LS Series 6). London: HMSO.

Gove, W.R. (1979). Sex differences in the epidemiology of mental disorder: evidence and explanations. In: Gomberg, E.S. and

Franks, C. (eds), *Gender and Disordered Behaviour: Sex Differences in Psychopathology*. New York: Brunner Hazel.
Graham, H. (1984). *Women, Health and the Family*. Brighton: Wheatsheaf.
Haavio-Mannila, E. (1986). Inequalities in health and gender. *Social Science and Medicine*, **22**: 141–9.
Judge, K. and Benzeval, M. (1993). Health inequalities: new concerns about the children of single mothers. *British Medical Journal*, **306**: 677–80.
Leviatan, U. and Cohen, J. (1985). Gender difference in life expectancy among kibbutz members. *Social Science and Medicine*, **21**: 545–51.
Macintyre, S. (1986). Health and Illness. In: Burgess, R. (ed.), *Key Variables in Social Investigation*. London: Routledge & Kegan Paul.
Matlin, M.W. (1993). *The Psychology of Women*, 2nd edn. London: Harcourt Brace Jovanovich.
Miles, A. (1988). *Women and Mental Illness*. Brighton: Wheatsheaf.
Miles, A. (1991). *Women, Health and Medicine*. Milton Keynes: Open University Press.
Moser, K., Pugh, H. and Goldblatt, P. (1988). Inequalities in women's health: looking at mortality differentials using an alternative approach. *British Medical Journal*, **296**: 1221–4.
Moser, K., Pugh, H. and Goldblatt, P. (1990). Mortality and the social classification of women. In: Goldblatt, P. (ed.), *Longitudinal Study 1971–81: Mortality and Social Organization* (OPCS LS Series 6). London: HMSO.
Office of Population, Censuses and Surveys (OPCS) (1990). *Standard Occupational Classification*, **1**. London: HMSO.
Office of Population, Censuses and Surveys (1991). *General Household Survey for 1989*, **20**: London: HMSO.
Ornstein, R. and Sobel, D. (1988). *The Healing Brain*. London: Macmillan.
Rahkonen, O., Lahelma, E., Karisto, A. and Manderbacka, K. (1993). Persisting health inequalities: social class differentials in illness in the Scandinavian countries. *Journal of Public Health Policy*, **14**: 66–81.
Shorter, E. (1984). *A History of Women's Bodies*. Harmondsworth: Penguin.
Stacey, M. and Olesen, V. (1993). Women, men and health. *Social Science and Medicine*, **36**: 1–5.
Stark, J. (1987). Health and social contacts. In: Cox, B.D. (ed.), *The Health and Lifestyle Survey*. London: Health-Promotion Research Trust.
Townsend, P., Phillimore, P and Beattie, A. (1988). *Health and Deprivation: Inequality in the North*. London: Croom Helm.
Tripp, P. and Crockett, R. (1994). *Children Living in Reordered Families*. Joseph Rowntree Foundation.
Verbrugge, L.M. (1986). From sneezes to adieux: stages of health for American men and women. *Social Science and Medicine*, **22**: 1195–1212.
Wadsworth, M.E.J. (1986). Serious illness in childhood and its association with later life achievement. In: Wilkinson, R.G. (ed.), *Class and Health: Research and Longitudinal Data*. London: Tavistock.
Waldron, J. (1976). Why do women live longer than men? *Social Science and Medicine*, **10**: 349–50.
Waldron, I. (1983). Sex differences in illness incidence, prognosis and mortality: issues and evidence. *Social Science and Medicine*, **17**: 1107–23.
Webb, C. (1986). Women as gynaecology patients and nurses. In: Webb, C. (ed.), *Feminist Practices in Women's Health Care*. Chichester: Wiley.
Whitehead, M. (1992). *The Health Divide*. In: Townsend, P. *et al.* (eds), *Inequalities in Health: The Black Report*, 2nd edn. Harmondsworth: Penguin.

Further Reading ▲ ▲ ▲

Oakley, A. (1993). *Essay on Women, Medicine and Health*. Edinburgh: Edinburgh University Press.
Doyal, L. (1995). *What Makes Women Sick: Gender and the Political Economy of Health*. Basingstoke: Macmillan.

9

Social Trends and Health: The Next Twenty Years

Sebastian Garman

LEARNING OBJECTIVES

After studying this chapter you should:

- Be able to discuss how changes in society have affected health trends
- Understand demographic trends and their impact
- Be able to describe the roles of informal carers with regard to social trends

INTRODUCTION

Social changes in the 1990s are confronting governments with difficult options and are transforming the work of health professionals and the lives of the people who use the services. This chapter is intended to introduce readers to some of these transformations and their likely consequences. In particular, the chapter focuses on the ageing structure of populations, changing family structures and the shifting dependency ratios. An awareness of the social and political factors that influence the decisions of health professionals is necessary to equip them to manage change in their careers.

CHANGES IN SOCIAL TRENDS

It seems generally accepted by sociologists that the enormous transformations of socio-economic structures implied in the shift from traditional rural societies based on agriculture to 'modern' societies based on industry, urban life and markets has been followed by a further reshaping of social structures and cultural styles. These major changes have been variously described as 'post-modernist', 'post-Fordist', 'post-industrial', or 'globalization', depending on which aspects – cultural, economic, or social – are being emphasized (Kumar, 1995; Fox, 1993; Hall *et al.*, 1992).

Industrialism and modernity implied the rise of urban life, a factory system of production, social organization and loyalty focused on the nation-state, the patriarchal nuclear family headed by a male wage-earner, and a belief in science and progress. Post-modernism implies, on the other hand, a restructured global industry beyond the control of individual nation-states, a movement away from the old factory-based heavy industries, a global mediation of information and styles by way of new electronic technologies, reawakened ethnic tensions as state boundaries are challenged, a transformation of gender roles, a plurality of family structures including rising divorce rates, and a loss of faith in the neutrality and objectivity of science as well as the inevitability of progress (Kumar, 1995).

Britain's continuing transformation can be seen in these terms. In the words of one authoritative observer, 'the institutional division of labour of prototypic industrialism was an essential triangle joining the family, the economy, and the state. Families had raised children, men had worked, women had run households. The economy produced, the family reproduced and consumed, and the state protected and redistributed' (Halsey, 1987, p. 12). All this is now in the throws of rapid change. A small but rapidly growing proportion of economic production is returning to the home for the first time since industrialization took place; employment is being redefined to include a much greater 'service element'; the family is producing fewer children and breaking up to become 'reconstituted' much more frequently; women are being incorporated into the economy and gender roles are being renegotiated; manual occupations are going into decline, and formal education becoming far more significant for employment prospects (Table 9.1).

Projections for the present decade (Griffin, 1990)

Table 9.1 *Trends in the UK family (Halsey, 1987)*

	1931	1951	1961	1966	1971	1976	1981	1985
Percentage of all women aged 16 or over economically active[a]	34[f]	35[g]	37[g]	42[g]	43[g]	47	48	49
Percentage of married women aged 16 or over economically active[a]	10[f]	22[g]	30[g]	38[g]	42[g]	49	49	52
Total period fertility rate[a, b]	..	2.16	2.78	2.78	2.40	1.72	1.79	1.78
Illegitimate births as a percentage of all births	5	5	6	8	8	9	13	19
Persons divorcing per 1000 married population[c]	-	3	2	3	6	10	12	13
Remarriages as a percentage of all marriages	11[a]	18[a]	15[a]	16[a]	20	31	34	35
One-person households as a percentage of all households[a]	7	11	12	15	18	21	22	24
Percentage of all men aged 16 or over economically active[a]	91[f]	88[g]	86[g]	84[g]	81[g]	79	76	74
Thousands of students[d] in part-time higher education[e]								
Men	..	..	107	115	142	168	207	212
Women	..	..	6	8	23	50	87	107
Aged 21 or over in:								
Non-advanced further education	..	..	..	..	..	2260	1986	2200
Adult education	..	..	..	..	1987	..	1169	1349
Part-time higher education[e]	..	..	..	..	..	201	236	269
Full-time higher education[e]	..	..	..	..	216	266	235	252

[a] Great Britain only.
[b] The average number of children which would be born per woman if women experienced the age specific fertility rates of the period in question throughout their child-bearing life-span.
[c] England and Wales only.
[d] Data are for academic years ending in the year shown.
[e] Includes Universities, Open University, and advanced courses in major establishments of further education.
[f] Aged 14 or over.
[g] Aged 15 or over.
Sources: British Labour Statistics Historical Abstract; Population Trends, Office of Population Censuses and Surveys; Department of Education and Science; Central Statistical Office.

suggested that these trends will continue. Ninety per cent of the one million new jobs in the 10-year period are expected to be done by women; one-person households will grow by more than a million, putting further strain on the supply of available housing for those in need; service industries will take an even greater share of total employment; and higher skill levels will be demanded. Recent statistics largely confirm this picture (CSO, 1994). The service sector continues to expand, and by 1991 more than a quarter of households consisted of one person living alone. Although women continue to take an increasing share of the labour market, a third of single women of working age were economically inactive in 1993 – more than twice the proportion of men.

INDUSTRIALISM, MODERNITY AND DISEASE

Populations from agrarian and rural societies of Europe before the industrial revolution, and much of the Third World today, are vulnerable to predominantly infectious diseases carried by water, food, air, or vectors such as fleas, mosquitoes or snails. Infant mortality tends to be high and men usually live longer than women. Agrarian societies are heavily dependent on the rhythm of the seasons, and distribution networks, especially on land, tend to be expensive and unreliable. Food shortages, therefore, are common, at times of harvest failure or in the 'hungry gap' of temperate climates, after the winter when stores are low but the early crops have yet to bear. Malnutrition and infectious diseases are closely associated (for useful introductions to this topic, see McKeown (1980) or Acheson and Hagard, (1984)).

Modernity and industrialism has been accompanied by a dramatic decline in deaths from infection in all countries that have been through the process. As nutrition and hygiene standards have improved with clean water supplies, cheap food and efficient distribution, the resistance of populations to disease in these areas seems to have improved. Even so, the major causes of death world-wide today are generally attributed to a combination of malnutrition and infection. In contrast, the major causes of death in advanced industrial countries are degenerative diseases such as cancer and those associated with the cardiovascular system.

The demographic transition and health

The movement from traditional agrarian societies to urban societies based on industrial production systems and labour markets has been accompanied by dramatic demographic shifts that are referred to as the 'demographic revolution'. This is a process by which populations move from high to low birth and mortality rates. Such a process is characterized by an ageing population structure as the number of children falls as a proportion of the total population and greater longevity is achieved. In the European Union, the number of births fell by 25% between 1960 and 1989 (Eurostat, 1991) and the infant mortality rate showed a spectacular decline from 34.8 per thousand live births in 1960 to an average of 8.2 in 1989. As a consequence of ageing population structures, the population of many European countries may even begin to decline.

The population of the United Kingdom is fairly typical of this process. Dramatic demographic change occurred between 1870 and the 1920s, when the average size of British families dropped from 5.8 to 2.2 children. Apart from a slight rise in 1960 to 2.4, it has continued to be below replacement levels at around 1.8 (Coleman and Salt, 1992).

The reasons for the change in birth rate are several, and largely related to the changing role of women. It is possible that fecundity is also a factor, since the human sperm count has halved in the last 25 years despite an apparent increase in the rate of sexual intercourse. But there have been dramatic and far-reaching changes in women's lives. The widespread acceptance of oral contraception has fundamentally influenced the balance of political power between the sexes since women for the first time control their own fertility. A slightly higher percentage of women are choosing to remain childless. More significantly, women are marrying later and delaying the birth of their first child. Moreover, social attitudes strongly suggest that a smaller family is preferred (Coleman and Salt, 1992). As the reasons people offer to explain that preference – such as the cost of a home mortgage and the necessity for two incomes to sustain family expenditure – are thought likely to persist, demographers are confident in projecting this trend forward. Since 1966 the proportion of women working has grown from 38% to 66% (Coleman and Salt, 1992). The globalization of the labour market and the changing pattern of industry towards electronics and the service sector, where female labour is often preferred, means that these changes are almost certain to continue.

In the recent past the UK population increase has been gradual, rising by about 10% between 1961 and 1991, from 52.8 million to 57.8 million. Over the next 35 years this increase is expected to tail off until zero growth is reached, first in Scotland (by the year 2000) and then in Wales (by the year 2015), and finally in the whole of the UK by the year 2030 (CSO, 1994), when the total population is expected to reach 62 million.

With a falling birth rate comes an ageing population structure. Between 1961 and 1991 the proportion of the population of the UK under 16 years fell from 25% to 20% and is expected to continue to decline to 18% by the year 2031. On the other hand, between 1961 and 1991 the proportion of the population aged 65 and over had risen from approximately 12% to nearly 16% and is expected to continue to rise to 22% by 2031 (Figure 9.1).

The 'demographic timebomb'

Those under 16 years of age and those over pensionable age are, together, referred to as the 'dependent population' by policy analysts, and their combined numbers expressed as a proportion of people of working age is known as 'the dependency ratio'. The ratio was 57 (out of every 100 of working age) in 1951, rose to 63 in 1991 and is expected to rise to 79 by the year 2031. Such an increase has serious implications, because the cost burden will have to be borne by an ever smaller proportion of the population. This has been dubbed the 'demographic timebomb'.

In part to alleviate the effects, it was announced by the government in 1993 that the age at which women

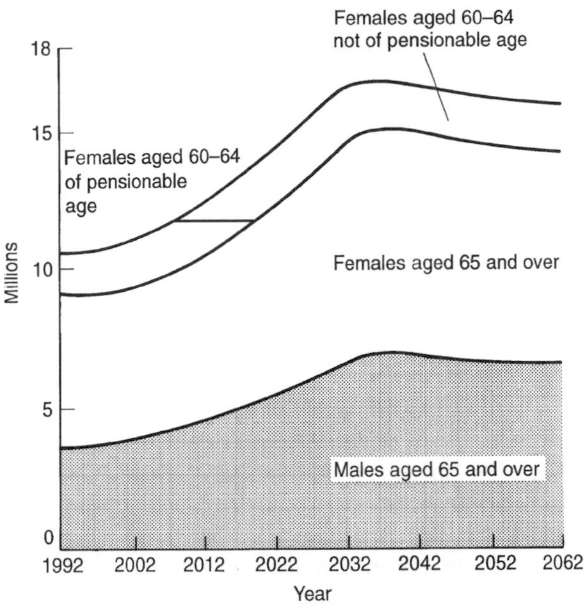

Figure 9.1 *Elderly dependency and population change (OPCS, 1994)*

receive a state pension, currently 60, is to be altered to 65 to match that of men. This change is to be phased in between the years 2010 and 2020. As a consequence the 'pensioner dependency ratio' (defined as the number of pensionable age per 100 people aged 16 and over but below pensionable age) is projected to rise much less steeply than would otherwise be the case. In 1992 the ratio was 30 per 100. With the change in the retirement age this ratio is expected to remain fairly constant until 2020, but after that it is expected to rise rapidly to 43 per hundred in 2038 (OPCS, 1994). It is often suggested, however, that such an alleviation will not be sufficient to counteract the other trends referred to above, in which case increasing demands upon the taxed working population will increase political pressures to abandon commitments to universal state pensions.

The implications of these changes on healthcare and the work of health professionals are already considerable, and will continue to put pressure on the managers of healthcare to implement programmes of continuous change. Because of the large age range of the retired population, it is useful to divide the category between the 'young elderly' (65–74) and the 'old elderly' (75 and over). After the rise of the last decade, the proportion of 'young elderly' is at present decreasing; and projections demonstrate that, although this decrease is temporary, the overall rise will not be great over the next three decades. In contrast, the projected increase in proportion of the 'old elderly' is dramatic, from 8.5% of the population in 1992, to 11% by 2011 and 13% by 2025 (OPCS, 1994). Since women live on average almost six years longer than men, and marry men younger than themselves, the resulting healthcare problems are increasingly gender-related. Most men die at home cared for by their wives; most women die alone.

Although the health problems of the population are becoming increasingly degenerative and chronic (Acheson and Hagard, 1984), owing to the ageing population structure and better living standards, it is important to emphasize that a large proportion of the 'old elderly' do maintain their independence in the community, relying on informal care only in times of acute crisis (Fennell *et al.*, 1988).

In the early part of this century old age was strongly linked with poverty (Victor, 1994). More recently attention has been drawn, particularly by market researchers and advertisers, to a large minority of pensioners who are as financially well off as employed people with families (Johnson and Falkingham, 1992) – because of, for example, the asset value of an unmortgaged home. Moreover, the incomes of pensioners as a group were 35% higher in real terms in 1991 than a decade earlier because the value of investments and occupational pensions had risen (OPCS, 1994). In an attempt to defuse the perceived consequences of the 'demographic timebomb', and in response to the greater wealth of pensioners, central government has attempted to slow the growth in proportion of national income devoted to state expenditure by encouraging a climate of individual responsibility and self-reliance through incentives for private expenditure in the health and welfare fields.

Learning Activity 1 ◆ ◆ ◆

Within (i) your own family and (ii) your social group, calculate the numbers of individuals who are under 16 and those who are over 65. Then consider the dependency ratios. Do they reflect recent trends?

COMMUNITY CARE AND THE ELDERLY

Before 1990, responsibility for community care was divided between social security (finances), social services (personal social services), health authorities (medical care), and the Department of the Environment (housing). Recent changes have been aimed at rationalizing this bureaucratic complexity whilst, at the same time, introducing a market discipline of budgets and the buying of services. A strong if more implicit policy aim is to reduce the level of dependency on the state by the elderly population. Thus real attempts have been made to reduce the population in residential homes (Tunnicliffe *et al.*, 1993).

From April 1993, local authorities became responsible for ensuring that services, including healthcare in its wider sense, are provided within appropriate budgets using both private and public sector resources. Local authorities have to collaborate with health and welfare professions to design multidisciplinary care packages and to attempt audit and quality monitoring. This care is now most likely to be in the private and voluntary sectors (Tunnicliffe *et al.*, 1993). The implications of these changes are wide-ranging. A small progress report (Collyer, 1993) suggests that individuals now complain of deficits in most aspects of their care. It has been suggested (Murphy, 1993) that one barrier to the changes remains the different styles of management of health and social service departments. One suggested solution is for common undergraduate training of health and welfare professionals.

General practitioners have expressed scepticism and dissatisfaction with the reforms (Murphy, 1993). A local survey in Croydon showed GPs to be dissatisfied because of an increased workload for minimal advantage, which mirrors the findings of a national study by the British Medical Association (Chew and Wilkin, 1994). The proportion of elderly on a GP's register has long been recognized as an indication of deprivation by primary healthcare workers (Jarman, 1983), and with continuing demographic change this is almost certain to grow in significance among the perceived problems of healthcare professionals.

Part of the problem is the assumption that the elderly are uniformly better off and capable of taking more responsibility for their own care. The elderly comprise a highly heterogeneous group and it is misleading to make blanket generalizations about their financial standing and health needs. The income of the retired is derived from four sources: state pension, occupational pension, savings (including investments) and earnings (Walker, 1993). At present two-thirds of this income is derived from public transfers (state pensions) and one-third from earnings and occupational pensions. As a proportion that income which is derived from employment is shrinking. Moreover, there has been a marked increase in the proportion of the total social security budget that goes to the elderly (42% in 1951, 59% in 1986), a rate of increase that seems to be greater than their increase in numbers; this may mean that more old people are becoming eligible, through poverty, for social security support.

Since the 1970s the value of the state pension has fallen in relative terms because it is tied to increasing prices rather than to the higher index of the growth in wages (Johnson and Falkingham, 1992). Because the greater part of the income of the retired derives from this source, it is difficult to see how the demographic transitions, combined with government policies focusing on more self-reliance, can do other than lead to an increasing slide of the elderly into poverty and exacerbated health problems. It is important to remember that both mortality and morbidity are correlated with wealth (Benzeval, 1995). Canadian evidence suggests that the wealthiest fifth of that population not only live more than six years longer than the poorest fifth, but also can expect to be free of disability for 14 years longer (Robine and Ritchie, 1991). A study in Newcastle of those who died prematurely also showed how poorer people on average are chronically sick or disabled for a much longer period (Phillimore, 1989).

Of course, home ownership is an important source of equity that can provide for additional income in later life. However, analyses of the pattern of home ownership shows a correlation with the socio-economic status of pre-retirement occupation, being mainly a phenomenon of the professional classes for older people. The elderly are twice as likely as the general population to live in rented accommodation. The houses they do own are on average less valuable, owing to geographical location or state of disrepair (Johnson and Falkingham, 1992).

INFORMAL CARERS AND SOCIAL TRENDS

Healthcare needs are normally met from informal sources. Carers for the sick, the disabled and the frail are mostly female (Oakley, 1974) and the assistance people receive from community social networks reflects such gender roles (Wenger, 1984). Although families do accept their responsibilities of care in principle (Wenger, 1984), and seem to maintain their links despite the increasing geographical and social mobility of members (Wilmott, 1986), there are important reasons for concern. It is likely that the needs of the ageing population will not be met by greater reliance on informal carers and 'the community' without more resources and commitment being demonstrated by the state to 'community' health support networks.

It is important to examine these trends in the context of recent health and community care policies. In 1986 the government-appointed Audit Commission warned that 'there are serious grounds for concern about the lack of progress in shifting the balance of services towards community care' (Audit Commission, 1986). Remarkable discrepancies were identified between different areas of Britain in home-help provision and the mix between private and voluntary residential accommodation for the elderly. There has been a dramatic rise in private residential and nursing homes since 1983 when, for the first time, central government allowed local authorities to make payments to private residential homes to care for elderly frail people. Both the British Medical Association and the Audit Commission drew attention to the distortions this was producing in 'the market', which seriously undermined the whole concept of community care by subsidising high-cost residential care while restricting the option of low-cost home support. Moreover, because the private residential homes were being built mainly in the south of England, the effect was the opposite of declared policy intentions by adding to the already unacceptable channelling of public funds to people in better-off regions.

Learning Activity 2 ◆ ◆ ◆

Speak to colleagues and friends to see if you can find examples of people experiencing problems or difficulties with coping with the care of the elderly. You may well have an example within your own family. Try to identify the major issues involved.

The National Health Service and Community Care Act (1993), as has been suggested above, was implemented in part to deal with these problems, but fears remain that the impetus of past policy confusion may prove difficult to remedy. As long ago as the Black Report (1980), there have been widespread calls by health professionals for a rational and cost-effective strategy of community health. This was to include reviews of hospital, residential and domiciliary care, as well as increasing community support with sheltered housing, community nursing services, and an expanded role for home-help services.

As the percentage of the population over 75 expands from 8.5% to 13% over the next 30 years, it remains unclear as to whether health standards can be maintained. Both policy and pragmatism suggest a reliance on informal carers, but without more support it is unclear whether they can meet the increasing demands. With more public education and greater practical support it is possible that they can. In a climate of increasing expectation of greater material wealth and individual freedom, it is unlikely that people have realized that, as one analyst has observed, 'the average young adult today faces life-long responsibilities towards elderly people which are greater than those bearing upon a similar individual in the early twentieth century' (Thompson, 1993).

There are some grounds for optimism. People do care about their elderly relatives (Lewis and Meredith, 1988) and make strenuous efforts to sustain their practical caring activities. A large proportion of women choose to work part-time to free themselves for other commitments, including caring for their family members (CSO, 1994). Moreover, the cohort who are now over retirement age (65–75 years) is more likely than its predecessor (85 and over) to have adult children who can take the role of carer (Lewis and Meredith, 1988).

In balance, however, without more evident support from community care networks the trends do not suggest much optimism. The rapid expansion of the 'old elderly' means that many either have no daughters, or have children who themselves are retired. The enormous increase in divorce and 'reconstituted families' means that, increasingly, women with responsibilities for the elderly are either having to care unaided, as single mothers, for their children or finding themselves in second marriages. It is not at all clear that the sense of obligation to the older generation is sustained under these conditions (Jeffreys, 1989). The number of elderly people living with their relatives continued to show a decrease, from 42% in 1961 to 18% in 1987. Until recently just over half of all carers for the chronically sick or disabled were spouses (Arber, 1986), but with the increasing longevity of women this proportion is not likely to be sustained. Both spouses (Miles, 1991) and children (Ory and Bond, 1989) report a high level of stress in caring for elderly dependants.

SUMMARY

Behavioural scientists have pointed out that advanced industrial societies are undergoing radical transformations that are both new in cultural style (post-modern) and different in socio-economic structure (post-industrial). This chapter has focused on certain aspects of change, in particular the ageing structure of populations, changing family structures, and shifting dependency ratios. Their likely consequences for perceptions of health and illness, and the delivery of health care and treatment, have been discussed.

Key Points ■ ■ ■

❐ Major changes are occurring in cultural styles and socio-economic structures.

❐ There is inter-dependence between social structural change and health.

❐ Demographic shifts and the ageing structure of populations have led to a reappraisal of health systems.

❐ There has been a change in dependency ratios, and an increased emphasis on community care.

❐ There are limitations and possibilities associated with the shift to community care.

References ▼ ▼ ▼

Acheson, D. and Hagard, S. (1984). *Health, Society and Medicine: An Introduction to Community Medicine*, 3rd edn. London: Blackwell.

Arber, S. (1991). Class, paid employment and family roles: making sense of structural disadvantage, gender and health status, *Social Science and Medicine*, **32**: 425–36.

Audit Commission Review (1990). *Caring for People: Community Care in the Next Decade and Beyond*, London: HMSO.

Benzeval, M., Judge, K. and Whitehead, M. (1995). *Tackling Health Inequalities: An Agenda for Action*. Poole, Dorset: King's Fund and BEBC.

Black, D. (1980). *Inequalities in Health: Report of a Research Working Group Chaired by Sir Douglas Black*, London: DHSS.

Central Statistical Office (1994). *Social Trends*, **24**. London: HMSO.

Chew, C. A. and Wilkin, D. (1994). Annual assessment of patients aged 75 and over. *British Journal of General Practice*. Jun. vol. 44, **33**: 263–267.

Coleman, D. and Salt. J. (1992). *The British Population: Patterns, Trends and Processes*. Oxford: Oxford University Press.

Collyer, M. (1993). *Community Care and Older People – Progress Report on Londonwide Monitoring of Unmet Need*. London: Age Concern.

Eurostat (1991). *A Social Portrait of Europe*. Brussels and Luxembourg: Office for Official Publications of the European Community.

Fennell, G., Phillipson, C. and Evers, H. (1988). *The Sociology of Old Age*. Milton Keynes: Open University Press.

Fox, N. (1993). *Postmodernism, Sociology and Health*. Buckingham: Open University Press.

Griffin, T. (1990). Social trends: the next twenty years. *Social Trends*, **20**. London: HMSO.

Hall, S., Held, D. and McGrew, T. (1992). *Modernity and its Future*. Oxford: Polity Press.

Halsey, A.H. (1987). Introduction. *Social Trends*, **17**. London: HMSO, 10–17.

Jarman, D. (1983). Identification of underprivileged areas. *British Medical Journal*, **286**: 1705–9,

Jeffreys, M. (1989). *Growing Old in the Twentieth Century*. London: Routledge.

Johnson, P. and Falkingham, J. (1992). *Ageing and Economic Welfare*. London: Sage.

Joshi, H. (1989). *The Changing Population of Britain*. Oxford: Blackwell.

Kumar, K. (1995). *From Post-Industrial to Postmodern Society*. Oxford: Blackwell.

Lewis, J. and Meredith, B. (1988). *Daughters Who Care*. London: Routledge.

McKeown, T. (1980). *The Role of Medicine: Dream, Mirage or Nemesis*, 2nd edn. Oxford: Blackwell.

Miles, A. (1991). *Women, Health and Medicine*. Milton Keynes: Open University Press.

Murphy, E. (1993). *Services for Elderly People: Annual Review of Health Care Policy*. London: King's Fund Institute.

Oakley, A. (1974). *Housewife*. London: Allen Lane.

Office of Population Censuses and Surveys (1994). *Population Trends*, **75**: 10–12.

Ory, M. and Bond, K. (1989). *Ageing and Health Care – Social Science and Policy Perspectives*. London: Routledge.

Phillimore, P. (1989). *Shortened Lives: Premature Death in North Tyneside* (Bristol Papers in Applied Social Studies 12). University of Bristol.

Robine, J.M. and Ritchie, K. (1991). Healthy life expectancy: evaluation of a global indicator of change in population health. *British Medical Journal*, **302**: 457–60.

Thompson, D. (1993). *Generations, Justice and the Aged in the 1990s* (Economic Equation Resource Paper). London: Age Concern.

Tunnicliffe, H., Coyle, G. and More, W. (1993). *ABC of Community Care: What Its Really All About*. Birmingham: PEPAR Publications.

Victor, C. (1994). *Old Age in Modern Society*. London: Chapman & Hall.

Walker, A. (1993). *The Responsibilities of the State and the Individual* (Economic Equation Resource Paper). London: Age Concern.

Wenger, C. (1984). *The Supportive Network: Coping with Old Age*. London: Allen & Unwin.

Wilmott, P. (1986). *Social Networks: Informal Care and the Public Policy* (Research Report 665). London: Policy Studies Institute.

Further Reading ▲ ▲ ▲

Coleman, D. and Salt, J. (1992). *The British Population: Patterns, Trends and Processes*. Oxford: Oxford University Press.

McCreadie, C. (1994). *Planning and updating community care plans*. Ageing Update Conference Proceedings. London: Age Concern Institute of Gerontology.

Wolfe, V. R. (1993). *The coming health crisis*. Chicago: Chicago University Press.

10

Epidemiology

David Marsland and Athena Leoussi

LEARNING OBJECTIVES

After studying this chapter you should:

- Understand the key concepts and the methods of the discipline of epidemiology
- Understand the importance of epidemiological knowledge and methods for the health professions

INTRODUCTION

Epidemiology is an important and useful discipline for health professionals. It draws on and synthesizes the knowledge produced by biologists, psychologists, sociologists, economists, and statisticians. It focuses this complicated knowledge on the practical task of describing and explaining patterns of health and illness. Epidemiology consists of concepts, principles and methods, for every disease and illness known. Because of the complexity of the subject it is useful to start with a clear definition:

> Epidemiology investigates patterns of health and illness and the forces which shape them.

To explore the meaning of this definition, it is useful to consider an example of epidemiological discovery (see Case Study 10.1). This case study displays the three key elements of epidemiology listed in Box 10.1.

Case Study

Case Study 10.1

In the mid-nineteenth century, London was struck by epidemic waves of cholera. Its causes were estabished and a remedy was found by means of epidemiological methods.

During the 1854 epidemic, described as 'the most terrible outbreak of cholera which ever occurred in this kingdom', John Snow (1813–58) collected the statistics of mortality from cholera and collated them to permit comparisons of death rates in areas supplied by different water supply companies. He was able to demonstrate that death rates in streets and houses supplied by one company were massively higher than elsewhere.

Then he undertook further and more detailed analysis of the figures, including careful comparisons designed to check out and eliminate other possible causes of the epidemic which had been suggested by theories different from his own. He also arranged for deliberate manipulation of the water supply in order to test out his hypotheses experimentally.

By these means, he proved conclusively that cholera was caused by water-borne infection. He thus demonstrated to the politicians and the people of London the necessity of public health measures to control the quality of water and to prevent its pollution (Winslow, 1980).

Box 10.1 *The three key elements of epidemiology*

- Identification of a statistical pattern of the distribution of a disease.
- Careful objective use of research designs and methods of statistical analysis.
- Systematic analysis of the pattern to discover statistical associations and causal links.

Epidemiology's mission falls into two parts, both aimed at controlling and preventing illness and optimizing the population's health. The first is to discover and describe patterns and variations in mortality, morbidity, handicap, and subjectively perceived health status. The second task is to make sense of these patterns, and to explain them.

PATTERNS OF HEALTH AND ILLNESS

Epidemiology does not deal directly with individual cases. It is essentially a statistical discipline, focusing on the patterning of health and illness in particular populations. The patterns investigated are defined in terms of incidence rates and prevalence rates of mortality and morbidity within different populations. The accuracy and validity of the descriptions of these patterns depends on the quality of the health indicators used. Careful analysis of these terms is essential for an adequate understanding.

Rates and epidemiology

Because epidemiological studies make comparisons and discover differences, the discipline deals not in absolute numbers but in rates. Some of the Key rates in epidemiology are birth rates, fertility rates, infant mortality rates, disease specific mortality rates, and survival and success rates in relation to treatments.

Suppose that we wish to investigate the changing pattern of fatal traffic accidents in Britain between 1900 and 1990. Between these two dates, the population has increased and the number of vehicles has increased enormously, as has the mileage driven. A comparison of the simple absolute figures would be completely misleading. Therefore a rate would be defined and calculated which could legitimately be compared – perhaps the number of deaths per year per vehicle mile.

As Rose and Barker (1986) state: 'Rates are the hallmark of epidemiology. For they form the basis of comparison between groups'. Most rates take the form:

$$\frac{\text{Numerator}}{\text{Denominator}} = \frac{\text{Frequency of observed event (illness, etc.).}}{\text{Total number among whom this event might occur.}}$$

Rates have to be expressed as proportions. Moreover, the denominator has to be correct and constant if comparisons are to be valid. Apparently interesting changes are often caused by errors with denominators. For example, if the number of sports injuries apparently increased dramatically, it would probably be because the number of people playing sport had increased, with the real *rate* of sports injury remaining constant or even actually decreasing.

Incidence and prevalence

All rates can be expressed as either incidence rates or prevalence rates. Great care must be taken not to confuse the two:

- The *incidence rate* is the proportion of a defined population developing a condition within a stated period.
- The *prevalence rate* is the proportion of a defined group having a condition at any one point in time.

Crude rates, specific rates, and standardization

All rates may be expressed as crude or specific rates. For example, the crude mortality rate is a measure of the death rate for the whole population. This usually needs refining to cause, age or sex specific rates (e.g. deaths from car accidents). The more refined and specific the rate, the more accurate and meaningful will comparisons over time or place become.

Rose and Barker (1986) suggest: 'Crude rates are not false, but they are often misleading, because they fail to take into account other variables, particularly age'. Thus a much higher crude death rate would be expected in Bournemouth, a retirement town where the average age may be 60+, than in Basildon, a new town with a youthful population. Age-specific death rates, standardized to take account of age variability, would be needed if a comparison of geriatric care in the two communities were to be performed.

The most familiar example of standardization is provided by unemployment figures. Regardless of other influences, unemployment in Britain tends to increase in the winter months and improve during the better weather. In order to facilitate comparisons throughout the year, the rates are standardized by means of a seasonal adjustment factor based on past trends. Similar adjustments and corrections are applied to many rates to make them more accurate and more genuinely comparable.

Classification

Rates, incidence and prevalence as technical concepts are of little value if observations and measurements are of poor quality. Health and healthcare variables must be defined and appropriate indicators must be used in their measurement. At the very beginning it is necessary to make the terminology and classification of diseases, illnesses and health conditions comprehensive and precise. The best current classification system is the World Health Organization's International Classification of Diseases (1992). This is used as the basis of all official health statistics.

Such classifications, and measurement systems based on them, need continuous revision and augmentation. Many topics are not covered, and new health problems are coming to light all the time. Wherever possible, researchers should use established, well-tested indicators whose validity and reliability have been demonstrated (Bowling, 1991, 1993).

DIMENSIONS OF HEALTH AND ILLNESS

There are four main dimensions of health and illness whose rates and patterning provide the focus of investigation. These are: mortality, morbidity, handicap, and felt condition.

Mortality: number of deaths in a period

Mortality is usually measured as the annual incidence of death per thousand or hundred thousand of a given population. From it is calculated *life expectancy*. As McNeill (1991) says, with life expectancy now so much increased in advanced societies, mortality rates are less useful indicators of health than they were earlier. Between 1846/50 and 1981/85 the crude death rate for Britain fell from 23.3 to 11.7 per cent.

Nevertheless, mortality rates are still basic and important data in epidemiological studies, especially versions more refined than the crude rate, and the relations between mortality rates and particular causes of death. Especially important and useful is the age-specific death rate, including rates for infant, neonatal and perinatal mortality. Other age-group death rates are important in relation to particular fields of study; examples are the mortality rate of the elderly in relation to hypothermia, or of the working-age population in relation to studies of stress and occupational health, or of teenagers in relation to suicide.

The major source of information for mortality rates is death certificates, which have been required in relation to every death in Britain since the 1840s. Britain is fortunate in having very reliable mortality statistics. Nevertheless there are problems. The cause of death recorded on the certificate is, except in suspicious circumstances, purely the judgement of one doctor. In addition to mistakes, there may sometimes be instances of 'disguises' – precipitating causes hidden by secondary

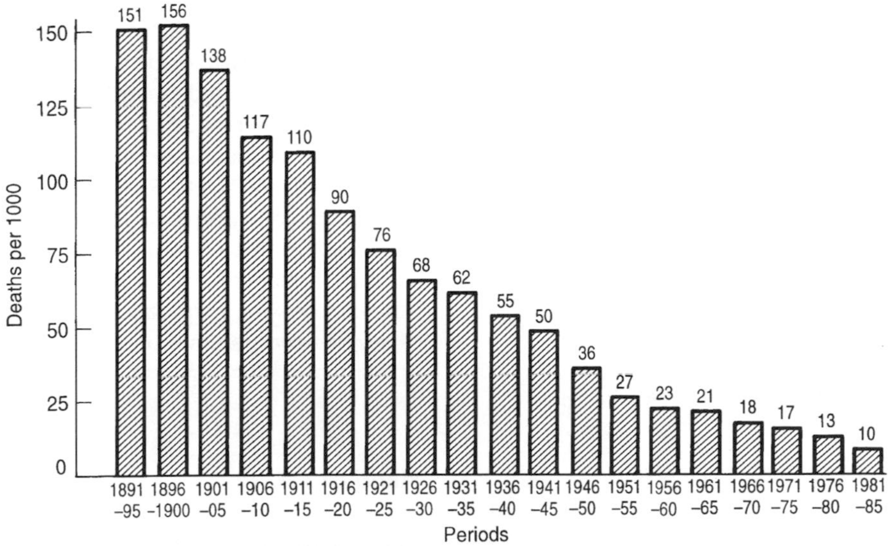

Figure 10.1 *Infant mortality: deaths at under one year per 1000 live births, England and Wales, derived from OPCS (1989)*

disease, and embarrassing causes cloaked in more respectable descriptions.

The general and continuing trend in Britain since the beginning of industrialization and modernization is for mortality rates to fall, and to become more and more homogeneous throughout the whole population; hence the improving life expectancy and rapidly increasing incidence of very old age. Today the over-85s are counted rather than the over-65s. Infant death rates – deaths of infants aged under one year per thousand live births – have followed a similar pattern on an even steeper curve of improvement, plunging from 150 per 1000 for the period 1846/75 to below 10 per 1000 in recent years. Details of this fundamental change in the population structure are set out in Figure 10.1.

Morbidity: diseases

Important variations in death rates do remain. This can be seen between income groups and occupations, in different countries, and between distinct causes of death. As infectious diseases are conquered, and standards of living and diet improve, mortality rates decrease, life expectancy lengthens, and healthcare has to focus on 'diseases of affluence' – cancer, heart disease, and mental illness – and on the needs of the elderly (see Table 10.1).

The primary sources of morbidity statistics are GP records, hospital records, the regular 10% In-Patient Hospital Enquiry, and specialized surveys (Abramson, 1990).

In general, British morbidity statistics are good compared with those of most other countries (Farmer and Miller, 1991). Current reforms in health and community care, the growth of screening, and the impact of the Acheson Report on Community Health (1988) – with its demand for coherent, regular health surveillance – should improve quality still further. However, psychiatric illness remains particularly difficult to measure, owing to changing understandings and conflicting interpretations of the data (Klerman, 1987).

There seem to be no general overall patterns of morbidity that can be identified, no equivalent of the secular decline in mortality rates. As rates for some conditions have decreased almost to vanishing point (tuberculosis, poliomyelitis, and rickets), others have soared (cancer, heart disease, motor accident injuries).

Table 10.1 *The overall pattern of morbidity: 'Key areas and targets' proposed in* Health of the Nation *(Department of Health, 1992)*

Causes of substantial mortality
- Coronary heart disease
- Stroke
- Cancers
- Accidents

Causes of substantial ill-health
- Mental health
- Diabetes
- Asthma

Factors that contribute to mortality, ill-health and healthy living
- Smoking
- Diet and alcohol
- Physical exercise

Areas where there is clear scope for improvement
- Health of pregnant women, infants and children
- Rehabilitation services for people with a disability
- Environmental quality

Areas where there is great potential for harm
- HIV/AIDS
- Other communicable diseases
- Food safety

Learning Activity 1 ◆ ◆ ◆

Scan the broadsheet daily and Sunday newspapers for the past month (or the past 6 months if you have access to a CD–ROM in your library). Find any articles that refer to epidemiology and epidemiological studies, and pick six that interest you. There will be quite a few to choose from – on the incidence and causes of cancer, heart disease, asthma, HIV/AIDS, etc. Read them carefully, and note down any problems you have with the terminology, the concepts, or the statistics included. Use your queries to guide your study of the rest of the chapter. You might also like to look out for television programmes on epidemiological topics.

Handicap

After mortality and general morbidity, handicap is the third major dimension of epidemiological focus.

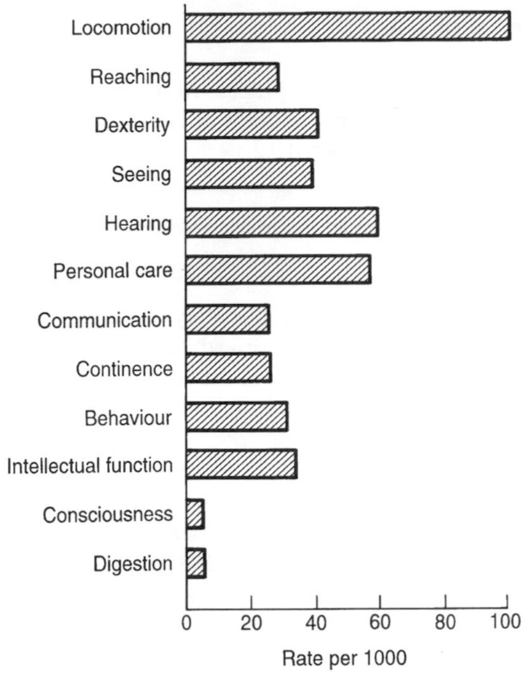

Figure 10.2 *Prevalence of adult (16+) disability: rate per 1000 of population, Great Britain, 1985, derived from OPCS (1988)*

Physical and mental handicap have long been neglected in healthcare. Despite recent improvements, neglect in care has been paralleled by under-development of research (Marsland *et al.*, 1994).

Handicap as a health concept is fraught with theoretical, conceptual and definitional problems. There is a vast range of conditions, from severe mental and physical handicaps, to moderate levels of deafness or blindness as part of the natural ageing process.

Further useful information on handicaps can be found in the publication *The Prevalence of Disability among Adults* (OPCS, 1988), which is based on an extensive national survey. Methodological backing is provided in another publication, the *Survey Research Methods Newsletter* (SCPR, 1989), which contains a valuable analysis of the International Classification of Impairments, Disabilities and Handicaps, an analysis of how changes in social policy affect the definition and meaning of disability, and a report of the methodology of the 1988 OPCS survey. For examples of the prevalence of disabilities in the UK, see Figure 10.2.

Felt condition

There is one further key dimension of epidemiological data which, although an aspect of morbidity, merits separate attention. This is self-reported health status or 'felt condition'. Increasingly the more objective data provided by medical records are being complemented by the results of studies which seek from respondents their own view of their past or current health.

Self-report studies of health are disclosing a somewhat worse and more complex picture of the health of the nation than is to be derived from the records. An important instance is provided by the health section of the official annual *General Household Survey* (see Table

Table 10.2 *Self-reported general health by age and sex (percentages)*

Self-reported general health	Age range							Totals
	16–24	25–34	35–44	45–54	55–64	65–74	75 and over	
Men								
Very good	37	48	43	40	23	30	13	36
Good	48	42	43	45	46	29	39	42
Fair	15	9	11	12	24	27	39	17
Bad	-	1	2	3	5	12	8	4
Very bad	-	0	1	0	1	2	1	1
Women								
Very good	36	41	40	36	30	20	16	33
Good	48	43	45	39	44	35	34	42
Fair	15	14	12	18	22	37	39	21
Bad	0	1	3	6	3	6	9	4
Very bad	0	1	0	1	1	3	2	1

Source: Health Survey for England 1991, Department of Health, 1993, p. 207.

10.2). Analysis of how ordinary people feel about their own health is a crucial dimension of epidemiological research (Jenkinson, 1994).

EXPLAINING PATTERNS OF HEALTH AND ILLNESS

The shaping forces

Influence processes affecting human conditions and behaviour are rarely simple. They usually involve long chains or multiple complexes of causal factors which have to be carefully disentangled. This is illustrated in Figure 10.3 – itself much simplified – of the interacting factors implicated in the causation of lung cancer. All of the distinct factors included in the diagram play some key role, and the direction of causal influence goes in several directions.

Bearing in mind that the idea of causality is quite complicated, a simple clarification could be that one factor might be associated with another factor without causing it. For example, rain-making ceremonies may, sometimes and coincidentally, be followed by rain. But they do not cause rain; the real cause of the rain is the operation of natural meteorological forces. Similar mistakes can be made by health researchers. To avoid mistakes, research studies have to be very carefully designed so as to disentangle genuine causes from irrelevant coincidences.

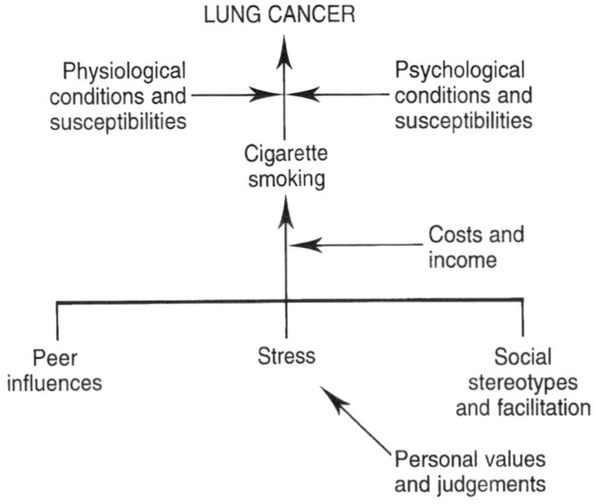

Figure 10.3 *Interacting factors causing cancer*

Potential pitfalls

There are three potential pitfalls which need to be avoided when explaining patterns of health and illness. These are described in Box 10.2.

Box 10.2 *Pitfalls to avoid in explaining patterns of health and illness*

- 'Crying wolf' by making explanatory claims too early, with insufficient evidence, or without careful qualifications about probabilities, statistical limitations, and causal complexities (Lee, 1994).
- Focusing explanations on deep-level causes that cannot be influenced at all, or on factors whose control would involve economic or social costs and counter-productive side-effects which would outweigh any likely benefits (Black, 1980)
- Being too cautious or too conservative, and as a result allowing a health problem to go out of control (Barker and Rose, 1990).

Multicausality of health and illness

Epidemiology explores the whole range of influences on health and illness – the impacts of biological, psychological and social forces and of the inter-relationships between them. Farmer and Miller (1991) give a useful picture of the complex explanatory resources of epidemiology (see Figure 10.4).

Figure 10.4 shows how epidemiologists must always take into account in their explanations of patterns of health and illness a wide range of distinct factors and their interactions. Mistakes occur if social and other environmental influences, pathogenic substances of all sorts, or the widely varying susceptibility of potential victims are neglected. Consider, for example, the current public debate about HIV/AIDS, or childhood leukaemia.

The relevant biophysical variables, which are relatively easy to isolate in the laboratory, are mostly well-defined, well-measured and well-understood. In consequence, the calculation of precise 'dose–response relationships' characterizing one-for-one relationships between a risk agent (such as mercury) and a health effect (here mercury poisoning) is relatively straightforward, allowing accurate computation of risk levels and coherent development of effective control measures.

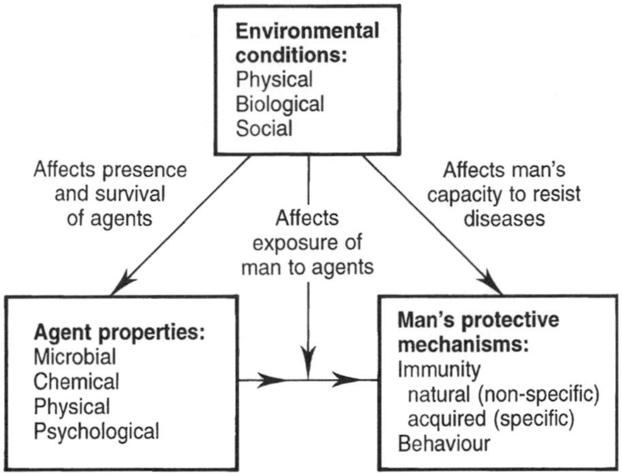

Figure 10.4 *Interactions of agent, host and the environment (Farmer and Miller, 1991)*

The psychosocial domain offers an almost complete contrast. Here the emphasis is on a mixture of qualitative and quantitative methods rather than purely quantitative methods. Hence these areas rarely answer established 'canons of epidemiological proof' (Bradford Hill, 1977). With social and cultural variables, the methodology is still very crude. As a result, epidemiologists' understanding of the considerable influence of social forces on patterns of health and illness is very much under-developed.

Table 10.3 sets out data on causes of death in different societies to explore whether health is worse in capitalist than in socialist societies. Hart's analysis refutes the hypothesis, but it also reveals graphically how little is known about the social causes of the simplest patterns of health and illness. Why, for example, is the Hungarian rate of suicide so enormously high compared with any of the others? Why is the British stomach cancer rate so low? It is quite easy to identify large differences in the patterning of health in different countries, explaining them is much harder. Consideration needs to be given to levels of economic development, standards of living, health policies, the political regime, variations in culture and basic values, educational standards, and many other factors. None of these is as yet clearly defined, carefully measured, or better than half-understood (Marsland, 1992).

Consider also Figure 10.5, which sets out mortality rates for adults in the six occupational class groupings. Here, compared with Table 10.3, there would seem to be a clear, definite finding about the patterning of health and illness: in accordance with the argument first presented in the Black Report (1980) on 'health inequalities', the enormous impact of poverty on health is demonstrated. But as Le Fanu (1993) shows, the effect is more modest and more complex than social scientists typically claim. In epidemiological terms, other factors besides 'poverty' are certainly involved – including biological susceptibilities, lifestyle choices, and behavioural patterns. The impact of poverty is probably rather modest.

Some sociologists would disagree with our conclusion (see Chapter 6). However, the sociological knowledge epidemiologists can draw on is still scientifically under-developed. Epidemiologists are currently working on clarifying the concept of poverty, on investigating the relative power of psychological and social forces, and on unravelling the key role of genetic influences on health and illness (Nesse and Williams, 1995; Marsland and Leoussi, 1996).

Table 10.3 *Causes of death* in different societies (Hart, 1985)*

	Czeckoslovakia	Hungary	Italy	Spain	England and Wales
All causes	108	108	90	90	93
Lung cancer	200	148	140	97	222
Stomach cancer	195	218	161	151	117
Circulatory disease (males)	128	238	98	107	102
Accidents (males)	240	230	200	179	119
Accidents (excluding traffic)	242	236	136	177	102
Suicide	240	374	59	46	76

* Standard mortality ratios (SMRs) derived from a base of England and Wales, 1951–1975 = 100

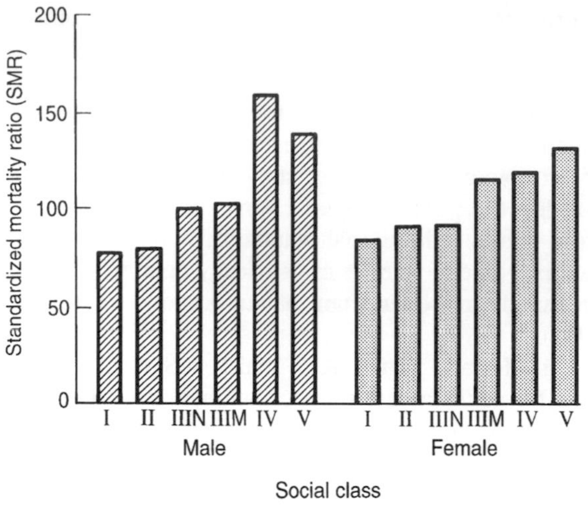

Figure 10.5 *Mortality by occupational class and age (Occupational Mortality 1970–72, HMSO, 1978)*

EPIDEMIOLOGICAL METHODS

Within the discipline of epidemiology there is a core of principles and methods (Beaglehole *et al.*, 1993). Broadly, three types of study may be identified: descriptive, analytic, and intervention (Farmer and Miller, 1991). Each method serves a different purpose, and frequently the detailed investigation of a disease involves undertaking several studies of different types.

> **Learning Activity 2 ◆ ◆ ◆**
>
> When you have read the rest of this section carefully, you should re-examine some of the research papers about health and illness you have read recently. Try to decide what sort of research design their authors used, and whether they were appropriate or adequate.

DESCRIPTIVE STUDIES

These discover the patterns of distribution of disease in the population. Correlations with factors influencing these patterns may be identified, but it is inappropriate to establish causality, or even definite linkage.

ANALYTIC STUDIES

These are carefully designed to test specific hypotheses. There are two main subtypes of analytic studies – cohort studies and case–control studies. The cohort study, the stronger of the two methods, has been developed for *prospectively* identifying causes and effects accurately without experimental intervention. Case–control studies are *retrospective*, studying people who have already been exposed to disease.

INTERVENTION STUDIES

These presume earlier descriptive and analytic studies of the same topic. They are concerned with assessing the efficacy and safety of healthcare interventions (such as treatment, prevention, control, and care delivery) and the comparative effectiveness of different interventions. The key research design for intervention studies is the clinical trial. Intervention studies take the form of field experiments, providing as a result reliable and precise conclusions about the details of cause and effect.

CHOOSING A RESEARCH DESIGN

DESCRIPTIVE STUDIES

Descriptive epidemiological studies adopt the simplest and most basic research design. By using comprehensive random sampling, an accurate, representative picture is produced of the incidence and prevalence of health and illness in particular populations. This is always the essential first step towards epidemiological understanding.

Descriptive studies can also generate *suggestions* and *tentative hypotheses* to explain the patterns they describe, but they can never provide trustworthy analyses of the causes and effects. For that, the stronger research design of analytic studies (cohort or case–control) and interventional studies are used.

COHORT STUDIES

Results must always be treated more tentatively than the experimental results of intervention studies. In a cohort study, a set of people identified by some hypothetically relevant characteristic is carefully studied prospectively (i.e. into the future), and the frequency of occurrence of the disease or illness condition being studied is observed. Comparison is made of the different rates of diseases in subgroups identified beforehand by the preselected characteristics. Allowing for the misleading effects of confounding variables (other characteristics which might spoil the comparison), the cohort design permits strong, confident inferences about the causes of disease and ill-health. Farmer and Miller use Sir Geoffrey Doll's famous

Table 10.4 *Cohort study data from Doll and Hill (1964)*

	Number in study	Died within 7 years	Death rate per 1000 over 7 years
Cigarette smokers	25 769	133	5.16
Non-smokers	5 439	3	0.55

Relative risk in cigarette smokers (5.16/0.55) = 9.38
Attributable risk in cigarette smokers (5.16 − 0.55) = 4.61 per 1000

studies of cancer to illustrate the power of cohort designs (see Table 10.4).

The researchers carefully selected appropriate samples of smokers and non-smokers, and then studied their lives over the following seven years. This enabled them to conclude that the much higher death rates among smokers could be securely attributed to the effects of smoking rather than to any other factors. The death rate was more than nine times higher among smokers (the relative risk), and the risk specifically attributable to smoking was as high as 4.6 per thousand. There are still no experimental data about the links between smoking and lung cancer, but Doll and Hill's epidemiological study in 1964 was so well designed that their conclusions about the key causal role of smoking in the causation of lung cancer is indisputable.

CASE–CONTROL STUDIES

These are less powerful than the cohort study. In contrast to cohort studies, case–control studies are retrospective. The focus is on people who are identified as already having the disease being studied. Histories of exposure to relevant harmful agents are taken by interviews, questionnaires, or from records. Then the same data are collected from a control group – people known not to have the disease, but in other ways as similar as possible. Identification of causes is then made by comparing the frequencies of influence factors in the two groups.

Case–control studies are much quicker and considerably cheaper than cohort studies. On the other hand, case–control studies are substantially less powerful and considerably less reliable than cohort studies. The selection of cases and matching controls has to be done with great skill, care and precision, otherwise the results can be entirely spurious and the study worthless.

Even at their best, case–control designs can never altogether exclude mistaken inferences, and they can never properly be used, as cohort study designs can, as a basis for calculating risk levels. Many recent instances of mistakes in epidemiology and of judgements that have been embarrassingly reversed after further investigation have been occasioned by over-easy reliance on case–control study designs. Cohort studies are in almost all instances to be preferred.

INTERVENTION STUDIES

Intervention studies are more powerful than even the best analytic studies. In the form of clinical trials organized as large-scale experiments, they provide reliable and precise analyses of the causes of health and illness conditions and of the impacts of agents on health and illness.

This approach does have drawbacks, however, as it is difficult, expensive, and fraught with severe ethical problems. Its application is strictly limited. It would hardly be acceptable to assign groups of people on a random basis to a lifetime of heavy smoking or to prolonged periods of unemployment to strengthen the understanding of causal effects!

Even so, clinical trials extended to a wide range of explanatory factors should provide answers to key questions in the long run. Ideally, epidemiological research should move, in relation to every kind of health and illness condition, from descriptive studies to analytic studies, and within this category from case–control to cohort studies, and beyond analytic studies into the clinical trial and social experimental arena of intervention studies.

SUMMARY

According to Rose and Barker (1986), 'No one would expect to understand a disease without knowledge of its clinical findings and pathology, but a surprising number of doctors remain ignorant of another important aspect – the study of disease in relation to populations.' The necessity for health professionals to fill this gap in their knowledge by understanding epidemiology is important. This involves:

- a thorough grasp of techniques of data collection and interpretation;
- familiarity with key technical concepts, particularly rates, incidence, prevalence, and types of research design;
- commitment to scientific rigour.

Epidemiology is able to contribute to the work of health professions by its relevance to public policy and to practical action. For example, four out of the six objectives specified in *The Health of the Nation* (Department of Health, 1991) require epidemiological data as a means of defining needs, and as evidence about the outcomes and effectiveness of healthcare.

If the quality of the NHS is to continue to improve, increasing attention will need to be given to epidemiological data. If healthcare professionals are to continue improving the effectiveness of their specialist professional interventions, they must equip themselves with a thorough understanding of the epidemiological perspective. An example of this trend is the introduction of evidence-based medicine.

Key Points

- Epidemiology requires and enables comparisons over time, place, and cases.
- Epidemiology provides a body of knowledge about patterns of distribution of health and illness.
- Epidemiology provides approaches and methods that offer a broad understanding of the causes and natural history of illnesses.
- Epidemiology supplies evidence for testing and challenging treatment and intervention strategies that may be merely conventional or rest purely on established power and status relations in healthcare teams.
- Epidemiology plays an increasingly important role in evaluation of the safety and usefulness of healthcare interventions.

References

Abramson, J.A. (1990). *Survey Methods in Community Medicine.* Edinburgh: Churchill Livingstone.

Acheson, D. (chairman) (1988). *Public Health in England: Report of the Committee of Enquiry into the Future of the Public Health Function.* London: HMSO.

Barker, D.J.P. and Rose, G. (1990). *Epidemiology in Medical Practice*, 4th edn. Edinburgh: Churchill Livingstone.

Beaglehole, R., Bonita, R. and Kjellstrom, T. (1993). *Basic Epidemiology.* Geneva: World Health Organization.

Black, D. (1980). *Inequalities in Health: Report of a Research Working Group Chaired by Sir Douglas Black.* London: HMSO.

Bowling, A. (1991). *Measuring Health.* Buckingham: Open University Press.

Bowling, A. (1993). *Measuring Disease.* Buckingham: Open University Press.

Bradford Hill, A. (1977). *A Short Textbook of Medical Statistics.* London: Edward Arnold.

Department of Health (1992). *The Health of the Nation.* London: HMSO.

Doll, R. and Hill, A. (1964). Mortality in relation to smoking. *British Medical Journal*, **1**: 1399–410 and 1460–7.

Farmer, R. and Miller, D. (1991). *Lecture Notes on Epidemiology and Public Health Medicine*, 3rd edn. Oxford: Blackwell.

Hart, N. (1985). *The Sociology of Health and Medicine.* Causeway Books. Ormskirk, Lancashire.

Jenkinson, C. (ed.) (1994). *Measuring Health and Medical Outcomes.* Buckingham: Open University Press.

Jones, D. (ed.) (1992). *Invisible Enemies: Epidemics and Plagues through History.* London: Channel 4 Television.

Klerman, G.L. (1987). Psychiatric epidemiology and mental health policy, In: Levine, S. and Lilienfeld, A. (eds), *Epidemiology and Health Policy.* London: Tavistock.

Lee, P. (1994). The need for caution in interpreting low-level risks reported by epidemiologists, In: Le Fanu, J. (ed.), *Preventionitis.* London: Social Affairs Units.

Le Fanu, J. (1993). *A Phantom Carnage: The Myth that Low Income Kills.* London: Social Affairs Unit.

Marsland, D. (1992). Methodological weakness in British social science, In: Cang, S. (ed.), *Festschrift for Elliot Jaques.* Wahsington DC, USA: Cason-Hall.

Marsland, D., Leoussi, A.S. and Norcross, P. (1994). Disability abated: audio-cassettes for the visually impaired. *Journal of the Royal Society of Health*, **114**: 312–15.

Marsland, D. and Leoussi, A.S. (in press). Social misconstruction: inattention to biology by sociologists. *American Sociologist.*

McNeill, P. (1991). *Society Today.* Basingstoke: Macmillan.

Nesse, R. and Williams, G.C. (1995). *Evolution and Healing.* London: Weidenfield & Nicholson.

Office of Population Censuses and Surveys (1988). *The Prevalence of Disability among Adults.* London: HMSO.

Office of Population Censuses and Surveys (1989). *Mortality Statistics 1841–1985.* London: HMSO.

Rose, G. and Barker, D.J.P. (1986). Epidemiology for the uninitiated. London: *British Medical Journal.*

SCPR (1989). *Survey Research Methods Newsletter*, autumn (Social and Community Planning Research).

Winslow, C.-E.A. (1980). *The Conquest of Epidemic Disease: A Chapter in the History of Ideas.* University of Wisconsin Press. Madison, Wisconsin, USA.

World Health Organization 1980: *International Classification of Impairments, Disabilities, and Handicaps.* Geneva: WHO.

World Health Organization 1992: *International Statistical Classification of Diseases and Health Related Problems*, 10th revision. Geneva: WHO.

Further Reading

Beaglehole, R. *et al.* (eds) (1993). *Basic Epidemiology.* Geneva: WHO.

Farmer, R. and Miller, D. (1991). *Lecture Notes on Epidemiology and Community Medicine*, 3rd edn. Oxford: Blackwell.

Levine, S. and Lilienfeld, A. (eds) (1987). *Epidemiology and Health Policy.* London: Tavistock.

11

Professions and Professionalism

Roger Gomm

LEARNING OBJECTIVES

After studying this chapter you should:

- Be able to recognise a 'professional' occupation as one which presents itself as expert and trustworthy with a rightful monopoly to certain desirable kinds of work
- Be able to describe three different pictures of the relationship between professional groups and the public interest
- Be in a position to discuss why multiprofessional 'teamwork' usually seems so difficult
- Be able to evaluate recent trends in social administration that are tending to erode the discretion, autonomy and influence enjoyed by professional groups

INTRODUCTION

'Professions allied to medicine' (PAMs) often represent themselves as members of 'professional' occupations. When this claim is made, individuals point to qualities such as the possession of rare skills, the trustworthiness of occupation members and a guarantee of good service to users of their service. All these are aspects of 'professionalism', but in the last resort, professions are occupations.

An important issue is how certain areas of work become defined as the kind done by a particular occupational group, and not by another. Why, for example, do dentists look after teeth, chiropodists and podiatrists look after feet, but the rest of the body is looked after by doctors? And what is it that makes the difference between the professions of chiropodist and podiatrist, or chiropodist and footcare assistant? The answer to this question is not to be found in the nature of feet, but in the way in which occupational groups jostle with each other to capture particular areas of work for themselves.

PROFESSIONAL TRAITS AND PROFESSIONAL CLAIMS

Attempts to define a truly 'professional' occupation usually generate lists of characteristics, such as that in Box 11.1.

Lists like this do capture something of the everyday notion of 'profession', but they always founder on the issue of how much of each characteristic an occupation has to show before it can be called a profession. Generously interpreted, the list in Box 11.1 might apply

Box 11.1 *Professional traits (based on Millerson, 1964)*

Professions are occupations:

- that have a philosophy of public service and altruism;
- that have skills based on theoretical knowledge derived from research;
- where members receive an extensive period of education and training prior to practising;
- where members are tested for their competence before being allowed to practise;
- where there is an explicit code of conduct for practice;
- where the occupational group is allowed to regulate itself.

to driving instructors, funeral directors, and even to highly skilled manual workers such as coalminers.

Listing traits misses a most important point about professionalism – namely, that professionalism is something that is *claimed*.

Licence and mandate

One answer to the question 'What is a profession?' is that it is an occupational group that *claims* to be a profession. Everett Hughes (1993) writes:

> 'An occupation consists in part in the implied or explicit *licence* that some people claim and are given to carry out certain activities rather different from those of other people and do so in exchange for money, goods, or services. Generally, if the people in the occupation have any sense of identity and solidarity, they will also claim a *mandate* to define – not merely for themselves, but for others as well – proper conduct with respect to matters concerning their work.'

This could be expressed more briefly as: 'We have the right to do this work: others don't (the licence). And we (and not others) have the right to say how it should be done (the mandate).'

Professions differ from other occupations in the degree to which they claim that their licences and mandates are 'for the public good'. Profession-claiming is easiest to see when an occupational group is attempting to keep outsiders out. For example, consider the following extract from *Therapy Weekly* (13 January 1994) under the headline 'Campaign steps up over physiotherapy title':

> 'Chartered physiotherapists have been asked to find examples of damage caused by people who are not chartered practising as physiotherapists. . . . They will be presented to the health secretary later this year by the Chartered Society for Physiotherapy in an effort to persuade ministers that a change in the law is needed to protect the public.'

The occupational groups most people think of as being 'professions' are those that have been able to achieve the best licences and mandates. Thus, for example, doctors, lawyers and nurses in the UK do have government backing by Acts of Parliament to achieve licences and mandates (see Box 11.2).

Other occupational groups who claim to be professionals, including the PAMs, have been much less successful in establishing such a monopoly. For most of the latter, only employment in the NHS requires state registration – private practice does not, and the regulation of these occupations is not with their professional associations but with a committee of Privy Council.

Box 11.2 *A strong mandate backed by Act of Parliament*

Professions can:

- monopolize certain areas of work as their own;
- prohibit others from doing that work;
- make impersonating a member of the profession a criminal offence;
- define for themselves and others how the work ought to be performed;
- select new entrants;
- define the curriculum and assessment for training;
- set and police codes of conduct for practice and discipline.

Look again at the list of 'professional traits' in Box 11.1, and the kind of bargaining with governments which goes on when an occupational group claims to be 'professional' can be seen. The occupational group, in effect, says to the government, 'it will serve the public interest if you allow us to develop or keep these traits'.

Professionalism has been represented as a persuasive argument used by some occupational groups in a struggle to secure a monopoly over certain desirable kinds of work. Is this mere rhetoric? There are two main questions to keep in mind. The first is whether the knowledge and expertise concentrated in a 'professional' group is really so special and esoteric that only a select few can acquire it and practise it. Bear in mind that most of the things that most professionals do, for most of their time, do not actually require the long periods of training they receive. Consider the following extract, again taken from *Therapy Weekly* (7 July 1994):

> 'I have heard it argued that only a qualified Occupational Therapist (OT) has the knowledge to assess for, and provide, bath aids. But this is professional nonsense in my view, and does nothing to enhance the status of our profession. . . . In social services, there is certainly a growing need for specialist OT skills which exceeds current staffing level. But there is also an overwhelming demand for low level support . . .' (Tim Barnes, Community Occupational Therapist)

Here a strategy common in professional politics can be seen; that of subcontracting mundane tasks to 'non-professional' workers, but retaining professional control over them.

The second question is whether and how far occupational groups can be trusted to regulate their own affairs 'for the public good'. If either, of these questions is answered in the negative, then professionalism just looks like a higher class version of the kinds of restrictive practices common among trade unions.

Professions and the social structure

There are three divergent answers to the question of whether professionalism is in the public interest.

TRUSTWORTHY PROFESSIONALS AND THE DIVISION OF LABOUR

One view is that most congenial to profession-claiming occupations themselves. Progress is seen in terms of the growth of knowledge. No one can know all there is to know, so specialization becomes inevitable. Professional occupations are one kind of necessary specialization. But expertise is power, and therefore it is necessary that expert groups deny themselves opportunities to exploit the less knowledgeable and do so by adopting a philosophy of public service and altruism – devising professional codes of conduct, recruiting only those of good moral character, and disciplining deviant members of the occupation. In this version, then, both the value of the expertise claimed by the occupational group, and the trustworthiness of the occupational group, tend to be taken for granted. This is a view of professional occupations widely held by sociologists until the 1960s, but less so today (e.g. see Parsons, 1952, pp. 439–54).

PROFESSIONALS AS MONOPOLISTS

George Bernard Shaw's claim that 'professions are conspiracies against the laity' sums up this view (Shaw, 1946). The professional group monopolizes some kinds of knowledge, codes it in difficult language, shrouds it in mystery, excludes other people from knowing it or practising it, creates a position for itself where members of the occupation benefit from the ignorance of other people, and makes people dependent on professionals by preventing them doing things for themselves (Illich, 1975). To hold this view it is not necessary to assume that professionals are knowingly manipulative and conspiratorial. Exactly the same effects might be created by professional groups genuinely believing that their practice was in the best interests of 'the laity'.

PROFESSIONS AS INSTRUMENTS OF POWER

A third view argues that occupational groups achieve their privileged positions in proportion to the extent to which they serve the interests of other powerful groups.

Marxist writers such as Terry Johnson (1972) or Vicente Navarro (1976) have viewed the professions in terms of the role they play in sustaining the power structure of capitalist societies. As Marxists, their view is that most power lies with those who own and control the means of production – finance capital, manufacturing plant, mass media companies, and so on – and that government action is limited to that which does not go against the interests of capital. They then argue that the most prestigious, well-paid and influential professional groups will be those that do most work in upholding the capitalist system. By this logic, the occupational groups which make up the 'professions allied to medicine' must be less useful to the capitalist class.

This line of argument is credible but only up to a point. Accountants and the lawyers engaged in company law are probably the best-paid professionals and they do serve the interests of capital in a very obvious way. But the argument becomes less compelling when doctors are considered, who are well paid and who are allowed a wider degree of self-regulation than are accountants. Navarro (1976) argues that the important role of doctors in capitalist societies is ideological: that the practice of medicine perpetuates the myth that illness and misery are just a matter of germs and injuries affecting individuals more or less at random. What this ideology pushes out of sight is the fact (and indeed it is a fact) that ill-health is very closely related to social class and a result of social inequality (Townsend *et al.*, 1988; Benzeval *et al.*, 1995). In ideological terms, medicine encourages people to believe that they are sick, rather than sick of capitalism: to go to the doctor, rather than to go to the barricades.

A further point made with regard to doctors is that, in the more developed countries of the world, they are the most important points of sale for pharmaceuticals (Thunhurst, 1982). So, perhaps their prestigious position derives from their relationship with this highly profitable capitalist industry. But this argument wears a little thin when it is realized that pharmaceutical companies actually make much higher rates of return in Third World countries where most drugs are sold direct to consumers without the intervention of doctors (Bodenheimer, 1984). Again, it has been argued that doctors play a crucial role maintaining a healthy workforce and in policing absenteeism from work to the benefit of employers. But in the UK, since the inception of the National Health Service, absenteeism from work backed by doctors' certificates has increased virtually every year.

Learning Activity 1 ◆ ◆ ◆

Review the last 6–10 editions of your own professional journal. Are you able to:

- Identify any articles that discuss factors affecting the standing of the profession?
- Find examples where your profession suggests they have achieved their status by licence and mandate?
- Isolate areas where education is trying to break down professional barriers?

Power and professionalism

The Marxist view on professionalism tends to fall down because it adopts an over-simple view of the distribution of power in modern societies. If, instead, matters are viewed in terms of there being many sources of power of which capital is only one, then questions can be asked about how professional groups gain and maintain their licences and mandates by pressure-group and political activity. Any week's supply of a quality newspaper will give you at least some examples of the politics of professionalism in action.

As acknowledged experts, professional groups have privileged access to the media. The government proposes some changes to the NHS; the media ring up the BMA or the RCN for a view. There is a documentary on youth crime; the media invite probation officers, social workers, psychiatrists and the like to give an opinion. And, of course, professional associations also make news by publishing reports, by distributing press-briefings, and so on. The views of representatives of professional occupations are not uncontested, but their views do usually feature in the way in which the mass media define what is going on and what ought to be done about it. Less publicly, most government legislation is preceded by a consultation period in which professional bodies give their comments, and if it is an important matter to them, lobby sympathetic MPs. This does not mean that governments take notice. But professional bodies do have an entrée to the parliamentary process which ordinary citizens do not.

Professionalism and social selection

The professionalization of an occupation has usually been accompanied by social selection. For example, the Nightingale revolution in nursing in the UK transformed the occupation from one that was open to women from lower class origins (and which was classified in the census together with 'domestic service') to a profession suitable for the daughters of gentlefolk (Abel-Smith, 1960).

Explicit selection on the basis of social class, gender and ethnicity is no longer characteristic of professional occupations; indeed, the latter two are against the law. Nonetheless, covert racial and sexual discrimination still seems to occur in acceptances for medical school places, and the need for high initial qualifications tends to discriminate against working class applicants. The way in which careers are structured tends to disadvantage women who have children. As a rule of thumb, it can be said that the better established, the better paid, and the more self-regulating an occupation, the more closed it is to lower class, female and ethnic minority entrants (Doyal, 1985; Stacey, 1988; Goss and Brown, 1991).

The fact that professional occupations are socially selective occupations has given rise to three kinds of observation. The first is that professionalization is one of the ways in which a social class, or a gender or an ethnic group stakes out desirable occupations for itself and keeps outsiders out. The second suggests that this social selectivity incapacitates professionals from understanding their clients, where their clients are from less favoured social groups. This line of argument does not rely on the social origins of professionals. Illich (1975) argues that training to become a professional is itself a training in incapacity; a training which changes the perceptions of the trainee so that, irrespective of their previous experience, they simply cannot understand things from the client's point of view.

The third observation is that because professional occupations are dominated by men, they operate to exert patriarchal forms of social control over women; for example by hospitalizing more women than men for mental illness (Busfield, 1986). Similar remarks are made about ethnic dominance (Littlewood and Lipsege,

1989); and, by definition, professionals are 'middle class'.

Interprofessional relations

That there is a legal category called 'professions allied to medicine' is witness to the fact that the doctors ('medicine') were first to organize themselves as a profession and other profession-claiming occupations had to develop in a field in which the doctors had already staked out the most desirable kinds of work for themselves. It is often the case that doctors behave as if they had the right to direct the activities of other profession-claiming groups. In fact, in the health service a great deal of the work of PAMs is part of a package where the overall coordination of activities is done by a doctor.

The superordinate power of doctors is a source of considerable resentment to PAMs when there are differences of opinion and the doctor's view prevails. Mention doctors to any member of the PAM occupations and it will not be long before he or she relates how doctors do not understand and do not respect the contribution which can be made by occupational therapy, or radiography, physiotherapy, or dietetics and so on. And this of course is true, because very few doctors *do* understand the practice or appreciate the philosophy of other occupational groups; they have been trained only as doctors, and the hallmark of professional training is exclusivity.

TRAINING FOR EXCLUSIVITY AND COMMITMENT

One of the most important objects of professional training is to get new entrants to the profession to think of themselves as very special kinds of people. Tutors track the progress of their students in terms of how far they have come to think and speak in a manner distinctive to their own professional group (Dingwall, 1977). Later, members of an occupational group tend to interact most closely with others of their kind, read the same journals and go to the same conferences. Training for occupational distinctiveness builds solidarity within the occupation, but at the cost of creating distance from and misunderstandings with other occupational groups. For OTs and physiotherapists this issue came to a head in 1994 with suggestions of a merger of the two occupational groups (*Therapy Weekly*, 1 December 1994):

> 'Delegates . . . clashed over the issue of generic therapists. Some claimed a combined OT and PT qualification was the only way forward for the professions. Others argued it would result in the decline of specialist skills.'

THE DIFFICULTIES OF TEAMWORK

Having divided the service users up into spheres of work for different occupational groups, there is then often an attempt to put them back together again through multidisciplinary teamwork. Training which encourages identification with one's own occupation, and occupationally distinctive ways of thinking, make it almost inevitable that interprofessional relationships in health and welfare will be fraught with misunderstandings and conflicts (Dalley, 1989). Many interdisciplinary 'teams' turn out to be made up of different kinds of practitioners working in parallel, rather than together.

Learning Activity 2 ◆ ◆ ◆

- Identify the characteristics of your own discipline which make it a profession.
- What methods has your profession used to achieve and maintain a professional status? Try to find evidence from the literature.
- By looking at newspapers, are you able to identify any erosion of professional power? This need not refer exclusively to health professions.
- Select an occasion which brings you together with members of other occupational groups. Try to observe what goes on. How far do the different occupational groups view matters in different ways, have different priorities, use different words, or the same words in different ways? How would you explain any differences you observe: as due to being trained differently, teaming with colleagues from the same occupational group, or as due to working for different agencies?
- Members of one occupational group often tell stories and jokes about members of another occupational group. Keep a note of these kinds of stories. What do these tellings say about 'them' and what do they say about 'us'.

THE BEGINNING OF THE END FOR PROFESSIONALISM ?

If professionalism refers first and foremost to the claim for autonomy and self-regulation, then there are two main sources of opposition to this. Firstly there is the state – or rather the politicians and the civil servants together with the public opinion and the pressure groups which influence government action. It is worth remembering that the best-established professional occupations established themselves as private practitioners, before the development of a large-scale state apparatus, and prior to the situation where most of the money for professional practice comes from government.

Secondly, there is opposition from the clients of profession-claiming workers. The last ten years or so have seen a considerable increase in consumer group activity by users of health and social services. This includes a much greater use of established agencies such as the Community Health Councils (ACHC, 1994) and the Health Service Commissioner or 'Ombudsman' (Health Service Commissioner, 1992), and the establishment of new ones such as Patients' Councils in long-stay hospitals (Gell, 1992), and of self-advocacy groups in the fields of learning disabilities and mental health (Campbell, 1992), together with a much more assertive stance from charities (such as MIND, MENCAP and Age Concern).

At the same time there have been reforms to health and social services, which have been designed explicitly by central government to give a stronger voice to the receivers of services. They include legislation such as the National Health Service and Community Care Act (1990), its Northern Ireland equivalent, Patient's Charters, and soon 'Community Care Charters', and new, easier to use complaints procedures. The NHS and Community Care Act allows individuals to be supported by independent advocates when they meet professionals.

All these initiatives encourage consumers to be assertive about what they want, and to complain when they don't get it. This serves to shift power away from professional occupations, and to limit their autonomy and room for manoeuvre. This 'consumerism' runs alongside other public policy initiatives which limit professional autonomy by bringing professional occupations more firmly under central government control, either directly or by imposing on them a management structure that operates according to central government dictat. So, for example, in NHS Trusts professionals have been brought much more firmly under the control of managers who are employed to run Trusts in a way modelled on commercial companies. Sackings of professional staff are becoming an increasingly important mode of discipline, by contrast with professional disciplinary procedures. 'Gagging' clauses are included in contracts to prevent staff from exercising their 'professional' freedom to speak out about malpractice. And in pursuit of more 'value for money', many tasks which were previously done by professional workers are being delegated to ancillary staff, trained 'on-the-job' through the new Scottish and National Vocational Training schemes (CCETSW, 1992a, b; City & Guilds, 1992a, b; SCOTVEC, 1992a, b).

In the contemporary situation, then, the autonomy, discretion and power of professionals is being eroded from two directions. On the one hand, individuals are being empowered to challenge professional dominance; and on the other hand, central government is dictating the work of professionals more closely. The main thrust of a profession claim is that professional autonomy serves the public interest. But, of course, managers, governments, and the receivers of services have their own ideas about what is in the public interest, and these do not necessarily coincide on each and every occasion with those of a profession-claiming occupation.

SUMMARY

'Profession' is a political term rather than a straightforward description of a particular kind of occupation. Occupational groups that claim to be professions are thereby making political claims for the freedom to regulate their own affairs. The usual basis for justifying this claim is that self-regulation will be in the 'public interest'. What is the public interest, however, is subject to wide differences of interpretation, and professionalism has been seen as self-serving, conspiratorial and socially exclusive. Governments across the world have been seeking to break the monopoly position of more powerful professional groups; to bring them more closely under government control; and to push down the price of professional services. At the same time, strident consumer movements have developed, calling for professionals to be more account-able to their clients. Historically the PAMs occupations have not been very successfully achieving the kind of professional autonomy enjoyed by doctors or lawyers. The current climate suggests that there will be even fewer opportunities to do this in the future.

Boundary disputes are a common feature of the politics of professionalism, often making for awkward working relationships between one occupational group and another. The PAMs, for instance, developed in a context already dominated by doctors, and they work in situations where what doctors decide often limits and sometimes determines what they do. Seeking to maintain independence from doctors has been an important aspect of the occupational politics of PAMs. Maintaining the boundaries of work between one PAM group and another has been an important issue, and currently all PAM groups feel threatened by initiatives to train 'non-professional' assistants, to take over some of the more routine tasks of these occupations.

Key Points

- A 'professional' occupation is one that presents itself as expert and trustworthy with a right to monopolize certain desirable types of work.
- Professions achieve their status by licence and mandate.
- Relationships between the professions and the public depend upon trust, division of labour and monopoly.
- Inherent within professional education is exclusivity which isolates one profession from another, producing potential difficulties with interdisciplinary teamwork.
- Professional power is being eroded by 'consumerism' and political 'pressure'

References

Abel-Smith, B. (1960). *A History of the Nursing Profession*. London: Heinemann.

Association of Community Health Councils for England and Wales (1994). *Annual Report 1993*. London: ACHC.

Benzeval, M., Judge, K. and Whitehead, M. (1995). *Tackling Inequality in Health*. London: King's Fund.

Bodenheimer, T. (1984). The transnational pharmaceutical industry and the health of the worlds' people. In: McKinlay J., (ed.), *Issues in the Political Economy of Health Care*. London: Tavistock.

Busfield, J. (1986). *Managing Madness: Changing Ideas and Practice*. London: Unwin Hyman.

Campbell, P. (1992). Mental health self-advocacy. In: Winn, L. (ed.), *Power to the People*. London: King's Fund, 69–78.

CCETSW (1992a). *Awards in Care at Level 2*. London: CCETSW.

CCETSW (1992b). *Awards in Care at Level 3*. London: CCETSW.

City & Guilds of London Institute (1992a). *Care NVQ Level 2*. London: CGLI.

City & Guilds of London Institute (1992b). *Care NVQ Level 3*. London: CGLI.

Dalley, G. (1989). Professional ideology or organisational tribalism? The health service–social work divide. In: Taylor, R. and Ford, J. (eds), *Social Work and Health Care*. London: Jessica Kingsley Publications.

Dingwall, R. (1977). *The Social Organisation of Health Visitor Training*. London: Croom Helm.

Doyal, L. (1985). Women and the National Health Service. In: Lewin, E. and Olesen, V. (eds), *Women, Health and Healing*. London: Tavistock.

Gell, C. (1992). User group involvement. In: Wynn L (ed.), *Power to the People*. London: King's Fund, 79–91.

Goss, S. and Brown, H. (1991). *Equal Opportunities for Women in the NHS*. London: NHS Executive/DoH.

Health Service Commissioner (1993). *Report of the Health Service Commissioner 1991–92*. London: HMSO.

Hughes, E. (1993). Licence and mandate. In: Walmsley, J. *et al.* (eds), *Health Welfare and Practice: Reflecting on Roles and Relationships*. London: Sage, 21–24.

Illich, I. (1975). *Medical Nemesis: The Expropriation of Health*. London: Calder & Boyars.

Johnson, T. (1972). *Professions and Power*. London: Macmillan.

Littlewood, R. and Lipsedge, M. (1989). *Aliens and Alienists: Ethnic Minorities and Psychiatry*. London: Unwin Hyman.

Millerson, G. (1964). *The Qualifying Associations: A Study of Professionalism*. London: Routledge.

Navarro, V. (1976). *Medicine under Capitalism*. London: Croom Helm.

Parsons, T. (1952). *The Social System*. London: Tavistock.

Scottish Vocational Educational Council (1992a). *Care Core Units: Level II*. Glasgow: SCOTVEC.

Scottish Vocational Educational Council (1992b). *Care Core Units: Level III*. Glasgow: SCOTVEC.

Shaw, G.B. (1946). Preface on doctors. In: Shaw, G.B., *The Doctor's Dilemma: A Tragedy* (first published 1906). Harmondsworth: Penguin.

Stacey, M. (1988). *The Sociology of Health and Healing: A Textbook*. London: Unwin Hyman.

Thunhurst, C. (1982). *It Makes You Sick: The Politics of the NHS*. London: Pluto Press.

Townsend, P., Davidson, N. and Whitehead, M. (1988). *Inequalities in Health: The Black Report and the Health Divide*. Harmondsworth: Penguin.

Further Reading

Dalley, G. (1989). Professional ideology or organisational tribalism? In: Taylor, R. and Ford, J. (eds), *Social Work and Health Care*. London: Jessica Kingsley Publications.

Higgins, R., Oldman, C. and Hunter, J. (1993). *Let's Work Together: Lessons for Collaboration Between Health and Social Services* (Working Paper 7). Leeds: Nuffield Institute for Health.

Soothill, K., Mackay, L. and Webb, C. (eds) (1995). *Interprofessional Relations in Health Care*. London: Arnold.

SECTION III

Psychological Development

12

Lifespan Development

Léonie Sugarman

LEARNING OBJECTIVES

After studying this chapter you should:

- Be able to describe the life-course in terms of key psychosocial processes
- Be able to compare different models of development
- Understand the main tenets of lifespan psychology
- Appreciate the implications of the lifespan perspective for personal and professional development.

INTRODUCTION

Since ill-health is frequently experienced and assessed in relation to a person's age or life stage, the concept of the life course is crucial to healthcare. Responses to illness or accident reflect past and present developments, and can have implications for the future course of life. The present chapter looks at personal change in general, and at developmental change in particular, from a lifespan perspective. Other theoretical frameworks for discussing development are covered in Chapters 1, 13 and 14.

Box 12.1 *Concepts for describing the life course*

- *Developmental tasks*: tasks arising at or about a particular point in the life course, successful resolution of which leads to healthy and successful growth in a particular society.
- *Life events*: markers that give shape and direction to our lives.
- *Transitions*: changes in assumptions about ourselves and the world, and consequent changes in our behaviour and/or relationships, triggered by life events.
- *Evolving life structure*: the underlying design of a person's life, and its pattern of change across time.

DESCRIBING THE LIFE COURSE

The psychology of lifespan development is concerned with 'the description, explanation, and modification of developmental processes in the human life course from conception to death' (Baltes *et al.*, 1980, p. 66). This is a gigantic task, rendered manageable through the use of a number of overarching or 'meta' concepts. Whilst there is no generally accepted list of such concepts, those summarized in Box 12.1 provide a framework for describing and thinking about the life course.

Developmental tasks

Developmental tasks (Havighurst, 1972; Oerter, 1986) are those tasks which, arising out of a combination of physical maturation, individual aspirations and cultural pressures, characterize a particular phase of the life course. Success in these tasks will usually facilitate and denote 'healthy and successful growth in our society' (Chickering and Havighurst, 1981). When physical maturation is the prime source of a developmental task – as, for example, with learning to walk – it may be possible to identify universal norms; but to the extent that social and cultural factors are implicated, it is likely that tasks will be specific to a certain social group, culture and/or historical era. For example, choice of occupation depends on such things as the structure of the labour market, the opportunities available locally, and the nature of the relationship between education and the world of work, as well as individual inclinations and aptitudes (Roberts and Parsell, 1992).

Developmental tasks operate as 'a kind of culturally specific guidance system' (Reinert, 1980, p. 17) in that they provide 'a prescriptive timetable for the ordering of life events' (Neugarten, 1977, p. 45). Many age norms, such as those concerning age of marriage, age at which education is complete, and age of retirement, are less constraining than in previous generations. Nonetheless, people still tend to operate in relation to a 'social clock' (Neugarten, 1979) against which they assess whether they are 'early', 'late' or 'on time' with regard to many developmental tasks. Deviations from age norms tend to attract both negative self-assessments and criticism from others.

Learning Activity 1 ◆ ◆ ◆

The aim is to define the norms for developmental tasks. Is there an age when people are too old or too young to:

- run a marathon?
- take a driving test?
- become a parent?
- embark on a career in healthcare?

How would you justify your answers? Compare the age limits you set with those of fellow students. If you know anyone (including yourself) who falls outside or near the edge of these age limits, what would be your opinion of their decision to do these things?

Life events

Life events are markers that give shape and direction to a person's life (Danish *et al.*, 1980). By our mid-thirties a person can typically list more than 30 or 40 significant life events that we have experienced (Hopson, 1981). At least 35 different dimensions have been used to describe and classify such events (Reese and Smyer, 1983) depending on the interests of the investigator. Brim and Ryff (1980) distinguished between:

- *event dimensions* – the objective characteristics of the event;
- *perception dimensions* – referring to the person's subjective impression or evaluation of the event;
- *effect dimensions* – the outcomes or consequences of events.

Brim and Ryff (1980) also developed a taxonomy of events based on:

- *likelihood of occurrence* – 'How likely is it that a particular event will happen to me?'
- *age-relatedness* – 'If it does happen, how sure can I be about when it will happen?'
- *prevalence* – 'How many other people will it happen to?'

Highest levels of stress tend to be associated with those life events that are involuntary, unfamiliar and unpredictable, and which demand large and rapid change (Hopson, 1981).

Learning Activity 2 ◆ ◆ ◆

- The following could be regarded as major life events: death of a relative; having an accident; getting married; moving house; passing/failing exams; getting divorced; falling out with a friend; starting work; having a baby.

Make a list of the main life events that have affected you. Compare and contrast these life events using the two sets of categories identified by Brim and Ryff (1980).

Transitions

Life events are transitions as well as markers. A transition occurs when 'an event or non-event results in a change in assumptions about oneself and the world, and thus requires a corresponding change in one's behaviour and relationships' (Schlossberg, 1981, p. 5).

The inclusion of 'non-events' in the foregoing definition recognizes that unfulfilled expectations (jobs not obtained, illnesses not succumbed to, for example) can trigger changes in people's image of themselves and their world as much as can the experience of events.

Other criteria denoting a transition are that the changes are lasting in their effect, take place over a relatively short period of time, and influence large areas of the life structure (Parkes, 1971; Connell and Furman, 1984). Having a heart attack, for example, even in the face of a history of heart trouble, would meet all these criteria.

Disruptions to people's accustomed ways of being and thinking about themselves tend to trigger a relatively predictable sequence of reactions and feelings – *the transition cycle* (Hopson and Adams, 1976) – which is similar to the familiar stages of bereavement: shock (manifested through denial and isolation), acknowledgement (reflected in anger and bargaining), depression, and acceptance (Kubler-Ross, 1970).

Learning Activity 3 ◆ ◆ ◆

From the list of your life events in Activity 2, identify one that you feel brought about some sort of change or transition in you. That is, how did it change your view of yourself, your world and your relationships with others?

Reflect on the period of transition:

- Was it emotionally difficult? Were its effects wide-ranging, or limited to one or two aspects of your life? Did it take long? Is it still happening? Do you or did you feel stress somewhere in the process of transition?

An evolving life structure

A portmanteau concept for examining the life course is that of the *life structure* (Levinson, 1986) – the underlying pattern or design of a person's life at a given time. It comprises not only the characteristics of the person, but also the person's relationships with the sociocultural world – people, things, places, institutions, and cultures. The life structure exists on the boundary between the person and the environment, a link between them, being part of both yet partially separate from them.

The life structure is not static, but evolves through an alternating series of structure-building and structure-changing (transitional) periods.

Transitional periods are times of reappraisal and decision-making, times 'to explore possibilities for change in the self and the world, and to move toward commitment to the crucial choices that form the basis for a new life structure' (Levinson, 1986, p. 7). They are often experienced as periods of upheaval, both frightening and exciting.

Structure-building phases are periods of consolidation, during which a person forms a new structure around the key choices they have made and 'pursue values and goals within this structure' (Levinson, 1986, p. 7). Whilst all structure-changing phases share similarities, as do all structure-building phases, each will also be characterized by particular developmental tasks.

Even the best-crafted life structures will become outmoded within five to ten years. Another structure-changing phase, itself lasting about five years, is heralded when the existing life structure can no longer accommodate changes in a person and their relations with the world. The concept of an evolving life-structure, and the notion of development through the resolution of developmental tasks, both focus attention on points of change in the life course and the events that trigger them.

Levinson's research identified developmental stages common to all his subjects (adult American males in four different occupations). However, it is generally accepted that structural, cultural and physical characteristics of the environment serve to differentiate human populations (Dowd, 1990), reducing the likelihood of identifying universal stages of development, especially beyond childhood (Gergen, 1980). Thus, the concept of the evolving life structure has greater general utility than the detailed descriptions of particular life stages.

Learning Activity 4 ◆ ◆ ◆

Draw a picture of your current life structure. Include such things as:

- your personal characteristics (e.g. shy, confident, optimistic, hard-working);
- roles (e.g. student, friend, lover);
- relationships (e.g. with parents, partner, sibling, teachers)
- institutions (e.g. college, church, club, hospital).

How stable is your life structure? Are there any parts undergoing significant change? Which elements are likely to change significantly in the future? Would you judge yourself to be in a structure-building or a structure-changing phase?

Of the four concepts discussed in this section, that of the life structure is the most general and overarching. Descriptions of the life structure at any particular point in time might include the developmental tasks engaged in, the life events that are occurring, and the transitions being worked through. Similarly, descriptions of developmental tasks include life events to be coped with and transitions to be managed. Life events provide a more externally focused, and transitions a more internally focused, approach to specific upheavals or discontinuities in the life course.

None of these concepts, however, provides a definition of what is meant by development. Judgements as to the quality of a life structure, the success of developmental task completion, the desirability of a life event, and the effectiveness of transition management all depend on the definition of development that is explicitly or implicitly adopted.

THE CONCEPT OF DEVELOPMENT

The picture of development that emerges from the discussion so far is one of the individual learning and benefiting from experience: accomplishing tasks characterizing different stages of the life course and on which later development, at least to some extent, rests; and working through the implications of significant life events to emerge a stronger, more mature, more 'developed' person.

Not all changes across the life span would be described as development. Rather, the concept of development centres on some *value-based notion of improvement*. Changes in amount and/or in quality are evaluated against an implicit or explicit notion of what constitutes the 'good' or the 'ideal'. Development is potentially never-ending; one is a developing, not a developed person. Thus, Kaplan (1983) defines development as movement in the direction of perfection.

It is a matter of opinion as to what constitutes 'perfection'; although descriptions, if not of perfection, then of such concepts as the fully functioning person (Rogers, 1967) or self-actualizing person (Maslow, 1970) do have a degree of similarity. Such concepts lack clear definition, but their tenor is reflected in Erikson's (1980) concept of *ego integrity* – the outcome, according to Erikson's model, of successfuly resolving life's final developmental crisis between ego integrity and despair. Ego integrity is the culmination and, to use Erikson's term, the ripe fruit of all earlier development. He identifies several indicators of ego integrity, the main characteristic of which is acceptance:

- acceptance of one's self and one's life, and freedom from excessive regret that it has not been different;
- acceptance that one's life is one's own responsibility;
- acceptance of and respect for the validity of world views different from one's own;
- acceptance of the smallness of one's place in the world, combined with a recognition of the reality of one's own contribution.

Prevalent in many accounts of the ultimate goal of development is the recognition that it refers to an ideal, not an attainable reality. 'The good life', writes Rogers (1967, p. 186), 'is a process, not a state of being. It is a direction, not a destination.'

There is, however, no single theory of lifespan development. Instead, there is a group of theoretical propositions which orient research and practice, and which 'together specify a coherent metatheoretical view on the nature of development' (Baltes, 1987, p. 612).

TENETS OF THE LIFESPAN APPROACH TO DEVELOPMENT

The details of a lifespan view of development are summarized in Box 12.2 and described more fully below.

Box 12.2 *Theoretical propositions on the nature of lifespan development (adapted from Baltes, 1987)*

Development is:

- *A lifelong process.* Development is not restricted to childhood. Both quantitative and qualitative development can occur at all stages of the life course.
- *Multidimensional and multidirectional.* Development occurs in a number of different domains, at different rates, and in a number of directions.
- *Variable.* An individual's developmental course shows plasticity – that is, it can be modified through life conditions and experiences.
- *Involves both gains and losses.* As well as involving growth and gain, development also involves coming to terms with decline and loss.
- *An interactive process.* Development is the outcome of interactions between individual and environment, both of which can influence its course.
- *Culturally and historically embedded.* Developmental rates and courses vary across different cultures and historical periods.

Development is a lifelong process

A lifespan perspective on development challenges the traditional assumption that childhood is the main, or only, period of growth and development. Exponential rates of social change – for example, increasing varieties of occupational histories and family patterns – have negated the view of adulthood as a period of stability. As a result, adulthood has become recognized as an important research topic, slotting into its place in the lifespan between the already established disciplines of developmental (that is, child) psychology and gerontology. Old age was always seen as a period of change, albeit characterized by decline and loss rather than growth. It was studied first from a primarily pathological perspective – with health problems, and physical and mental decline being the main focus of attention. Such a perspective is increasingly insufficient as more people live to a healthy and active old age (see Chapter 16).

The past emphasis on growth in childhood and decline in old age reflects the implicit assumption of a growth–maintenance–decline model of development which is generally applicable to biological and physical functioning, but which may not be appropriate for the psychological, social and spiritual realms. An example of this is the different labelling of similar processes in people of different ages. For example, when young or middle-aged professionals specialize and become expert in a particular area, this is applauded as 'career advancement'. However, when older people respond to decreasing energy and physical capacity by selecting and focusing on goals that are especially important to them, this is likely to be labelled more negatively as 'disengagement from society' (Cumming and Henry, 1961; Cumming, 1975). The lifespan perspective encourages a shift towards a more positive assessment of the processes accompanying ageing as, for example, when this so-called disengagement is relabelled 'selective optimization and compensation' (Baltes and Baltes, 1990).

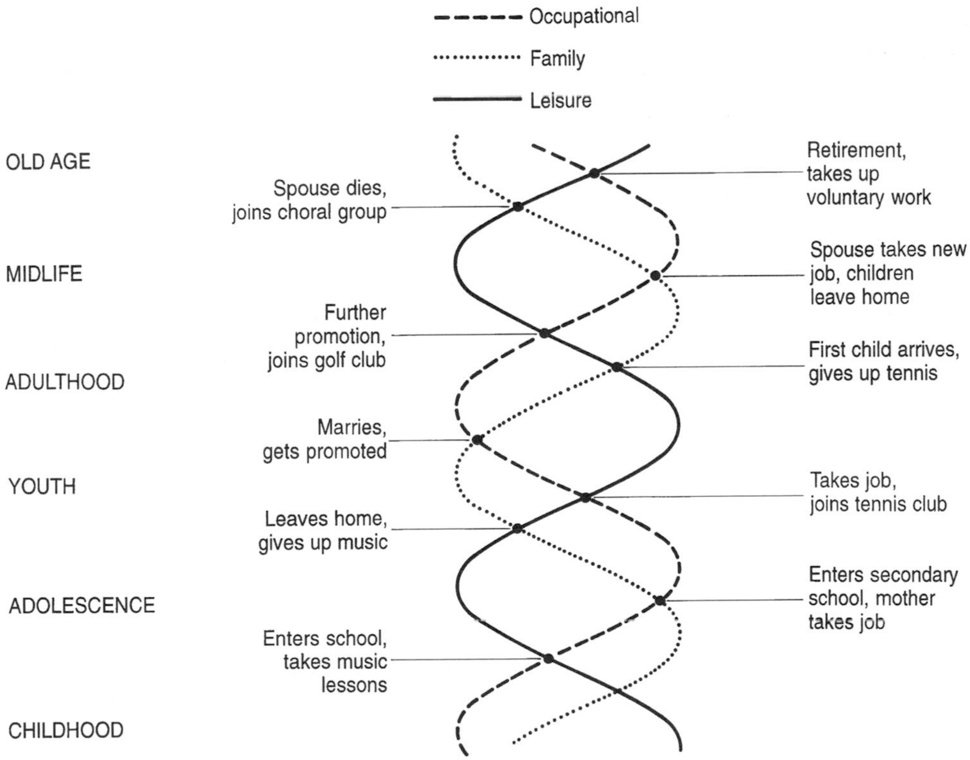

Figure 12.1 *Triple-helix model of personal careers (Rapaport and Rapaport, 1980)*

Development is multidimensional and multidirectional

Lifespan developmental psychology adopts a total lifespace, as well as a total lifespan perspective (Super, 1980). There are many different dimensions of development – intellectual, social, career, family, for example – each of which may follow a different developmental path. The relative saliency and demands of different elements of the lifespace will wax and wane over the years, generating qualitatively different life structures at different points in time.

Health issues, for example, may only become important and time-consuming in the wake of the experience of illness or accident in one's self or a significant other. For a while a person's life structure may revolve around hospitals and treatment programmes. If recovery follows, these concerns may recede into the background, although possibly still leaving a life structure significantly different from the one existing previously.

Development, therefore, is not necessarily an uninterrupted sequence of 'onward and upward' movement. Direction of change can vary. Development may take a number of forms. If a person's life course were depicted as a line across a page, with the horizontal dimension representing time and the vertical dimension representing the 'ups' and 'downs' of life, then the shape of the resulting curve would not be the same for all individuals. Both the degree of incline and the alterations in the direction of the line would denote the amount of change characterizing a particular life (Gergen, 1988).

It would be possible to draw different life lines for different aspects of life. Thus, Rapoport and Rapoport (1980) depicted work, family and leisure careers as an intertwining triple helix, with the separate strands interacting and combining at points where the lines meet – for example, giving up tennis (part of the leisure career) on the birth of a first child (part of the family career) (see Figure 12.1).

Learning Activity 5 ◆ ◆ ◆

Draw, in the manner of a temperature chart, lines to represent your own development along the dimensions listed below. Add any further dimensions that are significant for you. Note similarities and differences in the shape of the lines describing different dimensions. How would you account for these patterns? Compare your responses with others, again looking particularly for differences and similarities across different dimensions of development.

Physical ______________________

Emotional ______________________

Social ______________________

Intellectual ______________________

Career ______________________

Family ______________________

Spiritual ______________________

Others ______________________

Development shows plasticity

Not only is development multidimensional and multidirectional, but it is also, to a greater or lesser degree, modifiable through experience and circumstance. Thus, the rate, degree and nature of both physical and psychological development following a major car accident will vary according to the type of therapy received. This, in turn, will depend on variable factors such as the state of medical knowledge, the financial and social resources available, personal inclinations, and cultural norms.

In other words, development can show plasticity. The degree of potential variability will be different across different strands of development, some (e.g. career development) showing greater plasticity than others (e.g. perceptual development). The greater the plasticity of a strand of development, the less is the likelihood that a 'typical' developmental path can be identified.

Development involves both gains and losses

Lifespan developmental psychology recognizes that each step forward also entails loss. As babies grow their body proportions change and they lose the ability to suck their toes with ease – this is accepted as an inevitable part of growing up, and is not defined as decline. More generally, it may be that skills atrophy, alternatives are closed off, valued relationships are severed.

By the same token, losses may result in developmental gains, such as in the form of new opportunities or the development of coping skills. Longed-for transitions may turn out to be 'mixed blessings'; or, to coin another colloquialism, it may be that a particularly nasty cloud really does have a silver lining. Role exchange may be a more valuable concept than role loss or role gain (Schlossberg, 1981). Decision-making inevitably involves the weighing-up of pros and cons, and the rejection of some options.

Learning Activity 6 ◆ ◆ ◆

Write down and discuss what might be the personal gains and losses associated with the following developments:

- Starting school
- Learning to read
- Becoming a parent
- Developing CHD
- Being promoted
- Being made redundant
- Having asthma

Development is an outcome of individual–environment transactions

Traditionally, psychologists have identified the locus of development as within either the individual or the environment (Pervin and Lewis, 1978). This is the basis of the nature–nurture debate. Maturationalists emphasize the part played by 'nature', notably innate, maturational and hereditary factors. Humanistic psychologists see development as the emergence of an inner self or essence. These approaches enshrine an organic model of the person, whereby the individual is seen as the source of acts rather than a puppet acting out behaviours initiated by external forces. The environment inhibits or facilitates, but does not cause development. This perspective leads to the search for universal, invariant developmental paths.

By contrast, a learning-theory or social learning-theory perspective rests on a mechanistic model, emphasizing 'nurture' and focusing attention on the role of environmental factors in causing development (Bandura, 1989). Sociological perspectives which focus, for example, on the role of class and ethnicity also fall into this category. From this perspective development is seen as involving continual adjustment to external circumstances (Pearlin, 1982).

Taking a lifespan perspective tends to emphasize the limitations of both the organic and mechanistic models. Both are too simplistic (Reese, 1976) and need to be replaced by an interactive, contextual or systems view of an active organism as part of an active environment. Thus the nature–nurture debate is approached in terms of 'both–and' rather than 'either–or'. For example, children who are 'by nature' physically adventurous will tend to seek out situations which challenge their physical skills. In this way their inborn characteristics will be reinforced and enhanced by environmental experiences, further differentiating them from children who are 'by nature' more timid.

Learning Activity 7 ◆ ◆ ◆

The interaction of 'nature' and 'nurture'.

Make a list of some of your own strengths and skills. To what extent do you think these are a reflection of your inborn characteristics? Which have been most influenced by such environmental factors as parental encouragement, educational opportunities and community facilities? In what ways have they been influences?

Now think about your weaknesses and the things about which you would say 'I'm no good at that'. To what extent are these the result of lack of opportunity? Under what circumstances might these have been your strengths or skills?

Compare your thoughts with those of fellow students.

Development is culturally and historically embedded

Lifespan development is not determined purely by individual psychological factors. The individual can be seen as embedded in a hierarchical nest of social systems, which can each influence development (Bronfenbrenner, 1977).

At the broadest and most encompassing level are the general cultural carriers of the values and priorities of a particular society. These are largely reflected implicitly in such things as language and social mores – a society's 'unwritten rules'. The major institutions of society –

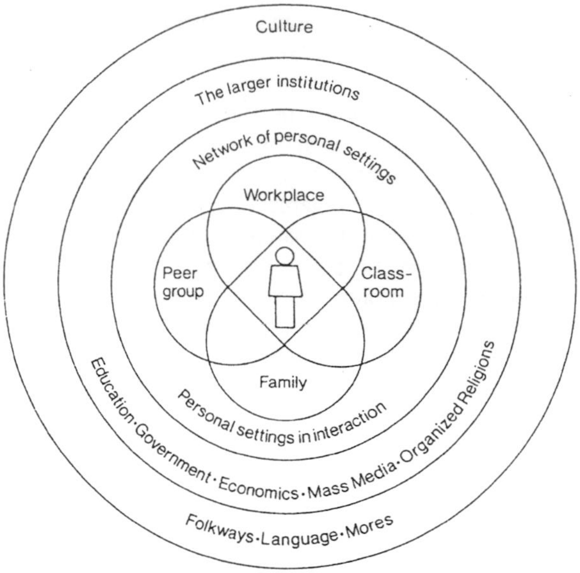

Figure 12.2 *A systems view of the development context (Egan and Cowan, 1979)*

education, government, health services, the mass media, and so on – comprise the next cultural system of influence. Then comes the network of interacting personal settings of which the individual is a part – the way what is happening in one area of life (career, for example) affects what happens in another area (leisure, let us say). At the most specific level of cultural or social influence is the interactions between individuals and their immediate physical and social environment. These relationships are shown in Figure 12.2.

Social and cultural environments change over time, both in terms of specific events such as wars or economic recession, which will be experienced by some generations but not by others, and in terms of general trends, such as technological developments or changing social attitudes. As a result, the life course of different generations will vary (Baltes *et al.*, 1980). Thus, the relationship between education and work changed as a result of industrialization, the raising of the school leaving age, and increasing opportunities for further and higher education. Whereas cultural differences highlight the inappropriateness of transferring concepts of development from one social group to another, historical differences serve to make the past an uncertain and unreliable guide to the future.

Taken together, this set of theoretical propositions provide a general framework for conceptualizing lifespan development. Perhaps best expressed metaphorically, the essence of the perspective can be seen as an attempt 'to capture a view of human development as a continuous and sometimes unpredictable voyage throughout life, sailing from seas that have become familiar into oceans as yet uncharted toward destinations to be imagined, defined, and redefined as the voyage proceeds, with occasional, often unpredictable, transformations of one's vessel and sailing skills and the oceans upon which one sails resulting from unforeseen circumstances' (Ford and Lerner, 1992, p. 47).

Learning Activity 8 ◆ ◆ ◆

How might historical and/or cultural factors affect the experience of the following life events:

a *Being unemployed*
- in the 1890s as opposed to the 1990s
- in rural Ireland as opposed to inner-city Britain
- for a 20-year-old male as opposed to a 45-year-old female.

b *Going to university*
- in the 1950s as opposed to the 1990s
- for working-class as opposed to middle-class students
- for school-leavers as opposed to mature students.

c *Being divorced*
- in the 1930s as opposed to the 1990s
- for women as opposed to men
- after 4 years as opposed to after 40 years of marriage.

d *Having a baby*
- in the 1920s as opposed to the 1990s
- at the age of 15 and at the age of 35 years
- in China and in Brazil.

IMPLICATIONS FOR HEALTH PROFESSIONALS

Adopting a lifespan perspective suggests a number of stances which can help health professionals enrich the quality of care offered to people of all ages and lifestages. Of particular importance is, firstly, the adoption of a developmental rather than a disease perspective on life events, including illness; and, secondly, a concern with intervention strategies that facilitate progress through the different stages in the process of coping with change.

Development not disease

It is to be expected that many people in the care of health professionals will be experiencing stressful life events. Furthermore, to the extent that people assume that development should be smooth and adulthood a period of stability, then almost any major life event is likely to be perceived as an undesirable disruption of what should be unruffled progress. From this viewpoint, disruptions to accustomed ways of being are to be avoided if possible, and if unavoidable, then the goal of intervention is to minimize their impact, and bring the person 'back on course' as soon as possible (Danish *et al.*, 1980).

By contrast, the lifespan perspective, with its 'bumpy ride' view of the life course, sees crises and upheavals as an inevitable and normal part of life. The intervention implication of this is to view the management of such crises as developmental tasks, enshrining opportunities as well as dangers. The challenge for health professionals is to help those in their care to adopt a similar perspective. This can be facilitated by viewing coping with trauma or illness as a process (Murgatroyd and Woolfe, 1982) with variable intervention implications.

Coping with change

The focus of the lifespan perspective on change over time encourages health professionals to adapt their interventions and style of working to the stage in the change process which those in their care have reached. During the initial period of shock or immobilization, a person is likely to feel 'frozen up', and may be unable to take in either the reality of the situation or information about such things as detailed treatment regimes. It is a time for patience and support. The phase of acknowledgement does not imply acceptance, and health professionals may be the butt of people's anger, frustration and resentment at what has happened to them. The tasks for the professional are to allow those in their care to express their feelings, and to 'be with' them, supporting them through both this phase and the period of depression likely to accompany their gradual realization of what has happened to them. The degree and duration of these phases of shock, acknowledgement and depression will vary depending on the impact of the illness or problem on the life structure. For events causing severe disruption it may be a process lasting weeks, months, or even years.

As people begin to accept and come to terms with what has happened, specific professional expertise can help them with the task of letting go of their old, outdated views of themselves, and also with the task of trying out new ways of being in the post-change reality. The need for empathic care continues throughout this process in order to help people make sense of what has happened. Only then can their new situation become fully integrated into their new life structure. This focus on integration draws attention to the contextual nature of development and coping. The person needs to be seen not only as a whole person, but as a whole person enmeshed within a network of relationships with people, things, places and ideas.

SUMMARY

Lifespan psychology argues that development continues throughout life and it proposes a set of psychosocial processes to describe development. By putting health and ill-health into a developmental perspective, health professionals are better able to assess and address some of the psychological and social issues that promote recovery. A final point to bear in mind is that issues of lifespan development concern health professionals as much as the people they serve.

Key Points ■ ■ ■

❑ The potential for development extends throughout the lifespan.

❑ The life structure is not static but evolving.

❑ Development is the result of transactions between the individual and his or her environment.

❑ Development is multidimensional and multidirectional.

❑ Life events have developmental potential.

❑ Achievement of developmental tasks can be crucial to well-being, social approval and subsequent achievements.

❑ Transitional periods are opportunities to develop new, more appropriate life structures in response to changes in the person or relationships to the world.

❑ Coping with illness or trauma is a process that takes time and is best helped by empathic support.

References ▼ ▼ ▼

Baltes, P.B. (1987). Theoretical propositions of life-span developmental psychology: on the dynamics between growth and decline. *Developmental Psychology*, **23**: 611–26.

Baltes, P.B. and Baltes, M.M. (1990). Psychological perspectives on successful aging: the model of selective optimization with compensation. In: Baltes, P.B. and Baltes, M.M. (eds), *Successful Aging: Perspectives from the Behavioral Sciences*. New York: Cambridge University Press.

Baltes, P.B., Reese, H.W. and Lipsitt, L.P. (1980). Life-span developmental psychology. *Annual Review of Psychology*, **31**: 65–110.

Bandura, A. (1989). Social cognitive theory. *Annals of Child Development*, **6**: 1–60.

Brim, O.G. and Ryff, C.D. (1980). On the properties of life events. In: Baltes, P.B. and Brim, O.G. (eds), *Life-span Development and Behavior*, vol. 3. New York: Academic Press.

Bronfenbrenner, U. (1977). Toward an experimental ecology of human development. *American Psychologist*, **32**: 513–31.

Chickering, A.W. and Havighurst, R.J. (1981). The life cycle. In: Chickering, A.W. *et al.* (eds), *The Modern American College: Responding to the New Realities of Diverse Students and a Changing Society*. San Francisco: Jossey Bass.

Connell, J.P. and Furman, W. (1984). The study of transitions. In: Emde, R.N. and Harmon R.J. (eds), *Continuities and Discontinuities in Development*. New York: Plenum.

Cumming, E. (1975). Engagement with an old theory. *International Journal of Aging and Human Development*, **6**: 187–91.

Cumming, E. and Henry, W. (1961). *Growing Old: The Process of Disengagement*. New York: Basic Books.

Danish, S.J. Smyer, M.A. and Nowak, C. (1980). Developmental intervention: enhancing life-event processes. In: Baltes, P.B. and Brim, O.G. (eds), *Life-span Development and Behavior*, vol. 3. New York: Academic Press.

Dowd, J.J. (1990). Ever since Durkheim: the socialization of human development. *Human Development*, **33**: 138–59.

Egan, G. and Cowan, M.A. (1979). *People in Systems: A Model for Development in the Human Services Professions and Education*. Monterey, CA: Brooks/Cole.

Erikson, E.H. (1980). *Identity and the Life Cycle: A Reissue*. New York: W.W. Norton.

Ford, D.H. and Lerner, R.M. (1992). *Developmental Systems Theory: An Integrative Approach*. London: Sage.

Gergen, K.J. (1980). The emerging crisis in life-span developmental theory. In: Baltes, P.B. and Brim, O.G. (eds), *Life-span Development and Behavior*, vol. 3. New York: Academic Press.

Gergen, M. (1988). Narrative structure in social explanation. In: Antaki, C. (ed.), *Analysing Everyday Explanation: A Casebook of Methods*. London: Sage.

Havighurst, R.J. (1972). *Developmental Tasks and Education*, 3rd edn. New York: David McKay.

Hopson, B. (1981). Response to papers by Schlossberg, Brammer and Abrego. *Counseling Psychologist*, **9**: 36–9.

Hopson, B. and Adams, J. (1976). Towards an understanding of transition: defining some boundaries of transition dynamics. In: Adams, J. *et al.* (eds), *Transition: Understanding and Managing Personal Change*. London: Martin Robertson.

Kaplan, B. (1983). A trio of trials. In: Lerner, R.M. (ed.), *Developmental Psychology: Historical and Philosophical Perspectives*. Hillsdale, NJ: Lawrence Erlbaum.

Kubler-Ross, E. (1970). *On Death and Dying*. London: Tavistock.

Levinson, D.J. (1986). A conception of adult development. *American Psychologist*, **42**: 3–13.

Maslow, A.H. (1970). *Toward a Psychology of Being*, 2nd edn. New York: Van Nostrand Reinhold.

Murgatroyd, S. and Woolfe, R. (1982). *Coping with Crisis: Understanding and Helping People in Need*. London: Harper & Row.

Neugarten, B.L. (1977). Adaptation and the life cycle. In: Schlossberg, N.K. and Entine, A.D. (eds), *Counselling Adults*. Monterey, CA: Brooks/Cole.

Neugarten, B.L. (1979). Time, age and the life cycle. *American Journal of Psychiatry*, **136**: 887–94.

Oerter, R. (1986). Developmental task through the life span: a new approach to an old concept. In Bates, P.B. *et al.* (eds), *Life-span Development and Behavior*, vol. 7. Hillsdale, NJ: Lawrence Erlbaum.

Parkes, C.M. (1971). Psycho-social transitions: a field for study. *Social Science and Medicine*, **5**: 101–15.

Pearlin, L.I. (1982). Discontinuities in the study of aging. In: Hareven, T.K. and Adams, K.J. (eds), *Aging and Life Course Transitions: An Interdisciplinary Perspective*. New York: Guilford Press.

Pervin, L.A. and Lewis, M. (1978). Overview of the internal–external issue. In: Pervin, L.A. and Lewis, M. (eds), *Perspectives on Interactional Psychology*. New York: Plenum.

Rapoport, R. and Rapoport, R. (1980). *Growing Through Life*. London: Harper & Row.

Reese, H.W. 1976: Conceptions of the active organism. *Human Development*, **19**: 108–19.

Reese, H.W. and Smyer, M.A. 1983: The dimensionalization of life events. In: Callahan, E.J. and McCluskey, K.A. (eds), *Life-span Developmental Psychology: Nonnormative Life Events*. New York: Academic Press.

Reinert, G. (1980). Educational psychology in the context of the human life span. In: Baltes, P.B. and Bri, O.G. (eds), *Life-span Development and Behavior*, vol. 3. New York: Academic Press.

Roberts, K. and Parsell, G. (1992). Entering the labour market in Britain: the survival of traditional opportunity structures. *Sociological Review*, **40**: 726–53.

Rogers, C.R. (1975). *On Becoming a Person*. London: Constable.

Schlossberg, N.K. (1981). A model for analyzing human adaptation to transition. *Counseling Psychologist*, **9**: 2–18.

Super, D.E. (1980). A life-span, life-space approach to career development. *Journal of Vocational Behavior*, **16**: 282–98.

Further Reading ▲ ▲ ▲

Bee, H. (1994). *Lifespan Development*. New York: HarperCollins.

Salmon, P. (1980). *Living in Time: A New Look at Personal Development*. London: Dent.

Schlossberg, N.K. Waters, E.B. and Goodman, J. (1995). *Counselling Adults in Transition: Linking Practice with Theory*. New York: Springer.

Sugarman, L. (1986). *Life-span Development: Concepts, Theories and Interventions*. London: Routledge.

Thomas, R.M. (ed.) (1990). *The Encyclopedia of Human Development and Education: Theory, Research and Studies*. Oxford: Pergamon Press.

13

Childhood and Adolescence

Jennie Lindon

LEARNING OBJECTIVES

After studying this chapter you should:

- Be aware of theories explaining why and how development takes place
- Appreciate patterns of normal development during childhood and adolescence
- Understand the applications of these ideas to the practice of healthcare

INTRODUCTION

Contact with the health services, and with medical procedures in particular, are likely to be experienced by children as unusual and possibly anxiety-provoking events. A broad knowledge of child and adolescent development can help health professionals engage effectively with babies, children and adolescents. This chapter provides a conceptual framework that can be developed by further reading and informed clinical practice.

DIMENSIONS OF CHILD DEVELOPMENT

There are a number of theories which try to explain how and why children develop. Most theories of development try to establish the influence on development of inherited characteristics (genetic factors) as opposed to children's experiences (environmental factors). Some theorists take uncompromising positions, explaining almost all of development through either genetic factors or environmental factors. Some considerable effort has gone into finding a means of quantifying the relative impact of inheritance versus experience; see, for example, Bee's descriptions of theories (1992).

The lifespan approach (see Chapter 13) and other interactionist theories avoid this debate by proposing that both genetics and environment contribute to the process of development, and in ways that are still not well understood.

The following introduction to the theories of child development can be supplemented with further reading, such as Bee (1992); Salkind (1985); Smith and Cowie (1991); Coleman and Hendry (1990) and Hill (1993).

Biological explanations

Theories rooted in human biology all emphasize the programming of the genetic code and physiological processes such as hormonal changes. These are used to explain the shared patterns in development as well as the differences between individuals. Experience is not discounted altogether but is believed to work within the powerful genetic framework.

Biological explanations of child development allow for individual differences in timing – for example, in the start of speech or the onset of puberty – but stress that the sequence will be basic to all children, since it is unfolding through maturation. Thus the temper tantrums of a 2-year-old or the mood swings of an adolescent would be seen as inevitable phases of development. Such a view can produce inappropriate feelings of guilt in parents or other carers, although an unhelpful consequence can be that adults feel that nothing they do will make any difference.

Genetic theories have been used to explain individual differences in temperament (Thomas and Chess, 1977) and differences between the sexes. There is considerable work, following on from Bowlby (see Anderson, 1972), on the concept of bonding to explain how and why babies form attachments, arguing that babies have an evolutionary need to form a close attachment to the mother within the early days and weeks of life.

However, see Schaffer (1990) critique of the research on bonding.

Explanations through learning

Most learning theorists do not totally reject biological or genetic factors. However, they see development as primarily a result of learning and so stress individual experiences rather than shared developmental sequences or stages. Learning theorists will explain similar patterns between children as caused by similar experiences. Development is shaped as a result of conditioning, of which there are two types.

- In *classical conditioning*, the co-occurrence of events at one time can lead to these events always being associated with each other in the future. For example, entering a hospital may always lead to crying because of a previously traumatic experience in the hospital.
- In *operant conditioning*, a behaviour is established as a result of its consequences in the past. For example, keeping still for the dentist results in a badge.

Learning theorists are sometimes called behaviourists because of this strong focus on what children, or adults, can be observed to do, rather than theoretical deductions about unobservable feelings or motivations.

SOCIAL LEARNING THEORY

This is an extension of learning theory. It tries to integrate the more internal processes of thought by proposing that childrens' interpretations of events change with experience and this different kind of understanding shapes how children subsequently behave. There is therefore a continuing interaction between what happens and the sense that a child makes of the event (Herbert, 1991).

In contrast to biological theories, learning theories stress the importance of how children are treated and imply that adults can consciously behave in more effective ways by allowing for the impact of their behaviour or the setting upon children. An over-simplistic analysis of cause and effect, however, can deny the complexity of children's experience and may discount the power of feelings for children and adults. An exclusive focus on behaviour may have no capacity to embrace a sense of pride or achievement in the child sitting still for the dentist, thereby discounting the power of internal motivation. The social learning approach has developed to encompass the impact of such experiences.

Learning Activity 1 ◆ ◆ ◆

If possible, observe a young child in the home when he or she is with different members of the extended family (e.g. mother, father, older sibling, grandparent).

a Do these members of the family behave differently towards the child?

b Does the child initiate different activities with them?

Personal development

Personality theories offer explanations which combine children's experiences (external) and their feelings (internal). It is proposed that children pass through a number of qualitatively different stages in personal development. Individuals' behaviour is affected both by their current stage and by the traces left on their personality by earlier stages. Past experience can influence present behaviour without the individual being fully aware of this. Some personality theories (e.g. Sugarman, 1986) view adolescence and adulthood as potentially continued development as individuals make conscious choices to resolve conflicts from the past, deal with current dilemmas and approach life choices from a different perspective.

The psychoanalytic tradition has sometimes focused more on the effects of traumatic events in early childhood rather than on positive experiences. Study of children whose childhoods have been marked by high levels of distress and trauma have nevertheless shown how experience affects individuals differently (Stallard and Law, 1994; Sylva, 1990).

The psychoanalytic approach (to development) was developed by Blos (1962). Although Freud and Blos's theories have received much criticism, Erikson's (1968) notion of psychosocial rather than sexual stages of development have attracted a lot of support. Erikson argued that developmental stages are characterized by age-determined social tasks. He thought that adolescence, rather than early childhood, was the most decisive period in personality formation and he describes adolescence as 'normative crisis'. Erikson's ideas have been developed further by Marcia (1980).

Other personality theorists have looked at the quality

of the parent–child relationship in terms of the attachment of the family members to the child, the attachment of the child to family members, and the interaction between child and family members (Graham, 1991).

In the context of health, an awareness of this range of theories can support a sensitivity to what can be the prime concerns of a child or young person.

Development through thinking

Cognitive theories of child development stress patterns that all children share. These are described as qualitatively different stages of children's capacity to process information and to make sense of the world. All children will pass through the same stages, although not necessarily at the same age, and individual differences emerge through the variation in how children understand and respond to events and objects. Behaviour is seen as the child's active attempt to explore, control and understand their environment. Their mistakes are often very informative as the errors illustrate how children are interpreting the world; see the many research studies reported in Grieve and Hughes (1990).

This approach to development has highlighted that adults can make erroneous assumptions about what children understand. Often adults do not take account of a child's need to explore; nor of their limited ability to see events from the same perspective as adults. Thus there is a need for clear communication with children in order to grasp their understanding and to appreciate that this is continuing to develop (Grieve and Hughes, 1990).

In the context of health, professionals need to consider not only that the understanding of children may be qualitatively different from that of adults, but that even young children will nevertheless be striving to make sense of any situation.

Systemic influences

Bronfenbrenner (1979, 1986) proposed what he called an *ecological approach* to child development, in which children can be seen as interacting within several, interlinking social systems, each of which have their own set of rules and expectations. The systems approach has become very influential in developmental psychology especially in the study of families. It is suggested that it is the child's experience of family relationships in particular which shape development. The set of relationships within a system, such as the family, are experienced differently by different individuals within the system, thus accounting for individual differences in development. For example, one child may be seen in the family as the 'clever' one whilst another as 'trouble'; these family beliefs become expectations and self-fulfilling prophecies for the children concerned.

In the context to health, children with problems – and this includes many common paediatric conditions – may sometimes be considered as the symptom-bearer for a family system which is dysfunctional. The interpretation is then that it is the system which is 'sick' and not the individual child. Sometimes an approach of treatment to the whole family may be appropriate (Lask, 1982).

All the psychosocial approaches challenge the biomedical view of the child as a passive organism at the mercy of some inevitable pathological process, and imply instead an active intelligent person with responses that must be incorporated into the description of any illness. Learning theories and systems theories challenge personality and cognitive approaches to childhood illness where a child is seen as an isolated individual. The former argue that to be adequately described illness must be seen in the context of a social world (see, for example, Shute and Paton's (1992) description of the complex social issues that can surround chronic childhood illness).

It is often argued that, in practice, getting to grips with these less clear-cut conceptualizations of illness will require too many resources. But it is training which is the issue, as a good assessment at the outset and intervention focused on relevant psychosocial issues could in the long term be more cost-effective than expensive or repetitive medical treatments.

PATTERNS OF DEVELOPMENT FROM BIRTH TO ADOLESCENCE

What is normal development?

This is a deceptively simple question about a complex issue. Objectivity can be clouded by one's personal experiences of childhood and family life, which are seen as normal and others as deviations from it. This section looks in detail at how children of different ages are likely to have developed, in particular their communication and understanding. For further reading, see for example Bee (1992).

Babies show individual differences from the earliest days, and so development cannot be described by specific milestones associated with exact timings in years and months. Yet children share the same general events of development, in a similar though not identical sequence. Disabling conditions, chronic illness or serious deprivation will exert an impact on the pattern and timing of development (Eiser, 1985; Garmezy and Rutter, 1985; Johnson, 1985; Lansdown, 1980). However, exact predictions are not feasible, even where two children may be diagnosed as having the same disability or have apparently been subjected to a similar level of deprivation.

Normal child development does not progress completely smoothly. For a period of time a child may not appear to be changing much and then a new skill emerges. Neither is normal development characterized by an absence of difficulties (see also Chapter 12). Minor frustrations can act as a positive challenge for a child to develop a skill, for instance to persist in turning wants into words.

Child development is more easily described by taking physical, intellectual, emotional and other changes separately. However, these different aspects interact in everyday development; for example, independent mobility between 6 and 14 months opens up a new world of interesting objects and spaces to explore. A consequence might then be bruises from tumbles as interest overrules any sense of potential danger. A further, very likely consequence can be frustration as adults prevent access to unsafe environments.

Developmental changes are filtered through the uniqueness of each child. Thus one 14-month-old may be a cautious explorer whereas another runs at top speed with little apparent awareness of obstacles or danger. But perhaps the more cautious child is also very persistent and complains loudly at being removed from a potential plaything, while the speedy toddler can be relatively easily distracted into another source of exploration (for a discussion of temperament, see Thomas and Chess (1977)).

Finally, development takes place in a family network which in turn is embedded in the traditions of particular cultures and subcultures. A child's skills and abilities are shaped by cultural expectations transmitted through parents and other important adults (see Lindon, 1994).

Physical growth and abilities

Numerous standard texts describe the general pattern and pace of physical development (e.g. Leach, 1993). It is important to point out, however, that – as with other aspects of development – physical development is affected by the child's social environment. Children who are encouraged by adults can be motivated to grow in self-reliance (Leach, 1993; Cobb, 1992). Four- and five-year-olds can be very capable, although they may still want help, especially if they are tired or distressed. Development of physical skills in middle childhood and adolescence depends a great deal on the activities they are offered and on the ability of adults to motivate involvement. Older children and adolescents may pursue physical activities for enjoyment and improved skill. They may, however, choose not to apply their potential and restrict themselves to relatively inactive pastimes. The level of self-reliance demonstrated by adolescents tends to depend on family beliefs about coaching young people towards a more adult role (Cobb, 1992).

Skills of communication

VERBAL COMMUNICATION

Very young babies are alert to information from all five senses. Some babies are evidently calmed by the sound of a familiar voice, and the ability to discriminate faces has been shown as early as a few days old; but the most consistent finding is at 3 months of age. Even during the first 6 months of life there are deliberate attempts at sound-making, and babies can copy sounds as well as facial expressions.

Older babies' sounds are more expressive, capturing the rhythm and pitch of speech, and they start to use supporting gestures and different tones of voice depending on mood. Familiar adults usually recognize real words and then short word combinations within a child's second year of life. Young children who are encouraged in their attempts to communicate by speech then go on to learn even more words and attempt new word combinations and then short phrases (Snow, 1977).

Children under five years become fluent in their spoken language, and children in bilingual families can have become fluent in more than one language. During these early years they make mistakes in choice of words, pronunciation or spoken grammar. Their mistakes tend to be logical and often result from taking the wrong word from a short sentence; for example, believing that an aeroplane is called 'sky' because the word was introduced in the short phrase 'there's a plane up in the sky'. They may overgeneralize grammatical rules, so 'bought' becomes 'buyed' (Karmiloff-Smith, 1994).

During the primary school years, children learn to deal with the written form of language through reading and writing.

NON-VERBAL COMMUNICATION

Children extract meaning from more than just the spoken words of others. They are alert to non-verbal forms of communication, sometimes called *body language*, and notice the message from gestures and facial expression (Karmiloff-Smith, 1994). Younger children often depend on non-verbal communication to complement half-understood words, but older children, like adults, still remain alert to body language. When messages conflict, children (like adolescents and adults) often trust the unspoken message. For instance, an unfriendly expression will carry more weight than friendly words.

Finally, children copy the style of communication that they observe around them. This imitation is noticeable in the breadth of their use of spoken language as well as non-verbal patterns of listening or interrupting and cultural traditions, for example, in eye contact or the use of touch in communication (Konner, 1991).

Intellectual development

Once a child communicates through spoken language, it can seem easier to ascertain their level of intellectual, or cognitive, development. Yet observation of younger children, and even babies, can show that non-speaking children are working hard to make sense of their world (Karmiloff-Smith, 1994). Young children will initiate homely rituals or find and offer a plaything. They are not only demonstrating how they remember what happened on previous occasions, but they have also developed working theories about how familiar adults are likely to behave and what may engage their attention.

Young children are usually interested in the world around them and extend their understanding through questions as much as by physical exploration. They are amassing a great deal of information while developing a conceptual framework in which to make sense of facts (Tizard and Hughes, 1984). Children's predictions are often reasonable deductions based on what they currently know and understand. They can make mistakes because of the gaps in their knowledge. For instance, a 4-year-old may have learned that a toy boat floats in the bath; the child generalizes from this and places a book in a bowl of water, to find that the book floats for only a while before sinking and is ruined by the soaking.

By the time children reach the age of five years they are capable of thinking and talking about events that are not happening in front of them. They have moved into a level of abstract thought and reasoning as they speculate about what may happen, and are able to use a range of abstract concepts such as relative size or number. Through middle childhood and into adolescence, children are substantially extending their knowledge base but are also developing and changing the cognitive framework in which they make sense of new information.

A child's underlying conceptual framework can be demonstrated by seeing how understanding changes with age. Historical facts, for example, are viewed differently as children's perception of time changes; scientific knowledge becomes understood as the result of controlled experimentation. Likewise, over the years children's understanding of health and illness develops, both in a more abstract way and as issues affect them personally. Children of different age groups tend to reach quite different conclusions about the cause of their illness; many of the youngest children may think they are ill as the result of some wrongdoing on their part, whilst older children have begun to develop concepts of no-fault illness. Older children may be as concerned about the social consequences of their ill-health as the medical ones (Bibace and Walsh, 1980; Bird and Podmore, 1990; Brewster, 1982).

It would appear that children's understanding can be hampered by lack of information or by misunderstandings that are not corrected. Sometimes adults prefer to believe that children are unable to understand issues which they themselves find difficult or distressing to communicate. On the other hand, parents will be in a better position to prepare their children and to make the best use of a service if they are given some information prior to an appointment. Studies suggest that depending on spoken messages alone may not be reliable; advice is best given in written as well as spoken communication. Mensah and Davies (1993) demonstrated the variation in parents' knowledge of their child's asthma medication, and Shute and Paton (1992) give examples of mishandling of medication by parents, for reasons that made sense to the parents themselves.

Social and emotional development

Forming a working relationship with a young person requires a recognition not only of what they know and understand but also what they feel. Babies and young children experience and express a range of emotions and are often responsive to the emotional state of their carers. They form strong attachments to a small number of familiar adults, not solely their mother, and to other children, both within and outside the family (Schaffer, 1985; Schaffer, 1990; Parke, 1981).

Children tend to be happier and more at ease with familiar figures. They can be distressed by separation from those they know and trust, especially under circumstances that are strange or upsetting. Children form friendships with other children, often but not always of a similar age, and such friendships become progressively more important through childhood. In adolescence, friends can become more influential than the views and preferences of parents (Cobb, 1992).

Through interaction with others, children develop a view of themselves and expectations of how other people are likely to behave. Their feelings can be hurt, as well as their sense of dignity, by dismissive or rude remarks. Both children and adolescents, much like adults, can become uncooperative with those whom they judge to be untrustworthy or disrespectful to them as individuals. With sensitive encouragement from adults, children become more able to talk about what they are feeling and sometimes to deal with strong feelings through words rather than physically. (See Perry (1994) on communicating with very young children in hospital; and Robertson and Robertson, 1989.)

Children develop a range of social skills based on beliefs about appropriate behaviour or communication in different situations. Such beliefs are based on experience and reflect family and cultural traditions. Older children and adolescents can have a detailed understanding of what is expected in a range of different situations. They have a broader life experience but they can feel as if they are an uneasy blend of child and near-adult. Moreover, lack of confidence or high levels of stress may lead to less than 'best' behaviour.

Children's distress may be expressed in a variety of ways, by crying, by attempts to get away, or by retreating in upon themselves. This might derive from anxiety, discomfort, embarrassment or pain. Babies and children have feelings, both emotional and in their physical reaction to discomfort and pain. It is counter-productive certainly in the long term to deny children's expressed feelings by arguing with a distressed child 'that doesn't hurt' or telling an embarrassed child not to be 'so silly'. An essential part of acknowledging children's feelings is showing respect for their bodies and sense of personal dignity – a point well described by Lansdown (1980).

Writing two decades after the Robertsons (1958, 1962), Lansdown (1980) describes in sensitive detail the confusion and distress that can strike a child when little or no attempt is made to explain what is happening or to reduce the number of new and changing faces in the medical personnel; or when every known homely ritual for the child has been overturned. He goes on to offer guidelines of good practice in communication with children, adolescents and parents.

Stressful circumstances are unlikely to elicit the best from anyone (Whaite and Ellis, 1987). Young children may need very definite reassurance in strange surroundings, and their feelings should be acknowledged and given the respect of simple explanations. The concerns of a wary or frightened child should never be dismissed because they do not fit adult logic. A piece of equipment can be very large and daunting to a child; bits of a machine that stick out can look threatening, or a noise may convince the child that a procedure will be very painful. Rational information will not help unless the child's feelings are acknowledged.

Whenever possible, coping strategies that might be used should be developed in consultation with the child. Many such strategies have been developed and used with considerable success (Shute and Paton, 1990; Palmer, 1994; Alderson, 1993). And all young service users deserve a clear acknowledgement of their efforts and forbearance; and children, although probably not those approaching adolescence, may also appreciate tokens of thanks such as stickers or badges.

Rodin (1983) reports on the development of educational material that might allay anxiety before a painful or uncomfortable procedure. Alderson (1993) wrote specifically of teenagers in hospital, and Palmer (1994) addresses this issue specifically with adolescent oncology patients. For instance, with explanation and information an older child can make an informed choice about options for pain relief.

In some situations parents' groups have been found to be a strong source of support and explanation for parents. Argles *et al.* (1994) describe a group for families attending a paediatric renal unit. Farrell (1994) describes support systems in the United States and Canada for families with critically ill children. Both Lansdown (1980) and Whaite and Ellis (1987) stress the positive

Learning Activity 2 ◆ ◆ ◆

The aim is to evaluate the management of distress in a child in a clinical situation. Recall a clinical situation (either personally experienced as a child yourself, or as a relative, or as an observer) where you feel that a child who was already distressed was upset further by poor management on the part of the professionals concerned.

a How was the distress manifesting itself?

b How did the professional respond to this, and with what consequences?

c What do you think was wrong with this approach?

d What could have been done differently in this situation?

Can you now describe another clinical incident where you feel that a child who was distressed was managed in a sensitive and effective manner?

If you are unable to recall either such incident, look out for one in the future and refer back to this exercise.

help that can be gained from parents meeting others going through a similar experience with their sons or daughters. Shute and Paton (1990) describe the often overlooked opportunity for children to support one another.

CARING FOR YOUNG PEOPLE

Children and young people are as much legitimate users of health services as their parents who accompany them. A number of studies look at how children and parents perceive the care that is offered and the quality of the information communicated (e.g. Cooper and Harpin, 1991; Hall and Stacey, 1979). Martin (1994), for example, describes how parents and children view the consultant's ward round.

Much of the research has concentrated on the experience of children admitted to hospital, but the development of good practice has extended to other parts of the health services. Mayall (1990), for example, describes the different views held by parents and by clinic staff about children and healthcare, raising the point that professionals in any service can become convinced that their perspective is also shared by the users, or that it should be.

Changes in healthcare practice

Belsen (1993) describes how care in hospital has improved over the last three decades, and in her opinion should continue to change, in response to the needs of developing children. The work of the Robertsons (1958, 1962) challenged the prevailing view that children's distress on admission to hospital was minimal. Further research and the pressure of organizations such as Action for Sick Children has encouraged health professionals to be far more aware that children who are ill remain first and foremost children. Therefore there are important developmental needs for such things as play, appropriate communication and the support of a familiar adult.

One of the most striking changes in hospital procedure has been to view parents as a positive help and important for the well-being of their children, rather than as a source of infection and interference. Belsen (1993) describes the changes in visiting hours and ease of access for parents of children admitted to hospital. Parents are usually allowed to remain until their child is under anaesthetic and to be the first face that the child sees on recovery. Any accompanying adult should not be excluded, except briefly for reasons of safety – for instance, taking X-rays where mother is pregnant.

Lansdown's (1980) descriptions highlight the conflict for the professional in trying to combine compassionate involvement with technical expertise. It is to be hoped that training to improve professionals' understanding of young people will enable them to find ways of resolving this conflict.

SUMMARY

Child and adolescent development is an extensive field of practice, theory and research. A chapter of this length can provide only an outline of the key issues, which can be developed through further reading. An equally valuable source of further knowledge can be gained through an alert and reflective approach to clinical practice. With caution, health professionals can continue to extend knowledge and understanding of children and adolescents and improve the standards of the service offered.

Key Points

- Development can be viewed from a number of different theoretical perspectives.
- Children's development can be described along a number of dimensions that are interconnected, not independent of each other.
- There are some typical patterns of development along these dimensions, but these are tempered by the individuality of the children and the environment in which they are developing.
- Children and adolescents are legitimate users of the health services and should be treated as individuals in a full awareness of their likely development.
- Professionals who are constructively critical of their own practice can improve the experience of young people receiving healthcare.

References

Alderson, P. (1993). *Teenagers in Hospital*. Action for Sick Children family information leaflet.

Anderson, J.W. (1972). Attachment behaviour out of doors. In: Blunton-Jones (ed.), *Ethological Studies of Child Behaviour.* Cambridge: Cambridge University Press.

Argles, J. *et al.* (1994). The parents' group: support for families attending a paediatric renal unit. *Maternal and Child Health*, **19**: 152–8.

Bee, H. (1992). *The Developing Child*, 6th edn. Harper Collins.

Belsen, P. (1993). Children in hospital. *Children in Society*, **7**: 196–210.

Bibace, R. and Walsh, N.E. (1980). Development of children's concepts of illness. *Pediatrics*, **66**: 912–17.

Bird, J.E. and Podmore, V.N. (1990). Children's understanding of health and illness. *Psychology and Health*, **4**: 175–85.

Brewster, A.B. (1982). Chronically ill hospitalized children's concepts of their illness. *Pediatrics*, **69**: 355–62.

Bronfenbrenner, U. (1979). *The Ecology of Human Development.* Cambridge, Mass: Harvard University Press.

Bronfenbrenner, U. (1986). Ecology of the family as a context for human development: research perspectives. *Developmental Psychology*, **22**: 723–42.

Cobb, N.J. (1992). *Adolescence – Continuity, Change and Diversity.* California: Mayfield Publishing.

Cooper, A. and Harpin, R. (1991). *This is Your Child: How Parents Experience the Medical World*. Oxford: Oxford University Press.

Coleman, J. and Hendry, L. (1990). *The Nature of Adolescence.* London: Routledge.

Eiser, C. (1985). *The Psychology of Childhood Illness*. New York: Springer-Verlag.

Erickson, E. (1968). *Identity: Youth and Crisis*. London: Faber.

Farrell, M. (1994). Support for parents of critically ill children. *Paediatric Nursing*, **6**(4): 16–18.

Garmezy, N. and Rutter, M. (1985). Acute reactions to stress. In: Rutter, M. and Hersov, L. (eds), *Child and Adolescent Psychiatry: Modern Approaches*. Oxford: Blackwell.

Graham, P. (1991). *Child Psychiatry: A Developmental Approach*, 2nd edn. Oxford: Oxford University Press.

Grieve, R. and Hughes, M. (eds) (1990). *Understanding Children.* Oxford: Basil Blackwell.

Hall, R. and Stacey, M. (1979). *Beyond Separation*. London: Routledge & Kegan Paul.

Herbert, M. (1991). *Clinical Child Psychology: Social Learning, Development and Behaviour.* Chichester: Wiley.

Hill, P. (1993). Recent advances in selected aspects of adolescent development. *Journal of Child Psychology and Psychiatry*, **34**: 69–100.

Johnson, S.B. (1985). The family and the child with chronic illness. In: Turk, D.C. and Kerns, R.D. (eds), *Health, Illness and Families*. New York: Wiley.

Karmiloff-Smith, A. (1994). *Baby It's You*. London: Ebury Press.

Konner, M. (1991). *Childhood*. New York: Little Brown.

Lansdown, R. (1980). *More than Sympathy: The Everyday Needs of Sick and Handicapped Children*. London: Tavistock.

Lask, B. (1982). Physical illness and the family. In: Bentorim, A. *et al.* (eds), *Family Therapy: Complementary Frameworks of Theory and Practice*. London: Academic Press.

Leach, P. (1993). *Baby and Child: From Birth to Age Five*. Harmonsworth: Penguin.

Lindon, J, (1994). *Child Development from Birth to Eight: A Practical Focus*. National Children's Bureau.

Marcia, J. (1980) Identity in adolescence. In: Adelson, J. (ed.), *Handbook of Adolescent Psychology*. New York: Wiley.

Martin, V. (1994). Viewing the round: parents' and children's perceptions of the consultant's ward round, *Child Health*, **1**: 196–201.

Mayall, B. (1990). Childcare and childhood. *Children and Society*, **4**: 374–85.

Mensah, E. and Davies, H. (1993). Do asthmatic children or their parents know the prescribed medicines and their actions? *Maternal and Child Health*, **18**: 324–26.

Palmer, S. (1994). Providing information to adolescent oncology patients. *Paediatric Nursing*, **6**(5): 18–22.

Parke, R. (1981). *Fathers*. Harvard: Harvard University Press.

Perry, J. (1994). Communicating with toddlers in hospital. *Paediatric Nursing*, **6**(5): 14–17.

Robertson, J. (1958). *Young Children in Hospital*. London: Tavistock.

Robertson, J. (1962). *Hospitals and Children: A Parent's Eye View.* London: Gallanz.

Robertson, J. and Robertson, J. (1989). *Separation and the Very Young*. Free Association Book.

Rodin, J. (1983). *Will This Hurt?* London: Royal Colege of Nursing.

Salkind, N.J. (1985). *Theories of Human Development.* Chichester: Wiley.

Schaffer, R. (1985). *Mothering*. Harvard: Harvard University Press.

Schaffer, H. (1990). *Making Decisions about Children: Psychological Questions and Answers*. Oxford: Blackwell.

Shute, R. and Paton, D. (1990). Childhood illness: the child as helper. In: Foot, H.C. *et al.* (eds), *Children Helping Children.* Chichester: Wiley.

Shute, R. and Paton, D. (1992). Understanding chronic childhood illness: towards an integrative approach, *The Psychologist*, **5**: 390–94.

Smith, P.K. and Cowie, H. (1991). *Understanding Children's Development*. Oxford: Blackwell.

Snow, C. (1977). The development of conversation between mothers and babies. *Journal of Child Language*, **4**: 1–22.

Stallard, P. and Law, F. (1994). The psychological effects of trauma on children. *Children and Society*, **8**(2): 89–97.

Sugarman, L. (1986). *Lifespan Development: Concepts, Theories and Interventions*. London: Methuen.

Sylva, K. (1990). Resilient children. *The Psychologist*, **3**: 244–5.

Thomas, A. and Chess, S. (1977). *Temperament and Development.* Brunner/Mazel.

Tizard, B. and Hughes, M. (1984). *Young Children Learning*. London: Fontana.

Whaite, A. and Ellis, J. (1987). *From Me to You: Advice for Parents of Children with Special Needs*. Baltimore: Williams & Wilkins.

Further Reading ▲ ▲ ▲

Carter, M. (1989). *You and Your Child in Hospital*. London: Methuen.

Goodyear, I. (1990). *Life Experiences, Development and Childhood Psychopathology*. Chichester: Wiley.

Jolly, J. (1991). *The Other Side of Paediatrics: A Guide to the Everyday Care of Sick Children*. Basingstoke: Macmillan.

Mayall, B. (1986). *Keeping Young Children Healthy*. London: Allen & Unwin.

Petrillo, M. and Sanger, S. (1980). *Emotional Care of Hospitalized Children: An Environmental Approach*. New York: Lippincott.

Woodroffe, C. and Glickman, M. (1993). Trends in child health. *Children and Society*, **7**: 49–63.

14

Midlife and Old Age

Carol Ann Sherrard

LEARNING OBJECTIVES

After studying this chapter you should:

- Have an appreciation of ageing as a biological, social and psychological process
- Be aware of how stereotypes influence others' views of older people, and their view of themselves
- Understand the communication pitfalls for older people
- Understand the psychological processes contributing to older people's well-being
- Appreciate how this knowledge can be applied to enhance interactions with older people in the health setting

INTRODUCTION

Often a person's first awareness of their own ageing comes from someone else's unexpected comment or action. A hairdresser may remark that one 'still has such beautiful hair'. A university lecturer first realized his ageing (at 55) when a young woman offered him a seat in a crowded tram (Vischer, 1966). Clearly ageing may be perceived by oneself differently from other people. Given that health professionals are often younger than the people receiving care, it becomes important to gain some understanding of development through middle and old age.

AGEING

It is usual for the words 'old' and 'elderly' to be firmly rejected as applying to oneself, at any age (Bultena and Powers, 1978; Mac Rae, 1990; Oswald, 1991). Keller *et al.* (1989) reported that about half of their sample of North Americans older than 70 considered themselves to be 'middle-aged'.

From midlife onward in modern societies, a number of conflicting social factors can act to separate a person's awareness of their age in years ('chronological age') from their 'social age' (others' view of their age status) (Neugarten, 1979; Karp, 1988). These include improved health and greater aspirations to health and prolonged youthfulness, the longer survival of parents (who may require care from their middle-aged children), and the accelerating pace of social change, which may leave middle-aged employees' skills redundant while they are still youthful.

To compound these confusing recent changes in the condition of midlife, a number of social psychological processes also add to the divergence of social image from self-image with ageing. These are *stereotyping*, *self-stereotyping*, and *self-enhancement*. Since these are social processes, they affect not only perceptions and beliefs, but also the communication between older and younger people.

Stereotyping

This is the blanket assignment of a specific set of supposed features to all members of a social category (Billig, 1985). The features can be evaluated negatively, positively (Ryan and Bartlett-Weikel, 1993) or compassionately (Revenson, 1989). This blanket assignment leads to selective expectation, perception and memory for these supposed features, and the filtering out of others. These cognitive effects make stereotypes self-perpetuating. Since they lead to faulty perceptions of individuals, they may also lead to inappropriate treatments. Stereotyping of the elderly as physically and cognitively weak is more likely among health workers, since they see many more sick than healthy elderly.

Ageism is a unique form of prejudice, in that given a normal life course, the self eventually comes within its range. Adelman *et al.* (1991) suggest that the partial awareness of this self-reference can lead to denial or trivialization of elderly needs for care by some health providers (Adelman *et al.*, 1991).

Learning Activity 1 ◆ ◆ ◆

Which of the following *stereotypical features* have you attributed to older people: hard of hearing; depressed or irritable; doddery; unfit; thrifty; mean; poor?

Self-stereotyping

Of course, older people are likely to have held negative stereotypes of the elderly when they themselves were young. If they continue to hold them as they age themselves, they may become prey to self-stereotyping and a negative self-image (Oswald, 1991). They may misattribute illness or cognitive symptoms to normal ageing processes, and underestimate their own capacities to function or to reacquire normal function (Gray, 1983; cited in Adelman *et al.*, 1991). Twining (1988) makes the important observation that elderly people under-report their symptoms of illness, accepting them as normal features of ageing.

Learning Activity 2 ◆ ◆ ◆

Collect evidence of self-stereotyping. Talk to adults ranging from 40 to 80+, asking the following set of questions:

a Do you have any ailments?/Have you been ill?/Do you have something physically wrong?
b What has caused this?/What is the reason?/Why have you got this?
c Is this normal for someone of your age?
d Will you get better?

Self-enhancement

On the other hand, Keller *et al.* (1989) and Stokes (1992) report that those elderly people who do not experience the ill-health and disability they stereotypically expect as normal in old age may come to see themselves as unusually youthful exceptions. Elderly people may stereotype their age-mates while using psychological defences to 'self-enhance', or maintain a positive self-image. Such defences include denial of ageing (Bultena and Powers, 1978; Stokes, 1992), alteration of the meaning of changes brought by ageing (Jerrome, 1989; Keller *et al.*, 1989), the distortion and exclusion from the self-concept of ageing-related experiences such as mishaps in traffic (Thomae, 1980), and 'downward social comparison' (comparison of the self with worse-off others; Bultena and Powers, 1978; Keller *et al.*, 1989; Suls and Wills, 1991; Sherrard, 1994). Some of these self-enhancement processes will be discussed later, in the discussion of old age and well-being.

FUNCTIONAL CAPACITIES

Physical changes

The best-documented functional change with ageing is slower reaction time. This is apparent already by age 40, in performance on complex tasks designed especially for experimental evaluation. However, with advancing age a slowing-down becomes evident in all types of activity, and the effect on designed experimental tasks is not removed when younger and older subjects are matched for intelligence, education and health status (Myerson *et al.*, 1989).

Ageing beyond maturity also brings degenerative changes in the joints and tissues, which may manifest in painful conditions beginning in middle age. A Swedish study by Bergenudd *et al.* (1988) found that shoulder pain in middle age could be related to low job satisfaction and physical workload, but not for all individuals.

There is gradual loss of sensitivity in vision, hearing, touch, taste and smell with ageing. However, as with the self-image, there may be little self-awareness of these changes (Rabbitt, 1990). Hearing loss is present in 65% of people over 65. Hearing loss can effect comprehension and memory during conversation, since cognitive resources must be diverted from these higher levels to the level of perception. Rabbitt (1990) reports that these 'knock-on' effects of hearing loss are greater in 70-year-olds than in those at 60 and 50, although a high IQ protects against them at all ages by affording spare cognitive resources. Old age therefore does not necessarily imply cognitive deficit, even though there is an overall pattern of decline. Improvements in health care, nutrition and education this century have impacted on this overall pattern so that later cohorts of elderly people show it to a lesser extent (Rabbitt, 1990).

Intellectual changes

Cognitive functions age at different rates. Skills built up by long practice, such as language and general knowledge, are more resistant to ageing than skills which depend on rapid processing of new information, on speed and accuracy of logical or arithmetical reasoning, or on spatial problem-solving. As a general picture, this difference between practised and relatively unconsolidated cognitive skills has been described as the maintenance of 'crystallized intelligence' but the gradual decline of 'fluid intelligence' with age (Horn, 1982). Rabbitt (1990) argues that such a picture makes it cognitively more economical for older people to adapt their existing skills to new needs, than to attempt to learn fundamentally new and complex skills.

Dementia

Relatively few people in their sixties are affected by dementia (approximately 2.5%), and only a minority of octogenarians (22%) manifest outright cognitive dysfunction (figures for USA; Charatan *et al.*, 1981). It should be noted, too, that dementia ranges widely from mild to severe impairment; consequently a diagnosis of dementia does not imply that the person's capacity is impaired across all functions.

COMMUNICATION PITFALLS

Stereotyping and changes in functional capacities are likely to lead to at least two major pitfalls in communication with older people:

- to simply assume that they view themselves as either old or impaired in function;
- to make these assumptions about older people oneself.

Learning Activity 3 ◆ ◆ ◆

Recall a clinical situation where you felt a person was treated in an ageist or condescending fashion by the professional concerned.

What was wrong with the approach? What could have been done differently?

If you are unable to recall such an incident, look out for one in the future and go through this exercise.

Such assumptions are clearly present in, for example, over-familiar or over-supportive forms of address to older people (Coupland *et al.*, 1991).

Consultation time

Equally though, there is the pitfall of not making allowances for the *possible* consequences of ageing. For example, elderly patients who really are frail may have delayed contacting their GP because of poor mobility or self-image. This may mean that, by the time contact is made, a catalogue of problems has built up such that the consultation time allowed is not long enough to discuss them adequately, even if deafness and comprehension problems have been taken into account. Extra consultation time should be allowed also because illnesses in the elderly may compound and obscure each other, and the sheer length of a lifetime's medical history may require the careful sifting out of important from less relevant information.

In spite of these requirements for extra consultation time, research by Radecki and others (1988) shows that doctors surprisingly spend no more time with elderly (75+) than with younger people at the first meeting, and spend less time in follow-up meetings. Although this was partly explained by more frequent follow-ups with the elderly person, this was a careful nationwide (USA) study which took into account and controlled for many other factors such as doctors' specialities, ages, workloads, and reliance on Medicare insurance billings. There were also wide geographic variations in consultation times which could not be explained. The effects of shorter consultation times on care outcomes are unknown, although these authors cite other work (Rubenstein *et al.*, 1984) indicating that attention to previously overlooked problems, and active efforts to treat the whole person, lead to fewer follow-up visits by the elderly person.

Content of communication

Communication is easier between people who have large areas of shared knowledge and understanding (Rogers and Bhowmik, 1970). Such areas can be shared membership in the major sociodemographic groupings of age, sex, class and race, in addition to minor ones such as occupation, place of residence, etc.

Since age is one of the major social groupings, the difference in age between the elderly person and the health worker may reduce rapport and efficiency of communication unless this difference is sensitively oriented to by the health professional. Such sensitivity ideally requires special training. Greene *et al.* (1987) found that doctors raised more medical than psychosocial topics with older than with younger people, while, conversely, older people were more likely to raise psychosocial topics with their doctor than were younger people. This finding suggests adverse effects on rapport of a non-shared age background, an effect also reported by Stewart (1983).

Third parties

Adelman *et al.* (1991) point out the frequent presence of a third person during interactions between elderly people and health professionals. This person may be passive and neutral or, if intervening, either supportive or negative toward the older person. In any case, the interaction is fundamentally different when a third person is present. Confidentiality becomes problematic, and there are sensitive issues such as sexual function or incontinence which cannot easily be broached in a triad. Adelman *et al.* (1991) recommend that the third person be allowed in only after a private session with the elderly person, and if the latter so wishes.

Learning Activity 4 ◆ ◆ ◆

Carry out a direct observation of an interaction between an older person and a health professional, to collect evidence of the following:

- stereotyping
- self-stereotyping
- self-enhancement
- physical decline
- intellectual decline
- communication pitfalls:
  - time
  - content mismatch
  - third-party role.

MIDDLE AGE

The years from 40 onwards are subject to important life changes, increasing demands and stresses. These life changes are both personal, due to lifecycle changes in close others such as children and parents (Helson and Wink, 1992), but also societal, as the pace of economic and technological change dramatically accelerates in modern societies (Abercrombie *et al.*, 1988).

There is also a sense in which important change becomes more perceptible by the middle years of life. After 40 years of experience, a vantage point is reached from where it is possible to discern patterns and long cycles of change. Depending on the individual and their social location, these life changes may be resolved and lead to a calmly accepted discontinuity of the present with the past; or they may not be resolved, and lead to a state of 'moral siege' in which the patterns of belief and behaviour which have given meaning to life up to the present are seen as coming under threat (McCulloch, 1985; cited by Stokes, 1992). Enforced early retirement from work, in contrast to retirement which is accepted, is a precursor of poor psychological adjustment in later life (Roos and Havens, 1991).

The majority of people become parents, and children generally leave the parental home when their parents are in their forties and fifties. During the same decades, the grandparents of these families may become ill or frail, with the responsibility for care falling on their middle-aged children. People in middle age may therefore be sandwiched between the demands of their adolescent children and their parents, while the removal of either set of demands may be accompanied by feelings of loss and grief. If the caring role left redundant by the departure of children is not filled by the needs of aged relatives, the time and energy released may be directed into new activities, especially by women (Helson and Wink, 1992).

Menopause

Recent research on the menopause (Hunter, 1996) concludes that women are unlikely to experience psychological symptoms around this time, unless they already have a history of such symptoms, or unless they are undergoing stressful life events such as broken relationships or bereavements. Modern research, by using improved methods such as larger samples, standardized measures, and controls for factors other than menopause itself, has largely overturned the negative medical image of the menopause.

There is still, though, a complex of popular negative beliefs about the psychological effects of menopause. These include poor memory and concentration, anxiety, irritability, and loss of energy and libido. These false beliefs may cause self-stereotyping, and suggest psychological symptoms to some women. However, as society becomes more educated and less prejudiced toward women, such negative beliefs are losing force.

Learning Activity 5 ◆ ◆ ◆

Carry out a survey of beliefs about the menopause amongst self, colleagues, menopausal women, middle-aged and older men and women, by asking them all 'What do you consider are the five main characteristics of the menopause?' Then:

a Classify these responses into physical and psychological.

b Make comparisons between the various groups of respondents (e.g. men versus women, young people versus post-menopausal women).

Predictors

As the more recent findings about menopause suggest, events and conditions in later life are likely to be responded to in ways that reflect previous experience and established patterns of behaviour. This is the view of several writers (e.g. Harrison, 1973; Thomae, 1976), and it suggests that psychological adjustment in early life would be a good predictor of adjustment in middle and old age.

While this is a reasonable suggestion, modern research demonstrating such linkages in specific ways is not easily available. This is no doubt due to the difficulty and expense of longitudinal research: obtaining large enough samples of respondents who can be followed over long enough time spans to collect the relevant information. There is, however, some cross-sectional research comparing age identities (whether one feels young, middle-aged or old) at different ages between 40 and 80+ (Logan *et al.*, 1992). This research

Learning Activity 6 ◆ ◆ ◆

The aim is to identify preconceptions of what features characterize age ('age is in the eye of the beholder'). Guess the ages of the next five adults you meet in clinical practice. On what evidence do you base your guesses? Discover the actual ages and reflect on any discrepancies in your guesses.

indicates that poor health can change a person's age identity from 'middle-aged' to 'old', but not from 'young' to 'middle-aged'. This is in line with the repeated finding in the research literature that poor health is strongly associated with an 'old' identity; but the finding that the transition from 'middle-aged' to 'old' is also associated with health, is new.

OLD AGE AND WELL-BEING

Older people cannot be regarded as a single undifferentiated group. Some gerontologists separate the over-65s into three distinct age bands: the 'young-old' (aged 65 to 74), the 'middle-old' (75 to 84) and the 'old-old' (85 and older).

Retirement

The 'young-old' are those nearest the transition of retirement from work. However, the popular concept of 'retirement stress' is similar to that of menopause; it is not a distinct psychological state determined uniquely by a developmental stage, rather it reflects other stressors. Bosse *et al.* (1991) found that retirement was rated as the least stressful event from a list of 31 events among retirees and their spouses who had retired within the past year. (The most stressful events were bereavements, or other relationship losses through interpersonal conflicts, or institutionalization of spouse or parent.) Although 30% found retirement stressful, this was related to poor health and financial problems rather than simply to the cessation of work, or to personality problems preventing adjustment. Adjustment to a low income in later life of course impacts on many direct and indirect aspects of well-being, including nutrition (Wardle *et al.*, 1991) and access to transport for social contacts (Cribier, 1980).

Surprisingly, daily life in retirement has been found not to have a very different activity structure from pre-retirement life. In particular, elderly housewives structure their time in much the same way as young ones. From a diary-based behaviour-mapping study in West Berlin, Baltes *et al.* (1990) suggest three possible explanations for this. Obligatory activities such as self- and household maintenance may be extended to fill gaps left by work and other pre-retirement activities. Or, the general slowing of activity with ageing (Salthouse, 1985) could extend the time needed for obligatory activities. Finally, it may be that obligatory activities bringing social contact, such as shopping, may be extended beyond necessity in order to maintain levels of contact.

Health

General health does decline with age, although the elderly as a whole are healthier than the general public assumes (Fitch and Slivinske, 1989). Wardle *et al.* (1991) report that 50% of people over 65 have some chronic illness. Nevertheless, Marshall noted in 1973 (cited in Fitch and Slivinske, 1989) that 70-year-olds could engage in about the same level of moderate activity as 40-year-olds, though they took longer to recuperate from demanding exertion. The majority of elderly report being able to carry on with normal activities, with some adjustments (US National Center for Health Statistics, 1979; cited in Fitch and Slivinske, 1989).

Psychological adjustment

While health is undoubtedly a major factor in well-being (Diener, 1984), there is considerable psychological leeway in the individual's response to it. It is necessary to consider certain psychological processes which are central to the understanding of ageing. Individuals have a remarkable capacity to adapt their interpretations of meaning (Dittman-Kohli, 1990), to adapt their goals (Rapkin and Fischer, 1992) and their self-image in response to changes in material circumstances. Health as assessed by elderly people themselves is more predictive of well-being (Okun, 1986; Rudinger and Thomae, 1990) and of successful ageing (Roos and Havens, 1991) than medically assessed health status.

Physical decline in itself is less important than its impact on preferred activities. Mullins and Hayslip (1986) found that a daily structure around productive and leisure activities was critical to maintain self-esteem in people over 60. Yet again, it is the extent to which elderly people themselves assess the meaning, the degree and quality of notions such as 'structure' and 'productive' that is important. These self-assessments can be subtly altered in response to physical and other changes in such a way that the changes are largely assimilated to a maintained positive self-image. This is the process of self-enhancement.

Carlsson *et al.* (1991) studied the psychological adjustment of 'the oldest old', a sample of non-institutionalized 85-year-olds living in Gothenburg, Sweden. They found seven categories of adjustment, ranging from the positive 'self-realizing' to the negative 'withdrawing'. While there was an overall relationship between adjustment and physical dependence on others, there was also very wide variation between individuals. Many of them did not experience any subjective dependence. Carlsson *et al.* (1991) conclude that physical decline alone could not explain the wide range of individual psychological adjustments they observed. The expected relationship between impairment and adjustment was even reversed in some cases – poorly adjusted people could be most affected by minor impairments, while any kind of physical impairment was of lesser importance to the better adjusted.

However, such flexibility of self-concept, while it may lead to denial of need or failure to acknowledge help, is not necessarily total. The partitioned and often contradictory nature of the self-concept is increasingly recognized in psychology (Crary *et al.*, 1989). Keller *et al.* (1989) noted that, although their elderly people evaluated the 'meaning of aging' as positive, when they were asked to specify and evaluate the specific changes associated with ageing they mentioned almost only negative ones (largely physical decline, and a general slowing down). They had also deliberately worked out strategies to cope with these changes, such as compensating for them, attempting to keep current levels of function, and involving other people.

This study shows, at a practical level, the respondents' clear awareness of ageing changes. Yet, at the same time, they made conscious use of a psychological adjustment strategy – that of downward social comparisons – as a way of enhancing their well-being. Downward social comparison is comparing the self with less fortunate others. Sherrard (1994) also found downward social comparison widely used to enhance well-being by elderly people, at the same time as they had a clear appreciation of the negative changes due to physical and cognitive decline (especially of memory), and to reduced income. Findings like these suggest the limits, or perhaps the selectivity, of psychological adjustment strategies.

Learning Activity 7 ◆ ◆ ◆

Ask an elderly person to draw, in the manner of a temperature chart, lines to represent their development along the dimensions listed below. Reflect on their description of their lifespan.

Family ______________________

Physical ______________________

Emotional ______________________

Social ______________________

Intellectual ______________________

Career ______________________

Spiritual ______________________

SUMMARY

Recent research on ageing shows a shift from concern with documenting the biologically based process of functional decline to a concern with variabilities in the overall pattern. There is also a welcome shift in attributing ageing 'problems' (such as retirement stress, menopause, empty-nest syndrome, social isolation) away from internal causes such as personality, biology or developmental schedule, to more realistically and societally conceived factors such as reduced income, social prejudice, changing demands due to life-changes in family members, and rapid social and technological change.

Variability in the overall pattern has biological, historical/social (Rabbitt, 1990) and psychological sources, and it demonstrates three important points:

- There are increasing numbers of exceptions to the objective pattern. Ageing is decelerating, and longevity and health of the aged are rapidly gaining in Western societies (Schaie, 1981).
- Individuals may deploy psychological processes that allow them, within certain limits, to maintain a positive self-image even when their objective condition has changed, and they are well aware of the changes at a practical level.
- Some individuals, however, may self-stereotype, and mistake the symptoms of illness for 'normal' ageing.

The generally positive, and not 'old' self-image of many elderly people shows that their normal expectation is to be viewed and treated as any other adult. The restriction of new learning to the sphere of well-practised skills indicates a rational strategy of 'cognitive economy' (Rabbitt, 1990), and self-enhancement can be seen as a rational strategy to maintain normal dignity in self-image and social interaction. The failure of others to meet this expectation may stem from stereotyping, and leads to communication pitfalls. Great sensitivity is required in making allowances for possible deficits in elderly people, while maintaining the features of normal adult-to-adult interaction.

Key Points ■ ■ ■

- ❒ There is individual variability in the patterns of ageing.
- ❒ Variability and adjustment problems have origins which are biological, psychological, and social.
- ❒ Longevity and health status are improving in Western societies.
- ❒ Self-assessment overrides objective measures of ageing.
- ❒ Older adults are living in a potentially ageist culture.

References ▼ ▼ ▼

Abercrombie, N., Warde, A., Soothill, K., Urry, J. and Walby, S. (1988). *Contemporary British Society.* Cambridge: Polity Press.

Adelman, R.D., Greene, M.G. and Charon, R. (1991). Issues in physician–elderly interaction. *Ageing and Society*, **11**: 127–48.

Baltes, M.M., Wahl, H. and Schmid-Furstoss, U. (1990). The daily life of elderly Germans: activity patterns, personal control, and functional health. In: Baltes, PB and Baltes, MM (eds), *Successful Ageing: Perspectives from the Social Sciences*. Cambridge: Cambridge University Press, 173–9.

Bergenudd, H., Lindgarde, F., Nilsson, B. and Petersson, C.J. (1988). Shoulder pain in middle age. *Clinical Orthopaedics and Related Research*, **231**: 234–7.

Billig, M. (1985). Prejudice, categorization and particularization: from a perceptual to a rhetorical approach. *European Journal of Social Psychology*, **15**: 79–103.

Bosse, R., Aldwin, C.M., Levenson, M.R. and Workman-Daniels, K. (1991). How stressful is retirement? Findings from the normative aging study. *Journal of Gerontology*, **46**: 9–14.

Bultena, G.L. and Powers, E.A. (1978). Denial of aging: age

identification and reference group orientations. *Journal of Gerontology*, **33**: 748–54.
Carlsson, M., Berg, S. and Wenestam, C. (1991). The oldest old: patterns of adjustment and dependence. *Scandinavian Journal of Caring Science*, **5**: 93–100.
Charatan, F.B., Sherman, F.T. and Libow, L.S. (eds) (1981). *The Core of Geriatric Medicine: A Guide for Students and Practitioners*. St Louis: CV Mosby, 59–84.
Coupland, N., Coupland, J. and Giles, H. (1991). *Language, Society and the Elderly*. Oxford: Blackwell.
Crary, L.M., Pazy, A. and Wolfe, D.M. (1989). Patterns of life structure and variability in self. *Human Relations*, **41**: 783–804.
Cribier, F. (1980). Changing retirement patterns: the experience of a cohort of Parisian salaried workers. *Ageing and Society*, **1**: 51–71.
Diener, E. (1984). Subjective well-being. *Psychological Bulletin*, **95**: 542–75.
Dittman-Kohli, F. (1990). The construction of meaning in old age: possibilities and constraints. *Ageing and Society*, **10**: 279–94.
Fitch, V.L. and Slivinske, L.R. (1989). Situational perceptions of control in the aged. In: Fry, P.S. (ed.), *Psychological Perspectives of Helplessness and Control in the Elderly*. Amsterdam: North-Holland, 155–86.
Greene, M., Hoffman, S., Charon, R. and Adelman, R. (1987). Psychosocial concerns in the medical encounter: a comparison of the interactions of doctors with their old and young patients. *The Gerontologist*, **27**: 164–8.
Harrison, P. (1973). Living with old age. *New Society*, Nov., 265–8.
Helson, R. and Wink, P. (1992). Personality change in women from the early 40s to the early 50s. *Psychology and Ageing*, **7**: 46–55.
Horn, J.L. (1982). The aging of human abilities. In: Wolman, BB (ed.), *Handbook of Developmental Psychology*. Englewood Cliffs, NJ: Prentice Hall, 847–70.
Hunter, M. (1996). Menopause. In: Niven, C.A. and Walker, A. (eds), *The Psychology of Reproduction. Vol 1: Reproductive Potential and Fertility Control*. London: Butterworth–Heinemann.
Jerrome, D. (1989). Virtue and vicissitude: the role of old people's clubs. In: Jeffreys, M. (ed.) *Growing Old in the Twentieth Century*. London: Routledge, 151–65.
Karp, D.A. (1988). A decade of reminders: changing age consciousness between fifty and sixty years old. *The Gerontologist*, **28**: 727–38.
Keller, M.L., Leventhal, E.A. and Larson, B. (1989). Aging: the lived experience. *International Journal of Aging and Human Development*. **29**: 67–82.
Logan, J.R., Ward, R. and Spitze, G. (1992). As old as you feel: age identity in middle and later life. *Social Forces*, **71**: 451–67.
Mac Rae, H. (1990). Older women and identity maintenance in later life. *Canadian Journal on Aging*, **9**: 248–67.
Mullins, D. and Hayslip, B. (1986). Structure of daily activities and self-efficacy. *Clinical Gerontologist*, **4**: 48–51.
Myerson, J., Hale, S., Hirschman, R., Hansen, C. and Christiansen, B. (1989). Global increase in response latencies by early middle age: complexity effects in individual performances. *Journal of the Experimental Analysis of Behavior*, **52**: 353–62.
Neugarten, B.L. (1979). Time, age, and the life cycle. *American Journal of Psychiatry*, **136**: 887–94.
Okun, M.A. (1986). Life satisfaction. In: Maddox, G.L. *et al.* (eds), *Encyclopedia of Aging*. New York: Springer, 399–401.
Oswald, F. (1991). Das personliche Altersbild alterer Menschen. *Zeitschrift fur Gerontologie*, **24**: 276–84.
Rabbitt, P. (1990). Applied cognitive gerontology: some problems, methodologies and data. *Applied Cognitive Psychology*, **4**: 225–46.
Radecki, S., Kane, R., Solomon, D., Mendenhall, R. and Beck, J. (1988). Do physicians spend less time with older patients? *Journal of the American Geriatrics Society*, **36**: 713–18.
Rapkin, B.D. and Fischer, K. (1992). Framing the construct of life satisfaction in terms of older adults' personal goals. *Psychology and Aging*, **7**: 138–49.
Revenson, T.A. (1989). Compassionate stereotyping of elderly patients by physicians: revising the social contact hypothesis. *Psychology and Aging*, **4**: 230–4.
Rogers, E. and Bhowmik, D. (1970). Homophily–heterophily relational concepts for communication research. *Public Opinion Quarterly*, **34**: 523–38.
Roos, N.P.. and Havens, B. (1991). Predictors of successful aging: a twelve-year study of Manitoba elderly. *American Journal of Public Health*, **81**: 63–8.
Rubenstein, L.Z., Josephson, K.R., Wieland, G.D. *et al.* (1984). Effectiveness of a geriatric evaluation unit: a randomized clinical trial. *New England Journal of Medicine*, **311**: 1664–70.
Rudinger, G. and Thomae, H. (1990). The Bonn longitudinal study of aging: coping, life adjustment and life satisfaction. In: Baltes, P.B. and Baltes, M.M. (eds), *Successful Aging: Perspectives from the Social Sciences*. Cambridge: Cambridge University Press, 265–95.
Ryan, K.M. and Bartlett-Weikel, K. (1993). Open-ended attributions for the performance of the elderly. *International Journal of Aging and Human Development*, **37**: 139–52.
Salthouse, T.A. (1985). Speed of behaviour and its implications for cognition. In: Birren, J.E. and Schaie, K.W. (eds), *Handbook of the Psychology of Aging*. New York: Van Nostrand Reinhold, 400–26.
Schaie, K.W. (1981). Psychological changes from midlife to early old age: implications for the maintenance of mental health. *American Journal of Orthopsychiatry*, **51**: 199.
Sherrard, C.A. (1994). Elderly wellbeing and the psychology of social comparisons. *Ageing and Society*, **14**: 341–56.
Stewart, M. (1983). Patient characteristics which are related to the doctor–patient interaction. *Family Practice*, **1**: 30–6.
Stokes, G. (1992). *On Being Old*. Falmer, Brighton: Falmer Press.
Suls, J. and Wills, T.A. (eds) (1991). *Social Comparison: Contemporary Theory and Research*. Hillsdale, NJ: Lawrence Erlbaum.
Thomae, H. (1976). *Patterns of Aging*. Basle: Karger.
Thomae, H. (1980). Personality and adjustment to aging. In: Birren, J.E. and Sloane, R.B. (eds), *Handbook of Mental Health and Ageing*. Englewood Cliffs, NJ: Prentice-Hall.
Twining, C. (1988). *Helping Older People: A Psychological Approach*. Chichester: Wiley.
Vischer, A.L. (1966). *On Growing Old*. London: Allen & Unwin.
Wardle, J., Blundell, J., Booth, D., Connolly, K., Shepherd, R. and Wright, P. (1991). Food, health and nutrition. *The Psychologist*, **5**(1): 35–8.

Further Reading ▲ ▲ ▲

Birren, J. and Warner Schaie, K. (1990). *Handbook of the Psychology of Ageing*, 3rd edn. New York: Academic Press.
Coupland, N., Coupland, J. and Giles, H. (1991). *Language, Society and the Elderly*. Oxford: Blackwell.
Gravell, R. (1988). *Communication Problems in Elderly People: Practical Approaches to Management*. London: Croom Helm.
Stokes, G. (1992). *On Being Old*. Falmer, Brighton: Falmer Press.
Twining, C. (1988). *Helping Older People: A Psychological Approach*. Chichester: Wiley.

SECTION IV

Interpersonal Issues

15

Perceiving People and Events

Martin F. Davies

LEARNING OBJECTIVES

After studying this chapter you should:

- Understand the processes underlying impression formation by relating these to personal experience
- Have a critical appreciation of research on impression formation
- Be able to apply an understanding of impression formation to clinical situations

INTRODUCTION

The work of health professionals involves a vast range and amount of interaction with others. Many of the social encounters can be brief and circumscribed by the technical duties to be performed, yet at the same time demanding of empathy or pastoral care.

This and the next chapter look at aspects of interpersonal behaviour which seem relevant to a healthcare situation. This chapter looks at how people perceive each other – more specifically, how first impressions are formed. The next chapter looks at how people explain and judge the behaviour of others. Without these processes meaningful social interaction could not take place.

IMPRESSION FORMATION

On meeting someone for the first time, a person observes a number of things about them:

- what they do (their actions);
- the context in which the actions occur;
- what they say (verbal behaviour);
- how they say it (non-verbal behaviour).

On the basis of these observations people then go beyond the information immediately available and make judgements about personality and character. Even with little information about somebody, a person still forms impressions about personality quite quickly and easily. First impressions are important because they influence the way one person feels and acts towards another. Research into impression formation has looked at how people infer characteristics such as personality from behaviour and how people organize different pieces of information about a person into a consistent, meaningful whole.

Inferring personal characteristics from behaviour

The classic research into impression formation was carried out in the 1940s but remains influential. Early work by Asch (1946) involved giving subjects a list of traits that described a particular person (actually a hypothetical person). The subjects then described their impressions and selected traits that they felt best described the person. The traits given to subjects at the outset to describe the person were the *stimulus* traits and the words that the subjects selected at the end were the *response* traits. Two stimulus lists were used which were identical except for the traits 'warm' (Group A) and 'cold' (Group B). Asch found that this simple warm–cold difference resulted in quite different impressions being formed of the stimulus person (see Box 15.1).

CENTRAL TRAITS

Asch argued that warm and cold trait adjectives were *central* traits, in that they had a strong influence on people's impressions. Differences on other trait dimensions did not seem to produce such large differences in

Box 15.1 *Asch's (1946) impression formation experiment*

List of stimulus traits presented to subjects	*Overall response or impression formed*
Group A	
Intelligent Skillful Industrious Warm Determined Practical Cautious	Talented but secure enough to be generous towards others
Group B	
Intelligent Skillful Industrious Cold Determined Practical Cautious	Talented but egocentric and selfish

impressions. For example, when *polite* versus *blunt* replaced *warm* versus *cold*, the two groups of subjects did not form impressions that were radically different. Asch further argued that whether a given trait was central or peripheral in the formation of an impression depended on its relationship with all the other traits in the list (the trait's *context*).

IMPLICIT PERSONALITY THEORY

Bruner and Tagiuri (1954) suggested that a person makes inferences about someone directly from their own *implicit theory of personality* – that is, their ideas about which personality traits go with other traits. For example, if they know a person is cold, they may automatically infer that the person is also unkind or hostile.

Wishner (1960) asked students to judge their teachers on a number of personality traits, and from these data the correlations or strength of relationships among the traits were calculated. Similar to Asch, Wishner found a correlation of 0.48 between ratings of warmth and imaginativeness. Wishner showed that if the relationships among traits is known, it is possible to predict subjects' selection of response traits from the stimulus traits; thus he provided a more objective definition of central traits: a trait is central if it correlates highly with the response traits. In this fashion, Wishner showed how people infer what traits are more or less related to other traits. Such a set of trait relationships is the perceiver's *implicit personality theory.*

It seems likely that people may initially acquire their implicit personality theory from observing actual co-occurrences amongst behaviours, but once such a theory is formed it may then serve to distort recalled relationships amongst behaviours observed subsequently. For example, although a person may learn that sociable behaviour does indeed co-occur with talkative and extrovert behaviour, they may subsequently tend to expect and recall a stronger association than actually exists. This debate highlights two more general points about person perception and impression formation:

- Impressions of others are determined partly by the actual characteristics of the other person. This can be called a *data-driven process.*
- Implicit personality theories can lead to the expectation and perception of characteristics that may not really be present in the other person. This can be called a *theory-driven process.*

Learning Activity 1 ◆ ◆ ◆

The aim is to identify your own implicit personality theory. Make a list of 10 people important in your life who you know quite well (e.g. parent, tutor, friend, sibling, colleague) and choose five traits from the list below which best describes each person:

- Outgoing/shy
- adjusted/maladjusted
- decisive/indecisive
- calm/excitable
- interested in others/self-absorbed
- cheerful/ill-humoured
- responsible/irresponsible
- considerate/inconsiderate
- independent/dependent.

Look at your responses and see if any traits typically occur together in different lists. If so, you have demonstrated part of your implicit personality theory. It also implies that once one trait is perceived in someone you tend to assume that they also possess the other trait.

Learning Activity 2 ◆ ◆ ◆

Ms Smith attends for a brief routine examination. She is middle-aged, well-spoken and smartly dressed. Her movements are relatively slow and shaky and she apologizes for keeping you waiting when she can see how busy you are. Towards the end of the examination she becomes very emotional but manages to contain her distress to enable you to finish. She tells you that she has just lost her purse and doesn't know how she can get home. She lives alone and can't think of anyone she might ring to come and fetch her as her family are not local and her neighbours are elderly. She accepts your offer of a cup of tea while she calms down, giving you time to arrange to see her to the bus stop with sufficient money to get home.

a Write down your overall impression of the woman.
b Choose five words which best describe her.
c Explain what information in the case description led you to your conclusions.

Organizing information into an impression

Most research on impression formation has concentrated on how people organize information to form an overall impression. Asch (1946) suggested two models of impression formation: additive and relational.

AN ADDITIVE MODEL

This predicts that the overall impression is based on the sum of the impressions of each individual piece of information about the person. The model is based on the notion that traits can be represented on particular *value dimensions*. Usually the dimension of interest in impression formation is an *evaluative* one (e.g. good–bad, likeable–dislikeable, positive–negative). Each piece of information is evaluated on its own for, say, likeability, and an overall impression of likeability is then obtained by adding up all the likeability values.

There are two basic additive models, the *summation* model and the *averaging* model. Both the summation and averaging models are based on a simple additive process. The summation model suggests that an impression is determined by the *total* likeability of the traits. The averaging model takes into account the number of traits so that the overall impression is based on the *average* likeability.

The difference between these two models is not trivial. For example, in terms of presenting a favourable image of oneself to others, the summation model suggests that a person should keep adding more and more positive information about self; whereas the averaging model suggests that they should not add weakly favourable information about self, otherwise this will dilute the impression.

Anderson (1965) extended Asch's ideas to produce first the *weighted average* model, which takes into account not only the likeability or favourability of the traits, but also how important they are or how heavily they are weighted for the perceiver. From this he developed a model of people's judgements based on the values and weights of the component items, called *integration theory* (Anderson, 1981). The theory has been used widely to predict judgements in a variety of areas, such as the guilt of defendants in jury trials (Ostrom *et al.*, 1978) and the choice of an opposite-sex partner in dating (Shanteau and Nagy, 1979) as well as impressions of personality.

A RELATIONAL MODEL

This suggests that the pieces of information are not seen as independent of each other, but rather are perceived as fitting into an organized whole called a *Gestalt*. The impression Gestalt is formed from the unique relationships among the traits. In this model, the overall impression is not easily predictable from knowing the likeability of each individual piece of information, since the likeability of any one piece of information is affected by the presence of other pieces of information.

So the trait *happy* may mean something different in the context of *stupid–silly* than in the context of *warm–relaxed.*

So Asch believed that trait terms actually change meaning in relation to one another. Another example, the mess ('untidiness') of the room of a great artist ('neurotic') could be explained by *creative eccentricity*, whereas the mess ('untidiness') of your room-mate (also 'neurotic') could be put down to their *sloppiness*. Thus the meaning of inconsistent information is changed to resolve the inconsistency. The change-of-meaning hypothesis seems quite straightforward, but it is difficult to test because it is difficult to measure not only change of meaning but also the different meanings of words themselves.

Change of meaning has often been studied by having subjects judge how much they like a particular trait alone and how much they like it when presented in the context of other traits. It is found that the context changes the evaluation of the trait (Anderson and Lampel, 1965). For example, the term *happy* is evaluated more positively alone than in the context of 'happy, stupid, insensitive'. Wyer and Watson (1969) proposed that change-of-meaning effects should be most pronounced for traits that can take on a wide range of evaluative meanings. Some traits have a relatively fixed meaning and cannot change their meaning in different contexts, whereas others have a more variable meaning and should be readily changed by context. For example, a trait such as *loyal* is generally positive, but it could range from extremely positive to extremely negative, depending on its context (e.g. the loyalty of Napoleon's troops versus the loyalty of Al Capone's hitmen); whereas a trait like *sincere* would be generally positive whatever the context. The change-of-meaning issue is interesting, but the debate about the interpretation of results has been rather technical – psychologists and linguists still have difficulty defining the psychological dimensions and processes underlying meaning and meaning change.

Learning Activity 3 ◆ ◆ ◆

Continuing the case study of Ms Smith in Activity 2: Later on, glancing through the hospital notes, you find that she has attended the drug dependency unit for at least 10 years. Intrigued by your discovery you read some of the case notes which describe her convictions as a confidence trickster; she is currently on probation for shoplifting. She lives in a hostel and has had five different addresses over the past two years.

a Choose *five* words which best describe the woman.
b In the light of the new information, write down your overall impression of her.
c Explain which information in the case description leads you to your present conclusions.
d Has your impression been changed in the light of the new information?
e Did you experience difficulties in forming an overall impression in the light of the new information?
f Did any of the traits chosen in Activity 2 change their meaning in the context of this new information or when paired with traits used in this exercise?
g Which model is best supported by your response – the additive or the relational?

Primacy–recency effects

A *primacy* effect is when information presented first is more influential in determining the final impression, and a *recency* effect is when information presented last is more influential. Asch had originally shown that when positive information is presented before negative information, the overall impression is more positive than when the reverse order is used.

These effects are explained differently by different models. Anderson's weighted-average model predicts that primacy effects are due to later information being given less weight than early information. This could be due to *attention decrement* – subjects get tired or bored and forget or pay less attention to later information – or that later information is *discounted* because it is inconsistent with the earlier information. The attention decrement hypothesis is supported best. Anderson and Hubert (1963) presented subjects with a list of trait adjectives to form an impression. Half the subjects were told that they would also be required to recall the adjectives at the end, whereas the other half were not expecting to have to recall the adjectives. The usual primacy effect was found in impressions for the no-recall group, but this disappeared in the recall group, because they had been asked to pay attention equally to all the adjectives.

In contrast, Asch's position was that primacy effects are due to a relational tendency – the initial information

Learning Activity 4 ◆ ◆ ◆

Do an experiment to demonstrate primacy effects. Using the case description in Activities 2 and 3, present some people firstly with the information in the notes, followed by the examination incident. Present things the other way round for some other people. After each presentation ask just the first three questions (in Activity 2).

a Compare the impression given in the second half of the experiment and see whether those given the hospital notes information first form an impression that is typically different from those given this information last. If so, how does it differ?
b Has your experiment shown a primacy effect?
c Which hypothesis is better supported by your findings – attention decrement or relational tendency?

sets up a directional feeling to which later information is assimilated.

ACCURACY IN PERSON PERCEPTION

The issue of accuracy in person perception has been concerned with what kinds of people make good judges of personality. This involves assessing the accuracy with which people ('judges') can estimate the personality of others, and measuring the characteristics of good versus poor judges of personality. One goal of early research was basically practical. If it could be discovered what made a good judge of others, people in important positions in social groups could be selected and trained to judge others accurately. This has become an important issue in personnel selection.

Early researchers looked for judges who could predict accurately the characteristics and behaviours of different people. Vernon (1993) identified three types of judges: good judges of the self, good judges of friends, and good judges of strangers. These results therefore suggest that accuracy in judging others is not a general trait, because it depends on the person being judged. However, Estes (1938) found that certain people possessed a general ability to judge others accurately (on all personality dimensions and for all actors). This general ability was associated with strong artistic interests, but not with any intelligence or personality factors. He also found that some personality dimensions (e.g. inhibition–impulsivity, apathy–intensity) were easier to judge accurately than others. Finally, some actors were more accurately judged than others. Thus in his review of over 50 studies on accuracy, Taft (1955) concluded that there was little evidence of a *general* ability to judge others accurately. People who were accurate on some dimensions and with some types of stimulus persons were not accurate on other dimensions and stimulus persons. In addition, accuracy was not consistently related to any personality characteristics of the judge.

It is conceivable that accuracy can never be established, because what criterion or standard of accuracy is appropriate? Vernon used test scores, Estes used the judgements of trained clinicians. Is one criterion better than another? Are the judgements of trained clinicians worse than scores on psychometric tests or subjects' own self-reports?

A number of major methodological issues were raised by Cronbach (1955). His comprehensive analysis made it difficult to study accuracy in person perception. With all the qualifications and technicalities involved in the accuracy question, researchers were put off investing the time and energy needed to calculate the different components of accuracy (computers were not readily available in 1955). It is important to note that Cronbach's critique did not imply that it is pointless investigating accuracy. Rather, he was suggesting that researchers should analyse *how* a good judge achieves accuracy.

The accuracy issue faded away for many years following Cronbach's analysis, and it is only recently that researchers have revived the question of accuracy in person perception. Kenny and Albright's (1987) social relations analysis deals with when and how people are accurate rather than who is accurate, and suggests separating accuracy into components rather than assessing overall accuracy. Swann (1984) has also argued against investigating global accuracy scores. He proposes that research should focus on 'circumscribed accuracy', where judgements are made about other people in the typical real-world settings in which we encounter them, rather than in the abstract and artificial situations of the laboratory experiment.

SUMMARY

It seems likely that impressions of others are based on a perceptual process in which observations are interpreted in the context of the perceiver's implicit personality theory. This serves to make some information more salient and permits the perceiver to go beyond the immediate information and infer general traits about the other person. This is an essential aspect of interpersonal relationships but not without its negative consequences such as prejudice and stereotyping.

Although psychologists have investigated how accurate people are in judging others, there is no evidence for a general ability to be an accurate judge. Rather, accuracy depends on what types of personality dimension are involved and on the type of person being judged.

Key Points ■ ■ ■

❏ First impressions are based on different sources of information gleaned from the interaction.

❏ Some information is selected as more important than others (central traits).

❏ This process of selection is in part guided by a person's own mental model of personality.

❏ People go beyond the immediate information given to infer personality traits.

❏ Impressions can be based on implicit personality theory or observation of behaviour, but are usually based on a mixture of the two.

❏ Debate continues about the processes involved in integrating information to produce an overall impression.

References ▼ ▼ ▼

Anderson, N.H. (1965). Adding versus averaging as a stimulus combination rule in impression formation. *Journal of Experimental Psychology*, **70**: 394–400.

Anderson, N.H. (1981). *Foundations of Information Integration Theory*. New York: Academic Press.

Anderson, N.H. and Hubert, S. (1963). Effects of concomitant verbal recall on order effects in personality impression formation. *Journal of Verbal Learning and Verbal Behaviour*, **2**: 379–91.

Anderson, N.H. and Lampel, A.K. (1965). Effect of context on ratings of personality traits. *Psychonomic Science*, **3**: 433–4.

Asch, S.E. (1946). Forming impressions of personality. *Journal of Abnormal and Social Psychology*, **41**: 258–90.

Bruner, J.S. and Tagiuri, R. (1954). The perception of people. In: Lindzey, G. (ed.), *Handbook of Social Psychology*, vol. 2. Reading, MA: Addison-Wesley, 634–54.

Cronbach, L.J. (1955). Processes affecting scores on 'understanding of others' and 'assumed similarity'. *Psychological Bulletin*, **52**: 177–93.

Estes, S.G. (1938). Judging personality from expressive behaviour. *Journal of Abnormal and Social Psychology*, **33**: 217–36.

Kenny, D. and Albright, L. (1987). Accuracy in interpersonal perception: a social relations analysis. *Psychological Bulletin*, **102**: 390–402.

Ostrom, T.M., Werner, C. and Saks, M.J. (1978). An integration theory analysis of jurors' presumptions of guilt or innocence. *Journal of Personality and Social Psychology*, **36**: 436–50.

Shanteau, J. and Nagy, G.F. (1979). Probability of acceptance in dating choice. *Journal of Personality and Social Psychology*, **37**: 522–33.

Swann, W.B. (1984). Quest for accuracy in person perception: matter of pragmatics. *Psychological Review*, **91**: 457–77.

Taft, R. (1955). The ability to judge people. *Psychological Bulletin*, **52**: 1–23.

Vernon, P.E. (1933). Some characteristics of the good judge of personality. *Journal of Social Psychology*, **4**: 42–58.

Wishner, J. (1960). Reanalysis of 'Impressions of personality'. *Psychological Review*, **67**: 96–112.

Wyer, R.S. and Watson, S.F. (1969). Context effects in impression formation. *Journal of Personality and Social Psychology*, **12**: 22–33.

Further Reading ▲ ▲ ▲

Brewer, M.B. and Crano, W.D. (1994). Forming impressions. In: *Social Psychology*. St Paul, MN: West Publishing.

Deaux, K., Dane, F.C. and Wrightsman, L.S. (1993). Understanding others: In: *Social Psychology in the 1990s*, 6th edn. Pacific Grove, CA: Brooks/Cole, 81–100.

Zebrowitz, L.A. (1990). The contents of social perception *and* Impression formation. In: *Social Perception*. Milton Keynes: Open University Press.

16

Explaining People and Events

Martin F. Davies

LEARNING OBJECTIVES

After studying this chapter you should:

- Appreciate the main concepts in attribution theory by relating these to clinical experience
- Have a critical appreciation of research into causal attribution
- Be able to apply some of the principles of attribution to common clinical situations

INTRODUCTION

In many situations the health professional has to be able to make rapid judgements about the behaviour of others, including what they say. Similarly the person receiving healthcare makes judgements – whereupon social discourse proceeds. The quality of this discourse determines the quality of their relationship and ultimately the quality of care. Thus in order for social intercourse to take place people need to make sense of each other's behaviour. This chapter looks at the psychological processes involved in understanding why other people act in the way they do. The study of this process within social psychology is called *causal attribution*, where identifying a cause for a given event or behaviour is to make an attribution.

Attribution theory has thrived for over 30 years. There have been three main developments in the classic theories or models of attribution (Heider, 1958; Jones and Davis, 1965; Kelley, 1967, 1972) (see Box 16.1).

These theories are cognitive and therefore assume a view of the person as an active information processor trying to make sense of their world. They present the perceiver as a fairly rational person; hence these models are referred to as *rational baseline* models.

However, research has shown that perceivers do not act like scientists, following detailed rules and formal models. Rather, they make attributions quickly, using much less information than the models suggest they should, and they show clear tendencies for certain sorts of explanation that are not predicted from the models.

Box 16.1 *The development of classic attribution theory*

• Heider (1958)	Person causes versus situational causes
• Jones and Davis (1965)	Observe behaviour ⇒ Infer intention ⇒ Attribute disposition Correspondent inferences versus non-correspondent inferences
• Kelley (1967, 1972)	Covariation versus configuration

NAIVE PSYCHOLOGY

Work on attribution theory began with Fritz Heider (1958), who believed that people's social behaviour depends on how they perceive and report their social world. He attempted to find out how ordinary people describe their social world in everyday terms, rather than how scientists, psychologists or philosophers explain events in terms of complex theories or models. Heider assumed that people want to understand their social world not simply out of idle curiosity or intellectual stimulation. People want to be able to anticipate the effects that their behaviour and other people's behaviour will have. Being able to predict events in this way might then help people to exert some control over events to make nice things happen and to avoid nasty things happening.

Person causes versus situational causes

Heider's contribution to attribution theory was not so much to produce a comprehensive theory as to outline many of the basic issues that were developed later.

He made a distinction between *person* and *situational* causes. Person causes are internal to the actor (the person doing the behaving) whereas situational causes are external to the actor. Take the example of a man going to a gym: a 'person' reason might be because he enjoys exercise; a 'situational' reason might be because friends asked him to go with them.

Heider was particularly interested in achievement situations – succeeding or failing. In his analysis, internal or person factors consist of one's motivation ('trying') and ability ('can') in achieving an outcome. For example, a man may have the ability to do gym exercises but without the motivation he won't succeed. However, external or situational forces also affect whether people succeed or fail. If an exercise or task is easy (a weak force), then they can probably succeed with just a little motivation and ability, but if the task is difficult (a strong force) they may not succeed even with a lot of ability and motivation. These ideas are relevant to how people deal with or manage ill-health, and disability in particular (see Chapter 5), where motivation to achieve a task can be critical.

Individuals differ in the extent to which they believe events are due to internal, personal causes or external, situational causes. Rotter (1966) suggested that some people believe they have the ability to control most events; he called these people *internals*. Other people, however, tend to believe that events are not under their control but are due to external forces such as luck, chance, or powerful others. He called these people *externals*. Rotter devized a locus of control scale for measuring internal versus external beliefs in control. For example, a person who agrees with the statement 'Promotions are earned through hard work and persistence' would be internal, whereas a person who agrees with the statement 'Making a lot of money is largely a matter of getting the right breaks' would be external.

Wallston *et al.* (1978) developed a locus of control measure specifically for health. Their measure comprises three subscales assessing the extent to which people attribute health/illness to *internal factors*, *powerful others*, or *chance*. An 'internal' item is 'If I get sick, it is my own behaviour which determines how soon I get well again'. A 'powerful other' item is 'Health professionals control my health'. A 'chance' item is 'If it's meant to be, I will stay healthy.'

Learning Activity 1 ◆ ◆ ◆

Reflect on *your own* beliefs about health by completing one of the *health locus of control measures*, such as that by Wallston *et al.* (1978). Compare your responses with those of others.

The fundamental attribution error

Heider's ideas have been elaborated by subsequent empirical work. Ross (1977) used the term 'fundamental attribution error' to describe the tendency to over-emphasize person attributions and to underemphasize situational attributions in explaining other people's behaviour. For example, Jones and Harris (1967), found that perceivers attribute attitudes to a speaker even when the speaker has been constrained to present a particular viewpoint – that is, when the speaker had little choice as to which side of an argument to give. Thus, they attach too little weight to the situational forces (instructions to argue one side of the issue) and too much weight to person/dispositional factors (the speaker's attitude).

Ross *et al.* (1977a) found a similar tendency for perceivers to fail to take account of the effects of social role in influencing behaviour. They randomly assigned subjects in a quiz game to be either questioners or contestants. The questioners were told to think up difficult questions from any area of knowledge. Both the contestants and the questioners overlooked the built-in advantage that the questioners had in demonstrating knowledgeability (i.e. selecting erudite questions from their own specialized areas of expertise), and so the questioners were rated as much more knowledgeable than the contestants.

What causes the fundamental attribution error? One explanation is that the actor's behaviour is perceived to be more *salient* than the situation. Heider had foreseen such an effect since there is a strong bond between the actor and the act. A second explanation is that there is a *social norm* for internality – internal attributions are looked on more favourably than external attributions (Jellison and Green, 1981). In societies that emphasize individualism and personal responsibility (such as Western societies), people are socialized into making internal attributions for behaviour. In societies that emphasize collectivism, however, the fundamental attribution error is much weaker or non-existent.

Actor–observer differences

Jones and Nisbett (1972) suggested that there is a pervasive tendency for actors to attribute their actions to situational requirements, whereas observers attribute the same actions to stable personal dispositions. This is not entirely surprising, given that actors have much more information about themselves than do observers. Actors know much more about their own past behaviours and how their behaviour changes across different situations. Thus, they may be more aware that the situation is rather unusual and that their behaviour departs from similar behaviour in previous situations; hence they make situational attributions. By contrast, observers do not have knowledge about previous behaviours and they assume greater consistency of behaviour; and hence they infer dispositional causes. In support of this, Nisbett *et al.* (1973) found that as familiarity of the other person increased (i.e. length of acquaintanceship with the other), so situational attributions for the other person's behaviour increased.

A second point is that actors and observers differ not only in the *amount* of information that they have, they also differ in information *processing*. Jones and Nisbett argued that the perceptual viewpoint or focus of actors is outwards on to the environment rather than on to the self. Thus, actors make situation attributions literally because they do not see themselves acting. By contrast, the focus of attention of observers is on the actor rather than on the situation, and so they make person attributions (Storms, 1973).

The implications of actor–observer differences can be quite important. For example, when a person appears not to have complied with treatment, this may be due to different interpretations about the same event. The person may blame the therapist for not giving clear instructions, whereas the therapist may blame the person for being unmotivated. They have different personal information and different perceptual viewpoints on the matter.

Self-serving biases

The self-serving bias is the tendency for people to take credit for success and deny responsibility for failure (Bradley, 1978). It is seen most clearly in experiments where some people are given feedback suggesting they have done well on a task whereas others are given feedback suggesting they have done badly. Success-feedback subjects tend to attribute their performance to internal factors such as high ability or motivation, so that their apparently good performance is given added shine by their attributions. Failure-feedback subjects tend to attribute their performance to external factors such as task difficulty or bad luck, so that their apparently poor performance is excused or justified. Similarly, the 'optimistic bias' is a tendency to believe that good things are more likely and bad things are less likely to happen to the self than to the average person; again this contributes to positive illusions about the self.

Self-serving biases can be quite adaptive, despite the fact that people are trying to fool others (and to some extent themselves) into believing an overinflated self-image. Attributing success to one's one efforts creates expectations that make it more likely that a person would attempt similar tasks in the future. A self-serving motivational bias can lead to people actually being more successful at tasks that they undertake. Taylor and Brown (1988) argue that self-enhancing perceptions are adaptive becase they tend to be associated with positive mental health. People who have positive illusions about themselves are happy and contented, care about others, and engage in productive and creative work – all criteria that are associated with successful life-adjustment.

Learning Activity 2 ◆ ◆ ◆

The aim is to explore attributional biases – to demonstrate the irrationality of causal attributions by identifying *self-serving biases* such as the 'optimistic bias'.

Rate the relative likelihood for yourself versus the average person (or perhaps the average health professional) of suffering from the following: drug addiction; suicide; venereal disease; alcoholism; lung cancer; kidney infection; diabetes; asthma; bronchitis. Use the following scale:

−3 = much less likely than average
−2 = less likely than average
−1 = slightly less likely than average
0 = average
+1 = slightly more likely than average
+2 = more likely than average
+3 = much more likely than average.

CORRESPONDENT INFERENCES

Following Heider's ideas came *correspondent inference* theory (Jones and Davis, 1965; Jones and McGillis, 1976) which was concerned with how people infer a particular disposition or characteristic from a person's actions or behaviour. It was argued that this is a two-stage process: first the perceiver has to establish the intention behind a given act, and from knowing someone's intentions the perceiver then makes inferences or value judgements about the person.

So, for example, if a person is observed going to the gym, it may be inferred that the person believes exercise to be worthwhile. However, the action may be attributed to something different, such as a means of socializing or of obeying someone else's instruction. In the first case the intention that is inferred is the desire to be fit, so the person is seen as 'health-conscious'; this is a correspondent inference because the same descriptive term is used for the act and for the disposition. In the second case the intention may be seen as the desire to please someone else; this is a non-correspondent inference.

Learning Activity 3 ◆ ◆ ◆

Think of a person you have met, either socially or professionally, whom you felt had probably been responsible (at least in part) for their ill-health. Consider the following questions in as much detail as possible:

a which *five* words best describe this person?
b On what evidence did you base your belief that the person's ill-health was internally caused?
c Did you have information about 'consequences'; 'social desirability'; 'expectancies'; and 'choice' (Jones and Davis) with regard to those actions which you felt were detrimental to their health.
d Which of Kelley's two models (covariation or configuration) best describe the reasoning processes used to make your internal attribution?
e Do you know whether the person concerned took any of the blame for their ill-health? If they did not, reflect on some explanations for this difference of opinion.

Inferring intention and disposition

Jones and Davis argued that to infer a particular intention to an actor depends on knowing a number of things about that person:

- *Consequences*. It has to be assumed that the actor knows the consequences of his or her action.
- *Social desirability*. People usually intend desirable outcomes. Therefore socially desirable outcomes are not informative about a person's intention or disposition. The most that can be inferred is that the person is normal – which is not saying anything very much. However, socially *undesirable* actions are more informative about intentions and dispositions because when people do not conform to group pressure it is more likely that they truly believe the views or actions they express.
- *Expectancies*. Jones and McGillis (1976) argued that only behaviours that *disconfirm expectancies* are truly informative about an actor. To know, for example, that a person values exercise sets up certain expectations and associations about his or her beliefs and character. It is notable, then, if the person acts in a way that is not expected.
- *Choice*. It has to be known whether the behaviour of the actor is constrained by situational forces or whether it occurs from the actor's free choice.

COVARIATION AND CONFIGURATION

As Box 16.1 showed, the next contribution to attribution theory came from Kelley (1967, 1972). He argued that attributions depend on the amount of information available to the perceiver:

- *Covariation*. The perceiver has information from multiple sources and can use this information to look for the 'covariation' of an observed effect (behaviour) with its possible causes.
- *Configuration*. The perceiver has only a single observation and must make an attribution from the 'configuration' or patterns of factors that are possible causes for the observed effect.

The covariation model

When the perceiver has information from a number of sources, Kelley suggests that the principle of covariation is used. In trying to understand the cause of some effect (behaviour), people observe its covariation with various

Box 16.2 *Kelley's covariation analysis*

Possible causes of reasons for a behaviour	Types of information required to attribute cause	Combinations responsible for specific attributions
Actor	Consensus information	Low consensus + Low distinctiveness + High consistency
Entity	Distinctiveness information	High consensus + High distinctiveness + High consistency
Circumstances	Consistency information	Low consistency

possible causes and attribute the behaviour to the cause with which it most closely covaries (see Box 16.2).

For example, if a certain woman keeps going on about how brilliant was the film she saw the other night, we can group possible causes into three general types:

- *The actor.* The woman may be undiscriminating and thinks all films are 'brilliant'.
- *The entity.* The film was, in fact, very good by any standards.
- *The circumstances.* The woman had a good time because of the company she was in, or it was on a big screen, or she had just had promotion at work.

Three types of information are required in order to identify the specific reason why the woman liked the film: whether other people like it ('consensus' information); how the woman reacts to other films ('distinctiveness information'); and, if the woman had seen the film before, whether she had liked it then ('consistency' information).

Kelley argued that each piece of information alone is insufficient to pinpoint a cause; it is the combination that is important. As Box 16.2 shows, he argued that distinct combinations are associated with particular attributions.

Single observation: the configuration model

Often, there is no access to the information needed to perform a covariance analysis or no time or motivation to carry out such an analysis. In these cases of incomplete data, Kelley suggests that attributions are made using *causal schemata.* These schemata are ready-made beliefs, conceptions, or theories – either learnt from experiences or from others – about how certain kinds of causes interact to produce a certain sort of effect.

One of the simplest schemata is the *multiple sufficient cause* (MSC), whereby any one of a number of causes is sufficient on its own to produce the effect. For example, a person's poor rehabilitation performance could be due to the extent of underlying pathology, personal problems, poor therapy, lack of effort, poor community support facilities, and so on. If a given cause is known to be present, other possible causes are discounted (the 'discounting principle'). Thus, if a person shows poor rehabilitation and it is known that the spouse died recently, other plausible causes such as poor therapy or support or lack of effort can be discounted. Kelley also suggested that a given cause is augmented if an effect occurs in the presence of some inhibitory cause (the 'augmentation principle'). Take the example of a person who lives across the other side of town yet turns up regularly for exercise classes and does well. The inhibitory force here is the amount of time, effort and inconvenience required to get to the clinic. Therefore it can be assumed that this person is probably better motivated than one who lives just down the road and who shows the same attendance and performance.

A second schema is the *multiple necessary cause* (MNC), whereby a number of causes must operate together to produce the effect (each cause on its own is not sufficient to produce the effect). Kelley suggested that this schema would be invoked to account for unusual or extreme effects. For example, to win a marathon race requires ability, effort, good training, proper diet, and so on.

The false-consensus effect

In practice people may not be as rational as Kelley's model suggests. In testing the model, McArthur (1972) showed that consensus information (how other people behave) is under-utilized in the process of attribution. This may be because perceivers prefer to rely on their own *self-generated* consensus information. This false consensus (or self-based consensus) is the tendency to see one's own behaviour as typical and to assume that under the same circumstances others would react the same way as oneself.

Ross *et al.* (1977b) demonstrated this effect by asking college students if they would walk around a college campus for 30 minutes wearing a large sandwich-board with the message 'Eat at Joe's'. Those who agreed to wear the sandwich-board estimated that 62% would also have agreed, whereas those who refused estimated that 67% would also have refused.

There are a number of explanations for this effect. One is that people tend to seek out the company of others who are similar to them and behave as they do. So, estimates of how others would behave is based on a biased sample of people (that is, people who have similar views to ourselves are more likely to come to mind when we estimate what others are like). Another possibility is that people need to believe that their behaviours are sound, sensible and appropriate, and so they attribute the same behaviours to others as a way of confirming this view.

The false-consensus effect has important implications for how people interpret social reality:

- The false-consensus effect may be one of the main ways by which people maintain that *their* attitudes and beliefs are correct.
- It may lead people to assume that there are a lot of others out there who feel the same way they do, which may not be the case.
- Under some conditions, the false-consensus effect may function as a justification for imposing one's own political, moral and religious beliefs on others. Thus, political leaders may believe that the electorate share their views when this is not so.

The false-consensus effect can be linked to groups and intergroup relations. People tend to believe that the views and values of their own group are more common and widespread than they really are. People who belong to a different group will therefore be seen as having not only different views and values, but views and values that are abnormal or wrong. A person's beliefs or implicit personality theories about groups ('stereotypes') can be influenced by false-consensus effects, and their evaluations and feelings about other groups ('prejudices') can be similarly influenced – usually in the direction of becoming more extreme (Brewer and Kramer, 1985). Via false-consensus effects, there will be a tendency for a professional group to believe that their attitudes, values and opinions are more widespread than they really are, and that they are more acceptable and reasonable than those of other groups (particularly lower-status groups). The more closely a person associates and identifies with a group, the stronger the false-consensus effect (because the views and attitudes of colleagues spring more readily to mind).

Learning Activity 4 ◆ ◆ ◆

The aim is to demonstrate how becoming a professional might encourage the false-consensus effect. Think of an incident when, because you were acting as a professional, you acted 'out of character' (that is, in a way you would not have expected yourself to act).

a What made you do this?
b List the main differences (if any) between your personal identity and your professional identity (i.e. how have you changed as a person since becoming a health professional?).
c What would you say have been the main influences on your development as a professional?
d Are there any things you see differently now that you have become a professional?
e What are the advantages and disadvantages to patients of your professional status?
f Can you foresee any obstacles to your professional growth in the future?

SUMMARY

Most research on attribution emphasizes cognitive explanations and phenomena, in keeping with the cognitive emphasis of the classic attribution theories. Many of the studies undertaken to test these theories have shown, however, that social perception is not a consistent and rational cognitive process; self-serving bias, for example, involves motivational processes. Ideas on attribution have therefore changed considerably since the early theories.

Heider assumed that people try to explain social events as accurately as possible in order to predict and control future events. Similarly, Kelley's covariation model assumes that the social perceiver applies certain principles in a careful (and laborious) search for the correct attribution. Such models present a picture of the social perceiver as a *scientist*, searching methodically for the truth.

Later work suggests that the social perceiver may not be as diligent as this analogy suggests. People take short-cuts and look for simple clues to the cause of an event. For example, they may attribute the cause of an event to people or things that catch their attention. Fiske and Taylor (1991) call this portrayal of the social perceiver the *cognitive miser* model.

With the self-serving bias, it could be said that the social perceiver seems to be more like a lawyer – not trying to find out the truth but trying to win the case and gaining public acclaim.

Key Points

- Attribution research adopts a view of the person as an active processor of information.
- Attribution, like other aspects of person perception, is based partly on observations and partly on preconceptions.
- An important distinction in accounting for someone's behaviour is between internal (person) causes and external (situational) causes.
- One classic theory suggests that people attempt to infer a disposition (e.g. a personality trait) to account for an observed act.
- Another classic theory suggests that people look for covariation between possible causes and observed effects.
- Research shows that the classic theories overestimate the extent to which people process information rationally and logically.
- The process of attribution can involve motivational and emotional factors and the use of cognitive short-cuts.

References

Bradley, G.W. (1978). Self-serving biases in the attribution process: a reexamination of the fact or fiction question. *Journal of Personality and Social Psychology*: **36**: 56–71.

Brewer, M.B. and Kramer, R.M. (1985). The psychology of intergroup attitudes and behaviour. *Annual Review of Psychology*: **36**: 219–43.

Fiske, S.T. and Taylor, S.E. (1991). *Social Cognition*. New York: McGraw-Hill.

Heider, F. (1958). *The Psychology of Interpersonal Relations*. New York: Wiley.

Jellison, J.M. and Green, J. (1981). A self-presentational approach to the fundamental attribution error: the norm of internality. *Journal of Personality and Social Psychology*: **40**: 643–9.

Jones, E.E. and Davis, K.E. (1965). From acts to dispositions: the attribution process in person perception. In: Berkowitz, L (ed.), *Advances in Experimental Social Psychology*: vol. 2. New York: Academic Press, 220–66.

Jones, E.E. and Harris, V.A. (1967). The attribution of attitudes. *Journal of Experimental Social Psychology*: **3**: 1–24.

Jones, E.E. and McGillis, D. (1976). Correspondent inferences and the attribution cube: a comparative reappraisal. In: Harvey, J.H. *et al.* (eds), *New Directions in Attribution Research*, vol. 1. Hillsdale, NJ: Lawrence Erlbaum, 389–420.

Jones, E.E. and Nisbett, R.E. (1972). The actor and the observer: divergent perceptions of the causes of behavior. In: Jones, E.E. *et al.* (eds), *Attribution: Perceiving the Causes of Behavior*. Morristown, NJ: General Learning Press, 79–94.

Kelley, H.H. (1967). Attribution theory in social psychology. In: Levine, D. (ed.), *Nebraska Symposium on Motivation*: vol. 15. Lincoln: University of Nebraska Press, 192–240.

Kelley, H.H. (1972): Causal schemata and the attribution process. In: Jones, E.E. *et al.* (eds), *Attribution: Perceiving the Causes of Behavior*. Morristown, NJ: General Learning Press, 151–74.

McArthur, L.Z. (1972). The how and what of why: some determinants and consequences of causal attribution. *Journal of Personality and Social Psychology*: **22**: 171–93.

Nisbett, R.E., Caputo, C., Legant, P. and Maracek, J. (1973). Behavior as seen by the actor and as seen by the observer. *Journal of Personality and Social Psychology*: **27**: 154–64.

Ross, L. (1977). The intuitive psychologist and his shortcomings: distortions in the attribution process. In: Berkowitz, L. (ed.), *Advances in Experimental Social Psychology*: vol. 10. New York: Academic Press, 174–221.

Ross, L., Amabile, T.M. and Steinmetz, J.L. (1977a). Social roles, social control, and biases in social-perception processes. *Journal of Personality and Social Psychology*: **35**: 485–94.

Ross, L., Greene, D. and House, P. (1977b). The 'false consensus effect': an egocentric bias in social perception and attribution processes. *Journal of Experimental Social Psychology*, **13**: 279–301.

Rotter, J.B. (1966). Generalized expectancies for internal versus external control of reinforcement. *Psychological Monographs*: **80** (1, whole no. 609).

Storms, M.D. (1973). Videotape and the attribution process: reversing actors' and observers' points of view. *Journal of Personality and Social Psychology*: **27**: 165–75.

Taylor, S.E. and Brown, J.D. (1988). Illusion and well-being: a social psychological perspective on mental health. *Psychological Bulletin*: **103**: 193–210.

Wallston, K.A., Wallston, B.S. and DeVellis, R. (1978). Development of the multidimensional Health Locus of Control Scales. *Health Education Monographs*: **6**: 161–70.

Further Reading ▲ ▲ ▲

Deaux, K., Dane, F.C. and Wrightsman, L.S. (1993). Understanding others. In: *Social Psychology in the 1990s*, 6th edn. Pacific Grove, CA: Brooks/Cole, 102–11.

Fiske, S.T. and Taylor, S.E. (1991). Attribution theory *and* Attribution theory: theoretical refinements. In: *Social Cognition*: 2nd edn. Maidenhead: McGraw-Hill.

Hewstone, M. and Antaki, C. (1988). Attribution theory and social explanations. In: Hewstone, M *et al*. (eds), *Introduction to Social Psychology*. Oxford: Blackwell, 111–41.

17

Social Influence

Valerie Kent

LEARNING OBJECTIVES

After studying this chapter you should:

- Be able to identify the main processes underlying conformity and compliance by relating these to your personal and clinical experience
- Have a critical appreciation of research on social influence processes
- Be able to apply your understanding of conformity and compliance to clinical situations

INTRODUCTION

Conforming to social norms is an important phenomenon both for social groups and for individuals. Group cohesion, social control, being accepted and liked and the provision of rules or codes of conduct are some of the more obvious consequences of conformity. In healthcare, treatment programmes often break down and cooperation with treatment may require people to make major long-term changes in their behaviour.

This chapter gives a brief history and contemporary review of research on social influence processes. The concepts of conformity and compliance are discussed, and normative and informational influence are explained. The impact of minorities on majorities is explored, as well as the importance of people's sense of social identity as a basis of influence.

CONFORMITY

The words 'conformity' and 'compliance' are used in everyday language. They may be used in a negative way, suggesting a rather sheep-like following of others, a passive yielding to pressure. They may conjure more positive images, such as showing a helpful acceptance of rules and expectations, fitting in so that a group can work smoothly. Sometimes conformity implies a rather boring lack of distinctiveness! When everyday words are used in social science they must be defined and used very clearly. Does conformity mean *being* like other people or *becoming* like them?

The generally accepted view is that conformity involves a *change* in someone's beliefs or behaviour because of perceived pressure from another person or group. Note the word *change*. Merely doing what everyone else does is not really conformity if it involves no change in behaviour. If all students attend lectures wearing clothes, this is not conformity. Acceptance of being clothed came about early in life and, anyway, clothes may be mutual adaptation to the weather! If, however, on joining a course they change their *style* of clothing to fit in better with other students, this, arguably, is conformity.

To take the example further, a mature student may decide to dress more casually than before, in order to be more like the others. This behaviour arises not because people have been hostile or insisted on conformity, but rather because the mature student has *felt* pressure to change. This pressure to change behaviour arises from the person's perceptions of the situation. These may be based on fact (as when the group really does demand change), or as above, based on the person's own wish to fit in. Even when the person only imagines the pressure, or misunderstands what is expected and does the wrong thing, changed behaviour is still conformity. People not only change their outward behaviour for public display; they may also change their underlying beliefs.

Learning Activity 1 ◆ ◆ ◆

Identify examples of conformity on your own part.

a Can you think of any times when you changed your behaviour in order to fit in with others?
b Did the pressure to change come from others, yourself or both?
c Were any of these changes in outward behaviour accompanied by changes in your beliefs?
d To what extent do you feel that your profession conforms to the biomedical model of care?

CLASSIC STUDIES OF CONFORMITY

Conformity has been demonstrated dramatically in a huge variety of social psychology experiments over the past 50 years.

Norm formation and change

A long tradition of research was started when Sherif (1935) decided to see what would happen when people made judgements with others present. He put two or three subjects, who did not know his hypothesis, into an entirely darkened room and showed them a pinpoint of light. Sherif knew that a visual illusion, the autokinetic effect, would make the light appear to move. He asked them to estimate, out loud, how far they thought it moved. What he found was that, although he did not ask them to agree, subjects in groups made judgements which converged. This demonstrated *norm formation* – there was no initial expected response as there might be in real-life small groups. Nonetheless, people seemed to feel pressure to shift their judgement to fit in with the others. Sherif (1936) found that when people were allowed to repeat the task alone, having done it with others, they were still influenced by the norm. They really believed the norm was the right answer. One person even thanked him for letting him repeat it because he had worried that he might have been influenced by the others, but now he was sure about the distance the light moved!

There are many real-life situations when people ask others what is going on, or use others' reactions to decide how they should behave. For example, people often fail to respond in emergencies because they assume that if it really *were* a crisis someone else would be doing something already. It is an ambiguous and unfamiliar situation in which a no-intervention norm may form. A victim is more likely to receive help if only one other person is present (Latane and Darley, 1970), and one of the reasons for this is pluralistic ignorance – people use each other's behaviour to define the situation and fail to see the emergency.

Majority pressure

Another famous social psychologist, Asch, felt that Sherif's findings were probably due to the use of a visual illusion. He believed that people would be far less influenced if there were a real right answer. To test this he did an experiment which, like Sherif's, has been copied, extended and developed ever since.

Asch (1951, 1956, 1958) used experimental confederates who answered questions according to a prearranged plan he had given. To the naive subjects the confederates seemed new to the experiment, like themselves. When a subject arrived to do the experiment he found other people there already and he (all the subjects were male) was asked to sit in the empty seat which was next to the end of a semicircle. They were told they were to do a perceptual task and would be asked to state their answers in the order they sat. Thus, the naive subject was 'set up' to answer next to last.

The task was straightforward. Subjects were shown a line and asked which of three other lines, A, B or C, was the same length (see Figure 17.1). They did many trials, using different lengths of lines. Most of the time all went smoothly. The discriminations were not difficult – control subjects who did the tests alone did not make mistakes. However, on certain critical trials,

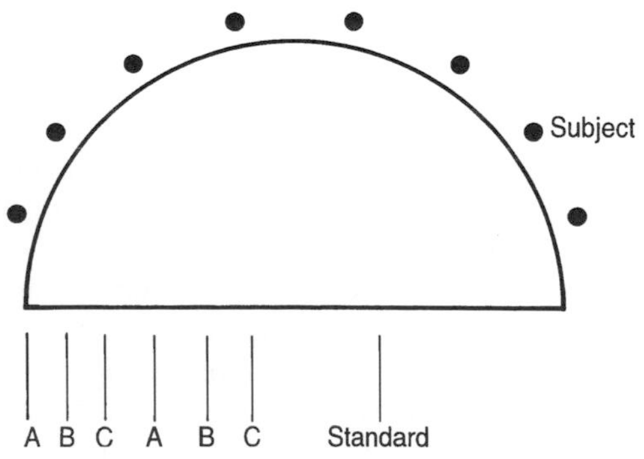

Figure 17.1 *The seating arrangement in Asch's experiment*

the accomplices of the experimenter gave a unanimous wrong answer. Confronted with this on several trials, while usually finding everyone agreed, Asch found that overall the naive subjects conformed about 34% of the time. There were individual differences. Some conformed often, others hardly ever. Afterwards some said that they must get their eyes checked or gave other explanations for their 'poor' performance. Others did what Asch called 'conscious conforming' – they were perfectly aware that they had only agreed because they had to state their responses openly. They did not really believe they were wrong. This was tested by Asch, who found that if after saying the answers out loud people were asked to write them down, there was a very much lower level of agreement. Public conformity is not necessarily private acceptance.

Conversely, if the lines were of very similar length, so the task was made more difficult, people were more likely to conform. In that sense, the experiment became more like Sherif's – the task was more ambiguous, the right answer less clear.

Schachter (1951) was also interested in the impact of majorities on minorities, in particular at how groups treated deviants. He introduced paid accomplices into real-life groups, telling them beforehand to behave in one of three different ways. He found that initially accomplices who were asked to deviate persistently from the group's position in a discussion had a lot of communication directed at them. When they kept on disagreeing they were ignored, receiving a much lower level of communication than accomplices who accepted or slid toward the group's position. In later elections for positions in the clubs, persistent deviants were not chosen, but those who changed their minds were included. This sort of research seemed to show the importance of conformity for the good functioning of a group, with penalties for not conforming. However, as Brown (1991) has pointed out, Schachter discarded some groups from his analysis because the persistent deviant persuaded the rest of the group – the minority influenced the majority (see later). Schachter simply thought they must in some way have not behaved normally.

Learning Activity 2 ◆ ◆ ◆

Identify different reasons for conformity.

a Can you think of an incident when you succumbed to pressure from others and found yourself expressing an opinion on an issue similar to theirs but actually different from the opinion you originally held?

b Reflecting on the incident, can you identify which, if any, of the following prompted you to change:

- You had no clear opinion in the first place.
- You didn't want to upset people (or the person) or draw attention to yourself.
- You could see their view as well as your own.
- There was no ideal stance, so it was best to support the majority.
- You wanted to fit in and be liked/accepted.
- The issue wasn't that important to you anyway.
- You just said you agreed but privately held on to your original opinion.
- You felt too uncomfortable being different.

SOCIAL INFLUENCE PROCESSES

The work of Sherif and Asch raises the question of why people change their behaviour and even their beliefs because of other people. It also raises the issues of why some people change more often than others and why some change only their public actions, while others appear to change their perceptions and beliefs. Commonsense suggests that the power of social influence lies in people's fear of punishment, of getting into trouble or being ostracized. Subsequent theory and research has shown this to be the case (e.g. Abrams and Hogg, 1990), but, in addition, a number of other pressures underlying social influence have been identified.

Social comparison

Festinger (1954) proposed a theory of social comparison suggesting that people constantly compare themselves with others to see if they are, as it were, on the right track. He went on to suggest that where it is difficult to understand physical reality, people become more dependent on social reality. Information gleaned from social comparison with others is used to make sense of the world. In the experiments cited above, people used others to make sense of what they were seeing. In Sherif's study there was no actual movement of the light, so this ambiguity would lead to the mutual dependence of subjects for information; hence the norm formation. Of course, although Sherif did not put pressure on them to agree, he used the expectation that if people see a light move there is a right answer in the real world. Not knowing they were in a world of illusion they used each other's ideas in order to be 'right'.

Social comparison processes are common in health and illness; the prognosis, even the diagnosis, of many chronic complaints is uncertain and in such circumstances people often resort to comparing their symptoms with those of fellow sufferers – sometimes this allays fears but sometimes it can lead to undue distress and anticipatory anxiety.

Learning Activity 3 ◆ ◆ ◆

State which of the following situations are likely to lead to the need for social comparison in order for people to check out the social reality and establish what is 'right': diagnosis of cancer; joining a club; going to the dentist; becoming a parent; learning to paint; shopping at the supermarket.

Of those to which you answered 'Yes', what features do these situations have in common? What is it about these situations that necessitates the process of social comparison?

Normative influence and informational influence

It is easy to imagine that social influence occurs because people deliberately pressurize others. However there are other fundamental reasons for social influence; what seems to be more important is that people want to be right and to act on what they believe to be good information. They also want to be liked, have social relationships, receive rewards and avoid being physically and emotionally hurt. Thus, Jones and Gerard (1967) argued that social influence derives from the fact that people are dependent on each other. They identified two types of dependency:

- *Effect dependence* – 'If you do that I will smack you/award you a medal/give an F grade/love you forever.' The other person delineates norms for behaviour and thereby exerts *normative* influence.
- *Information dependence* – 'If you do that you may fall over the cliff/burn yourself/pass your exams/reach the North Pole.' The other person provides relevant information and thereby exerts *informational* influence.

Compliance, identification and internalization

Kelman (1961) argued that there are three types of social influence. The processes of *compliance, identification* and *internalization* can all be responsible for changes in behaviour in certain circumstances; moreover, in practice they may all occur together but it is important to realize that they are logically distinct.

- *Compliance*: This means changing outward behaviour because someone else controls rewards and/or punishments. If the influencer cannot see the behaviour, then the change will not last. This is like Asch's 'conscious conformity', and depends on the power of the other to reward or punish.
- *Identification*: Here, the person changes behaviour in order to maintain a relationship with the influencer. This often means that the person wants to be liked, but not necessarily. For example, a person may hope their doctor finds them a sensible patient, but it is not the same as hoping they will be a friend. Here, behaviour will be maintained as long as the other appears to prefer it and the person wishes to maintain the relationship. The power of the influencer is known as *referent* power; that is, the extent to which they are regarded as a frame of reference for deciding what to do.
- *Internalization*: This entails a relatively enduring change of behaviour, based on believing that it is right, true, valid. It occurs when the influencer is seen as *credible*. To be credible, a person must be believed to be both expert and trustworthy.

Thus there are different reasons for changing behaviour. The only type of social influence that leads to long-term change is internalization, which becomes independent of the relationship with the original source. In Jones and Gerard's terms, it is based on *informational influence*. Both compliance and identification, on the other hand, are based on *effect dependence*; that is, on hoping that the other will *not* make the outcomes unpleasant, or *will* make them pleasant.

It is often the case that more than one influence process can be stimulated in any situation (a person may want to know *and* not want to look foolish to others, *or* be told off!). Moreover, both compliance and identification can be a consequence of normative influence, whereas internalization is a consequence of informational influence.

Power

This analysis of influence can be related to the five types of power described by French and Raven (1959). These are *reward* and *coercive* power (compliance); *referent* power, the person or group you look to as a frame of reference (identification); *expert* power (internalization). Finally there is *legitimate* power, where the person has authority because he or she is seen to have their position by legitimate means, such as winning an election or being appointed by open competition.

In the clinical setting, the professional may be perceived to have high status and coercive power: this may lead to instant compliance, for fear of the consequences or in order to be rewarded in some way. Friendlier approaches may still give rise only to apparent yielding, based on referent power. Only internalization will produce long-term change, because the clinician is seen as credible (expert and trustworthy) in providing help and advice for this person in the context of everyday life.

Learning Activity 4 ◆ ◆ ◆

Do we need to understand our own conformity first, in order to understand people's willingness to conform to treatment and care? For example, which of the social influence processes just described in the text best describe your adoption of a biomedical approach to your work:

- effect dependence?
- information dependence?
- compliance?
- identification?
- internalization?

How do you think this might affect your expectations of conformity in others?

Obedience

People usually obey because they believe that the other person has power to reward or punish them. Milgram's (1963, 1965, 1974) classic studies showed the extremes of behaviour that could be produced through the process of obedience. Essentially Milgram set up an experiment in which people were willing to administer electric shocks to others which they believed to be highly dangerous, if not fatal.

MILGRAM'S OBEDIENCE STUDIES

There were two roles in what was advertised as a study of learning; one participant was to act as teacher and the other as learner. They would be in adjacent rooms, the teacher asking questions and, if the learner was wrong, giving an electric shock. The severity of these shocks was to be increased steadily for each wrong answer. In fact, the draw was fixed, the learner was always the experimenter's accomplice. No shocks were ever delivered when the teacher pulled the lever, which was clearly labelled from zero and each 15 volts from 'slight shock', through 'danger: severe shock' to 450 volts, 'XXX'. The accomplice acted the part and as the level apparently increased, cried out, banged on the wall, begged that the shocks should stop, and at 450 volts, fell silent.

Many subjects protested but the researcher just told them that they must continue. Although psychiatrists before the study thought that perhaps 5% of people might deliver a fatal shock, 66% in fact did so. Naturally, subjects were distressed by what they believed they had done and by what they had discovered about themselves. It is here that the ethical controversy lies. Milgram did debrief them, comforting them and assuring them that they were just like everyone else who took part. It is doubtful that such a study would pass a modern ethics committee; nonetheless, it provided startling insight into people's willingness to be obedient. Even when repeated by a postgraduate student in a downtown office away from the authoritative of the university, almost half the subjects gave the maximum shock. The setting made a difference but the effect was still considerable.

The experiment was conducted with several variants. Where another person dissented (one of the researcher's assistants 'objected'), obedience was reduced dramatically. This suggests that people did not want to continue, as shown in their reported remarks, but felt they had to. People also disobeyed if the researcher was not physically present to check on them.

It was suggested earlier that it is difficult to disentangle

Learning Activity 5 ◆ ◆ ◆

The aim is to demonstrate the 'obedience' of people when in the 'patient role' at the mercy of health professionals (when cooperation becomes obedience). Consider, for example, the enormous trust needed for some procedures – even more so given that people often receive poor preparation/ information and that the procedure may be familiar to the professional but completely novel to those experiencing it.

Identify and discuss those procedures in your profession that do require obedience. Although people differ, on the whole do you get their cooperation through:

- blind obedience?
- ignorance or acceptance on their part of the dangers/pain/efficacy/prognosis/consequences, etc.?
- blind faith in medicine?
- passivity/dependence?

What does this say about the role and status of people in the care of health professionals?

compliance; identification and internalization. In Milgram's experiments, 'authority' had an effect. How much greater might this effect be in real life if obedience were also bound up with a person's own safety, job security or a desire to be admired by the other? A study by Martin *et al.* (1976) found that people were willing to use a training method on themselves which would deliver a loud noise. A substantial number obeyed in pulling a lever to a decibel level labelled as likely to cause permanent deafness in themselves. Thus through 'blind' obedience people may also hurt themselves. In summary, these obedience studies suggest that people may obey as a result of perceived status or power, but not only because they are frightened of what the experimenter might do to them. They may actually obey as a consequence of trying to use the information available to make sense of reality, trying at the same time not to lose face.

Automatic processing (heuristics)

'Making sense of reality' suggests that people do a lot of rational thinking. People do a lot of what appears to be thinking, but being constantly bombarded with so much information people often use short-cuts, not always realizing that they are not really processing the information. Langer (1989) has argued that people often are in a state of 'mindlessness'. When asked, for example, to lend a pencil – a small request – and the borrower has said 'please, I need to write', the lender may simply agree. While this is also a form of influence, it is rather automatic. The one person is not much concerned about the power of the other, nor if they are liked. They have simply learned a form of social exchange, a social script.

A larger request, however, might make people think about the implications of agreement. Instead of following the polite social script automatically (request plus explanation leads to help), they might bother to process both the request and the validity of the explanation and, depending on the outcome, comply or not.

People can delude themselves in other ways by automatic or peripheral (as opposed to central) processing, using rules-of-thumb (heuristics), while imagining that they have thought things through. At other times they use short cuts knowingly because they do not have enough information to go on. Behavioural style itself may lead to short-cuts. Nemeth and Wachtler (1974) showed how their experimental accomplice who was seen to 'choose' the head-of-table position for a discussion was more influential than when seen to be told to sit there. Chaiken *et al.* (1989) suggest, on the basis of their research, that people may accept information from someone who 'seems nice' or 'looks like an expert'.

Consider, for example, the unquestioning compliance to treatment from a specialist based not on information, comprehension or measured decision-making but on approval of the practitioner's manner and appearance.

Minority influence

The early studies on majority influence (e.g. Schachter, 1951) failed to identify minority influence, but for the past 25 years there has been much interest in how minorities affect majorities. If no such influence existed, how could social change ever happen? Leadership may be seen as a special case of minority influence, because leaders, like professionals, often have to persuade others to take on new ideas for the sake of innovation and development.

The many experiments carried out by Moscovici and his colleagues (1985) have shown how a minority can persuade the majority. Moscovici used a set-up like a reverse Asch experiment. He showed groups of subjects a series of bluish slides. Shade and light intensity were varied. People worked in groups of six. Two of the apparent subjects were actually accomplices, told to answer 'blue' to certain slides – Moscovici wanted to see the effect of this on the majority's colour judgements. The critical slides were labelled 'green' by 8% in the minority pressure condition, against 0.25% for control subjects; 32% changed at least one judgement.

Some studies addressed more real-life issues such as signing petitions from a minority group or discussions of feminism. An intriguing finding is that minority influence has a greater impact on people's private beliefs rather than on their public behaviour. This is the reverse of majority influence effects. People may be persuaded by the minority but do not like to say so in front of the majority.

However, eventually the time may come when people who have been privately doubting do admit their new views to others. Take the story of the Emperor's new clothes. Only when the Emperor paraded through the streets did a little boy see him and shout out that the Emperor had nothing on. Then everyone else, previously doubtful, started laughing. The fraud was revealed!

The minority effect appears to be achieved through the *behavioural style* of the minority. Majorities are convinced by minorities whose behaviour suggests that they:

- understand the causes of events;
- are consistent, and therefore have expertise;
- are honest, and therefore trustworthy;
- are therefore credible.

Minority influence, therefore, depends on informational influence. Because people want to understand, to predict events and behaviour, they may be susceptible to a minority or individual whose style seems to reflect expertise and trustworthiness. Minorities are most effective when consistently different on a particular issue, whilst maintaining fairness and reasonableness in other respects. Otherwise, people may regard the minority as deviant or an out-group whose views are of no relevance.

It is worth remembering that a clinician may be putting what is perceived to be a minority view to a person, given that the majority may comprise the many other people with whom he or she interacts in daily life. Rigidity, unfairness or seemingly bizarre views may lead to rejection of clinical suggestions. Equally, people may be unwilling to be seen to be persuaded to try a new regime in front of others but they may privately begin to change opinion.

Moscovici says that minority influence involves conversion, whereas majority influence leads to compliance. However, the distinction is not clear-cut. Minority influence is certainly dependent on informational influence, because people seeking to understand their world will only believe a minority which seems credible. This does not necessarily mean they are right. The work of Chaiken *et al.* (1989) on short-cuts in processing shows that even with informational influence people do not always think logically, but may process fairly automatically. While majorities may frighten people into complying, they often convince them also – if everyone else is doing something, perhaps they are right! The basic processes discussed earlier help to disentangle what is going on. The continuing academic dispute about whether minority and majority influence are different processes is continuing and need not be addressed here.

Social identity

Abrams and Hogg (1990) have used 'social identity theory' (Turner *et al.*, 1987) to explain conformity. People will change behaviour to fit in with the social category to which they think they belong. People have been shown to change their behaviour in *anticipation* of joining a group. Here, change cannot be due to pressure from group members. People like to act in a way which fits their view of themselves and the people they like to be with – their self-categorization. Behaviour should not, in this view, be regarded as various isolated acts. Behaviour reflects the person; asking someone to change behaviour may have far-reaching implications for their view of themselves and the groups with which they identify.

This perspective has important implications for health professionals who try to influence people in their care. Trying to change health behaviour or beliefs cannot be considered in isolation. The significance of the social context of influence has been mentioned many times in this chapter, particularly because new behaviour is normally carried out in everyday social settings. Social identity theory adds a new dimension. It underlines the idea that a behaviour is not like a solitary atom, floating about. The way a person acts is part of a whole substance, often reflecting who they believe they are. A clinician's promotion of new behaviours may seem unbelievable or unsustainable.

More than this, though, the influence attempts of health professionals may be seen as assaults on a person's very identity. At the least, a professional may be seen as failing to have any sense of who the person is or of the world in which they live. If this is so, influence attempts may be rejected. Consider the man who needs to stop drinking but whose entire social network resides in the pub, or the person who cannot receive blood or medication for religious reasons.

Comprehension of the message

If the target of influence is changed behaviour or beliefs, and there is no change, it may be wrongly assumed that the influence attempt has been resisted. Studies of compliance with physicians' suggestions have shown that people forget half of what they have been told within two hours (Ley, 1977), and that about half of what had been said was not understood in the first place (Ley *et al.*, 1976). Both forgetting and lack of initial comprehension may lead to *miscompliance*, although health professionals may too easily assume that people are simply refusing to follow instructions, and are showing *anticompliance* (Raven, 1988).

Most of the studies of communication in healthcare look at doctor–patient interactions. Many people would like their physicians to tell them more (Ley, 1988); people are more likely to do as the doctor recommends if they are satisfied that they and the doctor agree about their expectations and that their own expectations have been met during the appointment (Leventhal *et al.*, 1983). In order to produce improvements in communication, Ley (1982) suggested that instructions should be simplified, repeated by the doctor and the person, be specific rather than generalities, and written where possible. The issue of message content and comprehension of the message is also important in attitude change (see Chapter 18).

BEHAVIOUR CHANGE: LONG-TERM OR SHORT-TERM

Of all the processes discussed so far, the only one that leads to long-term change (independent of the influencing source) is informational influence via internalization.

Sometimes, of course, all that is wanted is immediate, short-term influence on behaviour; maybe to persuade someone to sign a petition or buy something or cooperate in a short procedure or treatment. Once done, the single act is irrevocable. Here, psychologists have learned from the tactics of the wider world of selling!

- *The foot-in-the-door technique.* By first persuading someone to agree to a small step, it is easier to get them to agree to a larger request. Freedman and Fraser (1966) found that women were more willing to have a large, ugly billboard in their garden, if two weeks earlier they had agreed to sign a petition for another person on a quite different issue.
- *The door-in-the-face strategy.* This does the opposite; a very large request is made and just before the door is slammed, metaphorically, the person makes a very much smaller request! This tactic gains greater compliance than just making the small request in the first place (Cialdini *et al.*, 1978).
- *Low ball.* The sales person suddenly introduces a detail which reduces the value of the original deal ('that doesn't include the wheels!'), after the customer has agreed a sale.

All these strategies may work for one-off compliance, which is all the salesperson needs. They may depend on people's self-image, wanting not to appear unreasonable to themselves or to the stranger who is actually acting unreasonably. Concern for the effects of such sales pressure led to changes in UK legislation so

Learning Activity 6 ◆ ◆ ◆

A professional who is asking (or expecting!) someone to behave in a way that is alien to their lifestyle and social identity could be said to be exerting *minority influence.*

a If you have experienced such situations, would you say that your influence attempts tended to result in (i) compliance, (ii) identification, or (iii) internalization?
b Were you aware of being in a minority?
c Would you say that your behavioural style tended to encourage internalization – i.e. was it consistent, credible, fair and honest?
d Were you *aware* of the differences between your view and theirs?
e How might you go about resolving such differences and ultimately persuade people to understand the need for change (informational influence) and carry out changes because they believe these to be valid and desirable (internalization)?

that there can be a 'cooling-off period'. These techniques are not so effective when people (including the reader!) are aware of them, have time to reflect on the value of their commitment, or where continuing commitment to change is needed.

The last point is important for clinical practice. People may agree to take a course of treatment in an interview with a therapist (short-term compliance) but will not follow it through when at home. The therapist's influence strategy may favour immediate behaviour change (agreement). However, the person may feel coerced, like a victim of high-pressure sales. Long-term belief change demands that professionals are seen as both trustworthy and expert. 'Expert' does not simply mean at their profession. They should also have enough knowledge and understanding of the person's home situation, habits and beliefs to offer a regimen that the person actually believes is workable and will be able to internalize.

SUMMARY

People are influenced because they try to make sense of the world. At the same time, they try to avoid negative events, such as being hurt or disliked; they seek positive outcomes, such as being rewarded or liked. Sometimes influence leads only to change in behaviour; in other circumstances it may also lead to a change in underlying beliefs.

Different types of influence are available to sources with different types of power. While it is often majorities who lead minorities to change, minorities can also be influential if they are seen as credible sources of information. Even when people try to process the information available to them they often use short-cuts, known as heuristics. A person's social identity is an important factor to be taken into account in the social influence process.

Key Points ■ ■ ■

- ☐ Conformity always involves a change in behaviour or beliefs.
- ☐ Conformity is important to the functioning of a social group.
- ☐ In uncertain situations people rely on a social reality.
- ☐ The processes fundamental to conformity and compliance are informational and normative influence; heuristics; and self-categorization.
- ☐ Compliance only lasts as long as a powerful other is present.
- ☐ Long-term change results from informational influence via internalization.
- ☐ Majority influence and minority influence rely on different processes.
- ☐ Minority influence leads to internalization.
- ☐ Majority influence may arise from compliance or normative pressures as well.

References ▼ ▼ ▼

Abrams, D. and Hogg, M.A. (1990). Social identification, self-categorization and social influence. *European Review of Social Psychology*, **1**: 195–228.

Asch, S.E. (1951). Effects of group pressure upon the modification and distortion of judgments. In: Guetzkow, H. (ed.), *Groups, Leadership and Men*. Pittsburgh, PA: Carnegie Press.

Asch, S.E. (1956). Studies of independence and conformity: a minority of one against a unanimous majority. *Psychological Monographs*, **70**.

Asch, S.E. (1958). Effects of group pressure upon modification and distortion of judgments. In: Maccoby, E.E. *et al.* (eds), *Readings in Social Psychology*, 3rd edn. New York: Holt, Rinehart & Winston, 174–82.

Brown, R. (1991). *Group Processes: Dynamics Within and Between Groups*, 2nd edn. Oxford: Blackwell.

Chaiken, S., Liberman, A. and Eagly, A.H. (1989). Heuristic and systematic information processing within and beyond the persuasion context. In: Uleman, J.S. and Bargh, J.A. (eds), *Unintended Thought*. New York: Guilford Press, 212–52.

Cialdini, R.B., Cacioppo, J.T., Bassett, R. and Miller, J.A. (1978). Low-ball procedure for producing compliance: commitment then cost. *Journal of Personality and Social Psychology*, **36**: 366–75.

Festinger, L. (1954). A theory of social comparison processes. *Human Relations*, **7**: 117–40.

Freedman, J.L. and Fraser, S.C. (1966). Compliance without pressure: the foot-in-the-door technique. *Journal of Personality and Social Psychology*, **4**: 195–202.

French, J.R.P. and Raven, B.H. (1959). The bases of social power. In: Cartwright, D. (ed.), *Studies in Social Power*. Ann Arbor: University of Michigan Press.

Jones, E.E. and Gerard, H.B. (1967). *Foundations of Social Psychology*. New York: Wiley.

Kelman, H.C. (1961). Processes of opinion change. *Public Opinion Quarterly*, **25**: 57–78.

Langer, E.J. (1989). Minding matters: the consequences of

mindlessness–mindfulness. In: Berkowitz, L. (ed.), *Advances in Experimental Social Psychology*: **22**: 137–74.

Latane, B. and Darley J.M. (1970). *The Unresponsive Bystander: Why Doesn't He Help?* New York: Appleton–Century–Crofts.

Leventhal, H., Zimmerman, R. and Gutmann, M. (1983). Compliance: a self-regulatory perspective. In: Gentry, D. (ed.), *A Handbook of Behavioral Medicine*. New York: Guilford Press.

Ley, P. (1977). Psychological studies of doctor–patient communication. In: Rochman, S. (ed.), *Contributions to Medical Psychology*, vol. 1. Oxford: Pergamon Press.

Ley, P. (1982). Giving information to patients. In: Eiser, J.R. (ed.), *Social Psychology and Behavioral Medicine*. New York: Wiley, 339–73.

Ley, P. (1988). *Communicating with Patients: Improving Communication, Satisfaction and Compliance*. London: Croom Helm.

Ley, P., Witworth, M.A., Skilbeck, C.E., Woodward, R., Pinsent, R.J., Pike, L.A., Clarkson, M.E. and Clark, P.B. (1976). Improving doctor–patient communications in general practice. *Journal of the Royal College of General Practitioners*, **26**: 720–4.

Martin, J.L., Lobb, B., Chapman, G.C. and Spillane, R. (1976). Obedience under conditions demanding self-immolation. *Human Relations*: **29**: 345–56.

Milgram, S. (1963). Behavioral study of obedience. *Journal of Abnormal and Social Psychology*, **67**: 371–8.

Milgram, S. (1965). Some conditions of obedience and disobedience to authority. *Human Relations*, **18**: 57–76.

Milgram, S. (1974). *Obedience to Authority*. New York: Harper & Row.

Moscovici, S. (1985). Social influence and conformity. In: Lindzey, G. and Aronson, E. (eds), *Handbook of Social Psychology*, vol. 2, 3rd edn. New York: Random House, 347–412.

Nemeth, C. and Wachtler, J. (1974). Creating the perceptions of consistency and confidence: a necessary condition for minority influence. *Sociometry*, **37**: 529–40.

Raven, B.H. (1988). Social power and compliance in health care. In: Maes, S. *et al.* (eds), *Topics in Health Psychology*. New York: Wiley, 229–44.

Schachter, S. (1951). Deviation, rejection and communication. *Journal of Abnormal and Social Psychology*, **46**: 190–207.

Sherif, M. (1935). A study of some social factors in perception. *Archives of Psychology*, **27** (187), 1–60.

Sherif, M. (1936). *The Psychology of Social Norms*. New York: Harper.

Turner, J.C., Hogg, M.A., Oakes, P.J., Reicher, S.D. and Wetherell, M.S. (1987). *Rediscovering the Social Group: A Self-Categorisation Theory*. Oxford: Blackwell.

Further Reading ▲ ▲ ▲

Aronson, E., Wilson, T.D. and Akert, R.M. (1994). *Social Psychology: The Heart and the Mind*. London: HarperCollins, 244–83.

Brigham, J.C. (1991). *Social Psychology*. New York: HarperCollins.

Brown, R. (1988). *Group Processes*. Oxford: Blackwell, 90–123.

Deaux, K., Dane, F.C. and Wrightsman, L.S. 1993: *Social Psychology in the 1990s*. Pacific Grove, CA: Brooks/Cole, 194–219.

Stroebe, W. and Stroebe, M.S. (1995). *Social Psychology and Health*.

Turner, J.C. (1991). *Social Influence*. Milton Keynes: Open University Press.

18

Attitudes

Valerie Kent

LEARNING OBJECTIVES

After studying this chapter you should:

- Be aware of the main theoretical developments in the understanding of attitudes and attitude change
- Be able to relate this understanding to personal and clinical experience
- Be familiar with common methods of measuring attitudes, appreciating the main pitfalls in measurement
- Be able to apply an understanding of the relationship between attitudes and behaviour to clinical situations
- Be able to apply some of the principles of persuasive communication to health-related attitudes and behaviour

INTRODUCTION

Attitudes towards health, illness, professionals, medicine, hospitals, oneself all affect how a person might respond to healthcare. So, too, do the attitudes of professionals affect their approach to working with people. This chapter examines the psychosocial processes involved in the formation, function and maintenance of attitudes. It also looks at their resistance to change, the mechanisms most likely to effect changes in attitude, and the relationships between attitudes and behaviour.

DEFINING ATTITUDES

The idea that the way people behave can be explained by their attitudes has a long history in social psychology. It has provoked controversies, partly over how attitudes should be defined and partly because of arguments about how they influence behaviour. Generally an attitude is seen to have three components:

- a *cognitive component*: what is known about the object of the attitude;
- an *emotional component*: what is felt about it;
- a *behavioural component*: how it is likely to be responded to.

Attitudes are one way of describing differences between individuals. Unlike 'personality' or 'intelligence', however, attitudes are more specific because they are directed towards something; that something may be a person, an event or even an abstact concept, such as the value of human life. Attitudes are assumed to be quite enduring because they are 'internalized' and can

Learning Activity 5 ◆ ◆ ◆

For each of the following, describe in a few words (i) your likely thoughts, (ii) your likely feelings, and (iii) your likely actions:

- euthanasia
- homeless young people
- squirrels in cities
- chemotherapy
- smacking children
- the rail network
- uniforms for health professionals
- homosexuality
- closure of hospitals.

give some idea of how a person may behave in the future (Aronson *et al.*, 1994). Thus those who seek to influence others often want attitudes to change so that any change in behaviour would be permanent and acted out independently without the presence of the original persuader – for example, changing someone's attitude to exercise and healthy living in the hope that this would lead to a permanent change in lifestyle.

In summary, therefore, there is a general consensus that an attitude 'consists of an enduring evaluation – positive or negative – of people, objects and ideas' (Aronson *et al.*, 1994).

FORMING ATTITUDES

Less is known about attitude formation than about how they are maintained or changed. This is because so many attitudes are a consequence of experience and socialization. It is very difficult to disentangle where many attitudes come from.

Attitudes that are based on cultural truisms may be susceptible to change because, when challenged, the individual is provoked into thinking about them (McGuire, 1964). On the other hand, some attitudes may be very resistant to change, especially if they have been learned through first-hand experience (Fazio and Zanna, 1981). It may thus be especially difficult to change attitudes about peoples' daily habits because these may have been acquired originally by learning to associate them with rewards or punishments ('a hug if you clean your teeth'). So attitudes towards activities that a person has learnt to enjoy – such as eating patterns, smoking, drinking, unsafe sex, driving, recreation – tend to be more firmly held than those acquired second-hand from other people (Fazio and Williams, 1986). Finally, attitudes that are accessible in memory (Fazio, 1990) or which are personally relevant are more likely to affect behaviour. People are more likely to think a matter through if the issue is especially important to the situation or to themselves.

THE FUNCTION OF ATTITUDES

Attitudes help to make sense of a complex world. Katz (1960) suggested that attitudes can serve four functions:

- A *knowledge function.* Attitudes put things into classes or categories and associate thoughts, feelings and actions. They are economical and they provide structure. Talking in general attitude terms helps people to communicate. Thus, instead of saying 'I like my dog; and your dog; and his dog; and Auntie's dog' a person can say just 'I like dogs'. The person may also like cats, gerbils and budgerigars and so might say 'I like many pets'. If lions, tigers, walruses and snakes are included, the person might declare instead a liking for the animal kingdom in general. At each level of classification, there would be expectations of what the person might do, such as own a dog, keep several pets, take wildlife photographs or campaign to save whales.
- A *utilitarian function.* Some attitudes are adopted to fit in with other people, at home, at work or in the wider society. This allows people to adjust to their social environment.
- A *value-expressive function.* Attitudes can reflect a wider value. For example, a person might not eat meat because of concern about their cholesterol level, but there may be other reasons. Perhaps the person is concerned about animal diseases such as BSE, but would eat meat otherwise. Perhaps they have a distaste for killing animals. Maybe it is part of their religion. In order to change an attitude rooted in an underlying value, it would be necessary first to understand the value and the perceived implications of any change in attitude or behaviour.
- An *ego-defensive function.* This is where an attitude is held because it protects one's ego or self-image. This has been particularly applied to *prejudice.* If a person holds a negative attitude because he or she feels threatened by a racial group, then the prejudicial attitude is not going to be changed merely by rational explanation. The need for ego defence would have to be dealt with, perhaps by another form of reassurance.

Although Katz's analysis was not a major thrust of research for many years, this *functionalist approach* has gained renewed support among current researchers. For example, Shavitt (1990) studied the affective base of some attitudes – that is, those rooted in emotions and feelings. These attitudes serve to reflect and express a person's underlying value system rather than accurate

Learning Activity 2 ◆ ◆ ◆

Think about the attitude you described towards one or two of the examples in Activity 1.

a Where did the attitude come from?
b Why do you keep this attitude?
c What would change it?

information about their world. He identified two reasons for holding an attitude:

- utilitarian reasons;
- social identity reasons.

Shavitt compared the effectiveness of advertising strategies towards different types of products. He argued that people buy some consumer products, such as coffee, for utilitarian reasons and hence attitudes towards them would be expected to be based on cognitive appraisal – how good the product was. Others were described by him as social identity products, such as greeting cards or perfume. These are more about values, feelings, the kind of person one wants to be.

Shavitt found that for utilitarian products, advertisements that used utilitarian messages emphasizing their practical advantages worked better than social identity messages. People had more favourable thoughts about them and had a higher level of intention to buy them. Conversely, for social identity products, affectively based messages that addressed people's values and worries about social identity were much more effective than utilitarian messages in producing both favourable thoughts and buying intentions. Thus Shavitt was able to show what Katz had originally predicted, that the strategy used to induce attitude change has to be tailored to the underlying reason for holding the attitude in the first place.

MEASURING ATTITUDES

Social psychologists have been devising ways of measuring attitudes since the 1920s. The method most widely used is the scaling system invented by Likert (1932). Here, a person is asked to indicate on a linear scale, labelled at each end, just where their own view lies. The labels at each end can vary according to what is needed (also see Chapter 24).

To do attitude scaling properly a statistical procedure – factor analysis – should be used to be sure that all the items in the questionnaire are actually measuring what they should. Devising attitude measures can be complex and expensive; it is useful to be able to use standardized scales where available rather than trying to invent new ones.

A common mistake in attitude research is to assume that the attitude measured would predict behaviour; however, this depends entirely upon the methodology used. One mistake is to try to seek a relationship between a very general attitude and a very specific action. For example, a study of the use of contraceptives by married women showed a very poor relationship between attitudes to contraception in general and the use of the birth control pill, whereas there was a very good correlation between pill use and attitudes specifically towards the pill (Davidson and Jaccard, 1979). A second mistake is to ask people to fill in an attitude questionnaire about something quite general, such as religion, but then ask only about a single behaviour, such as church attendance. Attitudes to dogs might be reflected in may behaviours: asking people

Learning Activity 3 ◆ ◆ ◆

The aim is to practise using *Likert Scales* to measure attitudes. Read the following statements about euthanasia and mark your feelings about these along the lines provided (in pencil).

Euthanasia can sometimes be justified

|______|______|______|______|______|______|

Strongly agree — Strongly disagree

A very dear relative in excruciating terminal pain asks for help to commit suicide

|______|______|______|______|______|______|

Would definitely help — Definitely would not help

The law in the UK should be changed to make euthanasia legal

|______|______|______|______|______|______|

Strongly agree — Strongly disagree

Score 7, 6, 5, 4, 3, 2, 1 from left to right on each scale. Add up all your scores to get an overall score of your attitude to euthanasia. The higher your score, the more you agree with euthanasia.

Remove your own marks and then ask other people to respond to the statements. Compare your attitude scores. If this is done in a group you could then discuss some of the beliefs and reasons for your views.

whether they pat or attract the attention of other people's dogs, or are interested to talk about dogs, or contribute to the dog's home, might all contribute to an idea of their dog-related attitudes. It is a methodological error to use only one act as a criterion rather than using a whole battery of behaviour (Fishbein and Ajzen, 1975). When multiple measures have been taken in this way, then an overall attitude score can be obtained simply by adding the responses on all the scales related to that attitude.

THE MAINTENANCE OF ATTITUDES AND ATTITUDE CHANGE

Early social psychologists looking at attitudes tried to devise grand theories, but as in other areas of psychology, more recent research has been concerned to try to describe accurately what does happen. Since the early 1980s the approach to attitudes and attitude change has been more pragmatic, looking at what works rather than making universal claims for one process.

Early work: consistency theories

Some early theories of the 1950s are called *consistency theories* because they assumed that people would prefer their feelings, thoughts and subsequent actions to be consistent. They did not mean that the three components of attitude should fit logically together, but rather that people should make their world fit together psycho-logically. That is, it may not have been rational but people would rationalize in order to convince themselves that they were being consistent.

COGNITIVE DISSONANCE THEORY

Festinger (1957) assumed that the need for consistency between what people believed and how they acted was a basic human drive like seeking water when thirsty. He argued that when deprived of consistency people would try to regain consonance: people experienced a drive-like state that was physiologically uncomfortable, so they would seek to reduce it. The name he gave this state was *cognitive dissonance.* Attitude change was one way in which people could regain consistency.

The first experiment to test this is another classic in social psychology. Festinger and Carlsmith (1959) claimed to demonstrate dissonance by showing that subjects who were paid only a small amount of money to lie to others about how interesting a boring job had been were more likely to rate the job favourably than were subjects who had been well paid to lie in this manner. Festinger argued that the money itself was consistent with the behaviour while the beliefs were not. There was therefore more dissonance if paid less and hence greater pressure for attitude change.

Whilst these ideas have been challenged, the findings were extremely influential at the time, not least because the ideas of *learning theory* were widely accepted. Learning theory would have predicted the opposite result because it assumed people would like whatever they associated with greater reward. This experiment therefore was a major breakthrough for cognitive theory in psychology.

Hundreds of experiments have been conducted in the wake of dissonance theory. Subsequent clarifications have shown that people persuaded to behave against their attitude in this way are more likely to change their attitude if they are publicly committed to the action and if it has implications for their self-concept, especially if they do not like the consequences of their behaviour. Most important of all was the widespread finding that people are more likely to change their attitudes if they believe that they themselves have freely chosen to act as they do. A number of studies showed that if people are given the choice to take part in experiments of this sort, then they show more attitude change than subjects who have simply been told they are expected to take part in the experiment.

Reactance

Brehm (1966) argued that if an attempt to persuade someone makes them feel that their freedom of action is being threatened, there is evidence that this heightens motivation to restore freedom of action. This he called *reactance.* It may lead to even more extreme, dug-in behaviour, rebelliousness, opposition, even refusing to maintain relationships with the influencer. The argument is based on the idea that the success of human evolution has its roots in flexibility of behaviour and the ability to respond in a novel and appropriate way. Threats to this freedom produce a profound reaction. The person is aroused and will try to restore the banned behaviour, to act to avoid future attacks on freedom, and perhaps to behave in an argumentative or eccentric fashion in order to affirm the right to maintain freedom of action.

These ideas arose at the same time as new developments in attribution theory, which argued that people try to understand the causes of events (see Chapter 20). The notion of freedom of choice implies that a person's perception of causes of events, including their own behaviour, is very important. People are more likely to change attitudes if they believe they have freely chosen to act in a certain way but not if it is seemingly forced upon them. This has important implications for attitudes to health where people's perceptions about the causes of their health and illness and related behaviours become relevant. For example, McGuire (1964) found that people were better able to resist persuasion if they had been encouraged to write their own arguments about tooth-cleaning rather than read someone else's.

Self-perception theory

Fitting well with the notions of causal attribution and freedom of choice, Bem (1972) argued that people did not have attitudes at all, in the sense that there was some internal, organized schema underlying their behaviour. He suggested that people behaved first and then decide why and what they feel about it afterwards – and probably only then if someone asks them. He said that people act according to the demands of the situation. If they cannot see any external demands they conclude that they must have had an attitude. Thus, if a person eats brown bread and is asked why, they may reflect that no one has made them eat it and so conclude that they like it.

Bem conducted a study based on Festinger and Carlsmith's work but merely asked observers to say whether the low-paid or high-paid subjects would prefer the boring job. Bem's subjects said people would be more positive in the low-pay condition. Bem said this was because they, like the people actually in the Festinger study, looked at the rewards. If there was a lot of money for the job, they concluded that they did it for the money. If they were paid very little the pay was not sufficient explanation, so they concluded that they must have liked the job. No dissonance, no consistency, no prior attitude.

Both dissonance theory and self-perception theory are now seen to be appropriate in different domains. Dissonance theory applies only when there is an existing attitude, whereas self-perception theory is better able to explain what is going on when an attitude is weak or ambiguous and the person cannot see an external explanation for their behaviour (Fazio *et al.*, 1977).

Learning Activity 4 ◆ ◆ ◆

The aim is to look at the processes involved in the maintenance and resistance to change of attitudes. A person who sees himself or herself as no longer able to do certain acts (e.g. work, walk, laugh) develops a self-image of being disabled. This image prevents activity and increases disability, and so the cycle goes on (i.e. 'No-one is stopping me from doing things, so it must be because I am incapable of doing things; therefore I am a disabled person and can only do very little.'). The person's attitude to activity is to avoid it to prevent damage, pain or accidents, etc. This is a negative attitude towards exercise.

a How could you go about challenging this attitude, based on the ideas of dissonance, reactance, self-perception?
b How might an exercise programme bring about a change in this person's attitude towards activity?
c If increased exercise changed his or her attitude towards exercise and their attitude towards themselves as disabled, how would the theories explain this?

Contemporary research

Today theoretical claims are far more limited because it is recognized that people are different and that the same person can act differently in different situations. Thus some people find it harder to modify attitudes; they may have a more rigid, authoritarian personality which tends to make them see the world in clear-cut categories, so they find it difficult to handle ambiguity and uncertainty. New ideas may be very threatening to their rigid world view. However, such people may be very susceptible to the influence of an individual whom they hold in high regard. Others actively seek information; they are prepared to accept inconsistency and doubt, rather than be certain but wrong! (Kruglanski, 1989). In some circumstances people do try to be consistent and some people are more concerned about this than others. It is also evident that some people are more aware of being inconsistent than others, because they are more objectively self-aware of their own behaviour and surroundings.

There is much evidence to confirm that people are aroused by inconsistency but only in some circumstances, particularly when they perceive themselves to have chosen to act inconsistently. For example, Croyle and Cooper (1983) found that a person who believes there is choice not to take part is more likely to change attitude after being asked to make a counter-attitudinal argument. They were able to show that there were arousal effects, as dissonance theory predicts; but if subjects were able to attribute their physiological arousal to some other cause than to the fact they had argued against their own position, then they appeared to do so. Those who had a good alternative explanation for their arousal did not change attitude. Thus 'freely chosen' inconsistency may lead to arousal, as Festinger predicted. However, there is a variety of ways to reduce arousal, including the person making a different attribution about why they felt aroused in the first place.

Others, such as Steele (1988), have shown that there are many ways to reduce the arousal in subjects in forced compliance studies, importantly by providing an alternative means of *self-affirmation*, since acting inconsistently undermines the self. People then do not change their attitudes – they do not need to!

Finally, Aronson *et al.* (1991) introduced the concept of *hypocrisy*. In a study of condom use they asked students to read a message about their use and then make a speech in favour of using condoms. In between the two procedures half the subjects were asked to discuss recent occasions when they had failed to use condoms. These people were much more likely to be using condoms regularly when questioned three months later, compared with those who had not had the 'hypocrisy' experience – they had been made to face their own inconsistency.

Learning Activity 5 ◆ ◆ ◆

The aim is to demonstrate that inconsistency between feeling beliefs and behavioural components (hypocrisy) is probably very common. Return to Activity 3, and reflect on how often there was inconsistency between beliefs about euthanasia being acceptable and unwillingness to be actually involved. If there is no inconsistency, then reflect on other attitudes (perhaps those in Activity 1) where you might think one thing but act quite inconsistently with this belief. For example, do people who think the rail network is important and valuable use a car in preference to a train even when the latter is available?

THE RELATIONSHIP BETWEEN ATTITUDES AND BEHAVIOUR

It may seem obvious that attitudes affect behaviour, and certainly this was assumed by social psychologists for a long time. There are three logical possibilities:

- Attitudes affect behaviour.
- Behaviour affects attitudes.
- There is no relationship between attitudes and behaviour.

Unfortunately, as so often in the social sciences, all the options appear to be true, to an extent, sometimes! It is therefore more useful to ask about the underlying processes – to understand how, why and when attitudes affect behaviour and when they do not.

There have been numerous studies showing occasions where people do not act consistently with their attitude, or where one attitude overrides another (LaPiere, 1934). What is clear is that any particular attitude is by no means the single cause of any particular behaviour. A person may like dogs, but that does not mean they will own one. Perhaps they cannot afford to feed it, or have no time to look after it; a family member may be allergic to dog fur, or they may simply not have got around to thinking about it. So, there are many other factors that affect what people do, and introducing a change in a person's behaviour is not all that is needed to change their attitudes, and vice versa.

Theory of planned behaviour

Ajzen (1985) has proposed a *theory of planned behaviour* to account for the link between attitudes and behaviour, developed from the *theory of reasoned action* (Ajzen and Fishbein, 1980). They argue that behaviour can be predicted from *behavioural intention*, which in turn is influenced by three factors:

- the person's attitude to the behaviour itself;
- subjective norms about the behaviour;
- their perceived control to carry out the behaviour.

For example, a person may intend to lose weight. The person believes that dieting would make that likely and values this (attitude); the person further believes that others, too, would do the same (norms). So the person may approve the action of dieting and feel it is supported by his or her perception of the norms, but still not believe it possible to eat less (perceived control).

In the end the positive attitude to weight loss is not reflected in the person's actions.

Social scripts

People may not always see that a situation is appropriate for acting out their attitudes. In many social situations they behave as they are expected to do, rather than as they feel or believe; attitudes are not expected to influence what they do. Thus therapists do not help only the people they like, nor do people usually walk out of a treatment session the moment they feel it is not helping. People act out 'social scripts', behaving as they feel the other person in the encounter expects them to. Everyday social interactions can thus proceed smoothly.

According to social script theorists (e.g. Abelson, 1981), there are many occasions when people do not use attitude information or even think about what they are doing. Abelson thought that there are many situations where a relationship between attitude and behaviour should not be expected. People may, with varying degrees of 'mindlessness' (Langer, 1989), act out a social script. This may also be an economical process in terms of information processing, although being overscripted may have detrimental effects for well-being, as shown in Langer and Rodin's (1976) study of the institutionalized elderly. They found that those with more encouragement to be 'mindful' required less medication, were healthier, happier, more sociable and lived longer.

Health beliefs and health behaviour

Attitudes towards health are currently being extensively investigated. In general it is best to identify these

Learning Activity 6 ◆ ◆ ◆

The aim is to explore the factors influencing the relationship between attitudes and behaviour. Find someone you know who wants to lose weight but cannot persevere with a diet. Analyse the psychological barriers to their dieting by finding out the following:

(attitude)	*a*	What is their attitude to dieting?
(subjective norms)	*b*	What do they believe others think about dieting in order to lose weight?
(perceived control)	*c*	What is their belief about being able to sustain a diet? ('the doctor should be able to control it'/'it's uncontrollable (fate)'/ 'others make it impossible to control it' (e.g. tempt with food)).
(social script)	*d*	What do they think others would think of them dieting?
	e	What would be the effects on others if they dieted?
	f	How would others respond to them if they dieted?
(locus of control)	*g*	Do they feel they are able to lose weight?
(benefits and barriers)	*h*	What might be the benefits of dieting?
	i	What might be the barriers to dieting?
(perceived vulnerability and severity)	*j*	How important is it to diet? How seriously overweight are they? Is their weight a serious problem? Does it really matter to their health?
(satisfaction and well-being)	*k*	What affects their satisfaction with the diet?
	l	How could they be made more satisfied with it?
	m	How generally well and happy do they feel?
	n	Would dieting make this better or worse?

attitudes by using measures specific to the health issue in question. For example, Bradley (1994) has developed a range of measures specifically for diabetes. A number of relevant aspects of health belief have been identified:

- *Locus of control* – who is perceived to have causal control over aspects of the condition and its treatment.
- *Benefits and barriers* involved in treatment.
- *Perceived severity* – people may not believe the problem is serious.
- *Perceived vulnerability* – the person may not perceive that it affects them.
- *Treatment satisfaction.*
- *Sense of well-being.*

The health beliefs model of the relationship between health attitudes and health behaviours is complex. Although it is called a model, which sounds exact, not much is yet known about the relative importance of its elements or of their interrelations. What is known is that health behaviours are more likely to be carried out when any of the health beliefs components are enhanced: when people feel more in control of their condition and its treatment; if they appreciate that they are vulnerable and the problem is serious; if they have a greater sense of well-being and are satisfied with their treatment; if they perceive the benefits of treatment to outweigh the barriers.

Kent *et al.* (1995) used Bradley's scales in a census study in Tobago. They found that people with tablet-controlled diabetes who regularly attended a clinic saw the benefits of treatment to be greater, and the barriers to be less, than people who chose to attend irregularly or not at all. Those in regular treatment also scored more highly on personal and medical control and on the foreseeability of outcomes, and were less likely to blame uncontrollable external factors for problems with their management of the condition. Thus, the health beliefs concepts help to show the other variables that may intervene between an attitude ('I want to control my diabetes') and appropriate behaviour (going to the clinic, following advice).

PERSUASIVE COMMUNICATION

There are many occasions in healthcare when it is important for the professional to attempt to alter someone's attitudes and behaviour. This puts the health professional in the role of persuader, so it is useful to have some understanding of the processes underlying persuasion.

Central versus peripheral cognitive processing

Petty and Cacioppo (1986a) argued that there are two routes to persuasion:

- The *central route* involves 'cognitive effort', or thinking about the message content. While change is difficult to achieve, it is long-lasting because the message is internalized.
- The *peripheral route*, where people do not really think about the message content and may accept it on superficial aspects such as a famous or attractive speaker. Peripheral processing may be especially likely when people are distracted or in a group.

Petty and Cacioppo (1986b) developed a model of attitude change based on the idea of 'elaboration likelihood'. This involves looking at the factors that affect thinking about the message and hence processing centrally. Similarly, Fazio (1990) argued that people are more likely to act in line with their attitudes if they have been 'primed', so that they have easy access to their store of memories on the subject. For example, certain words or pictures may evoke relevant thoughts, or perhaps just happy or sad thoughts, which bring certain attitudes to mind. They may evoke the feelings or the information they have about the attitude object. A lot of advertising uses priming.

In a similar vein, McGuire (1964) studied what he called 'inoculation'. He presented subjects with evidence, apparently from serious medical journals, that it is damaging to clean teeth. Some subjects were first given a small, inoculating dose of this argument but others were not. For those who had the small dose, the possibility that they would have to defend their views was raised, and they were less influenced especially if they had been asked to develop an argument to defend their views. This study sits well with recent cognitive theory on active information processing; for many beliefs, for example about smoking, people may have become almost immune to persuasive communications on the subject; they have developed so many 'psychological antibodies'!

Chaiken (1987) has argued that people sometimes rely on 'heuristics', which are rules-of-thumb used to short-cut processing when people are not motivated to process the arguments.

By processing centrally people would be trying to

work out the message for themselves. It may be quite easy to achieve attitude change in people when they are processing peripherally, but the change is not likely to be long-lasting or have implications for long-term behaviour.

Source, message and audience

McGuire (1985) reviewed the Yale studies of persuasion (Hovland *et al.*, 1953) which looked at the source of the message, its content and its audience. In general it is found that:

- The source will be more influential if perceived to be credible (expert and trustworthy) and attractive.
- The content of messages are more effective if they are not seen as direct influence attempts.
- If the audience is opposed to the message, both sides of the argument should be presented. If the audience is already broadly in favour, a one-sided argument works better. Audiences are likely to be influenced if they are mildly distracted.

These findings can be incorporated into more recent theories. For example, distraction reduces the likelihood of central processing and may enhance the use of heuristics, facilitating short-term change if the message is superficially attractive.

Fear appeal

Often it is suggested that health campaigns should emphasize danger or suffering to get people to change their behaviour. A glance at posters in general practice and out-patient waiting rooms, and at health education material in general, confirms this.

It has been apparent since Janis and Feshbach (1953) studied the effects of differing levels of 'fear appeal' that fear in itself does not work. They found that a moderate level of fear led to most behaviour change on dental hygiene. In the many years since, the evidence broadly supports this. Leventhal (1970) conducted many studies on the issue and concluded that, while fear may make people want to change, actual change occurs when they also have plenty of information and process it. It may be that fear leads to peripheral processing and short-term attitude change; it may even inhibit central processing in that people do not want to think about it.

There are individual differences in handling fear. Some people like to deal with it and they process centrally if the message contains specific suggestions to solve the problem. If there is no clear way to reduce the fear, or people prefer to avoid being afraid, they may only process peripherally and may reject or avoid the issue (Gleicher and Petty, 1992).

Learning Activity 7 ◆ ◆ ◆

How would you go about persuading the person in Activity 6 to diet or not diet, depending on what their analysis showed? Try to use all the processes first identified above: central versus peripheral processing; priming; inoculation; presentation of source and message; fear appeal.

SUMMARY

It appears that people actively try to make sense of their world and to survive in it as best they believe they can. At some times they are more active in processing information that at other times, and some people are also more concerned to be right than others. People like to feel they are making their own decisions and being sensible. They also survive in a social network. They will not always wish to act in accordance with their attitudes and may not always feel able to do so.

Attempts at achieving persuasion and attitude change must take into account the social network and the practical limitations of behaving in line with the expected attitude. Moreover, people like to maintain their self-esteem and will choose self-affirmation strategies when it is threatened. Behaviour change might indeed lead to a change in attitude if the person believes that he or she has freely chosen the behaviour.

If people can be encouraged to try some new behaviour and react positively, this may be internalized and have long-term effects. If they do not enjoy the experience or feel they have been forced to do it, then the effects will not endure. Fear appeals may be effective if they invoke a moderate level of fear and clear proposals for action.

Key Points ■ ■ ■

❑ Attitudes are more likely to persist and to relate to behaviour if they are accessible. This is more likely if they are personally relevant or learned through direct experience.

❑ People generally like to perceive themselves as consistent, although attitude change does not depend merely on perceived inconsistency.

❑ People like to maintain their self-esteem and will choose self-affirmation strategies when this is threatened, thus avoiding the need to change attitude.

❑ Behaviour change might lead to a change in attitude if a person believes he or she has freely chosen to behave.

❑ Persuading a person to do something which is inconsistent with their own beliefs and with those of the people they care about is not likely to bring about long-term change.

❑ Fear appeals may be effective if they motivate people to attend to the message and process it centrally.

❑ If people can be encouraged to try some new behaviour and react positively, this may be internalized and have long-term effects.

❑ Attitude change is more likely to endure if the material has been thought about-centrally processed.

References ▼ ▼ ▼

Abelson, R. (1981). Psychological status of the script concept. *American Psychologist*, **36**: 715–29.

Ajzen, I. (1985). From intentions to actions: a theory of planned behaviour. In: Kuhl, J. and Beckman, J. (eds), *Action-Control: From Cognition to Behaviour*. New York: Springer, 11–39.

Ajzen, I. and Fishbein, M. (1980). *Understanding Attitudes and Predicting Social Behaviour*. Englewood Cliffs, NJ: Prentice-Hall.

Aronson, E., Fried, C. and Stone, J. (1991). Overcoming denial and increasing the intention to use condoms through the induction of hypocrisy. *American Journal of Public Health*, **81**: 1636–8.

Aronson, E., Wilson, T.D. and Akert, R.M. (1994). *Social Psychology: The Heart and the Mind*. New York: HarperCollins.

Bem, D.J. (1972). Self-perception theory. In: Berkowitz, L. (ed.), *Advances in Experimental Social Psychology*, vol. 6. New York: Academic Press, 1–62.

Bradley, C. (ed.) (1994). *Handbook of Psychology and Diabetes*. Chur, Switzerland: Harwood Academic.

Brehm, J.W. (1966). *A Theory of Psychology Reactance*. New York: Academic Press.

Chaiken, S. (1987). The heuristic model of persuasion. In: Zanna, M.P., Olson, J.M. and Herman, C.P. (eds), *Social Influence: The Ontario Symposium*, vol. 5. Hillsdale, NJ: Lawrence Erlbaum, 3–39.

Croyle, R.T. and Cooper, J. (1983). Dissonance arousal: physiological evidence. *Journal of Personality and Social Psychology*, **45**: 782–91.

Davidson, A.R. and Jaccard, J.J. (1979). Variables that moderate the attitude–behaviour relation: results of a longitudinal survey. *Journal of Personality and Social Psychology*, **37**: 1364–76.

Fazio, R.H. (1990). Multiple processes by which attitudes guide behavior: the MODE model as an integrative framework. In: Zanna, M.P. (ed.), *Advances in Experimental Social Psychology*, vol. 23. New York: Academic Press, 75–109.

Fazio, R.H. and Williams, C.J. (1986). Attitude accessibility as a moderator of the attitude–perception and attitude–behavior relations. *Journal of Personality and Social Psychology*, **51**: 505–14.

Fazio, R.H. and Zanna, M. (1981). Direct experience and attitude–behaviour consistency. In: Berkowitz, L. (ed.), *Advances in Experimental Social Psychology*: vol. 14. New York: Academic Press, 161–202.

Fazio, R.H., Zanna, M.P. and Cooper, J. (1977). Dissonance and self-perception: an integrative view of each theory's proper domain of application. *Journal of Experimental Social Psychology*, **13**: 464–79.

Festinger, L. (1957). *A Theory of Cognitive Dissonance*. Stanford, CA: Stanford University Press.

Festinger, L. and Carlsmith, J.M. (1959). Cognitive consequences of forced compliance. *Journal of Abnormal and Social Psychology*, **58**: 203–11.

Fishbein, M. and Ajzen, I. (1975). *Belief, Attitude, Intention, and Behavior: An Introduction to Theory and Research*. Reading, MA: Addison–Wesley.

Gleicher, F. and Petty, R.E. (1992). Expectations of reassurance influence the nature of fear-stimulated attitude change. *Journal of Experimental Social Psychology*, **28**: 86–100.

Hovland, C.L., Janis, I. and Kelley, H.H. (1953). *Communication and Persuasion: Psychological Studies of Opinion Change*. New Haven, CT: Yale University Press.

Janis, I.L. and Feshbach, (1953). Effects of fear-arousing communications. *Journal of Abnormal and Social Psychology*, **48**: 78–92.

Katz, D. (1960). The functional approach to the study of attitudes. *Public Opinion Quarterly*, **24**: 163–204.

Kent, V., Hinkson, J. and Moore, C. (1995). Psychological factors in the management of diabetes mellitus: cost-effectiveness, locus of control and involvement in treatment. In: Pfeiffer, E.F. and Reaven, G.M. (eds), *Diabetes Care and Research in Europe*. Stuttgart: Georg Thieme Verlag.

Kruglanski, A.W. (1989). The psychology of being 'right': the problem of accuracy in social perception and cognition. *Psychological Bulletin*, **106**: 395–409.

Langer, E.L. (1989). Minding matters: the consequences of mindlessness–mindfulness. In: Berlowitz, L. (ed.), *Advances in Experimental Social Psychology*: vol. 22. San Diego, CA: Academic Press, 137–74.

Langer, E.J. and Rodin, J. (1976). The effects of choice and enhanced personal responsibility for the aged: a field experiment in an institutional setting. *Journal of Personality and Social Psychology*, **34**: 191–8.

LaPiere, R.T. (1934). Attitudes vs actions. *Social Forces*: **13**: 230–7.

Leventhal, H. (1970). Findings and theory in the study of fear communications. In: Berkowitz, L. (ed.), *Advances in Experimental Social Psychology*, vol. 5. New York: Academic Press, 119–86.

Likert, R. (1932). A technique for measuring attitudes. *Archives of Psychology*, **140**.

McGuire, W.J. (1964). Inducing resistance to persuasion. In: Berkowitz, L. (ed.), *Advances in Experimental Social Psychology*, vol. 1. New York: Academic Press, 191–229.

McGuire, W.J. (1985). Attitudes and attitude change. In: Lindzey, G. and Aronson, E. (eds), *Handbook of Social Psychology*, vol. 2, 3rd edn. New York: Random House, 233–346.

Petty, R.E. and Cacoppo, J.T. (1986a). *Communication and Persuasion:*

Central and Peripheral Routes to Attitude Change. New York: Springer-Verlag.

Petty, R.E. and Cacioppo, J.T. (1986b). The elaboration likelihood model of persuasion. In: Berkowitz, L. (ed.), *Advances in Experimental Social Psychology*, vol. 19. San Diego, CA: Academic Press, 123–205.

Shavitt, S. (1990). The role attitude objects in attitude function. *Journal of Experimental Social Psychology*, **26**: 124–48.

Steele, C.M. (1988). The psychology of self-affirmation: sustaining the integrity of the self. In: Berkowitz, L. (ed.), *Advances in Experimental Social Psychology*, vol. 21. Orlando FL: Academic Press, 261–302.

Further Reading ▲ ▲ ▲

Aronson, E., Wilson, T.D. and Akert, R.M. (1994). *Social Psychology: The Heart and the Mind*. New York: HarperCollins, 295–323.

Brewer, M.B. and Crano, W.D. (1994). *Social Psychology*. St Paul, MN: West Publishing, 23–104.

Deaux, K., Dane, F.C. and Wrightsman, L.S. (1993). *Social Psychology in the 1990s*, 6th edn. Pacific Grove, CA: Brooks/Cole, 144–91.

Hogg, M.A. and Vaughan, G. (1995). *Social Psychology: An Introduction*. London: Prentice–Hall/Harvester–Wheatsheaf.

Stroebe, W. and Stroebe, M.S. (1995). *Social Psychology and Health*.

SECTION V

Cognitive Processes

19

Assessing Brain Function

Andrew D. Worthington

LEARNING OBJECTIVES

After studying this chapter you should:

- Be able to describe brain dysfunction from different conceptual perspectives
- Understand the nature of recovery mechanisms and their relevence to assessment
- Be able to describe the key principles and methods of assessment of brain dysfunction
- Know how to plan the neuropsychological assessment of a clinical problem

INTRODUCTION

The assessment of brain function is often crucial to understanding the nature and course of neurological illness or injury. Neuropsychology seeks to understand the brain functions underlying psychological experiences ranging from specific skills like memory, vision and reading to emotional responses, personality and self-concept. The idea that a neuropsychological assessment of brain function is something to be undertaken in a psychologist's office is common but misguided. Although formal neuropsychological testing is probably the most sophisticated form of assessment, only a minority of people with brain injury will undergo this type of investigation. Appreciation of neuropsychology can enrich the experience of working with individuals who have suffered brain injury; moreover, investigating impaired abilities and areas of preserved skill can be instrumental to the effective management of people with brain injury.

BRAIN ORGANIZATION AND RECOVERY

Damage to the cerebral cortex and subcortical structures can arise through vascular insult, viral infection, tumours, degenerative disease and head injury, often causing severe long-term disability. Before looking at how neuropsychological assessment might be carried out, it is important first to gain an overview of how the brain is organized and of its capacity to recover spontaneously after insult.

Recovery has been variously defined in the clinical and animal literature. It has been used to mean a complete remission of symptoms, survival of life-threatening illness albeit with residual effects, or adaption to disability sufficient to allow resumption of premorbid roles. Almli and Finger (1988) reviewed current definitions and suggested that recovery from brain injury is ' . . . a theoretical construct that implies a complete regaining of identical functions that were lost or impaired after brain damage'. This definition requires that there be an initial deficit, which ought to be demonstrated on assessment. The all-or-none nature of this description precludes the possibility of stages, or degrees, of recovery, yet the notion of gradual recovery is clinically very important. Attempts to assess the degree of recovery requires accurate estimation of premorbid levels of functioning in addition to detailed assessment of current abilities.

A crucial issue concerning the brain's potential for recovery is the extent to which functions can be served by any neural area (equipotentiality), as opposed to the notion that it has highly specialized processing regions (localization). In fact, both concepts are valid. Cognitive skills tend to be associated with particular brain regions, but these specialized areas may be widely dispersed across the brain, giving rise to the idea of 'distributed functions'. However, these different concepts of brain organization are reflected in explanations of recovery processes (Finger *et al.*, 1988). Many physiological

Box 19.1 *Principles of recovery after brain damage, and possible underlying physiological processes*

Principle	Main process	Mediating processes
Diaschisis	Neural shock	Oedema Neurotoxins Ischaemia
Redundancy	Restitution	Denervation supersensitivity Rerouting of growing axons Collateral sprouting (reactive synaptogenesis)
Reorganization	Vicariation (substitution)	Rerouting of axons Collateral sprouting Biochemical adaptations
	Compensation	Relearning
Adaptation	Behavioural change	Relearning

processes have been proposed to explain psychological recovery (see Box 19.1).

Neural shock

Initial effects of cerebral insult, which accompany changes in consciousness, include temporary disruption to brain tissue surrounding the lesion ('neural shock'). This passive depression of activity was termed 'diaschisis' by the neurologist Von Monakov in 1914, a term still in occasional use. These transient deficits resolve as cerebral oedema in surrounding tissue subsides, briefly released neurotoxins are absorbed, or a vascular blockage is removed, as occurs in transient ischaemic attacks (TIAs).

Redundancy

Some proponents of the equipotentiality notion argue that behavioural improvements soon after injury confirm that large portions of brain tissue are effectively redundant for normal use but can be used to assume functions of damaged regions. However, one might expect little dysfunction to result if this were the case. Just because people can function reasonably well with damaged brain tissue does not mean that the damaged tissue did not perform a useful function.

Reorganization

Several mechanisms have been proposed for the possible reorganization of brain functions. Vicariation – the idea that one part of the brain could take over the work of another – is now untenable. Vicariation cannot be mediated by *gross* reorganization of neural pathways, but substitution is compatible with the concept of distributed functions. If specific cognitive functions are organized across brain regions, this allows for the possibility of new connections forming between neighbouring healthy neurones. But animal studies show that rerouting of axons, and biochemical adaptions to modify the effectiveness of existing synapses, usually requires a period of relearning in addition to spontaneous recovery processes.

Retraining is also an essential component of rehabilitation and the promotion of compensation to impairment. Compensation may also take the form of spontaneous behavioural adaptation to difficulties.

Learning Activity 1 ◆ ◆ ◆

Match the following *descriptions of recovery* with the processes of redundancy, adaptation, reorganization, and diaschisis:

a Other cognitive skills are brought in to achieve ends previously achieved by other skills.
b Areas of brain tissue return to normal soon after injury.
c Spare neurons become involved when others have been damaged.
d Other neurons relatively nearby are gradually programmed to take over a lost function.

There is much debate as to whether it is possible to separate the possible effects of different recovery mechanisms and whether they are actually designed to aid recovery at all. Researchers and clinicians are faced with the likelihood of both neuronal and behavioural recovery, without understanding the relationship between them.

DESCRIBING BRAIN DYSFUNCTION

Brain dysfunction has been described in three main ways:

- *neuropsychological* – in terms of clinical syndromes;
- *information processing* – in terms of cognitive processes thought to underlie dysfunction;
- *functional disability frameworks* – in terms of complex behavioural activity.

Neuropsychological classification

Traditional neuropsychological assessment is closely identified with the detection of 'syndromes', which Walsh (1987) defined as '. . . a unique constellation of signs and symptoms which occur together frequently enough to suggest a particular underlying process'. In the nineteenth century the neuropsychological syndrome was not only a co-occurrence of signs and symptoms but was thought by many to be localizable to particular regions of the brain. In 1861, Paul Broca described language impairment (aphasia) arising from damage to circumscribed regions of the left hemisphere. He is often credited with being the first to propose the notion that the left cerebral hemisphere is dominant for language. Subsequently, Wernicke (1874) and Lichthein (1885) produced elaborate schemes (the predecessors of modern information processing models) to account for different patterns of language disorder. Examples and explanations of some traditional neuropsychological classifications that are still widely used are shown in Box 19.2, and described in a little more clinical detail below.

MEMORY

Memory disorders can take many forms. A loss of memory for factual information (semantic memory) can occur in dementia or after viral encephalitis (Parkin and Leng, 1993). Amnesia is characterized by poor recall of events (episodic memory) in the context of good short-term memory and preserved factual recall. Amnesia commonly follows damage to the diencephalon (Butters and Stuss, 1989) or medial temporal lobe structures (Smith, 1989). When it is severe, a verbal short-term memory deficit can affect speech comprehension (McCarthy and Warrington, 1987). Verbal

Box 19.2 *Common neuropsychological syndromes*

Cognitive domain	Syndrome name	Description
Language	Broca's aphasia	Poor speech production
	Wernicke's aphasia	Speech comprehension deficit
	Conduction aphasia	Impaired repetition despite good comprehension and fluent speech
	Anomic aphasia	Selective naming disorder
Literacy	Alexia	Disorder of reading
	Agraphia	Impaired spelling or writing
Numbers	Acalculia	Disorder of arithmetic skills or number processing
Perception	Visual agnosia	Failure to recognize objects from their appearance
	Prosopagnosia	Inability to recognize familiar faces
	Simultanagnosia	Inability to perceive multiple stimuli simultaneously
Memory	Anterograde amnesia	Deficit in learning new information
	Retrograde amnesia	Impaired recall of premorbid events
Motor skills	Apraxia	Disorder of voluntary skilled movement

memory can be impaired selectively, usually following left hemisphere lesions, especially in the temporo-parietal regions (Smith, 1989).

LANGUAGE

Many people in the acute stages of illness may have problems producing any speech, or have particular difficulty with recalling names of people or objects (anomia). People may seem to stutter, hesitate and describe things in a roundabout way; this is known as a circumlocution. This disorder is sometimes called non-fluent dysphasia because the person's speech becomes laborious and very tiring as they search for words.

Another form of speech production disorder is characterized not by difficulty producing speech, but by production of inappropriate, sometimes nonsense, speech. A person may produce individual words correctly but the meaning (semantic content) of their speech is disjointed. For example, a man asked to name an object in front of him (an envelope) replied: 'is a peculiar missive for demanding a disperse'. This is sometimes called a fluent dysphasia because speech is produced fairly easily. Unfortunately, patients with this form of speech production difficulty often have comprehension problems and so are not aware of the meaningless content of much of their speech. These people can easily be mislabelled as difficult, unmotivated, confused or intellectually impaired, because of specific problems in understanding instructions.

Language comprehension problems have been termed 'receptive dysphasias', and speech production problems, fluent and non-fluent, are sometimes referred to as 'expressive dysphasias'. There are several other ways of classifying speech disorders and newer information processing models reject the older notions of fluent and non-fluent, and expressive and receptive disorders. Nevertheless they are a useful initial guide to the complexity of language dysfunctions (also see Walker (1992) and Code (1991)).

VISUAL PERCEPTION

It is important to distinguish between visual problems (poor visual activity, visual field loss), preliminary perceptual processes such as orientation and shape, and more complex visual perceptual processes. Impairment of basic perceptual processes such as discrimination of shape, colour and spatial location often follows occipital lobe damage (Warrington, 1986). More complex percep-

Box 19.3 *Visual perceptual disorders and their common anatomical associations*

Impairment	Description	Localization
Basic visual abilities		
Single point localization	Ability to see and point to individual elements	Junction of occipito-parietal boundary
Size, shape, length	Ability to discriminate objects accordingly	Bilateral occipital
Orientation	ability to judge relative orientation/ angles	Right parietal
Spatial search and selection	Scanning/identification of elements in a complex array	Right fronto-parietal
Apperceptive agnosia		
Visual segmentation and integration	Integration of features into objects and discrimination from background	Bilateral or right parietal
perceptual categorization	Ability to copy objects or match objects across viewpoints	Bilateral or right parietal
Associative agnosia		
Stored knowledge about objects	Ability to recognize, mime use of or match objects in terms of function	Left or bilateral temporal lobe

Box 19.4 *Examples of left visual neglect after right hemisphere stroke*

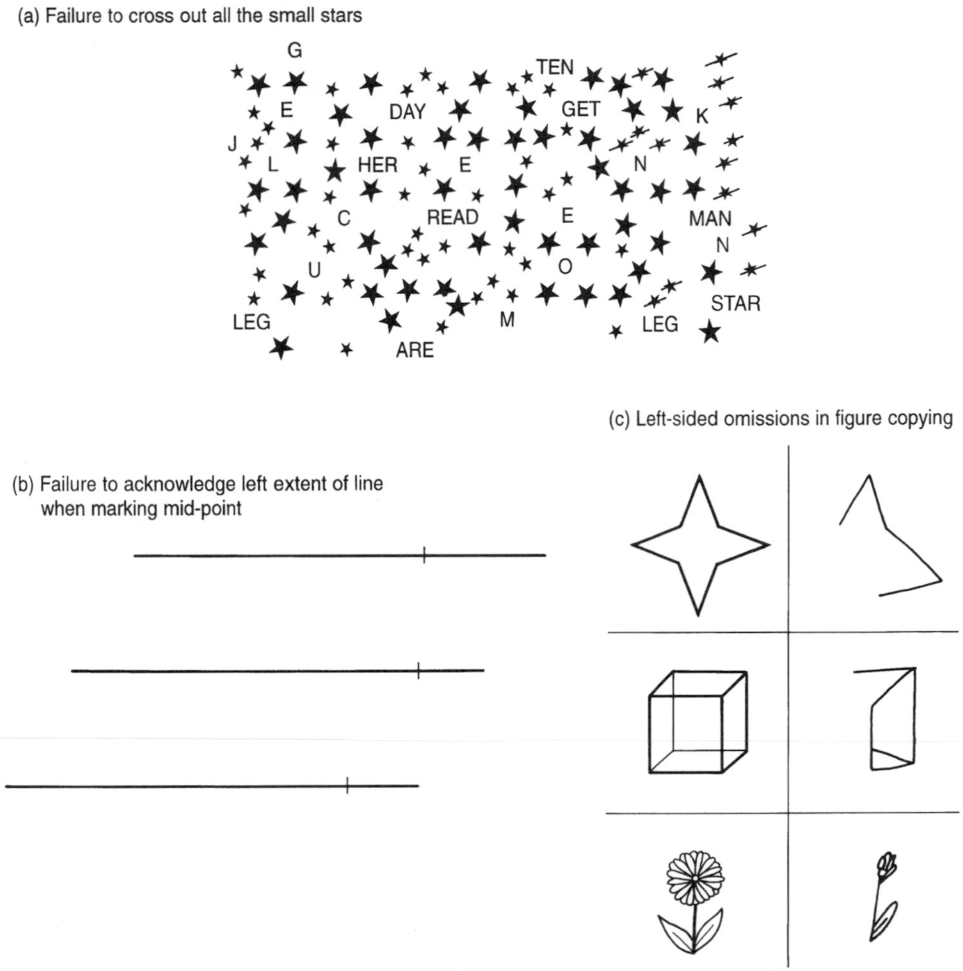

tual processing responsible for object recognition is associated with the temporo-parietal regions and a variety of visual perceptual and spatial disorders can be caused by right parietal damage (Warrington, 1982). Examples of common visual deficits and anatomical correlates are shown in Box 19.3.

The term 'visual agnosia' refers to a failure to recognize objects visually. Originally this included impairments due to poor visual perception (now occasionally referred to as 'apperceptive agnosia') which occur mostly after right hemisphere brain damage. Nowadays the term agnosia is used mainly to describe associative agnosia which more commonly follows left-sided posterior brain lesions. This kind of impairment has been called a 'percept stripped of its meaning' (Teuber, 1968). In other words, a person has adequate perceptual skills but fails to appreciate the functional significance of what is seen. Such a person faced with a potato-peeler, for instance, could copy it, recognize it again later and draw it from memory but would not have any idea of how to use it.

VISUAL NEGLECT

A specific deficit of visual attention, which is particularly common after stroke, is visuo-spatial neglect. This is a partial lack of attention, usually to one side of space or one side of an object, so that a person only sees, reads, draws or otherwise acknowledges an incomplete stimulus (Box 19.4). Visual neglect can follow right and left hemisphere damage (Stone *et al.*, 1991) but tends to be more severe and longer-lasting after right-sided brain lesions.

A distinction has been made between sensory neglect when a person reports seeing an incomplete object, and motor neglect when they produce (draw or copy) objects with features missing on one side (Pizzamilglio *et al.*, 1992). Visual neglect represents a significant impediment to functional recovery (Barer, 1990).

MOTOR SKILLS

The neuropsychological aspects of motor skills are the processes of preparation, planning and cognitive control of actions, rather than the apparatus of movement itself. Disorders of voluntary action are collectively known as 'dyspraxias'. These are amongst the least well understood areas of neuropsychology, and consequently assessment tends to be more descriptive.

Traditionally, two principal forms of dyspraxia have been recognized:

- *ideational dyspraxia* describes failures of voluntary action due to loss of knowledge about the uses of objects or the meanings of gestures. People with such problems may nevertheless be able to copy actions appropriately. Thus a person who has had a stroke may have 'lost' the action that accompanies being presented with a teapot. However, this person may well be able to execute and relearn a pouring motion successfully once it has been demonstrated by the therapist.
- *ideomotor dyspraxia* refers to an inability to execute the tasks properly, even when a person knows what they should do. These people may not benefit from demonstration as they already retain the concept of the action. However, they seem to have lost the capacity to translate the knowledge into a relevant set of instructions for the movement to take place. It is important to clarify whether a person has visual problems or physical restrictions before attributing difficulties in getting dressed, for instance, to dyspraxia.

EXECUTIVE FUNCTIONS

Probably the most enigmatic areas of the cerebral cortex in the history of neuropsychology have been the frontal lobes (Milner, 1982). The prefrontal cortex in particular is now believed to serve many different functions (Box 19.5). Cognitive operations affected by damage to the prefrontal regions may be simplified by describing them as essential to the control of behaviour.

A number of theories have been developed to encompass the diverse effects of frontal brain damage (Nauta, 1971; Damasio *et al.*, 1991). Perhaps the most promising of these is the notion that the frontal lobes serve to monitor how people allocate attention and effort to tasks, and how people respond to the external world (Shallice, 1988). If the system is disrupted, people can find that they too readily devote attention to any new information and therefore are unable to persist with a course of action, (i.e. they become very distractible).

Box 19.5 *Some suggested functions of the prefrontal cortex in humans, and the dysfunctions arising from acquired brain damage*

Cognitive skills	Function	Dysfunction
Memory	Judgements of recency	
	Memory for context	
	Validation of recollections	Confabulation
Attention	Sustained attention	Poor concentration
	Selective attention	Distractibility
Problem-solving	Planning	Disorganization
	Strategy formulation	
	Mental flexibility	Concreteness
Self-monitoring	Self-awareness	Loss of insight
	Error correction	Inaccuracy
Regulating behaviour	Activate action plans	Perseveration
		Lack of initiation
	Inhibit inappropriate behaviour	Impulsivity
		Environmental dependency

Schwartz *et al.* (1993) suggested ways to distinguish deficits of attentional control of action from the loss of conceptual knowledge that is typical of ideational dyspraxia. Attentional dysfunction may explain the impulsivity, poor planning and self-regulation problems associated with frontal lobe damage. Severely impaired people show a failure of internally driven control of their behaviour and are said to show an environmental-dependency syndrome (Lhermitte, 1986). Frontal dysfunction may also result in the opposite tendency (that is, a failure to inhibit actions when appropriate). In this case people become notoriously concrete in their thinking, inflexible in their problem-solving, and dogmatic and opinionated in social interaction. In extreme cases they may appear 'stuck' in a routine and repeat actions or phrases inappropriately (perseveration). Failure to regulate behaviour is often associated with poor insight into the difficulties, making these problems some of the most challenging in rehabilitation.

PROBLEMS WITH TRADITIONAL NEUROPSYCHOLOGICAL CLASSIFICATIONS

Despite the continued use of descriptive classifications in neuropsychology, these do present problems:

- Some skills are impaired and others left fairly intact after brain damage. It is now recognized that cognitive abilities are not neatly localized within the brain (for example, lesions of the left parietal lobe are commonly but not exclusively associated with spelling problems). Therefore the pattern of strengths and weaknesses evident on testing cannot be explained purely in terms of anatomical location.
- There is the problem of 'multiple determination', whereby the same result on an assessment can be obtained in various ways. For example, a person who cannot execute written instructions may have problems with visual word recognition, verbal comprehension, short-term memory, planning and sequencing skills or motor execution, not to mention peripheral sensory difficulties such as visual acuity and kinaesthetic impairment, or physical impediments. Thus an assessment that describes the problem as 'a difficulty following visual instructions', whilst objective, does not provide any insight into the reasons why this cannot be done; it gives no indication of where the cognitive failure lies.
- Any task may be achieved by different means. Detailed assessment of an apparently successful task performance still requires consideration of how a person attained their goal, and whether this reflects a conscious adjustment to disability or a process of partial recovery which is likely to change over time.

Nevertheless, the traditional neuropsychological classifications provide a useful summary of common patterns of performance. Often the first signs of difficulty occur to non-psychologists in the context of therapy sessions or medical investigations. In such cases accurate observation and description of a person's behaviour or performance serves as a valuable insight to guide more detailed assessment.

Information processing

In the latter half of this century cognitive science (which is concerned with studying cognitive skills in animals and machines) has been dominated by a perspective of the brain as an information processor. The advantage of an information processing approach to cognition is that it is concerned with processes underlying skilled performance rather than simply with whether or not a task is performed satisfactorily. In other words, it looks at why someone can or cannot

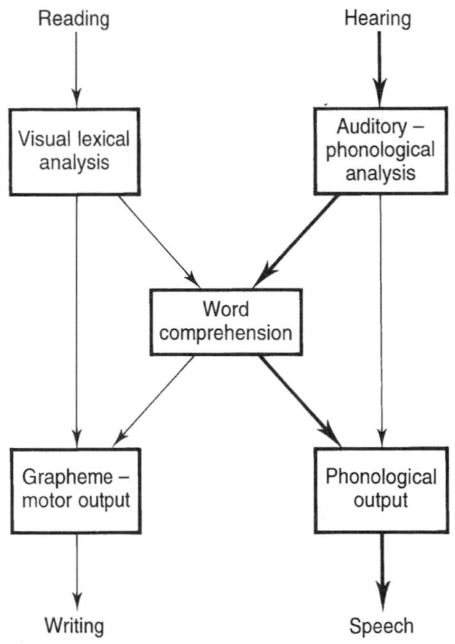

Figure 19.1 *An information processing model of stages in language processing – bold arrows define the processing pathway for understanding and repeating a spoken word*

execute a task rather than merely describing what they can or cannot do.

Information processing models describe the processes that are thought to underlie specific skills using 'box and arrow' diagrams. For example, Figure 19.1 illustrates some proposed processing stages involved in hearing a word, understanding it and repeating it. It is also possible to predict the kinds of errors resulting from damage to specific processing routes (Semenza *et al.*, 1988). Therefore these models suggest ways to understand patterns of cognitive performance in brain-injured persons.

This fortunate venture of cognitive psychology into the clinical realm was (and still is) motivated by the opportunities to learn more about normal human cognition by studying dysfunctions in the damaged brain. Subsequently, many conceptual models of cognitive abilities have been modified directly as a result of assessing people with brain injuries.

MODULARITY

The application of information processing models to understand brain dysfunction makes some assumptions about how cognitive processes operate (see Box 19.6). It is generally assumed that certain skills can be executed by semi-independent processing modules, without involving the whole brain or all psychological resources, and so they may be disrupted after injury without equivalent disruption to other skills (Fodor, 1983). Modular skills include, for example, reading, spoken language, visual perception, memory and motor abilities. Thus, a person with a poor visual memory may have good visual perceptual abilities. Similarly a person who has speech production problems may be able to understand perfectly well and may also be able to write intelligibly. Modularity is a way of understanding how some functions can be severely impaired with sometimes little impact on related processes.

DISASSOCIATIONS

When a person shows marked deficits on task A (e.g. object naming) but not task B (e.g. reading), a disassociation has been demonstrated. It may be that one task is generally more difficult than the other. However, if another person should show the opposite pattern, where performance on task A is superior to results on task B, then it is assumed that the two skills operate separately.

The combination of two opposite disassociations in task performance is known as a 'double disassociation'. By providing information about the relationship between different processes, the double disassociation allows psychologists to develop models of cognitive functioning (Olton, 1989). Whereas true disassociations require that one skill is entirely intact and the other is impaired, in clinical practice more often one encounters instances of relative disability where execution of two or more tasks is weak but performance on one task is more impaired than on the other (Miller, 1993).

Box 19.6 *Some core assumptions in the application of information processing models to assessment of brain function*

Key assumption	Description
Modularity	Mental operations are implemented as partially independent processing components
Subtractivity	Brain damage can selectively disrupt modular processes, leaving others intact
Dissociability	Modular processes can be inferred from patterns of task performance
Partial products	Patient errors are a result of normal processing up to the stage of the impairment
Single subject research	The appropriate level of data collection is individual cases, not group studies

Functional disability frameworks

These assessments look at complex functional skills like dressing, cooking, model-making and driving. They provide a useful summary of everyday problems and allow therapists to evaluate treatment success in meaningful activities (Giles, 1992). Models of functional disability tend to be descriptive in the sense that they conceptualize which activities people find difficult. This is often done in the form of observations of activities of daily living (ADLs). Unlike neuropsychological models which permit inferences about functional performance from impairments, disability frameworks assess skills directly and in different contexts (Katz, 1992). Laver and Powell (1995) recently published the Structured Observational Test of Function (SOTOF) which

Learning Activity 2 ◆ ◆ ◆

In the following list of dysfunctions, state which level or model of brain dysfunction seems appropriate (neuropsychological, information processing, or functional):

- unable to repeat short sentences
- retrograde amnesia
- communication difficulties
- self-monitoring deficit
- visual agnosia
- ideomotor dyspraxia
- inconsistent access to stored memories
- unable to find way around familiar routes.

combines observation of functional ability with assessment of underlying neuropsychological deficits.

These three models of brain dysfunctions are related in that they describe the same phenomena but at different levels of analysis. There is not a neat correspondence between the models because each has evolved from quite different knowledge bases, and for different reasons. Nevertheless, a 'dressing problem' at the functional disability level might be an 'ideomotor dysfunction' at a neuropsychological level and a 'failure to select or implement relevant action sequences' at an information processing level. Whilst it seems more sensible to be aware that, say, the dressing problem illustrates an underlying dyspraxia, information processing models do not provide the therapist with strategies to guide rehabilitation; and indeed the outcome at a functional level for retraining of specific cognitive skills identified by information processing models is disappointing (see Chapter 20).

Descriptions of dysfunction at each level have their own aims and all can serve a useful function depending on the purpose or nature of the question being asked. Assessments based on the different models tend to lead to different recommendations for treatment or rehabilitation. It has been argued, however, that sophisticated cognitive analyses can lead to recommendations for rehabilitation that could have been reached by much more obvious functional analysis and behavioural description and without any knowledge of information processing theory.

ASSESSMENT STRATEGIES

The psychological effects of injury to the brain may be:

- *direct* – a direct result of a brain region being damaged, affecting specific abilities such as speech, perception or emotional control, and sometimes causing increased aggression, tearfulness, or reduced motivation;
- *secondary* – secondary to brain injury, producing for example loss of self-esteem, depression, frustration or anxiety.

General principles

Before looking at specific methods, a number of general principles such as the purpose, timing and focus of the assessment must be mentioned.

PURPOSES OF ASSESSMENT

Traditional neuropsychological assessment to detect the presence of brain damage is no longer considered useful (Mapou, 1988). This is because brain damage is not a unitary concept; the extent of a brain lesion does not predict the nature or extent of a person's difficulties. Neuropsychology can still be an aid to diagnosis, but the development of imaging techniques means that this function is increasingly one of supplementing diagnostic information, rather than providing definitive answers.

Instead, neuropsychological assessment allows clinicians to hypothesize about possible underlying processing dysfunctions. More commonly, therefore, assessment is carried out when the diagnosis is already known, or strongly suspected; it helps to focus therapeutic efforts and provides a conceptual basis for evaluating treatment outcome. Box 19.7 shows the principal functions of neuropsychological assessment, some of which are discussed in detail by Miller (1992).

Box 19.7 *Principal functions of neuropsychological assessment*

- To provide diagnostic information
- To describe patterns of impairment
- To measure change or recovery
- To plan rehabilitation strategies
- To aid decision-making, such as whether to return to work or resume driving

Learning Activity 3 ◆ ◆ ◆

The remaining exercises in this chapter, which are all based on the following case study, will enable you to practice the process and techniques of neuropsychological assessment.

A young man was involved in a motorbike accident eight weeks ago. He was unconscious for 30 minutes. There is known damage to the left frontal region of his brain as well as complicated fractures of right tibia and fibula and right foot, but orthopaedic surgery is complete and progress is satisfactory. He needs to be fit enough for discharge, but so far he is very unstable on crutches and his general mobility and self-care skills are limited. He spends most of the day lying on his bed, sometimes looking at a paper or the television but more often than not he appears to be asleep. He is not cooperating with any aspect of his rehabilitation. Before the accident he worked as a computer engineer, he lived in a flat and had a girlfriend and a busy social life revolving around the rugby club. Neuropsychological assessment is required to gain a clearer understanding of his difficulties.

In this case example, identify what you believe are the *aims* of your assessment of this man.

TIMING OF ASSESSMENT

The reason for carrying out a cognitive assessment will affect when and how the assessment is undertaken. For example, a person with anoxic brain damage who is a problem to manage in hospital requires an early assessment of cognitive abilities. This may clarify any specific problems contributing to the difficult behaviour, such as impulsivity or poor short-term memory. Early assessment also allows prompt and appropriate management strategies to be developed by providing a framework for staff to understand the behaviour and a rationale for coping with it.

By contrast, in the case of a person who has recently suffered a stroke and has immediate physical and swallowing needs, a neuropsychological evaluation will be of limited relevance because the rate of cognitive recovery is slower. Assessment after several weeks may provide a better guide to immediate and future needs. In some cases an early cognitive assessment can usefully be undertaken, such as when a person's physiotherapy or occupational therapy is being undermined by apparent non-compliance.

Learning Activity 4 ◆ ◆ ◆

In the case example being studied, decide *when* the assessment needs to be done. Justify your answer.

FOCUSING ASSESSMENT

Assessments vary owing to the wide variety of tests available. The most useful assessments are those that answer a specific question. Thus, rather than investigating someone's current intellectual skills the issue could be reframed to ask whether there is evidence of deterioration since the last testing, or decline from what a person's history suggests was their previous level of functioning, or whether there is any improvement since medication was altered, or following surgery. Although the assessment might involve looking at a wide range of skills, the more specific the assessment question the better.

Learning Activity 5 ◆ ◆ ◆

In the case example being studied, what *question or questions* do you think need to be addressed in the assessment of this man?

Methods

A range of assessment methods can be used. The three discussed here are: cognitive tests; questionnaires and inventories; and behavioural monitoring.

COGNITIVE TESTING

Cognitive tests can investigate specific skills such as memory, language or problem-solving, deficits to which tend to occur after damage to particular brain regions, and more generalized functions that are sensitive to disruption after almost any cerebral insult.

Cognitive tests are only tools, so the skills lie in the tester. Unless a test is grounded in a systematic knowledge base, its application can be misleading or

Box 19.8 *Main forms of cognitive assessment*

Form of testing	Advantages	Disadvantages
Cognitive screening tests	Easy to administer	Superficial
Neuropsychological test batteries	Extensive; well standardized	Time-consuming; nothing assessed in detail
'Ecological' test batteries	Real-life tasks; in-depth assessment	Not useful diagnostically; focus on one skill only
Cognitive neuro-psychological tests	Theoretically derived; flexible administration	Conceptually complex; poor norms

even detrimental. There are a number of basic approaches to cognitive testing, summarized in Box 19.8.

Cognitive screening

Cognitive screening tests are designed to be administered by clinicians (usually non-psychologists) to provide a brief assessment of a person's mental capabilities. Hodges (1994) provides a good review of current screening tests. They tend to be short questions capable of being administered at a person's bedside, such as Hodkinson's (1972) mental test (see Box 19.9). They are particularly sensitive to disturbances in orientation, concentration and short-term memory and as such they are useful measures of cognitive state on acute hospital wards.

Box 19.9 *Hodkinson's mental test*

Score 1 point for each question answered correctly.

Question *Score*

- Age of patient
- Time (to nearest hour)
- Address given, for recall at end of test: 42 West Street
- Name of hospital (or area of town if at home)
- Year
- Date of birth of patient
- Current month
- Years of First World War
- Name of monarch (President in USA)
- Count backwards from 20 to 1 (no errors allowed, except self-corrected ones)

Score: ______ /10

Neuropsychological test batteries

These take several hours to complete and provide an extensive neuropsychological profile. They include the Halsted–Reitan and Luria–Nebraska batteries, common in the United States though never very popular in the UK (Lezak, 1983). British psychologists are more likely to use a combination of different tests in their armoury, including tests of IQ, memory, attention, speed, reading, visual perception and language. Crawford *et al.* (1992) provide a useful review of the tests most widely used. A summary of common cognitive tests is also provided in Box 19.10.

This approach requires that assessment be a systematic but flexible process. It is not possible to predict exactly which tests will be used in a given battery because the choice relies on preceding test results. Nevertheless there is a stock of popular basic tests; for example, the test used most widely in neuropsychology remains the Wechsler Adult Intelligence Scale–Revised (Wechsler, 1981), which contains 11 separate tasks divided into verbal and non-verbal tests. Although an IQ score tells very little about the kind of difficulties a person has, inconsistency in results across the individual subtests can provide useful clues to likely deficits, indicating where further testing is required (Warrington *et al.*, 1986).

Lack of UK standardization can be a problem for identifying relative strengths or the pattern of test results. It is less of a problem if changes within an individual's own scores over time are important, rather than how they compare with the general population. Norms may be useful for vocational guidance.

Box 19.10 *Summary of common cognitive tests*

Cognitive function	Test and source	Description
Intelligence	Wechsler Adult Intelligence Scale–Revised (WAIS-R) (Wechsler, 1981) Raven's Progressive Matrices (Raven, 1983)	Measures intelligence quotient (IQ) Verbal and non-verbal subtests Useful for basic screening Non-verbal reasoning tasks. Measures general ability. Useful for impaired; elderly people; limited intellecual ability
Premorbid intellectual abilities	National Adult Reading Test (NART) (Nelson and Willison, 1991)	Consists of irregular words list Tests reading skills which are reportedly resistant to brain damage
Short-term memory	Digit-span	Digits presented verbally or visually to be recalled immediately Tests short-term memory
Verbal-memory	Word lists Paired word-associates Sentences (Weschler, 1987; Coughlan and Hollows, 1985)	Presented verbally or visually Recalled immediately and after a delay Repeated to test learning Recognition test if recall fails
Non-verbal memory	Faces Complex figures Abstract designs Buildings and routes (Coughlan and Hollows, 1985)	Presented for immediate and delayed recall and/or recognition
General memory	Rivermead Behavioural Memory Test (Wilson *et al.*, 1985)	Tests verbal and non-verbal memory, learning, short- and long-term memory Useful as memory tasks approximate real-life situations
Recall processes	Recognition Memory Test (Warrington, 1984)	Covers verbal and non-verbal material Tests of immediate and delayed recall Tests of recognition of previously presented material Useful to identify problems of retrieval of stored material in both domains
Expressive language	Spontaneous speech Naming objects Repetition of words and sentences Reading aloud (Kay *et al.*, 1992)	
Receptive language (language comprehension)	Point to named objects Demonstrate object use (McNeil and Prescott, 1978)	Follow instructions of varying linguistic complexity
Expressive language and comprehension	Reading (Hillis and Caramazza, 1992) Writing (Ellis, 1988) Spelling (Patterson, 1988)	
Visual perception	Figure–ground Rotated figures Embedded figures (Warrington and James, 1991; Riddoch and Humphreys, 1993)	
Visual neglect	Line cancellation tasks	
Motor skills	Object use (e.g. pouring and brushing) Symbolic meaning (beckoning or hand-waving) Unfamiliar actions	Spontaneous or copied
Executive functions	Descriptive tasks (Parker and Crawford, 1992) Behavioural observation Cognitive Estimations Test (Shallice and Burgess, 1991)	

Domain-specific 'ecological' tests

These tests are designed to be administered by any relevant profession, in practice usually occupational therapists. They provide more realistic assessments of cognitive functioning in everyday situations. They include the Rivermead Behavioural Memory Test (Wilson *et al.*, 1985); the Rivermead Perceptual Battery (Whiting *et al.*, 1985); the Chessington Occupational Therapy Neurological Assessment Battery (Tyerman *et al.*, 1986); the Test of Everyday Attention (Robertson *et al.*, 1994); the Behavioural Inattention Test (Wilson *et al.*, 1987); and the Stroke Driver's Screening Test (Nouri and Lincoln, 1994).

Cognitive neuropsychological tests

These are a new breed of cognitive tests based on explicit theoretical models of the functions to be tested. Although not specifically for use by psychologists, their academic, rather than clinical, origins makes them difficult to use without some knowledge of cognitive psychology. If administered in their entirety they would take a considerable time to complete, but these tests are meant to provide a source of possible tasks for exploration. It is left to the clinician to decide which tasks are relevant for each person. Tests of this kind that are currently being developed include the Visual Object and Space Perception (VOSP) Battery (Warrington and James, 1991); the Psycholinguistic Assessment of Language Processing in Aphasia (PALPA) Battery (Kay *et al.*, 1992); the Birmingham Object Recognition Battery (BORB) (Riddoch and Humphreys, 1993); and the Johns Hopkins University Dyscalculia Battery (McCloskey *et al.*, 1991).

INTERPRETATION OF COGNITIVE TEST RESULTS

Faced with a number of test results, the interpretation of these is a process where the tester may ask a number of questions, for example:

- Has there been a generalized deterioration in cognitive skills since the brain insult?
- Are there specific deficits either in the absence of generalized deterioration or over and above it? So, for example, a typical pattern of scores for a person with a dementing illness may show a generalized deterioration in all cognitive skills from an estimated premorbid level, in addition to a particular deterioration of memory skills. On the other hand, a person with trauma damage to the right parietal area may have severe impairment of visuo-spatial skills but function at their premorbid level on other cognitive tests.
- What is the pattern of test results? A single test result cannot stand alone, it needs to be interpreted in the context of a person's other results.
- What was the *quality* of performance; not *what* a person can do (the test score) but *how* they go about doing it? Satisfactory test performance can be achieved in more than one way, thus is may have been through compensatory strategies, thereby masking a genuine impairment. In these circumstances, a test result might be misleading, so observation of the person's behaviour is an integral part of the testing procedure.

Learning Activity 6 ◆ ◆ ◆

Which of the following *cognitive functions* do you think need to be assessed in the case example being studied:

- general intellectual abilities?
- memory?
- language?
- motor skills?
- visual perception?
- executive/control function?

Learning Activity 7 ◆ ◆ ◆

In the case example being studied, test results showed that the man's general abilities were slightly lower than expected. He had mild verbal memory problems and mild executive problems in terms of planning and initiating behaviour. Behavioural observation during the assessment session showed that he often seemed to forget the purpose of the task and become side-tracked and concrete in his responses. He failed to initiate any conversation and on a few occasions seemed to confabulate answers and perseverate. He was cooperative and friendly when spoken to, although emotionally very flat and apathetic.

Interpret these results by giving a summary of what you think are the main cognitive problems and how these might account for his failure to rehabilitate.

Reducing the limitations of cognitive testing

There are at least three major limitations in cognitive testing:

- Performance is limited to the testing environment.
- Testing is time-constrained; it is a snapshot of how the person is performing in a given situation at a given time.
- Tests are based on hypothesized skills or processes that may have limited correspondence to real-life skills.

A number of safeguards can be built into the assessment strategy to try to reduce the impact of these problems.

- Good tests should have proved they have test–retest reliability during their development. This assumes consistency of test results over different testings. With this feature it becomes possible to monitor change within an individual over time where it is assumed that changes in scores reflect real changes in specific cognitive skills. However, this is a big assumption as test results can reflect non-specific factors such as mood and situational factors.
- Many tests have alternative forms, providing different sets of material to assess the same skill. Examples are forms A and B of the Coughlan and Hollows (1985) memory scale. This means people can be tested on more than one occasion if there is a suggestion that non-specific factors are affecting performance. The highest score would be used; and the information gained on the inconsistency in performance would be a valuable finding.
- Observing how somebody approaches a task is crucial. For example, a person may eventually learn a list of 12 words but may achieve this in a disorderly, apparently random fashion, suggesting problems in memory control processes. Behavioural monitoring is also a way of validating test results in real-life situations and seeing what everyday functions are affected by their skills deficit (see following sections).
- A number of tests, mentioned above, which emphasize more real-life skills have been developed. Examples are the Rivermead Behavioural Memory Test (Wilson *et al*., 1985) and the Behavioural Inattention Test (Wilson *et al*., 1987).

QUESTIONNAIRES, INVENTORIES AND INTERVIEWS

In any formal cognitive assessment a clinician will unearth results that either contradict what the person reports or which seem to conflict with the views of their family, and sometimes those of other staff. This may necessitate getting information over and above the test results in order to achieve a more accurate assessment. Questionnaires provide a useful means of assessing and quantifying subjectively reported difficulties.

Many instruments with adequate psychometric properties have been developed for assessing a variety of different functions. Amongst those used most widely are the Everday Memory Questionnaire (Sunderland *et al*., 1983), the Autobiographical Memory Interview (Kopelman *et al*., 1990), the Cognitive Failures Questionnaire (Broadbent *et al*., 1982), and the Hospital Anxiety and Depression Scale (Zigmond and Snaith, 1983).

Open-ended clinical interviews can provide much information about a person's cognitive and emotional state. These may be supplemented by the use of rating scales. Evaluations of functional ability may be carried out using the Extended ADL Scale (Barer and Nouri, 1989) or the Frenchay Activities Index (Wade, 1992), which include mobility, domestic and leisure activity. The SOTOF (Laver and Powell, 1995) represents a combination of neuropsychological and functional ratings.

Learning Activity 8 ◆ ◆ ◆

In the case example being studied, are there any other issues or further information you would wish to pursue to get a fuller understanding? If so, how might you go about getting this information?

If the information you gather confirms that there are other issues to be taken into account, how would the assessment change?

BEHAVIOURAL MONITORING

An important way of supplementing information is to observe and monitor behaviour, not least because of the limitations of a one-off assessment (Acker, 1986). Ideally, formal testing is supplemented with observation of daily activities. This is usually impractical, however, although it is sometimes helpful for a person/relative/key-worker to fill in a structured diary recording the critical problem (aggression, memory lapses, repetitive behaviour, etc.) for a set time period (see Box 19.11)

This is particularly crucial with people who are unable to meet the demands of formal cognitive

Box 19.11 *Self-monitoring checklist*

Date	Activity	No. of errors or 'action-slips' on task	No. of self-corrected errors	No. of errors corrected after prompting	No. of errors uncorrected	Time taken to complete task

assessment owing to behavioural difficulties or the severity of their brain damage. In such cases, assessment usually comprises systematic recording of behavioural routines over time (Jacobs, 1990). This is because severe damage to brain structures is often associated with a loss of executive control over residual cognitive abilities (Shallice and Burgess, 1991). This may lead to a failure to control strongly activated responses which may be demonstrated in characteristic patterns of behaviour such as impulsivity, aggression, distractibility, disinhibited and inappropriate actions. Alternatively, people who are severely injured may show low motivation, reduced sensitivity to reward, loss of libido, and failure to initiate activities, plan ahead or make decisions (thus showing difficulties in starting and maintaining action plans). These two forms of behavioural disturbance are underlain by severe cognitive impairment common after damage to the prefrontal regions of the frontal lobes of the brain. These issues are discussed more fully by Burgess and Wood (1990).

Learning Activity 9 ◆ ◆ ◆

The cognitive assessment in the case example showed a relatively short attention span, a tendency to be distracted, and difficulty in maintaining action plans. These are all typical of executive dysfunction. It was important to know how this was manifested in real, everyday life. Set up a monitoring sheet to assess these problems with a view to being able to use them as part of the rehabilitation process.

SUMMARY

The organization of cognitive functions within the brain is not completely understood but can be described at different levels of analysis. The three most commonly used models of brain organization are traditional neuropsychological, cognitive information processing, and functional. Each model has different implications for assessment, and in clinical practice neuropsychological and functional approaches have so far proved more useful for therapists. The brain has the capacity to recover some function spontaneously, although in many cases of brain injury this is incomplete. Therefore, systematic assessment of impaired and preserved cognitive abilities is necessary for planning effective rehabilitation and management of people with brain injury.

Key Points ■ ■ ■

- ❐ The organization of cognitive functions within the brain is not completely understood, and brain dysfunction is typically described at several different levels.
- ❐ There is not a simple correspondence between site of brain damage and loss of function.
- ❐ The neural mechanisms behind spontaneous recovery of function are understood in general terms but not in detail.
- ❐ Recovery of function can be enhanced by rehabilitation practices which accommodate/understand the nature of the underlying neuropsychological difficulties.
- ❐ Sound neuropsychological assessment is guided by a set of general principles as well as a range of assessment techniques.

References ▼ ▼ ▼

Acker, M.B. (1986). Relationships between test scores and everyday life functioning. In: Uzzell, B.P. and Gross, Y. (eds), *Clinical Neuropsychology of Intervention*. Boston: Martinus Nijhoff, 85–117.

Almli, C.R. and Finger, S. (1988). Toward a definition of recovery of function. In: Finger, S., LeVere, T.E., Almli, C.R. and Stein, D.G. (eds), *Brain Injury and Recovery: Theoretical and Controversial Issues*. New York: Plenum Press, 1–14.

Barer, D.H. (1990). The influence of visual and tactile inattention on predictions of recovery from acute stroke. *Quarterly Journal of Medicine*, **74**: 21–32.

Barer, D. and Nouri, F. (1989). Measurement of activities of daily living. *Clinical Rehabilitation*, **3**: 179–87.

Broadbent, D.E., Cooper, P.F., Fitzgerald, P. and Parkes, K.R. (1982). The cognitive failures questionnaire (CFQ) and its correlates. *British Journal of Clinical Psychology*, **21**: 1–16.

Burgess, P.W. and Wood, R.L. (1990). Neuropsychology of behaviour disorders following brain injury. In: Wood, R.L. (ed.), *Neurobehavioural Sequelae of Traumatic Brain Injury*. London: Taylor and Francis, 110–33.

Butters, N. and Stuss, D.T. (1989). Diencephalic amnesia. In: Boller, F. and Grafman, J. (eds), *Handbook of Neuropsychology*, vol. 3. Amsterdam: Elsevier.

Code, C. (1991). *The Characteristics of Aphasia*. Hove: Lawrence Erlbaum.

Coughlan, A.K. and Hollows, S. (1985). *The Adult Memory and*

Information Processing Battery. Leeds: St James University Hospital.

Crawford, J.R., Parker, D.M. and McKinlay, W.W. (1992). *A Handbook of Neuropsychological Assessment.* Hove: Lawrence Erlbaum.

Damasio, A.R., Tranel, D. and Damasio, H.C. (1991). Somatic markers and the guidance of behavior. In: Levin, H.S. *et al.* (eds), *Frontal Lobe Function and Dysfunction*, New York: Oxford University Press, 217–29.

Ellis, A.W. (1988). Modelling the writing process. In: Denes, G., Semenza, C. and Bisiacchi, P. (eds), *Perspectives on Cognitive Neuropsychology.* Hove: Lawrence Erlbaum, 189–212.

Fodor, J.A. (1983). *The Modularity of Mind.* Cambridge, Mass: Bradford/MIT.

Giles, G.M. (1992). A neurofunctional approach to rehabilitation following severe brain injury. In: Katz, N. (ed.), *Cognitive Rehabilitation Models for intervention in Occupational Therapy.* Stoneham, MA: Andover Medical, 195–218.

Hillis, A. and Caramazza, A. (1992). The reading process and its disorders. In: Margolin, D.I. (ed.), *Cognitive Neuropsychology in Clinical Practice.* New York: Oxford University Press, 229–62.

Hodges, J.R. (1994). *Cognitive Assessment for Clinicians.* Oxford: Oxford Medical.

Hodkinson, H.M. (1972). Evaluation of a mental test score for assessment of mental impairment in the elderly. *Age and Ageing*, **1**: 233–8.

Jacobs, H.E. (1990). Identifying post-traumatic behavior problems: data from psychosocial follow-up studies. In: Wood, R.L. (ed.), *Neurobehavioural Sequelae of Traumatic Brain Injury.* London: Taylor and Francis, 37–51.

Katz, N. (ed.) (1992). *Cognitive Rehabilitation: Models for Intervention in Occupational Therapy.* Stoneham, MA: Butterworth–Heinemann.

Kay, J., Lesser, R. and Coltheart, M. (1992). *Psycholinguistic Assessments of Language Processing in Aphasia (PALPA).* Hove: Lawrence Erlbaum.

Kopelman, M.D., Wilson, B.A. and Baddeley, A.D. (1990). *The Autobiographical Memory Interview.* Bury St Edmunds: Thames Valley Test Co.

Laver, A.J. and Powell, G.E. (1995). *The Structural Observational Test of Function.* Windsor: NFER–Nelson.

Lezak, M.D. (1983). *Neuropsychological Assessment*, 2nd edn. New York: Oxford University Press.

Lhermitte, F. (1986). Human Autonomy and the Frontal Lobes. II: Patient behavior in complex and social situations: the 'Environmental Dependency Syndrome'. *Annals of Neurology*, **19**: 335–43.

Mapou, R.L. (1988). Testing to detect brain damage: an alternative to what may no longer be useful. *Journal of Clinical and Experimental Neuropsychology*, **10**: 271–8.

McCarthy, R. and Warrington, E.K. (1987). Understanding: a function of short-term memory. *Brain*, **110**: 1565–78.

McCloskey, M., Aliminosa, D. and Macaruso, P. (1990). Theory-based assessment of acquired dyscalculia. *Brain and Cognition*, **17**: 285–308.

McNeil, M.R. and Prescott, T.E. (1978). *Revised Token Test.* Austin, Texas: PRO-ED Inc.

Miller, E. (1992). Some basic principles of neuropsychological assessment. In: Crawford, J.R. *et al.* (eds), *A Handbook of Neuropsychological Assessment.* Hove: Lawrence Erlbaum, 7–20.

Miller, E. (1993). Dissociating single cases in neuropsychology. *British Journal of Clinical Psychology*, **32**: 155–67.

Milner, B. (1982). Some cognitive effects of frontal lobe lesions in man. *Philosophical Transactions of the Royal Society of London B*, **298**: 211–26.

Nauta, W.J.H. (1971). The problem of the frontal lobe: a reinterpretation. *Journal of Psychiatric Research.* **8**: 167–87.

Nelson, H. and Willison, J. (1991). *National Adult Reading Test (NART).* Windsor: NFER–NELSON.

Nouri, F.M. and Lincoln, N.B. (1994). *Stroke Driver Screening Assessment.* Nottingham: Nottingham Rehab. Ltd.

Olton, D.S. (1989). Inferring psychological dissociations from experimental dissociations: the temporal context of episodic memory. In: Roediger, H.L. and Craik, F.I.M. (eds), *Varieties of Memory and Consciousness.* Hillsdale, NJ: Lawrence Erlbaum, 161–77.

Parker, D.M. and Crawford, J.R. (1992). Assessment of frontal lobe dysfunction. In: Crawford, J.R. *et al.* (eds), *A Handbook of Neuropsychological Assessment.* Hove: Lawrence Erlbaum, 267–91.

Parkin, A.J. and Leng, N.R.C. (1993). *Neuropsychology of the Amnesic Syndrome.* Hove: Lawrence Erlbaum.

Patterson, K. (1988). Acquired disorders of spelling. In: Denes, G. *et al.* (eds), *Perspectives on Cognitive Neuropsychology.* Hove: Lawrence Erlbaum, 213–30.

Pizzamiglio, L., Bergego, C., Halligan, P. *et al.* (1992). Factors affecting the clinical measurement of visuo-spatial neglect. *Behavioural Neurology*, **5**: 233–40.

Raven, J.C. (1983). *Standard Progressive Matrices.* Windsor: NFER-Nelson.

Riddoch, M.J. and Humphreys, G.W. (1993). *Birmingham Object Recognition Battery (BORB).* Hove: Lawrence Erlbaum.

Schwartz, M.F., Mayer, N.H., Fitzpatrick De Salme, E.J. and Montgomery, M.W. (1993). Cognitive theory and the study of everyday action disorders after brain damage. *Journal of Head Trauma Rehabilitation*, **8**: 59–72.

Semenza, C., Bisiacchi, P. and Rosenthal, V. (1988). A function for cognitive neuropsychology. In: Denes, G. *et al.* (eds), *Perspectives on Cognitive Neuropsychology.* Hove: Lawrence Erlbaum, 3–30.

Shallice, T. (1988). *From Neuropsychology to Mental Structure.* New York: Cambridge University Press.

Shallice, T. and Burgess, P. (1991). Higher-order cognitive impairments and frontal lesions in man. In: Levin, H.S. *et al.* (eds), *Frontal Lobe Function and Dysfunction.* New York: Oxford University Press, 125–38.

Smith, M.L. (1989). Memory disorders associated with temporal lobe lesions. In: Boller, F. and Grafman, J. (eds), *Handbook of Neuropsychology*, vol. 3. Amsterdam: Elsevier, 91–106.

Stone, S.P., Wilson, B., Wroot, A. *et al.* (1991). The assessment of visuo-spatial neglect after acute stroke. *Journal of Neurology, Neurosurgery and Psychiatry*, **54**: 345–50.

Sunderland, A., Harris, J.E. and Baddeley, A. (1983). Do laboratory tests predict everyday memory? A neuropsychological study. *Journal of Verbal Learning and Verbal Behaviour*, **22**: 341–57.

Teuber, H.L. (1968). Alteration of perception and memory in man. In: Weiskrantz, L. (ed.), *Analysis of Behavioural Change.* New York: Harper and Row.

Tyerman, R., Tyerman, A., Howard, P. and Hadfield, C. (1986). *The Chessington O.T. Neurological Assessment Battery.* Nottingham: Nottingham Rehab. Ltd.

Wade, D.T. (1992). *Measurement in Neurological Rehabilitation.* Oxford: Oxford University Press.

Walker, S. (1992). Assessment of language dysfunction. In: Crawford, J.R. *et al.* (eds), *A Handbook of Neuropsychological Assessment.* Hove: Lawrence Erlbaum, 177–222.

Walsh, K. (1987). *Neuropsychology: A Clinical Approach*, 2nd edn. Edinburgh: Churchill Livingstone.

Warrington, E.K. (1982). Neuropsychological studies of object recognition. *Philosophical Transactions of the Royal Society of London B*, **298**: 15–33.

Warrington, E.K. (1984). *Recognition Memory Test.* Windsor: NFER–Nelson.

Warrington, E.K. (1986). Visual deficits associated with occipital lobe lesions in man, *Experimental Brain Research Supplementum series II.* Berlin: Springer-Verlag.

Warrington, E.K. and James, M. (1991). *The Visual Object and Space Perception Battery.* Bury St Edmunds: Thames Valley Test Co.

Warrington, E.K., James, M. and Maciejewski, C. (1986). The WAIS as a lateralising and localising diagnostic instrument: a study of 656 patients with unilateral cerebral lesions. *Neuropsychologia*, **24**: 223–39.

Wechsler, D. (1981). *Wechsler Adult Intelligence Scale–Revised.* San Antonio, Texas: Psychological Corporation.

Wechsler, D. (1987). *Wechsler Memory Scale–Revised.* San Antonio, Texas: Psychological Corporation.

Whiting, S.E., Lincoln, N.B., Bhaunani, G. and Cockburn, J. (1985). *The Rivermead Perceptual Assessment Battery.* Windsor: NFER–Nelson.

Wilson, B., Cockburn, J. and Baddeley, A. (1985). *The Rivermead Behavioural Memory Test*. Reading: Thames Valley Test Co.
Wilson, B., Cockburn, J. and Halligan, P. (1987). *Behavioural Inattention Test*. Fareham, Hants: Thames Valley Test Co.
Zigmond, A.S. and Snaith, R.P. (1983). The Hospital Anxiety and Depression Scale. *Acta Psychiatrica Scandanavia*, **67**: 361–70.

Further Reading ▲ ▲ ▲

Crawford, J.R., Parker, D.M. and McKinlay, W.W. (1992). *A Handbook of Neuropsychological Assessment*. Hove: Lawrence Erlbaum.
Heilman, K.M. and Valenstein, E. (1993). *Clinical Neuropsychology*, 3rd edn. New York: Oxford University Press.
Luria, A.R. (1973). *The Working Brain*, Harmondsworth: Penguin.
Warrington, E.K. and McCarthy, R.A. (1990). *Cognitive Neuropsychology: A Clinical Approach*. San Diego: Academic Press.

20

Managing Brain Dysfunction

Andrew D. Worthington

LEARNING OBJECTIVES

After studying this chapter you should:

- Appreciate the positive and negative influence of cognitive, behavioural and emotional factors in neuropsychological rehabilitation
- Be able to apply key general principles in the design of a rehabilitation strategy
- Have a critical appreciation of common psychological techniques
- Be able to evaluate the outcome of individual (or group) rehabilitation strategies and techniques

INTRODUCTION

Advances in medical care mean that more people are now surviving severe brain damage and continuing their lives with some degree of disability. The extent of a person's recovery depends on several factors, including their age, the type and extent of cerebral damage and the onset of treatment. The type of brain injury sustained will also have implications for the length of time a person will continue to recover 'naturally'. The time course of recovery from a severe head injury, for example, is many years (Powell and Wilson, 1994), whereas optimum recovery from a stroke is often reached within the first six months. Although some recovery from brain damage takes place spontaneously, the natural recovery process can be assisted considerably by skilled therapeutic intervention.

NEUROPSYCHOLOGICAL REHABILITATION

Rehabilitation is a process of maximizing potential for recovery, succinctly described by Eames (1987) as: '. . . not to do with illness but moving from illness towards independence'. Its purpose, therefore, is to:

- *promote recovery* – '. . . the combined and co-ordinated use of medical, social, educational and vocational measures for training or re-training the individual to the highest level' (Ebrahim, 1990);
- *reduce disability* – 'a problem solving and educational process aimed at reducing the disability and handicap experienced by someone' (Wade, 1992).

Rehabilitation of physical function is covered elsewhere (Nichols, 1980; Corrigan and Maitland, 1983), but good assessment and management of the cognitive, behavioural and emotional consequences of cerebral dysfunction can be essential to intervention programmes (Cockburn, 1993; Evans, 1994). For example, Decety (1993) argued that greater attention to cognitive processes such as mental imagery in physiotherapy can assist in understanding the process of learning motor skills. A good example of a cognitive model being used in the treatment of functional problems is provided by Kasma *et al.* (1994). They describe a treatment programme for akinesia by training people with Parkinson's disease to turn in bed and rise from a chair. Twelve people were trained with videos, mental imagery and physical practice. They had to verbalize each stage of the action as it was performed, so that the movement changed from being taught to being self-instructed. After six one-hour sessions people with mild and moderate impairment made fewer errors executing the required actions.

Unfortunately, whilst the management of cognitive and behavioural impairments after brain injury can be crucial to rehabilitation outcome, in practice the majority of brain-injured people have inadequate access to specialized care in the rehabilitation phase. Murphy *et al.* (1990) examined the fate of severely head-injured people in north London across eleven District Health Authorities. Fewer than 15% of severely impaired people received any speech and language therapy or psychologist input. This state of affairs is probably typical of many health services across the country.

Management will inevitably improve as the behavioural and cognitive effects of brain injury are more widely appreciated. Memory impairment is often the most widely reported difficulty amongst brain-injured people, and learning ability is certainly an important aspect of cognitive rehabilitation. Yet some deficits (e.g. dyspraxia and perceptual dysfunctions) are difficult for sufferers to recognize though they can be severely disabling. Furthermore, reduction in self-awareness following damage to the frontal lobes of the brain means that people may often have little insight into their cognitive (and sometimes physical) problems. As the next section shows, current models of cognition take little account of motivation, awareness and self-concept which can be crucial to therapeutic outcome (Ben-Yishay and Diller, 1993). Nevertheless, the prospect is not entirely gloomy and it is encouraging to find psychologists and other health disciplines working together in clinical teams towards better understanding and management of brain dysfunction.

COMMON PROBLEMS IN THE MANAGEMENT OF BRAIN INJURY

Successful rehabilitation of specific impairments of a physical or cognitive nature is often influenced by a range of emotional–behavioural difficulties (see Box 20.1). The management of mediating factors like motivation and aggression is therefore crucial to positive therapeutic outcome. Strategies for managing potentially disruptive problems are discussed below.

Box 20.1 *Common emotional–behavioural problems in brain injury*

- Loss of insight
- Reduced motivation
- Aggression
- Disinhibition
- Epileptic seizures and learning difficulties

Loss of Insight

Damage to the frontal lobes of the brain often affects people's self-awareness. In extreme cases people may deny impairments such as hemiplegia or hemianopia (Bisiach *et al.*, 1986). This clinical syndrome is termed 'anosagnosia' and has been reported in association with dementia (Feher *et al.*, 1991), traumatic brain injury (Prigatano, 1991) and stroke (House and Hodges, 1988). Cutting (1978) reported denial of hemiplegia in 58% of people with left hemiplegia and in 14% of those with right hemiplegia. They made comments about their affected limbs 'disobeying them' or attributed possession of their limbs to other people. Clinically, limited insight may be associated with prolonged rehabilitation and poorer outcome (Youngjohn and Altman, 1989), although Malia *et al.* (1993) found no such relationship in people with traumatic brain injury. Fleming and Strong (1995) reviewed studies relating treatment outcome and self-awareness and suggested that increasing insight as people recover is associated with emotional distress.

Sometimes people report significant changes in their self-concept following brain injury. This may be related to physical impediments, but often it reflects changes in personality that can follow frontal lobe damage (Stuss, 1991). People usually benefit from education about the nature of their difficulties, although this may have to be demonstrated repeatedly in functional tasks. O'Brien *et al.* (1988) provide a session-by-session account of an educational approach for a man and his wife, following removal of a frontal lobe tumour. 'Insight-oriented' psychotherapeutic approaches sometimes facilitate personal adjustment to disability (Prigatano, 1987; Langer and Padrone, 1992), but successful adjustment also needs to incorporate the family and social context (Tyerman, 1991).

Reduced motivation

Reduction in motivation can result from organic brain damage to frontal and subcortical structures, or it can be due to depressed mood following brain injury. It is important to ascertain the cause in order to manage this problem successfully. Robinson *et al.* (1984) showed that depression was especially common in people with left frontal brain damage following stroke. Right frontal lesions were associated with apathy and indifference.

Depressed people may be underestimating their recovery potential or have unrealistic expectations about their speed of recovery. Education about the nature of brain damage and its psychological effects can help individuals' personal adjustment. Sometimes mood-elevating medication can be effective in raising mood sufficiently for patients to comply with treatment. Motivational problems arising directly from brain damage may also respond to medication. The drug bromocriptine, for example, is believed to enhance motivation by stimulating neurochemical dopamine pathways in the brain which mediate a person's sensitivity to reward (Eames, 1989; Zasler, 1992).

Behavioural strategies may be employed, such as providing unconditional positive reward in the first instance; a shaping procedure: approximating the desired performance until skills are acquired more accurately; or an intermittent reward schedule (see later). Very severely impaired people are often unable to appreciate abstract or long-term rewards and respond to immediate concrete reinforcements (e.g. tokens exchangeable for privileges). Eames and Wood (1985) followed up severely brain-injured people treated within a 'token-economy' regime. This strategy reduced difficult behaviour sufficiently for rehabilitation to take place, and was associated with long-term improvements in social behaviour.

Aggression

Aggression or agitation are common in the acute stages of brain injury owing to disruption to a number of neurochemical systems (Cassidy, 1990). Sudden explosive outbursts of aggression are associated with damage to medial temporal lobes or connected subcortical structures (Eames, 1990). Aggression can be treated by pharmacological means but this runs the risk of sedating the patient and thereby reducing potential to benefit from rehabilitation. Aggressive outbursts should be subject to a functional analysis to establish their nature more clearly (see Box 20.2). Instances of aggression may be precipitated by diurnal variation, staff shift changes, fatigue or stress.

Management strategies range from control and restraint techniques for dealing with physical outbursts; distraction or substitution methods which replace the aggressive behaviour with an incompatible response; 'talking down' an agitated person; and solving the problem which precipitated the aggression. Wesolowski (1988) has prepared a useful booklet for professionals on techniques for managing aggression after head injury.

Disinhibition

The effects of frontal lobe damage can include a loss of internal control over one's behaviour. People may be unable to inhibit their reactions to situations which provoke certain kinds of behaviour (e.g. sexual or aggressive acts). People say or do things which they may later realize were inappropriate. This can be managed in several ways.

- *Environmental manipulation* seeks to replace the situations that trigger disinhibited behaviour with stimuli that promote more acceptable actions. A simple example is changing mealtime seating arrangements to avoid person X (who repeats stereotyped phrases incessantly) irritating person Y (who cannot control anger).
- *Conditioning procedures* seek to change behaviour through new learning experiences. Wood (1990a) describes a number of techniques for achieving behavioural change (see Box 20.3). Alternatively, with persons of sufficient cognitive competence, it can be possible to train them to recognize the triggers and develop cognitive or behavioural coping

Box 20.2 *Components of a functional analysis of behaviour*

Events	Description	Therapeutic relevance
Antecedents	Triggers, cues, prompts (discriminative stimuli)	Information and events which increase the likelihood of a particular behaviour
Behaviour	Action to be changed in treatment	Defined explicitly in terms of constituent operations (lifting, touching, shouting, etc.)
Consequence	Events which follow the behaviour	Can be changed to increase or reduce likelihood of preceding behaviour recurring

Box 20.3 *Strategies for modifying behavioural problems after brain injury*

Method	Description	Implementation
Stimulus control		
Discrimination training	Increasing probability of behaviour in presence of one stimulus and decreasing if another stimulus present	Training stimuli are presented either simultaneously, or behaviour learned with one stimulus first
Chaining	Completion of one act cues next act in a sequence and is also reinforced by it	Used in forward and backward sequencing in functional skills training
Shaping	Reinforcement of successive approximations to desired behaviour	Used where desired behaviour rarely occurs
Response–Consequence Learning		
Time-out	Removal of positive rewards for brief time period	May involve absence of social interaction, attention or a separate time-out room
DRO (discriminative reinforcement of other behaviour)	Substitute a more acceptable and incompatible behaviour in place of undesirable behaviour	Usually involves attention and praise when alternative behaviour is observed
Response-cost	Relates consequences of actions to occurrence of behaviour, to reduce frequency of undesired behaviour	Tokens often used which people may lose or fail to earn

strategies to distract their attention and promote an alternative behaviour. Becker and Vakil (1993) describe the use of a behavioural approach with a young woman who became disinhibited following a head injury: structured controls enabled her to improve financial spending and budgeting skills, though her sexual behaviour remained disinhibited.

Impulsivity

People behave impulsively when the normal inhibitory influences of the cerebral cortex fail to effect control over behaviour. (Alcohol intoxication has a similar effect, as it reduces oxygen to the brain and thereby reduces cortical inhibition.) After brain injury people may suffer a chronic inability to exercise self-control. Impulsivity is one manifestation of this problem which threatens rehabilitation because people often fail to think about (and therefore learn) what they are doing. They can become inflexible in their reasoning and problem-solving because they do not plan ahead and anticipate events before acting.

Depending on the remaining cognitive abilities, management may involve conditioning procedures or educating the person about the difficulty and its causes. It may be helpful to introduce verbal cues to delay impulsive responses (such as counting to three) before starting on a course of action. Cognitive strategies that encourage verbal mediation of thought processes may also reduce impulsive behaviour (e.g. training the impulsive person in problem-solving exercises to think 'W-A-I-T: What Alternative Is There?').

Epileptic seizures and learning difficulties

The incidence of epilepsy after brain injury (post-traumatic epilepsy) ranges from 5% to 30% (Lishman, 1987), being more common in penetrating brain injuries or those requiring neurosurgery. The behavioural manifestations of epileptic seizures depend on the site or focus of the fit. Outburts of aggression or other forms of emotional behaviour are typically associated with seizures arising from temporal lobe structures. Milder 'petit-mal' seizures (absences) may occur undetected but can severely affect concentration and learning for the sufferer.

Box 20.4 *General principles of rehabilitation*

- Application of cognitive psychology
- Establishing therapeutic goals
- Baseline monitoring and evaluation
- Levels of intervention
- Generalization of training
- Maintenance of treatment gains

Evoked seizures have specific external triggers such as bright light or noise and constitute 5–6% of epilepsy cases. Interventions for managing evoked seizures have traditionally used conditioning methods (Forster, 1972). Most seizures, however, are precipitated by cognitive processing, which in turn disrupts the ability to carry out cognitive tasks. In addition to advances in pharmacological treatment, increasing emphasis is being placed on teaching self-management techniques to help people reduce arousal and learn control over seizure onset (Goldstein, 1990).

GENERAL PRINCIPLES OF REHABILITATION

Neurological rehabilitation is a multidisciplinary enterprise, each bringing its own expertise. There are, however, a number of general principles relevant to all health professionals (see Box 20.4).

The application of information processing models

Although information processing models have greatly influenced understanding of impairment after brain injury (see Chapter 19), the use of this approach in rehabilitation has received a cautious welcome. Wilson and Patterson (1990) argued that current information processing models are not particularly helpful to clinicians designing therapeutic interventions. Many sophisticated cognitive assessments lead to treatments that could have been employed without knowledge of an information processing model. For example, despite the sophistication of cognitive models of memory, external memory aids appear generally more successful in improving independence than cognitive-based strategies.

Box 20.5 *The value of cognitive models in rehabilitation*

Advantages
- Provide an explicit framework for assessing impaired cognition
- Provide a focus for treatment
- Restrict options for type of treatment appropriate

Disadvantages
- Several different models of similar processes
- No recognition of how impaired processes can be changed
- Models are skill-specific, and therapy is sensitive to general factors (motivation, fatigue, etc.)

Moreover, cognitive models of specific (modular) skills do not incorporate non-modular processes such as learning, motivation or self-concept, which are essential to therapeutic outcome. Rehabilitation is essentially a learning process, yet learning theory and models of specific cognitive process have traditionally developed separately. Therefore some neuropsychologists have suggested that cognitive models are necessary but not sufficient for rehabilitation (Hillis and Caramazza, 1994). The applicability of information processing models in rehabilitation is summarized in Box 20.5.

Establishing therapeutic goals

Treatment in rehabilitation is not usually prescribed by a therapist but based on a multidisciplinary assessment of the problems (Powell *et al.*, 1994). The results of the initial assessment are usually discussed with the individual concerned and a programme of remedial intervention is proposed. As cooperation and motivation are vital to positive outcome, it is important to discuss goals for therapy with the person, although people with cerebral damage are not always capable of the level of understanding or reasoning that this process requires. Poor insight into their difficulties is also a common feature of many brain-injured individuals. Therefore it is sometimes necessary to be more prescriptive in the initial intervention stages. However, Bergquist and Jacket (1993) report several useful strategies for non-directive goal-setting with brain-injured people.

Baseline monitoring and evaluation

Intervention programmes often incorporate review dates (every four weeks, for example) so that everybody involved knows that progress will be regularly monitored. This process has several advantages. It serves

Learning Activity 1 ◆ ◆ ◆

This is a goal-setting exercise. In order to achieve a goal it may be necessary to break it down into small, manageable steps. This is called a *hierarchy*, with the goal at the top. Only when one step has been well learned is the next one attempted. The steps (and even the goal) may need to be modified in the light of experience. When setting or agreeing goals, these should be *realistic, practical*, and *specific*.

Continue with the case example of the young male victim of a motorcycle accident you assessed in Chapter 19. He was shown to have difficulties stemming from damage to his left frontal region. These problems of executive control meant that he had difficulty in initiating activity, and once doing something he was easily distracted to the point where he did not carry out many of his action plans or those devised for him, but just drifted from one activity to another which caught his attention, or simply just ground to a halt. This made the execution of rehabilitation activities very erratic and, if left to his own devices, extremely unlikely to happen at all. In the light of this assessment:

a Draw up a number of goals that might assist the man's rehabilitation.
b Choose one goal and work out how it might be achieved. For example, a goal might be for him to carry out 5 minutes of exercise every hour. Bearing in mind his cognitive deficits, how could this or some other goal be broken down into achievable steps?

This goal-setting exercise is equally applicable to people whose dysfunction may be due mainly to secondary effects of brain damage – for example, lowered mood and motivation following a stroke. Here the need to maintain mobility as well as improve mood may require setting activity goals that can be devised only through discussion with the person concerned since their cooperation is the key.

Learning Activity 2 ◆ ◆ ◆

Design a monitoring sheet to record progress on the goal selected in Activity 1.

to provide the individual concerned with regular feedback about progress; it helps the therapist monitor changes over time which may be imperceptible from day to day. It also allows for treatment to be altered. This may occur because the intervention is ineffective for a particular individual, or if it is undesirable to continue with a treatment that is not producing positive results. Sometimes treatments are modified because the treatment goals change either as the patient improves or as the nature of the problems become clearer. For example, difficulties initially described by a patient as poor eyesight may later be found to occur specifically on reading and be attributed to a dyslexia, only for the therapist later to discover that it was *memory* for reading material, rather than reading skills themselves, that was impaired.

Levels of intervention

In 1980 the World Health Organization (WHO) developed a framework for classifying the consequences of illness. This model recognizes four levels at which problems may occur (see Box 20.6). In addition to assessing problems at these levels it is also possible to use this WHO model as a guide towards intervention.

Consider the following case. Mrs W develops visual perceptual problems as a result of stroke and has difficulties reading books and magazines that she previously enjoyed. This is especially important because the stroke has reduced her mobility to the extent that she cannot leave home unaccompanied and is trying to continue her typing job from home. An analysis of this shows that Mrs W has suffered a stroke (*pathology*) resulting in perceptual difficulties (*impairment*) which has restricted her reading skills (*disability*). This is threatening her ability to continue working, even in a limited capacity, in her present job (*handicap*).

Initial treatment would have been directed towards managing her stroke (e.g. thrombolytic drugs). However, in rehabilitation the focus of therapeutic intervention would change from a focus on pathology to an emphasis on the other levels of the model. For example, in the case of Mrs W:

- *An impairment-focused intervention* might take the form of a perceptual retraining programme to improve her visual perceptual analysis of the environment (e.g. Gordon *et al*., 1985).
- *A disability-focused intervention* might be to teach compensatory strategies such as encouraging the use

Box 20.6 *World Health Organization (1980) model of illness*

Classification	Definition	Levels of description
Pathology	Dysfunction of organ or organ system in the body (disease)	Genetic Biochemical Anatomical
Impairment	Neurophysiological and neuropsychological consequence of disease	Anatomical Physiological Psychological
Disability	Loss or disturbance of normal functioning of person in interaction with the environment (skills, abilities)	Psychological Functional
Handicap	Social or societal impact of changes resulting from illness, impairment or disability	Personal Social

of dictated rather than handwritten notes to transcribe.

- *A handicap-focused intervention* might be to find an alternative occupation, one more suited to Mrs W's post-stroke abilities.

Although different healthcare professions may operate at several levels in different cases, in practice doctors and radiographers (both diagnostic and therapeutic) tend to focus their efforts on pathology. This is crucial because if disease can be managed successfully at this level the resulting disabilities and handicaps are minimized. Psychologists tend to assess and treat cognitive dysfunctions at the impairment level, while physiotherapists and occupational therapists frequently assess and treat at the levels of disability and handicap.

Learning Activity 3 ◆ ◆ ◆

With reference to Activity 1, at what level of intervention (impairment, disability or handicap) is your chosen goal directed? Can you think of any goals that might be aimed at alleviating his executive problems at the two other levels of intervention?

Generalization

Generalization is the ability to apply or execute a skill in circumstances different from those in which the ability was taught. This notion is important to treatment for the following reasons:

- *Relevance*. It allows people (and their therapists) to feel confident that the treatment will be beneficial for the performance of meaningful activities outside the clinic.
- *Levels*. It is often assumed that interventions focused at one level such as pathology will benefit other levels. This assumption does not always hold. There may not be a direct relationship between the degree of impairment (e.g. speech problems) and resulting disability (communication difficulties).
- *Failures*. Ideally, impairment or disability-focused interventions would generalize towards reduction of the handicap (social impact) associated with illness. Unfortunately, many treatments do not generalize to other situations or tasks, or minimize handicap.

Poor generalization might be due to various factors. For instance, a person may be able to walk 400 metres in the outpatient gym but does not walk 200 metres to the corner shop. Motivational, emotional and social factors may prevent this (see Chapter 5 for a fuller discussion of disability). In addition, cognitive deficits may be problematic; for example, reduced motivation and initiative or impaired memory might undermine any practice of an outpatient exercise programme.

Generalization is particularly problematic for cognitive rehabilitation. As discussed later in the chapter, many cognitive techniques improve performance only on the tasks on which people were trained, but the gains do not generalize to related tasks or have significant social impact.

Attempts to increase generalization by using a transfer of training approach are popular with some

Learning Activity 4 ◆ ◆ ◆

Assuming that the goal you choose in Activity 1 was achieved successfully, how could you develop this strategy to:

a help execute other important activities?
b ensure that the activity continued on discharge?

occupational therapists. This involves training people on a range of tasks all using the same fundamental cognitive processes, with the aim of improving the underlying processes, not just task performance, sufficiently to generalize to other functional activities. However, this cannot guarantee success (Fanthome *et al.*, 1995). Toglia (1992) suggests that a multicontextual training strategy facilitates generalization. However, patients without the skills necessary to benefit from transfer training should be treated in functional settings.

Maintenance

Positive therapeutic outcome requires that improvements last long enough to be detected and measured. This is known as 'maintenance of treatment gains'. It is obviously important that a therapist can assume some progress will be made from one treatment session to the next. Often this requires a person to practise remedial techniques at home in between sessions. As already mentioned, this is not always realistic for people with reduced motivation or with initiation difficulties, or for people with severe memory deficits who may not recall details of treatment sessions.

Perhaps more importantly, treatment gains need to persist once an intervention has been concluded. Fortunately there are signs that some treatment techniques produce longer-lasting outcomes.

- *Errorless learning* – allowing somebody to learn without error involves presentation of increasing prompts/assistance until the task is performed successfully. Attempts to complete a task on a trial-and-error basis are discouraged. This technique has been useful in memory training (Wilson *et al.*, 1994) and physiotherapy. In re-education of gait after stroke, for example, a therapist would provide several verbal and physical prompts initially and progressively fade out assistance in successive treatment sessions.
- *Shaping* – involves gradually refining criteria for task success. Behaviours approximating the desired performance are rewarded until skills are acquired more accurately. Walking could be re-established by a series of therapy tasks of increasing gait control, such as maintaining a standing balance, followed by step-standing, weight-transference and walking. Once each stage can be achieved the goals change to the next task.
- *Intermittent reinforcement* – responding positively to or rewarding a desired behaviour every so often rather than every time it occurs. Although this may not be the quickest method to teach new skills, it offers 'protection' against subsequently poor maintenance, as people are used to the notion of executing a particular skill without the ever-present reinforcement (praise, etc.) typical of other teaching strategies. For example, a person may learn social skills by being rewarded after every two occasions, and later in treatment, every five occasions they are observed to be initiating social interaction. Rewards may be tangible (cigarettes, tokens), verbal (praise), or privileges (TV watching, an evening out).

Therefore, the appropriate degree of maintenance across time will depend on the nature of the intervention as well as on the cognitive abilities of the individual.

Learning Activity 5 ◆ ◆ ◆

Can you think how you might apply any of these three techniques to enhance the goal hierarchy devised in Activity 1?

COGNITIVE REHABILITATION

The previous sections have illustrated the application of behavioural techniques (based on learning theory) to tackle cognitive as well as behavioural problems arising from cognitive deficits. Less widespread but equally relevant are the treatment techniques based on cognitive information processing models.

Treatment techniques

Cognitive rehabilitation is difficult both to implement and to evaluate. It can involve the retraining of lost

Box 20.7 *Examples of techniques used in cognitive rehabilitation*

Dysfunction	Techniques	Source
Word-finding difficulty	Semantic and phonological cueing for noun retrieval Pictures for verb retrieval	Davis and Pring (1991) Mitchum and Berndt (1994)
Various communication problems	In a group setting: Structured television viewing Speech exercises Social Skills	Bollinger *et al.* (1993)
	Gestures and pictures	Johnson(1992)
Loss of reading due to visual field defects	Training eye movements using words on a moving screen	Kerkhoff *et al.* (1992)
Reading difficulties due to visual neglect	Visuo-motor cueing strategies	Worthington (1996)
Writing difficulties	Associating words with their meanings (semantic treatment) Combining letter sounds and writing non-words (phonological treatment)	Carlomagno *et al.* (1994)
	Semantic cues for irregular and ambiguous words	de Partz *et al.* (1992)
Information Learning	Repetition Vanishing cues	Butters and Glisky (1993) Glisky *et al.* (1986)
Verbal memory problems	Visual imagery (as a compensatory technique)	Stern and Stern (1989) Zenicus *et al.* (1990)
Verbal memory storage	Journal (for remembering past events) Diary (for remembering future events) (Both memory aids rather than cognitive-based strategies)	Fluharty and Priddy (1993) Moore *et al.* (1992) Burke *et al.* (1994)
Visual perception	Visual scanning, reading and copying, picture description Education and self-management approach	Pizzamiglio *et al.* (1992) Gianutsos and Matheson (1987)
Visual neglect	Verbal strategies to regulate visual attention when searching the environment	Robertson *et al.* (1988)
	Patching eye contralateral to the lesion and providing visual prompts	Butter and Kirsch (1992)
	Visual cueing in the form of sequences of numbers	Ishiai *et al.* (1990)
	Intermittent, cueing movements by the limb contralateral to the side of the brain lesion	Robertson and North (1992a, b, 1993)
Problem-solving deficits (executive dysfunction)	Task analysis leading to a checklist of actions	Burke *et al.* (1991)
	Practise at generating goal-directed ideas; evaluating information; drawing inferences	Von Cramon and Matthes-Von Cramon (1990, 1992)
Behavioural self-regulation	Regular verbal feedback on the appropriateness of behaviour	Burke *et al.* (1991)
Self-regulation of aggression	Cognitive remediation, personal counselling and group exercises	Ben-Yishay and Gold (1990)
	Cognitive–behavioural techniques: exposure combined with verbal strategies to find alternative responses	Burgess and Alderman (1990)
Ideomotor dyspraxia	Conductive education approach, using objects with goal-directed verbalization (e.g. 'grasp the cup')	Pilgrim and Humphreys (1994)

cognitive skills or the development of compensatory strategies to make up for cognitive deficits. Cognitive treatment techniques are being developed all the time alongside developments in information processing psychology. A variety of techniques have been tried (see Box 20.7) depending on the source of the difficulty. Thus, for example, a reading difficulty due to visual neglect would be approached in a different way from reading problems associated with central processing problems (Worthington, 1996).

Whilst it is not possible to go into detail of cognitive strategies relevant to particular deficits, the reader is referred to the following authors for rehabilitation methods in:

- *language* – Davis and Pring (1991), Bollinger *et al.* (1993), Mitchum and Berndt (1994);
- *memory* – Glisky *et al.* (1986); Stern and Stern (1989); Wilson and Moffat (1992);
- *visual perception* – Gordon *et al.* (1985); Edmans and Lincoln (1991); Toglia (1992);
- *visual neglect* – Robertson *et al.* (1988); Butter and Kirsch (1992); Robertson and North (1992b);
- *executive functions* – Burke *et al.* (1991); Sohlberg and Mateer (1989); Goldstein and Levin (1987);
- *behavioural self-regulation* – Alderman *et al.* (1995); Burke *et al.* (1991); Burgess and Alderman (1990);
- *motor control* – Pilgrim and Humphreys (1994); Miller (1986).

The success of cognitive techniques thus far has been limited because improvements gained in training on a specific task often fail to generalize outside the training session and to other tasks or functional levels.

To date, the most successful methods are those that use preserved cognitive skills to compensate for cognitive deficits, as in the use of external memory aids such as cues, lists and diaries. The attraction of these techniques is that they are based on models that are trying to understand how people change and on the process of intervention rather than the outcome. It is possible that future information processing models which take account of how people learn, such as those based on computerized neural networks, might be more influential.

The status of cognitive rehabilitation

Strategies for reducing behavioural difficulties are well-established compared with techniques for improving cognitive functioning. The effectiveness of the latter is a contentious issue. Opinions range from the deeply sceptical to the widely overoptimistic. Gianutsos (1991) reported that the discipline of cognitive rehabilitation had finally 'come of age', and Coltheart *et al.* (1994) claimed that the positive results of treatment studies were indisputable. By contrast, many commentators are cautious about the prospects of improving cognitive function. Their views can be summarized by Caramazza (1989), who argued that 'the promise of cognitive psychology as a guide for the choice of intervention strategies is still largely unfilled'. Nevertheless the potential exists to bring our increasing understanding of normal and dysfunctional cognition to bear on improving abilities after brain injury. Wood (1990b) summarized the present state of the art: 'A new generation of treatment methods is being developed which stands firmly on the rock of scientific theory and promises great advances in the scope and reputation of cognitive rehabilitation.'

EVALUATING REHABILITATION OUTCOME

In general, the management of problems after brain injury or illness continues to be practised with methods of uncertain effectiveness. The need to evaluate treatment techniques is widely recognized, but standard procedures for measuring treatment outcome are inappropriate in a clinical rehabilitative context. For instance, it is often difficult to claim that functional improvement is due to a particular intervention rather than to spontaneous recovery. It is not acceptable to withdraw and then reinstate treatments, as one can with some medications. The appropriate level of analysis of rehabilitation effectiveness is also unclear and debate focuses on the relative merits of group studies or single case designs. Nevertheless the value of single-subject research for studying effects of cognitive remediation is being increasingly recognized (Wilson, 1987).

One criterion for therapeutic success is the extent of generalization of treatment effects. In attempting to be 'scientific', many therapeutic studies eliminate potentially confounding variables – and thus much of the variability that is present in real life. Lack of generalization of positive improvement in training to functional settings is therefore unsurprising. Less rigid notions of what constitutes a scientific evaluation and the development of 'quasi-experimental designs' are a promising way forward in this rapidly developing field (Robertson, 1994).

Some of the more common difficulties in evaluating

Box 20.8 *Problems in evaluating the effects of rehabilitation*

Group designs
- Randomized, controlled studies are often impractical
- Dropout rates are rarely reported
- Group means conceal individual treatment effects, including failures
- Outcome measures are often inadequate

Single-case designs
- Reversal procedures are often impractical or inappropriate
- Treatments are too short to assess existence or maintenance of treatment effects
- The effects of cognitive intervention are difficult to separate from other aspects of therapy

interventions for people with brain injury are described in Box 20.8. Research on measuring the effects of rehabilitation (outcome research) is proliferating and there are a number of standardized scales available for evaluating psychological states (Peck and Shapiro, 1990) and health and functional abilities (Bowling, 1991). Further progress will require more replications of successful treatment studies in order to establish which methods are effective for which problems.

Learning Activity 6 ◆ ◆ ◆

Given the need for professionals to take a critical approach to clinical practice, design a study to evaluate the outcome of a particular rehabilitation strategy or technique using:

a a single case design;
b a group design.

Refer to Chapters 24 and 25 for further information on research design.

SUMMARY

The aim of rehabilitation is to minimize disability and optimize functional capacity. Frequently the direct and indirect psychological consequences of brain injury are poorly understood and can serve to undermine effective management. Systematic assessment and management of the cognitive, emotional and behavioural consequences of brain damage can help all aspects of its management.

Key Points ■ ■ ■

- ❒ The management of cognitive, emotional and behavioural impairments after brain injury is important where these might undermine other aspects of rehabilitation.
- ❒ Certain general principles need to be followed to ensure that the process of rehabilitation is systematic, focused, flexible and relevant.
- ❒ Behavioural techniques have been used effectively to tackle cognitive and behavioural problems arising from cognitive deficits.
- ❒ Information processing models and learning theory are valuable in providing a framework from which to develop rehabilitation strategies.
- ❒ To date, cognitive rehabilitation based on contemporary models of information processing have very limited clinical impact.
- ❒ Information processing models of cognition take little account of motivation, learning, awareness and self-concept, all of which can be crucial to therapeutic outcome.
- ❒ Cognitive, behavioural and emotional factors can have a positive role in neuropsychological rehabilitation, especially in the development of compensatory strategies and in adjustment to impairment.
- ❒ Evaluation of rehabilitation outcome is crucial to development in this field.

References ▼ ▼ ▼

Alderman, N., Fry, R.K. and Youngson, H.A. (1995). Improvement of self-monitoring skills, reduction of behaviour disturbance, and the dysexecutive syndrome: comparison of response cost and a new programme of self-monitoring training. *Neuropsychological Rehabilitation*, **5**: 193–221.

Becker, M.E. and Vakil, E. (1993). Behavioural psychotherapy of the frontal-lobe-injured patient in an outpatient setting. *Brain Injury*, **7**: 515–23.

Ben-Yishay, Y. and Diller, L. (1993). Cognitive remediation in traumatic brain injury: update and issues, *Archives of Physical Medicine and Rehabilitation*, **74**: 204–13.

Ben-Yishay, Y. and Gold, J. (1990). Therapeutic milieu approach to neuropsychological rehabilitation. In: Wood, R.Ll. (ed.), *Neurobehavioural Sequelae of Traumatic Brain Injury*. London: Taylor and Francis, 194–215.

Bergquist, T.F. and Jacket, M.P. (1993). Awareness and goal setting with the traumatically brain injured, *Brain Injury*, **7**: 275–82.

Bisiach, E. Vallar, G. Perani, D. *et al.* (1986). Unawareness of disease following lesions of the right hemisphere: anosagnosia for hemiplegia and anosagnosia for hemianopia. *Neuropsychologia*, **24**: 471–82.

Bollinger, R.L. Musson, N.D. and Holland, A.L. (1993). A study of group communication intervention with chronically aphasic persons. *Aphasiology*, **7**: 301–13.

Bowling, A. (1991). *Measuring Health*. Buckingham: Open University Press.

Burgess, P.W. and Alderman, N. (1990). Rehabilitation of dyscontrol syndromes following brain injury. In: Wood R.Ll. and Fussey, I. (eds), *Cognitive Rehabilitation in Perspective*. London: Taylor and Francis, 183–203.

Burke, W.H. Zenicus, A.H., Wesolowski, M.D. *et al.* (1991). Improving executive function disorders in brain-injured clients. *Brain Injury*, **5**: 241–52.

Burke, J.M. Danick, J.A., Bemis, B. *et al.* (1994). A process approach to memory book training for neurological patients. *Brain Injury*, **8**: 71–81.

Butter, C.M. and Kirsch, N. (1992). Combined and separate effects of the eye patching and visual stimulation on unilateral neglect following stroke. *Archives of Physical Medicine and Rehabilitation*. **73**: 1133–9.

Butters, M.A. and Glisky, E.L. (1993). Transfer of new learning in memory-impaired patients. *Journal of Clinical and Experimental Neuropsychology*, **15**: 219–30.

Caramazza, A. (1989). Cognitive neuropsychology and rehabilitation: an unfulfilled promise? In: Seron, X. and Deloche, G. (eds), *Cognitive Approaches in Neuropsychological Rehabilitation*, Hillsdale, NJ: Lawrence Erlbaum, 383–98.

Carlomagno, S., Iavarone, A. and Colombo, A. (1994). Cognitive approaches to writing rehabilitation: from single case to group studies. In: Riddoch, M.J. and Humphreys, G.W. (eds), *Cognitive Neuropsychology and Cognitive Rehabilitation*. Hove: Lawrence Erlbaum, 485–502.

Cassidy, J.W. (1990). Pharmacological treatment of post-traumatic behavioural disorders: aggression and disorders of mood. In Wood, R.Ll. (ed.), *Neurobehavioural Sequelae of Traumatic Brain Injury*. London: Taylor and Francis, 219–49.

Cockburn, J. (1993). Relevance of cognitive psychology and neuropsychology for physiotherapy practice. *Physiotherapy Theory and Practice*, **9**: 191–2.

Coltheart, M., Bates, A. and Castles, A. (1994). Cognitive Neuropsychology and Rehabilitation. In: Riddoch, M.J. and Humphreys, G.W. (eds), *Cognitive Neuropsychology and Cognitive Rehabilitation*. Hove: Lawrence Erlbaum, 17–37.

Corrigan, B. and Maitland, G.D. (1983). *Practical Orthopaedic Medicine*. Oxford: Butterworth-Heinemann.

Von Cramon, D.Y. and Matthes-Von Cramon, G. (1990). Frontal lobe dysfunctions in patients: therapeutical approaches. In: Wood, R.Ll. and Fussey, I. (eds), *Cognitive Rehabilitation in Perspective*. London: Taylor and Francis, 164–79.

Von Cramon, D.Y. and Matthes–Von Cramon (1992). Reflections of the treatment of brain-injured patients suffering from problem-solving disorders. *Neurological Rehabilitation*, **2**: 207–29.

Cutting, J. (1978). Study of anosagnosia. *Journal of Neurology, Neurosurgery and Psychiatry*, **41**: 548–55.

Davis, A. and Pring, T. (1991). Therapy for word-finding deficits: more on the effects of semantic and phonological approaches to treatment with dysphasic patients. *Neuropsychological Rehabilitation*, **1**: 135–45.

Decety, J. (1993). Should motor imagery be used in physiotherapy? Recent advances in cognitive neurosciences. *Physiotherapy Theory and Practice*, **9**: 193–203.

Eames, P. (1987). Head injury rehabilitation: time for a new look. *Clinical Rehabilitation*, **1**: 53–7.

Eames, P. (1989). The use of Sinemet and bromocriptine. *Brain Injury*, **3**: 319–20.

Eames, P. (1990). Organic bases of behaviour disorders after traumatic brain injury. In Wood, R.Ll. (ed.), *Neurobehavioural Sequelae of Traumatic Brain Injury*. London: Taylor and Francis, 134–50.

Eames, P. and Wood, R.Ll. (1985). Rehabilitation after severe brain injury: a follow-up study of a behaviour modification approach. *Journal of Neurology, Neurosurgery and Psychiatry*, **48**: 613–19.

Ebrahim, S. (1990). *Clinical Epidemiology of Stroke*. Oxford: Oxford University Press.

Edmans, J.A. and Lincoln, N.B. (1991). Treatment of visual perceptual deficits after stroke: single case studies on four patients with right hemiplegia. *British Journal of Occupational Therapy*, **54**: 139–44.

Evans, J. (1994). Physiotherapy as a clinical science: the role of single case research designs. *Physiotherapy Theory and Practice*, **10**: 65–8.

Fanthome, Y., Lincoln, N.B., Drummond, A.E.R. *et al.* (1995). The treatment of visual neglect using the transfer of training approach. *British Journal of Occupational Therapy*, **58**: 14–16.

Feher, E.P., Mahurin, R.K. Inbody, S.B. *et al.* (1991). Anosagnosia in Alzheimer's disease. *Neuropsychiatry, Neuropsychology and Behavioural Neurology*, **4**: 136–46.

Fleming, J. and Strong, J. (1995). Self-awareness of deficits following acquired brain injury: considerations for rehabilitation. *British Journal of Occupational Therapy*, **58**: 55–60.

Fluharty, G. and Priddy, D. (1993). Methods of increasing client acceptance of a memory book. *Brain Injury*, **7**: 85–8.

Forster, F.M. (1972). The classification and conditioning treatment of the reflex epilepsies. *International Journal of Neurology*, **9**: 73–86.

Gianutsos, R. (1991). Cognitive rehabilitation: a neuropsychological speciality comes of age. *Brain Injury*, **5**: 353–68.

Gianutsos, R. and Matheson, P. (1987). The rehabilitation of visual perceptual disorders attributable to brain injury. In: Meier, M.J. *et al.* (eds), *Neuropsychological Rehabilitation*. New York: Churchill Livingstone, 202–41.

Glisky, E.L. Schacter, D.L. and Tulving, E. (1986). Learning and retention of computer-related vocabulary in memory-impaired patients: method of vanishing cues. *Journal of Clinical and Experimental Neuropsychology*, **8**: 292–312.

Goldstein, L.H. (1990). Behavioural and cognitive-based treatment for epilepsy. *British Journal of Clinical Psychology*, **29**: 257–69.

Goldstein, F.C. and Levin, H.S. (1987). Disorders of reasoning and problem solving ability. In: Meier, M.J. *et al.* (eds), *Neuropsychological Rehabilitation*. New York: Churchill Livingstone, 327–54.

Gordon, W.A., Hibbard, M.R., Egelko, S. *et al.* 1985: Perceptual remediation in patients with right brain damage: a comprehensive program. *Archives of Physical Medicine and Rehabilitation*, **66**: 353–9.

Hillis, A.E. and Caramazza, A. (1994). Theories of lexical processing and rehabilitation of lexical deficits. In: Riddoch, M.J. and Humphreys, G.W. (eds), *Cognitive Neuropsychology and Cognitive Rehabilitation*. Hove: Lawrence Erlbaum.

House, A. and Hodges, J. (1988). Persistent denial of handicap after infarction of the right basal ganglia: a case study. *Journal of Neurology, Neurosurgery and Psychiatry*, **51**: 112–15.

Ishiai, S., Sugishita, M., Odajima, N. *et al.* (1990). Improvement of unilateral neglect with numbering. *Neurology*. **40**: 1395–8.

Johnsen, B. (1992). Aphasia and its relation to language and thinking: finding alternative ways for communication. *Scandanavian Journal of Rehabilitation Medicine Supplement*, **26**: 70–78.

Kasma, Y.P.T., Brouwer, W.H. and Lakke, J.P.W.F. (1994). Prevention of early immobility in patients with Parkinson's disease: a cognitive strategy training for turning in bed and rising from a chair. In: Riddoch, M.J. and Humphreys, G.W. (eds), *Cognitive Neuropsychology and Cognitive Rehabilitation*. Hove: Lawrence Erlbaum, 245–70.

Kerkhoff, G., Munsbinger, U., Eberle-Strauss, G. and Stogerer, E. (1992). Rehabilitation of hemianopic alexia in patients with postgeniculate visual field disorders. *Neuropsychological Rehabilitation*, **2**: 21–42.

Langer, K.G. and Padrone, F.J. (1992). Psychotherapeutic treatment of awareness in acute rehabilitation of traumatic brain injury. *Neuropsychological Rehabilitation*, **2**: 59–70.

Lishman, W.A. (1987). *Organic Psychiatry*, 2nd edn. Oxford: Blackwell.

Malia, K.B., Torode, S. and Powell, G.E. (1993). Insight and progress in rehabilitation after brain injury. *Clinical Rehabilitation*, **7**: 23–9.

Miller, N. (1986). *Dyspraxia and its Management*. London: Croom Helm.

Mitchum, C.C. and Berndt, R.S. (1994). Verb retrieval and sentence construction: effects of targeted intervention. In: Riddoch, M.J.

and Humphreys, G.W. (eds), *Cognitive Neuropsychology and Cognitive Rehabilitation*. Hove: Lawrence Erlbaum, 317–48.

Moore, M.M., White, O., Evans, E. and Mateer, C. (1992). Background and initial case studies into the effects of prospective memory training. *Brain Injury*, **6**: 129–38.

Murphy, L.D., McMillan, T.M., Greenwood, R.J. *et al.* (1990). Services for severely brain-injured patients in North London and environs. *Brain Injury*, **4**: 95–100.

Nichols, P.J.R. (ed.) (1980). *Rehabilitation Medicine*, 2nd edn. London: Butterworths.

O'Brien, K.P., Prigatano, G.P. and Pittman, H.W. (1988). Neurobehavioural education of a patient and spouse following right frontal oligodendroglioma excision. *Neuropsychology*, **2**: 145–59.

de Partz, M.-P., Seron, X. and der Linden, M.V. (1992). Re-education of a surface dysgraphia with a visual imagery strategy. *Cognitive Neuropsychology*, **9**: 369–401.

Peck, D.F. and Shapiro, C.M. (eds) (1990). *Measuring Human Problems: A Practical Guide*. Chichester: Wiley.

Pilgrim, E. and Humphreys, G.W. (1994). Rehabilitation of a case of ideomotor apraxia. In: Riddoch, M.J. and Humphreys, G.W. (eds), *Cognitive Neuropsychology and Cognitive Rehabilitation*. Hove: Lawrence Erlbaum, 271–85.

Pizzamiglio, L., Antonucci, G. *et al.* (1992). Cognitive rehabilitation of the hemineglect disorder in chronic patients with unilateral right brain damage. *Journal of Clinical and Experimental Neuropsychology*, **14**: 901–23.

Powell, G.E. and Wilson, S.L. (1994). Recovery curves for patients who have suffered very severe brain injury. *Clinical Rehabilitation*, **8**: 54–69.

Powell, T., Partridge, T., Nicholls, T. *et al.* (1994). An interdisciplinary approach to the rehabilitation of people with brain injury. *British Journal of Therapy and Rehabilitation*, **1**: 8–13.

Prigatano, G.P. (1987). Personality and psychosocial consequences after brain injury. In: Meier, M.J. *et al.* (eds), *Neuropsychological Rehabilitation*. New York: Churchill Livingstone, 355–78.

Prigatano, G.P. (1991). Disturbances of self-awareness of deficit after traumatic brain injury. In: Prigatano, G.P. and Schlacter, D.L. (eds), *Awareness of Deficit After Brain Injury*. New York: Oxford University Press, 111–26.

Robertson, I.H. (1994). Methodology in neuropsychological rehabilitation research. *Neuropsychological Rehabilitation*, **4**: 1–6.

Robertson, I., Gray, J. and McKenzie, S. (1988). Microcomputer-based cognitive rehabilitation of visual neglect: three multiple-baseline single-case studies. *Brain Injury*, **2**: 151–63.

Robertson, I.H. and North, N. (1992a). Spatio-motor cueing in unilateral left neglect: the role of hemispace, hand and motor activation. *Neuropsychologia*, **30**: 553–63.

Robertson, I.H. and North, N. (1992b). Spatio-motor cueing in unilateral neglect: three case studies of its therapeutic effects. *Journal of Neurology, Neurosurgery and Psychiatry*, **55**: 799–805.

Robertson, I.H. and North, N. (1993). Active and passive activation of left limbs: influence on visual and sensory neglect. *Neuropsychologia*, **31**: 293–300.

Robinson, R.G., Kubos, K.L., Starr, L.B. *et al.* (1984). Mood disorders in stroke patients: importance of lesion location. *Brain*, **107**: 81–93.

Sohlberg, M.M. and Mateer, C.A. (1989). *Introduction to Cognitive Rehabilitation Theory and Practice*. New York: Guilford Press.

Stern, J.M. and Stern, B. (1989). Visual imagery as a cognitive means of compensation for brain injury. *Brain Injury*, **3**: 413–19.

Stuss, D.T. (1991). Disturbance of self-awareness after frontal-system damage. In: Prigatano, G.P. and Schacter, D.L. (eds), *Awareness of Deficit After Brain Injury*. New York: Oxford University Press, 63–8.

Toglia, J.P. (1992). A dynamic interactional approach to cognitive rehabilitation. In: Katz, N. (ed.), *Cognitive Rehabilitation: Models for Intervention in Occupational Therapy*. Stoneham, MA: Andover Medical, 104–43.

Tyerman, A.D. (1991). Counselling in head injury. In: Davis, H. and Fallowfield, L. (eds), *Counselling and Communication in Healthcare*. Chichester: Wiley, 115–28.

Wade, D.T. (1992). *Measurement in Neurological Rehabilitation*. Oxford: Oxford University Press.

Wesolowski, M. (1988). *Head Injury Rehabilitation: Managing Anger and Aggression*. Houston: HDI Publishers.

Wilson, B.A. (1987). Single-case experimental designs in neuropsychological rehabilitation. *Journal of Clinical and Experimental Neuropsychology*, **9**: 527–44.

Wilson, B.A. and Patterson, K. (1990). Rehabilitation and cognitive neuropsychology: does cognitive psychology apply? *Applied Cognitive Psychology*, **4**: 247–60.

Wilson, B.A. and Moffatt, N. (eds) (1992). *Clinical Management of Memory Problems*, 2nd edn. London: Chapman and Hall.

Wilson, B.A., Baddeley, A., Evans, J. and Shiel, A. (1994). Errorless learning in the rehabilitation of memory-impaired people. *Neuropsychological Rehabilitation*, **4**: 307–26.

Wood, R.Ll. (1990a). Conditioning procedures in brain injury rehabilitation. In: Wood, R.Ll. (ed.), *Neurobehavioural Sequelae of Traumatic Brain Injury*. London: Taylor and Francis, 153–74.

Wood, R.Ll. (1990b). Towards a model of cognitive-rehabilitation. In: Wood, R.Ll. and Fussey, I. (eds), *Cognitive Rehabilitation in Perspective*. London: Taylor and Francis, 2–15.

World Health Organization (1980). *The International Classification of Impairment, Disabilities and Handicaps*. Geneva: WHO.

Worthington, A.D. (1996). Cueing strategies in neglect dyslexia, *Neuropsychological Rehabilitation* **6**: 1–17.

Youngjohn, F.R. and Altman, I.M. (1989). A performance-based group approach to the treatment of anosagnosia and denial. *Rehabilitation Psychology*, **34**: 217–22.

Zasler, N.D. (1992). Advances in neuropharmacological rehabilitation for brain dysfunction. *Brain Injury*. **6**: 1–14.

Zenicus, A., Wesolowski, M.D. and Burke, W.H. (1990). A comparison of four memory strategies with traumatically brain-injured clients. *Brain Injury*, **4**: 33–8.

Further Reading ▲ ▲ ▲

Christensen, A.-L. and Uzzell, B.P. (eds). *Brain Injury and Neuropsychological Rehabilitation*. Hillsdale, NJ: Lawrence Erlbaum.

Gordon, W.A. (ed.) (1993). *Advances in Stroke Rehabilitation*. Boston: Andover Medical.

Katz, N. (ed.) (1992). *Cognitive Rehabilitation: Models for Intervention in Occupational Therapy*. Stoneham, MA: Andover Medical.

Riddoch, M.J. and Humphreys, G.W. (eds) (1994). *Cognitive Neuropsychology and Cognitive Rehabilitation*. Hove: Lawrence Erlbaum.

Wood, R.L. and Fussey, I. (eds) (1990). *Cognitive Rehabilitation in Perspective*. London: Taylor and Francis.

SECTION VI

Ethics

21

Ethical Issues, Ethical Principles and Codes of Conduct

Jane Singleton

LEARNING OBJECTIVES

After studying this chapter you should:

- Be able to describe what ethical dilemmas are
- Understand when ethical issues arise, even implicitly
- Be able to isolate ethical dilemmas encountered in practice
- Recognize when ethical dilemmas involve the principles of autonomy beneficence, non-maleficence and justice
- Be able to reflect critically on the status and content of ethical codes of conduct
- Appreciate the need for critical reflection about ethical dilemmas

INTRODUCTION

Sensitivity to ethical issues is central to healthcare. The consultation with and treatment of individuals essentially involves a consideration of their rights, feelings and principles. The amount of time and financial resources allocated to an individual also raises ethical issues of the justice of distribution of resources. The length of time spent treating one individual is indicative of an evaluation of the importance of this case in comparison with others. Additionally, health professionals work in a team with their colleagues from the same profession and other members of the healthcare arena. Ethical issues arise by virtue of this necessary interaction when working with individuals referred to the healthcare system.

Sensitivity to the issues is fundamentally important. However, sensitivity needs to be accompanied by some knowledge of how to set about thinking about these dilemmas in order to assist decision-making. An uncritical reliance on professional codes of conduct is not adequate, and suggestions about how critical ethical reflection on these issues might be conducted needs to be considered.

WHAT ARE ETHICAL DILEMMAS?

Every day in the media, difficult ethical dilemmas that are the direct concern of healthcare are described. Here are some examples:

- Should a 60-year old woman be given infertility treatment to allow her to have a baby?
- Should a trauma victim be kept alive in order to donate organs?
- Should a doctor be allowed to assist someone who is terminally ill and in pain to die if that is their wish?
- Should individuals who are diagnosed as being in a persistent vegetative state be kept alive?
- Should genetic screening be allowed, with the consequent abortions if the embryo is not 'healthy'?

Ethical dilemmas are at their most harrowing when confronting issues of life and death, but they are not confined to these areas. In healthcare, ethical issues also arise from specific relationships that are involved (see Box 21.1). Some ethical issues involve just one of these relationships, but others are further complicated by conflicts between the requirements of more than one of the relationships. Also, ethical issues are not confined to duties arising from these relationships but also arise

Box 21.1 *Relationships within healthcare settings*

Relationships occur between:

- health professionals and the individual being examined/treated;
- health professionals and the relatives of the individual being examined/treated;
- different professionals within the healthcare team;
- individuals within the same profession in the healthcare team;
- the healthcare team and society as a whole.

with respect to possible conflicts between the requirements of codes of conduct and an individual's own moral evaluation of a situation.

An ethical dilemma occurs when a health professional is faced with a decision based on moral issues which requires him or her to consider what is 'right'. The health professional may be faced with a dilemma because all or none of the options seem to be 'right'. In this event it is important that the health professional has an ethical understanding and framework which will assist in a decision being made.

Learning Activity 1 ◆ ◆ ◆

Identify three or four ethical dilemmas from your own experience and/or practice.

Explicit examples of ethical dilemmas

Truth telling

Truth telling can raise ethical problems both in the relationship between healthcare professionals and the recipients of healthcare, and also in the relationship between different professions within the healthcare team. For example, there can be a conflict between the duty to tell the truth and a duty not to inflict unnecessary suffering. Other dilemmas involve different problems with respect to truth telling (see Case Study 21.1).

Case Study ◗ ◗ ◗

◗ *Case Study 21.1*

An individual who has undergone surgery for cancer, which at laporotomy was found to be inoperable, asks the physiotherapist how successful the operation was. Ought the physiotherapist to tell the individual the true diagnosis? In this case, the conflict arises between the dictates of the ethical code of conduct which states this information should only be given by the medical practitioner with overall responsibility for the individual, and the feeling that the individual has a right to know this diagnosis. This conflict might be solved relatively easily if the medical practitioner is contacted and gives the individual the information. However, if the medical practitioner feels non-disclosure is right and the physiotherapist considers the patient ought to be told, the conflict is unresolved.

Confidentiality

Ethical dilemmas can arise when healthcare professionals consider whether it is ever justifiable to divulge information given by an individual during an examination or treatment. In the case of radiographers, confidentiality is listed first in their professional code: 'radiographers must hold in confidence any information obtained through professional attendance on a patient' (1.1, Code of Professional Conduct; College of Radiographers, 1994). The Patient's Charter (1992) also emphasizes the importance of confidentiality by stating that you have the right 'to have access to your health records, and to know that those working for the NHS will, by law, keep their contents confidential'. Is this duty of confidentiality absolute or can it ever be overridden? This question is addressed in Chapter 23.

Consent

Surrounding the area of consent there are a host of issues which can give rise to ethical dilemmas. The Patient's Charter (1992) emphasizes the importance of informed consent as a right for individuals. An individual has a right 'to be given a clear explanation of any treatment proposed, including any risks and any alternatives, before you decide whether you will agree to the treatment'. If an individual refuses to assent to treatment that is considered to be in that individual's best interest, ought the treatment to be given? The refusal to accept a blood transfusion by a Jehovah's Witness might be one example.

Implicit examples of ethical dilemmas

There might be universal recognition that the examples above raise ethical problems, but there are also areas where ethical assumptions are made implicitly and are not always recognized as being present.

Recipients of healthcare

The use of the word 'patient' to refer to the recipients of healthcare carries with it value implications of dependency. Use of this term might make more acceptable a paternalistic approach to decision-making.

The term 'patient' is the one chosen by both the College of Radiographers and the Chartered Society of Physiotherapy in their codes of professional conduct. The common alternative is 'client', but arguably the business connotations of this beg important ethical questions. The use of 'client' might imply that it is acceptable for the availability of certain treatments to be based on the ability to pay just as business services are open to those who can afford them. The term 'client' is used by the British Association of Occupational Therapists in its code of professional conduct. Clearly, value issues need to be considered explicitly and not prejudged by virtue of the terminology that is employed.

The term used in this book, where possible, to replace the cumbersome 'recipients of healthcare' is 'individuals', since this is a more neutral term in this context.

Models of health

Another and connected area where ethical assumptions are made implicitly is in the model of health adopted. If a *biomedical model* (Beauchamp and Childress, 1983) is adopted, whereby the individual is viewed just as a body that is a complex machine in good or bad working order, this tends to lead to a paternalistic approach to decision-making. The medical practitioner will determine what is necessary to put the body back into good working order. Individuals will not be involved in the decision-making process since they will be viewed just as passive machines. This tendency is also apparent when, for example, health professionals refer to the condition rather than to an individual by saying 'the ankle in the corridor needs to be brought in'.

However, if a *biopsychosocial model* (Beauchamp and Childress, 1983) is adopted, which recognizes that thoughts and feelings that may influence our bodily state, then this will lend itself to a model of decision-making that involves the participation of the individual being treated. The individual will be viewed as an active participant whose thoughts and feelings must be reflected in the decision taken. It is an ethical question of importance to decide how decisions ought to be taken, and this question needs to be made explicit rather than implicitly accepted by virtue of a particular model of health that is adopted.

Health as a concept

Finally, it also needs to be recognized that the term 'healthy' itself is an evaluative term. What counts as a healthy state is dependent on how this state is evaluated and is not entailed by the state alone. For example, within the biomedical model a healthy state is one where the bodily machine is in good working order. However, from the perspective of the biopsychosocial model, the good working order of the body might not be enough to evaluate the state as healthy. This implicit evaluation in the use of the word 'healthy' was indicated in the list of dilemmas at the beginning of the chapter, when the question of genetic screening and the abortion of fetuses not considered to be healthy was used as an example.

The principles of non-maleficence, autonomy, beneficence and justice

Once the ethical questions have been recognized, an appropriate method for exploring them needs to be found. One such method would be to see whether there are any common principles that are being appealed to when these issues are considered. In examples concerning whether or not it is ever justifiable to tell a lie to an individual where telling the truth might be thought to cause great suffering, what principles might be employed?

In Case Study 21.1, the medical practitioner might well consider that the individual ought not to be told the truth because this would inflict unnecessary harm. The principle appealed to would be the *principle of non-maleficence* (see Box 21.2). However, the physiotherapist might consider this decision not justifiable by appealing to the *principle of autonomy*. The individual has asked for this information and to refuse it would deny him the opportunity of forming plans for the end of his life. His autonomy will be limited by incomplete information.

Case Study 21.2 illustrates possible conflicts that might arise between the application of the *Principle of*

Box 21.2 *Ethical principles*

- *The principle of non-maleficence*: One ought to do no harm.
- *The principle of autonomy*: In certain areas, an individual has a right to be self-governing.
- *The principle of beneficence*: The well-being or benefit of the individual ought to be promoted.
- *The principle of justice*: Equals ought to be considered equally.

Beneficence and the *Principle of Justice*. This example indicates a conflict arising, on the one hand, from the relationship between a healthcare practitioner and the individual seeking treatment, and, on the other hand, from the relationship that healthcare practitioners have to society at large.

Case Study

Case Study 21.2

A radiographer might feel the best way to achieve an accurate diagnosis of an individual's complaint would be by a scan MRI (magnetic resonance imaging). This course of action would be in conformity with the principle of beneficence. However, MRI examinations are expensive and limited resources, coupled with a consideration of the principle of justice, might lead to the conclusion that to spend so much money on this individual would be unfair to others seeking healthcare.

The four ethical principles appear to be at the heart of healthcare. Before discussing this in greater detail, it is necessary to understand more clearly just what these principles mean and the different justifications that can be provided for them. Are they all equally important, or is one more important than the others? Two different justifications and interpretations of these principles will be looked at in Chapter 22, and their centrality in specific ethical dilemmas will be illustrated in Chapter 23.

The necessity for undertaking this type of ethical analysis when faced with dilemmas in healthcare might be questioned. There are codes of conduct for the different healthcare professions, so perhaps the difficulties can be solved by appealing to the codes. It will be seen in the next section why appeal to codes of conduct will not be enough.

Codes of conduct

The codes of conduct for healthcare practitioners are intended as guides for professional behaviour. For example:

- The code of conduct for radiographers is designed 'to give advice and guidance to all practising members and those studying to gain qualification for state registration' (College of Radiographers, 1994).
- The code of conduct for physiotherapists is also intended as a guide for professional behaviour, although this point might be obscured by the use of the word 'rules' in this code (Chartered Society of Physiotherapy, 1992).
- The code of conduct for occupational therapists 'provides directions for occupational therapists and may be used by others to determine the standards of professional conduct which can be expected from occupational therapists and students' (BAOT, 1995).

These codes provide guidance on how professionals should behave towards recipients of healthcare, each other and society. However, they cannot be used as a substitute for critical ethical reflection on the kind of dilemmas that have been raised in this chapter, for a number of reasons.

First, when clauses are listed in these codes they are not given a hierarchical ordering. Therefore, in cases where the clauses conflict, no guidance is provided by the codes to resolve the conflict (see Case Study 21.3).

Case Study

Case Study 21.3

Radiographers: Clause 1.3 (College of Radiographers, 1994) states: 'Radiographers have a responsibility to promote and protect the dignity, privacy, autonomy and safety of all patients with whom they come into contact.' However, clause 3.3 of the same code states: 'Radiographers should work in a collaborative and cooperative manner with other members of the healthcare team.' If a physician in a healthcare team has decided that an individual should not be told the truth about their diagnosis, the code for radiographers gives no guidance on what the radiographer should do.

Promoting the autonomy of the individual being treated would appear to point towards disclosure, but collaborative and cooperative working relationships with other members of the healthcare team would seem to dictate non-disclosure. Critical ethical reflection will be required to examine this problem.

Physiotherapy: Interestingly, the code for physiotherapists is much more restrictive on this point. Rule 2 (Chartered Society of Physiotherapy, 1992) states: 'Chartered physiotherapists shall respect the rights, dignity and individual sensibilities of all their patients.' In elaborating this rule it is said that physiotherapists should inform their patients about treatment, giving them the opportunity to consent to or decline treatment. However, it is made clear in the discussion of Rule 6 (Confidentiality) that physiotherapists are not allowed to reveal an individual's diagnosis if the medical practitioner with overall responsibility for the individual has not disclosed this.

A second difficulty with relying on codes is that key terms used in their formulation require a critical analysis. It is important to know precisely what is involved in promoting and protecting patients' (radiographers, physiotherapists) or clients' (occupational therapists) autonomy, dignity and privacy. These key terms require critical ethical analysis to be understood and applied to specific cases.

A related point is that there is no explained underlying rationale to these codes. There is an implicit relation to ethical principles but no explicit account of the precise grounding of the codes. Without the philosophical underpinnings of these codes being made explicit, there is no way to assess adequately the resulting codes.

An even more fundamental shortcoming of these codes of practice is that they are not based on wide consultation with members of the community. For occupational therapists, the responsibility for compiling and revising the code is delegated to the College's Ethics Committee. Perhaps to avoid accusations of paternalistic elitism (Hull, 1981), the regulation of healthcare professions should be based on a contract with the community with public participation in the development of professional codes rather than with a self-regulatory committee (May, 1975).

Clearly, codes of conduct are necessary for all healthcare professionals as they set the boundaries, outline the ideals for practice and uphold standards of competence. However, they need to be looked at critically, and they cannot be used as a *substitute* for critical ethical reflection on ethical problems.

Learning Activity 2 ◆ ◆ ◆

Examine your professional code of conduct and isolate some problems that might arise if only codes of conduct are relied upon when attempting to resolve an ethical dilemma.

SUMMARY

This chapter has considered how all-pervasive ethical issues are. In addition to ethical dilemmas that are clearly recognizable, ethical issues are raised by less easily recognized situations. An example of this would be the term used to describe the recipients of healthcare. Many of these issues involve reference to benefiting or harming individuals, to an individual's autonomy, and to just dealings between individuals. Codes of professional conduct have something to say about these matters, but critical reflection is an essential prerequisite for decision-making in healthcare.

Key Points ■ ■ ■

- Ethical dilemmas can range from life or death situations, through the nature of specific relationships, to conflicts between codes of conduct and an individual's own moral evaluation of a situation.
- Ethical dilemmas can be explicit but many are implicit.
- There are four ethical principles: non-malefience, autonomy, beneficence and justice.
- Codes of professional conduct are guides and require careful consideration and reflection by practitioners.

References ▼ ▼ ▼

Beauchamp, T.L. and Childress, J.F. (1983). *Principles of Biomedical Ethics*, 2nd edn. New York: Oxford University Press.

British Association of Occupational Therapists (1995). *Code of Ethics and Professional Conduct.*

Chartered Society of Physiotherapy (1992). *Rules of Professional Conduct.*

College of Radiographers (1994). *Code of Professional Conduct.*

Hull, R.T. (1981). The function of professional codes of ethics. *Westminster Institute Review*, **1**(3): 12–14.

May, W.F. (1975). Code, covenant, contract, or philanthropy. *Hastings Center Report*, **5**: 29–38.

Patient's Charter (1992). London: HMSO.

Further Reading ▲ ▲ ▲

Muyskens, J.L. (1982). *Moral Problems in Nursing*. Totowa: Rowan & Littlefield.

Singleton, J. and McLaren, S.M. (1995). *Ethical Foundations of Health Care*. London: C.V. Mosby.

Veatch, R.M. (1981). *A Theory of Medical Ethics*. New York: Basic Books.

22

Justifications for Ethical Principles

Jane Singleton

LEARNING OBJECTIVES

After studying this chapter you should:

- Understand what consequentialist and deontological ethical theories are, and recognize when they are being applied
- Comprehend the justification for the principles of beneficence, non-maleficence, autonomy and justice, from within consequentialist and deontological frameworks
- Be able to describe when consequentialist or deontological justifications are being given for these principles, since this justification is often only implicit
- Be able to assess critically the relative merits of consequentialist and deontological ethical theories when applied to issues in healthcare

INTRODUCTION

An awareness of ethical dilemmas and when ethical issues arise is important, as has been shown in the previous chapter. There are different ways to reflect on these dilemmas and arrive at decisions, and one way is to assume that ethical dilemmas should be solved by seeking to achieve the best outcome possible. Ethical decisions are taken as a means towards reaching what is regarded as ultimately good.

Another approach to ethical decision-making that contrasts with this is to view ethics as a matter of obeying certain principles that are intrinsically right independently of the results of following them. The first approach might favour, for example, telling lies in certain instances if this will produce the best outcome, whereas the second approach might yield the claim that telling the truth is a principle that has binding force independent of the consequences of telling the truth.

In the previous chapter it was seen that many ethical dilemmas raise issues about *beneficence, non-maleficence, autonomy* and *justice*. This chapter examines the different interpretations that can be given of these principles from within these two approaches.

CONSEQUENTIALIST ETHICAL THEORIES

The concept that health professionals, when reflecting on ethical issues, ought to seek to achieve the best outcomes possible is known as *consequentialism* (Parfit, 1984). However, this view that there is one moral aim that outcomes be as good as possible is, as it stands, incomplete. If this position is to be accepted, then it is necessary to have some view about what would constitute a good outcome. What is to be taken as being fundamentally valuable or as having intrinsic worth? What consequences are we ultimately trying to achieve? (See Case Study 22.1.)

Case Study

Case Study 22.1

A circular issued by the Chartered Society of Physiotherapy (HC(77)33: 'Relationships between the medical and remedial professions') states: 'In asking for treatment by a therapist the doctor is clearly asking for the help of another trained professional, and the profession of medicine and the various therapies differ. It follows from this that the therapist has a duty and a consequential right to *decline* to perform any therapy which his professional training and expertise suggests is *actively harmful* to the patient.'

In cases to which this description would apply, the doctor is concerned to promote the well being of the individual and so is the physiotherapist. They are both appealing to the *principle of beneficence* but might hold differing views about how this benefit is to be achieved. In particular, appealing to the *principle of non-maleficence* – that is, one ought to do no harm – the physiotherapist ought not to perform any therapy which is likely to harm the individual.

In this case, the justification for appealing to these two principles seems to be based on the view that what we are trying to achieve is that outcomes be as good as possible (Parfit, 1984).

Hedonistic consequentialism

Hedonistic consequentialism is the doctrine that as much happiness be produced as possible. This classic statement of a consequentialist ethical theory was put forward by Bentham (1789) and later by Mill (1861). Both Bentham and Mill argued that the ultimate outcome to be achieved is happiness. Mill formulated this view in his famous Principle of Utility, which states: 'actions are right in proportion as they tend to promote happiness, wrong as they tend to produce the reverse of happiness. By happiness is intended pleasure, and the absence of pain; by unhappiness, pain and the privation of pleasure' (Mill, 1861, p. 257).

An advantage of this position is that it would appear to simplify ethical decision-making since all ethical decision-making, would amount to calculating the amount of pleasure and pain produced by alternative actions. Everything of value will have been reduced to a calculation about pleasure and pain. When this happens the position is described as one where all values are *commensurable*. Although this procedure might appear to simplify ethical decision-making, there is still the difficult task of determining how to measure sensations of pleasure and pain.

Interest or preference consequentialism

Owing to the difficulty of measuring sensations, contemporary consequentialists usually couple their consequentialist theories with a value theory different from the one put forward by Mill. They talk instead of good outcomes being those where the interests or preferences of those affected are maximized (Singer, 1993; Hare, 1981). By interests is meant anything an individual can desire. For example, individuals have an interest in avoiding pain, developing their abilities, and being able to pursue their life plans (Singer, 1993).

Although this position is easier to operate with than Mill's, important questions still need to be considered in conjunction with *interest or preference consequentialism*. For example, who exactly can be said to have an interest? Singer's elaboration of his theory makes it clear that not all members of the species homo sapiens can be said to have interests, and that many other species have interests just as strong if not stronger than some of the interests of our own species. Another problem will concern the measurement of conflicting interests. Both Singer and Hare propose that interest or preferences should be measured according to their strength, but how is this to be determined?

Despite these difficulties, there is a certain initial plausibility in the view that when faced with ethical issues what ought to be sought are solutions that will make outcomes as good as possible. This view is one rationale that can be provided for the principles of beneficence and non-maleficence.

Consequentialist justification of the principles of beneficence and non-maleficence

If these two principles are justified from within a consequentialist framework, a case can be made for saying that they are really not distinct principles at all but rather occur at opposite ends of a continuum (Frankena, 1973; see Box 22.1).

Beauchamp and Childress (1983) argue against this assimilation of the two principles because the range of application of the two principles is different. Whilst the

Box 22.1 *Beneficence and non-maleficence on a contimuum*

The principle of beneficence: The well-being or benefit of the individual ought to be promoted. This can be achieved by:

- increasing benefit
- removing harm
- preventing harm
- not harming.

The principle of non-maleficence: One ought to do no harm.

duty not to harm extends to everyone, we are not obliged to benefit everyone. Further, the principle of beneficence properly encompasses promoting benefit, removing harm and preventing harm since these are positive acts. However, to do no harm is an injunction to omit something and on this ground can be distinguished from the principle of beneficence.

The justifiability of drawing a distinction between acts and omissions will be considered in Chapter 23. However, this distinction is not morally important from within a consequentialist framework. This is because since the fundamental moral aim is that outcomes be as good as possible, it is irrelevant , other things being equal, whether these outcomes be produced by an action or an omission. This also has the implication that our duty to benefit might be much wider than it is commonly assumed to be.

Perhaps the most fundamental difficulty with these principles is to determine exactly what is to count as benefit and harm, and second, who is to assess this? In Case Study 22.1 both the doctor and physiotherapist were seeking to benefit the individual being treated but they had different views about what would be of benefit to that individual. What this highlights is that well-being and harm are evaluative terms and what will count as well-being and what will count as harm is dependent on who is making the evaluation. What a healthcare team considers to be of benefit for an individual receiving treatment might be very different from what that individual would regard as a benefit. The individuals life plans, spiritual beliefs, personal relationships, etc. will determine what is a benefit, and that may or may not coincide with the views of the healthcare team.

Frequently, clashes that arise between the principles of beneficence and non-maleficence, on the one hand, and the principle of autonomy on the other, are a result of a coupling of the former two principles with a paternalistic evaluation of well-being and harm. If, instead, these principles were coupled with the individuals own evaluation of what is a benefit and what is a harm, there is likely to be less conflict (Singleton and McLaren, 1995).

Consequentialist justification of the principle of autonomy

Autonomy has been defined as 'the capacity to think, decide, and act on the basis of such thought and decision freely and independently' (Gillon, 1990, p. 60). For adherents of consequentialist ethical theories, the principle of autonomy is not viewed as a fundamental right that individuals possess. The only justification for paying attention to the principle of autonomy will be if the consequences of acting in conformity with it are good. It is a derivative principle and not at the centre of a consequentialist approach which has as its linch-pin that outcomes be as good as possible. The principle of autonomy will only be supported to the extent that good outcomes can be achieved by allowing an individual to be self-governing in certain areas.

J.S. Mill's discussion of the principle of autonomy makes this point very clearly: 'The only purpose for which power can be rightfully exercised over any member of a civilized community, against his will, is to prevent harm to others. His own good, either physical or moral, is not a sufficient warrant . . . over himself, over his own body and mind, the individual is sovereign' (Mill, 1859, p. 68).

Mill's principle appears to give extensive liberty to individuals. They are to have autonomous control over their lives provided they do not harm others. This autonomy or liberty includes liberty:

- of thought and feeling, including the freedom to express and publish these thoughts;
- to choose life plans;
- to combine with others for a common purpose (Mill, 1859).

However, closer examination will reveal that in fact autonomy is quite a restrictive principle. Firstly, it is clear that it does not apply to everyone. Children and those who 'require being taken care of by others' are not included in the range of application of the principle. Mill relies on the law to determine what is to count as a child, which does not seem satisfactory. Rather, the ability to make autonomous decisions should depend on the characteristics of the individual concerned and the complexity of the decision that is required (Singleton and McLaren, 1995).

A further restriction implicit in Mill's principle becomes evident when we ask how far 'others' extend? Can an individual, for example, decide to pursue the life plan of drinking excessively? If, as a result, they require healthcare resources, this might be at the expense of someone else who also requires treatment. Many lifestyles that are adopted could also be said to harm those who might be distressed that someone has decided, for example, to take drugs.

The principle of autonomy is therefore restricted and is not fundamental within the consequentialist framework. The justification for adhering to it is that its promotion will increase utility. It is not a fundamental right that individuals possess (see Case Study 22.2).

Case Study ◗ ◗ ◗

◗ *Case Study 22.2*

Physiotherapy: Although the point is not made explicitly, the rules of professional conduct produced by the Chartered Society of Physiotherapy (1992) seem to imply that autonomy is a fundamental right. Rule 2 states that patients 'will be informed about and must be given the opportunity to consent to or to decline treatment proposals . . . Failure to warn a patient of the risks inherent in a procedure which is recommended may constitute a failure to respect the patient's right to make his own decisions.' Later in this chapter we shall examine a deontological theory that does give centrality to an individual's autonomy.

Radiography: The need to consider whether the principle of autonomy is a fundamental principle or not is also highlighted in the code of professional conduct issued by the College of Radiographers (1994). In clause 1.3 the following two claims are made: 'Radiographers should at all times act in such a way as to promote and safeguard the well being and interests of patients for whose care they are professionally accountable and ensure that by no action or omission on their part the patients' well-being or safety is placed at risk . . . Patients have a right to refuse treatment or examination and this right should be respected.' When considering the first part of this clause, it might well be considered in the professional judgement of the radiographer that a particular form of treatment is essential to an individual's well-being and that to omit treatment would place that individual at risk. However, it might be the case that the individual refuses this treatment and the second part of the clause would appear to require that the individual's decision should be respected. Critical ethical reflection is needed to clarify this important question.

Occupational therapy: The principle of autonomy is reflected in the code of ethics and professional conduct for occupational therapists (BAOT, 1995), where it is stated (2.1): 'Occupational therapists should at all times recognize and respect the autonomy of clients receiving their services, acknowledging their role in an episode of care, the need for client choice and the benefits of working in partnerships.'

Consequentialist justification of the principle of justice

An implication of taking the maximization of good outcomes as the central ethical goal is apparent in consequentialist justifications of the principle of justice. The formal statement of the principle of justice is that equals ought to be considered equally. However, although there might be agreement about this, when it comes to giving this principle some substance, there is a wide range of disagreement.

Singer (1993, p. 21) states what this principle means from within interest consequentialism: 'The essence of the principle of equal consideration of interests is that we give equal weight in our moral deliberations to the like interests of all those affected by our actions.' In other words, we are no longer talking about individuals being treated equally, but about interests. It could well be the case that the maximization of interest satisfaction could be at the expense of a very unequal treatment between individuals (see Case Study 22.3).

Case Study ◗ ◗ ◗

◗ *Case Study 22.3*

A consequentialist justification of justice has been considered in terms of the production of 'quality-adjusted life years' (QALYs) (Williams, 1985). A QALY takes a year of healthy life expectancy to be worth 1.0 and a year of unhealthy life expectancy to be worth less than 1.0, the precise value depending on how bad the quality of life is for the unhealthy person. In Singer's (1993) case, the principle that 'equals ought to be considered equally' becomes 'equal interests are to be considered equally' and here the claim is that QALYs are to be considered equally. Whilst recognizing decisions do have to be taken about the allocation of resources (see Chapter 23), this method appears to be inequitable for a number of reasons:

- The dimensions included in the concept of 'quality' are very restricted. They include physical mobility and freedom from pain and these evaluations were based on the responses of a limited number of people. (Williams, 1985).
- They fail to take account of an individual's own evaluation of quality and thus infringe an individual's autonomy (Brown *et al., 1992).*
- The autonomy of individuals will also be

infringed since the adoption of certain lifestyles will reduce the number of QALYs that can be produced; for example, treating a smoker for lung cancer (Lockwood, 1988).

- They are ageist, since the old will have less life expectancy than the young (Harris, 1988).
- They act to the disadvantage of those who require more than one treatment, since a lower QALY score will be registered.

A consequentialist justification of justice does not take into account the needs of different individuals. The prime concern is that QALYs be maximized or that interest satisfaction be maximized, but these outcomes are judged in isolation from which individuals receive these benefits. A fairer or more just way of proceeding would be to reinstate individuals at the centre of the principle of justice rather than considering what course of action would lead to a maximization of QALYs or interest satisfaction (Singleton and McLaren, 1995). A deontological justification of the principle of justice will have this effect, as will be seen in the next section.

DEONTOLOGICAL ETHICAL THEORIES

These theories hold that the rightness of an action is determined by the principle from which it is done. Case Study 22.4, reproduced from Chadwick and Tadd (1992), illustrates a consequentialist approach taken by healthcare workers, and this is contrasted with a deontological approach to this case.

Case Study

Case Study 22.4

An individual had been taking pentazocine for many years for chronic back pain. The healthcare team agreed that sterile water should be given instead, without the individual's knowledge, as it was believed that she was so addicted to this drug that it was difficult to know whether she really had pain or not. Despite her complaints of cramps, nausea and pain, the analgesia was gradually replaced with sterile water. After a few weeks, it became possible to control her pain with a milder and safer analgesic.

From a consequentialist perspective, the action of the healthcare workers would be right because this course of action resulted in the best outcome since a milder and safer analgesic was now being used. However, from within deontological theories, the rightness of actions is not determined by a consideration of consequences but is determined by the principle governing the action. In this case it would not be right to deceive the individual being treated since action on a principle that advocated deception would be wrong. This raises the question of how we are to determine which principles would make an action right and which would make it wrong.

The classic formulation of a deontological theory given by Kant provides a way of testing whether or not a proposed principle would in fact make an action right. He called the proposed test the 'categorical imperative', and it is first formulated as: 'Act only on that maxim through which you can at the same time will that it should become a universal law' (Kant, 1785, p. 84).

A maxim is just a rule or principle that is followed in action. For example, an individual who decides to commit suicide because life has become unbearable could be acting on the principle that life should be ended whenever it becomes too painful. Not all principles could pass the test incorporated in the categorical imperative and become universal laws. The principle just given about suicide would not pass this test and neither, according to Kant, would a principle of telling lies. In outline this means when someone tells a lie then they cannot will that everyone else will also tell lies. They cannot will that there be a universal law of lying, since if there were then their lie would not be believed. The efficacy of a lie is dependent on other people telling the truth.

Kant gives five different formulations of the categorical imperative, but it can be argued (O'Neill, 1989) that they amount to the same thing. The different formulations highlight the different aspects of the categorical imperative. For example, The Formula of the End in Itself states 'Act in such a way that you always treat humanity, . . . never simply as a means but always at the same time as an end' (Kant, 1785, p. 91). In Case Study 22.4, the individual taking the painkiller was being treated solely as a means towards a further end, namely, weaning from the drug. This is not legitimate since she is not being recognized as another individual who can also have ends. This principle of deception could not be universalized since this is not an end that the individual taking the painkiller would share. This position will be explained in greater detail when deontological justifications of the principles of beneficence, non-maleficence, autonomy and justice are considered.

Deontological justification of the principles of beneficence and non-maleficence

Unlike a consequentialist justification for these principles which places them on a continuum (see Box 22.1), a deontological justification of these two principles distinguishes them. Kant argues that the principle of non-maleficence is a *perfect duty* and the principle of beneficence an *imperfect duty*. Perfect duties are those that do not allow of any exceptions (Kant, 1785, p. 85). The principle of non-maleficence is one which allows no exceptions since it is a perfect duty. However, inclinations can be consulted in the case of the principle of beneficence. An individual can decide how to promote well-being; for example, well-being can be promoted by helping with famine relief in various parts of the world, or by doing social work at home.

Deontological justification of the principle of autonomy

Kant's justification of the principle of autonomy is given by him as 'the idea of the will of every rational being as a will which makes universal law' (Kant, 1785, p. 93). Individuals as rational beings exercise their autonomy by originating universal laws.

On the face of it this might seem to be a denial of autonomy. A restriction is being placed on principles of action to the effect that they must be universalizable. However, this is an erroneous impression. This is not an external restriction that is limiting autonomy, but rather the expression of autonomy requires action on principles that can be universalized. Rational action consists in making universal laws.

This last point connects with the point made above when discussing the Formula of the End in Itself. Other individuals are also authors of universal laws and this must be reflected in any principles upon which an individual acts. The recognition that other individuals are autonomous agents must not be lost sight of in daily practice. For example, within a radiography department there might be a tendency to forget that one is dealing with autonomous individuals by referring to individuals by their condition rather than directly. It is not uncommon to hear the individual referred to as 'the chest X-ray' or as 'a foot waiting in the corridor'.

IS THE PRINCIPLE OF AUTONOMY A FUNDAMENTAL RIGHT?

Unlike Mill, Kant is not arguing for the acceptance of the principle of autonomy on the ground that its adoption will lead to good consequences. Acting on principles that can become universal laws is not good because of the consequences this might achieve. Rather, acting on these principles is what makes an action morally right and it is this in which its rightness consists.

In summary, rational individuals exercise their autonomy by acting on principles that can be universalized, and this involves the recognition that other individuals are also autonomous agents and must be treated as such rather than as a means to a further end. They must be respected as autonomous individuals.

Deontological justification of the principle of justice

A largely deontological justification of a principle of justice has been given by John Rawls (1976). The proposal favoured by him is that the principles chosen should be be selected from behind a 'veil of ignorance'. This 'veil' would conceal an individual's position in society, the individual's natural attributes and the individual's social circumstances. These principles would be fair because they would not be based on accidental advantages that certain people might happen to possess. The following is the initial formulation of the principles he arrived at: 'First: each person is to have an equal right to the most extensive basic liberty compatible with a similar liberty for others. Second: social and economic inequalities are to be arranged so that they are both (a) reasonably expected to be to everyone's advantage, and (b) attached to positions and offices open to all' (Rawls, 1976, p. 60).

This first principle, which is a principle of liberty or autonomy, is intended to include freedoms such as thought, speech, political freedom and freedom to adopt different life plans. This principle has priority over the second one, since Rawls considers that autonomy is not to be sacrificed for greater social or economic advantage. The principle of autonomy is being taken to have intrinsic worth; it is being given a deontological justification and is not being justified on consequentialist grounds.

Within the second principle, (b) has priority over (a) so that just as the second principle does not come into play until the first is satisfied, so (a) is not considered until (b) is satisfied. The principles, therefore, that Rawls proposes have a hierarchical ordering and it is clear that the deontological first principle is fundamental. In the section that follows, an example from within healthcare will illustrate how this approach to a justification of the principle of justice differs from a consequentialist approach.

► AN EVALUATION OF CONSEQUENTIALIST AND DEONTOLOGICAL ETHICAL THEORIES

Perhaps the major point of difference between these two approaches is what is placed at the centre of each. For consequentialist theories, what has fundamental or intrinsic worth is the particular commodity that is taken to constitute a good outcome. As has been seen, it might be the maximization of happiness or interest or preference satisfaction or QALYs that is taken to be of ultimate value. In contrast, for deontological theories, individuals are at the centre. There are, for example, certain constraints on what individuals can do to each other even if it is thought that a good outcome in a consequentialist sense can be produced.

An implication of these different approaches in the area of justice can be seen in the example in Case Study 22.5 (Veatch, 1981; Singleton and McLaren, 1995).

Case Study ► ► ►

► *Case Study 22.5*

A proposal to spend more money on people with learning difficulties is being considered, by withdrawing them from large state-run institutions and housing them in smaller community-based homes. Is this a just way to spend some of the health budget? The claim is that the quality of life of these individuals will be greatly enhanced if they are rehoused in this way.

The alternative use for this money would be to spend it on healthcare for three other groups: predominantly normal children, adults of working age, and pregnant women who smoke. Many more children could be treated on this programme than on the former programme, and one result of healthcare for pregnant women would be fewer babies who will experience learning difficulties.

In order to arrive at a final decision about the just way to allocate resources in this sort of case, more information would be needed. However, the purpose of the example is to illustrate the different approaches that would be taken from within consequentialist theories and deontological theories. For example, if a QALY approach were adopted, the just way to distribute resources between these alternative proposals would depend on how many QALYs and their cost each approach would yield. The number and status of the individuals in the first programme are likely to yield less QALYs than in the second programme.

However, if an approach such as that suggested by Rawls were adopted, then it would become important to ensure that those at present in institutions have as much liberty as possible. Also, they are arguably part of the least advantaged section of society, so social and economic inequalities should be arranged to their greatest benefit. This approach might favour the first programme as the more just way to spend the resources in question. What this second approach illustrates is a concern for the needs of individuals and their equal treatment, rather than an equal consideration of QALYs abstracted from the individuals who are to be benefited.

These two different approaches will be seen at work in the next chapter when some specific areas of concern in healthcare will be examined.

Learning Activity 1 ◆ ◆ ◆

Apply a deontological approach and a consequentialist approach to three or four ethical dilemmas from your own practice. You might find it helpful to work through this process with a friend or colleague.

SUMMARY

An initial account has been given of two different approaches to ethical dilemmas that are characterized by consequentialist and deontological ethical theories. Often, the adoption of one or other of these approaches to ethical decision-making is not made explicit. An understanding of these possible approaches will assist critical ethical reflection about ethical dilemmas encountered in practice.

Key Points

- Two ethical theories have been considered: consequentialist and deontological.
- Within consequentialism two branches have been identified: hedonistic and interest/preference.
- Each theory is able to provide a framework for the justification of the four ethical principles.
- A comparison of the two theories highlights their core differences.

References

Bentham, J. (1789). An introduction to the principles of morals and legislation. In: Warnock, M. (ed.) (1968), *Utilitarianism of John Stuart Mill*. London: Fontana, 33–77.

Beauchamp, T.L. and Childress, J.F. (1983). *Principles of Biomedical Ethics*, 2nd edn. New York: Oxford University Press.

British Association of Occupational Therapists (1995). *Code of Ethics and Professional Conduct*.

Brown, J., Kitson, A. and McKnight, T. (1992). *Challenges in Caring: Explanation in Nursing and Ethics*. London: Chapman & Hall.

Chadwick, R. and Tadd, W. (1992). *Ethics and Nursing Practice*. Basingstoke: Macmillan.

Chartered Society of Physiotherapy (1992). *Rules of Professional Conduct*.

College of Radiographers (1994). *Code of Professional Conduct*.

Frankena, W.K. (1973). *Ethics*, 2nd edn. Englewood Cliffs, NJ: Prentice-Hall.

Gillon, R. (1990). *Philosophical Medical Ethics*. Chichester: Wiley.

Hare, R.M. (1981). *Moral Thinking: Its Levels, Method and Point*. Oxford: Oxford University Press.

Harris, J. (1988). More and better justice. In: Bell, J.M. and Mendus, S. (eds), *Philosophy and Medical Welfare*. Cambridge: Cambridge University Press.

Kant, I. (1785). Groundwork of the metaphysic of morals. In: Paton, H.J. (trans.) (1966), *The Moral Law*. London: Hutchinson.

Lockwood, M. (1988). Quality of life and resource allocation. In: Bell, J.M. and Mendus, S. (eds), *Philosophy and Medical Welfare*. Cambridge: Cambridge University Press.

Mill, J.S. (1859). On liberty. In: Himmelfarb, G. (ed.) (1985), *John Stuart Mill On Liberty*. Harmondsworth: Penguin, 59–187.

Mill, J.S. (1861). Utilitarianism. In: Warnock, M. (ed.) (1968), *Utilitarianism of John Stuart Mill*. London: Fontana, 251–321.

O'Neill, O. (1990). *Constructions of Reason: Explorations of Kant's Practical Philosophy*. New York: Cambridge University Press.

Parfit, D. (1984). *Reasons and Persons*. Oxford: Clarendon.

Rawls, J. (1976). *A Theory of Justice*. Oxford: Oxford University Press.

Singer, P. (1993). *Practical Ethics*, 2nd edn. New York: Cambridge University Press.

Singleton, J. and McLaren, S.M. (1995). *Ethical Foundations of Health Care*. London: C.V. Mosby.

Veatch, R.M. (1981). *A Theory of Medical Ethics*. New York: Basic Books.

Williams, A. (1985). Economics of coronary artery by pass grafting. *British Medical Journal*, **291**: 326–9.

Further Reading

Bell, J.M. and Mendus, S. (eds) (1988). *Philosophy and Medical Welfare*. Cambridge: Cambridge University Press.

23

Ethical Decision-Making

Jane Singleton

LEARNING OBJECTIVES

After studying this chapter you should:

- Be able to give an ethical analysis of dilemmas encountered in healthcare practice using the models described
- Be able to reflect critically on possible answers to the question of who should take ethical decisions in healthcare
- Understand the ethical underpinning of informed consent and the different factors that have to be considered for informed consent to be possible
- Be able to assess critically the justifications that can be provided for telling the truth, and evaluate the merits of possible exceptions to this principle
- Be able to assess critically the justifications that can be provided for a principle for the maintenance of confidentiality, and evaluate the merits of possible exceptions to this principle
- Appreciate the type of ethical analysis needed when reflecting on life and death issues
- Be in a position to apply the points discussed in the chapter to ethical dilemmas encountered by healthcare professionals

INTRODUCTION

The analysis of principles and the justifying frameworks of consequentialist and deontological theories discussed in the previous two chapters is designed to assist in the reflection on ethical problems that arise in healthcare. Clarification of the issues in this way should assist decision-making and increase the understanding that individuals have of different ethical views to their own. The development of skill in ethical analysis is an essential prerequisite for ethical decision-making. Case Study 23.1 is used to illustrate this process at work, and the discussion of the issues in the rest of the chapter will also provide further examples.

Case Study

Case Study 23.1

An individual has been referred by a medical practitioner to a physiotherapist for palliative treatment. Although the physiotherapist considers the treatment would be of benefit to this individual, scarce resources lead them to decline to perform any therapy. Is this decision justifiable?

ETHICAL PRINCIPLES IN DECISION-MAKING

The first step is to isolate the principles that are being implicitly appealed to in Case Study 23.1, then to look closely at the meaning and implications of the principle adopted by the physiotherapist. The analysis therefore goes like this:

- isolation of principles;
- meaning of principles;
- implications of principles;
- change or qualification of principles.

Isolation of the principle underpinning the physiotherapist's decision

Principle of beneficence

Presumably, the medical practitioner was appealing to the principle of beneficence when he referred this individual. The well-being of this individual ought to be promoted and it can be promoted by physiotherapy. Also, for the purposes of this example, it can be assumed that the individual concerned considers the treatment will be beneficial. After all, the Patient's Charter (1992) lists as one existing right, the right 'to be given a clear explanation of any treatment proposed, including any risks and any alternatives, before you decide whether you will agree to the treatment'. Finally, it is a further assumption of this example that the physiotherapist also believes the treatment will be of benefit to the individual.

Principle of justice

However, the physiotherapist overrides this principle of beneficence in favour of the principle of justice, the view of the physiotherapist being that giving this treatment is not justified in terms of available resources. A just distribution of resources would not include allocating resources to this treatment. This decision also overrides the principle of autonomy, the right to be self-governing, since the individual is not being given the treatment he wants.

Principle of non-maleficence

It might be argued that in refusing to treat this individual the physiotherapist is harming the individual, and thus violating the principle that one ought to do no harm. The physiotherapist might well argue here that there has been no positive act of harm, only an omission to do something. However, this defence will only work if it can be shown that there is a moral difference between acts and omissions. In this particular case, this position would be hard to defend because of the nature of the omission. A conscious evaluation of the case has been made and the decision not to treat would more accurately be described as an act of omission.

Not all omissions are of this sort. Some might be the result of forgetfulness; others arise because the alternatives that have been omitted have not even been considered. However, when an alternative has been considered and a decision is taken to omit treatment then this is more properly described as an act of omission.

The meaning of the physiotherapist's specific principle of justice

It is important to identify to what precise principle the physiotherapist is appealing when the treatment is denied. Presumably, it might be that, as the treatment is purely palliative and there are only sufficient resources for potentially curative treatments, then the curative treatments take priority.

However, what might justify this claim? A possible candidate might be the consequentialist claim that the consequences of spending money treating individuals who have a chance of their condition being cured are better than the consequences where treatment will not cure the condition but only provide a relief from the symptoms. Palliative treatment is not likely to receive a very high QALY score (Chapter 22) compared with potentially curative treatments.

It is not likely that this principle is being justified on deontological grounds. The individual seeking palliative treatment is going to continue suffering from their complaint and is arguably in greater need than the individual whose discomfort is temporary and will end after treatment.

Implications of this principle

At this point it is useful to consider the implications of adopting the specific principle appealed to by the physiotherapist as a basis for the decision taken. What would be the result if this principle were applied in other situations? For example, would acceptance of this principle mean that resources should be diverted away from, say, the hospice movement as only palliative care can be offered? Presumably, a consequentialist calculation would not justify many resources being devoted to the hospice movement as insufficient QALYs would be generated. The aspects of quality such as mobility, reduced pain, length of life and employment that have been used in the development of the QALY are not likely to favour the hospice movement.

Change or qualification of the physiotherapist's original principle

When these implications are pointed out, the physiotherapist might not wish to adhere to his or her original justification. This method of analysis has highlighted some of the implicit assumptions in the position taken, and indicated the implications that this justification could have for other cases. It does not provide a *formula* that can be used to generate ethical conclusions, but a *procedure* to assist critical reflection about the difficult dilemmas that are faced in healthcare. Other frameworks have been described in the literature (Griepp, 1992; Seedhouse, 1988).

Griepp's model accepts uncritically a deontological base for ethical decision-making, where individuals are regarded as ends in themselves. There is no discussion of the relative merits of a consequentialist framework. Also, whilst it emphasizes that decision-making is a collaborative process between the individual and healthcare team, it is only members of the healthcare team that consider the application of the ethical principles of autonomy, beneficence, non-maleficence and justice. Surely, if decision-making is to be truly collaborative and the autonomy of individuals as ends in themselves is to be fully recognized, then the application of these principles must not be limited to members of the healthcare profession.

Seedhouse suggests four different levels for comprehensive ethical deliberation, involving a consideration of:

- core rationale – the principles behind health work (creation of, and respect for autonomy);
- deontological layer – the duties of health professionals (truth-telling, non-maleficence, beneficence and promise-keeping);
- consequentialist layer – the beneficial outcomes of the proposed interventions;
- external considerations – external factors, such as codes of practice, resources and the law.

Learning Activity 1

Now that you have read the above example of ethical analysis, apply the same process to the principles that might guide the health professionals in case Studies 23.2 and 23.3.

Case Study

Case Study 23.2

A male occupational therapist needs to carry out a full dressing assessment on a young woman who is unable to dress herself. He is the only qualified OT available who is able to carry out this important assessment, but the young woman declines the assessment. From the OT's point of view the best outcome would be for the assessment to be undertaken, but from the perspective of the young woman the problems encountered dressing herself have to be set in the context of how important it is to her not to have this assessment undertaken by a male OT.

Case Study 23.3

In what is known as the Sidaway case, a medical practitioner failed to warn a woman of a 1 in 100 risk of damage associated with an operation on her spinal column. The damage occurred even though the risk was not great. The amount of information given to the woman was that accepted as proper by a responsible body of medical opinion. Conclusions about what would count as sufficient information for informed consent have therefore been deduced from this case.

WHO TAKES THE DECISION?

In the past, individuals seeking healthcare were not consulted in the decision-making process. The biomedical model of health lends support to this paternalistic approach to decision-making. The individual is viewed as a body which is in good or bad working order. However, the recognition that individuals have life plans and values of their own makes it imperative that decision-making be undertaken as a collaborative exercise between the individual and a team of healthcare professionals. Ellos (1990, pp. 171–2) writes: 'We should listen to patient preferences in terms of their own perceived quality of life. We should not be too aggressive in attempting to change or influence the patients' own life plans, goals and aims into which medical intervention fits as only one part or aspect.' The importance of recognizing an individual's life plans and values is illustrated in the examples in Case Study 23.4.

Case Study

Case Study 23.4

An occupational therapist might refuse to allow an individual to leave a closed group session to attend a ten-minute prayer meeting that is part of his or her religious beliefs. The cult to which the person belongs is considered a fringe group and is therefore viewed as not important. In another case, a physiotherapist has to treat a woman whose religious beliefs entail that she should expose her body only to another woman, and this factor needs to be reflected in any plans for treatment. Finally, a radiographer who needs an individual to starve before an examination needs to consider the person's perspective with respect to this request. Has this particular individual just been fasting as part of his or her religious beliefs?

The proposed interventions must be seen in the context of an individual's life plans and values and for this it is necessary that the decision-making process is a shared activity.

For this collaborative process of decision-making to work, there must be effective information exchange between the individual and members of the healthcare team. The issues of informed consent, truth-telling and confidentiality that are essential components in a model of decision-making as a collaborative process will therefore need to be examined. Another central factor in this approach is the need to be able to determine whether or not an individual has the required level of competence to reach a decision. How this might be determined will also be addressed. These decision-making factors will be examined in the differing contexts encountered in healthcare where ethical dilemmas arise.

INFORMED CONSENT

For there to be effective shared decision-making between individuals and those in healthcare, the self-governing nature of the individual needs to be reflected upon. The individual's autonomy needs to be respected, and this autonomy is limited if adequate information is not provided to allow a person to be self-governing. As Beauchamp and Childress (1983) write: 'The primary function of informed consent is the protection and promotion of individual autonomy.'

It has been shown in Chapter 22 that the principle of autonomy can be justified from within a deontological or consequentialist framework. The former framework gives intrinsic worth to the requirement to respect the autonomy of individuals. Individuals are to be treated as ends in themselves and as authors of moral principles. The consequentialist framework justifies the principle of autonomy on the grounds that it will produce good consequences. Since it is not valued in its own right, a consequentialist justification could yield the conclusion that it is justifiable to override a person's autonomy if the consequences would thereby be better.

Box 23.1 *Criteria for informed consent*

Criteria needed to assess an individual's competence to consent:

- outcome test
- status test
- the individual's capacity to understand the specific decision

Sufficient information must be given based on:

- professional practice standard
- reasonable person standard
- reasonable person standard plus the specific needs of the individual

The truth must be told according to:

- deontological justification
- consequentialist justification

Presentation of the information in respect to:

- timing
- type of materials

Type of informed consent:

- daily practice
- therapeutic research
- non-therapeutic research

For example, it might be judged that an individual dying of cancer may be happier if the true diagnosis is not revealed. This decision would clearly limit the individual's ability to take part in shared decision-making about the management of their case.

Criteria for informed consent

For informed consent to be valid there are a number of criteria that should be fufilled (see Box 23.1). The first set of criteria concern the individual who is required to make an autonomous decision.

CHARACTERISTICS FOR COMPETENCY TO CONSENT

The characteristics that an individual needs can only be considered contextually as they will depend on the complexity of the decision to be made. For example, the level of rationality and maturity necessary to take a decision about what to wear would not be so demanding as that required for a decision about whether or not to donate a kidney. This same point can be made in the case of people with learning difficulties when the degree of rationality and maturity required to make many simple everyday decisions might be present but this capability might not be deemed sufficient to take decisions – for example, about whether to undergo sterilization.

Given that there is this contextual variability, consideration should be given to what empirical criteria should be used to determine whether or not an individual does possess the ability to take decisions and give consent to a particular intervention.

CRITERIA FOR DETERMINING THE ABILITY TO GIVE CONSENT

The outcome test

This judges the ability of the individual by the decision they take (Kennedy, 1985). However, this has the potential for abuse, since if the carers disagree with the decision taken, this could be used as grounds for indicating that the individual was not capable of taking the decision and hence not competent to consent.

This abuse could occur if someone were using a consequentialist justification of autonomy, since it might be considered the best outcome would be achieved if the individual were not allowed to take such a decision. In addition, it is being assumed by the healthcarers that their evaluation of what is to count as the best outcome is better than that of the individual in question (refer back to Case Study 23.2).

The status test

If the outcome test is rejected, the ability to consent might be based on the status of the individual. Perhaps particular statuses carry with them certain capacities. However, unless a class has been defined in these terms then this would not follow. Also, even if it did, blanket inclusions or exclusions would not be appropriate since the competence required is dependent on the complexity of the decision required.

Ability to understand the specific decision

What seems to be needed is something along the lines of the individual's capacity to comprehend the nature and consequences of the required decision. This would involve not just considering this capacity in isolation but within the context of, for example, the individual's emotional state at the time the decision is required. However, difficult cases might still be encountered. What should be said about the decision of someone who satisfies these criteria but adopts a life plan that involves self-mutilation? This person's belief in God has led him or her to think that God requires these sacrifices in order to prevent even greater harm to the rest of humanity. This decision is consistent with their belief system and consistency would appear to be at least one of the marks of rationality.

HOW MUCH INFORMATION IS NEEDED FOR INFORMED CONSENT?

For an individual to give informed consent there needs to be sufficient information to allow an autonomous choice. But how is it to be determined what is to count as sufficient information? There are two widely discussed standards of disclosure.

The professional practice standard

The amount of information required to be disclosed is determined by the traditional practices of a professional community. More specifically, a health practitioner is not wrong to withhold information if other practitioners in the same area would generally agree that this was right. This view was taken in the UK in the Sidaway case in 1985, where the information adjured by the judges as reasonable was that accepted as proper by a responsible body of medical opinion, that is, by peer review (refer back to Case Study 23.3).

The objection to this standard is that it does not recognize the autonomy of individuals as something of intrinsic worth. Implicitly it rejects a deontological justification in favour of a consequentialist framework. The individual is being regarded as a means towards an end that the health practitioner considered will be in their best interests.

The reasonable person standard

This advocates that the amount of information required for informed consent is determined by reference to what a hypothetical reasonable person in this situation would consider to be sufficient. One of the advantages of this standard is that it emphasizes the role of the individual who has to take the decision to determine what will count as sufficient information. This is in opposition to the paternalistic approach incorporated in the first standard. It is closer to a recognition of the individuals' autonomy as something that has intrinsic worth and is thus operating from within a deontological framework.

Different decisions might be taken depending on which standard is applied (see Case Study 23.5).

Case Study ◗ ◗ ◗

◗ *Case Study 23.5*

Consider a case of giving information about a particular invasive procedure. It might be proposed to give a barium enema to an elderly individual suffering from terminal cancer. If the professional practice standard of disclosure were applied, then the details of the procedure would be described to the individual. However, if a reasonable person standard were applied then this information might be supplemented by information about what the function of this test might be and whether it is necessary.

The hypothetical reasonable person might wish to consider whether the results of this distressing examination are likely to be acted upon or whether the whole examination would just be an information gathering exercise.

The reasonable person standard plus the specific needs of the individual

Arguably, if the principle of autonomy is viewed as having intrinsic worth, then it is necessary to go even further than the reasonable person standard. In addition to what a reasonable person would require to know, it might also be necessary to provide additional information depending on the specific needs of the particular individual concerned. The justification for this is that the principle of autonomy is being given intrinsic worth and therefore enough information must be present for the individual to give informed consent

◗ TELLING THE TRUTH

A second element in the situation that needs to be present for informed consent is that the truth be told. Telling the truth can be justified on both deontological and consequentialist grounds.

For example, Kant would argue that a universal law of lying would not pass the test of the 'categorical imperative'. It is an absolute duty to tell the truth. While this might seem rather an extreme position, deontological frameworks have been suggested which retain the view that truth-telling has intrinsic worth without claiming that it is always an absolute duty to tell the truth (Ross, 1930). Truth-telling is regarded by Ross as a prima facie duty and when there is a conflict between prima facie duties then we shall have to reflect which one is our absolute duty.

Consequentialists, on the other hand, consider the effects of not telling the truth. For example, not telling the truth could lead to the destruction of trust, cooperation and interaction. However, it might be the case that in some instances it is considered that better consequences would be achieved if the truth were not told, and this is clearly a possibility if a consequentialist justification is adopted. If this were the case, then this would undermine the ability of the individual to give informed consent. The consequences from the perspective of the healthcarer are viewed as being better for the individual if that individual does not know the whole truth. Leslie (1954) writes: 'Deception is completely moral when it is used for the benefit of the patient.' It is claimed that 'therapeutic privilege' allows healthcarers to set aside the normal duty of disclosure in favour of what they take to be the best outcome for the individual being treated.

However, in this type of case it can be seen that the application of the principles of beneficence and nonmaleficence is being coupled with the carer's evaluation of what they consider would count as benefit or harm for the particular individual. As was recognized in the last chapter, benefit and harm are evaluative concepts and the evaluation of the carer might not coincide with that of the individual. The individual is not being allowed to make his own evaluation of benefits and harms if he is not being told the truth.

How the information is presented

A third point that needs to be considered is how the information is to be presented in order that an individual may exercise autonomy and give informed consent. Different individuals' capacities to comprehend will need to be considered when deciding on the timing and the presentation of the material. For example, are interviews or videos or brochures, etc. appropriate for this particular individual and at what stage should the information be presented? The importance of this point can be seen in Case Study 23.6.

Case Study

Case Study 23.6

A senior occupational therapist has been asked to make a splint for an elderly lady who has a compound fracture of the upper limb. The lady is nervous and apprehensive on attending the very open and busy OT department. The OT instructs the lady to take off her coat, jumper and vest so the whole of the upper limb is exposed. Asking for her consent to this procedure at this stage in such a public place would clearly be inappropriate.

When is informed consent necessary?

There has been much debate about when informed consent should be used to protect and promote an individual's autonomy. Gillon (1989) argues that in non-therapeutic research, where the benefit is intended for other individuals, the concept of informed consent is different from that of daily practice where the individual is not being used to benefit others. He writes (1989, p. 5): 'A "double standard" is not just acceptable but imperative.' That is, there are two different types of informed consent. One is appropriate for daily practice and therapeutic research, and the other is appropriate for non-therapeutic research. In the case of daily practice and therapeutic research, Gillon argues that implied consent is normal and proper.

However, this does not seem adequate to protect the individual's autonomy. Explicit, fully informed consent which Gillon accepts is necessary for non-therapeutic research is also necessary for therapeutic research and for daily practice. Gillon's distinction between daily practice and non-therapeutic research is based on who is to benefit and the fact that in daily practice a member of the healthcare team will only risk harm to an individual if that will benefit the individual overall. However, what needs to be recognized is that benefit and harm are evaluative terms, and protection and promotion of the autonomy of individuals requires that individuals be allowed to judge what they consider to be of benefit and what risks of harm they are prepared to take. For this to be possible, explicit, fully informed consent needs to be given to avoid the paternalistic evaluation of benefits and harms that are likely if Gillon's approach of 'implied consent' is adopted.

CONFIDENTIALITY

For decision-making to be a collaborative process, there must be trust that information disclosed by the individual seeking treatment will remain confidential. If this is not the case, individuals might be deterred from seeking help and might also be reluctant to disclose all the information necessary for effective decision-making.

The importance of maintaining confidentiality is recognized in the ethical codes governing practice. In the code for radiographers this requirement is listed first, and in the code for occupational therapists confidentiality is discussed in the second. However, it is only listed under Rule 6 in the code issued for physiotherapists.

The moral justification for confidentially lies with the principle of autonomy which can have a consequentialist or deontological justification. In certain areas individuals have a right to be self-governing, which is only possible when the individual has control over what can be known about him or her. In order to protect our privacy, there must be an assurance of confidentiality in the disclosure of information so that the individual retains control over personal information and access to that information (Beauchamp and Childress, 1983).

From a consequentialist perspective (Mill, 1859), the duty to maintain confidentiality is not a duty with intrinsic worth but is justified in terms of its consequences. It could thus be overridden to prevent harmful consequences. From a deontological perspective, the view taken may be that the duty to maintain confidentiality is a prima facie duty (Ross, 1930), which can be overridden in certain cases when it conflicts with other prima facie duties. Possible exceptions to the duty to maintain confidentiality are (see also Case Study 23.7):

- where the individual has given consent;
- for the purpose of communication of information within the healthcare team;
- where there is a legal requirement;
- where this is necessary to protect the health and safety of others.

Case Study ❱ ❱ ❱

❱ *Case Study 23.7*

An exception to confidentiality would appear to be the communication of information about an individual within the healthcare team when that is deemed to be in the individual's best interest. If access to medical/nursing records were denied to a physiotherapist treating an individual suffering from a neurological disorder who was vulnerable to the sudden onset of epileptic fits, then there would be the risk of accidental injury (Singleton and McLaren, 1995). In the codes of conduct for physiotherapy, radiography and occupational therapy, permission to disclose confidential information is allowable if there is a legal requirement to do so. However, the moral requirement to obey the law can be overridden – for example, to fulfil a responsibility to the individual being treated (Beauchamp and Childress, 1983, p. 235).

Although the maintenance of confidentiality is not an absolute duty, breaches of it require justification. The assurance that information will remain confidential is essential for cooperative, shared decision-making between recipients of healthcare and healthcare professionals.

For decision-making to be a truly collaborative process between the healthcare team and an individual, certain conditions need to be present to allow an individual to give informed consent to possible interventions. These conditions are:

- the characteristics of the individual who is required to consent;
- how much information is needed;
- telling the truth;
- how the information is presented;
- how the informed consent should be given;
- confidentiality.

Learning Activity 2 ◆ ◆ ◆

A psychiatrist disclosed information about an individual he was treating. This individual had an interest in making bombs and the psychiatrist disclosed this to the medical director of the hospital and to the Home Office (Brahams, 1988, p. 1503).

In the context of cases like this, consider in small groups the following questions:

◆ Is this breach of confidence really necessary to prevent harm to others?

◆ How likely is it that this harm will occur?

◆ How serious is the possible harm?

◆ Can this harm be prevented by other means rather than revealing confidential information?

❱ LIFE OR DEATH DILEMMAS

As well as these ethical issues in information exchange which are central to collaborative decision-making, there are also specific dilemmas that need to be considered to assist decision making. The two cases, in Case Study 23.8 illustrate the importance of reflecting on life and death issues.

Case Study ❱ ❱ ❱

❱ *Case Study 23.8*

A physiotherapist is giving treatment to an individual who is brain dead, in order that his organs may be used for transplant surgery. This is a difficult situation, particularly with respect to the relations the physiotherapist has with the individual's relatives.

A radiotherapy radiographer might be giving palliative treatment to an individual with spinal metastases. Although any decision to stop this treatment is one that is taken by the medical consultant, the radiographer might well feel that the quality of this individual's life is such that treatment ought not to be continued.

The scope of this chapter precludes an in-depth discussion of these cases and a detailed analysis of all the ethical issues surrounding death, but the following points indicate the problematic issues that need to be addressed (see Box 23.2).

Box 23.2 *Some problems to consider with life or death issues*

- What counts as death?
- How long should life be prolonged?
- Is it justifiable to forgo treatment and, if so, in what circumstances?
- Is euthanasia justifiable?

One of the problems highlighted by the first case is that, although the individual is brain dead, he is being treated as though he were alive. As the Danish Council of Ethics (Rix, 1990) has pointed out, brain death does not correspond with what individuals expect in their everyday experience of death. Ordinarily, an individual is not considered to have died while there is still respiration and heartbeat, which is compatible with brain death.

This discussion is part of the wider question of what exactly constitutes life and what counts as death (Lamb, 1985, 1990). Answers to these questions imply an evaluation of a certain state, and it is important that the evaluative nature of these definitions of life and death is made explicit.

In the second case, the question was raised about how long to prolong an individual's radiotherapy. Decisions concerning the prolongation of life can be viewed from within the wider context of other similar decisions, such as whether to forgo treatment or whether euthanasia is justifiable. In considering these questions, the Stanley Report (1992) pointed out the importance of considering them with respect to three classes of individuals:

- those who have decision-making capacity or have issued advance directives;
- those who have lost decision-making capacity and have not executed an advance directive;
- those who have never achieved decision-making capacity.

The first class of cases would clearly involve the principle of autonomy, since these are individuals capable of making decisions. The principles of beneficence and non-maleficence are also clearly relevant. In addition, the principle of justice has to be considered when taking decisions about the prolongation of life, since scarce resources might mean not every request for the prolongation of life can be granted. As has been seen in Chapter 22, interpretations of these principles within deontological or consequentialist frameworks might yield very different outcomes.

The last two groups of individuals distinguished in the Stanley Report will raise similar issues to those discussed above, except that in the case of the last group the principle of autonomy will not be applicable.

In the second group of individuals the application or not of the principle of autonomy will have to be carefully considered. The individuals could be regarded as not being autonomous. Alternatively, the recognition of their previous status as autonomous agents could be reflected by ascertaining from those who were close to them what their wishes might have been about these issues.

Finally, when considering questions about the prolongation (or not) of life, it is important to consider both duration and the quality of life (Singleton and Goodinson, 1989). This was recognized explicitly in the second example in Case Study 23.8, where the radiographer was concentrating on the quality of the individual's life. Guidelines issued by the British Medical Association (1993) about 'do not resuscitate' (DNR) orders recognize both the importance of acknowledging individual autonomy and the importance of quality-of-life considerations (see Box 23.3).

Box 23.3 *BMA guidelines for Do Not Resuscitate (DNR) orders*

The guidelines state that DNR decisions are to be considered when cardiopulmonary resuscitation (CPR) is:

- unlikely to be successful owing to the patient's condition;
- not in accord with the patient's wishes;
- likely to be followed by a length and quality of life which would not be acceptable to the patient.

SUMMARY

The foregoing examples of ethical dilemmas in life or death are intended to provide an illustration of the issues that would need to be considered when subjecting these problems to a critical ethical analysis. Coupled with the ethical issues in information exchange which are central to collaborative decision-making, this should provide at least a starting point for the critical ethical analysis that is necessary for healthcare professionals in the course of their practice.

Key Points ■ ■ ■

❏ Analysis of ethical dilemmas requires the decision-making principle involved to be isolated, then the meaning and implications of this principle to be considered.

❏ Informed consent requires a consideration of the individual's competence, amount of information required, truth-telling and presentation of information.

❏ For decision-making to be a collaborative process, the information disclosed by the individual should normally remain confidential.

❏ When viewing life or death dilemmas, there are important issues to be considered in a critical ethical analysis.

References ▼ ▼ ▼

Beauchamp, T.L. and Childress, J.F. (1983). *Principles of Biomedical Ethics*, 2nd edn. New York: Oxford University Press.

Brahams, D. (1988). A psychiatrist's duty of confidentiality. *Lancet*, **24**: 1503–4

British Association of Occupational Therapists (1995). *Code of Ethics and Professional Conduct*.

British Medical Association (1993). *Guidelines: Decisions Relating to Cardiopulmonary Resuscitation*. London: BMA.

Chartered Society of Physiotherapy (1992). *Rules of Professional Conduct*.

College of Radiographers (1994). *Code of Professional Conduct*.

Ellos, W.J. (1990). *Ethical Practice in Clinical Medicine*. London: Routledge.

Gillon, R. (1989). Medical treatment, medical research and informed consent. *Journal of Medical Ethics*, **15**: 3–5,11.

Griepp, M.E. (1992). Griepp's model of ethical decision-making. *Journal of Advanced Nursing*, **17**: 734–8.

Kennedy, I. (1985). The doctor, the pill, and the fifteen year old girl: a case study in medical ethics and law. In: Lockwood, M. (ed.), *Moral Dilemmas in Modern Medicine*. Oxford: Oxford University Press.

Lamb, D. (1985). *Brain Death and Ethics*. London: Croom Helm.

Lamb, D. (1990). *Transplants and Ethics*. London: Routledge.

Leslie, A. (1954). Ethics and the practice of placebo therapy. *American Journal of Medicine*, **16**: 854–62.

Mills, J.S. (1859). On liberty. In: Himmelfart, G. (ed.) (1985). *John Stuart Mills on Liberty*. Harmondsworth: Penguin, 59–187.

Patient's Charter. London: HMSO.

Rix, B. (1990). Danish ethics council rejects brain death as the criterion of death. *Journal of Medical Ethics*, **16**: 5–7.

Ross, W.D. (1930). *The Right and the Good*. Oxford: Clarendon.

Seedhouse, D. (1988). *Ethics: The Heart of Health Care*. Chichester: Wiley.

Singleton, J. and McLaren, S. (1995). *Ethical Foundations of Health Care*. London: C.V. Mosby.

Singleton, J. and Goodinson, S.M. (1989). Quality of life: a critical review of current concepts, measures and their clinical implications. *International Journal of Nursing Studies*, **26**: 327–41.

Stanley, J.M. (1992). Developing guidelines for decisions to forgo life-prolonging medical treatment. *Journal of Medical Ethics*, **18**(supplement).

Further Reading ▲ ▲ ▲

Rachels, J. (1986). *The End of Life*. Oxford: Oxford University Press.

Silverman, W.A. (1989). The myth of informed consent: in daily practice and in clinical trials. *Journal of Medical Ethics*, **15**: 6–11.

Thornton, H. (1994). Clinical trials: a brave new partnership? *Journal of Medical Ethics*, **20**: 19–22.

Veatch, R.M. (1981). *A Theory of Medical Ethics*. New York: Basic Books.

SECTION VII

Research and Evaluation

24

Approaches to Research

Jörg Huber and Nigel Reeve

LEARNING OBJECTIVES

After studying this chapter you should:

- Appreciate the nature and remit of empirical research
- Be aware of the main approaches to research
- Be able to understand research as a process

INTRODUCTION

Critical reflection on theory and clinical practice requires the application of a scientific approach. This and the following chapter provide a view of the nature of scientific research and a concise practical guide to the research process. In particular, this chapter highlights existing disagreements about the nature and remit of research, and describes the range of approaches available to health research.

THE NATURE OF EMPIRICAL RESEARCH

Scientific research is a systematic process of enquiry – a way of posing questions and answering them. As such it has some distinguishing characteristics:

- A scientific theory should be explicit and internally consistent. Statements must not contradict one another.
- Appropriate empirical evidence is required for the support of a theory. Theoretical statements need to agree with the data i.e. the theory must be external consistent.

This chapter will focus on empirical research that uses evidence in the form of data to answer questions. Other forms of scientific research that are just as important, such as theoretical research (e.g. so-called thought experiments, analysis of the logical status of theories) are beyond the scope of this chapter.

Empirical research should be *rigorous*. For this to be so, it must be well-planned so that potential sources of error are controlled and the research can be replicated. It is probably fair to say that for the last century or so, scientific knowledge has reigned supreme, and knowledge gained by other means such as the arts and religious faith has been seen as inferior. The aim of empirical research is to produce reliable knowledge based on empirical evidence or data (for a useful discussion see Ziman (1991)). Questions that can be posed and addressed by empirical research can be categorized under four headings.

DESCRIPTION – WHAT IS THE PHENOMENON UNDER INVESTIGATION LIKE?

The key to description is observation of the characteristics of the phenomenon under investigation (e.g. what are the characteristics of an asthma attack?). If the phenomenon has dynamic characteristics we may want to know what is going on – how is it changing? Observations are recorded (e.g. how many people suffer from asthma?).

UNDERSTANDING AND EXPLANATION – WHY IS IT HAPPENING AS IT IS?

Understanding means providing an explanation of an event in terms of what leads to that event. Seligman (1993) accounted for the longer life expectancy observed in those with an optimistic outlook on life by proposing that optimism leads to better health.

Such an explanation constitutes a theory – a set of conceptual statements which need to be mutually consistent, and agree with empirical evidence. A good theory should be parsimonious (as simple as possible), it should generalize to as wide a range of events as possible, and should be productive (predicting novel events). Frequently Newton's theory of gravity is seen as the yardstick for good theories, even in the social sciences.

PREDICTION – WHAT WILL HAPPEN?

Adequate understanding enables predictions to be made. For example, Seligman's theory on optimism successfully predicted which life-insurance sales representatives would stay in their jobs and who would leave (Seligman and Schulman, 1986). Adequate understanding also permits forecasting of the future (e.g. increases or decreases in the number of asthma sufferers as a result of changing atmospheric pollution levels). Successful predictions can provide further support for a theory.

PROBLEM-SOLVING – HOW CAN THINGS BE IMPROVED?

A traditional approach is that basic research must necessarily precede the application of findings to practical problems. For example, identification of a virus may lead to the development of a vaccine which can then be used in immunization programmes. While this approach is very successful in many instances, some problems (particularly practical ones) may suggest a different approach. Sometimes researchers consider possible applications right at the outset in order to, say, avoid the development of a medical treatment that would be prohibitively expensive.

Many problems tackled by the social sciences have an historical or cultural basis, in which case it is best to start investigations within the field of application. For example, it is unlikely to be useful to conduct a laboratory study of the acceptability of mixed-sex wards in hospitals.

Much social research has a direct policy orientation. Health campaigns and evaluation research can be integrated into action research which tries to promote healthy living while at the same time understanding what prevents people from adopting healthier lifestyles. (For details on action research as developed by Lewin, see Reason and Rowan (1981).

Integrating natural and behavioural sciences

It has been argued that the behavioural sciences cannot be 'true' science because the subject matter is *non-physical, context-specific,* and *subjective.* A very useful introductory text to these important but difficult problems has been written by the physicist John Ziman (1991).

NON-PHYSICAL PHENOMENA

For instance, can mental states or events be causes? Classical science, including Skinner's behaviourism, discounted mental states such as intentions or plans as possible causes of behaviour. Representatives of this outlook who attempt to explain all behaviour exclusively by recourse to material events such as neurophysiological processes call themselves *reductionists.* However, many scientists now accept mental states as causes. A good illustration of the causal role of mental states is the story of the horseman who, having unknowingly crossed the frozen Lake of Konstanz, was informed of the fact on arrival at a Swiss inn and consequently died from shock.

CONTEXT-SPECIFIC DATA

Can findings and theories be generalized when these are context-specific? Some social scientists (Harré *et al.*, 1985) have argued that generalization of results – which is common in the natural sciences – is not possible because social events are always bound by their historical and socio-cultural context. Others, who want to maintain the unitary nature of all science, want to incorporate historical and cultural factors into sociological and psychological theorizing.

Reductionists would argue that, ultimately, general principles will be found that apply to human beings just like any other biological species. Others think there is no problem at all because human beings are just another form of a biological entity to which the principles of the natural sciences apply. This issue is as yet unresolved.

SUBJECTIVE PHENOMENA

Can research paradigms apply across disciplinary boundaries? Many social scientists argue that the methods of the natural sciences – in particular, laboratory experiments – are inappropriate to social and psychological events because they exclude and deny the subjectivity of social experience. However, it is at least possible to consider subjective aspects of social experience in a laboratory (indeed there is a body of research on the experiment as a social setting). Nevertheless, critics of the natural science approach argue that this is not sufficient, and that the rich quality of subjective experience cannot be reduced to quantitative measurement under controlled conditions. Again, this issue is unresolved.

Scientific disasters, such as those linked to thalidomide, Bhopal and Chernobyl, have raised doubts about science as the ultimate and most reliable form of knowledge (Beck, 1992). Two solutions to this challenge (apart from denying it) can probably be distinguished – the rejection of science by certain groups (e.g. religious sects), and the extension and redefinition of scientific research by researchers championing qualitative research. The latter suggests a change in the remit of empirical research. Topics that traditionally were seen as inaccessible and inappropriate for empirical research have become a focus of qualitative research. An example is the content of consciousness, such as fantasies or magical thinking about healing, which has been considered to be an invalid topic for empirical behavioural research.

Integrative approaches

A number of authors have suggested integrative approaches. Probably the best-known is the *biopsychosocial model* (e.g. Sarafino, 1994). Somewhat more specific is *social action theory* (Ewart 1991). A more explicit attempt at integrating biological, psychological and social processes has been suggested by Hinde (1987) in his *model of levels of complexity*. Both Ewart and Hinde are potentially useful sources for the research practitioner.

The advantage of an integrative stance is that it helps to further interdisciplinary research. This is of particular importance in the health sciences, where for instance biomedical explanations of disease might be enriched by the incorporation of psychosocial processes.

APPROACHES TO RESEARCH

There are three main approaches to research, each with its traditional disciplinary associations:

- *The experimental approach* is most typical of biological and physiological research into health.
- *Surveys and questionnaires* are typical of psychological and epidemiological research.
- *Qualitative research* is most closely associated with sociological issues in health.

Although this is a simplified view, it is clear that many of the disciplinary divisions are artificial and may readily be abandoned in favour of a more integrated approach.

The experimental approach

Finding out which factors determine human behaviour requires active manipulation of the conditions surrounding the behaviour, in order to observe the effects. For example, the degree to which people are involved in their treatment planning can be manipulated (no involvement, detailed explanation of an exercise programme developed by a health worker, versus joint planning of an exercise programme) in order to see whether the level of involvement affects compliance.

Manipulation of conditions is more or less synonymous with experimentation. Furthermore, any conditions that are not of current interest, and which might affect the behaviour, need to be tightly controlled. This is the reason why experiments are often carried out in a laboratory. Hence a 'true experiment' is characterized by:

- manipulation of the conditions of interest (so there has to be a minimum of two conditions);
- control of all other conditions (such as the random allocation of subjects to conditions).

If control is perfect, findings from an experiment indicate *causal relationships* between independent and dependent variables.

CONFOUNDING VARIABLES

In reality, experimental control is rarely perfect, so that other variables contaminate the results. These *confounding variables* prevent definite conclusions being reached about causal relationships. One important source of confounding variables can be 'order effects' – a problem in experiments using repeated measures on the same subjects, as in medical drug trials.

QUASI-EXPERIMENTS AND FIELD EXPERIMENTS

Experiments can be classified in terms of their design (see Chapter 25). Additionally, there are many types of experiments that are not 'true' experiments. In a quasi-experiment (Campbell and Stanley, 1966), subjects are not randomly allocated to conditions – something that is frequently impossible or unethical in health research. Box 24.1 gives an example of a study where random allocation to regular and irregular physiotherapy groups would have been difficult or impossible.

A further distinction can be made between laboratory and field experiments. The latter afford less control, but are less artificial. This is an important advantage in the social and behavioural sciences.

In summary, the experimental approach affords high levels of control, and allows the identification of causal relationships. Reliable measurements tend to be more easily obtainable in comparison with other approaches.

Box 24.1 *Effects of long-term physiotherapy on disability in people with multiple sclerosis (MS)*

DeSouza and Worthington (1987) studied the long-term effects of physiotherapy on a group of 40 carefully selected people with MS over 18 months with four assessments (at 0, 6, 12, 18 months). While no explicit hypothesis was formulated, their introduction clearly suggests that they expected physiotherapy to be useful to these people. The functional ability of the individuals was assessed in various ways, including the index of Activities of Daily Living (ADL). Given that some of them attended physiotherapy more regularly than others, the group of 40 was divided into those who received most physiotherapy (14 people in regular attendance; upper 35%) and those who received least physiotherapy (14 people in irregular attendance; lower 35%). The two groups were similar regarding their neurological assessment, but using the Mann–Whitney U test (a non-parametric test) they could show that regular attenders improved, or deteriorated less than the irregular attenders.

This is fairly typical of study designs for looking at the long-term effects of a treatment programme. The design is longitudinal, using repeated measures of a number of functional ability assessment instruments. The comparison between the regular and irregular attenders is similar to experimental designs using an experiment and control groups. However, the study is not a true experiment because no conditions were manipulated and subjects were not randomly allocated to groups. This would have caused practical and ethical problems. A consequence of the chosen design is that we cannot be sure whether regular attendance is the cause of better outcomes – it is just possible that regular attendance is the consequence of being less impaired by MS.

The ADL is commonly used for measuring functional ability, and it is considered to be reliable. However, Bowling (1991) in a very useful handbook on instruments to measure health etc. doubted its validity. Frequently the choice of instruments is a compromise – few are both valid and reliable. Functional ability is only one aspect of health assessment; recently the incorporation of quality-of-life and well-being measures has become an important addition (Bowling, 1991, 1995).

The main problems, in particular with the laboratory experiment, are its artificiality and the demands it can impose on subjects. For further details and ways of dealing with some of these problems, see Harris (1986).

Surveys and questionnaires

A survey is defined as the collection of standardized information from a specific population – usually, but not necessarily, by means of a questionnaire or interview (Robson, 1993). Most surveys employ a set of questions to which participants respond according to the way they think, feel or behave, either in the present or in the past. However, a survey can also be based on behavioural observation. For example, Willems (1972) observed people whilst in a rehabilitation hospital and found they were more active and independent outside the actual treatment settings.

The aim of a survey is to accurately assess characteristics of whole populations of people. A population can be any clearly defined group, such as all members of a country, a town or a company workforce. It is rare to study all members of a population; usually a representative sample group is used. An example of a survey studying cancer screening behaviour is given in Box 24.2.

Survey research needs to deal with two main issues: sampling (dealt with in Chapter 25) and questionnaire design. The latter depends on the type of survey the researcher wants to carry out: face-to-face interviews, telephone surveys, street surveys, or postal surveys (for full details see Moser and Kalton (1971)). Face-to-face interviews can use longer questionnaires, more open-ended and complex questions, whereas a postal survey using a self-completion questionnaire needs to be shorter and ask very straightforward questions. In circumstances where respondents are highly motivated owing to their personal interest in the research topic, these rules may not apply and even a detailed and lengthy self-completion questionnaire may be acceptable.

There are two main issues affecting the choice of method – *intimacy* and *flexibility*. The level of intimacy afforded by different types of surveys has an important influence on a subject's motivation (talking to an interviewer is usually more motivating than filling in a questionnaire), and this affects the degree to which data of a very personal nature can be obtained. Skilled interviewers can obtain very personal information on difficult or sensitive issues (e.g. bereavement), but in

Box 24.2 *Do health beliefs predict women's cancer screening behaviour?*

A series of models have been suggested to explain women's cancer screening behaviour. This is just one example of many health behaviours that psychologists and sociologists have attempted to predict from demographic variables, health beliefs, and health locus of control.

Murray and McMillan (1993) assessed the usefulness of four sets of variables to predict breast self-examination (BSE) and attendance for cervical smears (ACS) in a survey of almost 400 women in Northern Ireland. Studies such as this should inform health promotion campaigns and policy – the identification of variables predicting health behaviours should help to target health promotion accordingly. Their main findings were that confidence in the practice of BSE was the best predictor of BSE, while lack of fear of the consequences of a cervical smear was the strongest predictor of ACS. The practical implications are straightforward, although not necessarily easy to implement – allowing women to practise BSE (e.g. using a model) should encourage BSE, while reducing fear of the consequences of a smear should increase attendance.

This survey used a self-completion questionnaire and employed sophisticated correlational analyses to investigate the relationships between a number of independent variables such as health beliefs and the dependent variables BSE and ACS. While the independent variables were measured at interval level, the dependent variables were nominal: a woman did or did not BSE (see levels of measurement in Chapter 25). When reading a paper like this, the uninitiated may find the results section difficult, even daunting, but it is important to be able to learn to read around the technical jargon and interpret papers, even if you do not fully grasp the methods or analysis – which in this case go well beyond the scope of this chapter. In this example a critical appraisal of the study rests not so much upon an understanding of statistics (except for a basic grasp of the nature of correlation and significance levels), but upon a technical knowledge about questionnaire design.

One shortcoming of the study is that Murray and McMillan did not discuss the possibility that, since none of the health beliefs predicted BSE, the health belief model should be discarded! However, the authors do provide important detail about the content of the health belief scales they used. For example, the component 'seriousness' has three items: (1) The thought of cancer scares me. (2) When I think about cancer I feel sick. (3) I am afraid to even think about cancer. It is a rule-of-thumb to construct scales consisting of at least three items which are all measuring the same thing or dimension – in this case the 'seriousness' of the condition. However, it is also recommended that the items should sample the whole domain of 'seriousness' (Kline, 1993). In this case items 1 and 3 can be considered to be identical, and item 2 perhaps taps another aspect of seriousness – feelings of sickness associated with thoughts of cancer. How can the measurement of seriousness be improved? You could consider incorporating items that cover the consequences of the condition for daily living or life expectancy (e.g. being unable to live an independent life). This would increase the coverage of the 'item pool'. Additionally the questionnaire items were taken from a North American study, which can lead to problems of wording and cultural difference. It is often necessary to adapt or standardize questionnaires in the country where they will be used before using them for research.

Finally, it should be pointed out that the prediction of BSE and ACS is rather weak. The results would be unsuitable for predicting which individual women would carry out BSE or ACS and which would not. Predictions can only be made at an aggregate level; i.e. what *percentage* of women are likely to carry out BSE or ACS.

some circumstances the personal presence may prevent disclosure of information (e.g. on sexual matters). Face-to-face interviews are most flexible, and create a more intimate setting, whereas postal self-completion questionnaires are least flexible and tend to be less appropriate for the collection of highly personal and emotive data.

Attention needs to be paid to the order of questions. They can be grouped according to topic, but sensitive issues should never be addressed in the very first questions. In addition, the form of the questions themselves has to be considered. Many different question formats are available, and in making the best choice, the required detail, accuracy and reliability of the information to be obtained are important considerations. Typical formats are:

- open-ended questions (e.g. 'In your view, what makes a good GP?');
- closed questions (e.g. 'How many times a week do you exercise?');
- rating scales (e.g. pain assessment ranging from 1, no pain at all, to 5, the worst possible pain; and attitude scales).

Two specific types of questionnaires are particularly important: *attitude scales* and *psychometric questionnaires*. The health belief model (see Box 24.2) uses attitude scales; the most popular format is the Likert scale which usually consists of 5 to 20 items containing evaluative statements, to which respondents express their level of agreement; e.g. respondents would express their agreement or disagreement with the statement 'Nurses on this ward care a lot about their patients' on a 5-point scale (ranging from 1 = strongly agree to 5 = strongly disagree). All items will be summed up to form a single score, which means that in order to form a scale all items must measure the same underlying dimension, such as 'Patients' perception of nursing care' (for details see Oppenheim (1992)).

Psychometric questionnaires measure personality characteristics such as extraversion or neuroticism, or quality of life. They are standardized, and should be highly reliable, and valid norms for populations should be available. This means it is then possible to compare study results with the norms of the wider population.

To summarize, the survey is useful for collecting large amounts of information from large numbers of people on their opinions and activities (past or present). However, questionnaire design is often a difficult task, and survey data can suffer from low reliability because of ambiguous, insensitive or intrusive questions.

Qualitative research

Good qualitative research is just as demanding as any other type of research. Qualitative research can reveal new insights into social phenomena, or issues that have not previously been researched. Qualitative techniques can also provide a systematic way of introducing a researcher to an unfamiliar field of research. In this sense qualitative research is frequently a forerunner to quantitative research. However, qualitative researchers dislike this subserving or preliminary role of their approach. Instead, they argue that qualitative methods are the best way to study the ways people construe social and political events around them.

Qualitative research covers a wide range of methods: case studies, ethnographic research, grounded theory, discourse and conversational analysis. This variety can be quite bewildering, but Silverman (1993) provided a good overview.

It is difficult to define the characteristics of qualitative research. To define it negatively as the avoidance of measurement and the rejection of quantification is not very satisfactory. Silverman (1993) suggested that qualitative research should focus on naturally occurring data concerning people in their normal content.

Qualitative methods that were developed some time ago, such as ethnographic research and case studies, tended to focus on very detailed descriptions and relied usually on interviews and observations in the field (see Box 24.3).

Grounded theory, as the name suggests, concentrates on developing a theoretical understanding grounded on interviews and behavioural observations (Strauss and Corbin, 1990). This reflects a recent shift in qualitative research towards a more theoretically driven understanding of data, such as the detailed analysis of power relationships in interactions. Examples are discourse analysis to study face-saving 'devices' in interviewer–interviewee interactions (e.g. Coyle, 1995), and conversational analysis to look at 'turn-taking' (e.g. Heath and Luff, 1993). Both of these transcript-based methods may include extra-linguistic features such as pauses, 'um's and 'ah's, and intonational emphases.

The *case study* is a strategy for doing research which involves an empirical investigation of a particular contemporary phenomenon or case within its real-life context, using multiple sources of evidence. It preserves the unitary character of the phenomenon or case (Robson, 1993). Mitchell (1983) suggested that case studies, rather than being purely descriptive, need to focus on an understanding of a case in theoretical terms (e.g. by providing explanations for changes).

The main criticisms of qualitative methods are the potential for researcher bias, the lack of explicit procedures to assess the reliability and validity of findings, and the often very small samples. All these problems are also familiar in quantitative research, but then explicit methods to assess and remedy them are available. A number of methods to increase the rigour of qualitative research have been suggested. These include the use of several researchers to compare their analyses (inter-rater reliability assessment) to overcome researcher bias (Wilson, 1995), negative case analysis (Robson, 1993) and theoretical sampling (Arber, 1993) to increase generalizability of findings.

The novice should look in great detail at examples of qualitative research and seek advice from someone experienced in such methods. As already stated, qualitative research can be very time-consuming, and it requires a liking for detailed in-depth analysis. The clearer, predefined structures of quantitative research can make it easier to hide a lack of theoretical reflection – something that can justify the misgivings that many qualitative researchers have towards quantitative research.

Box 24.3: *Qualitative research: Becoming a carer – an ethnographic study*

Ethnography is one example of qualitative research. It uses a range of methods including observation and interviews. It operates in the natural setting of those being observed or interviewed; the researcher should be appreciative of setting and its inhabitants. The work is driven by analytic ideas of understanding. Fuller details are given by Fielding (1993).

Taraborrelli (1993) studied the process of carer's careers amongst people who care for a relative suffering Alzheimer's disease. She gives a very useful account of how she went about using ethnography. She describes the details of getting access to carers of Alzheimer sufferers, her attendance of support groups, the keeping of a journal of notes and analytic memos, and the development of her theoretical ideas. She developed a taxonomy of three career paths:

- Those who adopt directly the carer's perspective. These individuals take what might be called a realistic perspective on the pressures and demands a carer is under.
- Those who take an innocent view or 'carry on as normal' and 'I must do it all' perspective. At some stage these carers get overwhelmed and start relying on support such as daycare.
- Those who reach a crisis point, leading them to opt out of the carer's role suddenly and completely. They seem to suffer some emotional or physical breakdown.

The information given by doctors etc. appears to be important in determining the career path of the carer. These findings are useful to the planning of support for carers.

Taraborrelli conveys very well the reflective attitude that is important in much of qualitative research. Qualitative research, if being done well, is very time-consuming. What she did is usually referred to as the development of grounded theory; that is, theory grounded in the setting and its participants, and on the data rather than preconceived ideas of the researcher.

How does this compare with quantitative research? Ideally quantitative research should be reflective, should take into account the context in which participants live or work, and should develop theory in accordance with the data. However, because quantitative research is so well established, and tools for collecting and analysing data are readily available, it is not only novices to research that forget that research is more than just the administration of tools (e.g. the unthinking distribution of poorly designed questionnaires). As a process of enquiry it requires the collection of evidence which is pertinent to the research question. Qualitative researchers are sometimes more reflective on these issues – a point that quantit researchers would do well to remind themselves of.

Combining approaches and techniques

Frequently, the relationship between qualitative and quantitative approaches is seen as being antagonistic. This view is not particularly helpful, nor does it reflect what often happens in practice. For example, in case studies experimental elements may be introduced to augment qualitative data, such as in longitudinal studies in which the manipulation of an experimental variable (perhaps a series of implementations and withdrawals of treatment) can provide important evidence of causal linkage between events and measured variables. Similarly, the survey approach may depart from the purely descriptive if samples are collected according to an experimental protocol that seeks to control variables, so that differences between groups or associations between variables may be investigated.

Qualitative information is often contextually important, especially in the study of human interactions, and may add important dimensions to otherwise purely quantitative studies. Rather than arguing whether qualitative or quantitative research is better, Carr and Kemmis (1986) suggest that scientific practice is not so much dependent on specific characteristics such as sample size, but on a process of critical and rational enquiry.

A MODEL OF THE RESEARCH PROCESS

The research process can be characterized by the phases through which the research proceeds to gain reliable knowledge, and the constraints which the researcher can or wants to impose on the research process (for more details see Graziano and Raulin (1989)).

Typically, research proceeds stepwise from a stage of gathering information and formulating questions, to a stage where an appropriate method is determined.

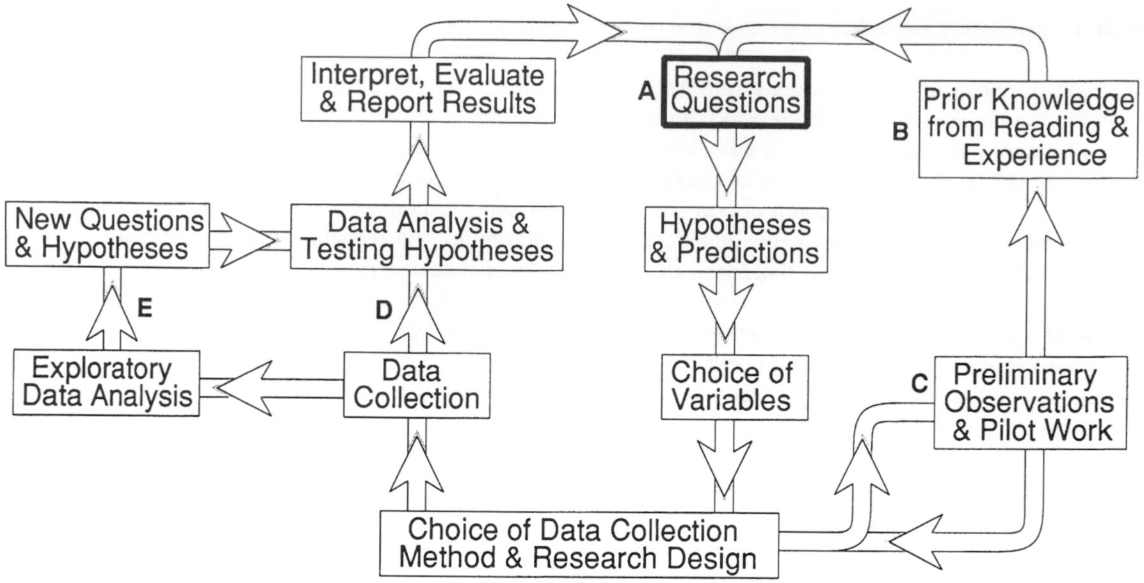

Figure 24.1 *Steps in the research process. Research usually begins with the formulation of one or more research questions (A), but these will almost always spring from prior knowledge (B) obtained in various ways. The results of preliminary observation or pilot work (C) are mainly used to modify and refine the research methods but may also contribute new information which changes prior knowledge and provokes a reformulation of research questions. Data analysis should primarily be confirmatory (D) – testing the hypotheses and predictions made. However, complex data sets may well show unanticipated patterns, and exploration of these (E) can raise new questions which may also be tested.*

Then follows the gathering of data and finally analysis, interpretation and conclusions. However, the order of the steps in the research process is not fixed; each may feed on the other in a circular process. For example, during the process of formulating questions for research your ideas will depend to some extent on what you know can be done (methodological constraints). Similarly, initial results of an enquiry may stimulate further analyses to answer additional questions (see Figure 24.1).

Earlier it was argued that empirical research is a systematic form of enquiry with each step in the research process organized on the basis of rational considerations. This process can be understood in terms of the level of constraints the researcher can and wants to impose. If little is known and a research question needs to be explored, low-constraint methods would be used – such as qualitative case studies. In contrast, a large amount of prior knowledge and theory-driven hypothesis testing will lead to high-constraint methods – such as laboratory-based experimentation. For further details see Box 24.4, and consult Graziano and Raulin (1989).

In applied research one attempts to impose few constraints. Hence a questionnaire-based survey may be used to determine the level of satisfaction with a specific health service programme, for example. Basic research requires higher levels of constraint by typically using laboratory-based experimentation. Conventionally, qualitative research, such as the case study approach, is seen as a low-constraint method. However, recent developments of very specific methods of data analysis, such as grounded theory, impose considerable constraints both on the quality of data required and the processes by which they are analysed (e.g. Strauss and Corbin, 1990).

SUMMARY

This chapter has provided an overview of the nature of research and some of the principal philosophical and methodological approaches to tackling research problems. Adopting a more integrative view of the research process can help to break down the constraints imposed by traditional disciplinary paradigms and so

Box 24.4 *Typical levels of constraint in empirical reseach (adapted from Graziano and Raulin, 1989)*

Level of constraint	Examples	Notes on examples
Low	Naturalistic observation	Observation of people or events as they occur in the 'real' world The researcher should avoid altering or controlling people or settings
	Ethnographic research	Observation of and interviews with people in their natural environment (see Box 24.3) Similar to naturalistic observation, but researcher usually becomes involved with people in the setting
Medium	Questionnaire survey	Quantitative questionnaires studying health beliefs and behaviours using highly structured measurement procedures that constrain the answers given by respondents
	Field experiments	Research is carried out in the subjects' environment but manipulations and controls are introduced Measurement procedures are likely to constrain possible responses
High	Standardized questionnaires	Similar to questionnaire surveys except that the questions are even more prestructured Typical examples are personality questionnaires and diagnostic questionnaires used in clinical psychology, psychiatry and quality of life assessment instruments
	Experimental research	This imposes the highest level of constraint, particularly in a true experiment which uses random allocation of subjects to conditions and is likely to be carried out in a laboratory

allow a more productive and reasoned approach to research in the health sciences. Whatever the research model, we have emphasized the rational and critical nature of the research process, the need for a careful formulation of research questions, the selection of appropriate research instruments and protocols, as well as a strict requirement for methodological rigour at all stages. This theme is followed through in the following chapter which contains a brief practical guide to setting about a research problem.

Key Points

- Theories must be internally and externally consistent.
- Empirical research is used to describe, explain, predict, or solve problems.
- There is controversy over the extent to which behavioural phenomena can be the subject of scientific enquiry.
- Quantitative and qualitative approaches can be complementary in practice.
- Main approaches of empirical research are experiment, the survey and qualitative research.
- Different approaches to data collection are traditionally associated with different approaches, but again these need not be mutually exclusive.
- Empirical research is an ongoing process of critical and rational enquiry.

References ▼ ▼ ▼

Arber, S. (1993). Designing samples. In: Gilbert, N. (ed.), *Researching Social Life*. London: Sage, 68–92.

Beck, U. (1992). *The Risk Society*. London: Sage.

Bowling, A. (1991). *Measuring Health*. Milton Keynes: Open University Press.

Bowling, A. (1995). *Measuring Disease*. Buckingham: Open University Press.

Campbell, D.T. and Stanley, J.C. (1966). *Experimental and Quasi-Experimental Designs for Research*. Chicago: Rand McNally.

Carr, W. and Kemmis, S. (1986). *Becoming Critical*. London: Falmer.

Coyle, A. (1995). Discourse analysis. In: Breakwell, G. *et al.* (eds), *Research Methods in Psychology*. London: Sage, 243–88.

DeSouza, L.H. and Worthington J.A. (1987). The effect of long-term physiotherapy on disability in multiple sclerosis. In: Rose, F.C. and Jones, R. (eds), *Multiple Sclerosis*. London: John Libbey, 155–64.

Ewart, C.K. (1991). Social action theory. *American Psychologist*, **64**: 931–46.

Fielding, N. (1993). Ethnography. In: Gilbert, N. (ed.), *Researching Social Life*. London: Sage, 154–71.

Graziano, A. and Raulin, M. (1989). *Research Methods*. Cambridge, Mass.: Harper & Row.

Harre, R., Clarke, D. and De Carlo N. (1985). *Motives and Mechanisms*. London: Methuen.

Harris, P. (1986). *Designing and Reporting Experiments*. Milton Keynes: Open University Press.

Heath, C. and Luff, P. (1993). Explicating face to face interaction. In: Gilbert, N. (ed.), *Researching Social Life*. London: Sage, 306–26.

Hinde, R. (1987). *Individuals, Relationships and Culture*. Cambridge: Cambridge University Press.

Kline, P. (1993). *Handbook of Psychological Testing*. London: Sage.

Mitchell, J.C. (1983). Case and situational analysis. *Sociological Review*, **31**: 187–211.

Moser, C.A. and Kalton, G. (1971). *Survey Methods in Social Investigation*, 2nd edn. London: Heinemann.

Murray, M. and McMillan, C. (1993). Health beliefs, locus of control, emotional control and women's cancer screening behaviour. *British Journal of Clinical Psychology*, **32**: 87–100.

Oppenheim, A.N. (1992). *Questionnaire Design, Interviewing and Attitude Measurement*, 2nd edn. London: Pinter.

Reason, P. and Rowan, J. (eds) (1981). *Human Enquiry: A Sourcebook of New Paradigm Research*. Chichester: Wiley.

Robson, C. (1993). *Real World Research*. Oxford: Blackwell.

Sarafino, E. (1994). *Health Psychology*, 2nd edn. Chichester: Wiley.

Seligman, M. (1993). *Learned Optimism*. New York: Pocket Books.

Seligman, M. and Schulman, P. (1986). Explanatory style as a predictor of performance as a life insurance agent. *Journal of Personality and Social Psychology*, **50**: 832–8.

Silverman, D. (1993). *Interpreting Qualitative Data*. London: Sage.

Strauss, A. and Corbin, J. (1990). *Basics of Qualitative Research*. London: Sage.

Taraborrelli, P. (1993). Becoming a carer. In: Gilbert, N. (ed.), *Researching Social Life*. London: Sage, 172–86.

Willems, E.P. (1972). The interface of the hospital environment and patient behavior. *Archives of Physical Medicine and Rehabilitation*, **53**: 115–22.

Wilson, M. (1995). Structuring qualitative data: multidimensional scalogram analysis. In: Breakwell, G. *et al.* (eds), *Research Methods in Psychology*. London: Sage, 259–73.

Ziman, J. (1991). *Reliable Knowledge*. Cambridge: Cambridge University Press.

Further Reading ▲ ▲ ▲

Graziano, A. and Raulin, M. (1989). *Research Methods*. Cambridge, Mass: Harper & Row.

Harris, P. (1986). *Designing and Reporting Experiments*. Milton Keynes: Open University Press.

Silverman, D. (1993). *Interpreting qualitative data*. London: Sage.

Vaus, D.A. de (1994). *Surveys in social research*, 3rd edition. London: UCL Press.

25

The Research Process: A Practical Guide

Nigel Reeve and Jörg Huber

LEARNING OBJECTIVES

After studying this chapter you should:

- Be able to formulate research questions
- Understand how to design and implement a research project
- Be aware of the different methods of analysing raw data
- Know how to present and interpret results and to evaluate a research project

INTRODUCTION

This chapter looks at the research process in detail, from the initial idea, through study design, measurement, analysis of data and interpretation of results. Particular emphasis has been laid on a practical guide to *hypothesis testing* and choosing statistical tests. Hypothesis testing is a standardized decision-making technique that is highly explicit. This makes it suitable for illustrating the need for rigour in the research process. Selected examples and guides to certain aspects of statistical analysis are given in boxes, allowing the reader to focus on important detail when needed.

IDENTIFYING A FOCUS FOR RESEARCH QUESTIONS

Research may be aimed directly at solving a practical problem (applied), or concerned with theoretical issues that do not have immediate practical application (pure). Although the stimulus for research may thus vary greatly, most research in the health domain involves the investigation of a nest of related questions, and often requires a blend of qualitative and quantitative information. It may help to keep a research journal to log possible study ideas, questions and problems.

An important first step in the research process is to clarify carefully the questions being asked and to consider the level of constraint (see Chapter 24) relevant to each. This will almost always entail an exploration of the relevant research literature, consultations with colleagues, and possibly pilot work to clarify the nature of the problem. Sometimes it may help to explore the opposite of the phenomenon to be studied (e.g. to examine empathic qualities in health workers it might be useful to examine the characteristics of individuals who rarely show empathy). For further details see Smith (1975, Chapter 3).

It is also very important to consider whether your research ideas are *ethical*. Try to anticipate possible ethical objections to the research, especially if tackling a sensitive issue. Any health-related study is likely to require approval from an ethical committee before it can be started, a process which can cause delays for the unwary.

Whether in qualitative or quantitative research, a good definition of the problem should include the following (Kerlinger, 1986):

- a statement on the expected relationships between variables, or features of the information gathered;
- a statement of the problem in the form of questions to be answered;
- the statement of the problem must at least imply the possibility of an empirical test (most relevant to the quantitative approach).

It is useful and often necessary (as in experimental research) to turn a research question into a hypothesis (see below). At this point it is also worth mentioning that in some publications a distinction is made between:

- a *conceptual hypothesis* – one expressed in general terms, such as 'Noise leads to increased levels of stress';
- an *operational hypothesis* – one expressed in terms of variables and their measurement procedures, such as 'Live rock music increases the pulse rate in adults' or 'Low-flying aircraft over a neighbourhood will increase sleep disturbances in residents'.

SAMPLING AND SUBJECTS

Populations and samples

A study *population* is the total number of subjects, objects or events from which your samples may be drawn (e.g. the male population of Liverpool, the total number of domestic violence incidents that occur in Greater London in a year). Measures that describe population characteristics are known as *parameters*. It is usually impractical to study the entire population, unless it is very small. Hence a *sample* is a more conveniently sized (but representative) subset of the population. *Statistics* are estimates of population parameters obtained from samples (see Figure 25.1).

A real problem in research is to ensure that a sample is a good representation of the study population. Ideally a sample should be large enough to represent all the variation found in the population and all items/subjects must have an equal chance of being included – as in a truly random sample. However, as well as being too small, sample sizes can be too large so that statistical tests find even the smallest of effects spuriously significant. See Moser and Kalton (1971) for guidance on survey sample sizes.

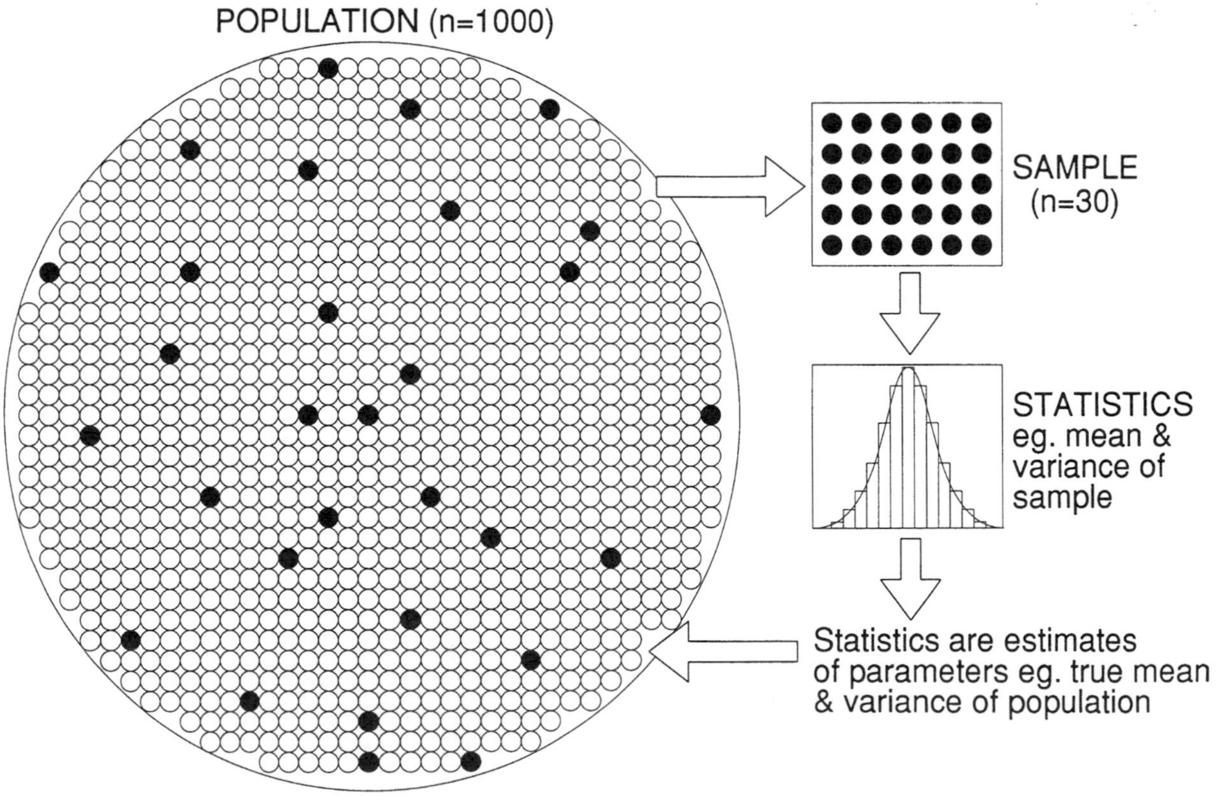

Figure 25.1 *Relationship between population, parameters, sample and statistics. A population is characterized by its parameters (variables such as height, weight, gender etc.) but is too large for all individuals to be measured. Instead, the characteristics of a representative sample of randomly picked individuals (black dots) are used to provide statistics (i.e. estimates of the population parameters)*

Table 25.1 *Summary of some common sampling strategies*

Method of sampling	Notes
Random sampling	All items in the selected population stand an equal chance of inclusion in the sample. Subjects usually chosen by random number
Systematic random sampling	Items included according to some regular pattern e.g. picks every 10th (or *n*th) individual or event, only the starting point is randomly chosen. This may be more convenient to administer than a truly random sample
Stratified sampling	A strategy that includes quotas of population subgroups ('strata') to ensure an adequate sample of each. Each stratum is randomly sampled. For example, a minority group may, by chance, be unrepresented in a random sample of 1000 people living in a town of 50 000 people. Stratified samples ensure that representative random samples of all relevant subgroups are included
Cluster sampling	Initially a convenient group is selected, but this is then sub-sampled randomly. Any generalization of findings outside the population actually sampled should be cautious or avoided altogether
Multistage subsampling	Initially based on a cluster of potential sampling frames (e.g. several suitable institutions or study areas). One of these is randomly chosen, then individuals are randomly chosen from within the chosen sampling frame (e.g. single institution or area). As with cluster sampling, generalization outside the population actually sampled should be avoided
Quota sampling	The sampling frame is restricted to a predetermined (targeted) sample composition (e.g. of specific age range, social class, gender, etc.). The sample biases allow generalization of findings only for the specific target group which is not representative of the wider population. Often used by market researchers in opinion surveys relating to targeted sales of products
Convenience sample	A sample group is selected purely on grounds of convenience. The group composition may be heavily biased and results should never be generalized. Generally an unsuitable method, but commonly used in pilot projects.

Sampling strategies

There are many sampling strategies designed to get around a variety of problems (see Table 25.1). For example, when sampling in the field, systematic random sampling can be a more practicable alternative to truly random sampling, and stratified sampling can be an important safeguard against excluding minority groups. Whatever the method chosen, researchers must always understand the limitations of a sample and never attempt to generalize findings beyond the population actually sampled.

Sampling problems

Survey studies are particularly prone to sampling problems (Moser and Kalton, 1971). Subjects may be hard to recruit if participation requires a significant effort (some questionnaires are very long) or if studying a rare phenomenon. In longitudinal studies, recruits may 'drop-out' part-way through. Possible sampling biases need to be anticipated (e.g. a high-street survey carried out during the day may exclude most of the working population). Some biases are unavoidable (e.g. if subjects are volunteers they may be self-selecting on certain criteria). Other problems are associated with confidentiality and access to sensitive data – so be aware of the Data Protection Act and follow appropriate ethical guidelines. A common source of bias is in the study of colleagues or one's workplace where, among other things, the politics of power relationships can introduce severe biases.

RESEARCH DESIGN

Even though the division is somewhat artificial, it is usually helpful to make a firm distinction between designs based on looking for differences between groups or samples and those looking for association between variables (Cohen and Holliday, 1982). To do so makes the subsequent choice of appropriate statistics much more straightforward (see statistics section below).

DESCRIPTIVE INVESTIGATIONS

These are non-experimental designs geared towards describing phenomena. Examples are a quantitative study to determine the normal range of body temperature of a population, or a qualitative study of the management of a hospital intensive care unit. Depending on the nature of the data collected, quasi-experimental analysis of differences between subgroups or associations between variables may be possible (see below).

COMPARING DIFFERENCES BETWEEN GROUPS

This is where a variable – which might be a treatment or a division into natural types such as gender or racial groups – is used to define sample groups and possible differences between them are investigated. This approach is most commonly associated with experimental studies where there is a control group and one or more treatment groups, but between-group comparisons are also important in quasi-experiments (where division into groups may follow data collection) and qualitative research. There are two main types of between-groups design:

- *Independent (unrelated) groups*. Two or more groups are created by random independent sampling of the study population (ideal), or by *post hoc* division of the sample on the basis of some variable (as in the MS study in Box 24.1 in the previous chapter).
- *Dependent (related or correlated) groups*. The two or more groups under study are linked by some factor which means that the values of one group are likely to influence the others (i.e. they are *correlated*). A very clear example is the use of repeated-measures designs for the measurement of change where subjects are measured under one set of conditions (e.g. before treatment) and then measured again after manipulation of, or observed change in, the independent variable (e.g. after treatment). Such designs are popular because they are frequently easier to run (fewer subjects are required) and subjects act as their own controls (individual characteristics which are difficult to control stay the same under all repeated conditions).

The second type of approach is common to many experiments studying psychological or medical treatments. For example, the effects of a drug and relaxation on hypertension may be studied on the same group of patients by giving the drugs at one time, and relaxation at another time. Such a situation is likely to lead to order effects where the first set of conditions exerts a modifying influence on the second; the subject may be more tired, or more hungry, in subsequent trials than in the first. One simple remedy is to counterbalance – half of the subjects will take the drug first, and the other half receive relaxation therapy first. In this way any order effects, which might still occur, at least do not all work in the same direction, and hence should cancel each other out.

ASSOCIATION BETWEEN VARIABLES (CORRELATIONAL DESIGNS)

These are normally associated with descriptive studies, where data (often consisting of numerous variables) are gathered and the researcher looks for correlations between certain variables (see Box 24.2 for an example). Correlational designs are also used in experimental situations where the level of a variable is manipulated and associated change in other variable(s) is investigated.

LONGITUDINAL DESIGNS

These are really an extension of a simple repeated-measures design (see above), where subjects or events are studied in order to investigate change over prolonged periods of time, in the same way as in some case studies (refer to Box 24.3).

Longitudinal designs may be a kind of extended dependent-groups design (see above), where subjects receive more than two sequential changes of treatments. They may also be correlational in nature, where the manipulation of an independent variable (e.g. drug dosage) over time provides associated change in a dependent variable (e.g. symptomatic relief). These designs usually make use of specialized analysis methods that are beyond the scope of this chapter but which are dealt with by Oppenheim (1992).

MEASUREMENT AND THE NATURE OF VARIABLES

Whatever the research question, a valid and reliable research tool is needed to yield the required data. The choice of research tool depends on many considerations, and there are numerous kinds including: structured interviews, questionnaires, psychometric tests, ethologically based records of observed behaviour, or instruments measuring physiological variables. The quantitative measures yielded by such tools may be very different, so a clear grasp of their nature is essential if descriptive and inferential statistics are to be used correctly in the analysis of results.

***Table 25.2** Summary of the four levels of measurement and their associated measures of central tendency and variation*

Level of measurement of the variable	Typical measures of central tendency	Typical measures of sample variation
Nominal level (classification into categories) Subjects, items or events are classified into defined mutually exclusive categories. Includes yes/no (dichotomous) type responses	*Mode*: the most commonly occurring category	Not usually applicable, although the number of categories showing counts is an expression of the number of categorized types (variation at a nominal level) found in the sample
Ordinal level (a scaled rank-order measurement) Measurements or scores ascribed to subjects (or objects) allow them to be ranked in a series ranging from highest to lowest. But the scores either do not indicate absolute quantities, or the scale intervals are not absolutely regular	*Mode*: the most commonly occurring score (or range of scores if data are grouped) *Median*: the middle value (50% of sample values lie above the median and 50% lie below it)	*Inter-quartile range (IQR)* The value of one quartile (25% of sample values) either side of a median encompasses 50% of sample values. The semi-interquartile range is half the IQR *Percentile* The value below which a specified percentage of sample values lie, e.g. 90% of values are below the 90th centile *Range of values* The difference between the highest and lowest sample values. Used to express total variation
Interval level (truly scaled measurement) Scores are ranged on a scale where the intervals are truly equal, allowing one to determine the exact separation between the individuals, objects or events in the study sample. The position of the zero value is relatively rather than absolutely determined on the scale *Ratio level* Interval level variables that include an absolute zero point and therefore can meaningfully be used in the calculation of an index or ratio – e.g. a rate (events/second), speed or an index of physical proportion.	All the above measures may be applicable as required, plus . . . *Mean*: the average of sample values i.e. the total of values divided by the number of values	All the above measures may be applicable as required, plus . . . *Standard deviation* The value of one s.d. either side of a mean includes 68.26% of sample values. The s.d. shares the same units as the mean and hence is the most common measure of variation if data are measured at interval or ratio level *Variance* A standard expresson of variation about the mean used as part of many statistical tests. Variance = s.d.^{2} *Coefficient of variation* The s.d. expressed as a percentage of the mean

Levels of measurement

The nature of a variable and the way in which it is measured fundamentally affect the kind of data obtained. Such issues are a key consideration in choosing an appropriate study design and subsequent analysis of results.

Four hierarchical *levels of measurement* can be usefully defined (see Table 25.2), ranging from the *nominal* level which makes the weakest assumptions, to the *ratio* level which makes the strongest assumptions about the data. When the level of measurement is uncertain, it is often best to take a conservative view and so avoid making too strong assumptions about your measurements.

NOMINAL LEVEL

Nominal level measures simply allow subjects, objects or events to be classified into mutually exclusive categories in the same way that a child's building blocks may be sorted into groups based on colour or shape.

However simple this may seem, great care must be taken to ensure that the categories are defined realistically, very carefully related to the study questions, and include all the study subjects: a catch-all category (e.g. 'other') may be needed.

Typical inferential statistics tests for such 'counts in categories' data include the several forms of *chi-squared test*. If such tests are to be used then it is essential that no individual, object or event can contribute more than once to the counts comprising any one sample. This is a common design error. Suppose that questionnaires were left in a waiting room for outpatients to complete before posting them anonymously into a box. The same patient might contribute repeatedly on several successive visits, biasing the responses. Another common problem is the confusion between 'counts in categories', often described as 'frequency' data, and other kinds of frequency measures. The number of times an event occurs (e.g. as in behavioural records) is also described as frequency data, but in this case it is a rate (number of events per unit time) and therefore a ratio level variable (see below).

ORDINAL LEVEL

Ordinal level measures allow the ranking of measurements obtained from subjects, objects or events, but the measurement scale does not represent regular or absolute values. Examples are a subjective rating scale of 1–5 to quantify observed levels of aggression, or Likert scales such as those designed to measure preference or agreement. Non-parametric statistics are usually most appropriate for ordinal level data because they avoid arithmetic operations (such as the calculation of means) which would be invalid without at least interval level data (see below).

A common error is to treat ordinal level measures as if they were interval level, and then to apply parametric tests (see below). This can only be justified when the variable has been shown to closely mimic an interval level variable (see below) and also satisfies the other criteria of parametric tests.

INTERVAL LEVEL

Interval level measures require a scale where the intervals are truly equal. So addition and subtraction may be used to determine relative differences between subjects, objects or events in the study sample. However, the zero value is not absolute (e.g. the Celsius and Fahrenheit temperature scales both have different arbitrary 'zero' values). Some psychometric scores, such as anxiety scores from Spielberger's State–Trait Anxiety Inventory (Spielberger *et al.*, 1983), can be argued to show a reliable enough scaling to be treated as interval level. Parametric tests require variables to be measured at no less than interval level, and hence are usually appropriate, provided that their other assumptions of the tests are also met (see below).

RATIO LEVEL

Ratio level measures are interval level variables that include an absolute zero point and therefore can be used meaningfully in the calculation of an index or ratio. Examples are a rate (events/second), direct counts, length, speed or an index of physical proportion. As with interval level measures, parametric tests are usually appropriate.

Types of variables and the nature of variation

Different variables may be quite dissimilar in the way that they vary.

- *Continuous variables*, like length, weight or temperature, are (at least in theory) able to take on any value on the measurement scale. The scale's resolution is only limited by measurement accuracy.
- *Discrete variables* are only able to vary in chunks. The clearest cases of discrete variables are dichotomous variables which are only able to take on one of two values (e.g. yes or no, present or absent).

DISTRIBUTIONS

Of fundamental importance to a researcher's choice of data analysis is the way in which any measurement varies in a population or sample; i.e. its distribution. Many statistical techniques (such as parametric tests) assume that population variables (parameters) are 'normally distributed' (see Box 25.1 for more details).

However, there are many circumstances in which the variable is not normally distributed. Some limiting factor may mean that the measure under study is not free to vary beyond certain limits – so-called 'floor' and 'ceiling' effects. Artificial floor or ceiling effects can be created by instruments (or other research tools) with a restrictive range of measurement. Similarly, proportions such as percentage values are by their nature unable to vary beyond the range 0 to 100%. Often in such cases, data will not show a normal distribution and may need to be transformed (see Box 25.1) before parametric statistics can be applied correctly. Alternatively, non-parametric statistical techniques may be used (see below).

Box 25.1 *The normal distribution, skewness and transformation*

1. The normal distribution. The distribution of a variable is the pattern of its variation in a population or sample. There are many theoretical distributions but a key one is the Normal distribution (Fig. 1). When plotted as a frequency histogram (e.g. Box 25.2, Fig. 4), the distribution of many population variables (e.g. measures of height, weight or performance) approximate well to a normal distribution in which most scores cluster around the mean (μ or 'mu') but the number of scores declines symmetrically towards the upper and lower extremes (the *tails*) of the distribution. Variation about the mean is usually described in terms of the standard deviation (σ or 'sigma'); i.e. $\pm 1\sigma$ on either side of the mean includes 68.26% of the population, $\pm 2\sigma$ includes 95.48%, $\pm 3\sigma$ includes 99.72% (Fig. 1). Note that the algebraic terms μ and σ are only used for the mean and standard deviation of the population, not the values obtained from samples.

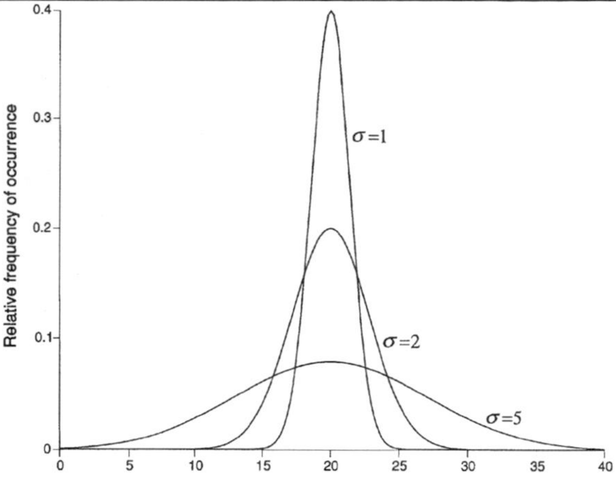

Fig. 2 *Graph showing three normal distribution curves each with a mean (μ) of 20 but with standard deviations (σ) of 1, 2 and 5*

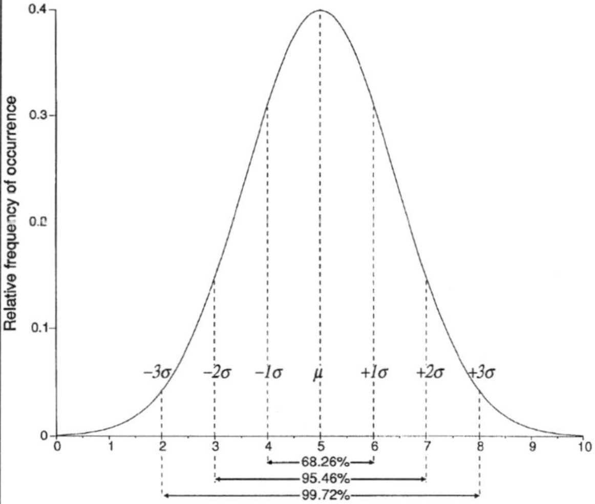

Fig. 1 *Graph showing a Normal distribution curve with standard deviations (plotted with Gauss's equation where* $\mu = 5$, $\sigma = 1$)

Truly normal distributions are always symmetrical and somewhat 'bell-shaped', but otherwise they may vary considerably according to the value of the mean (μ) and the standard deviation (σ) of the population (Fig. 2).

2. Skewness and transformation. All parametric tests (e.g. *t*-test, analysis of variance, Pearson's correlation etc.) require variables to be approximately normally distributed. However, data may be *skewed* (i.e. show an asymmetrical distribution) either negatively (to the left) or positively (to the right). One effect of skew is to separate out the mean, median and mode (measures of central tendency) which all have the same value in a truly Normal distribution (Fig. 3). Note that, where the distribution is skewed, the median is a more appropriate measure of central tendency because it is less affected by outlying extreme values than the mean.

Where data distributions are significantly skewed, the assumptions of parametric tests are no longer met and should not be used. In some cases, however, transformation may be used to correct the problem.

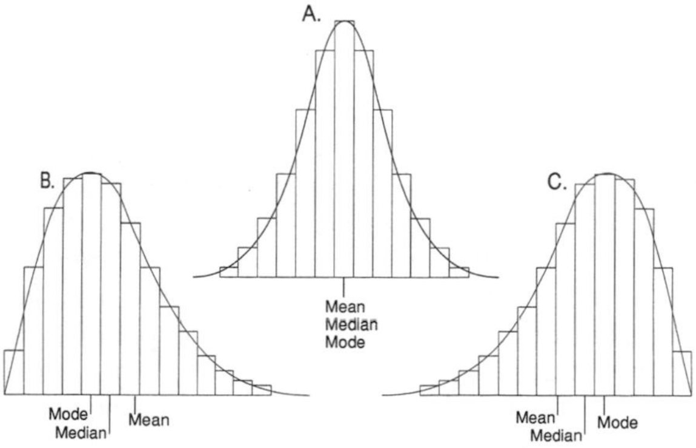

Fig. 3 *Hypothetical frequency histograms showing normal (A), negatively skewed (B) and postively skewed (C) distributions. Note the relative positions of the mean, median and mode*

Continued on page 270.

Box 25.1 *continued from page 269.*

Transformation is a process in which the data values are rescaled by applying a mathematical function e.g. square-root, logarithm etc. In many cases, data that are skewed or show too great a variance can be 'normalised' by an appropriate transformation – so allowing tests requiring normally distributed data to be used, e.g:-

a) **Logarithmic** transformation is a useful correction for data which (in the form of frequency histogram) show a negative skew and/or when the variance (σ^2) of the data is larger than its mean.

b) **Arcsine** transformation can be used as a correction when data values are proportions e.g. percentages which cannot vary below 0 or above 100. The distribution is thus liable to truncation at either end of the scale; so violating the normal distribution rule of tapering 'tails'.

Transforming data is not cheating, but a legitimate use of different measurement scales for statistical purposes. Nevertheless, transformations are easy to misapply and the advice of a statistician should usually be sought.

For the beginner wishing to avoid complex decisions there is a simple alternative. Untransformed non-normal data may be used in *non-parametric* tests. These have less stringent requirements than parametric tests and make no assumptions about the distribution of the data.

INDEPENDENT AND DEPENDENT VARIABLES

In most research designs, it is important to distinguish between the independent and dependent variables. If a variable (*A*) may be presumed to have a causal effect on another variable (*B*), then *A* is termed the independent variable (IV) and *B* the dependent variable (DV). In experimental studies, the researcher controls the independent variable(s) to investigate changes or differences in one or more dependent variables. For example:

- *A study of the effect of changing room temperature on subject's sweat production.* Room temperature presumably has a causal effect on sweat production; the reverse relationship is very unlikely. Hence the experimenter controls the room temperature (IV) to investigate its likely effect on sweat production (DV). Even if the study is not experimental but observational (room temperature changes are observed, not controlled) and related to changing sweat production, temperature remains the IV because of its likely causal relationship with sweating.
- *A study of difference in some variable, say scores of aggression, between groups* (e.g. two or more treatment groups with subjects randomly assigned to each, or gender groups). Aggression levels might well be influenced by treatment or gender, but the reverse – that aggression will either influence the random assignment of subjects to treatment group, or alter a subject's gender – can be discounted. Hence treatment and gender groups are the IVs and the aggression score is the DV.

However, in some observational studies, associations may be observed between variables but there is no clear causal relationship – the IV and DV cannot be distinguished. An example is in the study of MS reported in Box 24.1 of Chapter 24, where it is unclear whether regular attendance at therapy sessions is a cause or a result of improved mobility.

Validity and reliability of measures

In any study, it is crucial to consider whether the variables being measured really do allow the research hypothesis to be tested:

- *Validity* is the degree to which a variable is actually a true measure of what we think we are measuring or observing. For example, to assess a student's understanding of sociology, a test which just asks for the names of famous sociologists is unlikely to assess understanding. Such a test would not be valid.
- *Reliability* is an expression of consistency in measurements.

Note that a measure cannot be valid unless it is reliable, but a measure can be reliable without being a valid measure of the variable of interest (Graziano and Raulin, 1989).

Unreliability can be revealed and quantified by repeated remeasuring of the same subject, object or event. Poor reliability is often due to measurement errors resulting from procedural errors and/or a lack of standardization. Variation in the readings given by instruments can be due to insufficiently rigorous control of environmental variables (temperature, humidity, electricity supply etc. depending on the nature of the equipment). Variability may also result from inherent random effects not under the control of the researcher. Smith (1975) noted that if poor reliability appears to be due to errors of a consistent type, so that there are systematic rather than random errors, then the validity of the measures used should be questioned. See Kerlinger (1986) for a thorough but more advanced treatment of these topics.

Appraising a study design

When appraising a study design, a useful approach is to consider the following.

- *Control.* Is there adequate control of irrelevant and possibly confounding factors? Rigorously standardized conditions and procedures are an essential part of ensuring 'internal validity' in most experimental, observational and interview-based studies.
- *Replication.* Can observations be repeated with different but equivalent samples and equipment, by a different researcher following the same method? This implies the need to document carefully all methodological details. Successful replication of a study indicates that the findings are reliable.
- *Representativeness.* To what extent can the findings be generalized? Are the study sample, experimental conditions or the experimental variables representative of the 'outside-world'? This aspectof a design is known as external or 'ecological' validity.

DATA HANDLING

Descriptive statistics and data presentation

The intelligent use of descriptive statistics and clear, informative presentation of data are vital in any research report. Standard descriptive statistics (e.g. measures of central tendency and variation) are a universal 'language' which concisely and accurately reports the characteristics of the sample data.

As discussed in the measurement section above, different measures of central tendency (mean, median and mode) and variation are appropriate to different levels of measurement (see Table 25.2). Means and standard deviations are really only suitable for at least interval level variables; with ordinal level variables one may instead make use of a median with variability expressed as centiles or quartiles. With nominal level data, only the mode may be used.

Similarly, different graphical techniques are associated with the different levels of measurement. Pie charts and bar charts are appropriate for nominal level data, histograms and frequency polygons are for grouped data which have been measured at no less than ordinal level. Line graphs and scattergrams also require at least ordinal level data. See Box 25.2 for some examples.

A common source of error is the failure to distinguish clearly between nominal categories and ordinal scales. Confusion can result if the names given to nominal categories are ordered numerical values (e.g. categories 1 to 5). In such cases, it is good practice to ensure that the bars of bar charts are clearly separated along the *x*-axis to help to avoid such nominal data misleadingly appearing to represent a scale.

When presenting graphs, it is an important and useful convention to plot the independent variable along the *x*-axis and the dependent variable along the *y*-axis.

Inferential statistics and hypothesis testing

Inferential (inductive) tests are so-called because they use probability theory to make inferences (guesses) about population parameters from sample statistics. For example, by using body mass index (BMI) measures from two randomly drawn samples of men and women, one could draw conclusions about gender differences in obesity in the general population.

Inferential statistics (statistical tests) provide a ready-made standardized 'toolkit' of decision-making techniques. This allows one to judge objectively the significance of differences between study groups or association between variables. Statistical tests are not infallible; but the way they work, their characteristics, strengths and weakness, are well understood by other researchers.

FORMULATING A RESEARCH HYPOTHESIS

Initially, the researcher may have an idea about the nature of the phenomenon under investigation. In exploratory research this may be no more than a tentative hunch, but in experimental research the idea under investigation should be based firmly upon prior evidence. A scientific hypothesis is a concise statement regarding two or more variables linked by some relationship (adapted from Smith, 1975). This is a formalization of a more general research question.

For example, wondering whether an increased daily intake of vitamins would reduce the severity of viral illnesses would be too general to be a research hypothesis. A more useful starting point would be to design an experiment to investigate the possible effects of a specific vitamin supplement, say vitamin C, in reducing the symptoms of a specific viral illness (e.g. the common cold). Then the research hypothesis is:

Box 25.2 *A selection of basic graph types with notes on their use*

1. Pie and bar charts: For nominal level data. Pie charts are useful (Fig. 1) for simple presentations but unless data values are also displayed, it can be hard to visually compare the sizes of pie chart sectors – especially if distracting colours or shading are used.

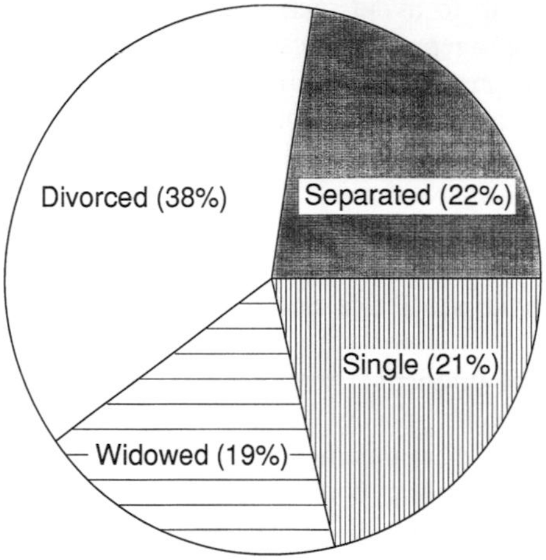

Fig. 1. *Pie chart showing the percentages of lone mothers in four categories of marital status (data for Britain, 1981, estiamted total n = 800 000). Source of data: Donaldson & Donaldson (1983)*

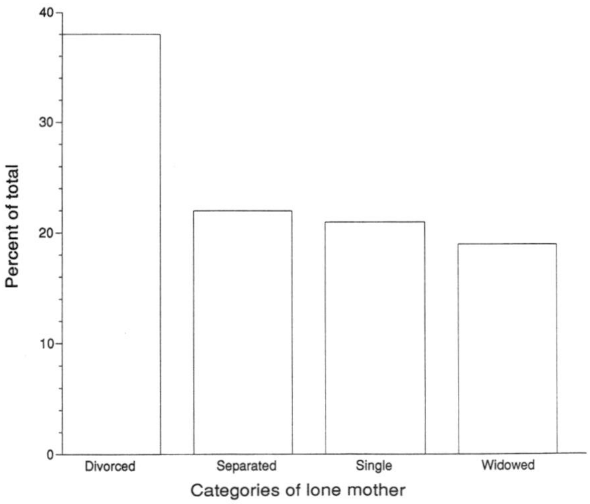

Fig. 2 *Bar chart showing the same data previously used in Fig. 1.*

However, presenting the same data as a bar chart (Fig. 2) makes the relative size of each group much easier to see.

The bars must be separated by gaps. This signals that the ordering of the categories along the *x*-axis is arbitrary and avoids confusion with histograms in which the *x*-axis has a directionally ordered true scale.

An advantage of bar charts over pie charts is that two or more different series of data can be simply displayed together for easy visual comparison (Fig. 3).

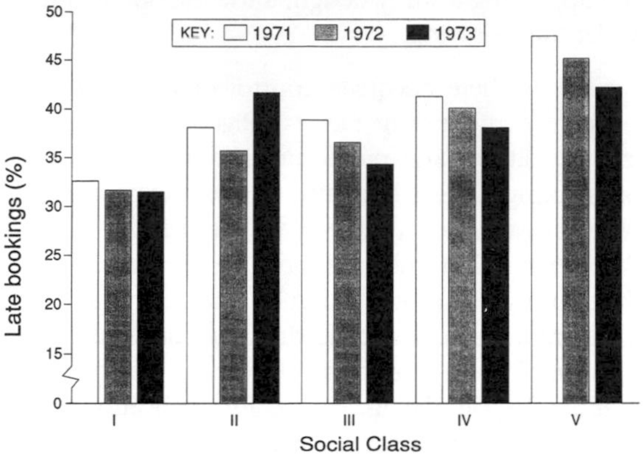

Fig. 3 *Percentage of married women in each social class making a first antenatal booking when over 20 weeks pregnant, Scotland 1971–1973. Source of data: Brotherston (1976); cited by Donaldson & Donaldson (1983)*

2. Histograms: Where data are scaled measurements at ordinal, interval or ratio level, histograms display the distribution of values in groups defined by intervals along the *x*-axis. The contiguous bars denote the underlying continuity of the *x*-axis scale (unlike bar charts).

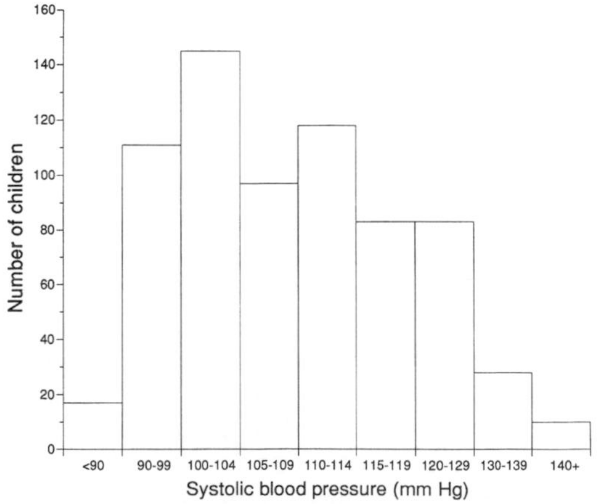

Fig. 4 *Histogram showing the distribution of the systolic blood pressure of 10-year-old children (n = 692). Source of data: Pollock et al. (1981); cited by Donaldson & Donaldson (1983)*

3. Line graphs: These are designed to show continuous change in ordinal, interval or ratio level measurements.

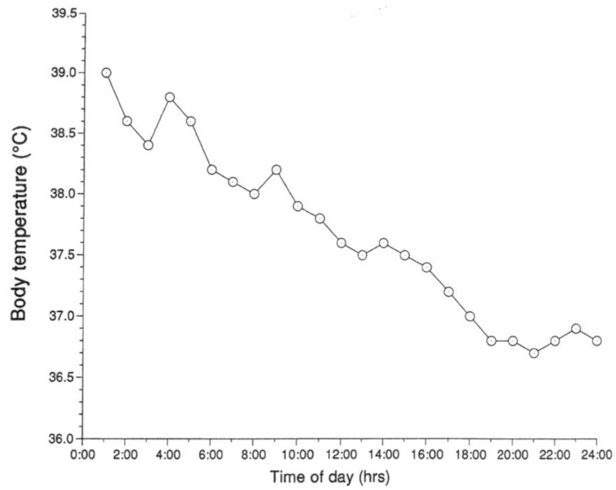

Fig. 5 *Line graph showing the change in body temperature of a patient over a 24-hour period (hypothetical data)*

4. Scatterplots: For ordinal, interval or ratio level data. As in line graphs, the axes are continuously scaled. Each point plotted represents an independent individual, object or event. Scatterplots are ideal for showing relationships between variables (Fig. 6, line fitted by linear regression).

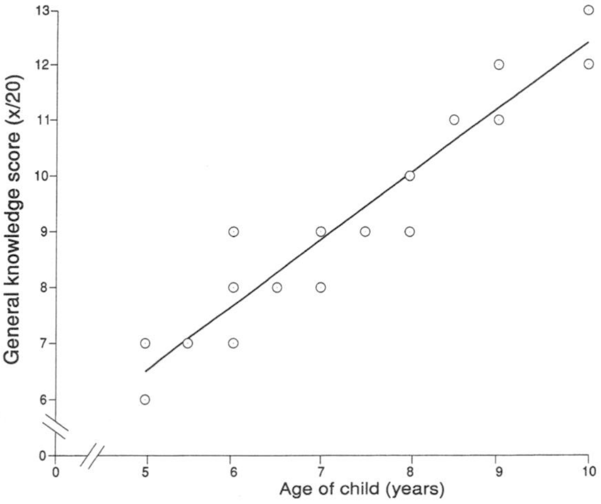

Fig. 6 *Hypothetical graph showing the relationship between age and general knowledge scores in a sample of 18 children*

Variable 1 (independent variable)	*Relationship*	*Variable 2 (dependent variable)*
Vitamin C dosage	will affect	Level of symptoms

The next step would be to decide the measurement methods and the units of measurement of the two variables. Vitamin C dosage could be measured in milligrams per kilogram of bodyweight per day, and a clinical rating scale could be devised to measure symptom severity.

It is useful to distinguish between the research hypothesis and the *null hypothesis* (H_0) which is the basis of statistical tests (see below) and which will assert a *lack* of relationship between the two (or more) variables. The null hypothesis states:

Variable 1 (independent variable)	*Relationship*	*Variable 2 (dependent variable)*
Vitamin C dosage	will not affect	Level of symptoms

The distinction between the research hypothesis and the null hypothesis can be used in all research contexts, including qualitative research. However, in experimental research one tends to refer to the research hypothesis as the experimental hypothesis.

CHOOSING A STATISTICAL TEST

For the novice, choosing the most appropriate test can seem daunting, especially after a brief glance at a fairly comprehensive choice-chart of tests (Figure 25.2). In fact, more discerning inspection will reveal that the choice of test follows logically from a simple series of carefully made decisions based on the kind of question being asked and the research design (see above), as well as the level of measurement of the variables and their pattern of variation (see above and Box 25.1). It is critical to remember that *all* statistical tests are designed to be *tests of hypotheses*. If your hypotheses are poorly formulated or your measurements or research design are unsound, then poor judgements will be the result – whether or not statistical tests are used.

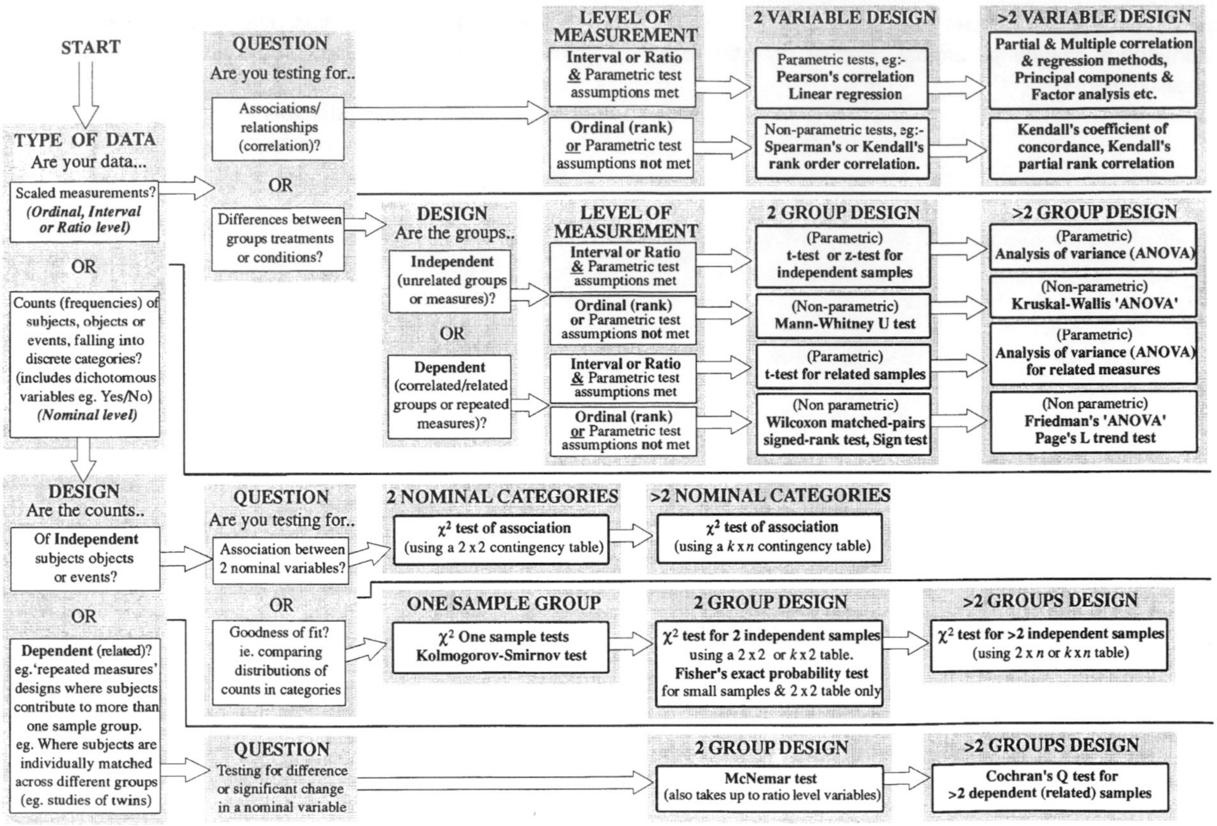

Figure 25.2 *A summary choice-chart for inferential statistical tests (from Reeve and Hewitt, 1995, unpublished)*

Parametric and non-parametric statistics

Parametric tests (e.g. *t*-test, *F*-test, analysis of variance) assume:

- an interval or ratio level of measurement;
- that the dependent variable is Normally distributed in the population (Box 25.1);
- that the sample size is big enough to reflect accurately a Normal distribution (the size will vary according to the nature of the variable and its variance.

However, in health research, data are often measured at less than interval level and/or may show non-Normal distributions. In such cases, especially if sample sizes are small, *non-parametric tests* (distribution-free tests) are usually appropriate. Although they often sound exotic (e.g. the Kolmogorov–Smirnov one-sample test), most are simple to use. Non-parametric statistics:

- make no assumptions about the distribution of population parameters;
- will accept data measured at less than interval level.

However, because they have less information to use, such tests are more conservative in their findings (less likely to show significance) than parametric tests. Nevertheless, when sample sizes are large, non-parametric test statistics may approximate very closely to those of parametric tests.

Chi-squared tests and their many derivatives are usually lumped in with non-parametric tests (e.g. Siegel and Castellan, 1988) because they require only a nominal level of measurement.

Although non-parametric tests are more suited than parametric tests to small sample sizes, the issue of exactly what is a small or large sample size with respect to any particular test is not an easy one to deal with at an introductory level. A useful discussion on the influence of sample size on the *power* of tests in relation to the size of the effect being measured may be found in Howell (1992). Overall, if you have sample sizes of less than around 10, or suspect that your sample is too small to be representative of the study population, you should consider the use of non-parametric tests and/or seek further advice.

The choice of test

To begin the test-choice process, state carefully the research question, including the variables and their units of measurement. Then follow the steps on the choice-chart in Figure 25.2, as in the following three examples.

Example 1: *Is there an association between alcohol dose (mg/kg) and reaction times (milliseconds) in a sample of 100 individuals?* Steps in the choice chart are:

- Both alcohol dose and reaction times are scaled measurements.
- The question is one of association between two variables.
- The level of measurement is ratio level and both variables are of the type that are typically Normally distributed in populations. Note that parametric tests require data to be Normally distributed, to be measured at interval or ratio level, and each variable should have a roughly similar variance (checked by using the variance ratio or *F*-test).
- The choice is a Pearson's correlation test.

Should one or both of the measures be ordinal level (e.g. the reaction times replaced by a drunkenness rating scale from 1 to 10), then the choice would be a Spearman's or Kendall's rank order correlation.

Example 2: *In the example study given in Box 24.1, the researchers asked whether there was a difference in the functional abilities (ADL scores) of MS sufferers between two groups – regular attenders for physiotherapy and irregular attenders?* Steps in the choice chart are:

- ADL is a scaled measure.
- The question is one of difference between two groups, regular and irregular attenders.
- Each treatment group is independent of the other; i.e. subjects from one group have no influence on, or association with, the ADL scores of the other group.
- The level of measurement of ADL is ordinal, so parametric assumptions are not met.
- The test choice is the Mann–Whitney U-test of difference between two independent groups.

Had the ADL been an interval level variable and the general assumptions of parametric tests been met, then a *t*-test for independent samples could have been used.

An alternative question might have been: *Is there a change in the ADL scores of MS sufferers from the first assessment to the last (after 18 months of physiotherapy)?* Most of the choices above would still be applicable, but because the same subjects would be measured twice, the pre- and post-physiotherapy groups would not be independent. The test choice would be a Wilcoxon matched-pairs signed-rank test.

Example 3: *In the example study given in Box 24.2, the researchers might have asked whether there was an association between whether or not (Yes or No) women carry out breast self-examinations (BSE) and whether or not (Yes or No) women attend for cervical smear tests?* Steps in the choice chart are:

- Both BSE and attendance are dichotomous variables (women either do or do not BSE or attend smear tests); i.e. they are nominal level variables.
- The question is one of association between two variables.
- Each nominal variable has two categories; hence the 2×2 chi-squared test of association is the choice.

INTERPRETING INFERENTIAL TEST RESULTS: SIGNIFICANCE AND *P* VALUES

All test results should be expressed in terms of acceptance or rejection of the null hypothesis (H_0) that there is no effect – i.e. no difference or no association (see above). It is the likelihood of H_0 being true that the test is determining, no more than that. The *test statistic* (the *t*-value or whatever) may be referred to tables which show critical values of the statistic at particular sample sizes (or degrees of freedom) for certain levels of significance.

These days, most computer statistics software packages will display significance levels after each test, without the need to refer to tables. The 'significance level', typically expressed as a *p*-value, is the remaining chance that H_0 is true. The smaller it is, the greater the chance that the effect being investigated is real (significant). Table 25.3 shows some typical conventions for denoting significance levels (the chance that the H_0 is true).

Often the significance level is expressed in terms of the confidence one has in rejecting H_0. Hence a 5% chance that H_0 is true becomes translated into a 95% confidence that H_0 can be rejected. The significance

Table 25.3 *Typical significance levels (i.e. the chance that H_0 is true)*

Less than 1 in 20	Less than 1 in 100	Less than 1 in 1000
< 5% $p < 0.05$ *	<1% $p < 0.01$ **	<0.1% $p < 0.001$ ***

level at which H_0 is rejected is conventionally taken to be $p = 0.05$ (95% confidence), but this is arbitrary and may not be exacting enough for many test situations. To illustrate this point, would you use a shampoo that might cause skin cancer in 5% of people?

There is no such thing as statistical proof! A test delivers *a judgement about what is probably true*, but that judgement is based not only on the data used but also on the assumptions underlying the mathematics of the test. This is why violations of test assumptions can produce false results. Even when the assumptions are met, errors of judgement (so-called Type I and Type II errors) are always possible. When a test falsely rejects H_0 it has committed a Type I error; if it wrongly fails to reject the H_0 it has committed a Type II error. Effectively p is the probability of a Type I error.

The use of computers in research

Although it is beyond the scope of this chapter to provide a review of hardware and software, readers should appreciate the wide range of research applications offered by computer-based technologies.

These include systems that can contribute to the logistical planning and costing of research, communications, literature searching and information retrieval. Word-processing and reference management programmes are valuable in all kinds of scientific reporting.

Specialist software to help design and produce questionnaires can be used with Optical Mark Recognition (OMR) systems that can automatically read and process information from box-ticking style questionnaires.

Computers, interfaced with measuring instruments, can be a valuable aid to behavioural and physiological monitoring.

Once data have been gathered, a wide range of data analysis, graph plotting and presentation software is available. Some studies may find that one of the many spreadsheets available (e.g. Excel, Lotus 1-2-3, Quattro) offers sufficient statistical analysis options, but more comprehensive packages (e.g. Minitab, SPSS, SAS) allow many more options, more control of data and more complex designs and analyses, as well as cross-tabulation and coding options more suited to qualitative research. Databases can also be useful for qualitative analysis.

Whatever software is used, on whatever kind of computer, one should pay special attention to the data formats being used. Data in the form of an ASCII file are universally transferable, but in practice this can be an unwieldy process. It is thus very important to check that text and data can be satisfactorily imported and exported to and from all the packages being used.

EVALUATING AND COMMUNICATING RESEARCH FINDINGS

Evaluating a research paper is an important skill needed in the development of research ideas and when reviewing the literature, but also when finalizing a report or paper. It is basically the same task as peer-reviewing an article for publication in a scientific journal. Sommer and Sommer (1991) provided guidelines for evaluating and reviewing a research paper (see Box 25.3); incidentally, the headings reflect the generally accepted structure for a research report as found in many scientific journals.

While there is no generally accepted format for a critique, it is probably a good idea to start with a brief overall summary of the paper and finish with an overall evaluation. Another useful source is Sternberg (1988), who also gives advice on the organization of literature reviews and the writing of project reports. In the end, the specific format of a critique is probably less important than good organization which ensures that the reader can follow the argument.

When communicating research findings it is necessary to be aware of their limitations. This is partricularly important when writing reports to policy-makers or those who attempt to utilize scientific findings for practical purposes, but are not interested in the details of the research itself. Unfortunately, researchers sometimes mix up statistical significance with practical significance (Cronbach, 1990) – for example a difference found between two groups of people may not be really useful or important in healthcare. Even small differences *can* be significant, and therefore of theoretical interest, if study samples are large. But in practice, only clearly identifiable differences tend to be relevant – such differences may lead to different diagnoses, different treatments or different needs. The example in Box 24.1 in the previous chapter suggests that regular physiotherapy makes a real difference to the development of MS. However, detailed reading of the research presented in Box 24.2 suggests that the effects there are relatively small, and are possibly of little relevance to health promotion.

Box 25.3 *Guidelines for evaluating and reviewing a research paper – a step-by-step approach for your critique (based on Sommer and Sommer, 1991)*

Introduction and background

A. Is the problem clearly stated?
   1. What questions are posed by the researchers?
   2. Are the hypotheses or goals of the study clearly stated?

B. Is the important background literature (earlier work in the field) included?

Research method

A. Are the methods appropriate to the goals of the study?
   1. Do they fit the question/hypotheses?
   2. Was the choice of methods dictated by the goals of the study, or simply a matter of expediency?

B. Is the sample appropriate, given the nature of the study (i.e. is it representative of the population of interest)?
   1. Were the participants selected in such a way as to avoid bias?
   2. Is it a special group whose characteristics may influence the outcome in particular ways?
   3. Does the sample make sense for the hypotheses being tested?
   4. Is the sample described in sufficient detail?

C. What variables are being measured?
   1. How are they measured; for example, a paper-and-pencil test, an open-ended questionnaire, a measure of time, counts of some activity, statistics from a government report, etc.?
   2. Are questionnaires, surveys, or tally sheets described in sufficient detail for the reader to judge their adequacy?
   3. Are laboratory instruments adequately described?
   4. In observational studies, is the selection and training of observers described?
   5. Is evidence of reliability presented (i.e. reliability of instruments, interrater reliability etc.)?

D. Does the procedure do what it is supposed to do?
   1. Is the logic of the procedure correct?
   2. Were all sources of bias (subject, experimenter, responder, interviewer, setting, etc.) eliminated or controlled?

Results (description of findings)

A. What answers were obtained to the questions posed?
   1. Are the findings clearly presented with adequate descriptive statistics (e.g. number of cases, mean, median, standard deviation, or range)?
   2. Are tables and graphs present and informative?
   3. Are the statistical tests (inferential statistics) appropriate to the data?

Discussion and conclusion

A. Are the findings correctly interpreted?
   1. Are the interpretations of the results based on these results?
   2. Is the level of generalization appropriate?
      a. Is it justified by the sample?
      b. Is it justified by the research design?
   3. Are procedural weaknesses noted?
   4. Are the limitations of the study discussed?
   5. Are the findings related to the literature?

B. Are conclusions drawn from the study?
   1. Are any practical implications noted?
   2. Do the researchers make specific suggestions for further research?

Key Points

- A key first step in the research process is to clarify carefully the questions being asked.
- In experiments the research question must be formulated as a hypothesis.
- Sampling methods should aim to ensure that a sample is a truly representative and unbiased subset of the population from which it is drawn.
- Findings based on a sample of a population only relate to that population.
- There are three main research designs: description, comparison, and correlation.
- The type of statistical analysis is constrained by the level of measurement and distribution of the data collected.
- Statistical tests do not provide proof, rather they are standard decision-making tools that provide a measure of probability.
- Stronger conclusions can be drawn from parametric tests than non-parametric tests but only if their stringent assumptions about the data are met.
- A critical appraisal of scientific literature requires an understanding of the methodology and analysis methods used.

References

Cohen, L. and Holliday, M. (1982). *Statistics for the Social Sciences.* New York: Harper & Row.

Cronbach, L.J. (1990). *Essentials of Psychological Testing,* 5th edn. New York: Harper & Row.

Donaldson, R.J. and Donaldson, L.J. (1983). Essential community medicine. Lancaster: MTP Press.

Graziano, A. and Raulin, M. (1989). *Research Methods.* Cambridge, Mass.: Harper & Row.

Howell, D.C. (1992). *Statistical Methods for Psychology,* 3rd edn. Massachusetts: PWS-Kent.

Kerlinger, F.N. (1986). *Foundations of Behavioral Research,* 3rd edn. Fort Worth: Harcourt Brace Jovanovich.

Moser, C.A. and Kalton, G. (1971). *Survey Methods in Social Investigation,* 2nd edn. London: Heinemann.

Oppenheim, A.N. (1992). *Questionnaire Design, Interviewing and Attitude Measurement,* 2nd edn. London: Pinter.

Siegel, S. and Castellan, N.J. (1988). *Nonparametric Statistics for the Behavioral Sciences,* 2nd edn. New York: McGraw-Hill.

Smith, HW (1975). *Strategies of Social Research.* Englewood Cliffs, NJ: Prentice-Hall.

Sommer, R. and Sommer, B. (1991). *A Practical Guide to Behavioural Research.* Oxford: Oxford University Press.

Spielberger, C.D., Gorsuch, R.L., Lushene, R., Vagg, P.R. and Jacobs, G.A. (1983). *Manual for the State–Trait Anxiety Inventory (Form Y).* Palo Alto, CA: Consulting Psychologists Press.

Sternberg, R. (1988). *The Psychologist's Companion,* 2nd edn. Cambridge: Cambridge University Press.

Further Reading

Cohen, L. and Holliday, M. (1982). *Statistics for the Social Sciences.* New York: Harper & Row.

Graziano, A. and Raulin, M. (1989). *Research Methods.* Cambridge, Mass.: Harper & Row.

Kerlinger, F.N. (1986). *Foundations of Behavioural Research,* 3rd edn. Fort Worth: Harcourt Brace Jovanovich.

Oppenheim, A.N. (1992). *Questionnaire Design, Interviewing and Attitude Measurement,* 2nd edn. London: Pinter.

Sommer, R. and Sommer, B. (1991). *A Practical Guide to Behavioural Research.* Oxford: Oxford University Press.

26

Principles of Health Promotion

Lesley Vernon

LEARNING OBJECTIVES

After studying this chapter you should:

- Be able to describe the diversity of the disciplines contributing to health promotion
- Be able to discuss the role of the 'new public health' in the development of health promotion in recent years
- Understand the value of interdisciplinary collaboration and partnership in the practice of health promotion
- Appreciate the political nature of health promotion

INTRODUCTION

In recent years, health promotion has become an important force in improving the quality and duration of peoples' lives (Catford, 1992). This is a result of a worldwide realization that a predominantly biomedical approach to health and healthcare has had little effect in reducing mortality and morbidity in preventable diseases (McKeowan, 1976; Morgan *et al.*, 1985).

In the UK it is acknowledged that the National Health Service has not had the effect that was originally intended, of reducing inequalities in health and access to healthcare. The form of healthcare now advocated by the World Health Organization is one based on an ecological systems model. As such, hospital-based medical care is seen as only part of a healthcare system that is combined with aspects of environmental health protection, personal prevention and primary healthcare (Luker and Ashton, 1991). Traditionally, the biomedical model of healthcare has been dominant in the education of everyone in the caring professions. However, because of the change in emphasis from intervention to prevention, health promotion is one of the disciplines that are now thought to be essential in the education of a new generation of healthcare workers.

A discussion on the meaning of health promotion will reveal that people's understanding of this concept differ. This is not surprising, as this confusion, at a conceptual level, is recognized by theorists and practitioners alike. It has been suggested that because health promotion means different things to different people, there may be as many definitions around as there are disciplines working in this arena (Anderson, 1983; Tones, 1984).

Learning Activity 1 ◆ ◆ ◆

You may already have a good idea of what health promotion is. However, discuss the concept with colleagues and friends to discover whether you share similar thoughts.

As a result of this growing interest in health promotion, a wide literature on the subject has developed. For example, Sutherland (1979) gives a clear account of its historical development; while Bunton and Macdonald (1992) show how the various subjects that constitute the knowledge base in health promotion, complement each other. This chapter aims to provide the reader with an overview of the structural and theoretical development of health promotion. This is in order to equip students with the beginnings of a sound framework for practice.

Box 26.1 *Six dimensions of health (Ewles and Simnett, 1992)*

PHYSICAL HEALTH	the mechanistic functioning of the body.
MENTAL HEALTH	the ability to think clearly and coherently.
EMOTIONAL HEALTH	the ability to recognise emotions such as fear, joy, grief and to express them appropriately. It is also associated with coping with the effects of emotions like stress and anxiety.
SOCIAL HEALTH	the ability to establish and maintain human relationships.
SPIRITUAL HEALTH	this may be associated with religious beliefs or ways of achieving peace of mind.
SOCIETAL HEALTH	this view of health moves away from the individual and recognizes that health is not attainable in an unhealthy society. People cannot be healthy if they cannot afford food and shelter and if they are so politically oppressed that basic human rights are denied (Ewles and Simnett 1992).

DEFINING HEALTH AND ILLNESS

Any discussion of the meaning of health promotion usually begins with an analysis of the concept of health. Over the past twenty years or so, studies have been carried out by researchers from various backgrounds in order to try to find a common definition that would help professionals to improve their practice. These studies have looked at health beliefs from the lay and professional perspectives.

The lay perspective

Herlizch investigated the beliefs of health and illness of middle-class people in France in 1973. Her conclusion was that her subjects thought of health as something 'internal', which they could control, and illness was associated with 'external' agents, beyond their control. Herlizch also identified three distinct themes which emerged from her data, which she described as:

- *health in a vacuum*: the absence of disease;
- *health as a resource*: the physical ability to maintain health and resist illness;
- *health as an equilibrium*: balance, harmony, the notion of well-being.

A similar study of elderly people in Aberdeen (Williams, 1983) identified similar dimensions in health.

Further studies in the UK (Pill and Stott, 1982; Calnan and Johnson, 1983; Blaxter, 1990) have concentrated on the relationship between health beliefs and social class. What emerges from these is that middle-class people have a more positive perception of health in that they tend to control their health by being active, keeping fit and using preventive health services. Working-class people tended to view health negatively, in terms of 'not being ill' and 'getting by' despite disease.

To summarize, from a lay perspective, there is no finite definition of health. People's views vary according to their age, social class, economic status and cultural background.

The professional perspective

Although professionals working in healthcare may be able to view health objectively, they too have no shared opinion on how to define health. As long ago as 1947 the World Health Organization defined health as 'a state of complete physical, mental and social well-being, rather than solely as absence of disease' (WHO, 1947). This definition is still frequently quoted and often accepted at face value, but there are many problems associated with it. The spiritual, societal and emotional aspects of health are addressed, but it is very idealistic and implies a static position. The dynamic nature of health is ignored.

In attempting to answer the questions in Activity 2, you may have added further dimensions to the WHO (1947) definition of health. Ewles and Simnett (1992) classify six dimensions of health (see Box 26.1).

Clearly, from both lay and professional perspectives health is a multidimensional concept. In reality none of these dimensions can be taken as discrete entities, they are interdependent. The main conclusion to be drawn from this discussion is that it is important for

Learning Activity 2 ◆ ◆ ◆

Consider the following questions:

- ◆ How many people do you know who would say that they think they are always in a 'complete state of physical, mental and social well-being'?
- ◆ Do you think that people who are physically disabled are unhealthy?
- ◆ Do you think that people who have a learning disability are unhealthy?
- ◆ Can people who have a disease for which there is no known cure feel well?
- ◆ Is someone who is a heavy drinker unhealthy?
- ◆ Are people who don't take any regular exercise unhealthy?
- ◆ Does wealth or poverty influence health?

practitioners, managers (policymakers) and the public to communicate their views, beliefs and understanding of health so that they can work together to promote health effectively (Edelman and Mandle, 1994).

DEFINING HEALTH PROMOTION

At its most simple level any interpretation of health promotion is dependent upon whether one adopts a 'structuralist' (collective) or 'individualist' (lifestyle) approach to health (Bunton and Macdonald, 1992). A 'structuralist' sees health as being determined by the environment in which people live and work. As such, health promotion has a political dimension. An 'individualist' sees health as being the responsibility of the individual, and dependent on the lifestyle that people adopt regardless of their environment.

Therefore, ill-health could be described, respectively, as the consequence of poverty and social deprivation, or of the unhealthy and harmful habits that people have, such as drinking and smoking too much, eating 'junk food', and not participating in any form of exercise.

Bunton and Macdonalds' explanation is useful in beginning to understand what is meant by health promotion. However, studies have repeatedly shown that interventions aimed at changing individual 'unhealthy lifestyles' and ignoring people's social life have been unsuccessful (Ewles and Simnett, 1990; Beattie, 1992; Williams *et al.*, 1993). All they do is induce feelings of rebelliousness and guilt, and for these reasons they have been called 'victim-blaming'. Therefore, further clarification of the concept is required. The rest of the chapter will be devoted to this task.

Health promotion is frequently described as a new discipline; this is not so. It has evolved from health education, which has its roots in the classical Greek view of health. This view is *holistic* and is described as the degree to which individuals are capable of achieving balance and harmony in their lives. Although, historically, health education was not the exclusive domain of health professionals, with the implementation of the 1974 National Health Service Act it was formally institutionalized within the NHS in the United Kingdom. From then on it became an essential part of practice (Rodmell and Watt, 1986; Nijuis and van der Maesen, 1994). However, people may only come into contact with health workers at certain times in their lives, such as in pregnancy, childhood and old age. The impact they can have in terms of traditional health education, which is about informing people on how to use services and improve compliance in treatment, is questionable (Ashton and Seymour, 1986).

THE 'NEW PUBLIC HEALTH'

It was as part of the shift in focus from a biomedical to a social and environmental model of health that the concept of health promotion emerged. This was in Canada in 1974. The then minister for health and welfare, Lalonde, produced his report *A New Perspective on the Health of Canadians*. This can best be described as the catalyst for the re-emergence of the nineteenth century public health movement in developed countries. The Lalonde Report introduced into public policy for the first time the notion that all causes of death and disease could be divided into four discrete elements:

- inadequacies in healthcare provision;
- lifestyle and behavioural factors;
- environmental pollution;
- biophysical characteristics.

The basic message was that critical improvements in the environment (structure) and in behaviour (lifestyle) could bring about a significant reduction in premature death. The aim of the New Public Health is to improve the health of populations. It goes beyond a recognition of the purely biological aspects of health and illness causation.

The Acheson Committee (1988) describes this as 'the art and science of preventing disease, prolonging life and promoting health through the organised efforts of society'. It views individuals in a social, cultural and physical environment which is the central conceptual base for health promotion (Kickbush, 1985). The New Public Health aims to enable interventions to be made that are based on 'common life situations and/or life chances of certain groups rather than on intervention aimed at specific diseases' (Kickbush, 1985). At international, national and local levels, it therefore involves the reorientation of public, corporate and health services through the creation of healthy public policies which are health-promoting. This means that policies should be proactive, focusing on prevention rather than cure.

The recurring themes in the literature are now on participation and collaboration. For the healthcare professional, participation means that it is not enough to decide on a form of treatment or care and give it, but that individuals should be actively involved in any decisions or choices that are made. Collaboration can be interpreted as lay people and professionals from different disciplines and organizations working together as equal partners in order to tackle health problems.

What is also emerging as a result of the growth of the public health movement is an increasing involvement by social scientists, community activists and educationalists in health promotion. This is because the disciplines underpinning the knowledge base of health promotion (natural sciences, social sciences, economics, ethics, epidemiology and the media) are similar to those supporting the various professions in health and social care. For these reasons, health promotion is described as the unifying thread that has brought these fields of study together, in an attempt to develop new approaches to improvement in health (Bunton and Macdonald, 1992).

HEALTH FOR ALL 2000

The desire for a new public health movement was expressed by a series of initiatives by the World Health Organization, the first of these being the WHO Assembly at Alma Ata (1978). This is where the concept of health promotion was formally introduced. Its main focus was a commitment to primary healthcare, community participation and intersectorial collaboration. All member countries were signatories to these principles of 'Health For All 2000'.

Following on from this, the international strategy was launched. Various nations of the world were banded into regions with their own specific targets to achieve. The UK is a member of the European region. The 38 European targets are aimed at improving both public and individual health.

In explaining the structure of these targets, the WHO (1985) defines the prerequisites for health (see Box 26.2). None of these can be achieved without strong political and public support. They also describe the aims of improvement in health along quality lines.

***Box 26.2** Prerequisites and aims of improvement in health (WHO, 1985)*

The prerequisites for health	The aims of improvement in health
A satisfying role in society	Equity in health
Peace	Adding life to years
Adequate food and income	Health to life
Safe water and sanitation	Years to life

Health promotion was defined as 'the process of enabling people to increase control over and improve their health'. In this context health is viewed rather as a resource for living rather than an end in itself (Ashton and Seymour, 1988). The WHO also describe health promotion as a:

> 'unifying concept for those who recognize the need for change in the ways and conditions of living in order to promote health. Health promotion represents a mediating strategy between people and their environments, synthesizing personal choice and social responsibility in health to create a healthier future' (WHO, 1984).

Publication of this document paved the way for a series of international conferences, the first being in Ottowa, Canada, in 1986. The result of this was the charter for action, namely the creation of:

- healthy public policy;
- supportive environments;
- strong community action;
- personal skills;
- reorientated health services (Kelly, 1990; Bunton and Macdonald, 1992).

The Ottowa Charter also stated three main aims which could be utilized by professionals in beginning the process of helping people to take control over their own lives. These are described advocacy, mediation and enablement. What is meant here is that any public policy should be designed in ways that have positive rather than negative consequences for health. The political obstacles to the adoption of healthy policies in agencies such as housing, agriculture, taxation and transport should be recognized and removed.

However, health promotion efforts cannot be the sole responsibility of governments; communities must be involved and empowered to take responsibility for health. To do this they need information and other resources in order to be able to identify their needs, set priorities and begin to work towards solutions to their problems.

Within the NHS this is being achieved, to some extent, by the work of the public health directorates in health authorities, which publish their annual reports based on an epidemiological data collection that utilizes quantitative and more sensitive qualitative methods. The aim is to plan and commission health services that reflect local needs, through what can be called 'community profiling' or 'community diagnosis'. The WHO's Healthy Cities Programme is a series of national networks based on the idea of multisectorial working or healthy alliances. The intention here is to bring together a small number of European cities to collaborate in working to produce models of good health promotion practice in urban environments. Ashton and Seymour (1986) provide a very thorough and illuminative analysis of their work in the Liverpool Healthy Cities project.

THE UK GOVERNMENT'S RESPONSE TO HEALTH PROMOTION

The shape of health promotion within the NHS has been determined through a series of White Papers: *Prevention and Health: Everybody's Business* (DHSS, 1976); the Griffiths Report (DHSS, 1983); *Promoting Better Health* (DoH, 1987), *Working for People* (DoH, 1989a); *Caring for Patients* (DoH, 1989b). The Griffiths Report was responsible for the introduction of general management principles into the NHS. The last two of these White Papers provided the framework for the NHS and Community Care Act 1990.

One of the main aims of this legislation, and in line with the Ottowa Charter, was for the UK government to place the issue of primary healthcare and health promotion on the political agenda. The NHS and Community Care Act (DoH, 1991) contains a number of key proposals for improving primary care. The main intention here was to shift the emphasis from an illness service, to one offering to prevent disease and disability. However, the preferred model is one that is general practitioner led and based on screening for individual risk factors and health and lifestyle advice which, it is argued, is not in keeping with the philosophy of the WHO (Williams *et al.*, 1993).

The new GP contract offers financial incentives for providing health promotion services. These incentives are banded according to the type of service offered. For example, a minimum fee is provided for checking the height, weight, blood pressure and urine of new patients. Further remuneration is offered for the provision of more formal clinics, such as for well women, diabetes, asthma and smoking cessation. The weaknesses inherent in this lifestyle approach to health promotion have already been addressed. However, it should also be made apparent here that the preference for this approach could be due to the fact that, because it has the merit of producing quantifiable results, it fits quite well within the market culture of the current NHS.

Having established that policy decisions in this country do not appear to entirely reflect the WHO philosophy of health promotion, it is necessary to revisit the definition and examine some of the problems associated with it. The main problem seems to be concerned not so much with the definition itself, but with the interpretation. For example, it can be argued that, although the WHO's definitions and approaches to health promotion acknowledge medicine as part of the process, the predominance of the social model of health and illness could also be limiting. An enthusiasm for de-medicalizing explanations for disease causation can lead to an unhelpful conflict between medical and social models of health and illness.

It is more useful to utilize Antonovsky's claim that behavioural and medical science should focus on system survival. In terms of health promotion, this means that critical questions should be asked about why particular individuals or societies are more able to withstand the effects of poor economic and social conditions, environmental pollution and self-harm. The debate between the social and medical model is irrelevant if the contributions made by medical and behavioural sciences are equal and emphasis is placed on system survival rather than breakdown (Kelly, 1990).

There are also problems associated with target-setting, regarding the orientation towards action for change in the future. For example, Kelly (1990) acknowledges the problems encountered by the Healthy Cities projects in devising indicators to measure future changes of state. By placing a target of a 15% reduction in a specific disease in a particular community by the year 2000, a future improved state of health is implied. However, community profiles often show that ordinary people are much more concerned with the problems of everyday life (Kelly, 1990).

There is also a view that the WHO's definition pays scant attention to the importance of the contribution of sciences of behavioural and social change, such as sociology, psychology and social psychology. While no one person can be an expert regarding the range and depth of knowledge in these disciplines, when any health promotion initiative is planned, regardless of the level, it is important that attention should be given to the models of behavioural and social change that will be utilized (Kelly, 1990).

The 'Health of a Nation'

With these factors in mind, it should be somewhat easier to view the emergence of the government's Green Paper (1991) and White Paper (1992) on the *Health of the Nation* in a more sympathetic light. The White Paper focuses on five key areas for change up to and beyond the year 2000 (see Box 26.3).

The document also identifies four 'risk factor' or target areas where strategies for change should be focused, these being:

***Box 26.3** Five key areas for change identified in* Health of the Nation

Heart disease and stroke
By the year 2000 reduce:

- heart disease death rates in people under 65 by at least 40%, and among people between 65 and 74 by at least 30%;
- the death rate from stroke among people under 75 by at least 40%;
- the number of people smoking by a third.

Cancer
By the year 2000 reduce:

- the number of people smoking by a third;
- the rate of breast cancer deaths among women invited for screening by at least 25%;
- the incidence of invasive cervical cancer by approximately 20%.

Mental illness

- Improve significantly the health, social functioning and quality of life of people who are mentally ill;
- By the year 2000 reduce the national suicide rate by 15%.

Sexual health
Reduce:

- the national incidence of gonorrhoea by at least 20% by 1995;
- the proportion of drug users who report needle sharing from a fifth in 1990 to no more than a tenth in 1997;
- by at least half the rate of conceptions amongst the under-16s by the year 2000.

Accidents
By 2005 reduce:

- the rates of accidental deaths among children and elderly people by a third;
- the rates of accidental deaths among young people aged 15 to 24 by at least a quarter.

Box 26.4 *Weaknesses identified by the RCN (1991) in response to the Health of the Nation Green Paper*

- Targets within some of the key areas are defined too narrowly.
- Targets where relevant should make provision for different levels of compliance for different ethnic groups, socio-economic groups or genders.
- Reducing the total incidence of disease in the nation is welcome, but attempts should be made to reduce differentials between groups.
- Resources must not be diverted from those areas where no targets are to be set.
- Targets should be finalized in the light of local circumstances, and the resources needed to make progress towards targets must be controlled locally.

- smoking;
- diet and nutrition;
- blood pressure;
- HIV/AIDS.

This strategy has been criticized by political opposition parties for ignoring the fact that poverty and inequalities in health still exist (Williams *et al.*, 1993). Professional organizations have been equally critical. The Royal College of Nursing, in response to the Green Paper identified several weaknesses in the document (see Box 26.4).

The White Paper does represent an advance in government thinking on public health issues, but it still tends to be disease-orientated. It is also long on descriptive analysis and short on outlining effective ways in which it can be implemented. For example, although a target of a 30% reduction in congenital heart disease and mortality from stroke is set, along with targets to reduce smoking to 22% and 21% of respective male and female populations, no suggestion is made regarding the financial and human resources required to achieve them.

The document also indicates an understanding of the relevance of a collaborative approach to health promotion. At both national and local levels, agencies are acknowledged as having a responsibility to work together to implement health promotion strategies. They should have clearly defined and common aims. The departments involved range from environment, transport, energy and education through to the Health and Safety Commission, local authorities and the voluntary sector. However, despite this shift, there is still a strong emphasis within the document on changing individual lifestyles and behaviour.

SUMMARY

Health promotion is about creating change. It is the responsibility of international, national and local governments and organizations to enable people to lead healthier lives, by creating environments which empower them to do so. A multiplicity of agencies and professionals with diverse philosophies and perceptions of health and health promotion are involved in this work. For these reasons it is an extremely challenging and complex discipline. Because of the conflict and lack of consensus regarding the meaning and intended outcomes of health promotion, it is often difficult for health professionals to identify how they can work effectively.

In order to begin to establish a framework for practice, it was stated at the beginning of this chapter that, at its simplest level, practice was determined on whether a structural or lifestyle approach was adopted. What emerges, though, is that at whatever level professionals are working, they cannot work in isolation. Communication is one of the major components of this discipline and notions of partnership and collaboration are the key themes.

The stance adopted in this chapter is that, by basing their philosophy for practice within this framework of 'health for all', health professionals – whether working in acute hospital or community settings – will begin to understand the roles and boundaries of the variety of disciplines working in this sphere. Conflicting value systems or ideologies should not be a barrier to progress. Ultimately this should have a significant effect on the quality of service and care being given, not only to the well, but to also those who are ill or chronically disabled.

Key Points ■ ■ ■

- ❐ Both lay and professional understanding of health promotion represents a wide spectrum of differing perspectives.
- ❐ The successful development of health promotion lies in interdisciplinary collaboration and partnership.
- ❐ Health promotion is a unifying concept which draws health disciplines together in an attempt to empower people to take control of their health.
- ❐ The political dimension of health promotion has major consequences.

References ▼ ▼ ▼

Acheson, D. (1988). *Public Health in England*. London: HMSO.

Anderson, R. (1983). *Health Promotion: An Overview*. Copenhagen: WHO.

Antonovsky, A. (1987). *Unraveling the mystery of health*. San Francisco: Tossey Bass.

Ashton, J. and Seymour (1988). *The New Public Health*. Milton Keynes: Open University Press.

Beattie, A. (1992). Knowledge and control in health promotion. In: Gabe, J. *et al.* (eds), *The Sociology of the Health Service*. London: Routledge.

Blaxter, M. (1990). *Health and Lifestyles*. London: Tavistock/ Routledge.

Bunton, R. and Macdonald, G. (eds) (1992). *Health Promotion: Disciplines and Diversity*. London: Routledge.

Calnan, M. and Johnson, B. (1983). Health, Health Risks & Inequalities: an exploratory study of women's perceptions. *Sociology of Health and Illness*, **7**(1), 55–75.

Catford, J. (1992). Vital signs of health promotion. In: Bunton, R. and Macdonald, G. (eds), *Health Promotion: Disciplines and Diversity*. London: Routledge, 1–6.

Department of Health (1987). *Promoting Better Health*. London: HMSO.

Department of Health (1989a). *Working for People*. London: HMSO.

Department of Health (1989b). *Caring for Patients*. London: HMSO.

Department of Health (1991). *NHS and Community Care Act*. London: HMSO.

Department of Health (1991/92). *The Health of the Nation* (Green and White Papers). London: HMSO.

Department of Health and Social Security (1976). *Prevention and Health: Everybodys Business*. London: HMSO.

Department of Health and Social Security (1983). *NHS Management Enquiry: The Griffiths Report*. London: HMSO.

Edelman, C. and Mandle, C. (1994). *Health Promotion Throughout the Lifespan*. London: C.V. Mosby.

Ewles, L. and Simnett, I. (1992). *Promoting Health: A Practical Guide to Health Education*. London: Scutari Press.

Herzlich, C. (1973). *Health and Illness*. London: Academic Press.

Kelly, M. (1990). The World Health Organization's definition of health promotion: three problems. *Health Bulletin*, **48**: 4 July.

Kickbush, I. (1988). In: Anderson, R. *et al.* (eds), *Health Behaviour Research and Health Promotion*. Oxford: Oxford University Press.

Lalonde, M. (1974). *A New Perspective on the Health of Canadians*. Ottowa: Information Canada.

Luker and Ashton (1991). Healthy cities? *Community Outlook*, 32–33.

McKeowan, T. (1976). *The Role of Medicine*. Oxford: Oxford University Press.

Morgan, M., Calnan, M. and Manning, N. (1985). *Sociological Approaches to Health and Medicine*. London: Croom Helm.

Nijuis, H. and van der Maesen, L. (1994). The philosophical foundations of public health: an invitation to debate. *Journal of Epidemiology and Community Health*, **48**: 1–3.

Pill, R. and Stott, N. (1982). Concepts of illness causation and responsibility: some preliminary data from a sample of working class mothers. *Social Science and Medicine*, 43–52.

Rodmell, S. and Watt, A. (1986). *The Politics of Health Education*. London: Routledge & Kegan Paul.

Royal College of Nursing (1991). *The Health of the Nation: A Response from the Royal College of Nursing*. London: RCN.

Sutherland, I. (ed.) (1979). *Health Education: Perspectives and Choices*. London: George, Allen & Unwin.

Tones, K. (1984). *The Notion of Health Promotion*. London: Health Education Authority.

Webb, P. (ed.) (1994). *Health Promotion and Patient Education: A Professionals Guide*. London: Chapman & Hall.

World Health Organization (1947). World Health Organization's constituion. *Chronicle of the WHO*, **1**: (3), 1.

World Health Organization (1978). *Report on the International Conference on Primary Health Care*, Alma Ata, 6–12 Sept. Geneva: WHO.

World Health Organization (1984). *Health Promotion* (European Monographs in Health and Health Education, 6). Copenhagen: WHO.

World Health Organization (1985). *Health Promotion: A Discussion Document on the Concept and Principles*. Copenhagen: WHO.

Williams, S. (1983). Concepts of Health: An analysis of Lay Logic. *Sociology*, **17**, 185–204.

Williams, S., Calnan, M., Cant, S. *et al.* (1993). All change in the NHS? Implications of the NHS reforms for primary care prevention. *Sociology of Health and Illness*, **15**: 43–66.

Further Reading ▲ ▲ ▲

Bunton, R. and MacDonald, G. (eds) (1992). *Health Promotion: Disciplines and Diversity*. London: Routledge.

Webb, P. (ed.) (1994). *Health Promotion and Patient Education: A Professional's Guide*. London: Chapman & Hall.

27

Health Promotion in Practice

Lesley Vernon

LEARNING OBJECTIVES

After studying this chapter you should:

- Be able to review critically the influence of dominant political thought in the application of health promotion principles
- Understand the importance of utilizing health promotion strategies in the context of professional practice
- Be able to discuss some of the problems associated with the implementation of effective health promotion strategies
- Be aware of the reasons for selecting appropriate methods for evaluating health promotion

INTRODUCTION

The controversial and challenging nature of health promotion, and some of the problems subsequently associated with this discipline, emerged in Chapter 26. It seems that this is because, within formal healthcare systems, the change in priority from curative to preventative services conflicts with traditional values and beliefs about healthcare. Downie *et al.* (1991) provide an analysis of the morals and values involved. The approach in this chapter is more pragmatic. This is achieved by explaining how the problems already identified in Chapter 26 may be overcome by the examination of the more popular health promotion models.

This will complete the framework initiated in the previous chapter, which will enable students to understand how important it is to work together in order to make a positive impact on the overall goal of health promotion.

PROBLEMS IN HEALTH PROMOTION

There are two main areas of concern within health promotion. The first problem is to do with resources and can be described as *distributive justice*, or the task of creating an economic balance between primary prevention, promotion and cure (Lambert and McPherson, 1993; Yeo, 1993). In short, in an ideal world where money was no object, there would be no problem in resourcing preventive services aiming to improve the health of populations over time. However, the reality is that these aims have to be considered in conjunction with current problems and can be summed up by asking such questions as:

> Given the choice, should we abandon help for some of those who are already sick in order to increase the future health of those who are well?
>
> (Lambert and McPherson, 1993)

The second problem is concerned with *intervention ethics*, which can be broken down into two more categories. These are the problems associated with devising appropriate strategies and questions about evaluation.

Selection of appropriate strategies

From a moral stance, health promotion interventions can be described as ranging from voluntary to non-voluntary to coercive. The methods used by professionals to try to change behaviour can be described as persuasive, manipulative and coercive (Faden, cited by Yeo (1993)). The problems encountered when using these methods is that they can be perceived negatively and construed as social engineering. The role of intervention ethics is to evaluate these strategies to ensure that their impact on people's freedom, choice, responsibility and health is not limited or offended (Yeo, 1993). This is not easy and issues of moral justification need to be considered.

For example, action to reduce motor vehicle accidents has concentrated on introducing legislation to reduce risk factors associated with lifestyle, such as the wearing of seat belts and speed restrictions (Locker, 1991). It can be argued that such legislation restricts an individual's freedom of choice and that less effort has been made to control advertising which displays images of cars and driving in a counterproductive way; speed is portrayed as being sexy, exciting and glamorous, the car is a status symbol. However, national government advertising campaigns to drive safely and wear seat belts failed to effect any behavioural change, but legislation has had an impact on reducing mortality and morbidity from road traffic accidents. What is significant here is that there was strong public support for legislation (Naidoo, in Rodmell and Watt (1986)). Therefore, in terms of moral justification, although legislation can restrict the freedom of some people, it is acceptable in that it is for the common good.

Coercion, the subtle manipulation of behaviours deemed unacceptable or unhealthy by professionals – such as smoking or exceeding sensible drinking limits – can be regarded as morally indefensible. The argument that this latter approach does make people aware of their health is not valid, especially when the foundations for the implementation of some strategies are unsupported by reliable empirical evidence (Lambert and McPherson, 1993). The current debate surrounding the validity of the research into safe drinking limits is one such example (Gronbaek *et al.*, 1994). The sort of questions that need to be asked in this context are:

- Who are the people who adopt unhealthy behaviours?
- What makes people adopt unhealthy behaviours?
- Why do some people and not others adopt unhealthy behaviours?

By trying to elicit answers to questions such as these, it should be possible to develop services that can support people through change.

Problems associated with evaluation

Evaluation is an essential part of any health promoting activity, being based on sound research principles that are incorporated into the planning process. However, methodological problems exist. In the UK, it would seem, this is because the philosophical foundations of health promotion are in conflict with those of the WHO. In the UK, policies indicate a preference for an individualistic approach to health promotion. In this context health evaluation is considered in short-term quantitative terms, related to the reduction of morbidity and mortality due to ill-health caused by damaging behaviour.

The WHO European strategy for 'health for all' states that in the year 2000 the difference in health status between countries and groups of people within countries should be reduced by at least 25% (Power, 1994). This should be achieved by improving the level of health of disadvantaged nations and groups. Because of this latter belief in the notion of a healthier future, health promotion evaluation should incorporate ways of measuring long-term social or behavioural change. This could be through action research and longitudinal studies.

The problems encountered in using these methods are associated with difficulties in controlling external variables such as the time lag involved in seeing the impact of various preventive strategies. For example, if a community physiotherapist sets up an exercise group in a local leisure centre as part of a community development programme to support a 'healthy heart' initiative, and there is a reduction in mortality and morbidity in coronary heart disease in that area, it does not follow that this initiative is the cause of that improvement. One of several other variables could have had an impact.

The lack of systematic evaluation in health promotion activities in the NHS is attributed, by some, to the fact that strategies do tend to be influenced by political ideology (Lambert and McPherson, 1993). However this is an unproductive and sterile argument. What has to be realized is that politics will always dominate what is evaluated and how and whether or not recommendations are acted upon (Downie *et al.*, 1991).

The lack of rigour in health promotion evaluation need not be perceived as a problem if methods are not viewed solely in quantitative terms. For example, Downie *et al.* (1991) appear to prefer a phenomenological approach based on a variety of methods, stating that they do not insist on experimental rigour in situations where it is not justified. Health promotion programmes should not be restricted to the demands of evaluators to 'carry out the plans no matter what'; they should rather be encouraged to develop to their full potential. The diversity of talent and expertise of the researchers and practitioners implementing these programmes should be acknowledged and developed.

PRACTICAL APPROACHES TO HEALTH PROMOTION

There is a debate regarding the adequacy of the theoretical foundations of health promotion. Models of health promotion are considered to be unscientific because their underlying philosophy is unsound. This may well be, as Rawson (1992) identifies, because theorists have either scrutinized other disciplines for a scientific foundation or concentrated on justifying the ideological basis of health promotion. However, it is recognized that most models have evolved from typologies that were devised by health educationalists, in order to help them provide some structure to their work. Consequently their perceptions are influenced by their practice orientations. In order to demonstrate this process, and to help readers to select the most appropriate approach for their particular discipline and level of practice, some of the models used most frequently will now be considered.

Early attempts to classify approaches to health promotion were made by health educationalists who wished to demonstrate the shift from individual to collective and societal action to improve health. Coutts and Hardy (1985) discuss five models of health promotion (see Box 27.1). These are similar to those of Ewles and Simnett (1986), who decline to use the word model and describe five 'approaches' (see Box 27.2).

Besides demonstrating the change in focus of the discipline from individual to collective action, Ewles and Simnett (1992) also identify the change in the professional's role from informer and educator, to facilitator, as power is transferred to the client. From a sociological perspective, Beattie (1992) is critical of these typologies. He feels that because they are not grounded in sociological theory it is not possible to test or develop them any further. However, Ewles and Simnett (1992) do give a descriptive account of their approaches, as well as a critical review of their relative strengths and weaknesses. It is also necessary to acknowledge that the methods they describe originated in health education. Consequently they are grounded in a range of theories of educational and social psychology.

Box 27.1 *Coutts and Hardy's five models of health promotion*

- The medical model
- The educational model
- The media model
- The community development model
- The political model

Beattie's concern regarding the lack of sociological analysis in health promotion led him to develop a theoretical model of health promotion based on C. W. Mills' (1959) system of cross-clarification and Bernstein's (1974) concept of codes and control (Figure 27.1).

This structural map defines the different strategies in terms of two bipolar dimensions, the mode of intervention and the focus of intervention. The authoritative/negotiated dimension compares with the debate regarding the paternalistic 'top-down' types of social intervention, versus the participatory or 'bottom-up' approaches (Ewles and Simnett, 1992; Beattie, 1992).

In his analysis of this model, Beattie describes the cluster of health persuasion techniques as having their origins in the nineteenth century temperance campaigns as well as the propaganda campaigns in the two world wars which focused on VD and better eating. These tactics are still popular with the government and the Health Education Authority (the first AIDS campaign being one such example), despite the dubious effects of these approaches (Beattie, 1992).

Strategies for legislative action for health originate from the nineteenth century public health movement. Again, Beattie gives useful examples of studies where these measures have had a dramatic influence on health, the most remarkable being the Clean Air Act in 1956. He continues to support this ecological approach at policy level in the adoption of no-smoking and healthy-eating policies. Added to this could be the current legislation being implemented regarding health and safety at work through recent EU directives, notably the manual handling policies. However, in this context, Beattie also warns that there are dangers of 'collective authoritarianism' if reform is focused too much on achieving health itself without considering the problems or needs of the wider community.

At an individual level, approaches used in personal counselling for health have their roots in the humanistic psychology of Carl Rogers (1969). Beattie highlights the contribution these techniques have had in agencies in the NHS and voluntary sector. He describes

Box 27.2 *Ewles and Simnett's five approaches to health promotion*

Approach	Aim	Intention	Method
• Medical	Freedom from medically defined disease	To prevent or ameliorate ill-health	Persuasion, for example: Women to use family planning clinics Middle-aged men to be screened for raised blood pressure
• Behaviour change	To change attitudes and behaviour	To adopt healthy lifestyles	Promoting the idea that smoking is antisocial and teaching people how to stop smoking
• Educational	To give knowledge and ensure understanding of health issues	Based on the notion that people will act on well-informed decisions	Information is as value-free as possible People encouraged to explore own values and attitudes and make their own decisions
• Client-centred	To work with clients so that they can identify what they want to know	For people to make their own decisions and choices according to their own value systems	The professional acts as facilitator, gradually withdrawing as the group becomes cohesive and productive
• Social change	To change the environment	To help people take control over thier own lives and make choice easier	Political and social action This may be aimed nationally at lobbying governments to reduce unemployment, or at a local level such as campaigning for healthy eating policies in a hospital or school

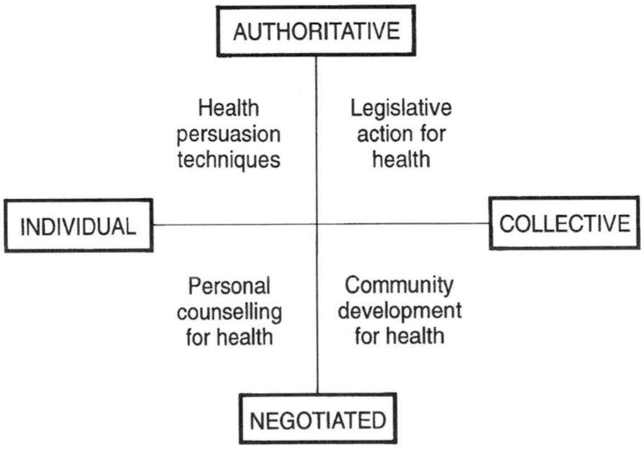

Figure 27.1 *The bipolar dimensions: mode of intervention (vertical) and focus of intervention (horizontal) according to Beattie* et al., *1992)*

their use in general practice, psychiatry and mental health nursing as well as the Family Planning Association and Relate. They have also been adopted in the professional training of teachers, healthcare professionals and social workers.

Beattie describes the community development or public health approach as the most recent, the strategies used here being self-help, community orientated health outreach and community action. He adds nothing more to description of this approach than Ewles and Simnett (1986). However, while acknowledging its dynamism, he concludes that it is debatable whether local action on its own without support at policy level can ever do more than 'achieve marginal victories in the face of larger social inequalities' (Craig *et al.*, 1982; cited by Beattie).

In the development of this construct, Beattie identifies how social enquiry can be of use in the

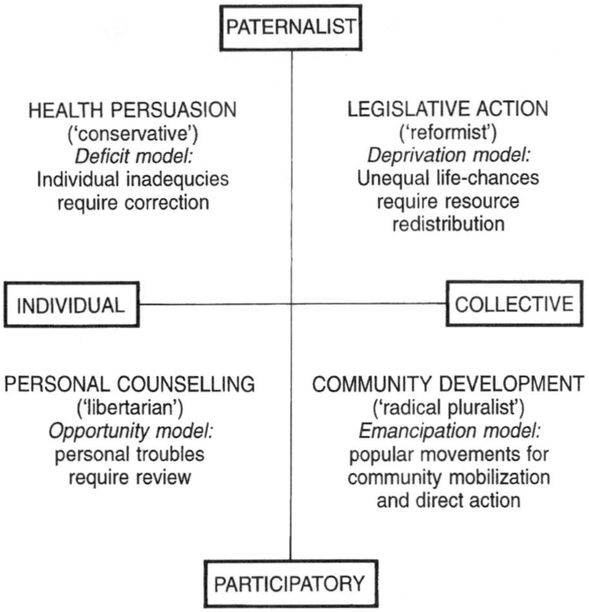

Figure 27.2 *Conflicting political philosophies in health promotion (adapted from Beattie* et al., *1992)*

Box 27.3 *Seven overlapping domains of health promotion (see Figure 27.3) aimed at prevention and promotion of positive health (Downie* et al., *1991)*

1. *Preventive services*: immunization, screening, case finding
2. *Preventive health education*: education to influence lifestyles plus encouragement to take up of services
3. *Preventive health protection*: fluoridation of water supplies
4. *Health education for preventive health protection*: lobbying for seat belt legislation
5. *Positive health education*: to influence behaviour, such as, encouraging productive leisure pursuits that promote fitness and well-being
6. *Positive health protection*: no-smoking policies in the workplace
7. *Health education aimed at positive health protection*: raising awareness and securing support for these measures at public and policy levels

future. Consequently, he highlights the conflicting policy debates within the field (Figure 27.2). Like other theorists (Rodmell and Watt, 1986; Rawson, 1992), he feels that because of the 'range of antagonistic value positions within a pluralist society' it is important to confront these issues so that we may work with such conflicts in a more open and constructive way (Beattie, 1992).

In recognition of the diversity of health promotion, as well as the fact that it had 'acquired so many meanings as to become meaningless', Tannahill (1985) developed a model for defining and 'doing health promotion' (Downie *et al.*, 1991). This is reproduced in Figure 27.3.

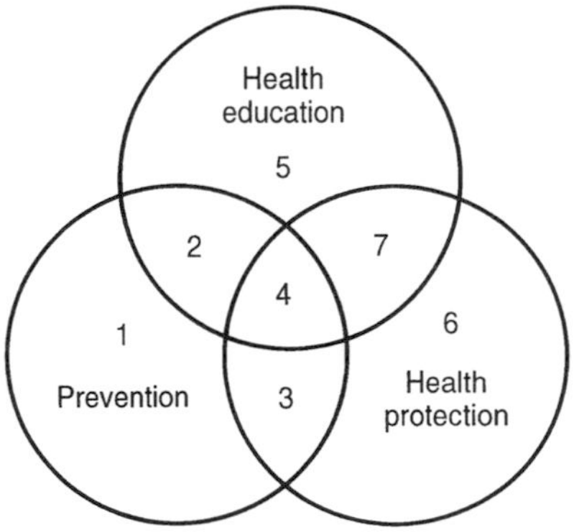

Figure 27.3 *Tannahill's model of health promotion (Downie* et al., *1991)*

A key factor influencing Tannahill's development of this model was Tones' (1984) concern that, ethically, health promotion could be interpreted as an attempt at 'social engineering' through the adoption of mass-media persuasion tactics. Tones argues that such approaches need to be accompanied by health education programmes that 'operate synergistically' with one another. Tannahill does not perceive health promotion in purely structuralist or individual terms, but rather as 'overlapping spheres of activity' which are not mutually exclusive. These spheres of health education, prevention and health protection all contribute to the 'goal of health promotion'. In order to represent a wide range of health promotion, seven domains are identified aimed at prevention and the promotion of positive health (see Box 27.3).

Clearly, Downie *et al.* (1991) see health education as being at the core of health promotion and not part of an evolutionary process. They also see communication as an essential element of these processes. At a planning level, in setting priorities for action they see community development as a major component of health promotion. In proposing their integrated approach to

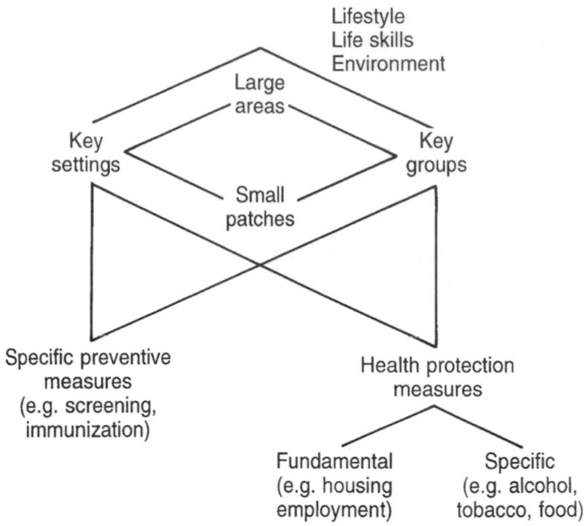

Figure 27.4 *Integrated health promotion planning (Downie* et al., *1991)*

health promotion planning (Figure 27.4), they view empowerment as an important theme, arguing that it is necessary for 'comprehensive programmes of health services and health protection' to be 'tailored to the needs of the people and places concerned'.

Here, Downie and colleagues appear to agree with the Research Unit in Health and Behavioural Change at Edinburgh University (1989). In their discussion of health promotion through community development they state that:

> changes in public health which require alteration or modification of individual habits will only happen through understanding of the nature and context of human behaviour. Health promotion and health education provide an outside climate which influences the direction of behaviour change, but they are unlikely to trigger such changes when based on a "rational approach". The most efficacious is community development. Only when people's lives become less strained, and adaptive and coping processes reasonably untaxed, will people be likely to think about changes in behaviour.

Learning Activity 1 ◆ ◆ ◆

You now have the opportunity to select the most appropriate tools for your work in health promotion.

a Within your area of clinical practice, identify a health promotion issue you would wish to address.

b Having chosen your topic, prepare and present one of the following:
- A teaching package for use on a one to one basis.
- A teaching package for a group of people.
- A plan for implementing change in your area.

c Discuss how you identified your problem/need (e.g. observation, demographic, epidemiological data collection, literature review). Consider whether this was a normative, felt or expressed need.

d Investigate whether there is any strategy within your organization that is attempting to address the issues you are concerned with. For example, you may have thought that nutrition was a focus for prevention of obesity, eating disorders, prevention of cancer and heart disease. Is there a healthy eating policy within your organization? How is this policy being implemented?

e Discuss an intended intervention with the relevant personnel (i.e. Chair of food committee, dietitian, health promotion officer). Could your work be part of an overall plan, or would it be an innovation?

f To translate a project into an operational activity you need to be aware of the professional and structural culture of your workplace. Points to consider are whether your colleagues are interested or motivated and what resources you have.

g Critically analyse and evaluate an intervention in terms of suitability of approaches and cost-effectiveness. Give reasons for perceived strengths and weaknesses, and suggest how improvements could be made. Your evaluation should also include the use of quantitative and qualitative methods such as questionnaires, interviews, self-evaluation, peer evaluation. How did your project fare in terms of long- and short-term change?

SUMMARY

The chapter has considered economic and moral issues regarding the successful implementation of health promotion principles. It appears essential for professionals to take account of the social and individual personal values of individuals as part of any needs assessment, prior to the planning and implementation of any activity. This needs to be done in conjunction with a close scrutiny of their own value systems.

In reviewing various approaches to health promotion, at a strategic level, it may not be appropriate to adopt one particular model or approach to health promotion. As has been demonstrated, there are areas of inter-relatedness and overlap. Therefore an eclectic approach may well be more helpful. Once the common aim or goal of any strategy has been determined, the appropriate tool or method can be utilized depending on the level and environment where the professional is working.

Finally, problems associated with evaluation have been discussed. In the UK, it appears that there is a conflict between the government philosophy and that of the WHO. In this context, evaluation is considered from a short-term quantitative perspective, related to the reduction of morbidity and mortality due to ill-health caused by damaging behaviour. As a result, evaluation of strategies aimed at reducing inequalities is limited. This is a pity, as much could be learned by identifying the strategies that are effective.

Although there are methodological complications associated with both action research and longitudinal studies, this does not mean to say that this structure should not be built into the plans for health promotion strategies. Theorists are critical of the foundations of knowledge in health promotion. Further systematic enquiry by practitioners, utilizing action research methodologies, is the only way that health promotion theory will develop. Health promotion is political, but this does not mean that conflicting value systems or ideologies should be a barrier to progress. These differences should be viewed as an opportunity for dynamic and innovative thought and progression.

Key Points

- Successful health promotion is determined by the needs, values and beliefs of individuals and communities.
- All health professionals should consider using the WHO philosophy 'health for all' as a framework for practice.
- Within health promotion there are dilemmas based on two main areas: resource allocation, plus the choice of strategies for interventions and their evaluation.
- All health professionals should be aware of the importance of health promotion strategies in the context of their professional practice.

References

Beattie, A. (1992). Knowledge and control in health promotion. In: Gabe, J *et al.* (eds), *The Sociology of the Health Service*. London: Routledge.

Bernstein, B. (1974). On the classification and framing of educational knowledge. In: *Class Codes and Control*, vol. 1. London: Routledge & Kegan Paul.

Coutts, L. and Hardy, L. (1985). *Teaching for Health: The Nurse as a Health Educator.* London: Churchill Livingstone.

Downie, R.S., Fyfe, C. and Tannahill, A. (1991). *Health Promotion: Models and Values*. Oxford: Oxford University Press.

Ewles, L. and Simnett, I. (1986). *Promoting Health: A Practical Guide to Health Education* 2nd edition. Chichester: Wiley.

Ewles, L. and Simnett, I. (1992). *Promoting Health: A Practical Guide to Health Education.* London: Scutari Press.

Faden, R. (1987). Ethical issues in government sponsored public health campaigns. *Health Education Quarterly,* **14:** 27–37.

Gronbaek, M., Deis, A., Sorensen, T. *et al.* (1994). Influence of sex, age, body mass index, and smoking on alcohol intake and mortality. *British Medical Journal,* **308:** 302–6.

Lambert, H. and McPherson, K. (1985). Disease prevention and health promotion. In: Davey, B. and Popay, J. (eds), *Dilemmas in Healthcare*. Ch. 9. Milton Keynes: Open University Press.

Locker, D. (1991). In: Scambler, G. (ed.) *Sociology as Applied to Medicine*. London: Baillière Tindall.

Mills, C.W. (1959). *The Sociological Imagination*. Oxford: Oxford University Press.

Power, C. (1994). Health and social inequality in Europe. *British Medical Journal,* **308:** 1153–6.

Rawson, D. (1992). The growth of health promotion theory and its rational construction: lessons from the philosophy of science. In: Bunton, R. and Macdonald, G. (eds), *Health Promotion: Disciplines and Diversity.* London: Routledge.

Research Unit in Health and Behavioural Change, University of Edinburgh (1989). *Changing the Public Health*. Chichester: Wiley.

Rodmell, S. and Watt, A. (1986). *The Politics of Health Education*. London: Routledge & Kegan Paul.

Rogers, C. (1969). *Freedom to Learn*. New York: Charles E. Merrill.

Tannahill, A. (1985). What is health promotion? *Health Education Journal,* **44:** 194–8.

Tones, K. (1984). *The Notion of Health Promotion*. London: Health Education Authority.

Yeo, T. (1993). Toward an ethic of empowerment. *Health Promotion International,* **8:** 225–35.

28

Evaluating Healthcare Systems

Armando Barrientos

LEARNING OBJECTIVES

After studying this chapter you should:

- Be able to describe the basic concepts needed to evaluate healthcare systems and their reform
- Know the main explanations for the escalation of healthcare costs
- Be able to outline and compare healthcare systems in the USA, the UK and Chile, with special reference to the private/public mix of healthcare financing and provision
- Be aware of the use of efficiency and equity criteria in the evaluation of healthcare systems

INTRODUCTION

Health professionals are today more aware than ever that operational decisions have important economic implications, and are constrained by economic factors. In the United Kingdom, the reform of the National Health Service (NHS) has been argued for on grounds of economic necessity and efficiency, and has worked in practice to make decisions more sensitive to economic considerations. This demands of health professionals that they develop a good understanding of the economic evaluation of different forms of provision and financing of healthcare.

This chapter has been designed to help you gain this understanding. The central issue in healthcare financing and provision is the appropriate mix of private and public, and so trends in healthcare expenditure costs are considered. It is then shown why this issue has come to dominate debate on healthcare. An international comparison of health systems provides a useful setting against which to discuss these issues. Health systems in the UK, the USA and Chile are outlined to draw out the key advantages and disadvantages of private and public systems. The chapter then sets out in more detail the criteria that can be used in evaluating health systems; in particular the notions of efficiency and equity are introduced and discussed. A final section focuses on the NHS Reforms and the important concept of 'quasi-markets'.

TRENDS IN HEALTH EXPENDITURE COSTS

The recent NHS reforms reflect a growing concern with the effectiveness of healthcare systems, and their costs. This concern arises from the sustained upward trend in health expenditure which most developed and developing economies experienced in the 1970s and 80s (McGuire *et al.*, 1988). Table 28.1 below provides figures for health expenditure in the UK and the USA for the years 1970 and 1983 as a proportion of gross domestic product (GDP), which is a measure of the sum total of resources generated by an economy in a year. The figures show the portion of resources devoted to healthcare in that particular year by the relevant country. This portion rose between 1970 and 1983 by 42.1% in the USA and by 37.7% in the UK.

Table 28.1 *Private and public health expenditures as a percentage of GDP for the USA and UK, 1970 and 1983 (OECD, 1985)*

	USA			UK		
	Total	Public	Private	Total	Public	Private
1970	7.6	2.8	4.8	4.5	3.9	0.6
1983	10.8	4.5	6.3	6.2	5.5	0.7

Reasons for the upward trend in health expenditures

Four explanations can account for this trend. *Demographic changes* are producing an older population, especially as the greater numbers born after the Second World War are now approaching late middle-age. The population aged 60 and over is set to rise as a proportion of the total population in the next decades. Other things being equal, an older population will make greater demands on healthcare resources (Johnson and Falkingham, 1992).

Economic development produces *rising incomes*, which are in turn associated with a more than proportionate rise in demand for healthcare. As income and standards of living improve, a greater proportion of any extra income will be spent on healthcare and other services that improve the 'quality of life'.

Productivity improvements are more difficult to achieve in services than in industry, particularly in labour-intensive sectors such as healthcare. Whereas rapid increases in productivity in car manufacturing and consumer durables have resulted in falling relative prices, improvements in productivity of that scale are hard to achieve in, say, heart surgery. This means that over time an economy will have to devote a greater proportion of its resources to healthcare.

Technological change in healthcare may require considerable investment, producing rising costs of provision (Newhouse, 1992).

While these four explanations show that a rise in healthcare expenditure is to be expected, it is the rise in the public component of that expenditure that has generated greatest concern. Table 28.1 also shows the breakdown of health expenditure by the public and private sectors. The UK and the USA are at different ends of the spectrum with regards to the mix of public and private provision: the private sector is dominant in the USA, while the public sector dominates in the UK. Yet public sector expenditures in health are rising faster than the total *in both countries*: the ratio of public to private expenditures in health rose, between 1970 and 1983, from 0.58 to 0.71 in the USA, and from 6.5 to 7.85 in the UK. It is this upward trend in public health expenditure which is the focus of debates on the reform of healthcare provision and financing.

Why public health expenditure has risen faster than overall health expenditure

The answer lies in the lack of strong incentives for 'cost containment' in public health systems. This can be illustrated in the following:

- The level of private health expenditure is dependent on the willingness of patients to pay for healthcare, and this is directly constrained by their income. But the level of expenditure in public healthcare is ultimately dependent on *voters*, who are constrained only collectively by the resources generated by the economy. Individually, voters may be only indirectly concerned with healthcare costs (McGuire *et al.*, 1988).
- In addition, and given the complexities of diagnosis and treatment in some areas of healthcare, demand for health resources is largely determined by health professionals, who themselves may be only indirectly concerned with costs (Mooney, 1994).

The argument is then made that the cost containment incentives present in private health expenditure are lacking in the public sector, so that costs in the latter tend to grow at a faster rate. The reform of the NHS is largely about introducing financial constraints in the provision and financing of healthcare.

THE PROVISION AND FINANCING OF HEALTHCARE

For the reasons discussed in the previous section, the public/private mix of healthcare provision and financing has been changing in the 1980s and early 90s with private provision and financing increasingly favoured. In this section the public/private mix is identified for three countries – the USA, the UK and Chile – and some general points are made.

In the *USA*, private financing and provision of healthcare is the norm. Healthcare is financed by a mixture of private insurance and direct charges to patients. An important development has been the growth of Health Maintenance Organizations (HMOs) which combine health insurance and healthcare provision. From the 1960s the US government has taken responsibility for the financing of healthcare for vulnerable groups. *Medicare* is a social insurance scheme covering the elderly, run by the federal government, while *Medicaid* is a non-contributory programme to finance healthcare for the poor.

Table 28.2 *NHS purchasers and providers*

Purchasers	Contract type	Providers
Private users	Cost-per-case	DHA directly managed units
District Health Authorities (DHAs)	Block	Self-managed trusts
Fund-holding GPs		Privately owned units

In the *UK*, the *NHS and Community Care Act 1990* introduced radical reforms into the NHS by splitting purchasers from providers, and creating an 'internal market' for healthcare. Purchasers of healthcare are the District Health Authorities (DHAs) and the fund-holding general practitioners (GPs), in addition to private individuals and companies. Providers are GPs and other independent units, Directly Managed Units under DHA control, and the new Self-Managed Trusts. Purchasers buy care from providers under two types of contracts: (i) a cost-per-case contract in which the units of care are specified and costed; or (ii) a block contract, by which providers agree to supply care for a fixed term and for a fixed-term fee (see Table 28.2) The expectation is that competition among providers, and the price signals generated, will lead to greater efficiency.

Chile provides an example of a rapid expansion of private provision and financing of healthcare (Miranda *et al.*, 1995). Until the 1970s, healthcare was provided by a national health service, while financing came from social insurance contributions paid to two separate bodies, one for blue-collar and one for white-collar workers. From 1979 onwards, reforms were introduced that had the objective of expanding the private provision and financing of healthcare. A minimum level of health insurance is mandated for workers and their dependants, which is financed by a contribution of 7% of earnings. This premium can be paid into the government-run health insurance programme, or to any of the private health insurance programmes. Within the private sector, workers can freely contract into more comprehensive insurance packages in exchange for a higher premium. Workers in the private sector and high-income workers in the government health programme can go to the healthcare provider of their choice, but they have to make up the difference between the insurance payment and the provider fees. Those who are unable to make contributions are covered by the government programme, but they are restricted to using the services provided by government-owned units.

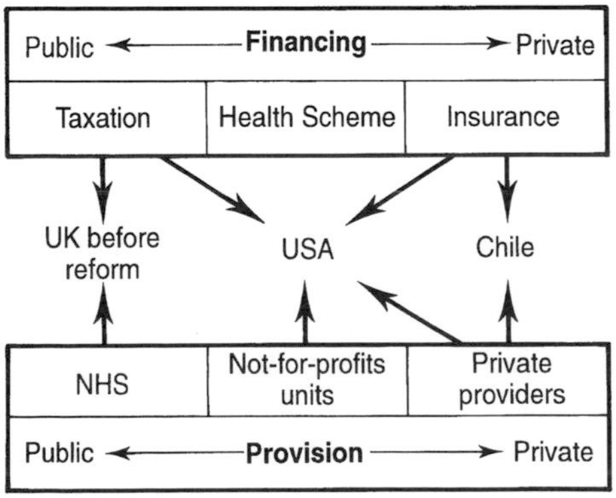

Figure 28.1 *The public/private mix of health financing and provision in the UK, the USA and Chile*

This brief description of healthcare systems in three countries shows that there are considerable variations. Each country has a different public/private mix of healthcare provision and financing. Figure 28.1 depicts these in a stylized form.

Learning Activity 1 ◆ ◆ ◆

As a useful exercise, consider the private/public mix existing in other countries with which you are familiar.

Having identified differences in healthcare provision and financing across countries, the next stage is to evaluate their relative effectiveness. The polar cases can be discussed first.

A purely public healthcare system corresponds to the situation in the UK before the recent reforms and to Chile before 1979. Healthcare is financed via taxation and provided by public non-profit-making bodies. The main disadvantage of a purely public healthcare system has been noted above. In the context of secular rises in demand for healthcare, none of the participants in the system have a stake in cost containment. The main advantages of a purely public system lie in its potential to exploit *economies of scale* in provision (economies that can be made by providing a service for large numbers of people, with for example a more intensive utilization of hospital equipment), to avoid marketing costs, and to focus on reducing inequalities in health provision (Barr, 1993) (see Box 28.1).

A purely private health system, based on private health insurance and private competitive provision, also has advantages and disadvantages. There are well-

Box 28.1 *Comparison of public and private healthcare systems*

Sector	Advantages	Disadvantages
Private	• Responsive to consumer preferences • Incentives for cost containment	• Adverse selection and moral hazard • Agency problems • Marketing costs
Public	• Economies of scale • Avoids marketing costs • Ensures minimum provision	• Lowcost containment incentives • Less responsive to consumer preferences

known reasons why a private insurance solution to the financing of healthcare is problematic (Barr, 1993). For the insurance solution to work it is required that the contingencies covered by insurance do not happen with certainty, and do not happen simultaneously to all the individuals covered.

Consider motor insurance as a useful analogy. High-risk groups such as young drivers or motorcyclists, face steeper insurance premiums because their risks are more certain – some insurance companies simply refuse to insure high-risk groups. With private health insurance, high-risk groups would find it difficult to find cover in cases of chronic illness, congenital diseases and age-related healthcare costs.

There are also information and incentive problems in contracting health insurance. 'Adverse selection' refers to a situation where, in the absence of hard facts about the insured, in order to calculate premiums insurance companies must guess the probabilities that contingencies covered will materialize. It is obvious that individuals keener to buy health insurance are also those more likely to incur healthcare costs, so that insurance companies will set premiums at high levels. But those sections of the population less likely to suffer from health problems are put off buying insurance, with the result that premiums rise even further. Eventually only high-risk groups will be in the market for insurance.

Insurance cover may provide individuals with incentives to behave recklessly; this is known as 'moral hazard'. Drivers of expensive cars with comprehensive insurance need not to be so careful about where to park, and by analogy those fully insured against healthcare costs may find less pressure to stop smoking. Cost sharing between the insurer and the insured may be a way of alleviating the moral hazard problem.

Learning Activity 2 ◆ ◆ ◆

Cost-sharing is a useful device through which insurance companies discourage small claims, and encourage careful behaviour. For example, a motorcar insurance policy can be obtained at a lower premium if the insured is prepared to pay the first £100 of any claim.

- ◆ Consider ways in which cost-sharing could be used in a healthcare context to achieve the same objectives.
- ◆ Are you able to find any examples of this model of cost-sharing being suggested or used in the health arena?

There are also problems in private provision where the type of healthcare, and its cost, are determined by the health professional on behalf of the individual. The health professional is here acting as the agent of the person, but in a private setting he or she must also act so as to fulfil personal objectives (Mooney, 1994). Such potential conflicts of interest are normally addressed by the regulatory standards enforced by the professional bodies examined elsewhere in the book.

Private healthcare systems also have the disadvantage, relative to a purely public system, that resources must be diverted to marketing and selling health services. Where marketing is aimed simply at preserving or expanding 'market share', and not to inform those in need of healthcare, the associated costs are difficult to justify. Health systems relying on private financing and provision also have advantages, though in recent reforms both in the UK and in Chile these have been overplayed. It is argued that competitive forces may lead to outcomes in terms of healthcare provision that are more efficient, in the sense that resources could be used more effectively and be deployed with a greater focus on people's needs. It is also

Learning Activity 3 ◆ ◆ ◆

- ◆ To what extent would competition among providers be an effective means of bringing the decisions of health professionals into line with the needs of individuals in their care?
- ◆ Consider this issue in the context of the specific service you are involved in providing.

argued that private health offers people greater freedom of choice. A different argument in favour of private healthcare is that a properly constituted price system may convey information more cheaply and effectively about producer costs and consumer preferences than their public counterparts (Hudson, 1994).

EVALUATING HEALTHCARE SYSTEMS

Economics identifies two main criteria that can be used to evaluate institutions: efficiency and equity (Barr, 1993). *Economic efficiency* includes three interconnected concepts:

- *Technical efficiency* is attained where the optimal combination of inputs to production (technologies) is used.
- *Productive efficiency* applies to firms that produce a given quantity of resources at the lowest cost per unit.
- *Exchange efficiency* applies to markets in which the preferences of consumers match the costs of producing goods and services at the margin.

Overall, providers are efficient if they are sensitive to consumer preferences, choose the optimal technology, and produce at the lowest average cost. Economic theory claims that competitive forces within a market setting ensure that only the efficient providers survive, and thus efficiency will follow.

Equity criteria are more difficult to pin down, as there are different ways in which healthcare provision and financing may be said to be equitable (Mooney, 1992). One interpretation emphasizes *access* to healthcare: provision would be equitable if everyone had equal access to health services. A second interpretation concentrates on *minimum standards*: healthcare provision is just if there are standards below which no one, regardless of income or status, is allowed to fall. It is clear that public healthcare systems are more likely to ensure minimum standards for all, and that private systems by themselves would be hard-pressed to satisfy this criterion. In the case of the USA and Chile, private healthcare must be supplemented by government provision for the more vulnerable sections of society. Although the UK healthcare system would perform better on this criterion, regional and socio-economic disparities in both access and provision exist (Le Grand, 1982).

THE NHS REFORMS: A QUASI-MARKET IN HEALTH

What kind of healthcare system will the NHS reforms produce for the UK? The 1991 reforms are intended to create an 'internal market' within the NHS, and to extend opportunities for private sector involvement. Le Grand and Bartlett (1993) describe the resulting framework for healthcare provision as a 'quasi-market' – that is, nearly but not quite a market.

Although the financing of healthcare, and an important portion of provision, remain public, the separation of purchasers from providers is expected to induce behaviour and outcomes similar to those observed in private health systems.

In this quasi-market, purchasers have the responsibility to assess healthcare needs and the cost-effectiveness of service provision, and to monitor quality. Purchasers are expected to be more sensitive to people's needs and preferences, and at the same time ensure cost-effectiveness. Using the concepts introduced in the previous section, they are expected to ensure both exchange and productive efficiency, while at the same time securing minimum standards. Providers, on the other hand, will compete for service provision contracts and will need to consider carefully their decisions about what services to provide, at which price, and the appropriate contractual platform. Using the terminology of the previous section, providers will be forced to ensure technical and productive efficiency.

Whether in the purchaser or provider role, health professionals will need to be attuned to the economic and financial background of their operational decisions, and to develop their awareness of the relative effectiveness and desirability of different forms of healthcare financing and provision.

Learning Activity 4 ◆ ◆ ◆

- With reference to your area of professional practice, list the advantages and disadvantages of the purchaser/provider model of health delivery.
- How are the outcomes of healthcare delivery measured and rationalized?

SUMMARY

Healthcare expenditures show a sustained upward trend, with public expenditures on health rising faster than the total. There are a number of explanations for this, all of which indicate that this upward trend is likely to continue into the future.

Attention has focused on the effectiveness and cost of healthcare provision, and on its financing. Comparisons of healthcare provision and financing across countries indicate a great diversity in healthcare systems, and in their private/public mix. Private and public provision and financing of healthcare have advantages and disadvantages that can be identified with the help of economic analysis. In particular, the concepts of efficiency and equity can provide criteria to evaluate healthcare systems. In the UK, the NHS reforms are aimed to create an internal market, and to enhance opportunities for private sector involvement. The resulting framework of healthcare and provision has been described as a 'quasi-market' in health.

Key Points ■ ■ ■

- Trend changes in health expenditure costs raise issues concerning the effectiveness of healthcare systems, and their costs.
- There are four main explanations for the upward trend in health expenditure.
- Public health expenditure has risen faster then overall expenditure owing to the lack of strong incentives for 'cost containment' in public health systems.
- International comparisons of healthcare systems demonstrate considerable variations in system design and in the financing of these systems.
- Health economics identifies two main criteria for the evaluation of institutions: efficiency and equity.
- The NHS reforms have produced a quasi-market in health.

References ▼ ▼ ▼

Barr, N. (1993). *The Economics of the Welfare State*, 2nd edn. London: Oxford University Press.

Johnson, P. and Falkingham, J. (1992). *Ageing and Economic Welfare*. London: Sage.

Le Grand, J. (1982). *The Strategy of Equality: Redistribution and the Social Services*. London: George Allen & Unwin.

Le Grand, J. and Bartlett, W. (1993). *Quasi-Markets and Social Policy*, London: Macmillan.

McGuire, A., Henderson, J. and Mooney, G. (1988). *The Economics of Health Care: An Introductory Text*. London: Routledge & Kegan Paul.

Miranda, E., Scarpaci, J. and Irarrazaval, I. (1995). A decade of HMOs in Chile: market behaviour, consumer choice and the state. *Health and Place*, **1**: 55–9.

Mooney, G. (1992). *Economics, Medicine and Health Care*, 2nd edn. London: Harvester Wheatsheaf.

Mooney, G. (1994). *Key Issues in Health Economics*. London: Harvester Wheatsheaf.

Newhouse, J.P. (1992). Medical care costs: how much welfare loss? *Journal of Economic Perspectives*, **6**: 3–21.

OECD (1985). *Measuring Health Care 1960–1983: Expenditure, Costs and Performance*. Paris: OECD.

Oxford Review of Economic Policy (1989). *Health*, **5**: 1.

Further Reading ▲ ▲ ▲

Barr, N. (1993). *The Economies of the Welfare State*, 2nd edn. London: Oxford University Press.

Hudson, B. (1994). *Making Sense of Markets in Health and Social Care*. Sunderland: Business Education Publishers.

Le Grand, J. and Bartlett, W. (1993). *Quasi-Markets and Social Policy*. London: Macmillan.

McGuire, A., Henderson, J. and Mooney, G. (1988). *The Economics of Health Care: An Introductory Text*. London: Routledge & Kegan Paul.

Mooney, G. (1992). *Economics, Medicine and Health Care*, 2nd edn. London: Harvester Wheatsheaf.

Mooney, G. (1994). *Key Issues in Health Economics*. London: Harvester Wheatsheaf.

29

Quality Assurance and Professional Competence

Nikki Rochford

LEARNING OBJECTIVES

After studying this chapter you should:

- Be able to describe the term 'quality assurance'
- Be able to discuss the role of quality assurance in practice
- Know how to incorporate quality assurance into clinical practice
- Understand who has responsibilty for quality assurance

INTRODUCTION

The term 'quality assurance' has rapidly become part of the language of healthcare professionals. However, it can mean many things to many people and so be a source of confusion – its perceived officiousness creating a barrier to greater understanding. Mention of quality assurance is met by some with groans, by others with resignation and possibly by the majority with non-comprehension. All this can have the effect of making individuals avoid its consideration or believe it to be another's responsibility, that of managers or audit departments.

This chapter aims to demystify the term and to show that quality assurance should be a normal and welcome part of practice.

CONCEPTS OF QUALITY ASSURANCE

The process of assessing the quality of any product or service involves making judgements of that product or service in relation to a standard or set of standards. When buying any kind of consumer good it is normal to consider whether or not the product is of a high standard, whether it is good value for money and appropriate to needs, and whether it is efficient in performing the task for which it has been purchased. Before deciding to buy any item most consumers will evaluate how their prospective purchase fulfils these criteria and will make their decision accordingly.

In a healthcare setting, considerations of 'quality' are not dissimilar. However, it is almost impossible to arrive at a precise definition of what it is that constitutes the 'quality' of a particular healthcare product or service. Quality is dependent upon a number of different attributes of that product or service (Wright and Whittington, 1992) and likely to include:

- access
- relevance
- effectiveness
- equity
- efficiency
- economy
- social acceptability
- satisfaction.

In other words, a quality service is one that is not compromised by undue limits of time, distance or cost. Is one that meets the needs of its client group and supplies them fairly and impartially, making the best use of resources and avoiding unnecessary waste. It also satisfies the reasonable expectations of the client, society as a whole and the provider (Wright and Whittington, 1992).

Assessment of quality requires that a product or service be judged against a set of *standards*. A standard is simply some desired and attainable level of performance, but this standard is only meaningful if actual performance can be compared against some measurable criterion or criteria (Castledine, 1983; Gruchy and Rogers, 1990). It is only when the provider can ascertain, with a fair degree of certainty, that such standards have been met that they can promise to provide a particular quality of service. Such a promise is an assurance of quality. *Assurance* of quality requires the continual measurement of provision with respect to the set standard.

However, the process of *quality assurance* does not involve simply the combination of these two component terms, since this would only require the setting of standards and the measurement of the degree to which these standards are met (*quality assessment*). For a service to assure quality its provision must be appropriate, the service provided must meet the requirements of those to whom it is directed.

Hopkins (1993) defines appropriate care as "the selection, from the body of available interventions that have been shown to be efficacious for a disorder, of the intervention that is most likely to produce the outcomes desired by the individual patient". The standards to be attained must be appropriate to the individual and encompass knowledge of recent development of interventions. As such, standards cannot be set in stone but must change and develop to meet the challenge of expanding knowledge and expertise within the health field and changes in the requirements of service users.

Quality assurance is thus a continually evolving cyclical process within which services are provided and restructured to meet the changing needs of the 'client group' effectively and efficiently. It is useful to consider this process as a perpetually revolving wheel (see Figure 29.1).

The wheel symbolizes movement that has no beginning or end. Equally, quality assurance is not an event to be completed but a process that should be an integral part of daily individual treatment and service provision.

Within a service, quality assurance operates as a system of interlocking, interdependent wheels. Individual members of a department evaluate and develop their practice, using their own standards and those of others to develop and monitor the practice of the department. Departments work with other departments to evaluate and develop a service . . . and so on. In this way the process ensures accountability from the most junior to most senior levels of the service. The process relies upon and begins with the front line health professionals responsibility for quality assurance; it is this that identifies the centre of the wheel and the reason for its existence – the 'client'.

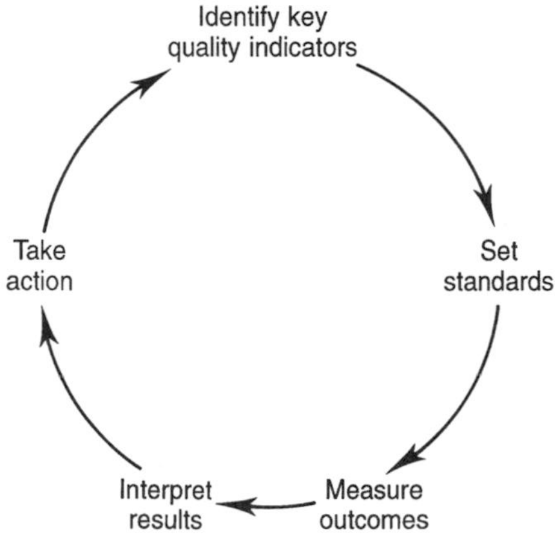

Figure 29.1 *A quality wheel*

It is this last point that is the central key to an understanding of quality assurance – that it is about assuring quality of service for the user. This process cannot take place without consideration of customer views, opinions and needs. It is these that initially drive the wheel and which power its perpetual motion.

Competence and quality

'The hallmark of a profession is its responsibility for the quality and competence of its members'. Holmes Report (1986).

For many years academics have debated which attributes a profession should encompass (Greenwood, 1957; Goode, 1969). Ellis (1988) suggests the following: skill and practices that are particular to that profession, background training and education. The profession should also be responsible for the 'review and generation' of this knowledge and should therefore be 'research based'. Ellis continues to explain that the totality of this package may be termed 'competence'.

The Concise Oxford Dictionary defines competent as 'adequately qualified'. This implies that some degree of standard must be met to achieve competence. A healthcare student must pass certain assessments and be deemed to be of a sufficient standard in order to be considered able to practise. These standards have to be defined so that they can be assessed and met. The competence of the qualified professional is less easy to define.

Ellis (1988) suggests that competence should include the 'total of observable behaviours that occur in professional practice, categorised and specified into measurable standards'; and furthermore, that it will also refer to 'unobservable attributes, capacities, dispositions, attitudes and values that the professional should have and that these must surface and be detectable as behaviour'. All of these are much more difficult to assess than is the case when assessing the academic performance of a student. A useful analogy is that of the learner driver who must be assessed before being judged competent to drive a car; however, once 'qualified', how is that drivers competence assessed? By the number of accidents they have, or do not have? By the fact that they drive regularly? Or because their eyesight is still good?

It might be assumed that the drivers competence has been maintained because he or she has passed the driving test and is still practising. This is obviously not sufficient for the healthcare professional who has a responsibility to service users and service managers. It is necessary for that person to be able to display competence; standards have to be set and the performance of the professional has to be assessed in terms of those standards.

Professional standards

Most professionals work to agreed standards set out by the governing body of their profession. Standards are also set out within a contract of employment. The basis for all standards, however, must be that the interventions provided to people are the most appropriate and effective. Outcomes should be considered as the standards upon which the competence of the professional is measured. Given this, it is necessary that the healthcare professional monitors the outcomes of interventions and alters the intervention as is suggested by that monitoring (Grimmer and Dibden, 1992). It is questionable that without this process a profession can credibly consider itself competent.

Therefore quality assurance must not be considered as an intrusive management tool, a bureaucratic, pen-pushing task or even as unnecessary. It has to be the core upon which competence and professionalism are based.

The responsibility for quality assurance has to lie with each individual healthcare professional. It is essential that individual practice is monitored and developed (Hopkins, 1993). Equally, a professional has a responsibility to change behaviours in response to feedback (Nosworthy *et al.*, 1989) and to maintain a current level of knowledge so that patients may be offered the most appropriate interventions (Hopkins, 1993; Grimmer and Dibden, 1992).

Responsibility also lies with service managers. Many quality assurance processes can only be performed on a departmental level, and it is necessary to coordinate these activities with other services and to communicate and inform all staff regarding the process. The benefits of the activity should be made clear (Saunders, 1984), since quality assurance can fail if there is staff resistance, misunderstanding or lack of education and support (Forquer and Anderson, 1982; Williamson, 1991). Staff should be given access, in terms of time and resources, to continuing education; not only regarding the quality assurance process but also to allow the furthering of their own professional development. This last point cannot be over-emphasized as it is central to the concept of competence and therefore to quality assurance itself.

Learning Activity 1 ◆ ◆ ◆

Identify five areas within your own profession that have been subject to quality assurance.

HISTORICAL PERSPECTIVES

Hippocrates was perhaps the first healthcare professional to consider quality assurance. He recorded his observations of poor-quality care and made recommendations for improvement; 25 centuries later Florence Nightingale employed the same method. In the sixteenth century the Royal College of Physicians made reference in its founding charter to the need to 'uphold standards for public benefit' (Wright and Whittington, 1992). In America in 1915, Dr Ernest Codman reviewed his patients one year after discharge from hospital to assess the efficacy of treatment and later founded the End Results Hospital. Shortly afterwards, the American College of Surgeons emphasized the need to 'analyse, review and evaluate, and where necessary, improve the quality of clinical practice' (cited in Saunders, 1984).

However, while there was a continuation of these quality initiatives they remained isolated and the responsibility of individual practitioners. Formalizing the necessary setting of standards and evaluation of services has been a more recent initiative and has, to a very large extent, been due to the changing attitudes and greater knowledge of consumers increasing their power to affect change within the health service (OKeefe and Patterson, 1985).

British healthcare professionals have lagged behind those in the USA, Canada, Australia and New Zealand, where accreditation has encouraged hospital and state initiatives (Sale, 1990). Ellis and Whittington (1993) suggest that there was no explicit reference to quality assurance before 1980 in Britain, although the Royal College of Nursings 'Standards of Care' project was set up in 1965 (Royal College of Nursing, 1989). In the early 1980s, both the Griffiths report (DHSS, 1983) and the World Health Organization (WHO, 1985) highlighted the need for systematic quality assurance. In 1983 the Royal College of General Practitioners outlined their Quality Initiative. Radiographers have, because they work with ionizing radiation, a strong background of national and European regulations and standards by which they practise and have been at the forefront in the production of quality assurance programmes (WHO 1982, HMSO 1988, HMSO 1990, IRCP 1990, Commission of the EC 1989, Watkinson *et al.* 1993). The other health professions have been a little slower in developing guidelines and standards, these being produced by the College of Occupational Therapists, the Chartered Society of Physiotherapy and the College of Speech and Language Therapists in 1989, 1990 and 1991 respectively.

Learning Activity 2 ◆ ◆ ◆

Search out your own professional standards as issued by your professional body.

This activity has coincided with the publication of several government reports. The most powerful of these, the 1989 'Working for Patients' working paper, outlined the need for high-quality, cost-effective services and recommended the establishment of formal systems of 'medical audit' for both hospital and community care (DoH, 1989).

Additionally, healthcare reorganizations introduced in 1991 (NHS and Community Care Act) have had a powerful impact on quality assurance. The separation of purchaser and provider roles within health and social services has created opportunities for competition, providers having to compete with each other to win contracts from the purchasers. Within this 'internal market' it was envisioned that contracts between purchasers and providers would include explicit standards against which the quality of the service could be measured.

In 1991 the government launched the Patients Charter, which has the explicit aim of giving service users the opportunity to influence the quality of service they receive. This is to be achieved both directly, by means of complaints procedures and satisfaction surveys etc., and indirectly, by introducing the opportunity for patient choice.

This recent legislation has ensured that quality assurance has to be on the top of the agenda for every healthcare service. That we should provide, and show that we provide, good quality services are now a mandatory aspect of this legislation. The service receiver is highlighted by legislation as having a central role in this process. There is, however, wide variation in the commitment to, and enthusiasm for, this process by healthcare professionals (Shaw, 1990). As yet, there is little evidence that quality assurance standards are consistently being set and measured by providers or that patients have any real choice.

An unprecedented opportunity for service providers to set standards of healthcare and for them to develop methods by which quality of care can be assured is currently available. If healthcare professionals, in consultation with service users, do not set standards that they believe truly reflect good quality of care, there is a danger that these standards will be set by others and that price and not quality may dominate the contracting process (Williamson, 1991).

THE QUALITY ASSURANCE PROCESS

Many practical examples of quality assurance methods exist. These include *criteria mapping* (Shimeld, 1983; Law *et al.*, 1989), *audit* (Merral *et al.*, 1991), *occupational therapy review* (Ostrow, 1983), *physiotherapy assessment* (Nosworthy *et al.*, 1989), *flow sheet mapping* (Saunders, 1984), and *radiology equipment review* (Watkinson *et al.*, 1983; Watkinson, 1985). All these methods have a common underlying process, and so each stage of this quality assurance process will be explained in the

Box 29.1 *The eight stages of a quality cycle*

1. Determination of the area for consideration
2. Establishing standards
3. Determination of measurement tools
4. Data collection
5. Analysis and interpretation of data
6. Determination of the appropriate course of action
7. Implementation of action
8. Monitoring the effects of action

remainder of this section. The aim is to help the reader in making the choices required for each stage of the activity. To achieve this the basic quality circle is expanded to include eight stages (see Box 29.1).

Within this quality assurance cycle is nested a subsidiary process, the *quality correction cycle* – stages five to eight. This can be used, when the quality assurance cycle has been established, for regular monitoring of performance. It is important to note that, while the latter cycle may be useful, it is essential that the process is regularly completed throughout all of the stages to ensure that the initial areas for consideration remain appropriate. To allow a quality assurance circle function, three important assumptions must be made:

- The service has an understood statement of intent (i.e. a mission statement).
- All staff working within the service are aware of the mission statement.
- The service has a clear understanding of its target client group.

Box 29.2 *Stages in a quality circle using outpatient waiting times as an example (Ostrow and Kaufman, 1981)*

Stage 1: Key feature – outpatient waiting times

Stage 2: Statement of standard – patients should be seen by a qualified health professional for an initial assessment or examination within 6 weeks of receipt by the health professional of a referral

Stage 3: Measurement tool – receptionist's appointment book

Stage 4: Data collection – date of referral and date of first appointment

Stage 5: Data analysis and interpretation – number of referrals waiting 6 weeks or longer for an initial assessment or examination

Stage 6: Determination of action – increased productivity of staff

Stage 7: Implementation of actions – pare down number of hours spent on rounds and meetings; streamline documentation procedures

Stage 8: Monitoring the effects of the actions – review whether actions have achieved the desired outcomes

In order to more clearly illustrate the practical working of the quality assurance process, the above is an example which uses outpatient waiting time as a quality indicator (see Box 29.2).

DETERMINATION OF THE AREA FOR CONSIDERATION

Key areas for consideration are those that specify the quality of a service. These must be measurable and achievable, and make sense to users, purchasers and providers. It is important when deciding these 'key quality features' (Ovretveit, 1992) that appropriate consultation occurs. Quality assurance should be an individual process, as well as a departmental and a service-wide initiative. The amount of consultation will vary with each of these stages. For an individual practitioner, perhaps working in private practice, consultation with patients, support staff and the appropriate professional body may be sufficient. For a departmental initiative, however, it is necessary to consult with patients, staff, other departments and the organization's managers to ensure that the key quality features reflect the mission statement of the organization.

An effective way of doing this is by means of a *quality circle*, which is a process by which staff at every layer in an organization work together as a team to improve the quality of the service. The quality circle also creates a useful forum within which conflict can be dealt with. It is naive to believe that indicators of quality may be the same for each member of the group. Service users may perceive quality in terms of individual treatment, while providers may view it as concerning adequately kept records. The quality circle enables all the interested parties to discuss the relative importance of these different indicators and to reach a consensus regarding the key indicators to be used.

An enterprising expansion of the quality circle is the five-point approach described by Shimeld (1982) (see Figure 29.2). Here the central quality circle is reported to by five subsidiary circles: credentialing, audit, utilization, clinical activities and continuing education. Such an extended process ensures that all staff are involved and that the wide scope of activities required for comprehensive quality assurance are included.

Having selected the team and established the groups with whom consultation is needed, it is necessary to 'brainstorm' the key features that, to the members of the quality circle, encompass quality. These may be waiting times, amount of information given, record-keeping, assessments etc. It is important at this stage that key quality features are received from all members of the group so that the standards that are

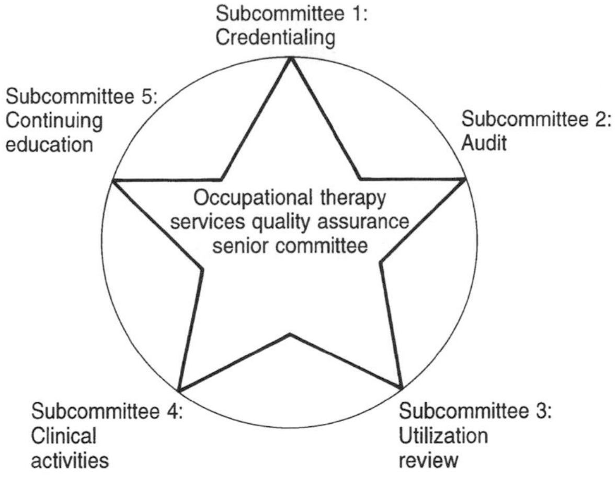

Figure 29.2 *A quality circle (Shimeld, 1982)*

consequently set do not reflect only the views of the health service workers, managers or users.

Having established all the features that contribute to quality, it is essential to prioritize them. Many quality assurance programmes flounder not because of the process itself but because too many areas are chosen for consideration. Only the most important key areas should be chosen for the next stage of standard-setting. The danger of choosing too many areas can be that the amount of work generated for an already busy staff can be too great which may result in the essential processes of re-evaluation and action-taking never occurring. It is possible that when a few standards have been set and these are regularly being re-evaluated, others may be identified, allowing the process to grow and develop with the support of the staff group.

This group should also be responsible for the organization of the quality assurance cycle. It is not enough to set standards if this information is not disseminated, if the procedures are not in place for the total process, if key staff necessary for the process are not available or sufficiently trained, or if staff do not have the authority necessary to take the appropriate action when this is identified. The importance of detailing the basic organizational infrastructure at this stage cannot be over-emphasized.

ESTABLISHING STANDARDS

Once the key features have been identified, standards need to be established. A standard is a specified expectation of staff, described in terms of an activity or outcome against which their level of performance can be compared with a defined measure or indicator (Ovretveit, 1992). Standards should be set out in statement form. These should be specific and measurable, since if a standard does not relate to a measure it cannot be used to assess quality. For example, 'patients should be seen as soon as possible' is an ambiguous statement and allows no opportunity to measure performance. Similarly, standards should be easily understood, by both clients of a service and the service providers. Finally, the standards set must be achievable. If they are not then opportunity for the service to succeed is diminished, which may demoralize service providers and encourage all participants to lose confidence in the quality assurance process.

This is not to say that low standards should be set initially. It should always be borne in mind that the standards set are always interim ones which, as the quality assurance process progresses, move towards an ideal or optimum. Equally, it is important that standards are not reset at a lower level if they are not met. The quality correction cycle must be used to establish the reasons for failure to meet standards and to allow corrective action to be taken.

DETERMINATION OF MEASUREMENT TOOLS

This is often a stumbling ground for many healthcare professionals who feel that measurement implies the use of purely quantitative methods. Many standards, such as waiting times, easily lend themselves to measurement and therefore are often chosen. The challenge is to measure the more intangible constructs that indicate quality of service: these may be politeness, information, or a relaxed atmosphere. There are many methods that enable us to measure these, the best-known being the satisfaction survey. These are valid and appropriate methods of measuring quality and should not be readily dismissed.

The most important points to consider when choosing a measuring tool are:

- whether or not it measures the construct specified by the standard;
- whether you have the available skills within the department to develop such a tool (and analyse the data generated);
- how frequently measurement will occur; and
- whether the measurement tool will be simple to use and welcomed by staff and patients.

A complicated tool may have the perverse ability of adversely affecting staff and user satisfaction and so their perception of the quality of the service as a whole.

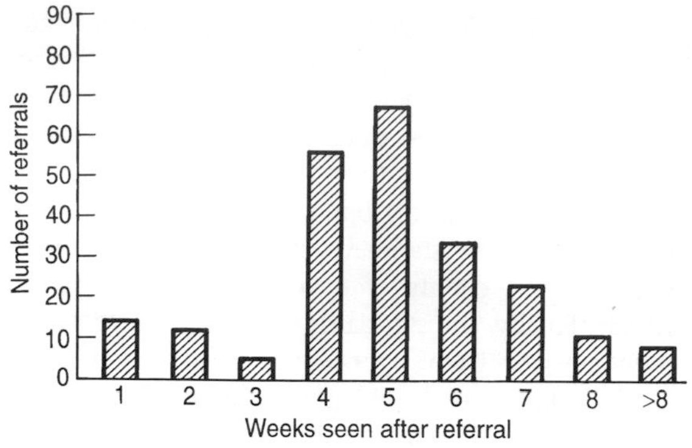

Figure 29.3 *Histogram illustrating the length of time between referral and assessment*

DATA COLLECTION
Simplicity is the most important factor here. The data generated must be collected in an easily retrieved and uncomplicated format that naturally becomes part of staff's daily routine. An arduous data collection process that appears to reduce the time available for patient contact will not be welcomed by the majority. Compliance will be poor and consequently the data collected suspect. Again, it is important to emphasize that the quality of the service should not be compromised by attempts to measure that quality.

ANALYSIS AND INTERPRETATION OF DATA
Data should be presented in an easily understood format. Graphs, pie charts and histograms are useful in this context (see Figure 29.3).

Many sophisticated statistical tests may only be understood by those with research expertise and should be avoided. Quality assurance is a practical process that should be readily understood and appreciated by all concerned – especially the individuals using the service.

DETERMINATION OF THE APPROPRIATE COURSES OF ACTION
This is obviously dependent upon the results collected. If the standard has not been met, the reasons for this failure must be established. Causes of failure can be many and various, and so it will be necessary for the quality circle to meet together to ensure that all reasons can be considered. It might be the case that the initial standards need to be reviewed at this stage to ensure that they were set appropriately and realistically. A review of histograms of the results are useful as they enable the group to look at those highest results that will affect an average. It may be that these have a common theme – longer waiting times on a particular day, for example – which may be resolved by rearranging the weekly calendar and thus positively affecting the overall mean of results.

IMPLEMENTATION OF ACTION
Actions should be implemented as soon as possible after data analysis, and an appropriate meeting of the quality circle arranged at which the actions can be reviewed.

MONITORING THE EFFECTS OF ACTIONS
Regular meetings of the quality circle should be scheduled to monitor the effects of actions. If corrective action, taken in response to a failure to meet a standard, has had little or no effect, then further reasons for failure should be considered and appropriate action implemented

When the data collected meet the standards set, the work of the quality circle is not completed. Rather the process should again be initiated after reconsideration of the original standards. It should be considered how these standards can be raised in an attempt to improve quality. Similarly, new key indicators can be selected for inclusion in a new quality cycle.

Learning Activity 3 ◆ ◆ ◆

- Find out who is in charge of quality assurance within your department. Ask them to outline what is happening with regard to quality assurance.
- Identify an area that you think would benefit from quality assurance in your practice, and identify the stages that would be necesssary to carry out a quality circle process on it.

SUMMARY

Quality assurance should not be perceived as 'more paperwork' – it is an integral part of the process of care, not an addition to it. It is an extension of the normal procedure of assessment, intervention, reassessment, and further intervention based on reassessment. Quality assurance is the formalization of this procedure, so that the indicators used in assessment and reassessment have some objective meanings (both for the practitioner and the individual attending for examination or treatment), so that these indicators are easily and effectively measured and, most importantly, so that goals are set to permit further improvement.

A final word should be said about the role of the team. No practitioner works independently of others. Relationships are formed within a healthcare team, with the individual being treated as the focus of their work. Whilst quality assurance can be practised by each individual professional, the process is most effective when agreed and negotiated within that team, the delivery site, the professional community as a whole and the social community served by the team. Only then can a process of quality assurance be said to be in the interests of the community served by an establishment, and thus to truly focus on those areas felt to be important by all its members.

Key Points

- Assessing the quality of any product or service involves making judgements of that product or service in relation to a standard or set of standards.
- Quality assurance is a continually evolving cyclical process within which services are provided and restructured to meet the changing needs of a client group effectively and efficiently.
- The quality assurance process is the responsibility of each health professional, thus forming a cohesive team approach to the setting of 'client-centred' standards.
- Health professionals work to agreed standards set out by the governing body of their profession.
- The quality assurance cycle has specific stages agreed by participants which need to be implemented for successful quality assurance.

References

Castledine, G. (1983). In the best possible care. *Nursing Mirror*, **156**(19), 22.

College of Radiographers (1992). *Guidelines for the Introduction of a Quality Assurance Programme in a Diagnostic Imaging Department*. London: College of Radiographers

Department of Health (1989). *Working for Patients: Medical Audit*. (Working Paper 6). London: HMSO.

Department of Health (1991). NHS and Community Care Act. London: HMSO.

Department of Health and Social Security (1983). *National Health Service Management Enquiry: The Griffiths Report*. London: HMSO.

Ellis, R. (1988). *Professional Competence and Quality Assurance in the Caring Professions*. London: Chapman & Hall.

Forquer, S.L. and Anderson, T.B. (1982). A concerns based approach to the implementation of quality assurance systems. *QRB*, **8**: 14–19.

Goode, W. (1969). *The Theoretical Limits of Professionalization. The Semi-Professions and their Organization*. New York: Free Press.

Greenwood, E. (1957). Attributes of a Profession. *Social Work*, **2**: 44–55.

Grimmer, K.A. and Dibden, M. (1992). Marketing and quality assurance: the two faces of Janus. *Australian Clinical Review*, **12**: 38.

Gruchy, C. and Rogers, L.G. (1990). Quality Assurance: the current challenge. *Canadian Journal of Occupational Therapy*, **57**: 109–15.

Holmes Report (1986). *Tomorrow's Teachers*. East Lansing, Michigan, USA: Holmes Group Inc.

Hopkins, A. (1993). What do we mean by appropriate healthcare? Report of a working group prepared for the Director of research and development of the NHS Management Executive. *Quality in Health Care*, **2**: 117–23.

Law, M, Ryan, B. and Townsend, B. (1989). Criteria mapping: a method of quality assurance. *American Journal of Occupational Therapy*, **43**: 104–9.

Merral, A., Patel, R. and Taylor, J. (1991). *Audit for the Therapy Professions*. Keele: Mercia Publications.

Nosworthy, J.C. Calea, M. and McCoy, A.T. (1989). Quality assurance: standard physiotherapy assessment forms and computerisation *Australian Clinical Review*, **9**(9), 46–8.

O'Keefe, M. and Patterson, P. (1985). The marketing of physiotherapy services. *Australian Journal of Physiotherapy*, **31**: 31–2.

Ostrow, P.C. (1983). Quality assurance requirements of the Joint Commission on Accreditation of Hospitals. *American Journal of Occupational Therapy*, **37**: 27–31.

Ovretveit, J. (1992). *Health Service Quality: An Introduction to Quality Methods for Health Services*. London: Blackwell Scientific.

Royal College of General Practitioners (1983). The Quality Initiative. *Journal of the Royal College of General Practitioners*, **33**: 523–4.

Royal College of Nursing (1989). *A Framework for Quality, RCN Standards of Care Project*. London: RCN.

Saunders, B. (1984). Muriel Driver Memorial Lecture 1984. Quality Assurance – reflections on a wave. *Canadian Journal of Occupational Therapy*, **51**: 161–70.

Shaw, M. (1990). *Medical Audit: A Hospital Handbook*. London: King's Fund.

Shimeld, A. (1983). A clinical demonstration program in quality assurance. *American Journal of Occupational Therapy*, **37**: 32–5.

Watkinson, S., Shaw, M., Moores, B.M. and Eddleston, E. (1983). Quality assurance: a practical programme. *Radiography*, **49**(578), 27–54.

Watkinson, S.A. (1985). Economic aspects of quality assurance. *Radiography*, **51**(597), 133–40.

Williamson, J. (1991). Providing quality care. *Health Services Management*, **Feb.**, 18–23.

World Health Organization (1985). *The Principles of Quality*

Assurance (European Reports and Studies 94). Copenhagan: WHO.
Wright, C.C. and Whittington, D. (1992). *Quality Assurance: An Introduction for Health Care Professionals*. London: Churchill Livingstone.

Further Reading ▲ ▲ ▲

Ellis, R. (1988). *Professional Competence and Quality Assurance in the Caring Professions*. London: Chapman & Hall.
Ovretveit, J. (1992). *Health Service Quality: An Introduction to Quality Methods for Health Services*. London: Blackwell Scientific.
Sale, D. (1990). *Quality Assurance*. London: Macmillan Education.
Wright, C.C. and Whittington, D. (1992). *Quality Assurance: An Introduction for Health Care Professionals*. London: Churchill Livingstone.

Index

Page numbers in *italic* refer to tables or illustrations; **bold** type indicates a major subject section.